Business Law

Sixth Edition

George Getz, J.D.
Member of the New York Bar
Adjunct Professor of Business Law
Florida Atlantic University
Boca Raton, Florida

Karen S. Romito
Archbishop Mitty High School
San Jose, California

Glencoe Publishing Company
Mission Hills, California

Consultants

Janie G. Blankenship
Assistant Professor, Business Administration
Delmar College
Corpus Christi, Texas

Don L. Crawford
Chairman, Administrative Systems
and Business Education
West Georgia College
Carrollton, Georgia

Nancy A. Leathers
Instructor, Business Education Department
Hart High School
Newhall, California

Loretta Stewart
Specialist, Business and Office Education
Jefferson County Public Schools
Louisville, Kentucky

Bonnie Bray Hopson
Assistant Professor, Business Education
The University of Georgia
Athens, Georgia

Photographs:
Alpha Photos page 148; American Stock Photos 431; Apple Computer 195, 305; BART 82; Comstock 188, 607; Liane Enkelis 284; FPG 575; Tony Freeman 38, 63, 295, 309, 324, 336, 339, 344; Glencoe Photo Library 207, 244, 371, 569; Bruce Hilliard 366, 384, 646; Richard Hutchings 232, 482, 485, 502, 601; Los Angeles County Fire Department 93; Los Angeles Superior Court 237; Stephen McBrady 110, 412, 545, 550, 585; National Archives 6; New York Stock Exchange 641; Tom Pantages 152; Photo Researchers 3; Port of New York 331; Karen Stafford Rantzman 61, 277; H. Armstrong Roberts 303; James Shaffer 97, 179; Elliot Varner Smith 265; The Stockmarket 57, 99, 122, 183, 296; Texas Stock 108, 495, 516, 556, 612; Woodfin Camp 75, 351, 419, 452, 599, 605.

Cover Photo:
Arnold Gore/FPG

Illustrations:
Ellen Stern

Send all inquiries to:
Glencoe Publishing Company
15319 Chatsworth Street, P.O. Box 9509
Mission Hills, CA 91345-9509

ISBN 0-02-831651-7

2 3 4 5 6 7 8 9   92 91 90 89 88

CONTENTS

PREFACE

The sixth edition of *Business Law* provides a working knowledge and understanding of legal principles that affect our daily lives as workers, consumers, and citizens. The text deals with important rules of conduct concerned with earning a living and acquiring goods and services. Underlying these two objectives are a wide variety of legal principles that must be observed and complied with by all producers or consumers.

The new edition of *Business Law* has been heavily revised, updated, and expanded. A new unit has been added, focusing closely on consumer protection and credit. There is also a new chapter on social insurance, and the information on the basic functions of our legal system has been considerably lengthened.

While many of the popular features of previous editions have been retained and improved, a significant number of new features have been incorporated. Each chapter now begins with "You Be The Judge," two fact-situation case problems, which serve to stimulate interest and provoke discussion about the legal principles to be studied. After reading the chapter, students are asked to review the cases and to think about their earlier decisions in light of their new learning. Correct decisions are provided at the end of the chapter so that students can perform a self-check.

The textual instruction is reinforced by "Problems" and "Examples." New legal principles are introduced by case problems that are then immediately solved and explained. The explanations are brief but concise, often accompanied by realistic examples that further clarify the points of law under discussion. The textual instruction is also supported by abundant photographs, line drawings, legal forms, and charts.

Each of the 46 chapters in the text contains one of three special boxed features: "Living Under the Law" includes topics of current consumer interest; "Careers in the Law" describes the duties of various careers in the legal field, as well as any personal or educational requirements; and "Law in the News" consists of actual newspaper clippings that deal with current legal concerns.

In addition to the review of "You Be The Judge," each chapter concludes with four student assignments: "Understanding What You Have Read" reviews the substantive law presented in the textual instruction; "Building Your Legal Vocabulary" reinforces important legal terms in three different exercise formats—matching, multiple-choice, and sentence completion; "Applying Legal Principles" presents hypothetical case problems; and "Analyzing Court Cases" features three actual adjudicated cases from federal and state appellate courts.

A strong focus is placed on mastering basic legal terms and concepts. All the important legal terms given in the text are highlighted for ease of recognition and carefully defined in simply stated language. In addition to the "Building Your Legal Vocabulary" activity at the end of each chapter, there is an extensive Glossary of almost 700 legal terms at the end of the text.

The sixth edition of *Business Law* is complemented by three supplementary components. The *Student Workbook* contains four different worksheets for every chapter in the text: vocabulary activities (in the form of crossword puzzles), objective questions, short-answer case problems, and applications (such as analyzing newspaper articles and completing legal forms).

The *Teacher's Manual and Key* includes a full methodology for teaching the program; complete lesson plans with objectives, teaching suggestions, and enrichment activities for each chapter; and an answer key.

Completely new to the program is the *Teacher's Resource Book,* which features student handouts, additional activities, the testing program (comprising achievement tests for each unit and cumulative review case problems), 44 transparency masters, and a simulation of a trial.

The authors wish to thank all the people who have helped to produce this new edition. We are particularly grateful to Linn Van Meter-Drew, Stewart Cusimano, John True, and our team of consultants. We would also like to express our special appreciation to Neal Saunders, editorial director for business education at Glencoe, Mary Lorenz, and all the staff at Glencoe for their invaluable assistance.

George Getz
Boca Raton, Florida

Karen S. Romito
San Jose, California

Business Law

UNIT 1

LAW AND SOCIETY

LEARNING OBJECTIVES

After you have studied this unit, you should be able to:

- Show how a respect and understanding of the law contribute to smoother personal, family, and work relationships.

- Give reasons why law is essential in maintaining social control.

- List the main sources of law and describe its historical development and classification.

- Identify the proper court to hear and decide a given legal dispute.

- Point out the differences between torts and crimes and the legal consequences of common torts and crimes.

CHAPTER 1

Nature and Classification of Law

YOU BE THE JUDGE

Think about these cases.
If you were the judge, how would you decide each case?

1

Matagorda was being terrorized by the James Gang. A sheriff sent to clean up the town killed one gang member and arrested two others. At the trial, the defense lawyer asked for the release of the captured gang members. He claimed they hadn't known any laws other than their own rules were enforceable in the area. Was his claim correct?

2

A small town called Nogales sits on the border between the United States and Mexico. City police in Nogales arrested a gang of Mexican youths for disturbing the peace, a violation of a United States law. The youths claimed that they should be set free because they had not violated Mexican law. Do you agree?

WHAT IS LAW?

Human beings do not exist independently of other humans. We are drawn by nature toward living in communities, or societies. Those communities thrive only when the people in them are able to get along with one another. If each person in a community had a unique set of rules to live by, conflicts between individuals or between groups of people would continually arise.

Sets of rules have gradually been established to insure peaceful relationships between groups of people. These rules are known as *laws*. **Law** can be defined as the body of principles that governs our conduct with other individuals and with the government.

A **government** is a collection of people or an organization that has been chosen to serve the government's citizens. That organization is empowered to make and enforce the laws that allow people to coexist peacefully. Because there are many people in any given government, that government is a stronger source of law enforcement than is any individual. Indeed, without government, law enforcement is impossible. Similarly, without law enforcement, laws are rendered useless.

WHY WE HAVE LAWS

The laws that govern our relationships are not intended merely to control the way we, as individuals, behave. They are also intended to control the way we are treated by other individuals, by government, and by businesses. Laws are useful because they guarantee us the freedom to pursue our constitutional rights. They also specify that we must allow the same opportunity to others, both singly and collectively. This means that while we have certain rights and privileges, we also have a responsibility to others not to violate their rights. These rights and protections extend to individuals as well as to society, and they apply to both personal and public property. They are also used to promote social programs that benefit society as a whole.

It's important to know that ignorance of the law is not a legitimate excuse for violating it. Citizens are presumed to be responsible for the law they live under. Using the defense "I didn't know it was illegal" is not acceptable.

HISTORICAL DEVELOPMENT OF OUR LAWS

To help understand how we arrived at the set of laws we use today, let's take a look at the laws used in some earlier societies. The rules established by those societies are important sources of our current law.

The legal systems of the Hebrews, Greeks, and Romans used written laws. The foundation of Hebrew law was the Ten Commandments. The Greek legal system was based on the principles of democracy. Although the Greeks had no trained judges or lawyers, trials were conducted by juries chosen by the people. The Romans, however, placed greater emphasis on formal law. The Romans developed a system of written law in the form of codes that are still in use today.

Common Law

People who moved from one part of Europe to another carried with them the systems of law established in their former communities. When new settlements formed, the groups merged their legal systems and began to practice a composite of those systems. The body of legal rules developed in England is known as the **common law.**

Common law is based on accepted customs and traditions of the English people. An outstanding characteristic of common law is the practice of deciding cases by following **precedent** (a previous decision). This is done by preserving the legal principles developed by early English courts and applying those same principles when disputes of a similar nature arise.

A particular kind of common law, known as the **law merchant,** was established among traders and merchants during the Middle Ages. The English adopted the law merchant as the part of their common law that governs business transactions.

It was natural for England's American colonies to adopt the laws to which the colonists had been accustomed in England. Even after gaining independence from England, early American settlers continued to use the common law to govern themselves. With one exception, all of our states today make common law the basis of their laws. Louisiana, formerly part of the French empire, bases its laws on the Code Napoléon. This is a codification of French laws completed during the rule of Napoleon Bonaparte.

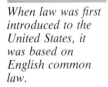

When law was first introduced to the United States, it was based on English common law.

LIVING UNDER THE LAW

Differences Between Civil Law and Common Law

Law is often classified by source as *civil law,* from the Roman civil law, and as *common law,* which is based on the English common law. It is significant that Roman civil law is the basis of law in all western European countries *except* Great Britain. The British may have developed their own legal system based on the feudal law of medieval England because of their isolation from the continent. While civil law countries codified their laws, English and American common law follows precedents that stem almost entirely from the decisions of judges in actual trials.

Besides this fundamental difference between the two legal systems, there are several important substantive and procedural differences. For example, while the common law makes a sharp distinction between real and personal property, the civil law regards property as either personal or real, without distinction. Also, for a contract to be valid, the common law requires that promises be supported by a valuable consideration. Under the civil law, however, there is no need for consid-

eration to make a contract enforceable. More important, while the Bill of Rights in our Constitution is recognized as a guarantee of an individual's fundamental rights, such rights don't exist under civil law.

The jury system is required under the United States Constitution for both civil and criminal cases. After the French Revolution, most European countries adopted a modified jury system, but only for criminal cases. Under the European system, a majority vote is sufficient for conviction or acquittal. Judges vote with the jury. If a victim demands money compensation from a convicted criminal, a judge alone may decide on the amount of compensation.

It's difficult to say which of the two legal systems is superior. Both are outstanding examples of a great achievement in the development of human beings. It is quite possible that some day, in a united world, a general law might evolve that would incorporate the best features of both systems.

Equity Law

At common law, the only compensation or relief (known as a **remedy**) available to injured parties was the payment of money. In some cases, however, an injured party could be fairly compensated only by means of some nonmonetary relief. Because of cases such as these, **courts of equity** arose. Judges in these courts made their decisions solely on the basis of what was fair and just in the particular cases before them. Those decisions became precedents, and the collection of precedents from courts of equity constitutes today's **equity law.**

One important principle of equity law is known as **specific performance.** This principle requires that an agreement be carried out under its original terms if there is no other way to compensate the victim fairly.

EXAMPLE

Mueller signed a contract to sell a Van Gogh painting to Sorenson. After accepting Sorenson's check, Mueller changed his mind and returned the money. Sorenson sued to force Mueller to sell her the painting. The return of her money couldn't compensate her for the loss of ownership of the painting. The court granted Sorenson the specific performance she had requested.

UNITED STATES LAW TODAY

When our nation's founders wrote the Declaration of Independence, they established a system based on the rights of human beings rather than on the rights of British subjects. This concept—that the rights of the individual exist without regard to will or authority of any kind—was a new concept in building a foundation for government. Since the establishment of our country, its citizens have continued to try to define the "rights of human beings."

EXAMPLE

In the 1950s and 1960s, a civil rights movement took place in this country. This movement resulted in the Civil Rights Act of 1964, which prohibits discrimination against people because of their race, color, religion, or national origin. Since its enactment, the Civil Rights Act has changed the level of opportunity for many people.

The concept of human rights has changed considerably since the Declaration of Independence and the establishment of the Constitution. Law is an expression of constantly changing social forces. As such, it is a living, fluid entity that is influenced by the world in which it functions. It has been argued that the greatest single feature of the United States Constitution is that it includes a provision for change based on the pressures of events. The Constitution can be amended to respond to changes in politics, technology, moral standards, international relations, economics, and other circumstances. The only underlying requirement for constitutional change is that any changes made must maintain the dignity and freedom of human life.

CLASSIFICATION OF TODAY'S LAW

Let's look at some of the ways in which our laws are classified. The most basic classification is by source (origin).

Classification by Source

Figure 1.1 illustrates the five primary sources of today's laws: constitutional law, statute law, case law, administrative law, and international law.

Constitutional Law

The United States Constitution defines the powers and limitations of the federal government by means of **constitutional law.** This is the basic law of the land. States also have constitutions that define the powers and limitations of state government. No state constitution, however, may conflict with

Figure 1.1
Sources of Today's Law

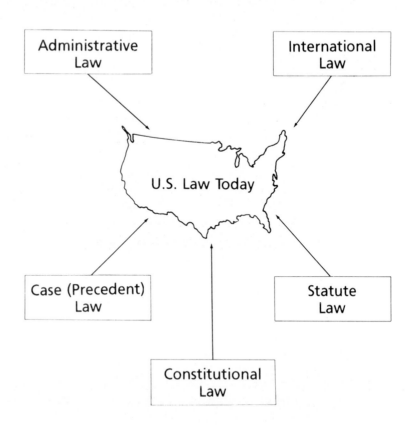

the federal constitution or with any proper federal law. The federal constitution and all state constitutions must respect the rights of all persons.

Powers not specifically granted to the federal government belong to the states. The states, on the one hand, have exclusive power to regulate **intrastate commerce** (commerce within their borders) or to punish crimes committed within their borders. The federal government, on the other hand, has exclusive power to regulate **interstate commerce** (commerce between states), to control foreign affairs, and to coin money.

Ng is arrested in Nevada for leaving the state of California while on bail for a statutory crime. Because Ng crossed state boundaries, his trial for the offense of leaving the state while on bail would be held in a federal court.

Statute Law

Statute law refers to laws passed by legislative bodies to keep pace with economic and social changes. These laws work within the framework of federal and state constitutions. They may be enacted by the United States Congress, by state legislatures, by local bodies such as city or town councils, or by county boards of supervisors.

The city of Santa Fe, New Mexico, has a statute requiring all pets to be restrained. Cats are exempt from this regulation because of the nature of their behavior.

One important feature of statute law is that any time a particular common law conflicts with an established statute law, the statute law always supersedes, or replaces, the common law.

Statute laws passed by local bodies are known as **ordinances,** or local laws. Ordinances are enforceable if they are not in violation of federal or state constitutions.

Because of major differences among the laws of the various states, especially laws concerning business transactions, most states have adopted **uniform laws.** These laws are uniform, or the same, from state to state. They aim to define the rights and duties of business people who deal across state lines. At present, almost all of the states have adopted the **Uniform Commercial Code (UCC).** The UCC replaces some of the more important uniform statutes governing business transactions.

Case Law

Some court cases raise points of law that are not covered by any existing law. Cases such as these reveal a need for a new application or interpretation of law. The court decisions in these cases become common law. The body of laws created in this manner is called **case law.** Although these laws can be changed by statute or by later court decisions, they do have the force of law.

Administrative Law

A special kind of law has been developed to meet the needs of our complex modern society. Legislatures are unable to give detailed attention to every situation that appears to need careful monitoring. As a result, they create regulatory or administrative agencies to help them in the task of governing. These agencies are given the authority to make laws and to administer and enforce those laws. Laws passed by regulatory agencies such as the Food and Drug Administration (FDA), the Internal Revenue Service (IRS), and state public utilities commissions form what is called **administrative law.** Administrative laws have the force of statute law. The agencies have the power to try cases and to make legal decisions within the limits set by the legislatures. Appeals may be taken from decisions of administrative agencies to the proper courts.

Sjoberg ran a nonprofit corporation for the benefit of blind people. When the corporation failed to file the proper income tax forms, the IRS placed a lien on Sjoberg's house. She appealed to a federal court, asking to be released from the lien because the corporation was run by volunteers who had made a mistake. The court allowed Sjoberg to repair the mistake and released her from her liability to the IRS.

International Law

International law regulates the conduct of one nation or its citizens toward another nation or its citizens.

International law prohibits any nation at war from firing on the ships of a neutral nation unless those ships are carrying war materials to an enemy. The purpose of this law is to protect the lives and property of innocent people.

Figure 1.2
An Event with
Criminal and Civil
Consequences

Event	Wrongful Action	Remedy
1. Schmidt steals Wallen's car.	The crime of theft	The state may prosecute Schmidt in criminal court.
2. During a police chase, Schmidt smashes Wallen's car into Okuni's car.	The tort of damaging the property of another	Wallen and Okuni may both file action in civil court to recover the cost of repairs to their cars.

When an event involves a question of which nation's law should prevail, the prevailing law will be that of the country in which the event occurred.

Classification by Nature

In our legal system, laws are classified as either criminal or civil in nature, depending on the situation. This is the most popular class distinction used in law today.

Trial of a legal action occurs in either a criminal or a civil court, each of which has its own set of rules and procedures. It is important to remember that sometimes the same event (such as an auto accident) may have both criminal and civil consequences. Figure 1.2 illustrates such an event and its consequences.

Criminal Law

Criminal law is the branch of law by which society protects itself against public wrongs by providing punishment for those who commit the wrongs. In each case, the government represents society against the accused party. A **crime** can be defined as any action for which the law provides a punishment.

EXAMPLE

Souza steals some jewelry. After her arrest for theft, she may be brought to trial by the state. If she is convicted, a prison sentence may be the imposed punishment.

Civil Law

Disputes of a noncriminal nature between two or more parties—either individuals or businesses—are the basis of **civil law.** Civil law is generally applied in one of three areas: contracts, property, and torts.

Contracts is a branch of civil law concerned with agreements that voluntarily create legal obligations (duties). Contract law also regulates special agreements covering sales of goods or real estate, agency, and the dealings of business organizations. The study of contracts forms a major part of the study of business law.

EXAMPLE

Suzynski and Campo agreed to purchase a house from Chow. Suzynski fails to carry out his part of the agreement, and Chow sues both parties. This case would be heard in civil court.

Property is a type of contract law governing the possession and transfer of personal or real property through gift, purchase, or inheritance. It may be subdivided into bodies of law such as bailments and probate.

Arnez was to inherit her grandfather's home, but her brother contested the will. This case will be tried in a civil court under property law.

The branch of civil law called **torts** deals with private wrongs committed by one person against another or against his or her property.

During a golf game, Royce carelessly strikes Silvera with a golf club and injures him. Royce has committed a tort. A civil court will probably order Royce to pay monetary damages to Silvera.

Classification by Function

Law can also be classified as **substantive law** or **procedural law.** Substantive law creates, defines, and establishes the rights and duties of individuals. Procedural law is the set of rules that determines the process of enforcing those rights and duties.

Crawford is arrested for speeding through an intersection. The substantive law that applies to this action states that the speed limit in an intersection is fifteen miles per hour. The procedural law related to the action is the fine or sentence imposed on the driver as a penalty for breaking the law.

Business Law

Business law regulates the business transactions of individuals and business organizations. Unlike common law or statute law, it is not a separate and distinct system of law. Rather, it is a group of laws derived from many sources, especially from the law merchant.

Laws relating to business transactions are constantly changing in response to changes in technology and methods of doing business. The Uniform Commercial Code (UCC) is the most standardized application of the form of law known as business law.

Now that you have begun to discover how our current laws developed, you will need to know how to use those laws. The application of the law begins with our judicial system. That system consists of courts, law enforcement agencies, and other important institutions. You will learn more about applying the law in Chapter 2.

Chapter 1 Review

"YOU BE THE JUDGE" REVIEW

Look again at the "You Be the Judge" cases given at the beginning of this chapter. Would you decide them differently now, after your study of the chapter?

Correct Decisions

1. No. The lawyer's claim is incorrect. Ignorance of the law is no excuse for violating it. The town of Matagorda was governed by the laws of the federal territory of which it was a part. However, before the sheriff arrived to enforce the laws of the territory, those laws were meaningless.
2. Cases involving international borders are often difficult to resolve because of the potential for harm to diplomatic relations between the countries. Sometimes a special government, made up of law enforcement people from both countries, presides over disputes. The solution of this case might be determined by the part of town in which the event occurred. Generally, citizens of one country who are visiting another country are subject to the laws of the country they are *in,* not the laws of the country in which they have citizenship.

UNDERSTANDING WHAT YOU HAVE READ

1. What would happen to society without law?
2. What purpose does law serve?
3. Briefly trace the historical development of our laws.
4. What is the basic difference between criminal law and civil law?
5. What new concept was devised by the authors of our Declaration of Independence?
6. What is the difference between constitutional law and statute law?
7. Which early societies had legal systems with written laws?
8. Why was the law merchant established?
9. Why were courts of equity established?
10. Who represents society against a party accused of a crime?

BUILDING YOUR LEGAL VOCABULARY

Match each of these legal terms with its correct definition from the list that follows. Write your answers on a separate sheet of paper.

administrative law
common law
constitutional law
crime

equity law
interstate commerce
ordinances

precedent
statute law
torts

1. a legal decision on which later decisions are based
2. law created to provide nonmonetary relief to injured parties
3. law passed by legislative bodies
4. laws passed by local bodies
5. a system of law developed in England, based on customs and traditions
6. a public wrong for which the law provides punishment
7. the basic law of the land
8. trade between businesses in different states
9. rules with the force of law, made by governmental agencies
10. the branch of civil law that deals with private wrongs committed against another or against another's property

APPLYING LEGAL PRINCIPLES

1. The legislature of a certain state passed a law providing that no person shall be allowed to work in stated occupations for more than eight hours a day. Is this common law or statute law? Give a reason for your answer.
2. Chong, a cashier at the First State Bank, stole a large sum of money from the bank. Will she be tried under civil law or criminal law?
3. Blum sprayed a potent weed killer on her lawn. Because of her carelessness in applying the spray, the weed killer fell on a hedge and flower bed in the yard of her neighbor, Valle. Valle's hedge and all of his flowers were killed. Would Valle seek relief under civil law or under criminal law?
4. Wosch drove her car at 65 miles per hour on a city street in violation of the local 40-mph speed limit. While doing so, she ran into Rivera's car and damaged it badly. Did Wosch violate a civil law? Did she violate a criminal law? State your reasons in each case.

5. The Securities and Exchange Commission (SEC) regulates the sale of shares of stock by certain corporations. The commission ordered Whitney Electronics Company to stop misrepresenting its past earnings in published statements. Which specific branch of law is involved?

6. Varma paid Rontiro $50 for an option to buy a car. The option was to be good until September 30. On September 26, Rontiro sold the car to Johanssen. Is Varma's claim against Rontiro a case for civil or criminal court?

7. Vail applied to a state licensing agency for a license to sell real estate. Even though she believed she had met all of the state requirements for the license, the agency denied Vail's application. Does she have any rights?

8. The Federal Trade Commission (FTC) found a sugar refining firm guilty of deceptive advertising. The firm disagreed with the commission's decision. What legal steps may the firm take?

9. A neighbor's lawsuit charged that Tanaka had committed acts that were not permitted under common law. Tanaka asked to have the charges dropped on the grounds that statutes had been passed making these acts permissible. Would Tanaka be found guilty under the common law?

10. In a written contract, Morris agreed to sell fifty acres of land to Norton at $2,500 per acre. Later, Morris refused to give Norton a deed to the property. Norton maintains that money damages will not compensate her for the loss of the land. What are Norton's rights?

ANALYZING COURT CASES

1. The common law of Massachusetts on a certain point had been clearly established by usage and precedent for more than two hundred years. Then the legislature of that state passed an act on the same subject. This act was clearly in conflict with the well-established common law. In a later lawsuit involving this point, which law governs: the common law or the statute law? (*15A Corpus Juris Secundum*, Section 13)

2. A certain lawsuit arose in New York and was being tried in a federal court in New York. One party in the suit claimed that the court should apply the common law of the United States. The other party claimed that the common law of the state of New York should be applied. Who is right? (*15A Corpus Juris Secundum*, Section 16)

3. Dumont stole a credit card and obtained merchandise by signing a sales slip in the name of the cardholder. He was prosecuted for the offense under the laws of the state of Oregon. Was Dumont prosecuted under the common law or statute law? Would the case be tried under civil law or criminal law? (*Oregon v. Dumont*, 471 P. 2d 847)

CHAPTER 2

Court Systems and Procedures

YOU BE THE JUDGE

Think about these cases.
If you were the judge, how would you decide each case?

1

Christiansen was injured when she was thrown from a horse she rented from Salusteri's stables. Salusteri refused to pay Christiansen's medical costs. Can Christiansen recover her costs? From whom?

2

Mendez and Travis were caught by the police while trying to steal a television from Carrillo's home. During the theft, Carrillo's house and TV were damaged. Who is liable for the damage to Carrillo's property? In what court would Carrillo seek relief?

WHAT IS A COURT?

A famous legal writer named Blackstone once defined a court as a "place where justice is judicially administered." The term **court** refers to a place, or an assembly, where laws are interpreted and applied. A court is established by government to hear and decide matters brought to it. The official who decides matters brought before the court and guides court decisions is a **judge.** Legal writers often use the terms *court* and *judge* interchangeably.

The role of a court is to enforce legal rights and duties. It does this by determining the facts of a case and then applying the proper legal principles to the case. A case is brought to a civil court by a party who claims to have been injured by another party in a private matter. A case is brought to a criminal court by government, which claims that society has been injured by a stated party. A court hears the facts in a case, determines responsibility for any injuries, and then assigns a suitable penalty or award.

The court system of the United States differs from that of any other nation. We have 51 separate court systems—the federal system and 50 state systems. Each of these functions independently of the others. Federal courts enforce the provisions of the Constitution and laws passed by Congress and federal agencies. State courts enforce state constitution provisions and laws passed by state legislatures.

Jurisdiction of the Courts

PROBLEM

> **1.** Weinberg, a resident of the state of New York, seeks to collect a sum of money from Ong. Ong resides in New Jersey. Weinberg files a lawsuit against Ong in a civil court in New York. Does the New York civil court have jurisdiction in the case?

The **jurisdiction** of a court is its authority to decide certain types of cases. A court's jurisdiction is often limited by the amount of money involved and the subject matter of the suit. It is *always* limited by geographical considerations. Thus, in Problem 1, a civil court in New York has no jurisdiction over a suit against a resident of New Jersey. Weinberg would have to file suit against Ong in a civil court in New Jersey.

A court of **original jurisdiction** is a court that has authority to hear a case for the first time. This court is also called a **trial court.** Courts of **general jurisdiction** are typically permitted to hear a wide range of cases. Courts of **limited jurisdiction** are specialty courts, designed to hear only one particular type of case. These include probate courts, juvenile courts, and traffic courts.

Trial Courts

The trial court, or court of original jurisdiction, is often a court of limited jurisdiction. Examples of trial courts with limited jurisdiction include small claims courts, traffic courts, and tax courts. If the decision of a trial court is not satisfactory to both parties, an **appellate court** may be asked to review the decision.

Appellate Courts

An appellate court, also known as a court of appeals, does not retry cases or hear original **testimony** (oral statements made while under oath). Its only function is to review decisions made by lower courts. Appellate court decisions are based solely on written records (called **transcripts**) of the trial court proceedings. A court of appeals may also ask the parties in a dispute to prepare written arguments (known as **briefs**) or to make oral presentations for the court to consider. These arguments are intended to help the court determine the validity of the lower court's decisions on various points of law.

If an appellate court disagrees with a lower court's decision, it will usually order the lower court to hold a new trial or to enter a new judgment.

Courts of Highest Authority

The highest court of authority in the federal court system is the United States Supreme Court. Each state also has a court of highest authority, usually called a state supreme court. Supreme courts hear appeals from lower court decisions and have a limited amount of original jurisdiction. They hear very few of the cases they are requested to hear, usually allowing lower appellate court decisions to stand. The cases they do hear are those that involve important social issues or set precedents.

THE FEDERAL COURT SYSTEM

The United States Constitution, in Article III, Section 1, makes provision for a system of courts. The Constitution expressly provides that there be a federal Supreme Court and such other, lower courts as Congress may see fit to establish. Acting on this authority, Congress has established United States District Courts and United States Courts of Appeals. It has also established special courts such as the U.S. Court of Claims, the U.S. Tax Court, the U.S. Customs Court, and the U.S. Bankruptcy Court. The structure of the federal court system is depicted in Figure 2.1.

United States District Courts

At the lowest level of the federal court system are the U.S. District Courts. There are 91 of these, each having jurisdiction over a particular geographic

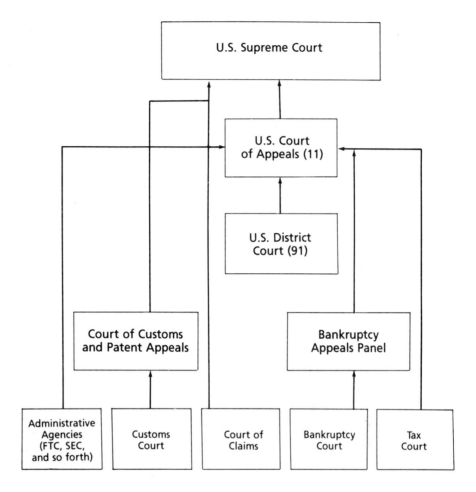

section of the United States or its territories. U.S. District Courts have original jurisdiction, which means that they are the first federal courts to hear cases. In some situations, a U.S. District Court is the *only* court in which a case may be tried. Its subject-matter jurisdiction covers cases involving a fine, penalty, or forfeiture under federal law; admiralty and maritime cases; and cases arising under patent and copyright laws. This court may also hear claims in which the amount in controversy is more than $10,000 and the parties to the suit reside in different states.

EXAMPLE

McDonnell, a resident of Oklahoma, entered into an agreement with Yager, a resident of Nebraska. McDonnell paid Yager $17,500 for some cattle, which Yager was to deliver to Mc-Donnell's ranch. When Yager failed to deliver the cattle, Mc-Donnell brought suit in U.S. District Court.

United States Courts of Appeals

A U.S. Court of Appeals may be found in each of eleven **circuits,** or geographical areas. Most cases reviewed by these courts are on appeal from U.S. District Courts or from certain federal agencies. The Federal Trade Commission, the Securities and Exchange Commission, and the National Labor Relations Board are some of the agencies whose decisions may be appealed to a U.S. Court of Appeals.

United States Supreme Court

There is only one U.S. Supreme Court, located in Washington, D.C. The Supreme Court has both **original** and **appellate jurisdiction.** Its original jurisdiction applies to disputes between states or between a state and the United States and to cases involving foreign ambassadors or other ministers. The Court rarely uses its original jurisdiction, however.

The Supreme Court's appellate jurisdiction extends to appeals from lower federal courts and from state supreme courts. The appellate jurisdiction of the Court is subject to the control of Congress. Traditionally, however, Congress has allowed the Court to limit its own appellate jurisdiction. Every year, the Supreme Court is asked to review many thousands of lower court decisions. It would be impossible for the Court to hear all of those cases. Thus, the Court decides to review only those cases that involve issues of great significance to the public or questions of constitutionality.

EXAMPLE

> The U.S. Supreme Court was asked to review a case involving a dispute between special-interest groups over land use in Texas. The Court refused to hear the case, saying that it wasn't an issue affecting the national welfare.

There are nine U.S. Supreme Court justices (judges). These people are appointed by the President with the consent of the Senate. They serve on the Court for life, and they may be removed only by impeachment.

Special Federal Courts

The special federal courts have very limited jurisdiction in terms of subject matter. The U.S. Court of Claims, for example, hears only cases involving claims against the federal government. The titles of the other special courts reflect their jurisdictions. These special courts appeal to their own special appeals courts (in customs or bankruptcy cases), to the U.S. Court of Appeals, or directly to the U.S. Supreme Court. Figure 2.2 summarizes the jurisdictions of the various federal courts.

Figure 2.2
Jurisdiction of the
Federal Courts

Court	Jurisdiction
U.S. District Court	Original (cases with federal fines, penalties, or forfeitures; disputes between residents of different states, involving more than $10,000; admiralty/maritime cases; patent/copyright cases)
Administrative Agencies	Original (limited to cases specific to the agencies' authority)
Tax Court	Original (limited to federal tax cases only)
Bankruptcy Court	Original (limited to bankruptcy proceedings only)
Bankruptcy Appeals Panel	Appellate (limited to reviews of bankruptcy proceedings)
Court of Appeals	Appellate (hears appeals from district, tax, and bankruptcy courts and from some rulings of administrative agencies)
Customs Court	Original (limited to customs issues only)
Court of Customs and Patent Appeals	Appellate (hears appeals from customs court and patent cases)
Court of Claims	Original and appellate (limited to claims against the federal government)
U.S. Supreme Court	Original and appellate

THE STATE COURT SYSTEM

Each state has its own court system, and those systems vary from state to state. A typical state court system includes four levels of courts, as shown in Figure 2.3. These are the local courts, general trial courts, intermediate courts of appeals, and a state supreme court.

Figure 2.3
A Typical State
Court System

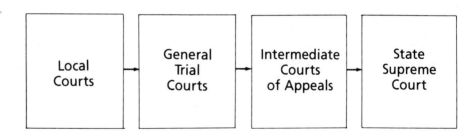

Local Courts

The general structure of the local court system remains fairly consistent from state to state. Local courts usually have very limited subject-matter jurisdiction. Yet these courts handle most of the judicial load for the states' populations.

The most popular civil courts are small claims courts. These courts handle civil claims that are regarded as minor in terms of their dollar amounts. The maximum dollar amount of a claim made in a small claims court varies by state, but it may range from several hundred to several thousand dollars. In these courts there are no juries, and attorneys aren't needed. A judge's ruling is final.

Other local courts are police courts (for minor criminal offenses), traffic courts, and justice's courts. Appeals from local court decisions are generally taken to an intermediate appellate court.

General Trial Courts

State general trial courts have original and general jurisdiction. These courts are variously called circuit courts, superior courts, district courts, courts of common pleas, or municipal courts. Specialized courts of limited subject-matter jurisdiction are also found at this level. These include family courts, juvenile courts, probate courts, and criminal courts. In some states, general trial courts may hear appeals from local court decisions.

Intermediate Courts of Appeals

States with large populations have an intermediate level of appellate courts. Their role is to relieve the burden of the state supreme court. Without appellate courts, the supreme court of a populous state would have to hear a tremendous number of cases. Appeals from state appellate courts are taken to the state supreme court.

State Supreme Courts

The role of a state supreme court is to determine the final outcome of any issue disputed within the state's borders. Unless the matter is of national interest or of interpretation of the United States Constitution, there is no appeal from a state supreme court decision.

OUT-OF-COURT SETTLEMENT The parties involved in a dispute often attempt to avoid the time and expense of a trial. An attempt to reconcile legal differences out of court is made through **mediation** or **arbitration**. A *mediator* is an independent third party who tries to find a fair solution to a dispute. The solution must be one to which both parties will *voluntarily* agree. An *arbitrator* performs the same function as a mediator, but both parties in a dispute *must* accept the decision of an arbitrator. Provision for arbitration in the event of a dispute is often included in the original agreement between the parties.

COURT PROCEDURES

> **2.** Aquine purchased Van de Kamp's automobile after relying on statements made by Van de Kamp. Those statements proved to be false and misleading. As a result, Aquine suffered a financial loss of $3,500. What are her legal rights?

When a dispute cannot be settled out of court, the party who claims to have been injured may apply to the proper court for relief. The legal term for a court action or lawsuit is **litigation.** There are standard procedures for beginning a court action.

The party who brings the suit (or files the action) is known as the **plaintiff.** The party against whom the suit is brought is called the **defendant.** In a criminal action, the state (the government) is the plaintiff, called the **prosecution.** In Problem 2, Aquine may file a civil suit to recover money damages from Van de Kamp. If the false statements made by Van de Kamp amount to criminal fraud, Aquine may enlist the aid of a public official (district attorney) in prosecuting Van de Kamp in a separate criminal action.

The Pleadings

An action is begun by filing a **complaint,** or **declaration,** with the clerk of the proper court. This document states the specific charges being made and briefly outlines the facts supporting the need for a lawsuit. In a civil suit, the defendant is then served with a **summons** (see Figure 2.4). A summons is the process by which a defendant is brought under the control of the court, and it is sometimes simply called **process.** It gives notice to the defendant that an action has been filed. Usually, a summons must be delivered directly to the defendant. Some states, however, permit a summons to be left with a family member of a minimum age. The summons may or may not include a copy of the complaint. If it does not, the defendant can request a copy of the complaint from the court clerk.

The defendant must file a written **answer** to the complaint (make an appearance in the case) within the time stated in the summons. Sometimes the defendant's answer neither admits nor denies the plaintiff's statements. In this event, the defendant leaves the plaintiff with the **burden of proof** (responsibility for establishing guilt) for the trial. In some cases, the plaintiff then must submit a **reply** to the facts stated in the defendant's answer.

Figure 2.4
A Summons

SUMMONS
(CITACION JUDICIAL)

NOTICE TO DEFENDANT: *(Aviso a Acusado)*

FOR COURT USE ONLY
(SOLO PARA USO DE LA CORTE)

ELLA TIMMONS

YOU ARE BEING SUED BY PLAINTIFF:
(A Ud. le está demandando)

ADAM BAINBRIDGE

You have *30 CALENDAR DAYS* after this summons is served on you to file a typewritten response at this court.

A letter or phone call will not protect you; your typewritten response must be in proper legal form if you want the court to hear your case.

If you do not file your response on time, you may lose the case, and your wages, money and property may be taken without further warning from the court.

There are other legal requirements: You may want to call an attorney right away. If you do not know an attorney, you may call an attorney referral service or a legal aid office (listed in the phone book).

Después de que le entreguen esta citación judicial usted tiene un plazo de 30 DIAS CALENDARIOS para presentar una respuesta escrita a máquina en esta corte.

Una carta o una llamada telefónica no le ofrecerá protección; su respuesta escrita a máquina tiene que cumplir con las formalidades legales apropiadas si usted quiere que la corte escuche su caso.

Si usted no presenta su respuesta a tiempo, puede perder el caso, y le pueden quitar su salario, su dinero y otras cosas de su propiedad sin aviso adicional por parte de la corte.

Existen otros requisitos legales. Puede que usted quiera llamar a un abogado inmediatamente. Si no conoce a un abogado, puede llamar a un servicio de referencia de abogados o a una oficina de ayuda legal (vea el directorio telefónico).

The name and address of the court is: *(El nombre y dirección de la corte es)*

CASE NUMBER: *(Número del Caso)*
145876

VENTURA COUNTY SUPERIOR COURT
33873 VISTA DEL RIO
CAMARILLO, CA 93010

The name, address, and telephone number of plaintiff's attorney, or plaintiff without an attorney, is:
(El nombre, la dirección y el número de teléfono del abogado del demandante, o del demandante que no tiene abogado, es)

HIRAM SHARP
50 EAST FLAGLER STREET
CAMARILLO, CA 93010
(805) 693-7103

DATE: 11/14/--   Frank S. Zolin,   Clerk, by Timothy Reilly   , Deputy
(Fecha)   *(Actuario)*   *(Delegado)*

[SEAL]

NOTICE TO THE PERSON SERVED: You are served
1. [X] as an individual defendant.
2. [ ] as the person sued under the fictitious name of *(specify)*:

3. [ ] on behalf of *(specify)*:

under: [ ] CCP 416.10 (corporation)   [ ] CCP 416.60 (minor)
       [ ] CCP 416.20 (defunct corporation)   [ ] CCP 416.70 (conservatee)
       [ ] CCP 416.40 (association or partnership) [ ] CCP 416.90 (individual)
       [ ] other:
4. [ ] by personal delivery on *(date)*:

The complaint, the answer, and the reply are collectively known as **pleadings.** Pleadings serve a twofold purpose: (1) they inform the parties of their claims against each other; and (2) they narrow down the points of dispute (issues) between the parties. Ordinarily, only those disputed points that are issues according to the pleadings will be considered at the trial.

The Trial

After the pleadings have been filed with the court and the issues have been determined, the case is set for trial. If the defendant fails to appear or answer, the plaintiff may obtain a **judgment by default.** This will be allowed if the court is satisfied with the proof of the statements in the complaint.

If the issues relate only to questions of law, the case may be decided by a judge alone. If the issues raise questions of fact, the case may be tried by a judge and a **jury.** A jury is a group of impartial people who are chosen by the attorneys for the parties through a special jury selection process. The role of a jury is to determine questions of fact in a case, under the guidance of a judge. Whether a jury trial is to be held may depend on the nature of the case, the court in which it is filed, or the wishes of the parties involved. When a jury is determined to be necessary, its members are selected and sworn. Then the parties, usually through attorneys, outline the nature of the case and what they expect to prove.

PROBLEM

3. During a business conversation held by Webber, Carnero, and Macklin, Webber made slanderous remarks about Macklin. Macklin served a summons and complaint on Webber and subpoenaed Carnero as a witness. Carnero, however, disregarded the subpoena and refused to testify. Will Carnero be punished legally for not appearing in court?

During a trial, both parties to a lawsuit give testimony to try to prove their claims. They also may include the testimony of witnesses who have knowledge of the facts. To make certain that a witness will attend and testify, a written order called a **subpoena** is served on the witness. A subpoena commands the witness to appear in court at a definite time and place. A witness who ignores a subpoena is subject to penalties for **contempt of court.** In Problem 3, Carnero would be subject to a fine or imprisonment, or both, for disregarding the subpoena served on him.

In addition to the oral testimony of witnesses, the parties may introduce **physical evidence** (proof of facts). Evidence may take the form of written documents, photographs, or various objects.

After all the testimony and evidence have been given, the attorneys for the parties address the court. They sum up their cases by reviewing and analyzing the facts presented at the trial. If the trial is before a jury, the judge then charges (instructs) the jury as to the law that must be applied in the case. The jury retires to a jury room to discuss the facts of the case and to weigh the testimony and evidence offered by both sides. When the jury has reached a decision, it returns to the courtroom. The jury foreman (a juror chosen by fellow jurors) announces the jury's **verdict** (decision).

A judge may set aside a jury verdict if it is contrary to the law and the evidence. A jury verdict that is satisfactory, however, becomes the basis for the court's judgment. If the case is being tried by a judge alone, without benefit of a jury, the judge's decision is a judgment rather than a verdict.

A judgment may provide that a sum of money is due from one party to the other. If the successful party is unable to collect the money, a public official such as a sheriff, marshal, or bailiff may be asked to seize some of the judgment debtor's property to satisfy the debt. This procedure is known as **execution.** It is begun by means of a document called a **writ of execution,** which authorizes the public official to make the seizure. Statutes vary as to which property is exempt from execution. An unsatisfied judgment remains a **lien** (a charge) against the judgment debtor for a certain time period. That period varies from five years to an unlimited number of years, depending on the state in which the judgment was rendered.

CAREERS IN LAW

Lawyer

In order to become a lawyer, a person must acquire a college degree and then complete three years of postgraduate education in law. At the end of those three years, the law student receives a J.D. (Juris Doctorate) degree. This degree, however, does not allow the student to practice law. The student must still pass the bar examination given by the state in which he or she wants to practice. (A lawyer who wants to practice in several states is usually required to take a bar exam in each of those states. States, however, may agree to respect one another's bar exams as their own, thereby eliminating the need for qualified petitioners to take multiple exams.)

By passing a bar exam, the student becomes a member of the state's bar association and is free to practice law. As with medical careers, there are many law specialties from which to choose.

Corporate lawyers are usually specialists in contracts and liabilities. They also advise management on the potential corporate effects of various laws. Some large corporations have several teams of lawyers, with each team providing expert advice on a specific topic. These topics include environmental responsibility, taxes and investments, product liability, contract negotiations, and merger and antitrust issues.

Lawyers also specialize in areas such as criminal law, personal injury law, divorce and family law, probate law, insurance law, and tax law. All of these lawyers spend time in court, although some make more court appearances than others.

Appealing a Court Decision

If one of the parties to a lawsuit disagrees with a court decision, that party may file an appeal with an appellate court. The appellate court examines the record of the proceedings from the lower court to see if there was an error of law. It reviews the pleadings, the testimony, and the judge's charge to the jury. The attorneys for the parties may provide written **briefs** (arguments) and argue orally before the court to help the court make a decision. If the appellate court agrees with the lower court's decision, it affirms (approves) that decision. If it does not agree with the lower court's decision, however, it sets aside or reverses the action of the lower court. The case may then be sent back to the lower court with directions to hold a new trial or to enter a new judgment.

Opinions and Citations

PROBLEM

> **4.** You and a fellow law student were discussing the right of a building contractor to recover the contract price where he had not completely performed the contract. It was suggested that you study the case of *Thomas Haverty Co. v. Jones*, 185 Cal. 285. What is the meaning of this reference?

The judges of an appellate court often give legal reasons for their decisions to affirm or reverse the judgment of a lower court. These legal reasons form the **opinion** of the court. Court decisions or opinions are published in book form by each state and by the federal government. The volumes are known as **reports.** Great numbers of these reports have been published over the years. Thus, it is important that a student of law learn how to use a **citation** to locate desired cases. A citation, as in Problem 4, is a reference to a published court opinion. It consists of the names of the parties to the suit, the number of the volume, the name of the series of volumes or reports, and the page number of the report in which the opinion is printed. Thus, *Thomas Haverty Co. v. Jones*, 185 Cal. 285 refers to a report covering the case of Thomas Haverty Co. **versus** (against) Jones. The report appears in Volume 185 of the official reports of the Supreme Court of the State of California, on page 285.

In addition to supporting cases, authoritative law texts are sometimes cited. These are referred to by the name of the author, the title of the text, and the page number on which the citation is found. For example, a citation to an authority on the subject of sales of personal property might read: *Williston on Contracts*, page 688.

This chapter has given you a basic understanding of the way our court system supports the law. In Chapter 3, you will look at the different kinds of laws established to encourage peaceful coexistence among its citizens.

Chapter 2 Review

"YOU BE THE JUDGE" REVIEW

Look again at the "You Be the Judge" cases given at the beginning of this chapter. Would you decide them differently now, after your study of the chapter?

Correct Decisions

1. Most states would allow Christiansen to recover her medical costs from Salusteri. A local court will determine whether the facts of the case should allow her to collect from Salusteri.
2. Mendez and Travis are liable for the damage to Carrillo's property. Carrillo would be permitted to file a civil complaint against them after any criminal charges had been dealt with. Depending on the dollar amount of the damage, Carrillo would seek relief either in a small claims court or in a general trial court of the state in which he lives.

UNDERSTANDING WHAT YOU HAVE READ

1. What is the function of courts?
2. Distinguish between original and appellate jurisdiction.
3. What is the structure of our federal court system?
4. Which is the only court established by the United States Constitution?
5. What is the structure of a typical state court system?
6. What is the difference between a complaint and a summons?
7. To what does the term *process* refer in a civil suit?
8. What two purposes do pleadings serve?
9. List three types of pleadings commonly used in court actions.
10. Why are citations needed?

BUILDING YOUR LEGAL VOCABULARY

From this list, select the legal term that belongs in the blank in each sentence below. Write your answers on a separate sheet of paper.

answer	citation	opinion
appellate jurisdiction	jurisdiction	plaintiff
arbitration	litigation	versus
burden of proof		

1. The legal reasons given by an appellate court for its decision are stated in a court ⅏⅏⅏⅏⅏ .
2. A defendant's response to a complaint is a/an ⅏⅏⅏⅏⅏ .
3. The ⅏⅏⅏⅏⅏ of a court specifies what types of cases it may hear.
4. The ⅏⅏⅏⅏⅏ for statements made in a complaint lies with the plaintiff.
5. ⅏⅏⅏⅏⅏ is a method of out-of-court settlement in which the parties are bound by a decision of a third party.
6. The party who originates a lawsuit is called the ⅏⅏⅏⅏⅏ .
7. The legal term for court actions is ⅏⅏⅏⅏⅏ .
8. The Latin word meaning *against* is ⅏⅏⅏⅏⅏ .
9. A ⅏⅏⅏⅏⅏ helps to locate a particular court decision.
10. A court that has only ⅏⅏⅏⅏⅏ does not hear original testimony or accept new evidence.

APPLYING LEGAL PRINCIPLES

1. Cahn violated a traffic regulation. In which court in your state would he be tried?
2. Held was arrested by agents of the Federal Bureau of Investigation and charged with the crime of kidnapping. Which court would have jurisdiction of this case?
3. The Chamber of Commerce of a certain state maintains that a minimum-wage law passed by the legislature violates the provisions of the United States Constitution. What route would the appeal of this case follow?
4. Hill is defeated in an action against her in a U.S. District Court. She wishes to appeal the decision of this court to a higher court. To which federal court should she apply?
5. The Miller Corporation disputed an order issued by the Securities and Exchange Commission. The order required the corporation to make certain changes in its prospectus describing a new stock issue. Does the corporation have a legal right to appeal the decision of the SEC? To which court should the appeal be taken if such a legal right exists?

6. Zoza served a summons on Allen in a suit to recover $1,000 he claimed Allen owed him. On the day set for trial, Allen failed to appear in court. He had previously filed an answer, however, denying that he owed any money to Zoza. What are Zoza's legal rights?

7. Westrum is served with a subpoena commanding her to appear as a witness in the case of *Viggiano v. Corsa.* Westrum ignores the subpoena and fails to appear in court. What action may the court take against her?

8. Wall is dissatisfied with the verdict of the jury in a case in which he appeared as a defendant. What legal right is available to Wall?

9. O'Neill commences a lawsuit against Wu by serving a summons on Wu's son. Wu applies to the court named in the summons for a dismissal of the service on the ground that it was improperly made. How should the court decide Wu's application for dismissal?

10. In the trial of a negligence case, the jury brought in a verdict for the injured plaintiff in the amount of $125,000. Judge Wise, before whom the case was tried, feels that the verdict is excessive. What action may the judge take?

11. Atkins was successful in a suit against Riva and received judgment for $5,500. How should Atkins proceed to collect the money?

ANALYZING COURT CASES

1. Casanova sued Paramount-Richards Theatre, Inc., for damages for personal injuries. The injuries occurred when Casanova fell while descending a stairway in the balcony of Paramount's theater. Paramount offered evidence of a lack of similar accidents over five years' operation of the theater, during which the balcony was used by many people. Was this evidence admissible? (*Casanova v. Paramount-Richards Theatre, Inc.*, 16 So. 2d 444)

2. Weber, a passenger, sued Chicago, Rhode Island & Pennsylvania Railway Co. for an injury that occurred as a result of a train derailment. Weber introduced evidence showing that he had been a passenger, that a derailment had occurred, and that he had been injured. The railroad company introduced evidence showing that the wreck had been caused by an insane person who wanted to see the wreck. Who has the burden of proof in this case? (*Weber v. Chicago, R.I. & P. Railway Co.*, 151 N.W. 852)

3. Williams was prosecuted for a robbery committed in Dade County, Florida. Before the trial, Williams was served with a notice to produce an alibi, and the court impaneled a six-person jury. Williams was convicted of the crime but appealed his conviction on the ground that his constitutional rights had been violated. Was his claim legally correct? (*Williams v. Florida*, 90 S. Ct. 1893)

CHAPTER 3

Crimes and Criminal Procedures

Think about these cases.
If you were the judge, how would you decide each case?

1

Carey, under the influence of liquor, drives her automobile in a reckless manner. As a result, she runs down and seriously injures a pedestrian. What action may be taken against Carey?

2

Jimenez, unable to pay his debts, sets fire to his business property in order to collect the insurance money. Who should take action against Jimenez?

WHAT IS A CRIME?

The government, known as "the state," is responsible for preserving law and order and protecting the lives and property of all of its citizens. In order to carry out its responsibilities, the state enacts laws. As mentioned in Chapter 1, criminal laws are the regulations enacted to protect society from the wrongful acts of individuals.

A crime is any wrongful act for which the law prescribes punishment. It is an action that directly or indirectly interferes with—or tends to interfere with—the fundamental rights of the community as a whole. A **tort,** in contrast, is a private wrong, committed against an individual rather than against the community. We will discuss torts in more detail in Chapter 4.

The state specifies the punishment to be imposed on anyone who commits a crime. That punishment may consist of a fine, imprisonment, or both. For certain criminal acts, the punishment may even be death.

People accused of performing criminal acts are prosecuted by a representative of the state, known as the attorney general, or the district attorney. The office of the attorney general or district attorney usually employs many lawyers, each of whom is assigned to cases.

Classification of Crimes

Crimes are often classified by the seriousness of the offense. Using this classification method, there are three basic types of crimes: treason, felonies, and misdemeanors.

Treason

Treason consists of committing an act of war against the United States or of giving aid to an enemy of the United States. Because of its potential for causing harm to all citizens, treason is the most serious crime that can be committed.

Felonies

PROBLEM

> **1.** O'Meara and Wann were caught stealing a fur coat from a fashionable department store. A tag on the coat indicated its price to be $5,000. The thieves were charged with the felony of grand theft. Their defense was that they had committed the crime of shoplifting, which was a misdemeanor. Of what crime were they guilty?

A **felony** is a crime of a serious nature, for which the punishment is death or imprisonment in a state or federal prison for more than one year. The seriousness of a crime and the punishment for it are specified by the state. In Problem 1, O'Meara and Wann's defense is not valid. The $5,000 value of the fur coat increased the seriousness of their crime from the misdemeanor of shoplifting to the felony of grand theft.

Some examples of felonies are kidnapping, murder, arson, rape, robbery, perjury, burglary, embezzlement, bribery, and drug dealing.

Misdemeanors

A **misdemeanor** is a less serious crime than a felony. The penalty for a misdemeanor is usually a fine or a sentence to county or city jail for less than one year, or sometimes both. Speeding, petty theft, shoplifting, and public drunkenness are some examples of misdemeanors.

Some states have created a new class of misdemeanor called an **infraction.** An infraction is a misdemeanor of a less serious nature, such as a parking violation or jaywalking.

Common Crimes

Some crimes—such as larceny, embezzlement, arson, and so on—occur quite often. The punishment for these crimes varies from state to state.

Larceny

PROBLEM

> **2.** Catlin came home and surprised two men who had broken into her apartment and were attempting to steal her jewelry. In their shocked state, the thieves forced Catlin into a closet at gunpoint. Of what crime are the two men guilty?

Larceny is the wrongful taking of someone's personal property with the intention of keeping the property from its rightful owner. Larceny can be classified as either a felony or a misdemeanor, depending on the circumstances of the act and the value of what was taken.

Another common name for larceny is **theft.** Burglary and robbery are two kinds of theft. **Burglary** is breaking into and entering the dwelling of another with intent to commit a crime. **Robbery** is taking away property from the immediate presence or possession of another by means of force or with the threat of harm. The essential difference between burglary and robbery is the threat of personal harm that accompanies a robbery. Thus, the men in Problem 2 are guilty of robbery. If Catlin had not returned home and been forced into her closet, the thieves would have been guilty of burglary.

Receipt or Possession of Stolen Property

A person who believes certain property to be stolen and yet accepts that property with the intention of keeping it from its rightful owner has committed a criminal act. That crime is called **receipt or possession of**

What crime is about to be committed?

stolen property. Courts usually will not accept the excuse that the possessor didn't know the property was stolen. If the possessor can *prove,* however, that the property was acquired in good faith—with the belief that the goods were legitimate—the courts will dismiss the criminal charges.

Embezzlement

Embezzlement is the unlawful taking of money or property by someone who was entrusted to look after the money or goods. Crimes of this nature are often performed by employees who handle money or who have access to a firm's financial records.

Arson

Arson is the willful and malicious setting of a fire. Most states have special statutes applying to the deliberate destruction of a building by fire in order to collect insurance benefits.

Bribery

A person who offers or gives a public official anything of value in order to influence an official action is guilty of the crime of **bribery.** Many states have expanded the concept of bribery to include payments made to athletes to influence the outcome of a game or score, and commercial bribery. **Commercial bribery** is making a gift of substantial value to an agent of a company in order to induce the agent to do business with the giftgiver.

Pai needed the county building inspector's approval of some remodeling work she had done on an apartment building she owned. The work had been done incorrectly, and Pai could not rent the apartments unless she had the inspector's approval. To influence the inspector to approve the defective work, Pai gave him a "gift" of a trip to Hawaii. When prosecuted, Pai was found guilty of bribery.

Extortion

Extortion, or *blackmail,* is the acquisition of money, property, or other benefit from another through threat or the use of force. Kidnapping is a well-known form of extortion.

In 1932, the son of Anne and Charles Lindbergh was kidnapped and a ransom was demanded. Although the ransom was paid to the extortionists, the child was murdered.

Drug-Related Crimes

The use, sale, transportation, and possession of illegal drugs are all considered **drug-related crimes.** Addictive drugs, such as heroin and cocaine, are illegal in all states.

In 1970, the federal government passed the **Controlled Substances Act.** This act created a pattern of fairly similar state laws that made specific drug- and alcohol-related activities illegal. Because many studies indicate that drug abusers are responsible for a large percentage of other criminal acts, drug-related crimes are being dealt with more and more harshly in courts across the country.

Driving While Intoxicated

The operation of a motor vehicle while under the influence of alcohol is the crime of **driving while intoxicated** (known to police as *DWI*). In most states, the concept of intoxication has been expanded to include any form of drug-induced intoxication.

Diaz drove away from a party where she had gotten "high" on marijuana. She hit several parked cars and crashed into a tree. Diaz can be held criminally liable for operating a motor vehicle under the influence of an illegal substance.

Criminal Mischief

One who deliberately causes damage to the property of another is guilty of **criminal mischief** (also known as *vandalism*). This crime can be either a felony or a misdemeanor, depending on the extent of the damage.

Conspiracy

PROBLEM

> **3.** Schoenfeld and Magnin were the only two dealers of a certain type of car in the city. They secretly agreed to increase the prices they charged for the cars they sold. Are they guilty of a crime?

Conspiracy is an agreement between two or more parties to commit a criminal act. The criminal act can be one that is illegal by law, or a legal act that has been made illegal by circumstances. These agreements are typically secret. If discovered, however, they are classified either as felonies or misdemeanors, depending on the circumstances. In Problem 3, Schoenfeld and Magnin are guilty of conspiracy. Their secret arrangement to increase the prices they charged for cars was an illegal price-fixing agreement.

Forgery

Forgery is the changing or creation of a legal or valuable document in order to deceive another person. Forgery is often performed in order to obtain the rights, money, or property of another person. Common instances of forgery include forged signatures on checks and on driver's licenses.

Perjury

Perjury is the act of telling a lie while under oath in a court of law. It is a felony.

EXAMPLE

> Albano was serving as a witness at the robbery trial of his friend Madden. While under oath, Albano stated that he and Madden had been together in another town on the night the robbery took place. Actually, Albano had not even seen Madden on the night of the robbery. Albano's lie is perjury, and he is subject to criminal prosecution for the felony.

CRIMINAL PROCEDURES

Many people are involved in the activities of our criminal justice system. Most of those people are employees (representatives) of government. There are two special groups, however, which play central roles in the enforcement of our criminal justice system. Those groups are law enforcement agencies (both local and federal) and the courts.

The Role of Law Enforcement Agencies

The role of law enforcement agencies is actively to protect society. Officers such as police, sheriffs, marshals, and federal agents are directly involved in the apprehension of criminals and in the investigation of crimes.

The act of taking a suspected criminal into custody is called an **arrest.** Someone who has been arrested has been accused of a crime. People who have been accused of crimes are entitled to **due process of law.** This means that they are due the full protection of the law, including a fair trial to determine guilt or innocence.

The Rights of the Accused

The law has clearly established certain rights to protect people who are accused of crimes. These rights fall into four main categories: (1) rights prior to arrest; (2) rights during and immediately following arrest; (3) rights while in custody; and (4) rights during the trial.

Rights Prior to Arrest. Unless law enforcement officers actually witness a crime in process, they may not search for or seize any evidence without a warrant from a judge. Also, an arrest cannot be made unless the arresting officers have reasonable grounds for believing the accused committed a crime.

Rights During and Immediately Following Arrest. An arrested person has the right to remain silent and must be warned that anything he or she

Jury Duty

Our legal system relies for support on the willingness of citizens to accept responsibility. Cooperating when called for jury duty is an important way in which to help enforce our system of justice.

Jury selection is accomplished in this manner: A list of prospective jurors is drawn up from lists of registered voters, licensed drivers, and property taxpayers. A panel of candidates is then selected at random from the list. Prospective jurors are notified to appear in court, where they are questioned by the judge or by attorneys for both parties. If a potential juror's answers to the questions are acceptable, that person will be placed on the jury. As soon as an acceptable group of jurors has been selected, the jury is sworn.

Remember, if you are called, do your duty!

says could be used against the person in court. (This process is called "Mirandizing." It is named after a Supreme Court decision in a case in which the accused had not been advised of these important rights.) The accused also has the right to have a lawyer present during questioning, the right to make a telephone call, and the right not to be forced into making a confession. If the accused cannot afford to hire an attorney, a **public defender** will be assigned to the case. A public defender is a lawyer provided by the state to defend someone who cannot afford to hire a private attorney.

Rights While in Custody. An accused person in custody has the rights to protection and to reasonable treatment and must be told what criminal charges are being made against him or her. The accused may have a lawyer present during each step of the proceedings. In most instances, the accused has a right to be released on a reasonable **bail** or after pledging to return for trial. (Bail is money or property provided by the accused to obtain temporary release from custody. It serves as a guarantee that the accused will show up for trial.) The accused has a right to a fair preliminary hearing on the evidence and the right to know when and where the trial will take place.

Rights During the Trial. The accused must be given a fair and impartial trial. The elements of a fair and impartial trial are very clearly stated by the law.

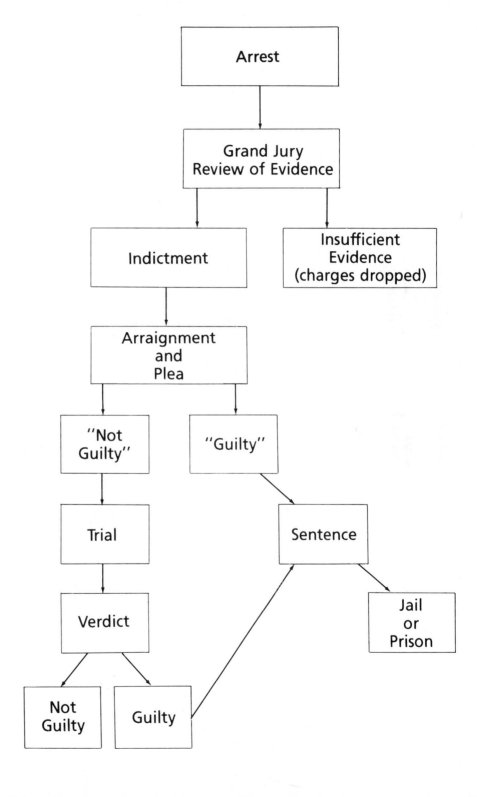

Figure 3.1
The Criminal
Justice System

The trial of the accused must take place as soon as possible after the arrest. It must be public, and it also must be heard before an unbiased judge and an impartial jury. At the trial, the accused must be allowed to appear in person and to have witnesses appear to testify in his or her behalf. The accused must be allowed to question prosecution witnesses and must be offered the opportunity to testify in his or her own behalf. Evidence that was obtained illegally may not be used in the trial.

If a trial results in a verdict of innocence for the accused, he or she may not be tried again on the same charge. If the trial results in a **conviction** (a finding of guilt), the punishment given the accused may not be cruel or unusual. The accused may appeal a conviction to a higher court.

The Role of the Courts

It is the courts' role to protect the rights of the accused until guilt is proven. The typical path of an accused party through the criminal justice system is depicted in Figure 3.1. This illustration shows the steps our courts take to assure that justice is rendered to an accused party.

Most states require the government to prepare a formal accusation of a specific crime before a trial takes place. That charge is prepared by the prosecutor or, in the case of a serious crime, by a **grand jury.** A grand jury is composed of people from the community who decide (1) whether a crime has been committed, and (2) whether there is enough evidence to support the prosecution of the accused. The formal accusation prepared by a grand jury is called an **indictment.** If a grand jury (or a prosecutor) finds that there is insufficient evidence to formally accuse the person who has been arrested for the crime, that person is set free.

After a formal accusation has been made, the accused must be arraigned. An **arraignment** is an appearance before a judge in which the charges are stated to the defendant. At an arraignment, the accused is offered a chance to enter a plea of guilty or not guilty. If a guilty plea is made, the judge examines the facts of the case and sentences the criminal according to the law. If the accused pleads not guilty, the case is scheduled for trial. The schedule used by a court is called a **court docket.**

At the end of the trial, a verdict is handed down from the court. If the defendant is found to be innocent, the charges are dismissed. If he or she is convicted of the crime, a sentence is rendered. A judge is usually responsible for determining an appropriate sentence, although some states allow juries to recommend sentences. After a criminal has been sentenced, he or she is placed into the hands of correctional officials for the time period stated in the sentence.

You now have some familiarity with the criminal justice system of the United States. There is another system of justice used in this country, too. That is the civil justice system, which we will discuss next.

Chapter 3 Review

"YOU BE THE JUDGE" REVIEW

Look again at the "You Be the Judge" cases given at the beginning of this chapter. Would you decide them differently now, after your study of the chapter?

Correct Decisions

1. Carey is subject to criminal prosecution for the crime of driving while intoxicated. The pedestrian whom she injured may also seek tort damages in a civil suit against Carey.

2. The state should prosecute Jimenez for the crime of arson.

UNDERSTANDING WHAT YOU HAVE READ

1. What is the purpose of criminal laws?
2. What are the three basic types of crimes?
3. What is the punishment for felonies?
4. List and describe four types of felonies.
5. Distinguish between robbery and burglary.
6. How is embezzlement different from robbery?
7. Distinguish between bribery and commercial bribery.
8. How has the concept of intoxication been changed by most states?
9. What does a grand jury do?
10. What is the purpose of an arraignment?

BUILDING YOUR LEGAL VOCABULARY

Choose the legal term that will correctly complete each definition below. Write your answers on a separate sheet of paper.

1. A charge made by a grand jury is a/an
   a. verdict.
   b. conspiracy.
   c. indictment.
2. Kidnapping is a form of
   a. burglary.
   b. extortion.
   c. embezzlement.
3. The crime of drunken driving is known by police as
   a. criminal mischief.
   b. DWI.
   c. an infraction.

4. One state representative who prosecutes criminals is the
   a. bailiff.
   b. public defender.
   c. district attorney.
5. The act of falsifying a legal document with intent to deceive is called
   a. forgery.
   b. bribery.
   c. due process of law.

APPLYING LEGAL PRINCIPLES

1. Ahern was arrested for smoking a cigarette on a public bus in disregard of a posted notice forbidding smoking. Will she be charged with having committed a felony or a misdemeanor?
2. Corbus was arrested and charged with possessing stolen property. The grand jury investigating the case learned that the evidence of stolen property had been taken from Corbus's home without a warrant. Should the grand jury insist that the case go to trial?
3. Hua, an accountant, made a mistake on a firm's accounting records. In order to cover the mistake, Hua "rearranged" the figures to look as if the money had been spent elsewhere. Then he transferred the amount of the error to his own account. With what crime should Hua be charged?
4. Alderson's car was damaged in a minor auto accident. While preparing an insurance claim for the damages, she altered the estimate for repairs so that it exceeded the actual cost of repairs. As a result, Alderson received more money for repairs than their actual cost. What crime has she committed?
5. Zybrinski was arrested for driving while intoxicated. He demanded a lawyer but had no money to pay for one. Who will handle the case for the defense?
6. Wayman was arrested for grand theft. Under what process will she be informed of the charges contained in the indictment?

7. Cuthbert was accused of selling drugs to high school students. After her arrest, she expressed fear of retaliation from other prisoners awaiting trial if she were to plead guilty. Can the court offer her protective custody while she awaits trial?

8. During a huge warehouse sale, a stereo salesperson accused a teenager of stealing a tapedeck. A police officer arrested the teenager and took him to the public station without advising him of his rights. Does the teenager have the right to ask that the case be thrown out?

9. Braithwaite sent her mother a letter containing a picture of her new baby. The mother's neighbor intercepted the letter as it was being delivered and told the mother that she must pay $10 to get the letter. Is this a crime? If so, what is the nature of the crime?

10. Dominguez, a citizen of the United States, was caught in the act of sending classified documents to the Soviet embassy in Washington, D.C. What kind of crime is this? How serious is it?

ANALYZING COURT CASES

1. The defendant entered a gas station at night, after it was closed, and removed the cash box from a soft-drink vending machine. He was caught and prosecuted for burglarizing a "warehouse." Should he be convicted? (*Koonce v. Kentucky*, 452 S.W. 2d 822)

2. The defendant was tried and convicted of the crime of forgery. The prosecution proved that he had forged the name "Hillyard Motors" as the drawer of a check. The defendant appealed on the ground that signing a trade or assumed name had no legal effect. Therefore, he claimed that he was not guilty of forgery. Was his claim correct? (*Washington v. Morse*, 234 P. 2d 478)

3. The defendant obtained possession of stolen property. At the time he acquired the goods, he did not know that they were stolen. Later, however, he did learn of this fact. Despite this knowledge, he decided to keep the goods. Subsequently, he was charged with the crime of receiving stolen goods. Defense counsel claimed that because the defendant did not know the goods were stolen at the time he acquired them, he was not guilty. Was the defendant guilty of the crime of receiving stolen goods? (*California v. Scaggs*, 314 P. 2d 793)

CHAPTER 4

Torts and Civil Procedures

YOU BE THE JUDGE

Think about these cases.
If you were the judge, how would you decide each case?

1

While entering a public bus, Anderson accidentally stepped on Wozniak's foot. Wozniak became very angry and struck Anderson, causing the latter painful injuries. What kind of legal offense has Wozniak committed? What are Anderson's rights against Wozniak?

2

Onizuwa sent a suit to a dry cleaner to be cleaned. The cleaning firm scorched the jacket badly, making it unfit for further wear. What are Onizuwa's rights against the dry cleaner?

WHAT IS A TORT?

In our daily activities, we have certain duties to one another that are imposed by law and must be respected. For example, the Constitution guarantees freedom of speech and freedom of the press. That guarantee not only entitles us to those rights but also imposes on us an obligation not to interfere with the same rights of others. If one person causes injury to another by failing to respect that person's rights or security, the wrongdoer has violated the civil law. As noted in Chapter 3, that violation is a tort. When a tort occurs, the injured party has the right to sue the wrongdoer for **damages.** Damages are awarded by civil courts to repay an injured party for any loss suffered as the result of a tort.

A tort may be defined as a civil wrong or violation of a duty imposed by law. It is a private wrong, inflicted on a specific party rather than on society as a whole. An event that is a tort may also be a crime, or an offense against society in general. If this is true, separate legal actions may arise from that event. The state may file a criminal action against the wrongdoer, and the injured party may file a civil (tort) action against the wrongdoer.

EXAMPLE

> Wei was killed by a drunk driver. The state prosecuted the driver in a criminal action for driving while intoxicated. Wei's widow brought suit in civil court for damages for wrongful death.

Elements of a Tort

A tort may be caused by a voluntary or an involuntary personal act. It may be malicous and intentional, or it may be due to negligence or disregard for the rights of others. Thus there are two elements in every tort: (1) a wrongful act or failure to obey the law, and (2) an injury to some person. Note that sometimes an event can occur in which there is injury but no tort.

EXAMPLE

> Henderson's Grocery was forced out of business by DeWhitt's Supermarket when DeWhitt's introduced an aggressive, but fair, advertising and pricing policy. Although Henderson's was injured, no tort occurred because there was no wrongful act.

COMMON TORTS

Most torts fall into three general categories: (1) wrongs affecting another's freedom and safety; (2) wrongs affecting another's possession and ownership of property; and (3) wrongs affecting another's reputation.

LIVING UNDER THE LAW

Ways to Select a Good Attorney

The Kees were having a lot of trouble with their temperamental landlady. She refused to make necessary repairs to the plumbing in the Kees' apartment and threatened to evict them if they complained to the local authorities. The Kees needed a legal advisor, but they didn't know how to choose one.

Sound familiar? There are thousands of people like the Kees. Experts offer the following suggestions for finding a lawyer competent to deal with problems similar to those encountered by the Kees.

1. Begin by asking trusted friends or neighbors for a recommendation.
2. For a simple case, such as that of the Kees family, try a low-cost legal clinic.
3. If your legal difficulty requires a specialist in a complex area— such as tax, trust, or trial work—

consider consulting a certified specialist. A bar association referral might help.
4. Visit the lawyer's office and see how you get along. Expect to pay for this consultation.
5. Check with your state's bar association to find out whether the lawyer has been reported for an ethics violation.
6. Finally, settle in writing the fees and legal costs you will be expected to pay. Will you have to pay a retainer fee in advance? Will there be an hourly charge, or will your attorney get a percentage of your recovery in a damage suit?

You need not be deprived of a legal remedy if you have a just cause. Remember, get a competent lawyer to represent you.

Wrongs Affecting Freedom and Safety

Negligence

Negligence is a failure to use the skill or care necessary to prevent injury to other persons or property.

EXAMPLE

Jennings left her skateboard on a sidewalk in front of her home. A passerby tripped over the skateboard and suffered several broken bones. Jennings is responsible for her tort of negligence.

The tort of negligence is called **malpractice** when it is committed by such people as medical doctors and lawyers. These people are legally obligated to carry out their professional duties with the care and skill commonly employed by capable and reasonably prudent people engaged in the same type of business. Failure to do so constitutes malpractice.

Assault and Battery

> **1.** Myers, a six-year-old boy, threatened to beat up Agar, a high school football player. Is this a tort?

An **assault** is a threat made with the intention of causing bodily injury to another by force or violence. The threat must indicate a real or apparent ability on the part of the person making it to harm another. It must also put the threatened person in reasonable fear of physical injury. Mere words are insufficient to constitute an assault. A **battery** is the wrongful touching of the person or clothing of another as a result of an assault. A battery always includes an assault. An assault and battery may also constitute a crime punishable by the state. In Problem 1, Myers is not physically capable of beating up Agar, so no assault occurred. Thus, no tort has been committed.

False Arrest/Imprisonment

A law enforcement official who detains a person without probable cause for the detention has committed the tort of **false arrest. False imprisonment** is the act of unlawfully detaining a person or forcing a person to remain somewhere against his or her will.

> Rowen was stopped by a store's security guard and escorted to the store manager's office. She was then forced to wait in the manager's office until the police arrived. When Rowen asked why she had been detained, she was told that the store was spot-checking for shoplifters. Because there was no probable cause for her detention, Rowen can sue the store management for the tort of false imprisonment.

Wrongful Death

If a wrongful act results in the death of another, the wrongdoer can be sued for damages for **wrongful death,** even though there was no intent to kill. Many events in which the tort of wrongful death occurs, such as robbery or driving under the influence of alcohol or drugs, are also crimes. In these cases, both criminal and civil actions may be brought against the wrongdoer.

Wrongs Affecting Possession and Ownership of Property

Trespass

The right to possess property without unlawful disturbance from others is granted by law. The infringement on this right is called **trespass.** Usually, this involves the wrongful entry onto, or use of, the land of another.

> Shorofsky dumped trash onto Ventura's land. Ventura sued to recover damages for trespass. Shorofsky lost the suit and was required to pay the cost of having the trash cleaned up.

Nuisance

Nuisance is wrongful interference with another's possession and enjoyment of his or her property, or with the health or comfort of another. The tort of nuisance is usually classified as either *public* or *private.* A private nuisance affects only one party. A public nuisance affects the general public.

> The Keenes played loud music over their stereo between midnight and 2:00 A.M. The Harrises, who lived four houses down from the Keenes, called the police to complain about the Keenes' music. The police went to the Keenes' home and asked them to stop creating a public nuisance.

Fraud

The tort of **fraud** consists of a misrepresentation made with intent to deceive. Fraud most commonly occurs when someone falsely represents a product or service in order to sell to or contract with another person. In our discussion of defective agreements in Chapter 9, we will look at fraud in more detail.

> You purchased a personal computer from a dealer who assured you that it was brand new. After you used the computer, you discovered that it was actually a rebuilt model. The dealer was guilty of fraud. You may file a civil action to recover damages from the dealer.

Conversion

Conversion is the tort version of the crime of larceny. It consists of the wrongful taking and use of the personal property of another. If an innocent party buys stolen goods that are later identified by their rightful owner, the purchaser is guilty of conversion if the goods are not returned to the rightful owner.

Nova bought a television set from Zinn, believing that the set belonged to Zinn. When Osborne saw the TV, however, she claimed it to be hers and proved her claim by identifying a hidden serial number. Nova refused to return the set to Osborne because he had paid Zinn for it. Nova is guilty of conversion.

Invasion of Privacy

2.   Hertzog was refused a bank's credit card because of an illness that had no effect on his ability to pay his debts. The bank information was based on a medical report from Hertzog's doctor, which Hertzog had not authorized. Has the doctor committed a tort?

The tort of **invasion of privacy** requires both the unwelcome or unlawful intrusion into one's private life and the result of causing outrage, mental suffering, or humiliation. This tort causes major concern today because of the wide-ranging use of computers and databases to store and transfer personal information. Many businesses keep records on computer systems to which other firms have access. This networking of information can occasionally cause the release of confidential data to a party who was not originally authorized to have that data. If this causes injury, the injured party may attempt to recover damages either from the unauthorized user or from the owner of the computer system.

An insurance company accidentally made privileged information accessible to a major lending institution. The lender revoked several accounts on the basis of information it obtained from these records. The people whose accounts were affected may sue to recover their losses from the insurance company.

In Problem 2, Hertzog can sue his doctor for damages relating to his inability to obtain credit. The doctor is responsible for invading Hertzog's privacy by revealing medical records without Hertzog's authorization.

Interference with Business Relations and Contracts

One of a person's fundamental rights is to engage in a trade or business. If this right is wrongfully interfered with, the tort of **interference with business relations and contracts** has occurred. The party who interfered is responsible for any damages suffered by the victim as a result of the interference. The wrongdoer may also be the target of an **injunction,** a court order to do or to stop doing something.

The Orchard Nursery and its competitor, the Vintage Association, both planned to bid on a large landscaping contract for the city in which both businesses were located. Just prior to the deadline for bid submission, Orchard discovered that it had been misinformed by Vintage on the terms of the bid proposal. As a result, Orchard's bid was worthless. Orchard sued Vintage for damages and requested that an injunction be issued to keep Vintage from bidding on the contract. Orchard was awarded damages amounting to the loss it had sustained, and Vintage was prohibited by injunction from contracting with the city for one year.

Wrongs Affecting Reputation

Defamation

> **3.** Prouet was engaged in a conversation with several business friends. Speaking of a competitor, Prouet commented, "Jurgensen is a deadbeat and a bankrupt. I wouldn't sell her any goods on credit." Jurgensen was informed of this statement and seeks to hold Prouet responsible for damages for slander. Will she succeed?

A false and intentionally communicated statement that brings hatred, disgrace, ridicule, or contempt on another person is known as **defamation.** If the statement is communicated by word of mouth or gestures, it is called **slander.** If it is communicated in writing, printing, or pictures, it is known as **libel.**

In order to constitute the tort of slander or libel, several elements are required: (1) The false statement must have been communicated or published (a third party must have heard or read the damaging words); (2) the statement must have brought hatred, disgrace, ridicule, or contempt on another; (3) the statement must have been made without justification (without legal excuse or privilege); and (4) damage must have resulted from the statement.

There are three major exceptions to these requirements. First, a statement made by the judge or witnesses during a court proceeding is regarded as privileged and not defamatory. Second, when a statement falsely charges that a person committed a crime, damage usually need not be shown. Third, if a false statement is so belittling as to tend to injure a person in trade or business, actual damage need not be shown. This last exception is illustrated in Problem 3. Jurgensen will succeed in her action against Prouet.

Liability for Torts

> **4.** Formsby stored an old car on jacks in his driveway, although this violated a city ordinance. Betina's daughter was injured when the car fell on her leg. Can Betina recover damages from Formsby, even though the event occurred on Formsby's property?

Liability is another word for responsibility. It is the legal assignment of responsibility for a given act or omission. Liability for a wrongful event includes liability for the natural or foreseeable result of the event. In Problem 4, Formsby could have foreseen that the car might fall and injure someone. Therefore, he is liable to Betina for damages.

Generally, all adults and businesses and most minors are liable for their torts. The law considers minors over the age of fourteen to be fully responsible for their torts. Minors between the ages of seven and fourteen are liable for their torts if it can be clearly shown that they can distinguish between right and wrong. Minors who are under seven years of age usually are not liable for any torts they commit.

Special Forms of Tort Liability

Depending on the situation, tort liability may be of several special types. These include vicarious liability, absolute liability, and strict liability.

Vicarious Liability. Responsibility for the wrongful acts or omissions of another is called **vicarious liability.** Some state statutes hold parents responsible under vicarious liability for certain tort damages caused by their minor children. Employers are also responsible under vicarious liability for torts committed by their employees during the course of their employment. Employers' liabilities will be covered more fully in Chapter 40.

Absolute Liability. A special kind of liability has been established for torts arising from activities which, although dangerous by nature, are

Minors under seven years of age are not usually liable for any torts they commit.

Mona Lisa

desirable and necessary. **Absolute liability** is the responsibility for injuries that result from legal but dangerous actions, in spite of precautionary measures and extreme diligence.

> Rawson Company uses highly flammable gases in its welding business. Rawson employees were using an acetylene tank while working in the Benassis' home. Even though all possible care had been taken, the acetylene tank exploded and damaged the Benassis' house. Under absolute liability, the Benassis may recover damages from Rawson Company.

Strict Liability. Under **strict liability,** manufacturers are responsible for consumer injuries caused by defective products. To win a suit for damages under strict liability, a consumer must prove that the product in question was dangerously faulty. Many auto and toy manufacturers have recalled defective products because of their strict liability to provide safe goods to consumers. The concept of strict liability will be discussed further in Chapter 19.

Common Defenses in Tort Actions

The situations that comprise the subjects of civil lawsuits are often the result of a combination of actions or events. Because of this, certain defenses in tort actions have become common.

In response to charges of tort through negligence, defendants often claim that the plaintiff's negligence contributed to the event in which the injury occurred. This defense is called **contributory negligence.**

> Leone drove through a stop sign at a reckless speed. Snyder had stopped and was carefully proceeding through the intersection when she was broadsided by Leone. Snyder filed a civil action against Leone to recover damages for negligence. As part of her defense, Leone claimed that Snyder's failure to stop when she saw Leone constituted contributory negligence.

In a case where the plaintiff is proved to have contributed to the injury, he or she may be prohibited under the contributory negligence theory from recovering any damages. In some states, however, the law will weigh the relative responsibility for fault in tort actions for negligence. This is called the **comparative negligence** theory. In cases where both the plaintiff and the defendant are proved negligent, damages are awarded according to the amount of negligence each party brought to the event. These are called **comparative damages.**

CIVIL PROCEDURES

To bring a tort action, the party who claims to have been injured files a complaint with the court. The court advises the defendant of the suit by means of a summons, in which the defendant is also instructed to answer the charges. After the defendant has filed an answer, a **pretrial hearing** is scheduled.

While the parties are preparing for trial, the court assists them in **discovery.** This is an exchange of information intended to eliminate surprises from the opposing parties at the trial. During this time, the parties may also ask the judge for rulings on various points of law. These requests are called **motions.** Motions are court documents that help the parties to focus on the issues of the case.

The primary purpose of a pretrial hearing is to finally determine the issues of an action. The judge and the attorneys for both parties attend this hearing, and the parties may attend. Many civil suits are settled at this point in order to avoid the time and expense involved with a trial. If a case is not settled, it goes to trial.

Damages

The amount of money to be awarded to an injured party in a tort action can be difficult to measure. In the case of wrongful death, for example, there is no truly fair way to repay the party who claims to have been injured. The courts must nevertheless determine a monetary award in an attempt to compensate the injured party.

The damages awarded in a tort action usually take one of two forms. The first form is known as **compensatory** (or actual) **damages.** The amount of compensatory damages is the actual dollar amount of the loss suffered. This may consist of medical expenses, repair bills, or other documented examples of loss.

The second common form of money damages is called **punitive** (exemplary) **damages.** These are awarded to an injured party who proves that the wrongdoer *deliberately intended* to cause harm. Punitive damages are, in effect, a fine levied against the wrongdoer as punishment. They are also intended to serve as an example to deter others from committing the same offense.

EXAMPLE

United Chemical Co. was found guilty of illegal dumping of toxic waste in a tort action brought by the city in which the dumping took place. The court ordered United to pay punitive damages of $100,000 to the city. The sizable penalty was intended to punish United and to deter other firms from attempting to dump toxic waste illegally.

A pretrial hearing is often held in an attempt to settle a civil suit before it goes to trial.

As mentioned earlier, comparative damages are sometimes awarded in tort actions for negligence. Damages awarded in tort cases involving contracts are discussed further in Chapter 16.

In this unit you have seen how our society protects itself by means of laws and a system for enforcing those laws. Unit 2 will introduce you to contracts—the foundation of business law—and show you how our system of justice respects and enforces agreements made between citizens.

Chapter 4 Review

"YOU BE THE JUDGE" REVIEW

Look again at the "You Be the Judge" cases given at the beginning of this chapter. Would you decide them differently now, after your study of the chapter?

Correct Decisions

1. Wozniak has committed the tort of assault and battery. Anderson may attempt to recover damages from Wozniak in a civil court action.

2. Onizuwa may file a tort action against the dry cleaner to recover damages for the destroyed jacket. The suit would probably be appropriate for a small claims court.

UNDERSTANDING WHAT YOU HAVE READ

1. How is a tort different from a crime?
2. What are the two elements of every tort?
3. Who is responsible for torts?
4. Distinguish between assault and battery.
5. Describe a common instance of the tort of negligence.
6. How does strict liability differ from absolute liability?
7. Describe the two forms of defamation.
8. Name and describe two common defenses to tort actions for negligence.
9. Under what circumstances does the tort of fraud most commonly occur?
10. Why is discovery important?

BUILDING YOUR LEGAL VOCABULARY

From this list, select the legal term that belongs in the blank in each sentence below. Write your answers on a separate sheet of paper.

battery	injunction	punitive damages
comparative negligence	invasion of privacy	trespass
conversion	pretrial hearing	vicarious liability
false arrest		

1. The tort of ▓▓▓▓▓ is of special concern today because of the wide-ranging use of computers for storage and transfer of personal information.
2. The tort of ▓▓▓▓▓ is the civil equivalent of the crime of larceny.
3. Unlawful disturbance of another's possession of property is called ▓▓▓▓▓.
4. There can be no ▓▓▓▓▓ without assault.
5. A ▓▓▓▓▓ is designed to clarify the issues in a case and may help to settle the case without trial.
6. Under the principle of ▓▓▓▓▓, courts weigh the relative responsibility of the parties in negligence actions.
7. An ▓▓▓▓▓ is a court order to do or to stop doing something.
8. A police officer who detains a person without probable cause may be guilty of the tort of ▓▓▓▓▓.
9. In some states, employers are responsible for the torts of their employees under the principle of ▓▓▓▓▓.
10. Damages designed to make an example of or to punish a wrongdoer for intentional torts are called ▓▓▓▓▓.

APPLYING LEGAL PRINCIPLES

1. Peterson placed her furniture and household goods in storage for several months. After paying the storage charges, Peterson requested that her personal property be delivered to her. The storage company, however, wrongfully refused to do so. What are Peterson's rights?
2. During an argument over politics, Hook angrily shoved Rankow. Rankow stumbled and fell, suffering painful injuries. What are Rankow's rights?
3. While driving her car, Barrero negligently injured a pedestrian who was lawfully crossing a street. What are the pedestrian's rights?
4. "Wilks is a shyster lawyer," said Bergstrom to several people engaged in a conversation with him. Wilks learned of this statement and brought suit against Bergstrom for slander. Will he succeed?
5. Without obtaining Asher's permission, Ojeda shot and killed a deer on Asher's estate. Is Ojeda guilty of any tort? Discuss the reason for your answer.

6. Wilkinson burned a large heap of trash in his backyard, causing a pall of smoke to hang over the crowded neighborhood. His neighbors complained that Wilkinson's trash burning constituted a nuisance. Were they legally correct?

7. Rheinauer's twelve-year-old daughter rode her bicycle over the flower garden of a neighbor. The neighbor sued Rheinauer for damages. In a state in which parents may be responsible for their minor children's torts, what kind of liability does Rheinauer have?

8. If the daughter in Problem 7 were 15 years old, who would be liable for her tort?

9. As the result of an auto accident with Patel, Winder incurred a total of $6,000 in actual expenses. She filed a civil action against Patel in an attempt to recover these expenses. Under the principle of comparative negligence, the court found Winder to be partly at fault for the accident. If her liability was determined to be 25 percent of the total liability in the case, what amount of damages would Winder be awarded from Patel? What are these damages called?

10. Stone filed a tort action against Novotny, claiming damages for negligence. Novotny ignored the court summons to answer Stone's complaint and failed to appear in court. What kind of judgment might Stone receive? Under what circumstances might the court award that judgment?

ANALYZING COURT CASES

1. Gallick, an employee of the Baltimore and Ohio Railroad, sued the railroad for negligence. Gallick claimed that the railroad had allowed a stagnant pool of water, which attracted vermin and insects, to remain on its property. While working near the pool, Gallick was bitten by an insect. When the bite became infected, Gallick lost both of his legs. The railroad claimed that the injury was unforeseeable and that there was no negligence on its part. For whom was judgment rendered? (*Gallick v. Baltimore and Ohio Railroad Co.*, 372 U.S. 108)

2. Durgin Snow Publishing Co. published an article in which Powers was described as a "classic example of typical Yankee thrift." In support of this statement, the article related how Powers—at the age of 35—was busily engaged in making his own funeral casket and planning to dig a hole in which to place it. Powers brought suit against the publishing company, claiming that the statements were libelous. In its defense, the publishing company claimed that the article was written in jest. Was the defense good? (*Powers v. Durgin Snow Publishing Co.*, 144 A. 2d 194)

3. A patient decided to submit to an operation on her right ear after consulting with her family doctor and with a skilled surgeon. The surgeon administered an anesthetic and then examined both of the patient's ears. The examination indicated that the left ear was more seriously diseased than the right. After consulting with the family doctor, the surgeon operated on the patient's left ear. The operation was skillfully performed. The right ear was not operated on. The patient sued the surgeon for assault and battery. Should the surgeon be liable? (*Mohr v. Williams*, 95 Minn. 261, 104 N.W. 12)

UNIT 2

MAKING CONTRACTS

CHAPTERS

LEARNING OBJECTIVES

After you have studied this unit, you should be able to:

- Identify various types of contracts entered into by parties.

- Distinguish between a valid offer resulting in a contract and mere preliminary negotiations or invitations to do business.

- List several ways in which an offer may be ended before acceptance.

- State whether an agreement is based on the genuine consent of the parties.

- Identify people who have limited capacity or total incapacity to enter into binding contracts.

- Identify situations in which minors may contract.

- Analyze a given fact situation and identify the type of illegality and its effect on the agreement.

- State whether a given agreement is based on a valuable consideration.

- Determine whether a given contract must be oral or written in order to be enforceable.

- Describe the rights acquired and the duties assumed by a third party to whom a contract has been assigned.

- Identify the methods by which a contract is discharged or terminated.

- Choose an appropriate legal remedy for use by a party injured by a breach of contract.

CHAPTER 5

Nature and Classification of Contracts

YOU BE THE JUDGE

Think about these cases.
If you were the judge, how would you decide each case?

1

Dunn promised to lend his motorcycle to his friend Garcia. Later, Dunn changed his mind and refused to let Garcia have the motorcycle. Can Garcia force Dunn to lend him the motorcycle?

2

Bentley found a wallet on the sidewalk as she returned home from a class. The wallet contained $100 in cash and several credit cards. Is Bentley obligated to return the wallet to its rightful owner?

WHAT IS A CONTRACT?

We must rely on one another for basic necessities such as food, clothing, housing, and medical care. But how can we be sure that others will supply the things we need when we need them?

Long ago, people discovered a very simple means of doing this. They exchanged *promises.* One person would promise to give something of value in exchange for a promise to receive something of value from another person. The first person needed something that the second person owned. These exchanges of promises came to be known as *agreements.* Gradually, they became so important in the lives of the people that the law began to recognize and enforce them. For example, if a party to an agreement wrongfully failed to keep a promise, a court could compel that person to do so. The court could also require a wrongdoer to repay any money loss the injured party could prove in court.

As society became more complex, people made many different kinds of agreements. The law found it impossible to enforce all of them. To solve this problem, limits were placed on the kinds of agreements that would be enforceable by law. The Greeks, for example, adopted the rule that only agreements sworn to by the parties were legally enforceable. In other ancient societies a special ritual or a written agreement was needed. Today, our courts usually enforce *only those agreements relating to a business transaction and considered useful to society as a whole.* The courts say that these agreements create legal obligations, which they will enforce. The name given to a promise or agreement that creates legal obligations enforceable at law is **contract.**

How Contracts Are Made

PROBLEM

> **1.** Powell read a newspaper ad offering ski boots at half-price at a local sporting goods store. She went to the store and bought a pair of the half-price boots. Did Powell enter into a legal agreement?

Every business activity involves a contract. If you buy a VCR, hire a mechanic to service your car, or leave your watch at a jeweler's for repairs, you have entered into a contract. These contracts are just as binding as contracts to rent an apartment, sell a home, or buy raw materials for manufacture into finished goods. In Problem 1, Powell has entered into a legally binding sales contract with the sporting goods store.

There can never be fewer than two parties to a contract. There may, however, be more than one person on each side. Contracts may be made during face-to-face conversations, over the telephone, or by an exchange of letters or telegrams.

In most cases, a contract made orally or through actions is just as binding as one made in writing. However, you will learn later that some contracts *must* be made in writing in order to be enforceable. Examples of these include agreements for the sale of land or real property. Formal written contracts, such as leases and deeds, are often prepared by lawyers.

Social Agreements

In law, the term *agreement* is a broader term than *contract.* Agreements of a nonbusiness nature are not particularly important to society in general. Therefore, they are not legally enforceable. This type of agreement is known as a **social agreement.**

> Whelan invited Jung to a party. Jung promised to go but failed to do so. There was no legal obligation on Jung's part to go to the party. It was a mere social agreement, with which the law is not concerned.

Illegal Agreements

The term *agreement* may also include a type that is definitely harmful to society. This type of agreement is known as an **illegal agreement.** Examples include an agreement to commit a crime or an agreement to violate a statute forbidding gambling. Illegal agreements are not recognized by the law. Therefore, they are not enforceable.

Elements of an Enforceable Contract

You have just seen that our courts will refuse to recognize social and illegal agreements. The courts also will not enforce a contract that lacks certain elements or fails to meet certain requirements. There are four essential elements in an enforceable contract, as shown in Figure 5.1. Those elements are (1) mutual assent, (2) consideration, (3) competent parties, and (4) legal purpose.

These four elements are required in order to enforce all *simple* contracts. A fifth element—the requirement that a contract be in written form—applies to certain types of contracts. We will study those contracts in Chapter 13.

Mutual Assent

The minds of the parties to a contract must "meet." This meeting of the minds is called **mutual assent** (agreement). Suppose I offered you a blank videotape for $1, and you quickly replied, "I'll take it!" In this instance, our minds have met and a contract between us has been formed. The law will enforce this contract if necessary. We will learn more about mutual assent in Chapters 6–9.

Figure 5.1
Elements of an
Enforceable
Contract

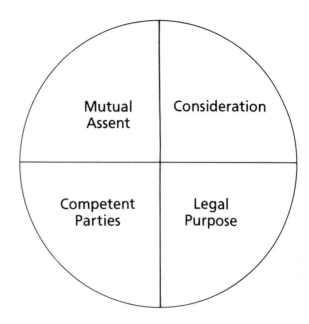

Consideration

Both parties to an agreement must give **consideration** (something of value) in order for the contract to be enforceable. The law looks with disfavor on an exchange of promises in which one party gets "something for nothing." If your uncle, for example, promises you a new car for your high school graduation and then fails to give it to you, there is nothing you can do about it legally. You did not give your uncle something of value (consideration) in exchange for his promise. In Chapter 10, we will discuss consideration in more detail.

Competent Parties

A person who is capable of entering into a contractual agreement is called a **competent party.** The law does not automatically recognize everyone as a competent party. For example, most states do not recognize minors as being competent to enter into contracts. State statutes on the subject of contractual age vary. In many states, the contractual age is 18; in other states, the parties must be 21 years of age in order to enter into a contract. There are other people, such as individuals known to be insane, who sometimes are even less competent than minors. We will talk further about the competence of parties to a contract in Chapter 11.

Legal Purpose

You have already learned that an agreement considered harmful to society is not enforceable. In other words, an enforceable contract must have a **legal purpose.** There are so many examples of illegal agreements that we shall postpone discussing them until Chapter 12.

Should You Buy A Service Contract?

When you buy a car, an appliance, or some electronic equipment, you're likely to get a "sales pitch" to buy a service contract. You are told that this contract will cover repairs if the product breaks down in the first year or so after your purchase. "Why take a chance?" the salesperson might say. "An extended-service contract will protect you and give you peace of mind at a cost of just pennies a day!"

Today, service contracts are sold on everything from automobiles to cameras. Increasing numbers of manufacturers, retailers, and independent service-contract firms have entered the business. Why? You guessed it: There's a large profit to be made from the sale of service contracts. One expert estimates that the service contract is one of the most profitable "options" that dealers sell. Actually, studies have shown that buyers are better off if they put money aside and pay cash for service calls.

If you decide to buy a service contract, study the document before you sign. Ask questions if you don't understand the terms. Here are a few questions you should ask.

1. What does the service contract cover that isn't already covered by the warranty? Compare the two. Is the additional coverage worth the extra expense?
2. How reliable is the company that backs the contract? Does it have sufficient reserves to cover claims?
3. Will there be costs other than the cost of the contract? What additional expenses, deductibles, or other exclusions are mentioned in the contract?
4. Can the contract be canceled? If you return the product, can you get your money back?
5. Where can you get service? Must you take the product back to the dealer from whom you bought it?

You should use good judgment in deciding whether to buy a service contract. Don't be rushed into signing. Remember, most people don't get back more than they put into anything.

CLASSIFICA-TION OF CONTRACTS   Contracts may be divided into five different classes or groups. There are (1) formal and simple contracts, (2) express and implied contracts, (3) executed and executory contracts, (4) bilateral and unilateral contracts, and (5) valid, void, voidable, and unenforceable contracts.

Formal and Simple Contracts

A **formal contract** is one that is in writing and under seal. A deed is one example of such a contract. Originally, a seal was an impression on wax that served as a person's signature. A seal was required under common law. Today, however, the courts recognize various signs or marks that may serve as a seal. For example, the letters *L.S.* (*locus sigilli,* or "place of the seal") may serve as a seal when they follow the name of a person or a corporation. In recent years, the legal effect of the seal has been reduced by statutes, court decisions, and the Uniform Commercial Code.

A contract not under seal is called a **simple** (informal) **contract.** It may be oral or written.

Express and Implied Contracts

A simple contract created by oral or written statements of the intentions of the parties is known as an **express contract.** As a general rule, most contracts are made by express (direct, specific) agreement.

An **implied contract** is one in which the intentions of the parties may be judged from their acts rather than from written or spoken words.

EXAMPLE

> Keller mowed King's lawn without having been asked by King to do so. King watched Keller do the work and did not try to stop him. An implied contract arose between the parties to pay Keller a reasonable sum for the work he performed.

Quasi Contracts

There is another form of an implied contract that, strictly speaking, is not a contract at all. This type of agreement is called a **quasi contract.** A true contract is intentionally entered into by the parties. A quasi contract, in contrast, is created by law to render justice to an innocent party. It resembles a true contract because it imposes a legal obligation on a party who is required to perform it.

EXAMPLE

> An automatic teller machine (ATM) was installed outside the First Federal Savings and Loan Bank. Jenkowski, a depositor, attempted to use the machine to withdraw $100. Instead, the machine gave her $1,000. The court said that Jenkowski had been "unjustly enriched" and, under quasi contract, must return $900 to the bank.

Executed and Executory Contracts

An **executed contract** is one whose terms have been completely carried out by the parties. For example, Huth sold some lumber to Jackson. Huth delivered the lumber and Jackson paid for it. The contract was executed.

An **executory contract** is one in which some act remains to be done on the part of one or both parties. Using the example given for an executed contract, assume that Huth delivered the lumber but Jackson did not pay for it. In this case, the contract would be considered executed on Huth's part and executory on Jackson's part.

Bilateral and Unilateral Contracts

A **bilateral contract** arises through an exchange of mutual promises. This is the usual type of contract. A bilateral contract is formed as soon as promises are exchanged between the parties.

Peters promised to sell a used truck to Manning for $2,000. Manning promised to pay Peters $2,000 for the truck. A bilateral contract was formed.

While a bilateral contract involves an exchange of promises, a **unilateral contract** arises by exchanging a promise for an act or an act for a promise.

Hull said to Barnes, "I'll give you $25 if you will remove the snow from my driveway." By *completing* the removal of the snow, Barnes has created a unilateral contract.

Valid, Void, Voidable, and Unenforceable Contracts

A contract that contains all the essential elements noted earlier is said to be a **valid contract.** This type of agreement is enforceable in a court of law. If a written contract is not required, omission of any *one* of the essential elements makes the agreement a **void agreement.** A void agreement has no legal effect and is not recognized by the law. Assume, however, that the law requires an agreement to be written, but it is made orally or through actions. An agreement such as this is legally regarded as an **unenforceable contract.** If either party raises an objection to it, the contract will not be enforced by the courts.

As noted earlier, an agreement made with a party who is not competent to enter into certain types of contracts is a **voidable contract.** It may be avoided at the option of the incompetent party. An agreement may also be avoided by a party who has been defrauded, or by one who was forced to sign an agreement against his or her will. "Voidable" means that one of the parties to a contract may choose to carry out the terms of the contract, or may choose not to do so (avoid the contract).

Wells purchased Janeiro's home after Janeiro represented that it was "in good condition and free of termites." Soon after moving in, Wells found that termites had weakened several wooden beams. The contract is voidable on Wells' part because of Janeiro's fraud.

In this chapter you have learned what a contract is and the kinds of contracts the law enforces. In Chapter 6 we will discuss the nature of a legally enforceable offer to contract.

Chapter 5 Review

"YOU BE THE JUDGE" REVIEW

Look again at the "You Be the Judge" cases given at the beginning of this chapter. Would you decide them differently now, after your study of the chapter?

Correct Decisions

1. No. A promise that is not based on a consideration is not legally binding.
2. Yes. A quasi contract arose when Bentley picked up the wallet. She is obligated to return the wallet to its rightful owner, if possible.

UNDERSTANDING WHAT YOU HAVE READ

1. Why is a study of business law important to you as a citizen and consumer?
2. In the past week, you engaged in a number of activities that involved exchanging promises with others. Make a list of the most important of those activities. Which of these activities do you believe to be business agreements or contracts? Which activities are merely social agreements?
3. Without looking at the book, define the term *contract.* Then compare your definition with the one given in this chapter.
4. Give several common examples of illegal agreements. Why are they regarded as illegal?
5. What are the essential elements of an enforceable contract? Explain one of these essentials.
6. Must all contracts be made in writing? Give reasons for your answer.
7. What is meant by the term *quasi contract?* Give an example of a quasi contract from your own personal experience.
8. Explain each of these classes or groups of contracts:
   a. formal and simple contracts
   b. express and implied contracts
   c. executed and executory contracts
   d. bilateral and unilateral contracts
   e. valid, void, voidable, and unenforceable contracts

BUILDING YOUR LEGAL VOCABULARY

Match each of these legal terms with its correct definition from the list that follows. Write your answers on a separate sheet of paper.

consideration   express contract   quasi contract
contract   formal contract   unenforceable contract
executed contract mutual assent   voidable contract
executory contract

1. a contract in which something remains to be done
2. a contract that the law will not enforce
3. a price bargained for and paid for a promise
4. a meeting of the minds
5. a contract in which the parties have made oral or written statements of their intentions
6. a binding agreement creating legal obligations
7. a contract that may be avoided by one or more parties
8. a contract under seal
9. a contract that has been completely performed
10. a contract implied in law

APPLYING LEGAL PRINCIPLES

1. Classify each of these agreements as contract, social agreement, illegal agreement, or quasi contract. State the legal reason for your classification in each case.
   a. Bailey purchases a new washing machine for $389.
   b. Chang hires a taxi to take him to a friend's home.
   c. Abeel bets Condon $10 that the Chicago Bears will defeat the College All-Stars in a preseason football game.
   d. Ames finds a $50 bill in a book belonging to Weiss.
   e. Washington borrows a book on auto mechanics from a public library.
   f. Parks is treated by a local physician who is not licensed to practice in the state.
   g. Cole leaves a stereo receiver at Hi-Tek Electronics for repair.
   h. Truong rents an apartment at 1700 Park Boulevard, Utica, New York.
   i. Warren checks a suitcase into the check room of the Terminal Bus Company.
   j. After passing a physical exam, Rizzo obtains a life insurance policy from Lenox Insurance Company.

k. Milton, an important witness in a criminal trial, is offered $500 not to testify. She agrees and does not testify.

l. Swedberg and Thurman agree to go fishing.

m. Arnold sells her summer bungalow to Shay for $59,500.

n. Lewis invites Makris to his home to play cards. Makris accepts the invitation.

o. You mistakenly give a grocery clerk a $20 bill to pay for some goods, thinking it is a $10 bill.

p. Gomez promises to pay Johnston $1,000 if Johnston will paint Gomez's house.

2. Daum orally offered to pay an auto mechanic $45 for testing a used car Daum was about to buy from a dealer. The mechanic agreed and tested the car. Daum paid him $45 in cash for his services. Was the agreement between the parties (a) formal or informal; (b) express or implied; (c) executed or executory; (d) bilateral or unilateral; (e) valid, void, voidable, or unenforceable?

3. Specify which essential element of a contract is missing in each of these situations:

a. Erdman promised to lend her portable stereo to Braun. Erdman later changes her mind and refuses to let Braun have the stereo.

b. Baxter, a shopowner, promises to pay Mellon, a police officer, $40 if he will "keep a sharp lookout for burglars" while he is on duty. Mellon agrees to do so.

c. Ramos wrote a letter to a camping supplies dealer asking about the price of a four-person tent. The company replies by sending Ramos the tent.

d. Jensen, a person known to be insane, agrees to purchase a computer printer for $900 from McGrath.

ANALYZING COURT CASES

1. Hertz, a former tenant of Ficus, brought an action in quasi contract against Ficus. The action was an attempt to recover some money Hertz spent to remodel a restaurant lounge owned by Ficus. The remodeling expenses were made while a lease contract was being negotiated and with the full knowledge and consent of Ficus. Later, Hertz was evicted from the premises for failure to pay rent. Should Hertz recover? (*Hertz v. Ficus*, 567 P. 2d 1)

2. School District sent a teaching contract to the plaintiff, enclosing a copy of the school calendar for the year. The plaintiff and other teachers brought an action against School District to prevent the district from holding classes on three dates noted in the calendar as holidays. The district claimed that the calendar was not part of the contract and could be changed. Who should have judgment? (*Adamick v. Ferguson-Florissant School District*, 483 S.W. 2d 548)

3. Martha Parker raised Louis Twiford as a foster son from the time he was very young. He lived with her until he was married and moved to his own house. During the next few years, Parker became very ill and Twiford took care of her. After her death, Twiford made a claim against Waterfield, Parker's executor, for the reasonable value of his services. Was he entitled to recover? (*Twiford v. Waterfield*, 83 S.E. 2d 548)

The Offer

Think about these cases.
If you were the judge, how would you decide each case?

1

O'Toole wrote to Correa as follows: "Will you sell your motorboat? If so, please state your lowest cash price." Correa replied, "Lowest cash price is $25,000." Was Correa's reply an offer?

2

In the *Morning Herald,* Arnold advertised a reward of $100 for the return of his lost briefcase. Pinson read the ad and began to look for the briefcase. Was an offer communicated to Pinson?

WHAT IS AN OFFER?

In Chapter 5 we learned that the law will not enforce business agreements unless they contain certain essentials. Mutual assent (meeting of the minds) was one of those essentials. To indicate mutual assent, one party, known as the **offeror,** must make an **offer** (a proposal) to another party, known as the **offeree.**

> **1.** Pearlman phoned Arthur and asked whether Arthur wanted to sell his car. Arthur replied, "I might sell it if I could get $4,000 for it." Pearlman replied, "I'll give you $4,000 for the car." Did a contract arise between the parties?

The proposal or offer made by the offeror is a promise that something shall be done or happen, or shall not be done or happen, if the offeree complies with the conditions stated in the offer. If the offeree agrees to the proposal exactly as it is made, an acceptance takes place. When this happens, a contract arises between the parties.

In Problem 1, Arthur was merely replying to an inquiry when he stated that he might sell the car if he could get $4,000 for it. His reply was not a promise or offer to sell the car to Pearlman. When Pearlman said that she was willing to pay $4,000, she was not accepting an offer. In fact, she was making an offer to purchase the car from Arthur. Since Arthur did not reply, no meeting of the minds took place. Thus, there was no mutual assent.

> **2.** Assume in Problem 1 that Arthur said, "I'll sell you my car for $4,000," and Pearlman replied, "I'll give you $4,000 for it." Would a contract arise between the parties?

Arthur's statement in Problem 2 constituted a definite offer, and Pearlman's reply indicated a willingness to comply with the terms of the offer. The minds of the parties met, and a contract was created.

REQUIRE-MENTS OF A VALID OFFER

Not every proposal made by an offeror is legally regarded as an offer. As a result of centuries of experience, the courts now apply three tests to an offer to determine if it is valid. The following are the three requirements of a valid offer: (1) it must be intended by the offeror; (2) it must be definite; and (3) it must be communicated to the offeree.

LIVING UNDER THE LAW

When Do You Need a Lawyer?

It is much easier to prevent trouble than to get out of trouble once you're in it. Most people have a family doctor, dentist, grocer, and so forth. But those same people see little need for a family lawyer. A skilled family lawyer, however, could come in handy if you knew when to use his or her services.

You should always consult a lawyer when you are ready to write a will, especially one with a trust provision. Having a lawyer draw up your will may prevent family squabbles and court actions.

Has your status changed in any way? You may need the help of an attorney due to changes that occur in your life. These changes include marriage, the birth of children, the purchase of a home, a divorce, or a death in the family.

You may need a lawyer when you enter into contracts. Promises—whether spoken, written, or implied—are binding if they are supported by a valuable consideration. A lawyer can help to make sure that you don't offer or accept such promises without knowing what you are getting into.

Are you expecting to buy or sell real or personal property? A lawyer can look for flaws in the papers *before* you part with money or sign anything involving big money or long-term debts.

Most people wait for trouble to strike before seeing a lawyer. Remember, however, that an ounce of prevention is worth a pound of cure.

Offer Intended by the Offeror

> **3.**   Gray says to Unaka, "I hope to sell my typewriter for $300." Does Gray's statement constitute an offer?

Gray's proposal in this problem is not an offer that Unaka may accept. Gray is only expressing a wish or desire to do something in the future. It is clear that she does not wish to assume a legal obligation to Unaka at the time of making the statement. The courts judge the intention of the offeror from what is said and done, not from what the offeror actually means to say or do. If this weren't so, a claim could always be made that the offeror's public statement and private meaning were not the same and that no binding contract, therefore, existed.

If an offeror is not serious or is emotionally upset when making a proposal, it is evident that there is no intention that the statement be binding.

> Perez jokingly offers LaBonte a $10 bill in exchange for a quarter. LaBonte, knowing that Perez is not serious, says, "I accept." Since LaBonte knew that Perez was just joking and that no serious offer was actually intended, Perez's proposal does not constitute an offer.

It is, however, unsafe for an offeror to make offers jokingly. The offeree may believe them to be intended as offers, and the courts may agree with this view.

Advertisements

> **4.** A department store placed this ad in a local newspaper: "SPECIAL SALE—TOMORROW ONLY! MEN'S ATHLETIC SHOES $28, REDUCED FROM $40." Is this advertisement an offer?

Familiar examples of statements made by offerors and not intended as offers are found in newspaper ads (as in Problem 4). These offers also may be found in announcements such as circulars, form letters, and catalogs. They are merely invitations to the people reading them to make offers for the advertised articles. Buyers often fail to understand the practical reason for this rule, but advertisers can't be expected to sell to everyone who reads their advertising material. As a matter of good business practice, however, no reputable business firm would refuse to sell goods at advertised prices unless the goods were impossible to supply. This might occur if the stock on hand had been sold out. Business people realize that to disappoint customers is to cause a loss of goodwill—something they are constantly trying to build up.

A recognized exception to the rule that advertisements are not offers is a **general offer of reward.** This offer is made to the general public. It is actually addressed to the first person who, by performing the act required with knowledge of the offer of reward, creates an agreement.

A general offer of reward

EXAMPLE

Hoyle advertised in *The New York Times* that she would pay $100 to anyone who found and returned her lost dog. Jeffers read the ad, began to search for the dog, found it, and returned it to Hoyle. An agreement was created between Hoyle and Jeffers when Jeffers returned the dog.

Auctions

PROBLEM

5. At an auction sale of jewelry and silverware, the first item put up for sale was an antique ruby pendant. Was this an offer made by the auctioneer?

In presenting goods for sale to the highest bidder, an auctioneer is not making an offer. The presentation is for the purpose of inviting offers from individuals in the audience. Similarly, if a city or state advertises for bids on the construction of a public improvement, it is not making an offer. It is asking contractors to submit offers stating the lowest price at which they will agree to do the work.

Definite Offer

> **6.** Denton says to Fenn, "I'll sell you a camera." Denton owns three different types of cameras at various prices. Has an offer been made?

If an offer is not definite (clear and complete), the courts say that the minds of the parties cannot meet to form an agreement. In Problem 6, Denton has not made it legally possible for Fenn to accept. He has failed to specify a particular camera at a definite price. However, had he said, "I'll sell you my X camera for $75," he would have made a definite proposal that Fenn could accept.

There are instances under the Uniform Commercial Code when an offer to sell goods will be regarded as definite although one or more important terms are not included. You will learn more about such offers in Chapter 17.

Offer Communicated to the Offeree

Although a proposal is definite and the offeror intends to be bound by it, it is not as yet an acceptable offer. It must still be communicated or made known to the offeree. An offer may be communicated in writing, orally, or by actions.

> Alecci sat down in a manicurist's chair, and the manicurist began to work on Alecci's nails. Nothing was said by either of them. Alecci has communicated an offer by her actions rather than by her written or spoken words.

Naturally, an agreement cannot arise if the offeree has not received the offer and has no knowledge of its terms.

> Craig Electronics Co. sent a letter to Freeman stating that it would sell her a "famous" brand of radio for $90 and would give her six months in which to pay. The letter was lost in the mail. Because Freeman did not receive the letter and could not have known of the offer's terms, no agreement arose.

Public transportation firms and public utilities, such as telephone, gas, and electric companies, are offerors of their services to any who may accept.

When you decide to ride a subway system, an agreement has been formed between you and the subway system.

They are legally obligated by the nature of their business to serve the public. They cannot choose those with whom they wish to deal. When a proper applicant indicates acceptance of the use of the offered public facilities, an agreement is formed.

PROBLEM

> **7.** Tian published a notice in the newspaper, offering a reward of $1,000 for information leading to the recovery of a valuable painting stolen from his home. The following day, a neighbor gave information to Tian that led to the arrest of the thief and to the recovery of the painting. Klein, the neighbor, was unaware of the reward offer when she gave her information to Tian. Was the offer of reward communicated to Klein?

Most states follow the common law rule that a reward is not payable unless the offeree knew of the offer. In Problem 7, since Klein did not know of the reward, the offer was not communicated to her. In the majority of states, Klein would not be permitted to claim the reward. Some states, however, would permit Klein to recover the reward on the ground that she really acted in the interest of the offeror.

You have now seen what it takes to make an offer valid. But what happens to a valid offer after it has been made? We will address that question in Chapter 7.

Chapter 6 Review

"YOU BE THE JUDGE" REVIEW

Look again at the "You Be the Judge" cases given at the beginning of this chapter. Would you decide them differently now, after your study of the chapter?

Correct Decisions

1. No. A mere reply to an inquiry is not an offer.

2. Yes. A general offer of reward is effective as to anyone who has knowledge of the reward and acts on it.

UNDERSTANDING WHAT YOU HAVE READ

1. How is a bilateral offer accepted?
2. How is a unilateral offer accepted?
3. Describe the three requirements of a valid offer.
4. Is an offer made in jest or under great emotional excitement a valid offer? Why or why not?
5. Is an advertisement an offer? Why or why not?
6. What other forms of announcements of goods for sale are not offers?
7. Who makes the offer at an auction?
8. What is a general offer of reward? Give an example.
9. When is an agreement formed between an applicant and a public transportation or utility firm?
10. How may an offer be communicated? Give an example.

BUILDING YOUR LEGAL VOCABULARY

Match each of these legal terms with its correct definition from the list that follows. Write your answers on a separate sheet of paper.

advertisement   legal obligation   offeror
auction   offer   public utility firm
communicated offer   offeree   reward
general offer of reward

1. an expression of willingness to enter into a contract
2. an offer addressed to the general public, which can be accepted by anyone with knowledge of the offer
3. an invitation to the public to make offers to purchase goods or services
4. an offer which is made known to the offeree
5. the person to whom an offer is made
6. a company that is legally obligated to serve the public
7. a public sale of property to the highest bidder
8. something offered or given for some service or achievement
9. the person who makes an offer
10. a duty to do or refrain from doing something required by law

---

APPLYING LEGAL PRINCIPLES

In these problems, state whether or not a valid offer has been made. Give legal reasons for your answers.

1. Ainsworth asks Malone, "Will you give me $7,000 for my Model T Ford?"
2. Sanchez stops at an alteration shop and leaves some skirts to be altered.
3. Sain, a chef, phones a grocer and asks him to send over two dozen of his best grapefruit.
4. Adelman, the owner of a large portion of land, offers to sell an acre of her land for $50,000.
5. Gaines offers Hsieh a position as a data-entry clerk at a salary of $190 for a 35-hour week.
6. Simms receives a form letter from a clothing store, offering him a $400 suit for $199.
7. An auctioneer displays an Oriental rug before a gathering in an auction shop.
8. The town of Elmcrest advertises for bids for the construction, as per specifications, of a highway.
9. At the request of a customer, a store clerk quotes the prices of certain models of televisions.

10. Guzman puts a notice in the town post office, offering a reward of $50 for the return of his 12-speed bicycle.

11. Bennett sees a newspaper ad placed by City Tele-Video. The ad reads:

> **TODAY ONLY**
> Great Rock Videocassettes!
> $39.95 each
> Huge Selection!

Bennett buys a round-trip bus ticket for $14, goes to City Tele-Video, and asks to see the advertised videocassettes. She is told, "We are sold out."

12. Elkin says to Aguirre, "I'll sell you my computer printer for $1,400." Swift, a third party, says, "I'll take it at that price."

13. Goodman Tire Co. mails a letter to Ahmed, offering to sell him four truck tires for $220, payable within six months from the purchase date. The letter containing the offer never reaches Ahmed.

14. Petri writes a letter to Hare offering to sell a two-year-old set of encyclopedias for $600. Hare receives the letter and places it in her desk without reading it.

15. Loser publishes a newspaper ad offering a reward of $250 for the return of his lost overcoat and briefcase. Finder reads the notice in the paper, finds the lost articles, and returns them to Loser.

16. Assume in Problem 15 that Finder returns the overcoat and briefcase to Loser without knowing of the reward.

17. When her new moped, which cost $200, fails to start, Clark becomes very angry and blurts out, "I'll sell this stupid thing for $1." Heuser, who is standing by, replies, "I'll take it for $1." Is there a valid contract between the parties?

ANALYZING COURT CASES

1. Owen wrote to Tunison, asking if Tunison would sell his store for $6,000. Tunison replied, "It would not be possible for me to sell unless I received $16,000 cash." Owen replied, "Accept your offer." Tunison denied that there was a contract. In whose favor should the court rule? (*Owen v. Tunison*, 131 Maine 42, 158 A. 926)

2. Haseltine sent postcards to a number of builders, inviting them to bid on the construction of a large building. Among the bids received, Leslie's was the lowest. He claimed that he was entitled to the contract because he had submitted the lowest bid. Was Leslie entitled to the contract? (*Leslie v. Haseltine*, 25 A. 886)

3. The Great Minneapolis Surplus Store advertised in a newspaper that a stole worth $139.50 would be sold for $1. The advertisement stated, "First come, first served." Lefkowitz, the first person to appear at the store, wanted to buy the stole. The store refused to sell it to him on the ground that the offer was open only to women. Lefkowitz sued the store for $138.50. Was the ad an offer that was accepted by Lefkowitz? (*Lefkowitz v. Great Minneapolis Surplus Store*, 84 S.E. 2d 516)

CHAPTER 7

Termination of the Offer

Think about these cases.
If you were the judge, how would you decide each case?

1

Tillman attended an auction and bid $5,000 for an antique clock. Before the auctioneer's hammer fell, Tillman yelled, "I withdraw my offer!" Nevertheless, the auctioneer pointed to Tillman and said, "Sold to this gentleman for $5,000." Did a contract arise?

2

On September 5, Krane orally offered to buy Chan's home for $125,000. Chan said that she could not give an immediate answer. Six months later, Chan wrote to Krane saying, "I accept your offer per the terms stated on September 5." Did a contract arise between Krane and Chan?

HOW DOES AN OFFER END?

An offer that has been properly communicated to the offeree may be terminated (ended) in any of several ways. It may be terminated by (1) revocation by the offeror, (2) lapse or expiration of time, (3) rejection by the offeree, (4) counteroffer by the offeree, (5) death or disability of either party, and (6) illegality or impossibility by operation of law.

Revocation by the Offeror

> **1.** During a conversation, Spencer offered to sell Leanos a portable electronic typewriter for $150. While Leanos was deciding whether to accept, Spencer suddenly said, "I withdraw my offer. I don't want to sell it." Did he have the right to withdraw the offer?

An offeror may withdraw an offer at any time before the offeree accepts. However, the offeror must notify the offeree of such **revocation** (withdrawal) of the offer. This can be done (as in Problem 1) by means of a direct statement, such as "I withdraw my offer." It also can be done by sending a letter or telegram informing the offeree that the offer is no longer open. Even indirect notice of withdrawal is legally considered binding, as long as the offeree learns that someone else has accepted the offer.

> Nowak offered her sailboard to Adams for $100. Adams went to Nowak's home to accept but found Baylson standing outside. Baylson told Adams that he had just entered into an agreement with Nowak to buy the sailboard and was waiting for Nowak to get it. When Nowak arrived, and before anyone had a chance to speak, Adams said to Nowak, "I'll take your sailboard." There is no contract between Adams and Nowak. Adams learned indirectly that the offer was no longer in existence before she accepted.

Public Revocation

The rule that notice of revocation must be communicated to the offeree before acceptance does not apply to revocation of an offer made to the public. In such a case, a notice of withdrawal published in the same way in which the offer was made is sufficient. This is true even though the offeree does not see the notice or know of it.

LAW IN THE NEWS

Study: Mediation Helps Spare Court System

United Press International

WASHINGTON—New ways to mediate legal disputes last year spared more than 13,000 citizens in three U.S. municipalities from courtroom battles, saving money for them and for taxpayers, according to a Justice Department study released yesterday.

"Multidoor courthouse programs"—an experimental system to resolve grievances without resorting to court trials—were assessed in Houston, Tulsa, Okla., and the District of Columbia for the study, sponsored by the American Bar Association.

"A dispute with the city over a water bill or a fistfight over parking in your neighbor's driveway should not go to an already overburdened court if mediation can be arranged," said James Stewart, director of the National Institute of Justice, a Justice Department agency.

In the study, a former assistant attorney general, Maurice Rosenberg, described the projects as "letting the forum fit the fuss."

Larry Ray, director of the Standing Committee on Dispute Resolution for the ABA, said mediation solves the problems about 95 percent of the time.

Based on 1,200 interviews over 18 months in the three municipalities, the study found that 83 percent of those who used the arbitration centers found them satisfactory and 82 percent said they would use them again. Only 59 percent, however, said the centers "helped" to resolve their grievances.

Ray said many people thought the centers would intervene directly in their complaints. None of the programs handled serious criminal matters or civil disputes involving substantial sums of money.

All three programs handled substantial caseloads, the study showed, including domestic assaults, consumer disputes, and citizen complaints.

A citizen may bring his complaint to a center, where a specialist will review it and advise on whether it should be mediated, prosecuted, or passed to another agency, such as the Better Business Bureau.

The centers, on the average, cost about $140,000 a year to run, Ray said.

In the three municipalities, about half the cases were resolved at the time of follow-up interviews, the study said, and 14 percent are pending.

Slocum advertised a reward for the return of her lost portfolio, which contained important papers. Later, she inserted an announcement revoking the offer. Fluss, who read the offer of reward but did not see the notice of revocation, returned the papers and the case. Fluss is not entitled to the reward. The offer had been effectively revoked before he returned the items to Slocum.

Revocation of Option Contracts

2. On June 5, Baker orally offered to sell Valencia an outboard motor for $200 and gave Valencia five days in which to accept. On June 7, Baker notified Valencia that he had sold the motor for $225. Valencia thereupon informed Baker that since he had until June 10 to accept, he wished to accept the offer at $200 and would hold Baker liable. Is Baker liable to Valencia?

Even though the offeree is allowed a certain time in which to accept, the offeror may revoke an offer provided the notice of revocation reaches the offeree before acceptance is made. This general rule has been modified by statutes in some states in cases where the offer is *made in writing and signed by the offeror.* Such statutes usually provide that the offeror may not revoke a written offer that states it is irrevocable for a specified time. If no time is specified in the written offer, it may not be revoked before the expiration of a reasonable time, even though no consideration has been paid to keep the offer open. The Uniform Commerical Code adopts this change in the case of *firm offers* made by merchants to buy or sell goods (see Chapter 17). In Problem 2, Baker is not liable to Valencia. No consideration was paid to keep the offer open, and the offer was not in writing.

In all states an offer may be kept open for a given time if the offeree gives some consideration to the offeror for holding the offer open. The consideration usually consists of a sum of money. The right purchased is known as an **option,** and the agreement between the parties is called an **option contract.** During the option period, the offeror cannot revoke the offer. The option contract may provide that the consideration paid by the offeree is to be applied toward the purchase price if the offer is accepted. Usually, if the offeree fails to accept the offer within the given time, the offeror may keep the money paid for the option.

> If Valencia, in Problem 2, had paid $10 or any sum to keep the offer open for the five days, Baker could not revoke the offer during the option period.

Lapse or Expiration of Time

PROBLEM

> **3.** The manager of a school baseball team sent an offer to an out-of-town team to play an exhibition game on a certain day. The letter requested an acceptance by May 15. No acceptance was received until May 29. Did the acceptance create a contract?

An offer does not remain open indefinitely. If the offeror has given the offeree a definite period of time in which to accept, the offer lapses or expires if it is not accepted within the stated time. Once the offer is terminated, the offeree cannot revive it by attempting an acceptance. In Problem 3, an acceptance was not received by the requested date of May 15. Thus, the offer lapsed or expired as of May 16. The letter of acceptance received by the offeror on May 29 was meaningless.

An offeree may purchase a right (called an option) to keep an offer open for a stated time.

If no definite period is stated during which an offer will be kept open, it will lapse after the passage of a reasonable time. The question of what is a reasonable time depends on all the circumstances surrounding the offer, including the nature of the subject matter. For example, an offer to sell shares of stock which fluctuate in price constantly will usually lapse if not accepted immediately. An offer made orally usually lapses when the conversation between the parties ends, unless otherwise indicated by the offeror.

Rejection by the Offeree

4. Harlow Company offered to employ Rinaldi as traffic manager in its shipping department. Rinaldi replied, "Thank you for your generous offer, but I can't take advantage of it at the present time." What is the effect of Rinaldi's reply on the offer made to her?

The refusal of an offeree to accept an offer is called a **rejection.** An offer is rejected when the offeree indicates by words or conduct an unwillingness to accept it. The effect of a rejection is to terminate the offer, as in Problem 4. Rinaldi's reply is a rejection of Harlow's offer. Any attempt by her to accept it later merely amounts to a new offer by her to Harlow Company, the original offeror.

A direct notice of rejection is effective when it is received by the offeror. Informal notice from some third party that the offeree has no intention of accepting is not an effective rejection of the offer.

Counteroffer by the Offeree

5. Yee offered to sell Johnson a tractor for $12,000. Johnson said that he would give $10,000 for it, but Yee refused the offer. Johnson then said, "All right, I'll give you the $12,000 you asked." Must Yee sell the tractor to Johnson?

If the acceptance differs from the terms of the offer, it is said to be a **counteroffer,** and its effect is to terminate the original offer. In Problem 5, Johnson is in effect saying to Yee, "I reject your original offer, and instead I am making you a different offer." Yee's original offer is terminated, and Johnson's offer is a counteroffer that Yee may either accept or reject. Since Yee rejected the counteroffer, no contract arose between the parties.

A counteroffer may arise without a direct contradiction of the terms of the original offer. Instead of offering $10,000 for the tractor, Johnson might have stated that he was willing to pay $12,000 for the tractor provided that Yee had the tractor repainted. Such a statement is a counteroffer if Yee did not mention repainting the tractor in his original offer.

Suppose that after Yee made his offer to sell the tractor to Johnson for $12,000, Johnson replied, "Won't you take less?" Such a reply would not be a counteroffer. Both parties knew and intended that Johnson's response was not to be regarded as a definite rejection of the original offer. It was merely a request for further information. Johnson would still have the power to create a contract on the original terms laid down by Yee.

Death or Insanity

> **6.** On June 15, Kraft mailed an offer to Beder to buy Beder's camper for $2,200. Beder accepted the offer on June 19 and mailed her letter of acceptance the same day. Unknown to Beder, Kraft had died on June 16. Did Beder's acceptance create a contract?

An offer terminates, as a matter of law, when either the offeror or the offeree dies or becomes insane (mental death) before acceptance. It is important to remember that *death or insanity terminates an offer, not a contract.* As a general rule, death, insanity, or disability does not excuse performance of contracts, except those for personal services. This topic will be studied in a later chapter. In Problem 6, the offer terminated on June 16 upon Kraft's death. Beder's acceptance on June 19 had no legal value.

Illegality or Impossibility

> **7.** Torrez offered in writing to sell her lake cabin to Cortina for $52,000. Before Cortina accepted the offer, the cabin was destroyed by fire without the knowledge of either party. Did Cortina's acceptance create a contract?

Destruction of the subject matter of the offer without the knowledge of either party terminates the offer as a matter of law. Notice of this event need not be given to the offeree. The offer ends instantaneously, since a contract cannot arise without one of its essentials—subject matter. Cortina's acceptance in Problem 7 was of no legal significance since the cabin had been destroyed before his acceptance. The same rule applies to offers

When this house was destroyed by fire without the knowledge of either party, the agreement between the parties was terminated.

that were legal when made but became illegal by legislative or other action before the offeree had accepted.

A drug manufacturer offered to sell a quantity of new weight-reducing pills to Wilton Pharmacy. Before Wilton had accepted the offer, the Food and Drug Administration declared the pill to be harmful for human use and forbade its sale. The offer automatically terminated when its illegality was declared by the government agency. Thus, the offer was no longer open for acceptance by the offeree.

In this chapter you have learned the ways in which termination of an offer takes place. There are also legal requirements for the valid acceptance of an offer. We will discuss them next, in Chapter 8.

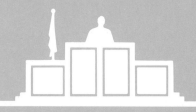

Chapter 7 Review

"YOU BE THE JUDGE" REVIEW

Look again at the "You Be the Judge" cases given at the beginning of this chapter. Would you decide them differently now, after your study of the chapter?

Correct Decisions

1. No. A bid made at an auction is an offer. It may be revoked at any time before the auctioneer's hammer falls to indicate acceptance.

2. No. An offer expires if not accepted within a stated time, or within a reasonable time if no time is stated. Under the circumstances of this case, six months is an unreasonable amount of time.

UNDERSTANDING WHAT YOU HAVE READ

1. List six ways in which an offer may terminate.
2. How may notice of revocation be given to an offeree?
3. What may an offeree do to keep an offer open for a stated period of time?
4. Under what circumstances may an offer lapse?
5. What is the effect of a counteroffer on the original offer?
6. How does the death or disability of either party affect an offer?
7. Give an example of the termination of an offer by illegality.
8. Give an example of the termination of an offer by impossibility.

BUILDING YOUR LEGAL VOCABULARY

Choose the legal term that will correctly complete each definition below. Write your answers on a separate sheet of paper.

1. A withdrawal of an offer is a/an
   a. revocation.
   b. option.
   c. expiration.
2. An agreement in which an offeree gives some consideration to the offeror for holding an offer open for a given time is a/an
   a. unenforceable contract.
   b. social agreement.
   c. option contract.
3. An offeree's refusal to accept an offer is called a
   a. lapse of time.
   b. firm offer.
   c. rejection.
4. An acceptance that differs from the terms of the offer is a
   a. quasi contract.
   b. counteroffer.
   c. revocation.
5. The right an offeree purchases from an offeror to keep an offer open for a given time is a/an
   a. counteroffer.
   b. rejection.
   c. option.

APPLYING LEGAL PRINCIPLES

1. Sayles told Stein, "I'll sell you that lot in town for $30,000. Let me know your decision in five days." The next day, Sayles notified Stein that the offer was withdrawn. May Sayles withdraw her offer before the expiration of the five-day period?
2. Lacy advertised a reward of $100 for the return of his lost college ring. Later, he inserted an announcement revoking the offer. Flair, who read the original offer of reward but did not see the notice of revocation, found and returned the ring. Was Flair entitled to collect the reward?
3. Abe offered to sell Kizik a refrigerator for $550 and gave Kizik five days in which to accept. Two days after making the offer, Abe sold the refrigerator to Connors. Kizik learned of the sale through Connors and, before the five days had expired, sent a letter of acceptance to Abe. Was there a contract between Abe and Kizik?
4. McManus called Ross and offered to sell her a used power lawnmower for $95. McManus promised to keep the offer open for ten days. Ross promptly mailed a check for $10 to McManus.

purchase price if Ross decided to accept the offer. Four days later, McManus notified Ross that he had withdrawn the offer and had sold the mower to Durkin. Was McManus within his legal rights in doing so?

5. On June 8, Espinoza mailed a letter to Underhill, stating, "I'll sell you my Mustang convertible for $6,000. The offer will be open for ten days." Underhill wrote a letter of acceptance to Espinoza but forgot to mail the letter until after the ten days had passed. What effect did this have on Espinoza's offer?

6. Assume the same facts as in Problem 5, except that Underhill mailed her acceptance on June 10 without knowing that Espinoza had died on June 9. Would there be a contract?

7. Gerber called Smythe, offering to repair Smythe's color television for $95. Smythe replied, "I can get it fixed for $65. Thank you for calling." What is the legal effect of Smythe's reply?

8. Hsu wrote to Brinton, offering to sell him a used Nautilus machine for $900 cash. Brinton wrote immediately accepting the offer if Hsu would take in payment a check for $100 and a 90-day promissory note for the balance. Did Brinton's acceptance result in a contract?

9. Boggs said to Ferraro, "I'll sell you that watch for $45." Ferraro replied, "I'll give you $25 for it." Boggs said, "No, I can't take $25." Ferraro answered, "Well, then here's $45." Boggs refused to let Ferraro have the watch. Is there a binding contract?

10. Lac offered to build a public garage for Goldstein Parking Co. on a lot owned by Goldstein in Marion County. Before Goldstein accepted Lac's offer, the county government passed a rezoning ordinance. The law forbade the construction of public garages anywhere within the county limits. Lac now claims that his offer was automatically revoked. Is Lac legally correct?

ANALYZING COURT CASES

1. The owner of a business made an offer to sell an interest in the business for a specified price. The potential buyer wrote back, agreeing to the terms of the offer and stating that payment would be made in 30 days, after the transaction was completed. Did a contract arise between the parties? (*Sassomon v. Littlejohn*, 129 S.E. 2d 124)

2. Ramsey offered to sell certain real estate to Herndon and gave him until January 15 to accept the offer. Herndon was trying to arrange a loan so that he could purchase the property. Ramsey was aware of Herndon's actions. Herndon failed to complete his loan arrangements by January 15, and Ramsey sold the property to Armstrong. On January 17,

Herndon completed the loan transaction and notified Ramsey. At that point, Ramsey informed Herndon of the sale to Armstrong. Herndon brought suit against Ramsey for damages for breach of contract. Will Herndon succeed? (*Herndon v. Ramsey*, 38 P. 2d 44)

3. Achenbach owned six $500 corporate bonds. Kurtz Bros. offered to buy them from him. Six years after the receipt of this offer, Achenbach died. The administrator of his estate accepted the offer and sued Kurtz Bros. when it refused to perform the contract. Was there a contract? (*Achenbach v. Kurtz*, 159 A. 718)

CHAPTER 8

Acceptance of the Offer

YOU BE THE JUDGE

Think about these cases.
If you were the judge, how would you decide each case?

1

Maguire wrote to Joers, "I offer you my teak desk for $200. If I don't hear from you in three days, I'll assume that you accept." He received no answer from Joers in the time stated. Was there an acceptance?

2

A book you had not ordered was sent to you by mail. You had never dealt with the firm that sent the book. You laid the book aside and made no effort to reply to the firm. Are you liable for payment for the book?

WHAT IS AN ACCEPTANCE?

An **acceptance** is an offeree's expression of willingness to be bound by the terms of an offer. To be valid, an acceptance must meet three requirements: (1) it must be made only by the intended offeree; (2) it must agree with the terms of the offer; and (3) it must be communicated to the offeror.

> **1.** Patterson offered Sherk an extension ladder for $90, but Sherk politely refused. Carnet, who was present, said, "Here's the money. I'll take it." Was the offer communicated to Carnet?

An offer is effective only as to the person to whom it was intended to be communicated. It is not transferable by the offeree to another person. In Problem 1, Patterson has a right to choose the person with whom she will deal. Therefore, no contract resulted from Carnet's reply.

The customer has accepted the offer made by the salesperson.

Acceptance in Agreement with the Terms of the Offer

> **2.** Baum sent an offer to Gonzalez by messenger. The offer stated that if Gonzalez agreed with its terms he was to give his reply to the messenger. Gonzalez wrote, "I'm glad to avail myself of your offer," and gave the signed note to the messenger. Did Gonzalez accept Baum's offer?

An acceptance must agree with the terms of the offer. An offer may contain provisions setting the time, place, and manner of acceptance by the offeree. If the acceptance is to be legally effective, these provisions must be strictly observed by the offeree. Where an offer calls for the receipt of the acceptance by a certain time, no contract will arise unless the acceptance is received by the offeror in time. In Problem 2, Gonzalez accepted Baum's offer in the manner described in the offer. A binding contract resulted when Gonzalez gave the acceptance to the messenger.

Acceptance Communicated to the Offeror

> **3.** Strong wrote to Mason, offering her a position as a buyer on a salary-and-commission basis. Mason planned to accept, but through carelessness, she forgot to mail her letter of acceptance. Was there an acceptance?

We learned in Chapter 6 that the minds of the parties must meet through offer and acceptance. One of the requirements of the offer was that it must be communicated to the offeree. The acceptance of an offer must also be communicated to the offeror to be effective. The communication may take place by words or by actions, depending on the terms of the offer. An offeree's mere mental determination to accept is not sufficient to create a contract. In Problem 3, Mason, by failing to mail her letter of acceptance, could not create a contract with Strong.

Communication in a Bilateral Contract

> **4.** Heming said to Osterberg, "If you will promise to repair my garage for $1,750, you may go ahead right away." Osterberg did not reply. The next day, however, without communicating with Heming, he bought the lumber needed to repair the garage. Did Osterberg's action constitute an acceptance?

LIVING UNDER THE LAW

Bringing An Action in Small Claims Court

There may be one or more occasions in your life when you feel that you have a just cause for a small claims lawsuit. If this should happen, you can save a lot of time and trouble if you know how to bring the action. Here are some useful steps to follow:

- Decide the amount of your claim. If it exceeds the small claims court's jurisdiction, you will have to sue in a higher court.
- Determine exactly whom you should sue. You are allowed to sue an individual or a corporation. In either case, you need to state the exact name and address of the other party. If you sue a corporation, you will also need the exact name of one of the firm's officers, on whom a summons and other court documents can be served. A corporation's full name can be obtained from an official of the state in which the corporation is incorporated or doing business.
- File your suit with the office of the clerk of the small claims court. The clerk will help you file the suit if you choose not to hire an attorney.
- If you can't speak English, bring an English-speaking friend with you to translate for you.
- You will be required to pay a fee for filing the suit. The amount of the fee

will depend on the amount of your claim. In most cases, however, the fee is under $10. You must pay another fee for having the sheriff's office serve process on the party you are suing.
- Some small claims courts have a pretrial conference. At this time, the judge will ask both parties if they are willing to settle the case out of court. If not, the case will be scheduled for trial. You do not need witnesses, but you should bring any written evidence that will help you prove your case. If the facts of your case are complicated, it may be to your advantage to get an attorney. If you can't afford one, the local Legal Aid Society or a lawyer referral service may be able to help you.

In a **bilateral contract,** a promise is exchanged for a promise. The offeree's acceptance in this type of contract must be communicated by means of a return promise. Action is not usually sufficient to create a contract. Some courts have held that a contract is formed if the act is fully completed within the time the offer would have remained open for a return promise. In Problem 4, Osterberg's action in buying the lumber is not an effective acceptance of the offer. He did not comply with Heming's request for a return promise.

Unordered Goods.   Because of a federal law, all unordered goods (books, magazines, tickets, and so forth) sent *by mail* may be treated as gifts by the recipients of the goods. However, the law does not apply to goods sent by mail by a charitable organization seeking contributions. Nor does it apply to unordered goods sent by mail and clearly marked "free samples."

PROBLEM

> **5.**   Danton Distributors sent a book to Lee by United Delivery Service. A bill for $19.95 was enclosed. Lee had not ordered the book. Nevertheless, she read the book and loaned it to her friends. Did Lee's conduct constitute an acceptance?

In Problem 5, Lee's conduct in reading the book and lending it to her friends clearly indicates that she intended to keep it. Most states regard such actions as an **exercise of ownership** over the goods and an acceptance of the offer. Lee would be liable for the purchase price.

Suppose, however, that Lee had received the unordered book by mail rather than by a delivery service. In that event, there would be no acceptance. Lee may treat the unordered book as a gift and is required neither to pay for the book nor to return it to Danton Distributors.

Silence as Acceptance.   When an offeree is not obligated to reply, acceptance cannot be implied from a failure to answer. *Silence does not usually constitute acceptance,* unless the offeree has by previous conduct indicated that silence means acceptance.

EXAMPLE

> Hobbs had sent fabric to Massasoit Co. on five previous occasions. Each time, the firm accepted and paid for the fabric. Hobbs later sent additional fabric to Massasoit, which the company held without paying Hobbs for it. After several months, Massasoit accidentally destroyed the fabric. Hobbs sued the firm for the price of the fabric. The firm claimed that it had never accepted Hobbs' offer, and thus there was no contract to pay the purchase price. The firm is liable for the purchase price of the additional fabric because the parties had previously treated silence as an acceptance.

The Uniform Commerical Code states that, in special cases and under certain conditions, silence may constitute an acceptance. These cases involve transactions *between merchants* for the sale of goods. You will study the UCC in Chapter 17.

Communication in a Unilateral Contract

> **6.** The city of Pottsville offered a reward of $5,000 for the capture of a certain criminal suspect. Haley, with knowledge of this offer, captured the suspect and turned her over to the Pottsville police. Is Haley entitled to the reward?

In a **unilateral contract,** an acceptance must be made by performance of a requested act. In this type of agreement, a contract arises as soon as the requested act is performed by the offeree. Unless the offer specifically provides for notice, the offeree need not notify the offeror that the act has been performed. In Problem 6, Haley accepted the offer by completing the requested act. Therefore, he is entitled to the reward.

Under the UCC, the rule regarding notice is changed in the case of performance of contracts for the sale and shipment of goods. We will discuss this further in Chapter 17.

> **7.** Pena, a house painter, painted Abel's fence. Abel watched Pena paint the fence and said nothing. Was there an acceptance of the services by Abel?

A person may perform a service with the expectation of being paid for it under circumstances that would lead any reasonable person to believe that compensation is expected. In this event, the person who performs the service has made an offer. If the offeree passes up a chance to reject the offered service and takes the benefits from it (as Abel did in Problem 7), the offer is regarded as accepted.

METHODS OF COMMUNI-CATING ACCEPTANCE

> **8.** Beck mailed to Akagi an offer to sell a used truck for $1,500. Akagi immediately mailed a properly stamped and addressed letter of acceptance. The letter, however, was lost in the mail and was never received by Beck. Did a contract arise between the parties?

We have seen that an acceptance of a bilateral contract must be a return promise from the offeree. If the offeree fails to communicate the promise to the offeror, the acceptance is not effective and no contract arises. When the parties are dealing face to face, a contract comes into existence when the words or acts are spoken or performed. If the parties are dealing over the phone, the contract arises when the offeree speaks the words of acceptance into the phone.

Suppose the parties use a method of communication such as the mail, the telegraph, or electronic mail. In that event, courts distinguish between a **stipulated means of communication** and an **authorized means of communication.** If the offeror states in the offer that the offeree *must* use a certain means of communication, the means is regarded as stipulated. No contract will arise unless the stipulated means is used by the offeree. In contrast, if the offeror states that the offeree *may* use this means of communication or fails to mention any means, the method of communication is authorized. An acceptance by an authorized means of communication is effective when it is sent. For example, if the offer is received in the mail, the offeree is authorized to use the mail to communicate the acceptance. A contract arises as soon as the letter of acceptance, properly stamped and addressed, is mailed. If the offer is received by telegram, a contract arises as soon as the telegram of acceptance (charges prepaid) is left with the telegraph company. However, any other means of communication, such as electronic mail, may be used if it is as fast or faster than the authorized means. In this event, the means of communication that is as fast or faster than the authorized means also is considered to be an authorized means.

In Problem 8, a contract arose between Beck and Akagi despite the fact that Beck never received Akagi's acceptance. Akagi used an authorized means of acceptance, and a contract came into existence when Akagi dropped the letter of acceptance into a mailbox.

When an acceptance is sent by a means of communication not authorized by the offeror, it is not effective until it is *received* by the offeror. Of course, the risk is on the offeree until the acceptance reaches the offeror.

EXAMPLE

Golov wired an offer of employment to Lester. Lester accepted in a letter sent by mail. When Golov received Lester's letter, a contract came into existence. If Golov had not received the letter of acceptance, no contract would have been formed.

As you have now seen, the requirements for a valid offer and a valid acceptance all focus on mutual assent. In Chapter 9 we will study defective agreements—those agreements in which the minds of the parties do not meet.

Chapter 8 Review

Look again at the "You Be the Judge" cases given at the beginning of this chapter. Would you decide them differently now, after your study of the chapter?

Correct Decisions

1. No. As a general rule, silence does not constitute acceptance.
2. No. People who receive unordered goods through the mail may treat the goods as gifts. The goods do not have to be paid for or returned to the sender.

UNDERSTANDING WHAT YOU HAVE READ

1. Why is an acceptance necessary?
2. List three requirements of a valid acceptance.
3. Give an original example of acceptance of an offer by words or actions.
4. Give an original example showing how silence may sometimes constitute an acceptance of an offer.
5. Give an original example of an acceptance of an offer by performance of a requested act.
6. "An acceptance must be communicated to the offeror where the offer requires a promise." Explain this principle of law by giving an original example.
7. If an authorized acceptance is mailed in response to an offer received by mail, when does a contract arise? Why?
8. If an offeree accepted by mail an offer that had been made in a telegram, when would a contract arise?
9. A mailed offer stipulates that an acceptance be made by telegram. When does a contract arise?
10. An offeror does not receive an authorized acceptance that creates a contract. What would you advise the offeror to do in future transactions?

BUILDING YOUR LEGAL VOCABULARY

Match each of these legal terms with its correct definition from the list that follows. Write your answers on a separate sheet of paper.

acceptance

acceptance in a manner other than that of the offer

authorized means of communication

bilateral contract

exercise of ownership

intended offeree

promise

silence as acceptance

stipulated means of communication

unilateral contract

1. an exchange of a promise for a promise
2. conduct by an offeree indicating an intention to keep unordered goods
3. an offeree's expression of willingness to comply with the terms of an offer
4. a means of communication that an offeree *may* use to accept an offer
5. the exchange of a promise for an act or an act for a promise
6. the person to whom an offeror directs an offer
7. generally not considered an effective manner of acceptance
8. acceptance that is not valid until it has been received by the offeror
9. a statement that one will do or refrain from doing something specified
10. a means of communication that an offeree *must* use to accept an offer

APPLYING LEGAL PRINCIPLES

1. Aldrich, a builder, advertised for bids on a certain construction job. Ikeda, a general contractor, submitted the lowest bid. Aldrich then wrote to Ikeda, "You are the lowest bidder. Come on down to my office." Was there a contract?
2. Jalbert offered to sell 1,000 yards of fabric to Lane at $5 per yard. Lane replied, "That's a fair price. You can deliver the goods to my warehouse. I'll pay you in three equal monthly installments." Was a binding contract created?
3. Bolling offered to sell Keats electrical fixtures at a stated price. Keats answered, "I accept your offer. I hope that if you can arrange to deliver the fixtures in installments of 25 fixtures per week, you will do so." Did Keats' reply constitute an acceptance?
4. Paperback Book Co. mailed MacDougal a book that she had not ordered. Mac-Dougal had never previously dealt with this firm. A letter enclosed with the book stated that if MacDougal enjoyed

the book, she could buy it at a special price. If not, she could return the book at the firm's expense. MacDougal laid the book aside and made no reply to the firm's letter. Was she liable for payment for the book?

5. Hernandez wrote to Wales, offering to sell her an antique chest for $15,000. She added that unless she heard from Wales within the next four days, she would conclude that Wales had accepted. Wales failed to make any reply. Was there a contract?

6. Zimble said to Martin, "I'll give you $10 if you deliver these stock certificates to 30 Wall Street." Martin promised to do so. Is there a contract?

7. Varela wrote to Eppes as follows: "If you will promise to develop that software for $2,500, you may have the job." Eppes did not reply. On the day after receiving the letter, however, without communicating with Varela, Eppes began the work. Was Eppes' action an acceptance of Varela's offer?

8. Curry, in New York, mailed a letter to Heller in Los Angeles. The letter contained an offer to sell the 25″ color TV sets for $495 each. Heller immediately mailed a letter of acceptance to Curry. Shortly thereafter, Heller sent a telegram to Curry, withdrawing the acceptance. Heller's telegram reached Curry three days before the acceptance arrived. Curry sued Heller for breach of contract. Should she succeed?

9. Abraham mailed an offer to Hexner without specifying how Hexner was to accept the offer. Hexner promptly sent an acceptance by messenger. The messenger delivered the acceptance to Abraham. Is there a contract?

10. a. Daly telegraphed an offer to Corn and requested a prompt reply. Corn accepted by electronic mail, and Daly received the letter before a telegram would have arrived. Does Corn's acceptance create a contract?

  b. If Daly had not received the electronic mail letter, would there be a contract?

ANALYZING COURT CASES

1. Miyakawa sued to recover a prize he claimed he won in a bowling contest sponsored by Bowlerama of Texas. For several months before the contest, Bowlerama posted house rules for the contest. The rules stated that contestants would be eligible for the prize only if their scores were kept by scorers se-lected by a clerk in charge of a control desk. Miyakawa ignored the house rules and kept his own scores. He claimed at the end of the contest that he had the highest scores and was entitled to the prize. Do you agree? (*Bowlerama v. Miyakawa*, 449 S.W. 2d 357)

2. The Great A&P Tea Co. rented a store from Geary. On February 25, the firm wrote Geary offering to sign a new lease for an additional year, beginning May 1. At 10:30 A.M. on March 7, Geary wrote a letter to A&P accepting the offer and enclosing a lease for the additional year. On the same day at 1:30 P.M., A&P mailed Geary a letter withdrawing the offer to sign the new lease. Both parties received the other's letter the following day. Was there an effective acceptance of the offer to make a lease? (*Geary v. Great A&P Tea Co.*, 10 N.E. 2d 350)

3. An insurance broker had for many years written fire insurance policies on Ehrlich's house. As a matter of fact, whenever a fire policy was about to expire, the broker sent Ehrlich a renewal policy and a bill for the premium. Ehrlich promptly paid the premium. On December 22, Ehrlich's fire insurance policy expired. On that day, the broker sent him a renewal policy issued by National Union Fire Insurance Company, with a bill for the premium. Ehrlich kept the policy for two months. Then, in response to a demand by the broker for payment, Ehrlich rejected the policy. National Union sued for the premium due for the two months' period, claiming that Ehrlich's retention of the policy implied an acceptance. Is the insurance company legally correct in its claim? (*National Union Fire Insurance Co. v. Ehrlich*, 203 N.Y.S. 434)

Defective Agreements

Think about these cases.
If you were the judge, how would you decide each case?

1

Bloomquist agreed to buy a lot on Hilton Street in a large city. There were two streets with that name in the city. Bloomquist meant one street, and the seller meant another. Is the agreement binding?

2

Both the buyer and the seller of a stamp honestly believed it was of small value. Actually, the stamp turned out to be extremely rare and valuable. Is the transaction binding?

DEFECTS OF ASSENT

1. Boaz offered to sell his car to Hablanian for $9,000. When making his offer, Boaz stated that he had driven the car only 10,000 miles. Actually, he had driven it 50,000 miles and had turned back the odometer reading. Relying on Boaz's statement, Hablanian bought the car. Soon, though, she discovered that she had been deceived. Hablanian offered to return the car and demanded a refund of the $9,000 she had paid. Will she succeed?

We have seen that agreements arise out of a true meeting of the minds of the parties. Frequently, one or both parties give their consent through a misunderstanding, or through an error about a **material** (important) **fact**

If a mutual mistake is made by these two parties concerning the identity of the tape player, the agreement will be void.

concerning the agreement. Such a misunderstanding or error may or may not constitute a **mistake** that makes the contract void. Cases may also arise where a party is forced to enter into an agreement unwillingly. The forced agreement of the party may result either from threats of violence, called **duress,** or from unfair persuasion, known as **undue influence.** Sometimes a party is induced to enter into an agreement through false and misleading statements made by another. As you learned in Chapter 4, a false and misleading statement made with intent to deceive is known as **fraud.** In Problem 1, Boaz's false representation about the car's mileage is fraudulent. Hablanian should succeed in an action against Boaz.

Mistake, duress, undue influence, and fraud prevent real assent and make an agreement defective. In this chapter, we will study the effect of these factors on an agreement.

Mistakes

As a general rule, mistakes have no legal effect on agreements. Some mistakes, however, make an agreement void or voidable. Mistakes may be bilateral **(mutual)** or **unilateral** (made only by one party).

If one party is mistaken about the value or quality of the subject matter, that party will still be bound to the agreement. Also, a party who makes an error in expressing or in understanding the terms of an agreement or in estimating the *legal* effect of an agreement will still be bound. There are, however, at least four types of mistakes that *do* prevent real assent: (1) a mutual (bilateral) mistake about the existence of the subject matter of the agreement; (2) a mutual mistake about the identity of the subject matter; (3) a unilateral mistake about the nature of the agreement; and (4) a unilateral mistake about the person with whom the agreement is made.

Mutual Mistake about the Existence of the Subject Matter

PROBLEM

> **2.** DeFazio agreed to buy Liang's sailboat, which was stored in a boathouse at Liang's summer home. Unknown to either party, the boathouse and sailboat were completely destroyed by fire the day before the agreement was made. What are the legal rights of the parties?

If, unknown to either party, the subject matter ceases to exist before or at the time the agreement is made, the agreement is void. Mutual mistake about the existence of the subject matter prevents an agreement from arising. In Problem 2, neither DeFazio nor Liang knew at the time the agreement was made that the sailboat had been destroyed. The existence of the sailboat was essential to the validity of the agreement.

Mutual Mistake about the Identity of the Subject Matter

3. Halliday contracted to sell a painting for $950. She believed the painting to be the work of an unimportant painter. The buyer, however, believed the painting to be the work of an obscure eighteenth-century Dutch painter. Actually, the painting was the work of a famous French artist and was valued at $50,000. May Halliday avoid the contract on discovering the actual facts?

When both parties are mistaken about the true identity of the subject matter of the agreement, there is no meeting of the minds. Therefore, the resulting agreement is void. Neither party in Problem 3 was aware that the painting was a masterpiece worth considerably more than the contract price. The mistake about the nature of the painting was mutual.

Mistake about the Nature of the Agreement

A unilateral mistake about the nature of a transaction usually results from fraud practiced on the mistaken party by the other party. Where a mistake of one party is fraudulently caused and taken advantage of by another, the mistaken party may avoid the agreement.

Duress may consist of unlawful detention of goods.

Taylor, an illiterate man, entered into a contract for the sale of some antique furniture he owned. He signed some papers that the buyer prepared and read to Taylor as a bill of sale for the antiques. Actually, the papers represented a transfer of the deed to Taylor's house to the buyer. Taylor may avoid the agreement because the document he signed was misrepresented to him as a bill of sale for antique furniture.

Mistake about the Person with Whom the Agreement Is Made

4. Navis sent an order for stationery supplies to her usual supplier, Kates. Unknown to Navis, Kates had sold his business to Mickel. The new owner, Mickel, sent the supplies to Navis. When Navis discovered the true facts, however, she refused to accept the supplies. Must Navis accept the shipment?

Real assent in an agreement is lacking if one party doesn't know that a substitute has taken the place of the other party. This is the case in Problem 4. Navis has a right to select those with whom she will do business. Under the circumstances, she does not have to accept the shipment from Mickel. Where the parties deal face to face, however, a contract is not affected by one party's mistake about the identity of the other.

Duress

5. Jastrow delivered some goods to Fast Freight Company for shipment to his warehouse at an agreed rate. After transporting the goods, Fast Freight refused to deliver the shipment to the warehouse. The firm demanded that Jastrow pay an additional charge, over and above what he had originally agreed to pay. In order to get possession of the goods, Jastrow paid the extra charge. He then brought suit against Fast Freight to recover. Will he succeed?

The law will help a party who is forced, through a threat of bodily or other harm, to perform some act that he or she would not have performed otherwise. In the case of contracts, a party so treated may avoid the agreement because of duress. Duress deprives a party of the right to enter into an agreement willingly.

There is no simple way to determine whether a contract was made under duress. The courts treat each case as an individual problem that must be decided according to the facts and surrounding circumstances. Usually, the courts will consider the circumstances of each case from these three standpoints: (1) Was the wrongful act directed against the contracting party or the party's near relatives? (2) Did the wrongful act induce the contracting party to enter into the agreement against his or her free will? (3) Was the wrongful act committed by the other party to the contract or by someone acting for that party?

Duress may consist not only of threats of bodily harm but also of unlawful detention of goods, as in Problem 5. Fast Freight's holding of Jastrow's goods in order to force him to pay an unreasonable charge constitutes "duress of goods." Duress is not present if a party threatens to do something that he or she has a legal right to do, such as bringing a civil suit against another party in order to collect a debt.

EXAMPLE

Farino threatened to bring a civil action against Sigoloff to collect some money Sigoloff owed her. The money was several months overdue. Sigoloff agreed to pay the money immediately if Farino would refrain from suing him. When Sigoloff failed to pay, Farino brought suit, and Sigoloff pleaded duress as his defense. Sigoloff's defense is improper because Farino had a legal right to sue to recover the debt.

Duress may be present when a person is forced to pay money in order to avoid a threat of criminal prosecution. If criminal liability is reasonably possible, however, many courts refuse to find duress in this instance.

Undue Influence

PROBLEM

6. Bricker, seriously ill, was persuaded by his lawyer to transfer to her 100 shares of Paragon Steel common stock. The stock was worth a large sum of money. After Bricker recovered from his illness, he brought suit to get his stock back from the lawyer. Should he be successful?

Undue influence is the improper use of one's position of trust in relation to another in order to gain an unfair economic advantage over that person. It results from the use of unfair persuasion to induce another to enter into an agreement. Where the parties bear a special or close relationship to each other, undue influence is presumed to exist. This is true in the

Undue Influence and Wills

In a recent case, Rosen made a will leaving his entire estate of a million dollars to his niece and nephew. Sometime later, he developed a terminal illness and was quite sick for about two years. Just before his death, Rosen went into a long-term health-care facility. There he was cared for primarily by one nurse. At a point when Rosen's condition was somewhat improved, the nurse bought a will form and had Rosen sign a new will, leaving most of his estate to the nurse. The nurse asked two of his friends to witness the will, and they did so despite the fact that Rosen was under heavy sedation at the time.

When the will was offered for probate, Rosen's niece and nephew contested the will. They claimed that it was drawn when Rosen was of unsound mind and acting under undue influence. The probate court agreed with them and set aside the will.

Generally, probate courts look carefully at certain wills. They ask questions such as these: Did a beneficiary have a confidential relationship with the maker of the will? If so, did the beneficiary profit substantially from the will? Did he or she use unfair methods in getting the will made? Affirmative answers to these questions will cause the will to be excluded from probate.

Undue influence is not the same as lack of mental capacity. A person of unsound mind cannot make a will at all. That person is incapable of knowing the objects of his or her bounty or the extent of the property being willed. A person who makes a will under undue influence, however, may have capacity; but because of unfair persuasion, such a person is prevented from exercising his or her own free will.

case of agreements between parents and children, husbands and wives, lawyers and clients, guardians and wards, and doctors and patients.

Like duress, undue influence makes the agreement voidable at the option of the injured party. The lawyer in Problem 6 would have to show that the transaction with Bricker was fair and reasonable in order to overcome the presumption of undue influence. If she fails to do so, Bricker will be successful.

Mere persuasion or high-pressure sales tactics are not ordinarily regarded as undue influence.

Fraud

> **7.** Hoffman bought an Oriental rug after the dealer represented that it was two hundred years old. After paying for the rug, Hoffman discovered that it was actually a new and much less valuable rug. What are Hoffman's legal rights?

As we have seen, some mistakes result from misrepresentation and tricks practiced by one party in order to gain an unfair advantage over the other. In each instance, the intentional misstatement or concealment of an important fact induced the other party to enter into the agreement. To avoid an agreement such as this, the injured party may choose to sue for fraud instead of claiming mistake. In order to prove fraud, the injured party must show the following four elements: (1) the other party falsely represented or concealed a material fact; (2) the other party knew the representation was false or made it in reckless disregard of its truth; (3) the other party intended the injured party to rely on the false representation; and (4) the injured party relied on the false representation and subsequently suffered a loss.

False Representation or Concealment of a Material Fact

The parties to an agreement have a right to rely on the truth and accuracy of the statements that caused them to enter into an agreement. Not every statement, however, may be the basis of fraud. The statement must relate to an important or material fact that exists now or has existed in the past. It must not be a *mere belief or opinion.* A statement such as "This stock will double in price within a year" is an opinion rather than a statement of fact. A buyer has no right to rely on opinions or "sales talk" as the equivalent of factual statements. In Problem 7, however, the dealer's representation to Hoffman that the Oriental rug was old was a factual statement on which Hoffman had a right to rely. The statement was also material and related to an existing fact.

A basis for fraud often arises from what a party intentionally conceals or fails to disclose rather than from what the party says or represents. Such conduct by either party is the legal equivalent of a false representation. Therefore, it enables the innocent party to avoid the agreement.

> Arman purchased and received goods from Acme Sales Co. on credit. At the time the agreement was made, Arman was hopelessly in debt and had no intention of paying for the goods. Arman's deliberate concealment of an existing material fact is the legal equivalent of a false representation.

A false representation may also consist of acts or tricks intended to deceive.

Knowledge of Falsity or Reckless Disregard of the Truth

PROBLEM

> **8.** Boyd, a stranger to you, seeks to borrow $3,000 from the First Traders Bank. Since Boyd has no established credit rating, you vouch for her credit as a favor to Gant, a mutual friend. Relying on your representation, the bank lends the money to Boyd, who turns out to be a swindler. The First Traders Bank brings an action against you for fraud. Are you liable?

If the person who made the statement knew it to be false or made it carelessly (without determining whether it was true), a basis for fraud is present. In Problem 8, you would be held liable for your reckless misrepresentation to First Traders Bank. You pretended to have knowledge of Boyd's financial responsibility when you actually had none.

Intention of Other Party's Reliance

PROBLEM

> **9.** Hurley submitted a false statement to a consumer credit agency about his financial condition. He then ordered $5,000 worth of goods from Enriquez Corp. Enriquez checked Hurley's credit with the agency and, relying on the information the agency furnished, shipped Hurley's order to him on 90 days' credit. When Hurley failed to pay, Enriquez discovered the true facts and brought suit against Hurley for fraud. Is Enriquez Corp.'s action proper?

As well as being knowingly false, a representation must be made with intent to deceive or mislead the other party. *Intention to deceive* distinguishes fraud from misrepresentation. Otherwise, both are governed by the same legal principles. It is not necessary, however, that the false representation be made directly to the intended victim. It is sufficient if the victim obtains the information through another source, such as the credit agency in Problem 9. Hurley is liable to Enriquez Corp., or to anyone who relied and acted on the accuracy of the information Hurley supplied to the credit agency.

Reliance by a Party Who Suffers a Loss

10. Tiao offered Whistler an air conditioner and stated that she had bought it new only four years earlier. Whistler, however, knew that the air conditioner was ten years old. May Whistler later avoid the contract on the ground of fraud?

A false representation must actually deceive the person for whom it is intended. That person must be induced to enter into an agreement on the basis of the false representation. Otherwise, there is no fraud. In Problem 10, Whistler knew the air conditioner was ten years old but still thought it was a desirable purchase. Thus, she could not have relied on Tiao's false statement. Since Whistler wasn't deceived by Tiao's misrepresentation, she cannot later claim fraud.

Remedies for Fraud

11. When Cain falsely represented to Benja that he had "inside" information that Rent-A-Car Co. would soon pay an extra dividend on its stock, Benja bought 100 shares of the stock at $15 per share. Shortly after, Benja resold it at a profit. Then he discovered that Cain's representation had been false. Is Benja entitled to recover damages if he sues Cain for fraud?

Fraud renders a contract voidable by the injured party. Of the several legal remedies available to the victim, there are two that are of primary importance. First, the injured party may **rescind** (cancel) the contract. The act of rescinding is called **rescission.** If this remedy is chosen, the defrauded party must return or offer to return any consideration received and then sue to recover any consideration paid. Second, the injured party may **affirm** (decide to carry out) the contract and then sue for any money loss. The act of affirming is known as **affirmance.**

Whichever remedy is chosen, the defrauded party must act with reasonable speed after discovering the fraud. Delay may **bar** (prohibit) a recovery. To recover damages, the injured party must show what money loss was actually suffered as a result of the fraud. Failure to prove a money loss results in no recovery of damages. In Problem 11, Benja actually made a profit from the resale of the stock. Undoubtedly, he would be unable to prove that he suffered any damages as a result of Cain's fraud.

This chapter has explained how mutual assent—one of the four elements of an enforceable contract—may be defective. Chapter 10 will explore consideration, another required element of a valid contract.

Chapter 9 Review

"YOU BE THE JUDGE" REVIEW

Look again at the "You Be the Judge" cases given at the beginning of this chapter. Would you decide them differently now, after your study of the chapter?

Correct Decisions

1. No. Mutual mistake as to the identity of the subject matter of the agreement makes the agreement void.

2. Yes. Since both parties were equally uninformed about the true value of the stamp, there was a mutual mistake as to its quality. The contract is binding.

UNDERSTANDING WHAT YOU HAVE READ

1. List four types of defects that prevent a true meeting of the minds of contracting parties.
2. Give original examples and the effect on the agreement of each of the following mistakes:
   a. mutual mistake as to the existence of the subject matter
   b. mutual mistake as to the identity of the subject matter
   c. mistake as to the nature of the agreement
   d. mistake as to the person with whom the agreement is made
3. Give an original example of an agreement in which duress is present.

4. What three conditions are needed to constitute duress?
5. What is the effect of duress on an agreement?
6. Give an original example of an agreement in which undue influence plays a role.
7. List four types of confidential relationships where undue influence may be presumed to exist.
8. What is the effect of undue influence on an agreement?
9. a. List four elements of fraud.
   b. What is the effect of fraud on an agreement?
10. What two important remedies for fraud are available to the injured party?

BUILDING YOUR LEGAL VOCABULARY

From this list, select the legal term that belongs in the blank in each sentence below. Write your answers on a separate sheet of paper.

affirm	mistake	rescind
duress	mutual mistake	undue influence
fraud	remedy	unilateral mistake
material fact		

1. A simple belief in the existence of a fact when it does not exist is a ▓▓▓▓▓▓▓.
2. To ▓▓▓▓▓▓▓ an agreement is to cancel it.
3. ▓▓▓▓▓▓▓ is a threat of violence or other harm that deprives a person of free will.
4. An error made by one party to an agreement is called a ▓▓▓▓▓▓▓.
5. To take unfair advantage of someone in a confidential relationship is to exert ▓▓▓▓▓▓▓ on that person.
6. One who misrepresents a fact with intent to deceive another has committed ▓▓▓▓▓▓▓.
7. A ▓▓▓▓▓▓▓ is an error made by both parties to an agreement.
8. An important representation or term of an agreement is a ▓▓▓▓▓▓▓.
9. A ▓▓▓▓▓▓▓ is a legal action taken by an injured party to obtain satisfaction.
10. A party who upholds an agreement or maintains it as true is said to ▓▓▓▓▓▓▓ the agreement.

APPLYING LEGAL PRINCIPLES

1. Mayo agreed to buy a camera from Haddad for $200. Unknown to either party, Haddad's daughter had dropped and destroyed the camera the day before the agreement was made. Is the contract binding?

2. Evans found a very valuable bracelet. Without knowing its true value, she sold it to Bowman for $5. Bowman, equally uninformed about the value of the bracelet, took it to an appraiser. The appraiser told Bowman that the bracelet was worth $5,000. When Evans learned of the true facts, she sought to have her agreement with Bowman declared void. Should she succeed?

3. Janik sold a valuable gem to Watson for $650. After the sale, Janik discovered that she had misread the price tag, which showed a price of $1,650. Janik immediately brought suit against Watson for $1,000. Is she entitled to judgment?

4. Fong chose and bought a dining room set from Arlington Furniture Co. He thought the furniture was made of mahogany, but it actually was made of maple. Because of the mistake, Fong offered to return the furniture and de-

manded a refund of his money. Must the furniture company comply with Fong's demands?

5. Paiva, employed by National City Bank, embezzled $30,000 of the bank's funds. The bank's officials threatened to send her to prison unless her parents transferred to the bank certain real estate worth about $60,000. Paiva's parents transferred the property to the bank. Now they seek to have the transfer set aside on the ground of duress. Will the parents be successful?

6. Ottoboni, who was suffering from a serious chronic disease, relied on her doctor for business advice. On the doctor's recommendation, Ottoboni signed a contract to buy a house and lot in which the doctor owned a half-interest. The price paid for the property was quite a bit more than its actual market value. Shortly thereafter, Ottoboni died. Her husband, as executor of her estate, sought to void the agreement because of undue influence. Under what circumstances would he succeed?

7. While negotiating the sale of a racehorse to Lynn, Tyson stated that his horse was a two-year-old with bright prospects of becoming a champion. Lynn, an experienced horse trainer, examined the horse. He found that the horse was actually four years old and was suffering from a disease that usually causes lameness. Lynn nevertheless bought the horse for $1,000. He soon became dissatisfied with the horse's performance, however, and sought to rescind the agreement because of fraud. Is Lynn entitled to rescind the agreement?

8. Markell bought land from an agent who represented the owner. The agent told Markell that the land was capable of producing an income of $7,500 per year. Actually, the land produced an income of only $4,500 per year. Does Markell have a right to cancel the contract because of fraud?

9. The agent of a public utility firm presented a paper to Iguchi, a landowner, and asked him to sign it. The agent stated that the paper was a receipt for an electric meter installed in Iguchi's home. Iguchi couldn't read the paper because he had just broken his eyeglasses. He nevertheless signed the document. Actually, the paper was a grant of a right-of-way across Iguchi's property, on which the utility firm intended to install utility poles. When Iguchi learned of the true nature of the paper he had signed, he sought to avoid the agreement on the ground of fraud. Should he be successful?

ANALYZING COURT CASES

1. Jacobs bought a new car from Lowell Perkins Agency. As part of the deal, she traded in her old car. Jacobs incorrectly believed that she would not have to pay any sales tax on the purchase of the new car. Lowell informed her that under state law, she was liable for the sales tax. Jacobs refused to pay the tax and sued to recover her traded-in car. Should she succeed? (*Lowell Perkins Agency, Inc. v. Jacobs*, 469 S.W. 2d 89)

2. Grant bought a new apartment building from a developer named Morris for $525,000. After Grant had owned the building for two years, he sought to rescind the contract, claiming mutual mistake. The defects that were the basis of Grant's claim could be remedied for $5,000. In your opinion, should the court rescind the contract? (*Grant v. Morris*, 498 P. 2d 336)

3. On February 9, Tucker bought a car from Central Motors. He relied on a representation made by Central Motors that the car was the latest model available on the market. On February 10, Tucker learned from a reliable source that the statement that the car was the latest model was false. However, Tucker continued to drive the car. On April 7, after putting more than 1,000 miles on the car, Tucker sought to set the contract aside for fraud. Was he entitled to do so? (*Tucker v. Central Motors*, 57 So. 2d 40)

Consideration

Think about these cases.
If you were the judge, how would you decide each case?

1

Finer rescued Zane from a house that was burning. In gratitude, Zane promised to pay Finer $1,000 as a reward for saving her life. Is Zane's promise legally enforceable?

2

Kefalis owed Quinn $500, due on March 1. Quinn agreed to take $400 in full settlement of the debt if Kefalis would pay it on January 2. Would such a payment discharge the debt?

WHAT IS CONSIDER-ATION?

Suppose your uncle said, "I promise to give you $5,000 on your eighteenth birthday." Can you legally enforce this promise when you reach your eighteenth birthday? What kind of promises will the law recognize as binding? Historically, no legal system ever devised enforced all promises. Yet some promises are of such importance to society that they must be enforced. In fact, the law regards these promises as creating *legal obligations* on the part of the people who make them to perform as agreed.

In order to separate legally enforceable promises from those that are not enforceable, the law uses the measuring device known as consideration. This means that there must be something given or received in exchange for a promise. Simply stated, this means "If you do something for me, I'll do something for you." When applying this test to your uncle's promise to give you $5,000 on your eighteenth birthday, we can see that the promise is unenforceable. You promised nothing, did nothing, and gave up nothing in exchange for the promise. In other words, there was no consideration for your uncle's promise. Therefore, there was no binding agreement to pay the money to you.

Consideration has been defined in various ways by legal scholars. One definition states that consideration consists of what the **promisor** (the person who makes a promise) demands and receives for the promise. Another definition describes consideration as the "price bargained for and paid for a promise." The person to whom the promise is made is called the **promisee.** The promisee who relies on the promise may bind it (that is, furnish consideration) in one of three ways. The promisee may (1) perform an act that he or she is not legally bound to do; (2) refrain (forbear) from doing something that he or she is otherwise free to do; or (3) make a return promise to do or refrain from doing what the promisor demands.

Performed Acts as Consideration

Suppose we modify our earlier illustration. Suppose your uncle said, "I promise to give you $5,000 on your eighteenth birthday, if you will graduate from high school." If you do graduate after relying on your uncle's promise, can you then enforce his promise? Yes, you can. There is a binding contract between you and your uncle. In exchange for his promise to give you the money, you performed the act your uncle requested—graduating from high school. The law regards your *performed act* as the consideration for your uncle's promise. By performing the requested act, you did something you were not otherwise bound to do. It is important to remember that your uncle specifically requested an *act* as the consideration (a unilateral offer). Therefore, a *mere promise* by you to graduate from high school would have been insufficient.

Forbearance as Consideration

What else may constitute consideration besides performed acts? Suppose Rice promises her daughter, who is seventeen, that she will pay her $1,000 if she will refrain from riding motorcycles until her twenty-second birthday. The daughter does refrain from riding motorcycles, and on her twenty-second birthday she claims the money. The mother refuses to pay, stating that there is no consideration for her promise. Can the daughter legally compel her mother to pay? She can. The daughter refrained from doing something she had a legal right to do—to ride motorcycles. By her **forbearance** (refraining from doing something she has a legal right to do), the daughter has provided consideration for the mother's promise.

A Return Promise as Consideration

Noonan writes to Trinh, "I'll sell you my station wagon for $8,000." Trinh replies, "OK, I'll take it." Is there a contract? If so, what is the consideration? In answer to the first question, there is a contract. To answer the second question, Noonan's promise to turn over the station wagon to Trinh is supported by the consideration of Trinh's *promised act* to pay $8,000 for it. Thus, a counterpromise requested by the promisor can be just as effective as the actual *doing* of the thing to constitute the necessary consideration for the promisor's promise.

NECESSITY FOR CONSID- ERATION

PROBLEM

> **1.** Hamilton gave $1,000 to Romero as a gift. Later, Hamilton demanded a return of the $1,000 on the ground that Romero gave no consideration for the gift. May Hamilton recover the money?

We have seen that courts will not enforce promises unless the promisee gives something of value to the promisor as consideration. If the rule were otherwise, the promisee would be getting "something for nothing." From earliest times, courts have sought to prevent this undesirable result. If, in Problem 1, Hamilton had merely promised to give Romero $1,000 and then changed her mind, Romero could not legally force Hamilton to give him the money. Romero had not given Hamilton any consideration in return for Hamilton's promise. The facts indicate, however, that the money had already been paid to Romero when Hamilton sought to get it back. In such cases the courts have said repeatedly that consideration is not necessary. This is because the gift was fully executed, and there was no longer a promise in existence that had to be supported by a consideration. Hamilton, therefore, would be unable to recover the $1,000 she gave Romero.

The rule that an executed gift needs no consideration applies with equal effect in the case of an executed contract. It is important to remember that *consideration is necessary only in case of an executory gift or in an executory contract.*

ADEQUACY OF CONSIDER- ATION

2. Mizzoni had a grand piano worth $10,000. He needed money badly and offered to sell the piano to Cranford for $9,000. Cranford refused the offer. Gradually, Mizzoni lowered his price until $4,000 was reached, and Cranford accepted that offer. Then, before the piano was delivered to Cranford, Mizzoni received a better offer from another person. He accepted the better offer and refused to carry out his contract with Cranford. Mizzoni claimed that Cranford's consideration was inadequate. Is Mizzoni liable to pay damages to Cranford for failure to carry out his part of the contract?

In the absence of fraud, duress, and undue influence, a court usually will not inquire into the value or sufficiency of the consideration. An exception to this rule occurs in cases where a promise is made to give "money for less money" or "goods for less goods." For example, a promise to pay $10 for $5 this afternoon or to give ten gallons of gas for five gallons of the identical grade and price are both unenforceable for lack of consideration. However, where the units exchanged are not identical, courts will not interfere unless the transaction is tainted with fraud, duress, undue influence, or some other serious defect. In Problem 2, the units exchanged (a piano and $4,000) were not identical. Mizzoni will be bound by the bargain he made with Cranford. Another example of a situation in which the units exchanged are not identical is the case of a buyer who pays $10 for an article normally selling for $5.

An exception to the rule—that courts usually will not concern themselves with the adequacy of consideration—occurs in the case of sales contracts. The Uniform Commercial Code has given the courts the power to deal directly with unjust sales contracts. If a sales contract or any part of it is found to have been unjust or unreasonable at the time it was made, the court may refuse to enforce the contract or the unjust part.

Existing Legal Obligations

3. McKenna agreed to build a swimming pool for Foresman for $15,000. After beginning the work, McKenna discovered a layer of solid rock. As a result, he had to do a great deal more blasting at additional cost. McKenna refused to go ahead with the work unless Foresman promised to pay him an extra $2,000. Foresman orally promised to pay. Is Foresman's promise legally binding?

Is Mr. Randall liable?

Contract Obligations

A party to a contract frequently does or promises to do something that he or she is already legally obligated to do. In these cases the law does not regard the act or promise as a valid consideration. This is because the other party to the contract is receiving no more than he or she was already entitled to receive. In Problem 3, for example, McKenna was under a legal duty to build the swimming pool for $15,000. His later promise to complete the work for an additional $2,000 is not a valid consideration for Foresman's promise to pay.

Some states have modified the rule that doing or promising to do something one is already obligated to do is not a valid consideration for a promise to pay extra compensation. In these states, if the promise to pay the extra compensation is made *in writing* and signed by the party making the promise, no consideration is necessary.

Some courts have held that where unforeseen difficulties arise after the original contract was made, a promise to pay additional compensation is binding. The justification for this is that the parties rescinded the old contract and formed a new one.

Public Obligations

A promise, *whether written or oral,* to pay someone for doing what he or she is already bound by law to do is against public policy. This type of agreement would be void.

EXAMPLE

A witness in a lawsuit refused to testify to what she had seen and heard. Pereira, the plaintiff, orally offered the witness $200 if she would testify. The witness then agreed to testify. Pereira's oral promise is not binding and would not be binding if the promise were made in writing. Every citizen is legally required to testify to the truth.

This principle is particularly applicable to promises made by public officials such as legislators, law enforcement officers, and court officials.

Partial Payments of Debts

PROBLEM

4.   Nisbet owes Wilder $500. Neither party questions nor disputes the amount owed. On the due date, Nisbet pays Wilder $250, and Wilder orally agrees to accept the $250 in full payment of the debt. Later, Wilder brings an action to recover the balance. What are the parties' legal rights?

Most states hold that a promise to pay less than an undisputed amount owed or actual payment of part of a debt will not discharge the debtor's liability to pay the rest of the debt. The debtor is already legally obligated to pay the full sum. Nothing is given up in return for the creditor's promise to forego the balance of the debt. Since there is no consideration for the creditor's promise, the agreement to pay a smaller sum is not legally enforceable. In Problem 4, Wilder can recover the balance of the debt from Nisbet.

Partial Payments Plus a New Consideration

PROBLEM

5.   Assume in Problem 4 that Nisbet gives Wilder $250 plus a used microwave oven. Wilder agrees to accept the money and the microwave in full settlement of the debt. Is the debt legally discharged?

When a debtor agrees to give or gives the creditor a smaller sum plus an additional consideration other than money, the courts consider the debt to be discharged. The object or service given instead of a money payment is valid consideration for the release of the debt. Any legal consideration except "money for less money" is sufficient to discharge a debt. Nisbet's debt in Problem 5 is legally discharged.

Assume, however, that a debtor pays or promises to pay a smaller sum *before the debt is due* or *at a place other than the one agreed on.* In this event, the debtor furnishes a valid consideration for the creditor's promise to forego payment of the balance of the debt.

> Landau borrows $1,000 from DiBiase. She is to repay the money to DiBiase when he is in New York. DiBiase has to cancel his trip to New York, however. He agrees to accept $800 in full settlement of the debt if Landau will deliver the money to him in Boston. If Landau does so, the debt is discharged.

Written Releases of Debts

> **6.** Assume in Problem 4 that Nisbet pays Wilder $250. Then he obtains from Wilder a properly executed General Release instrument. Is the debt discharged?

A written release of part or all of a debt as an executed gift needs no consideration. The gift is usually made by means of a written document known as a **General Release** (see Figure 10.1), under seal. In some states, however, *any written instrument that is a total or partial release of all claims or obligations is valid without consideration or a seal.* The written release in Problem 6 would discharge Nisbet's debt.

Disputed Debts

The rule that payment of part of a debt will not cancel the entire debt because of lack of consideration applies only when the amount is past due and is definite and certain. However, when there is an honest dispute as to the amount due, the law will recognize an agreement to pay less than the sum claimed. This situation typically occurs when a fee for a service is not determined before the work is done. The payment of less than the sum claimed will cancel the debt without a new consideration.

Figure 10.1
A General Release
(courtesy of
Seminole Paper
and Printing
Company)

GENERAL RELEASE

RAMCO FORM 22

Know All Men By These Presents:

That.....I....., MEREDITH VARDARO
(I, We)

first party, for and in consideration of the sum of One Thousand ($1,000)
Dollars, or other valuable considerations, received from or on behalf of

RICHARD RODGERS

second party, the receipt whereof is hereby acknowledged.

(Wherever used herein the terms "first party" and "second party" shall include singular and plural, heirs, legal representatives, and assigns of individuals, and the successors and assigns of corporations, wherever the context so admits or requires.)

HEREBY remise, release, acquit, satisfy, and forever discharge the said second party, of and from all, and all manner of action and actions, cause and causes of action, suits, debts, dues, sums of money, accounts, reckonings, bonds, bills, specialties, covenants, contracts, controversies, agreements, promises, variances, trespasses, damages, judgments, executions, claims and demands whatsoever, in law or in equity, which said first party ever had, now has, or which any personal representative, successor, heir or assign of said first party, hereafter can, shall or may have, against said second party, for, upon or by reason of any matter, cause or thing whatsoever, from the beginning of the world to the day of these presents.

In Witness Whereof, I have hereunto set my hand and seal this 15th day of August , A. D., 19--

Signed, sealed and delivered in presence of:
Henrietta Azcuy

.... L.S.

.... L.S.

STATE OF FLORIDA,
COUNTY OF Palm Beach

I HEREBY CERTIFY that on this day, before me, an officer duly authorized in the State aforesaid and in the County aforesaid to take acknowledgments, personally appeared
MEREDITH VARDARO
to me known to be the person described in and who executed the foregoing instrument and she acknowledged before me that she executed the same.

WITNESS my hand and official seal in the County and State last aforesaid this 15th day of August A. D. 19--

This Instrument prepared by: Henrietta Azcuy
Address 1234 Palm Drive
Palm Beach, FL 33480

Smothers claimed that Kasabian owed him $600 for repairing Kasabian's roof. Kasabian, however, claimed that the services were worth only $300. Smothers continued to insist that his services were worth $600, while Kasabian remained convinced that $300 was a reasonable figure. They compromised on $450, and Smothers received a check for that amount. Smothers may not claim later that Kasabian still owes him $150. Kasabian's payment of $450 canceled the debt.

Forbearance from Suing

7. Halsey negligently injured Muniz in a machine-shop accident. Muniz threatened to sue Halsey unless he paid her $500 within 60 days to compensate her for her injuries. Halsey promised to pay the money but later refused to do so. He claimed that there was no consideration for his promise. What are the legal rights of the parties?

An injured party may honestly believe that a legal claim against another could be successfully maintained in court. In this event, a promise to forbear or refrain from bringing suit on the claim is a valid consideration for a promise to pay a sum of money in settlement of the claim. Actually, the injured party refrains or forbears from doing something that is permitted by law—suing to recover for injuries sustained. In Problem 7, Halsey would be legally liable on his promise to pay $500 to Muniz. However, forbearance or a promise to forbear from doing what one cannot legally do is no consideration.

Promises Based on a Past Consideration

8. Sher was pinned inside her car as the result of an auto accident. Van Dyke, a passing motorist, rescued Sher. Sher then promised to pay Van Dyke $100 for his services. She later refused to pay, however, claiming lack of consideration as her defense. Is Sher's defense legally correct?

A promise or an act is not legally regarded as consideration unless it is given or performed at the same time that the contract is made. Promises made and acts completed before any request has been made for them are said to be **past considerations.** These promises and acts are not recognized

How to Be a Good Witness

As a witness in a lawsuit, you have a very important duty to perform. Your testimony is important not only to the party for whom you appear but to the American justice system as well. Remember that in order for a judge and jury to make a correct decision all of the evidence must be presented to them truthfully and accurately by cooperative witnesses.

Often, witnesses who have given oral or written statements before the trial are called to testify again at the trial. Many witnesses consider this to be unnecessary. But our court procedures require the presence of the witness at the trial in order to obtain testimony under oath and to allow the witness to be questioned by all parties.

As in every undertaking, there is a right way and a wrong way to be a good witness. These suggestions should be helpful to you in case you are called.

- Go over the facts of the case carefully in your mind before going to court to testify.
- Tell the *truth* when testifying. Your sole duty is to tell it like you saw it.

- Answer the questions put to you clearly and loudly enough to be heard by everyone.
- Don't memorize your testimony. It will sound rehearsed and lack the ring of truth.
- Listen carefully when you are being questioned. If you don't hear the question, ask that it be repeated. If you don't understand it, ask that it be rephrased.
- Answer only the questions asked you. Don't volunteer any information.
- If you make a mistake in answering a question, correct it immediately.
- Don't argue with the lawyer asking the questions.
- If an objection is made to a question put to you or if the judge interrupts, stop your testimony immediately.
- Finally, don't try to be someone you're not. Be yourself, and be natural. If you simply tell the truth, you'll be a fine witness.

by the law. In Problem 8, Van Dyke cannot collect the $100 from Sher. His rescue efforts weren't performed in reliance on or in exchange for any previous request or promise on the part of Sher. At the time when Sher promised to pay $100, Van Dyke performed no act and made no return promise in exchange. Sher's defense is legally correct.

WHEN CONSIDERATION IS UNNECESSARY

There are some exceptions to the rule that promises must be supported by consideration. A promise to pay a debt for which the debtor is no longer liable because too much time has passed needs no consideration. This rule touches upon the concept of *statutes of limitations,* which we will discuss further in Chapter 16. Also, a bankrupt debtor's promise to pay a debt that was discharged in the bankruptcy proceedings does not require consideration. Both of these exceptions will be discussed more fully later in the text. A third exception arises in the case of charitable subscriptions or pledges.

Charitable Subscriptions

We have seen that a mere promise to make a gift is not enforceable for lack of consideration. Courts have made exceptions, however, of promises made to organizations that rely on voluntary gifts. These organizations include religious, charitable, educational, and similar institutions. The courts will enforce subscription promises or pledges regardless of consideration when the organization has incurred obligations while relying on the promises. The principle that governs these promises is called **promissory estoppel.** This principle bars a party from taking back certain types of promises on which another party has relied.

EXAMPLE

> Sykes signed a pledge form promising to donate $1,000 to the Whitfield College Building Fund. The college's trustees, relying on the subscriptions received, contracted for architectural and other services. Sykes later refused to pay the money she had pledged. A court will hold Sykes liable on her contract to donate funds, based on the promissory estoppel principle.

The principle of promissory estoppel may also be applied in situations where a promisor makes a promise that a reasonable person would expect a promisee to rely and act on. Courts will enforce such promises without consideration in order to promote fair dealing or to avoid injustice.

As you have seen, consideration and mutual assent go hand in hand toward the formation of a valid contract. But there are two other elements needed to create an agreement that is legally enforceable. We will study one of those—competent parties—next.

Chapter 10 Review

"YOU BE THE JUDGE" REVIEW

Look again at the "You Be the Judge" cases given at the beginning of this chapter. Would you decide them differently now, after your study of the chapter?

Correct Decisions

1. No. Zane's promise is based on a past consideration, which is legally insufficient to support a present promise to pay a reward.

2. Yes. Payment of a smaller sum ahead of the due date is sufficient consideration to discharge a larger debt.

UNDERSTANDING WHAT YOU HAVE READ

1. Is consideration the inducement to a contract? Explain.
2. Why is consideration necessary?
3. What is the courts' present attitude toward the problem of adequacy of consideration?
4. When is a promise to pay extra compensation to one who is legally obligated to complete a contract binding? Give an example.
5. Under what circumstances may a debt be discharged by payment of part of the original debt?
6. Is consideration needed to bind a promise to pay a public official a sum of money for performance of duty?
7. "Refraining or forbearing from bringing a suit upon a claim is a valid consideration." Explain this statement and give an example of such a situation.
8. If there is an honest dispute as to the amount due, will an agreement to pay a smaller sum be binding? Why?
9. Why is a past consideration inadequate to support a present promise?
10. Under what circumstances will courts tend to uphold voluntary pledges for charitable purposes?

BUILDING YOUR LEGAL VOCABULARY

Choose the legal term that will correctly complete each definition below. Write your answers on a separate sheet of paper.

1. The party who pays the price bargained for a promise is the
   a. offeror.
   b. promisee.
   c. promisor.
2. The written document that frees a party from the requirement to pay part or all of a debt is called a/an
   a. General Release.
   b. court order.
   c. charitable subscription.
3. A delay in enforcing one's rights is known as
   a. promissory estoppel.
   b. a disputed debt.
   c. forbearance.
4. The legal principle that enforces promises or pledges made to organizations that rely on voluntary gifts is
   a. promissory estoppel.
   b. forbearance.
   c. rescission.
5. Promises made and acts completed before any request is made for them are called
   a. counterpromises.
   b. public obligations.
   c. past considerations.

APPLYING LEGAL PRINCIPLES

1. Valenzuela promised to give Beale his car, and Beale promised to accept it. Valenzuela gave the keys to Cale and asked her to give them to Beale. Valenzuela then changed his mind and got the keys back from Cale. Is Beale entitled to the car?
2. Luce gave Hoffer an old vase that she found in her attic. Shortly afterward, Luce learned that the vase was a valuable antique. Luce demanded its return, claiming lack of consideration. Was Luce entitled to have the vase returned to her?
3. Yang promised $3,000 to his niece Jenny if she would go back to college and complete her engineering degree. Jenny did go back to school and obtained her degree. Her uncle then refused to pay her the $3,000, however, claiming that there was no consideration for his promise. Is Yang's promise legally binding?
4. Subris, a clothing manufacturer, promised to pay Novello $150 a month. In return, Novello agreed to refrain from interfering with deliveries made by Subris's truck drivers to retail customers. Is Subris's promise legally binding?

5. James sold Booth a video camera for $1,400. Later, Booth found that the value of the camera was only about $1,100. Did Booth have a claim against James for $300?

6. Carew hired Van Ness to build a patio for $1,500. Van Ness found that the job would cost him more than he had estimated. He threatened to stop work unless Carew promised to pay him an additional $400. Carew did promise to do so, but on completion of the work Carew refused to pay more than the original $1,500. May Van Ness legally compel Carew to pay the extra $400?

7. Kisor owed Richman $100. When the debt was due, Kisor offered to pay Richman $65 in full settlement. Richman agreed to take it. May she legally collect $35 if she changes her mind?

8. Billing owed Haller $400. When the debt became due, Billing had only $200 in cash. He asked Haller if he would accept the $200 and a radio, worth about $75, as full payment. Haller agreed. Is the entire debt canceled?

9. Danzig owed Nunez a debt of $300, due on May 28. Nunez agreed to accept $250 from Danzig on May 1 and to cancel the entire debt. Danzig did pay Nunez the $250 on May 1. May Nunez hold Danzig liable for the balance of the debt?

10. Cass promised Tatarian that if Tatarian would pay part of her past-due debt to him, he would cancel the remainder of the debt. Tatarian paid the partial amount requested by Cass and received a written release for the balance. Cass later sued for the balance of the debt. Will he collect?

11. Haines received a bill from Reynes TV Repair for repair service amounting to $155. Haines refused to pay, claiming that she owed only $110. Finally, Haines and the company agreed to settle for $130. After the settlement, Reynes TV Repair found that the original statement had been correct and sought to collect the additional $25. Did the company have a legally enforceable claim against Haines?

12. Suarez incurred a doctor's bill of $500 for treatment of injuries she received after being struck by a car. The owner of the car promised Suarez $400 if she wouldn't sue him for the cost of the treatment. Suarez agreed and did not bring suit. Was the agreement binding?

13. Robertson's brother Quentin had been very ill for two months. His hospital bill amounted to $40,000. As Quentin was being released from the hospital, Robertson promised to pay the bill. Later, however, Robertson refused to pay, claiming lack of consideration as her defense. Was Robertson legally obligated to pay the bill?

14. Foley promised to donate $500 to the building fund of Trinity Baptist Church for the purpose of building a new daycare center. The church's trustees, relying on the promised donations, bought some land on which to build the center. Foley later refused to make his donation, claiming that there was no consideration for his promise. Was Foley bound?

ANALYZING COURT CASES

1. Hoffman wanted to acquire a franchise to operate a Red Owl grocery store. Red Owl was a corporation that maintained a system of chain stores. Hoffman was told by an agent of Red Owl that he could have a franchise if he sold his bakery in Wautoma, acquired a certain tract of land in Chilton, and put up the sum of $25,000. Hoffman complied with the agent's request but was refused a franchise. He sued the corporation, which raised the defense of no consideration and no binding contract to give him a franchise. Was the defense proper? (*Hoffman v. Red Owl Stores, Inc.*, 133 N.W. 2d 267)

2. Pankow was employed by Engineering Associates, Inc., for several years. At Engineering's request, Pankow signed a paper stating that he would not work for any of Engineering's competitors for a period of five years after leaving Engineering's employment. Was this contract binding on Pankow? (*Engineering Associates, Inc. v. Pankow*, 150 S.E. 2d 56)

3. Ida Melnick and her husband Samuel were passengers on a flight of National Air Lines from New York to Philadelphia. Upon arrival, Samuel discovered that his wife's suitcase, containing property belonging to both of them and valued at $1,677, was missing. Under the tariff rules in effect, National Air Lines' liability for lost baggage was limited to $100 unless the passenger had declared a higher value and paid an extra charge. The Melnicks had done neither. Accordingly, National sent them a check for $100, on the back of which was written:

   "In indorsement of this check, I hereby discharge National Air Lines . . . from any and all claims and demands which I now have or may hereafter have on account of incident involving lost baggage which occurred on or about. . . ."

   Samuel Melnick crossed out the above notation and cashed the check. Then the Melnicks filed a suit against National Air Lines to recover the remaining value of their belongings, claiming lack of consideration. Are they entitled to recover? (*Melnick v. National Air Lines*, 150 A. 2d 566)

CHAPTER 11

Minors and Legal Competency

YOU BE THE JUDGE

Think about these cases.
If you were the judge, how would you decide each case?

1

Dyer, seventeen, bought a computer from Tec-Help. Shortly after her eighteenth birthday, Dyer sold the computer. Then Dyer decided to avoid the contract and demanded a return of the price she paid for the computer. Tec-Help refused to return the money and claimed that Dyer couldn't avoid the contract. Who was right?

2

Chu, sixteen, was hurt in a football game. A doctor was called to the scene to set Chu's broken leg. Later, the doctor sent a bill for $100 for services rendered. Chu refused to pay the bill, claiming that, as a minor, he wasn't liable. Assuming the charge was reasonable, can the doctor hold Chu liable for payment of the bill?

CAPACITY TO CONTRACT

At the beginning of this unit, we learned that at least two parties are essential to create a contract. If these parties have the ability to acquire legal rights and can assume legal responsibility for their acts, they are said to have **capacity to contract.** Capacity to contract makes them *competent* parties. A competent party, therefore, as noted in Chapter 5, is one who has the capacity to enter into binding contracts.

A person who is incompetent to contract usually lacks capacity because of age, mental condition, or some statutory limitation. Incompetent persons may be minors (people under a certain legal age for making contracts), persons of unsound mind, people under the influence of alcohol or drugs, imprisoned persons, and enemy aliens.

Competency of Minors

> **1.** Byrd, fifteen, bought a basketball at a local sporting goods store. If Byrd changed her mind the next day and returned the basketball, is the store legally required to refund her money?

A **minor**—sometimes referred to legally as an **infant**—is a person who has not reached the age of full maturity of mind and judgment. Because the law regards a minor as too inexperienced to enter into business deals on equal terms with adults, a minor is given the special protection of the law. As a protective measure, the law sometimes permits the minor to avoid a sales contract with an adult. The minor may do this by returning the purchased goods and getting his or her money back. In Problem 1, Byrd may legally avoid her contract for the purchase of the basketball. On returning the ball, she would be entitled to a refund of her money.

> **2.** Pashos, seventeen, agreed to buy a used all-terrain vehicle for $495 from Harkness. Pashos paid $25 as a deposit and agreed to pay the balance when he picked up the ATV the following Friday. When Pashos appeared with the money, Harkness told him that he had changed his mind about selling the ATV and offered to return Pashos's deposit. Was Harkness within his legal rights?

Since early times, the law has automatically considered people under 21 years of age to be minors. Thus, they have not been thought capable of entering into any but a few contracts. In some states this is still true. The Twenty-sixth Amendment to the Constitution, however, grants to people eighteen and older the right to vote. Since that amendment's adoption, most states have passed laws that give people eighteen and older the right to make contracts, to sue and be sued, and to make wills. In some states, married minors are permitted to contract as adults. Legally, a minor becomes competent to contract on the *day before* his or her eighteenth birthday. A person is said to have reached **majority** on that day.

If a minor enters into a contract with an adult, the minor in certain cases may avoid or refuse to perform it. The contract is said to be **voidable** at the option of the minor. Remember, *voidable* means that *one* party to a contract (a minor, for example) may avoid or declare the contract at an end. Although a minor may avoid a contract with an adult, the adult is bound if the minor is willing to carry out the contract's terms. In Problem 2, therefore, Harkness may not avoid his contract with Pashos if Pashos is willing to be bound by it.

A Minor's Liability for Necessaries

Certain contracts made by a minor relate to things needed to sustain his or her life and well-being or that of the minor's dependent family. The law recognizes these needs, which are known as **necessaries.** Usually, necessaries include food, clothing, medical care, shelter, basic education, and equipment with which to earn a living. Whether articles or services constitute necessaries for a particular minor depends on the minor's age, financial condition, and social standing in the community. Membership in an exclusive country club, for example, may be a necessary for a wealthy minor.

> While her parents were out of town, Vaiella became very ill with the flu. She drove to a health-care clinic and engaged a doctor's services for an examination, diagnosis, and treatment. Because health care is a necessary service, the doctor who treated Vaiella has a valid claim for services rendered.

A minor is liable in quasi contract for the *fair or reasonable value* of necessaries supplied, regardless of the contract price. Also, the minor is liable only for the necessaries supplied and delivered. If someone legally responsible for the minor keeps the minor well supplied with necessaries, the minor is not liable on contracts for the purchase of additional so-called necessaries.

> Anders, sixteen, was a member of a well-to-do family. His parents kept him adequately supplied with clothes. While his parents were away on a short trip, Anders went to a tailor and ordered a new winter coat. May Anders later refuse to take the coat? Yes. Since he was already well supplied with clothes, he is not liable on the contract unless the tailor can prove otherwise.

A Minor's Disaffirmance of Voidable Contracts

PROBLEM

3. Rosenthal, seventeen, bought a fine collection of domestic and foreign stamps for $2,500. Shortly before her eighteenth birthday, Rosenthal returned the collection to the dealer and asked for her money back. What are Rosenthal's legal rights?

A minor may avoid contracts that the law considers voidable. The procedure by which this is done is called **disaffirmance.** Voidable contracts usually involve nonnecessaries (luxuries) or goods and services bought for ornamental or pleasure purposes. They may also relate to purchases of goods with which the minor is already sufficiently supplied. At various times, courts have decided that cars, racehorses, jewelry, liquor, tobacco, and pleasure trips are not necessaries for minors.

A minor may choose to disaffirm voidable contracts at any time before reaching the age of majority. In that case, the purchased goods still in the minor's possession must be returned. However, the right to disaffirm a contract does not depend on the minor's ability to return the purchased goods. In some states a minor is allowed to disaffirm on return of the article and to recover the purchase price minus wear and tear on the article. In Problem 3, Rosenthal was within her legal rights in returning the collection before her eighteenth birthday. The dealer would be obligated to refund Rosenthal's money.

A minor may also exercise the right to disaffirm a voidable contract *within a reasonable time after attaining majority.* What constitutes a reasonable time depends on the circumstances of each case. It is a question of fact that a jury would be called on to decide. A reasonable time within which to disaffirm a contract for the purchase of expensive jewelry would undoubtedly differ from that for a purchase of corporate stock. The price of expensive jewelry changes much less rapidly than the price of corporate stock may change.

EXAMPLE

Assume in Problem 3 that Rosenthal returned the collection to the dealer within two weeks *after* her eighteenth birthday. Rosenthal would be entitled to get her money back because she disaffirmed the contract within a reasonable time. If, however, Rosenthal had waited for six months or a year after reaching her majority, she might no longer have had the right to disaffirm the contract.

If a minor fails to disaffirm voidable contracts on reaching majority, these contracts are legally deemed to have been *affirmed* or *ratified.* This approval method is called **affirmance**, or **ratification.** It is important to remember that affirmance or ratification may take place only after the minor has reached majority. Affirmance may be indicated by an express promise to perform the contract. It also may be indicated by actions showing an intention on the minor's part to be bound on the contract.

> Shortly after reaching his majority, Romagosa sold to Sams a stereo radio he had bought while still a minor. Romagosa may no longer disaffirm the contract with the dealer from whom he bought the radio. By selling the radio to Sams, Romagosa indicated that he was willing to be bound on the original contract.

A minor may not legally affirm part of a voidable contract and disaffirm the rest. The entire contract must be ratified or rejected.

> DeFeo bought a boat with an outboard motor. She was a minor at the time of the purchase. A week after her eighteenth birthday, she returned the motor and offered to pay for the boat. DeFeo is not legally permitted to do so. If she chooses to disaffirm, she must return both the boat and the motor.

A minor must wait until reaching majority before disaffirming a contract involving real property.

Misrepresentation of Age by a Minor

> **4.** Igusa, seventeen, asked to see some pins in a jewelry store. The jeweler asked her age, and Igusa said that she was twenty. She then bought a gold and diamond pin from the jeweler for $400, to be picked up in a few days. Later, she refused to take the pin. Is Igusa bound to fulfill her contract?

Even though a minor deliberately misrepresents his or her age, the minor may still disaffirm a voidable contract. In some states, however, an adult who is taken advantage of unfairly in this way by a minor may hold the minor liable for deceit. In those states the adult may collect money damages from the minor for any loss incurred as a result of the minor's falsehood. In Problem 4, Igusa would have a legal right to disaffirm her contract to buy the pin. The jeweler, however, could hold her liable for any damages suffered because of Igusa's misrepresentation. When a dealer has reason to believe that the customer is a minor, the consent of the minor's parents—preferably in writing—should be obtained. If the parents consent to the transaction, they will be bound.

CAREERS IN LAW

Legal Secretary

The broadest use of the term *legal secretary* refers to anyone who performs secretarial duties as an employee of a law office. Generally, the phrase has come to refer to someone whose professional secretarial experience includes dealing with legal procedures and documents.

The duties of a legal secretary vary, depending on the employer and the kind of law practiced by the office's attorneys. Those duties typically include the preparation of legal documents such as contracts of all kinds, depositions, wills and estate plans, documents of incorporation, prenuptial agreements and divorce documents, and appellate briefs. Other duties may include research of precedent cases, the recording of documents with court officials, and proofreading.

Because virtually all legal documents are typed, a legal secretary must have excellent keyboarding skills. Most law offices today use word processing systems to generate the large volume of documents required in court actions. Many legal secretaries also must have excellent stenography or dictation skills. Legal secretaries are required to be diplomatic, discreet, and professional at all times.

Salaries paid to legal secretaries are usually higher than the salaries of secretaries who are not involved in the legal profession. The specialized knowledge of legal secretaries makes them very valuable to their employers. If you have the appropriate skills, this career can be a very rewarding one.

A Minor's Contracts Under Statutes

PROBLEM

> **5.** Silber, a minor, contracted to buy a van to be used in a business in which he was engaged. May Silber later avoid the contract?

A minor is bound by contracts made under the authority of a statute. In some states a minor fifteen years of age or over may make a valid contract of life insurance. In a few states, a minor eighteen years of age may not disaffirm a reasonable contract made in connection with a business in which he or she is engaged. In Problem 5, Silber would be bound on his contract in states that validate a minor's business contracts. In California, a minor is bound by a contract to provide services as an actor or as a sports professional, if the contract has been approved by a court. In many states, a minor is allowed by statute to deposit funds in a bank and to draw checks against those funds. Of course, minors who enlist in the armed forces must carry out their part of the contract. Eighteen-year-old people now have the right to vote, and in many states they can make valid wills and serve on juries. In most states, however, the minimum age for buying alcoholic beverages is still 21.

Others Who Lack Capacity to Contract

PROBLEM

> **6.** Wolcott had been adjudged insane, and a guardian had been appointed by the court to take care of her property. Shortly thereafter, Wolcott entered into a contract for the purchase of land. Is the contract voidable?

The incompetence of minors is due to their age. Other people may have limited contractual capacity because of an unsound mind or because of some statutory disability. These include insane people, people under the influence of drugs or alcohol, people in prisons, and enemy aliens.

Usually, the liability of an insane person is the same as that of a minor. However, a person who has been officially declared by a court to be insane cannot contract even for necessaries. That person may act only through a court-appointed representative, known as a **guardian.** A guardian is a person who is legally responsible for the care of an incompetent or of the incompetent's property. In Problem 6, the contract made by Wolcott is voidable.

Sometimes a person under the influence of alcohol or other drugs may avoid a contract. This is true when at the time of contracting, the person's mental capacity to understand the nature of the transaction was lacking.

During imprisonment, a person's civil rights are suspended. Most states do not allow prisoners to sue for breach of contract. About a quarter of the states have enacted **civil death statutes** that prohibit convicts from contracting for any purpose. Some states allow prisoners to enter into valid contracts to transfer title to real estate.

Courts usually recognize that an alien has a right to contract. If the United States is at war with the alien's country, however, the alien is known as an **enemy alien.** An enemy alien's rights to contract are suspended at the outbreak of war. Generally, an enemy alien is also denied the right to sue on an existing contract until the war is over.

Competent parties, as you have now seen, are just as essential to the creation of a valid contract as are mutual assent and consideration. One final element is needed, however, in order to make a contract enforceable at law. That element is legal purpose, and we shall study it next in Chapter 12.

Chapter 11 Review

"YOU BE THE JUDGE" REVIEW

Look again at the "You Be the Judge" cases given at the beginning of this chapter. Would you decide them differently now, after your study of the chapter?

Correct Decisions

1. Tec-Help was right. By selling the computer after reaching her majority, Dyer ratified her contract. She could no longer disaffirm it.

2. Yes. Medical care is regarded as a necessary for which a minor is liable. Since the fee was reasonable, Chu must pay it.

UNDERSTANDING WHAT YOU HAVE READ

1. Who is a minor?
2. Exactly when is a minor usually regarded to be of legal age?
3. What contracts made with a minor are legally enforceable?
4. When is a minor liable on a contract for necessaries?
5. May an adult avoid a contract made with a minor? Explain.
6. When may a minor disaffirm a voidable contract? Give an example.
7. May ratification take place before the minor has reached majority?
8. What is the legal effect of a minor's misrepresentation of age?
9. List at least five types of contracts that minors may enter into under statutory authority.
10. Name four types of people, other than minors, who are not competent to contract.

BUILDING YOUR LEGAL VOCABULARY

From this list, select the legal term that belongs in the blank in each sentence below. Write your answers on a separate sheet of paper.

capacity to contract	guardian	necessaries
civil death statutes	infant	ratification
disaffirmance	majority	voidable contract
enemy alien		

1. A ▌▌▌▌▌▌▌▌▌ is a court-appointed representative who is legally responsible for the care of an incompetent or of the incompetent's property.
2. The ability to acquire legal rights and assume legal responsibility for one's acts is called ▌▌▌▌▌▌▌▌▌.
3. The status of a person who has reached the age at which he or she becomes competent to contract is known legally as ▌▌▌▌▌▌▌▌▌.
4. ▌▌▌▌▌▌▌▌▌ is the process by which a minor affirms or approves a voidable agreement by failing to disaffirm it after becoming competent to contract.
5. Another legal term used to describe a minor is ▌▌▌▌▌▌▌▌▌.
6. Laws that prohibit convicted people from contracting for any purpose are known as ▌▌▌▌▌▌▌▌▌.
7. Things needed to sustain the life and well-being of a minor or of the minor's dependent family are called ▌▌▌▌▌▌▌▌▌.
8. The procedure by which a minor may avoid contracts that the law considers voidable is ▌▌▌▌▌▌▌▌▌.
9. A foreign resident of the United States becomes an ▌▌▌▌▌▌▌▌▌ when the United States is at war with the foreigner's country.
10. An agreement that may be declared at an end by one party is called a ▌▌▌▌▌▌▌▌▌.

APPLYING LEGAL PRINCIPLES

1. Gottlieb, a minor, was given $200 to buy needed clothing. She bought the clothes at a department store and received good value for her money. At the same time, she bought the store's finest portable stereo radio with $80 of her own savings. Several days later, Gottlieb decided to return all of her purchases and get her money back. Is the store legally obligated to take all the goods back?
2. A dealer sold and delivered a VCR to Kwan. Later, discovering that Kwan was a minor, the dealer sought to avoid the contract and recover the VCR. Will the dealer be successful?

3. Huston, sixteen, told Hermida that he was eighteen when he bought a camera from Hermida for $175. Three weeks later, Huston returned the camera and demanded his money back. Will he succeed?

4. One week before her eighteenth birthday, Sills bought a tapedeck from Accurate Electronics for $250 cash. On the day after her birthday, Sills returned the tapedeck and asked for a refund of her money. She stated that she had received another tapedeck as a birthday present. Could Sills disaffirm her contract?

5. Three months before his eighteenth birthday, Florez bought a boat for $7,500. He agreed in writing to pay $500 down and the balance in monthly payments of $200 each. After making twelve payments, Florez tried to return the boat and have his money refunded. Was he within his legal rights in returning the boat and getting a refund of his money?

6. Curtis, a minor, bought a movie camera and a projector. Shortly after reaching his majority, he decided to keep the movie camera and to return the projector. Is Curtis entitled to do so?

7. Gibeault, a minor, bought a personal computer from Trong. After Gibeault became eighteen, she sold the computer to Xavier. May Gibeault disaffirm her contract with Trong on the ground that she was a minor when she made it?

8. Lezec was declared insane, and the court appointed a guardian for him. Later, Lezec entered into an agreement for the purchase of some airline tickets. Was this agreement binding on Lezec?

9. Breuner was convicted of a felony and sentenced to prison. While in prison she hired an attorney to help her obtain a parole. The attorney succeeded in getting Breuner's parole. Breuner then refused to pay the attorney's bill on the ground that an imprisoned person has no capacity to contract. Do you agree with Breuner's claim?

ANALYZING COURT CASES

1. Rose appeared to be over 21, the age of majority at the time the parties entered into their contract. He bought a car from Sheehan Buick. Later, claiming that there were certain defects in the car, Rose sought to return the car and to avoid the contract. In addition, Rose informed Sheehan Buick that he was under 21 at the time of the sale. Sheehan claimed that the defects were minor. May Rose avoid his contract? (*Rose v. Sheehan Buick*, 204 So. 2d 903)

2. Stuhl, twenty, bought flight tickets from Eastern Airlines, Inc., and issued checks in payment. The checks were not honored by the bank on which they were drawn. Eastern filed suit against Stuhl to recover the price of the tickets. Five months after attaining his majority, Stuhl answered the complaint by disaffirming the contract for which the checks had been issued. May Stuhl disaffirm the contract? (*Eastern Airlines, Inc., v. Stuhl*, 65 Misc. 2d 901; 318 N.Y.S. 2d 996)

3. Spaulding was a minor living with his wife and child. He bought several items of household goods and furniture from New England Furniture Company on a conditional sales contract. The purchase price, including service charges, amounted to $1,431.09. Spaulding paid the furniture company $388 and then defaulted on his contract. After the furniture company had repossessed the goods and furniture, Spaulding brought an action against the firm to recover his $388 payment. The furniture company contended that the items purchased were necessaries and that Spaulding could not disaffirm the contract. Was this contention correct? (*Spaulding v. New England Furniture Company*, 147 A. 2d 916)

Legal Purpose

Think about these cases.
If you were the judge, how would you decide each case?

1

A golf club advertised that it would pay $5,000 to anyone shooting a hole-in-one. Gordon paid the $5 entry fee and made a hole-in-one. The club refused to pay the $5,000. When Gordon sued for breach of contract, the club claimed it was an illegal gambling contract and therefore void. Was this claim legally correct?

2

The owner of a grocery store sold his entire business. As part of the sales contract, he agreed not to re-engage in the grocery business anywhere in the country for a period of ten years. Is the agreement valid?

ILLEGAL AGREEMENTS

As well as being based on mutual assent, consideration, and competent parties, an agreement must have a legal purpose. If the purpose of the agreement is the performance of an illegal act, the agreement is therefore unenforceable.

> Rawls was a police court judge. Hirshberg promised to pay Rawls $300 if Rawls would dismiss a reckless-driving charge against Hirshberg. Rawls agreed to do so. Rawls cannot legally enforce Hirshberg's promise because the agreement is illegal. It tends to interfere with the proper administration of justice and is harmful to society.

Agreements may be illegal because they are specifically declared to be so by statute. Thus, statutes in nearly all states provide that gambling or wagering contracts are illegal. Statutes also provide that agreements for excessive interest and agreements with unlicensed persons are illegal.

An agreement may require the performance of an act that is harmful to the public welfare. This type of agreement is said to be against the best interests of the people or against public policy. Therefore, it is illegal. Examples include (1) agreements in unreasonable restraint of trade; (2) agreements in unreasonable restraint of marriage; (3) agreements that tend to interfere with public service; and (4) agreements that tend to obstruct justice.

Gambling or Wagering Agreements

> **1.** Burr bet Aiello $100 that the home team would win a certain football game. The home team won, and Burr collected the $100. Later, Aiello sued to recover the money she had lost. Will she be successful?

An agreement that calls for a payment or a transfer of something valuable to another on the happening of an uncertain event is illegal. This kind of agreement is known as a **gambling** or **wagering agreement.** Most states have declared gambling agreements to be illegal. The courts in these states will refuse to aid either party seeking to recover money paid under such an agreement. In some states, the loser or another interested party designated by statute may sue to recover a paid bet or a bet placed in the hands of a stakeholder. The object of statutes such as these is to discourage gambling by making it difficult for the winner to keep the winnings. In Problem 1, Aiello would not be allowed to sue in most states for the money she lost in the wager.

Some states, such as New York, California, Florida, Illinois, and Maryland, permit supervised legal betting. Commonly, this is betting in **pari-mutuels** (a pool in which people who bet on competitors finishing in the first three places share the total amount bet minus a percentage for the management) at racetracks. Also, about half of the states now have legalized **lotteries.** Lotteries are supervised games of chance in which some consideration is paid for a chance to win a prize.

Agreements Involving Excessive Interest

PROBLEM

> **2.** Villa borrowed $500 from Lantine. He gave Lantine a note promising to repay the money in two months, with interest at 50%. When the note fell due, Villa refused to pay the principal or interest. Can Lantine collect?

Statutes in nearly all states prescribe a maximum interest rate or charge that lenders may impose on borrowers. This statutory rate, which varies by state, is called the **contract rate of interest.** When the parties fail to specify an interest rate to be charged, statutes in most states declare a **legal rate of interest.** Typically, a state's contract rate of interest and the legal rate differ.

A lender who charges a borrower more than the contract rate of interest is guilty of **usury.** In states that have usury laws, Lantine, in Problem 2, would be guilty of usury.

Penalties for usury vary among the states. In some states there is no penalty at all. Other states require usurers to forfeit interest or even double interest. In many others, the usurious lender forfeits only the interest that exceeds the statutory maximum. In a few states, the lender forfeits the principal as well as the interest.

Usury laws in most states offer little protection to consumers who buy goods on credit. In fact, the **"Time Price" doctrine** developed by the courts exempts all sales credit transactions from the general usury laws. State legislatures have also enacted laws allowing loans to be made at rates in excess of the usury rate. The best-known of these laws is the **Uniform Small Loan Law.** This law requires the lender to be licensed and limits both the amount and the length of time of the loan. Other state statutes exempting lenders from usury laws are installment loan laws and industrial loan laws. These laws govern lenders such as full-service banks, credit unions, and savings and loan associations. Finally, some state laws deal with specific aspects of consumer credit transactions, such as disclosure of the actual cost of credit (truth-in-lending) to consumers. The federal **Truth-in-Lending Act** of 1969 requires full disclosure of the terms of substantially all consumer credit transactions. Among other things, this act requires lenders to state the loan finance charge in terms of an annual percentage. We will discuss the Truth-in-Lending Act in more detail in Chapter 22.

States adopting disclosure laws similar to the Truth-in-Lending Act may substitute their own laws for the federal law. States may also adopt the **Uniform Commercial Credit Code (UCCC)** in place of either the federal act or their own laws. Only a small number of states have adopted the UCCC.

Agreements with Unlicensed Persons

PROBLEM

3. Quill, a doctor who was not licensed by the state in which she was practicing medicine, treated a patient. The patient refused to pay the doctor. What rights does Quill have?

State laws require people in certain occupations to be licensed in order to do business legally. These people include doctors, nurses, lawyers, pharmacists, real estate and insurance agents, electricians, plumbers, and beauticians. The object of licensing laws is to protect the public from incompetent and untrustworthy people who may offer their services. A contract made with an unlicensed person is illegal and void. Any consideration paid to such a person may be recovered. In Problem 3, Quill would be unable to recover her fee.

A license may be required simply for the purpose of raising revenue. In that event, an agreement made with an unlicensed person is generally regarded as binding.

Many states require doctors to be licensed if work is to be done legally.

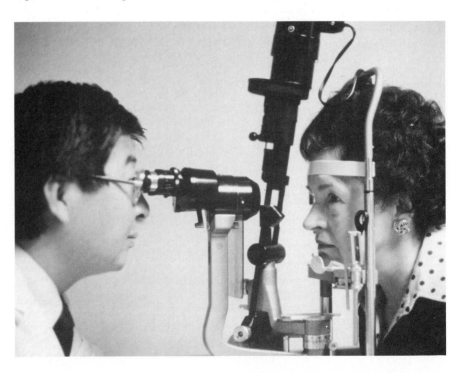

Agreements in Restraint of Trade

> **4.** Brewster sold his entire stock of hardware and fixtures to Singh for $90,000. It was agreed that Brewster wouldn't open another hardware store in the entire country for the next five years. A month later, Brewster opened another hardware store in the next block. Singh filed suit. What are the rights of the parties?

The agreement described in Problem 4 is an unreasonable restraint of trade because it is not reasonably limited in *time* and *space.* Therefore, it is void as being against public policy. Such agreements tend to prevent free and natural competition and usually result in higher prices to the public.

To determine whether a restraint is reasonable or unreasonable, courts today inquire into the extent of the protection needed by the purchaser. They also consider the interests of the public. The nature and size of the business and the extent of its market are helpful factors in deciding how much protection to give the buyer. Courts usually give more consideration to space provisions than to time provisions. In Problem 4, if Brewster had agreed not to open a hardware store within a certain part of the city, the agreement probably would have been valid. It would have provided Singh with adequate protection without interfering with the public.

Agreements in Restraint of Marriage

> **5.** An uncle promised in writing to give his eighteen-year-old niece $5,000 if she would refrain from marrying until she was 21. Shortly after reaching 21, the niece married and claimed the $5,000. The uncle refused to pay, claiming that the agreement was illegal. Is the uncle legally correct?

It is the policy of the law to encourage marriages. Any agreement that unreasonably restricts marriage is void because it is against public policy. The law, however, won't interfere with agreements that place reasonable restrictions on marriage. This was the situation in Problem 5. If the uncle had obtained a promise from the niece that she would *never* marry, the agreement would have been void. The uncle's restriction would have been unreasonable.

Agreements Interfering with Public Service

Agreements that tend to interfere with public service are illegal because they are against public policy.

Ward paid her congressional representative $500. In return, the representative was to secure for Ward an appointment as Internal Revenue Service agent in a certain city. The appointment was not made. Ward has no legal right to recover the money. In addition, the corrupt conduct of the representative would be subject to investigation by the House of Representatives.

Other agreements that interfere with public service include payments to legislators in order to influence legislation and payments to obtain public employment.

Agreements Obstructing Justice

6. Dorn agreed to conceal a crime committed by Trainor. Trainor promised to pay Dorn $5,000. Can Dorn enforce this agreement?

An agreement to conceal a crime, as in Problem 6, is illegal because it is against public policy. This type of agreement tends to obstruct the proper administration of justice. Other examples are agreements to encourage lawsuits, to lie on a witness stand, or to bribe jurors or judges.

OTHER ILLEGAL AGREEMENTS

7. Gutierrez agreed to pay Waller, a professional basketball player, $1,000 to "throw" an important playoff game. Waller intentionally played poorly and his team lost. May Waller collect the $1,000 from Gutierrez?

In addition to the agreements just discussed, there are many other illegal agreements. Examples include agreements that limit production, control prices, and limit competition. Others are agreements to commit crimes or to induce others to commit them. An agreement not to prosecute someone who has committed a crime is also illegal.

In Problem 7, Waller is guilty of accepting a bribe. Gutierrez is guilty of the statutory crime of bribing a professional athlete. Both parties are guilty of a crime punishable by a fine and a prison term.

An agreement to "throw" a professional game is illegal.

Many states have statutes that forbid work and business dealing on Sunday, except when the activity relates to necessary or charitable matters. Necessary matters include actions needed to protect the lives, health, and property of members of the community. However, Sunday agreements that don't relate to necessary or charitable matters and are to be performed on a weekday are valid. All contracts and business deals made and performed on a legal holiday other than Sunday are valid.

EFFECT OF ILLEGALITY

PROBLEM

8. Veit bought 100 shares of XYZ Corporation common stock. Unknown to Veit, the stock had not been registered with the Securities and Exchange Commission (SEC) as required by federal law. Is Veit entitled to return the stock and get his money back?

The courts usually won't aid either party when a contract is illegal. This is true when the illegal contract has been fully performed or when neither party has done anything to carry out the illegal purpose. Courts make exceptions, however, in cases where one party is induced to make an illegal agreement through fraud, duress, or undue influence. The injured party in such a case may receive the court's help in avoiding the illegal agreement.

How to Guard Against Credit Card Fraud

Every consumer pays for credit card fraud in higher prices. The fact that one is not personally defrauded makes no difference. Authorities on criminal behavior say that theft is the most obvious form of credit card fraud. But theft is not the only way in which fraud occurs. A more sophisticated type of credit card fraud takes place when the card number (not the card itself) is used without the card owner's permission. This can happen in a number of ways, including these:

- A phone caller says, "Do you want to qualify for a special vacation trip to Bermuda, at a terrific discount? Just give us your credit card number and its expiration date."
- A dishonest employee makes an extra imprint from your credit card for his or her use or illegally uses discarded receipts or carbons to obtain card numbers.

Here are some "DOs" and "DON'Ts" to help you protect yourself against credit card fraud.

DOs

- Sign your new cards on receipt from the issuer.
- Carry the credit cards separately from your wallet.
- Avoid signing a blank receipt or bill.
- Destroy all carbons and incorrect receipts.
- Open the monthly statements promptly and compare charges with your card receipts.
- Promptly report in writing any questionable charges to your account.

DON'Ts

- Never lend your card(s) to anyone.
- Never leave your cards lying around.
- Never put your card number on the outside of an envelope or on a postcard.
- Never give your card number to a phone caller unless you are talking to a representative of a reputable firm. Suppose your credit card is stolen. In that event, use the credit card company's toll-free number to notify the firm immediately. Legally, once you report the loss you have no further liability for unauthorized charges. In any event, you are not liable for more than $50 per card under federal law.

Stock market transactions are regulated by the Securities and Exchange Commission.

Another exception occurs in an agreement that violates a law passed for the protection of one of the parties. This is the case in Problem 8. The **Securities and Exchange Commission (SEC)** is the agency that administers federal laws dealing with stocks, bonds, and similar instruments. SEC registration of corporate stock is required for the protection of the public. A person who unknowingly buys unregistered stock may avoid the agreement and recover any money paid.

Some agreements contain several promises, some of which are legal and others illegal. Courts will separate the promises in these agreements and attempt to enforce the legal provisions. If the promises can't be separated, the entire agreement is unenforceable.

EXAMPLE

Satomi, a merchant, agreed to sell Phillips a camera for $225 and a rifle for $350. Phillips did not have a permit to buy a rifle, although the permit was required by state law. The agreement with respect to the camera is enforceable, but the sale of the rifle is illegal. If Satomi had charged Phillips $575 for both items without specifying the price of each, the entire contract would have been unenforceable.

Now that you are familiar with the four elements of an enforceable contract, let's move on to a study of the forms that contracts may take. Chapter 13 will explore oral and written contracts and the Statute of Frauds.

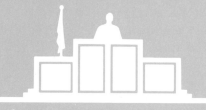

Chapter 12 Review

"YOU BE THE JUDGE" REVIEW

Look again at the "You Be the Judge" cases given at the beginning of this chapter. Would you decide them differently now, after your study of the chapter?

Correct Decisions

1. No. The court said this was not a gambling contract. Whether a person would make a hole-in-one was primarily a matter of skill. The contract did not depend on luck or chance alone.

2. No. The agreement is void because it creates an unreasonable restraint of trade. The restrictions of time and space are both unreasonable.

UNDERSTANDING WHAT YOU HAVE READ

1. Which agreements are usually regarded as illegal by statute? Give an example of one such agreement.
2. Name four types of agreements that are illegal because they are contrary to public policy.
3. What is a gambling or wagering agreement?
4. May the loser of a bet or wager recover the lost money?
5. What is the difference between a contract rate of interest and a legal rate of interest?
6. Describe each of these exceptions to state usury laws:
   a. Uniform Small-Loan Law
   b. installment loan laws
   c. federal Truth-in-Lending Act

7. Why are certain occupations required to be licensed? List at least six occupations that must be licensed in your state.
8. Give an example of an unreasonable restraint of trade.
9. Give an example of each of the following:
   a. an agreement interfering with public service
   b. an agreement obstructing justice
   c. an agreement in restraint of marriage
10. Under what circumstances will a court help a party to avoid an illegal agreement?

BUILDING YOUR LEGAL VOCABULARY

Choose the legal term that will correctly complete each definition below. Write your answers on a separate sheet of paper.

1. An agreement that calls for a payment or a transfer of something valuable to another on the happening of an uncertain event is a/an
   a. agreement in restraint of trade.
   b. gambling or wagering agreement.
   c. agreement that interferes with public service.

2. The federal law that requires full disclosure of the terms of substantially all consumer credit transactions is the
   a. Uniform Small Loan Law.
   b. Truth-in-Lending Act.
   c. "Time Price" doctrine.

3. The statutory maximum interest rate that lenders may impose on borrowers is the
   a. contract rate of interest.
   b. usury rate of interest.
   c. legal rate of interest.

4. Lenders who charge borrowers more than the contract rate of interest are guilty of
   a. obstruction of justice.
   b. usury.
   c. truth-in-lending violations.

5. Supervised games of chance in which some consideration is paid for a chance to win a prize are known as
   a. pari-mutuels.
   b. auctions.
   c. lotteries.

APPLYING LEGAL PRINCIPLES

1. Osinski and Dasho entered into an agreement. Osinski would pitch baseballs to Dasho and would pay Dasho $100 if Dasho hit one ball of every eight over the fence. If Dasho failed to do so, he was to pay Osinski $100. Is the agreement valid?

2. Aaron borrowed $500 from her friend Endres. Endres asked Aaron to write a promissory note with interest at 20%. Since Aaron needed the money, she complied with Endres's request. On the due date, Aaron refused to pay anything. Was she within her rights according to the law of your state?

3. A statute required electricians to be licensed. Klayman, without getting a license, installed new wiring for Akiba. When Akiba failed to pay Klayman the agreed price, Klayman brought suit to collect. Is Klayman entitled to judgment?

4. Comet Theater Enterprises engaged Cartwright to supervise the construction of a new theater. When the job was done, Comet paid Cartwright's fee and then sued to get it back. Comet claimed that Cartwright was not a licensed contractor. Will Comet be successful?

5. Weinfeld sold her pharmacy to Indelicato. Weinfeld signed an agreement stating that she would not engage in the pharmacy business on the same block for six months. Was Weinfeld legally bound by this agreement?

6. Janazzo sold her catering business in Miami, Florida, to Lacarno. The written agreement between the parties provided that Janazzo wouldn't engage in a similar business anywhere in Florida for five years. Six months later, Janazzo opened a catering business within a mile of Lacarno's shop. Does Lacarno have a legal claim against Janazzo?

7. Zonis, a baker, promised to supply the mayor of the city with free baked goods for a year if a local ordinance favorable to Zonis were passed by the city council. Would this agreement be binding on Zonis?

8. Hu charged Updike with stealing $500 from Hu's cash register. When Hu agreed not to prosecute Updike criminally, Updike gave Hu a promissory note for the amount claimed to have been stolen. Is Updike liable on the note?

9. Rodriguez, a candidate for public office, promised to pay Yaffee $100 if Yaffee would vote for him. Yaffee did so and claimed the $100, but Rodriguez refused to pay her. Can Yaffee collect?

10. Frey promised her nephew $25,000 if he would never marry. The nephew, as a result, never married. When Frye died, the nephew attempted to collect from his aunt's estate. Will he be successful?

11. Ellman promised to pay Harter $10,000 if Harter would destroy evidence that the district attorney needed to convict Ellman of a crime. If Harter agrees, is she entitled to collect from Ellman?

12. Strum operated a car wash in a certain city. A state law prohibited Sunday work except "works of necessity." Strum was prosecuted for operating a car wash on Sunday. In his defense, he claimed that since state laws required drivers to keep their lights, windshields, and license plates clean, his work was one of necessity. Was the car wash a work of necessity?

ANALYZING COURT CASES

1. Mohr, a broker, sued Miesen, a customer, for money paid by Mohr in certain stock transactions. The parties had agreed that the purchases and sales made by Mohr for Miesen should not result in an actual transfer of stocks. Rather, in each case the contract should be adjusted by the payment of money by Miesen if the transaction proved to be a losing one, or to Miesen if the transaction was a winning one. Mohr paid out for Miesen more than he took in for him. Can Mohr recover this money? (*Mohr v. Miesen*, 47 Minn. 228)

2. Lally owned and operated a barber shop in Rockville, Connecticut. He sold the business to Mattis. The sales contract contained a clause stating that Lally would not engage in the barbering business for five years in Rockville or within a radius of one mile from Market Street in Rockville. Thereafter, Lally claimed that this clause constituted an unreasonable restraint of trade and was invalid. Is Lally's contention correct? (*Mattis v. Lally*, 82 A. 2d 155)

3. Grannas and his partner bought some heavy equipment from Aggregates Equipment on the installment plan. They agreed to pay in 36 monthly installments. The monthly installments included a "credit service charge" of $11,713.44. Aggregates assigned the contract to Equipment Finance, Inc. When Grannas stopped making payments, Equipment Finance brought suit against him and his partner. Grannas defended the action by claiming usury. Was Grannas's defense proper? (*Equipment Finance, Inc. v. Grannas*, 218 A. 2d 81)

CHAPTER 13

Form of Contracts

Think about these cases.
If you were the judge, how would you decide each case?

1

Samuels orally agreed to sell her summer home to Furtado for $45,000. Furtado gave Samuels $5,000 as a down payment. Later, Samuels refused to deliver the deed to the property. She claimed that the contract should have been in writing. Was Samuels legally correct?

2

An oral contract between Lee City and A-1 Ambulance Co. provided that A-1 would furnish ambulance service at the city's request. If the person served did not pay A-1's fees, the city agreed to pay them. When a person did not pay for the service and the city refused to pay, A-1 sued the city. Was the city liable?

ORAL AND WRITTEN CONTRACTS

You have learned that a contract made orally or by actions of the parties is usually just as binding as one made in writing. This is true of simple contracts such as purchasing a newspaper, making a phone call, getting a haircut, and many other agreements. Even important contracts involving large sums of money are made over the phone.

There are several reasons, however, why important contracts should be made in writing. If the terms of a contract are stated in written form, each party knows exactly what those terms are. Also, the chances of a future dispute over an agreement are lessened if the contract is in writing. If a dispute does occur, it is much easier for either party to prove the terms of a written contract than those of an oral one. Of course, if the parties have no disagreement and are satisfied with an oral contract, the law will not interfere. Figure 13.1 is a sample of a written contract.

PROBLEM

> **1.** Hahn orally agreed to work for Phath for sixteen months at a salary of $1,800 per month. At the end of six months, Hahn was fired because Phath wasn't pleased with his work. Hahn claims that Phath had no legal right to fire him. Phath claims that the contract is not binding because it wasn't in writing. Who is right?

Problem 1 is an example of a contract that should have been made in writing. In fact, statute law in nearly all states says that a contract that cannot be completed within one year from the time it is made must be made in writing to be enforceable. Legally, Phath is correct in her claim that the contract isn't binding because it was made orally.

In addition to an employment contract for more than a year, there are other important contracts that must be made in writing to be legally enforceable. We will study these contracts in detail in this chapter.

STATUTE OF FRAUDS

Over 250 years ago, the English Parliament recognized that certain contracts should be put in writing. In lawsuits involving those contracts, the courts found that they had to put up with a lot of **perjury** (false testimony) and intentional misrepresentation of facts (fraud). To remedy this problem, Parliament passed the famous **Statute of Frauds.** Since English law is the basis of American law, nearly every state has adopted the Statute of Frauds, with some changes. In Problem 1, Phath probably claimed that the agreement with Hahn was unenforceable because the Statute of Frauds requires such a contract to be in writing.

The Statute of Frauds *applies only to contracts that have not been fully performed by the parties* **(executory contracts).** The statute requires the following types of contracts to be written in order to be enforceable:

1. a contract that, by its terms, cannot be performed within one year from the date it is made;
2. a contract for the sale of real property or any interest in real property, or for the lease of real property for more than a year;
3. a contract to answer for the debt or default of another;
4. a contract in consideration of marriage; and
5. a contract made by an estate's executor or administrator to pay an estate debt out of his or her own funds.

The Statute of Frauds also applies to contracts for the sale of goods worth more than $500. These contracts will be discussed in detail in Chapter 17.

Figure 13.1
A Written Contract

THIS AGREEMENT, made the 12th day of May, 19--, by and between CRESTWOOD REALTY CORPORATION of Crestwood, Texas, and hereinafter called the OWNER, and JAMES M. LEW, hereinafter called the ARCHITECT,
WITNESSETH, that whereas the Owner intends to build a one-family dwelling in Crestwood, Texas, of approximately 16,500 cubic feet in volume, and will furnish a survey of the property to the Architect,
NOW, THEREFORE, the Owner and the Architect, for the considerations hereinafter named, agree as follows:

The Architect agrees to perform for the above-named work the following professional services:

Prepare plans and specifications suitable for the construction of said dwelling and for obtaining the approval of local building authorities having legal jurisdiction. Architect will furnish three sets of plans and specifications to Owner. Additional sets will be furnished to Owner at cost.

The Owner agrees to pay the Architect the sum of Three Thousand Dollars ($3,000), payable as follows:

As a retainer upon signing of this agreement	$1,000
When preliminary designs and plans are approved	$1,000
When plans and specifications are completed and three sets are furnished to Owner	$1,000

The Owner and the Architect further agree that the Standard Conditions of Agreement between Owner and Architect as now published by the American Institute of Architects shall be part of this Agreement insofar as they are applicable hereto.

The Owner and the Architect hereby agree to the full performance of the convenants contained herein.

IN WITNESS WHEREOF, the said parties have executed this Agreement on the day and year first above written.

CRESTWOOD REALTY CORPORATION

Martin D. Ulwich
Witness

Barbara M. Bono ____ President

Clara Barlow
Witness

James M. Lew ____ Architect

Contracts Impossible to Perform Within a Year

The employment contract that was the subject of Problem 1 is an example of a contract that cannot, by its terms, be performed within a year of the date it was made. But read the facts of the next problem carefully.

> **2.** On January 2, Kent orally agreed to build a cabin for Michaelo for $47,000. The work was to be completed by May 1 of the following year. Is the contract enforceable?

Courts judge the enforceability of contracts under the Statute of Frauds not by *actual performance* within a year, but by the *possibility of performance* within a year. Thus, the employment contract noted in Problem 1 makes it *impossible* to carry out the purpose of the oral agreement in less than sixteen months. The contract is therefore unenforceable under the Statute of Frauds. In Problem 2, however, the contract's terms make it *possible* to complete the contract in less than a year from the time it was made. This is true even though the parties thought that complete performance would take more than a year. The Statute of Frauds does not apply in Problem 2, and the oral contract is enforceable. Applied examples of this section of the Statute of Frauds will be discussed later in the book.

Contracts Dealing with Real Property

> **3.** Odian orally agreed to sell her land to Gianino for $50,000. If Odian later refuses to perform her part of the contract, what rights does Gianino have?

The Statute of Frauds also provides that contracts for the sale of **realty** (land and anything permanently attached to land) must be in writing. Things permanently attached to land include buildings, growing trees, and minerals. Deeds, mortgages, and leases for more than a year are regarded as interests in real property. In Problem 3, Gianino could not enforce his contract against Odian. The contract should have been made in writing. You will study this provision of the Statute of Frauds again in later chapters.

Contracts to Answer for Debts or Defaults of Others

> **4.** Hittel's Clothing Store sold a suit to Markham for $325. Gohan orally agreed to pay for his friend's suit if Markham failed to pay. Is Gohan's oral promise enforceable if Markham fails to pay for the suit?

A promise to pay money or transfer property to another in consideration of marriage must be in writing to be enforceable.

The Statute of Frauds provides that the promise of one person to answer for the debt or **default** (failure to perform) of another must be in writing to be enforceable. In Problem 4, the clothing store cannot legally force Gohan to pay for the suit. His promise to pay *Markham's debt* was not made in writing. However, a party who orally promises to pay for goods delivered to another legally assumes the debt. An oral promise such as this is enforceable against the person who made the promise.

> Assume that Gohan, in Problem 4, had said, "Let Markham have the suit and send the bill to me." In this case, Gohan legally assumed the $325 debt for the suit and may be held liable for payment for the suit. The debt was not Markham's, but was Gohan's *own debt*.

Contracts in Consideration of Marriage

> **5.**   Houseman said to Donaldson, "If you'll marry me, I'll buy you a brand new Ferrari." After their marriage, Houseman refused to buy the car. Is his oral promise enforceable?

A promise to pay money or to transfer property to another in consideration of marriage is not binding unless it is written. In Problem 5, Houseman's oral promise is not enforceable. This provision of the Statute of Frauds does not apply, however, to mutual promises to marry. In that case, each promise serves as the consideration for the other.

Contracts of Estate Executors or Administrators

An estate executor's or administrator's promise to pay a debt of the **decedent** (the person who died) out of his or her own funds must be made in writing under the Statute of Frauds. This requirement actually gives the **executor** or administrator more time to decide whether to pay someone else's debt.

Simmons, the executor of David's estate, orally promised to pay David's funeral expenses out of her own funds. Simmons's oral promise is unenforceable. If she had promised to pay the funeral expenses using estate funds, though, the promise would have been enforceable and the Statute of Frauds would not have applied.

Figure 13.2
A Written
Memorandum
Sufficient to Satisfy
the Statute of Frauds

> Elmsford, New York
> September 1, 19--
>
> ELMSFORD LANDSCAPING AND JEANINE COUCH hereby agree as follows:
>
> ELMSFORD LANDSCAPING agrees to build a flagstone terrace for JEANINE COUCH at her residence, 52 Locust Drive, Elmsford, New York, for the sum of $1,850. The dimensions of the terrace are to be 20 feet in length by 15 feet in width and 4 inches in thickness. All material used is to be of good quality, conforming with standard specifications of the American Society for Testing Materials.
>
> ELMSFORD LANDSCAPING
>
> By _Joseph Ventana_
> President
>
> _Jeanine Couch_
> Jeanine Couch

Content of the Written Document

To comply with the Statute of Frauds, it is necessary to furnish written proof of the contracts we just discussed. This proof may take the form of a written agreement, note, or **memorandum** signed by the party against whom the contract is to be enforced (see Figure 13.2).

The memorandum need not be in any particular form, but it must contain every essential provision of the agreement. It may consist of a series of letters or telegrams that, when put together, show at least these items: names of the contracting parties; the consideration; the subject matter

LIVING UNDER THE LAW

Before You Sign

When you sign a business or other legal document, you start a chain of legal events that may be difficult to control. The following are some practical suggestions to avoid trouble:

- Be sure you know what you are signing and how it will bind you.
- Read EVERYTHING in a document, including the fine print. Remember, you won't be able to enforce a word-of-mouth promise if it contradicts what has been printed or typed.
- Check the details, including dates, prices, names, and terms. It's what the paper *actually says,* not what you *thought it said,* that counts legally. Be sure the language clearly states your desires.
- If you co-sign a note or indorse a check, you may wind up paying it if the party primarily liable fails to pay.
- The law may require special formalities when you sign certain papers. For example, at least two witnesses must sign a will in the presence of each other and the maker of the will. If you sign, you may have to testify to that effect in court.
- You may buy a car, an appliance, or some other goods on an installment sales contract. The property is not yours until you make the last payment. If you miss a payment, the seller may take back the goods and keep your past payments.
- ALWAYS KEEP A COPY OF WHAT YOU SIGNED. Don't allow anyone to talk you out of your copy.

involved; and the signature of the party assuming the obligation of his or her authorized agent.

When a contract is made in writing, future difficulties about its terms are avoided. If, for example, one of the parties dies, the contract's terms may still be determined from the written document.

Parol Evidence Rule

6. Valdez obtained a franchise from Excelsior Motors to engage in business as an auto dealer in Rockland, Ohio. A written contract identified a specific location in Rockland for the dealership. Later, Valdez claimed that during the negotiations for the franchise, Excelsior had orally agreed to move the dealership to a better location in the city. Was Excelsior liable for damages for having failed to keep this promise?

Once the parties have reached an oral agreement and then reduced it to writing, they are bound by the terms of the written agreement. The law assumes that when parties put an agreement in writing, all their *prior oral agreements* merge into the written form. Unwritten evidence that tends to contradict the written terms is not permitted during a lawsuit. This is known as the **parol** (oral) **evidence rule.** Because of this rule, Valdez in Problem 6 will not be allowed to introduce evidence of Excelsior's oral promise to relocate the dealership. This promise should have been included in the written contract.

However, the parol evidence rule does not prevent proof of a *new* oral or written contract that changes the terms of the earlier contract. Also, there are several exceptions to the parol evidence rule that allow certain oral evidence in a lawsuit seeking to enforce a written contract. First, oral proof is allowed to show that a contract is invalid because of fraud, lack of consideration, or some other defect. Second, oral proof may be included to clear up ambiguous (uncertain) or obscure terms. If a contract contains words that might mean one of several things, there is no way to prove what the parties intended except by oral evidence. Third, oral proof of *subsequent modifications* of a contract may be presented. Clear proof of the later agreement—which may be in oral or written form—is allowed if consideration is present. This last exception does not apply to the sale of goods under the Uniform Commercial Code.

This study of the Statute of Frauds has shown you the basic forms in which the rights and duties of contracting parties must be expressed. The next chapter will show you how the parties' rights and duties may be transferred to others.

Chapter 13 Review

"YOU BE THE JUDGE" REVIEW

Look again at the "You Be the Judge" cases given at the beginning of this chapter. Would you decide them differently now, after your study of the chapter?

Correct Decisions

1. Yes. Under the Statute of Frauds, a contract for the sale of realty must be in writing to be enforceable.

2. No. A promise to pay the debt of another must be in writing to be enforceable under the Statute of Frauds.

UNDERSTANDING WHAT YOU HAVE READ

1. Why should all important contracts be made in writing?
2. What is the purpose of the Statute of Frauds?
3. List five types of contracts that must be in writing to be enforceable under the Statute of Frauds.
4. Give an example of each of the following contracts:
   a. a contract that cannot be performed within a year from the time it is made
   b. a contract that may be performed within a year, although the time stated in the contract is for a period beyond a year
   c. a promise made by an executor to pay an estate debt out of his or her own funds
5. Give an example of each of the following contracts:
   a. a promise to pay the debt of another person
   b. a promise to pay one's own debt
6. Give an example of real property.
7. What must a note or memorandum contain in order to satisfy the requirements of the Statute of Frauds?
8. List at least four practical suggestions to give someone who is about to sign a contract.
9. What is the parol evidence rule? Give an example of its application.
10. List four exceptions to the parol evidence rule.

BUILDING YOUR LEGAL VOCABULARY

From this list, select the legal term that belongs in the blank in each sentence below. Write your answers on a separate sheet of paper.

decedent	memorandum	perjury
default	parol	realty
executor	parol evidence rule	Statute of Frauds
executory contract		

1. A written statement signed by the party against whom enforcement is sought is a ▯▯▯▯▯▯▯▯▯▯▯.
2. One who willfully swears falsely in court is guilty of ▯▯▯▯▯▯▯▯▯▯▯▯.
3. A ▯▯▯▯▯▯▯▯▯▯ is a failure to perform.
4. The law that requires certain contracts to be written is called the ▯▯▯▯▯▯▯▯▯▯.
5. The term ▯▯▯▯▯▯▯▯▯▯ refers to land and anything permanently attached to the land.
6. Another word for "oral" is ▯▯▯▯▯▯▯▯▯▯.
7. A contract that has not been fully performed by the parties is an ▯▯▯▯▯▯▯▯▯▯▯.
8. The ▯▯▯▯▯▯▯▯▯▯ states that oral proof tending to contradict the written terms of a contract may not be allowed during a lawsuit.
9. ▯▯▯▯▯▯▯▯▯▯ is the legal term for a person who has died.
10. The person appointed to administer the will of a party is an ▯▯▯▯▯▯▯▯▯▯.

APPLYING LEGAL PRINCIPLES

1. Conti orally leased an apartment to Ryan for a period of three years. Ryan lived in the apartment for a year and then moved. Is Ryan liable for breach of contract if he pleads the Statute of Frauds as a defense?
2. Assume the same facts as in Problem 1 except that the lease was for a single year. Would Ryan be liable on the oral contract?
3. DiLeo agreed orally to build a bridge for a developer and to complete the work within twenty months. The firm later canceled the contract. When DiLeo sued, the firm claimed that the contract was unenforceable because it wasn't in writing. Is the claim a valid one?
4. On October 17, Melendez orally employed Ianizzi for a year's work, to begin the following Monday. Ianizzi was fired in February of the following year. She sued Melendez for breach of her employment contract. Melendez pleaded the Statute of Frauds as a defense. Is this a good defense?
5. Kwok orally agreed to sell his winter ski cabin to Huston for $58,000. Before

receiving a down payment from Huston, Kwok refused to complete the deal. He claimed that he was not bound on the oral contract. Is Kwok's claim legally correct?

6. Patrick, a mine manager, planned to quit his job because his employers didn't pay his salary regularly. Duncan, a creditor of the mining company, realized Patrick's worth to the business. She orally promised Patrick that she would see that his salary was paid promptly if he wouldn't quit his job. Later, when Patrick sought to enforce Duncan's promise, Duncan claimed that her oral promise was not binding under the Statute of Frauds. Do you agree with her?

7. Bigley orally promised Hurlburt that she would transfer to him the title to certain real estate if he would promise to marry her. After they were married, Bigley refused to transfer the property to her husband. Can Hurlburt enforce the oral agreement?

8. Ellis orally agreed to sell his farm to Thoms. Ellis gave Thoms a memorandum that stated, "On this date I hereby agree to sell and transfer my farm, Sunny Acres, to Thoms for $50,000 cash. Dated: November 1, 19—. Signed: Theodore Ellis." Does this memorandum comply with the requirements of the Statute of Frauds?

ANALYZING COURT CASES

1. Williams promised to give her cousin, Robinson, her home in her will if he would leave his home and take care of her. Robinson did as Williams requested, but Williams failed to will the property to Robinson. Robinson sued for breach of the oral contract to give him the property. Was his claim barred by the Statute of Frauds? (*Williams v. Robinson*, 476 S.W. 2d 1)

2. Gardner bought a used car from City Dodge. A salesperson orally represented to Gardner that the car had never been wrecked. Gardner signed a sales agreement that said: "No other agreement, promise, or understanding of any kind pertaining to this purchase will be recognized." When Gardner discovered the car in fact had been wrecked, he returned it to City Dodge. Then he re-

scinded the contract, claiming fraud and deceit. In a suit by City Dodge, can Gardner introduce evidence of the salesperson's oral representation? (*City Dodge, Inc. v. Gardner*, 208 S.E. 2d 794)

3. Lewis orally agreed to sell certain land to Starlin for $4,500. Starlin gave Lewis a check for $1,000 and promised to pay the balance at the rate of $500 a year. The parties agreed to enter into a written contract later, but never did so. The $1,000 check from Starlin contained the notation: "Payment land." Later, Starlin brought an action to recover the $1,000. He claimed the agreement was unenforceable under the Statute of Frauds. Lewis, however, claimed the notation was a sufficient memorandum to satisfy the statute. Who was entitled to judgment? (*Lewis v. Starlin*, 267 P. 2d 127)

CHAPTER 14

Assignment
of
Contracts

Think about these cases.
If you were the judge, how would you decide each case?

1

Carrido has an employment contract with Eastern Supply Company. She earned $500 in wages for the past week. She assigned her claim for the wages to Vance in payment of a debt she owed Vance. Eastern, however, refused to pay the $500 to Vance. Is Eastern liable to Vance?

2

Janosik, a well-known artist, accepted from Noiles a commission to sculpt a statue of Thomas Jefferson. Then Janosik asked an assistant to sculpt the statue. Does Noiles, who ordered the statue and relied on Janosik to make it, have to accept the statue made by Janosik's assistant?

TRANSFER OF RIGHTS AND OBLIGATIONS

When parties enter into a binding contract, they usually acquire rights and assume obligations. Ordinarily, only the two parties acquire **rights** and **obligations.** However, consider the facts in this problem.

> **1.** Diep agreed to buy from Koch 100 gallons of fuel oil at 75 cents a gallon. Payment was to be made in cash on delivery. Diep assigned the contract to Cornell. Must Koch deliver the fuel oil to Cornell?

The rights and obligations of Diep and Koch in Problem 1 may be summarized as follows:

DIEP	KOCH
RIGHT To receive 100 gallons of fuel oil from Koch	RIGHT To receive $75 from Diep after delivering the goods
OBLIGATION To pay Koch $75 as the purchase price after receiving the oil	OBLIGATION To deliver 100 gallons of fuel oil to Diep

The law permits both parties to transfer or to sell their rights under a contract to a third party. It is important to know that *rights relating to money or to property may be transferred.* Therefore, Diep may legally transfer to Cornell her right to receive 100 gallons of fuel oil from Koch. Koch, too, may transfer his right—the right to receive $75 from Diep after delivering the goods to her. Such a transfer is known legally as an **assignment** (see Figure 14.1). The party who assigns rights under a contract is known as the **assignor.** The third party to whom rights are assigned is known as the **assignee.** Generally, any acts or words, *whether spoken or written,* that show an intention to assign will be regarded as an assignment.

Although the parties to a contract may assign their rights, it is inaccurate to say that they also may assign their obligations without the consent of the other party. Obligations or duties under a contract are usually transferred only by **delegation.** Delegation is entrusting a duty to another for performance. When duties are delegated, the original party (assignor) remains liable if the duties are not properly performed by the third party. This basic principle is expressed in the Uniform Commercial Code. In contracts for the sale of goods, the Code states that an assignment of "the contract" or of "all my rights under the contract" is an assignment of the rights and a delegation of the duties of the assignor. Acceptance of the assignment by the assignee constitutes a promise to perform the duties acquired under the contract. This promise is enforceable either by the assignor or by the other party to the original contract. In addition, the UCC repeats the principle that *a party who delegates duties under a contract remains liable for proper performance by the assignee.*

Figure 14.1
An Assignment

> ASSIGNMENT
>
> KNOW ALL MEN BY THESE PRESENTS:
>
> That I, JOHN P. CORCORAN, residing at 1131 39th Street, New York, New York, in consideration of ($1) paid by JUDITH A. BENIQUEZ, residing at 24379 Riverdale Parkway, New York, New York (herein called "the Assignee"), hereby assign to the Assignee all my right, title, and interest in the monies due me from HENRY ORMOND, for work, labor, and services as a carpenter performed by me, between May 1, 19--, and May 31, 19--, which services were performed at the request of said HENRY ORMOND, and were of the agreed value of two thousand, two hundred dollars ($2,200).
>
> IN WITNESS WHEREOF, I have hereunto set my hand and seal this 1st day of June, 19--.
>
> *John P. Corcoran* _____ (L.S.)

Referring again to Problem 1, Diep may not legally assign her obligation to pay Koch $75 for the fuel oil. She may, however, delegate this duty to Cornell. If Cornell fails to pay Koch, however, Koch could look to Diep for payment. Similarly, Koch may delegate to another his duty to deliver 100 gallons of fuel oil to Diep. Koch will remain liable, however, if this duty is improperly performed.

If the assignment of the contract will change materially what Koch is to do or to receive under the contract, the assignment can't be made without Koch's consent.

EXAMPLE

> Assume that, as a result of Diep's assignment of the contract, Koch is required to deliver a smaller quantity of oil than originally agreed to, or must deliver the oil to a distant point. In this event, there is a material change in the performance of the contract, to Koch's disadvantage. Diep will have to obtain Koch's consent to the assignment, or it will be invalid.

The Uniform Commercial Code recognizes this common-law rule. The UCC states that "unless otherwise agreed, all rights of either seller or buyer can be assigned except where the assignment would materially change the duty of the other party, or increase materially the burden of risk imposed on him by his contract."

A person's rights under a contract may not be assigned if such an assignment is prohibited by law or by the terms of the contract. However, the UCC states that such a prohibition in a sales contract is to be interpreted as applying only to the *delegation of the assignor's duties.* This is so unless the circumstances clearly show that the parties also meant to prohibit the assignment of rights.

Can the surgeon delegate his personal service duties without the patient's consent?

Personal Service Contracts

> **2.** Sanders, a prominent surgeon, agreed to perform a kidney operation on Ishii for $6,500. On the day of the operation, Sanders had to go out of town. In his place he sent Tigges, an equally well-known surgeon. Must Ishii accept Dr. Tigges's services?

The duties under a contract may involve personal trust and confidence or special skill, knowledge, and judgment. In this case, performance of the duties may not be delegated to a third party without the consent of both parties to the original contract. In Problem 2, Ishii need not accept the services of Dr. Tigges. It is obvious that Ishii selected Dr. Sanders because of his personal skill and reputation. Without Ishii's consent, Dr. Sanders will not be permitted to remake the contract by delegating his performance to Dr. Tigges.

When a contract calls for the performance of **standardized** (merely mechanical) **duties,** the performance may be delegated to others. Duties such as these might include sweeping a sidewalk, painting a fence, or greasing a car. As mentioned earlier, the person who delegates such duties remains liable for their proper performance.

An employer's right to the personal services of an employee may not be assigned without the employee's consent. If this rule were otherwise, an employer could change the terms of an employment contract without consulting the employee.

Alvarez, a fashion designer, was under a three-year contract to work for Dionne, Inc. Dionne sold all its assets, including the contract with Alvarez, to Sasona Fashions. Alvarez does not have to work for Sasona unless he so desires, because the right to his services is personal. Therefore, the right is not assignable without Alvarez's consent.

Similarly, an employee's personal service duties may not be delegated without the consent of the recipient of the services. Continuing the example, Alvarez may not delegate his duties under the contract to another designer unless Sasona consents to the arrangement. This rule applies to all professional people whose services require special skill, knowledge, and judgment.

Rights of the Assignee

3. Link sold a microwave oven to Imhoff for $175, representing it to be new. As a matter of fact, the microwave was used. Link assigned his claim for the $175 due him to DeSoto. When De-Soto tried to collect, Imhoff refused to pay, claiming that she had been defrauded in the deal. Is Imhoff's claim good against De-Soto?

Unless the contract provides otherwise, an assignment gives to the assignee no better title or rights than those the assignor had. The assignee is legally said to "stand in the shoes of the assignor." Any valid claim or defense that the third party could make against the assignor may be made against the assignee. Thus, DeSoto in Problem 3 obtained no better rights than his assignor, Link, had. Imhoff may legally rely on the defense of fraud against DeSoto if DeSoto brings suit to collect the $175. DeSoto now has a claim against Link for breach of the warranty that Link's representation to Imhoff was true and free from defenses.

Notice of Assignment

4. Ecker, a landlord, assigned to Taft a claim for $700 rent due from one of Ecker's tenants. The tenant, who was not notified of the assignment, paid the $700 to Ecker. Shortly thereafter, Ecker moved to another state. Does Taft have any rights against the tenant?

LAW IN THE NEWS

Houses Approves Privacy Measure to Help Electronic Communications

Associated Press

WASHINGTON—Moving to bring the federal wiretap law into the modern age of communications, the House yesterday passed and sent to the White House a bill to protect the privacy of electronic communications.

The bill, approved by voice vote, passed the Senate in the same manner Wednesday night.

The legislation would prevent eavesdropping on communications such as electronic mail, computer-to-computer data transmissions, remote computing services, private video conferences and cellular car phones.

Meanwhile, Congress was working on a final version of a computer crime bill. It would penalize those convicted of stealing or maliciously damaging information in computers belonging to the federal government, financial institutions with federal insurance and securities brokers.

The bill also would apply to those who, without authorization, access computers across state lines and who traffic in computer access passwords.

The computer crime measure has passed both houses with only slight differences.

The eavesdropping bill would modernize current wiretap law, which only pro-tects against interception of voice transmissions heard by the ear.

The new bill not only would protect new forms of communications, but would establish clear standards for law enforcement agencies to obtain access, through warrants, to electronic communications and records.

The Senate bill, but not the House version, would toughen penalties against video pirates such as "Captain Midnight," a man who briefly jammed a satellite television signal to broadcast a protest of cable signal scrambling.

The assignee should notify the debtor of the assignment in order to be protected from any fraudulent action on the part of the assignor. If the debtor doesn't know about the assignment and pays the debt to the assignor, the debtor is discharged from any further liability. The assignee, of course, would have a legal claim against the assignor for any money so paid.

When a person dies, all contracts remain in force except those of a personal nature.

Assignment by Operation of Law

> **5.** Hartley is a business person who has entered into a number of contracts. She suddenly dies. What legal disposition is made of her contracts?

When a person dies, the representative of that person's estate is bound by operation of law to perform all contracts not of a personal nature that had been entered into by the deceased while alive. The representative may be an executor, executrix, or administrator. In Problem 5, Hartley's personal representative is bound to perform any of Hartley's contracts that are not of a personal nature. We will discuss this topic in more detail in Chapter 44.

An **assignment by operation of law** also takes place when a person becomes bankrupt. In such a case, a trustee in bankruptcy takes over the bankrupt's contracts. The trustee then enforces those contracts for the benefit of the creditors.

This chapter has shown you the effect of assignment and delegation on the rights and duties of contracting parties. Chapter 15 will delve into the ways in which contractual rights and duties may be ended by the parties or by events beyond their control.

Chapter 14 Review

"YOU BE THE JUDGE" REVIEW

Look again at the "You Be the Judge" cases given at the beginning of this chapter. Would you decide them differently now, after your study of the chapter?

Correct Decisions

1. Yes. Rights to money or property may be assigned. The debtor, Eastern Supply Company, must honor the assignment.
2. No. A contract for personal services in- volving special skill, knowledge, and judgment may not be assigned. Noiles has a right to personal performance by Janosik.

UNDERSTANDING WHAT YOU HAVE READ

1. Give an example of an assignment.
2. Must an assignment be made in writing?
3. What rights under a contract may be assigned?
4. What obligations or duties under a contract may *not* be delegated?
5. What should an assignee do to protect his or her interest under an assigned contract?
6. Has the assignee a better title than the assignor? Give an example.
7. State whether the rights arising out of each of these contracts are *assignable.* Give a reason for your decision in each case.
   a. a right to receive money
   b. a right to receive the services of an artist
   c. a right to buy goods on credit
   d. a right to collect the proceeds of an insurance policy
   e. a right to transfer a lease to a third party
8. In which of the following contracts may the obligations be *delegated?* State a reason for your decision in each case.
   a. an obligation to build a bridge
   b. an obligation to supply coal
   c. an obligation to dig a ditch
   d. an obligation to audit a set of accounting books
   e. an obligation to paint a portrait
   f. an obligation to perform the duties of a bank teller

BUILDING YOUR LEGAL VOCABULARY

Match each of these legal terms with its correct definition from the list that follows. Write your answers on a separate sheet of paper.

assignee
assignment
assignment by operation of law
assignor

delegation
notice of assignment
obligations

professional services
rights
standardized duties

1. legal duties not to interfere with the rights of others
2. the manner in which rights and sometimes duties are transferred to another without that person's act or cooperation
3. a process by which contract rights are transferred to another
4. obligations that do not involve special skill, knowledge, and judgment
5. one who transfers contract rights
6. the notification that the assignee should give to the debtor

7. nonassignable contractual duties that involve trust and confidence or special skill, knowledge, and judgment
8. one to whom contract rights are transferred
9. legal claims that an owner of an interest has to prevent others from interfering in that interest
10. a transfer of contractual duties to another, with responsibility for performance remaining with the transferor

APPLYING LEGAL PRINCIPLES

1. Peale, the owner of a large service station, agreed to grease Albrecht's car for $10.
   a. What are Peale's rights under the contract? What are his duties?
   b. What are Albrecht's rights under the contract? What are her duties?
   c. Assume that Peale is very busy and tells his assistant to do the work. Does Peale have the right to delegate his duties under the contract?
   d. Assume that the assistant does a poor job and damages the car. What rights does Albrecht have?

2. Bonilla contracted to build a home for the Conleys for $130,000. Bonilla hired Rios to install the plumbing, McPhail to do the plastering, and Martini to do the carpentry work. Did Bonilla have a right to delegate his duties under the contract to other contractors, without the Conleys' consent? Who would be responsible for poor workmanship?
3. Surabian agrees to pay $450 for Okabe's stereo system. Okabe delivers the system to Surabian and assigns her right to collect the $450 to DeJong. Must Surabian pay DeJong?

4. According to the terms of a written agreement, Slawson contracts to sell Dumar a teak TV/VCR cabinet. Dumar is to pay Slawson cash on delivery. Before delivery, Dumar assigns his contract to Zimmer. Must Slawson deliver the cabinet to Zimmer?

5. Assume in Problem 4 that Zimmer fails to pay for the cabinet. May Slawson recover from Dumar?

6. Wyse agreed to act as secretary to Frost at a salary of $425 a week. After working two months, Wyse obtained a better position and assigned her contract to Ingalls. Ingalls then presented himself to Frost, ready to work. Frost refused to take Ingalls as his new secretary. What principle of law covers this situation?

7. Cosme was owed $3,500 on a variety of accounts. Since she needed money, she sold the accounts to a collection agency. The collection firm notified all debtors of the assignment. Blake, one of the debtors whose account was purchased, objected to the assignment. He claimed that he had the right to choose those with whom he did business, and he refused to pay the collection agency. Must Blake pay the agency?

8. Dao, a famous portrait painter, agreed to paint Inman's portrait for $1,000. Before the portrait was finished, Inman died. Dao now claims that the executrix of Inman's estate must permit him to finish the portrait and pay his fee. Dao bases his claim on the fact that the executrix has acquired all the rights that the deceased had under the contract. Do you agree?

9. A creditor assigned to a third party a claim for $800 for services rendered. The debtor, who was not notified of the assignment, paid the $800 to the creditor. Can the third party collect another $800 from the debtor?

10. McCallum installed new electrical wiring in Wing's home. McCallum did not have a license to do electrical work and was barred by local law from suing for the contract price for such work. McCallum assigned his claim against Wing to Crea, who then sued Wing for the amount due McCallum. Will Crea succeed?

ANALYZING COURT CASES

1. Smith, who owned the Avalon Apartments, sold individual apartments under contracts. Each contract required the buyer to pay an extra $15 per month for hot and cold water, heat, refrigeration, taxes, and fire insurance. Smith assigned his interest in the apartment building and under the various contracts to Roberts. She failed to pay the taxes on the building. Radley and other tenants of the building sued Smith and Roberts to compel them to pay the taxes. The court dismissed the action against Smith and rendered judgment against Roberts. Was the court justified in doing so? (*Radley v. Smith*, 313 P. 2d 465)

2. A special agent acting for the partnership of Saunders & Davis ordered 100 pairs of "all wool redyed serge" pants at $9.50 a pair from Falcon Sportswear. The order specified that the goods were to be shipped as per sample displayed, subject to the approval of the firm. After the goods were shipped, and without obtaining the partners' approval, Falcon assigned the account to William Eiselin & Co. When the goods arrived, Saunders & Davis rejected the shipment because it didn't conform to the sample. In an action brought against them by William Eiselin & Co., the partners claimed that they were entitled to set up the same defenses against the assignee, Eiselin, as they could have claimed against the assignor, Falcon. Are the partners legally justified in their claim? (*William Eiselin & Co. v. Saunders*, 58 S.E. 2d 614)

3. Page was a construction contractor who borrowed money from Bailey to finance various jobs. Under the terms of a written contract between them, Page agreed to repay the borrowed money from a new government construction job on which Page was bidding. Did this agreement constitute an assignment of Page's rights under the contract? (*Page v. Bailey*, 290 F. 2d 483)

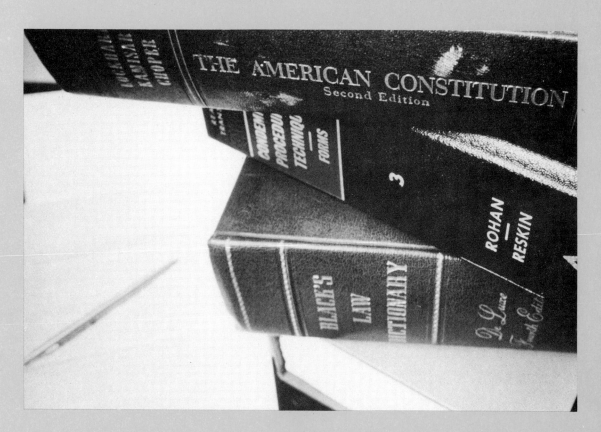

Termination of Contracts

Think about these cases.
If you were the judge, how would you decide each case?

1

Bronstein contracted with Zale Furniture to manufacture kitchen chairs for Zale. A fire in Bronstein's factory, however, prevented him from making the chairs. Bronstein claims that the contract is discharged because of impossibility of performance. Zale claims that Bronstein is not excused from performance. Who is right?

2

Martinez offered her personal check to La Foret Restaurant in payment of a bill. La Foret refused to accept the check, claiming that checks are not legal tender. Is La Foret right?

184

METHODS OF TERMINATION

In Chapter 14 we emphasized that a binding contract gives the parties rights and requires them to assume certain duties. We also said that obligations under a contract may sometimes be delegated to others. The party who originally promised to perform the duties must carry out that promise or see to it that the assignee does. In other words, obligations or duties under a contract are terminated when the parties do what they have promised to do. Legally, this type of discharge of a contract is called **termination by performance.**

Although a contract is usually terminated by performance, the rights and duties of the parties may be discharged in other ways. These include (1) impossibility of performance, (2) material alteration, (3) agreement of the parties, and (4) breach (see Chapter 16).

Performance

If one of the parties to a contract has performed the required duties, that party is discharged from further performance. It then becomes the duty of the other party to do what has been agreed on.

Westwood entered into a written contract to build a two-car garage for Idov for $23,000. Westwood built the garage as specified. By completing his duty under the contract, Westwood was discharged from further performance. Idov now has the duty to do what he agreed to do—pay Westwood $23,000.

When both parties have carried out their promises, the contract is at an end. Contracts usually indicate when, where, and how performance is to take place. If the contract does not state the time of performance, a reasonable time is understood.

Performance by Paying Money or Rendering Services

1. Fujii entered into a written agreement to construct a new wing for the Olsens' house. Fujii built the wing according to specifications. The Olsens tendered payment, but Fujii refused to accept the money. He claimed that it was insufficient because the job was more difficult than he had anticipated. What effect does the tender have on the Olsens' obligation?

An offer to perform an obligation is legally called a **tender.** It may be an offer to pay money or an offer to do some other act, such as delivering goods or rendering services. If a correct tender of money is made and refused, as

Crackdown on Bill Collectors

The phone rang at 3:30 A.M. A young woman was told by a bill collector, "Tell your father to pay up or he will go to jail." The young woman's father owed the creditor $35 for a pair of slippers he had bought.

This is only one of thousands of complaints received by the Federal Trade Commission since the passage of the Fair Debt Collection Practices Act. This act is intended to stop bill collectors from approaching debtors' bosses, threatening violence or imprisonment, impersonating police officers, and making dunning phone calls in the middle of the night.

The act does not apply to all businesses that grant credit. The following are exempt from its provisions: stores, hospitals, banks, credit unions, and other businesses that handle their own collections. The law is aimed mainly at agencies that specialize in collecting money for others.

Under the law, the agencies have five working days to send the debtor written notice of the amount of the debt and the name of the claiming creditor. The notice must also state that the collector assumes the debt to be valid unless the debtor contests it in writing within 30 days of receipt of the notice.

A collection agency may contact a debtor's friends or employer only to locate the debtor. The agency may not disclose the fact that the individual owes a debt or phone the debtor while at work if the employer does not permit such calls. A collector who violates the act is liable for the debtor's legal fees and may have to pay damages of up to $1,000. Any loss suffered by a debtor as a result of harassment (such as the loss of a job) can also be recovered. The Federal Trade Commission is responsible for enforcement of the Fair Debt Collection Practices Act.

in Problem 1, the party making the tender is *not* discharged from the debt. But that party won't be liable for interest on the debt or for the costs of any suit brought to recover the debt. If a correct tender of goods or services is made and refused, the party making the tender is usually released from the obligation and may sue for breach of contract.

Tender, whether of money, goods, or services, must be made at the time, place, and in the manner specified. Where these are not specified, the tender must be made in a reasonable manner.

Checks are not considered legal tender.

Legal Tender.   Where a contract calls for payment of money, payment must be made in **legal tender.** In 1933 Congress passed a bill that provides that "all coins and currencies of the U.S. . . . heretofore or hereafter coined or issued shall be legal tender for debts, public and private."

Suppose, in Problem 1, that the Olsens had tendered payment in two-dollar bills. Would Fujii have the right to refuse acceptance? No. Two-dollar bills are legal tender, although they are rare. Fujii has no legal right to refuse the Olsens' tender.

Other customary methods of payment, such as checks (either certified or uncertified) do not constitute legal tender. If tender that is not legal is accepted, it binds the party accepting it.

Substantial Performance

> **2.** Carreno installed a central air-conditioning system in Kilo's home. Carreno guaranteed that every part of the house would be cooled to 65 degrees when the outside temperature reached 90 degrees. When a test showed that the temperature in one bedroom could not be lowered below 67 degrees, Kilo refused to pay the contract price. She claimed that Carreno had breached the contract. Is her claim correct?

Substantial performance of a contract is assumed to have taken place when a defect is of a minor nature and performance was accomplished honestly and in good faith. This rule is usually applied by the courts in lawsuits involving building or construction contracts. It is important to remember that the rule of substantial performance applies only when the contractor does not *intentionally* depart from the terms of the contract. In Problem 2, Kilo will have to pay the contract price, less any money spent to have the defect fixed.

Substantial performance is an issue that occurs most often in construction contracts.

Impossibility of Performance

> **3.** Pomeroy contracted to make and deliver 10,000 pairs of shoes to Ripkin by October 1. A strike by Pomeroy's employees prevented her from fulfilling her contract. Ripkin then sued Pomeroy for breach of contract. Pomeroy claimed that the contract was terminated by impossibility of performance. Was her defense good?

When a contract is undertaken without any stated exceptions, it must be performed or damages must be paid. Generally, the fact that performance has become more difficult since the contract was made or will result in great hardship to a promisor will not excuse performance. The impossibility of performance must be due to an event that the parties could not have foreseen and provided against when they entered into the contract. In Problem 3, Pomeroy's performance has become much more difficult because of the strike, but it is not impossible. She may buy the shoes elsewhere and deliver them to Ripkin as agreed. Events such as strikes, fires, floods, difficulty in obtaining materials or skilled labor, and so forth, may *seem* to be good excuses for performance. However, these events will not terminate a contract because of impossibility unless the parties have expressly provided in their contract for such termination.

There are three situations in which courts *will* excuse a promisor on the ground of impossibility, even though no such provision is made in the contract. They are (1) destruction of the subject matter essential to the performance; (2) a change in the law that makes the performance illegal; and (3) the death or disability of the promisor. In addition, some courts *may* excuse a promisor because the performance has been economically frustrated.

Destruction of the Subject Matter

> **4.** Call agreed to sell to Li the entire crop of apples growing in his orchard. After the agreement was made, a sudden frost killed the crop. Call claimed that the contract was terminated because of impossibility of performance. Was his claim legally correct?

Performance of a contract often depends on the *continued existence* of specific subject matter. In that case, the destruction of the subject matter without the promisor's fault will terminate the contract. In Problem 4, performance of the contract is obviously impossible because the crop of apples ceased to exist before the contract was performed. Clearly, Li contracted for Call's apples and not for apples from some other orchard. It would be unfair to hold Call liable for nonperformance in this case. Therefore, the contract was terminated because of impossibility.

Death or Disability

PROBLEM

> **5.** Brace, a noted lecturer, was engaged to speak before a luncheon club. She missed a train, however, and was unable to keep her engagement. At considerable cost to herself, she sent an equally prominent lecturer to speak in her place. When the lecturer appeared, the club refused to let her speak. The club also refused to refund Brace's expenses. Does Brace have a claim against the club?

In a contract for personal services, impossibility of performance because of the serious illness or death of the promisor will usually discharge the contract. In Problem 5, Brace is not excused from performing her contract because she caused her own inability to perform by missing the train. Moreover, she will be unable to collect her expenses from the luncheon club.

Economic Frustration

There is a tendency today for some courts to excuse performance on the ground of **economic frustration,** as distinguished from impossibility. The economic frustration doctrine is applied by the courts when performance can be done only at an unreasonable cost.

EXAMPLE

> Santoro leased a building for three years for the purpose of manufacturing textiles. After occupying the building for two years, it was completely destroyed by fire. Some courts will discharge Santoro from liability for the remaining period of the lease because the purpose of the lease has been frustrated.

Material Alteration

PROBLEM

> **6.** Golman signed a contract to employ Green as advertising manager for one year, beginning April 25. Fraudulently, and without Golman's permission, Green changed the date to February 25. How does the alteration affect the contract?

Material alteration by a party to an agreement gives the other party the right to terminate the contract. An alteration is material if it changes the rights or duties of the parties and is made intentionally. A change in the amount, time, or place of payment, or in the rate of interest, is a material alteration. In Problem 6, Green's action relieves Golman of any responsibility for the performance of the contract.

Agreement of the Parties

A contract is created by mutual agreement, and it may be terminated in the same way. A contract that has not been performed by either party may be terminated by agreement. The consideration for the agreement to terminate is the release of each party by the other.

EXAMPLE

> Herman agreed to build a concrete sidewalk for Krause in front of Krause's store. Later, Krause decided that he didn't want a sidewalk, and Herman released Krause from the agreement. The release terminates the contract because neither party had performed any contractual duties.

The parties may also provide that an agreement is to terminate on the occurrence of a stated event or after the expiration of a stated period of time.

Novation

PROBLEM

> 7. Calenda and Barnicle, parties to a contract, agree to substitute a third party, Diamante, in Barnicle's place. What is the legal effect of such an arrangement?

When a new party is substituted for one of the original parties to a contract, the original contract is terminated. A new contract, called a **novation,** arises between the new parties. In Problem 7, the contract between Calenda and Barnicle was discharged when Diamante replaced Barnicle. A new contract arose between Calenda and Diamante. Diamante is now entitled to receive benefits from the performance of the novation. She is also obligated to carry out the duties that Barnicle would have had to perform.

This chapter has detailed four methods of terminating contracts: termination by performance, by impossibility of performance, by agreement, and by material alteration. Next we'll take a look at the fifth termination method—failure to perform.

Chapter 15 Review

"YOU BE THE JUDGE" REVIEW

Look again at the "You Be the Judge" cases given at the beginning of this chapter. Would you decide them differently now, after your study of the chapter?

Correct Decisions

1. Zale is right. When a party's performance is prevented by a fire, that party is not excused because of impossibility. A clause should have been included in the contract to excuse performance in case of fire.

2. Yes. Checks are not legal tender and need not be accepted in payment of debts. Only United States currency is legal tender.

UNDERSTANDING WHAT YOU HAVE READ

1. Name five ways in which a contract may be terminated.
2. Impossibility of performance usually does not excuse failure to perform a contract. (For example, strikes, fires, and floods will not ordinarily terminate a contract.) List three exceptions to this general rule.
3. How may a party to a contract protect himself or herself against the legal effects of unforeseen events such as fires and strikes?
4. What is the effect of a refusal to accept correct tender of money?
5. What is the effect of a refusal to accept correct tender of goods or services?
6. When is a contract considered *substantially performed?*
7. Give an example of a material alteration of a contract.
8. Give an example of the termination of a contract by agreement of the parties.
9. Give an example of the termination of a contract by economic frustration.
10. Give an example of a novation.

BUILDING YOUR LEGAL VOCABULARY

Choose the legal term that will correctly complete each definition below. Write your answers on a separate sheet of paper.

1. A contractor who performs in good faith may recover the contract price, less damages for defective work, under the doctrine of
   a. partial performance.
   b. substantial performance.
   c. unforeseen events.
2. An intentional change made by a party, which alters the parties' rights and duties, is a
   a. material fact.
   b. tender of performance.
   c. material alteration.
3. United States coins and currencies, acceptable in payment of debts, are known as
   a. legal tender.
   b. tender.
   c. necessaries.
4. The doctrine that excuses performance when performance becomes impracticable or unreasonable is
   a. termination by performance.
   b. promissory estoppel.
   c. economic frustration.
5. A new contract formed after the substitution of a third party for one of the original parties is a/an
   a. delegation.
   b. option contract.
   c. novation.

APPLYING LEGAL PRINCIPLES

1. Bruno agreed to repair Raines's porch for $400. Bruno arrived with his tools and materials, but Raines refused to let him work. She didn't give a satisfactory reason for her refusal. Two weeks later, Raines called Bruno and asked him to begin the repairs. Bruno, however, stated that he would be busy elsewhere for the next six weeks. Raines threatened to sue Bruno for breach of contract. Would she succeed in such an action?

2. Farrell agreed to sell Epstein a dozen ties for $88. The terms of the agreement were cash on delivery. When Farrell delivered the ties, Epstein tendered a $100 check and asked for change. Farrell declined the tender and later sold the ties to another person for $96. Epstein brought suit. Will he succeed?

3. If, in Problem 2, Epstein had tendered a certified check for $88, would your answer be the same?

4. Canoso built a house for the Brinds. The house was built according to specifications, except that the light fixture in one room wasn't exactly the kind called for in the contract. The Brinds refused to pay Canoso any part of the contract price until the fixture was changed. Were they justified in this refusal?

5. Sontag Company contracted with Talley Construction to furnish steel window frames for a new office building. Before the frames were delivered, a fire destroyed the Sontag manufacturing plant, preventing Sontag from fulfilling the contract. Talley claimed that Sontag must provide the frames under the terms of the contract. Is Talley's claim correct?

6. Would your answer to Problem 5 be the same if Sontag's failure to perform were caused by a strike?

7. How would you answer Problem 5 if the window frames were of a special type, made only by Sontag and not obtainable elsewhere?

8. Mack agreed in writing to build an addition on the front of Fulton's house. Shortly after the contract was made, but before construction was begun, a city ordinance was passed making such an addition illegal. Mack withdrew from the contract, and Fulton sued for breach of contract. Should Fulton succeed?

9. Carson entered into a contract to sell Fenway's house at auction on May 15. On the morning of May 15, Carson was seriously injured in an accident. Thus, she did not appear at the auction. Is she liable?

10. Vo engaged Fox to act as production manager for a period of two years, beginning March 1, at a stated salary. Fraudulently, and without Vo's knowledge, Fox changed the contract to read "for a period of three years." What is the legal effect of Fox's action on the contract?

11. Ralston agreed to paint Griffin's house for $2,500. Neither party had acted when they mutually agreed to cancel the agreement. What is the effect of the agreement to cancel on the agreement to paint the house?

12. Best and Collins entered into a contract. Before any performance had taken place, they agreed that Dhanda should take Best's place. If Dhanda fails to perform, can Collins hold Best liable on the old contract?

ANALYZING COURT CASES

1. A contractor was hired to open-air sandblast a building. The sand caused damage to some machinery located on adjacent land. A court order was obtained against the contractor, requiring him to take certain precautions to prevent further damage. The contractor refused to complete the job, claiming that he was discharged from his contract because it was impossible for him to work. Was his claim legally correct? (*Savage v. Kiewit*, 432 P. 2d 519)

2. A woman and a man signed a contract on the day before their marriage.

Several months after they were married, the husband, without any objections from his wife, destroyed the contract by burning it in an oven. After the husband died, the wife claimed that the contract was still in force. Was she correct? (*In re Reed's Estate*, 414 S.W. 2d 283)

3. Garner, who leased a building from Ellingson, applied to the city for a permit to repair the building. He intended to use the building as a theater and bookstore. The building permit was refused unless a sprinkler system was installed in the rented building and in an adjacent building. The adjacent building was also owned by Ellingson. Garner was willing to install a sprinkler system in the rented building, but Ellingson refused to install a system in the adjacent building. Garner sued Ellingson, claiming that the lease was not binding because of commercial frustration and requesting a recovery of rent that he had paid in advance. Was Garner entitled to recover? (*Garner v. Ellingson*, 501 P. 2d 22)

CHAPTER 16

Breach
of
Contract

Think about these cases.
If you were the judge, how would you decide each case?

1

Dolan, a production manager, was employed under a three-year written contract at an annual salary of $45,000. Without cause, she was discharged at the end of a year. What are her legal rights?

2

You agree to buy an antique chair from Estevez. Later, Estevez refuses to deliver the chair to you as agreed. Can you compel him to do so?

WHAT IS A BREACH OF CONTRACT?

Performance, impossibility of performance, material alteration, and mutual agreement are not the only ways to terminate a contract. Often a party to a contract fails to perform the duties required under a contract. This failure to perform is regarded by the law as a **breach** (breaking) **of contract.**

REMEDIES FOR BREACH

> **1.** Liebman agreed in writing to act as personnel manager for Southern Electronics for a period of a year at a salary of $50,000. She worked for Southern for six months and then left to take a position paying a higher salary. What are the rights of Southern Electronics?

When a breach has been committed, the injured party does not have to perform the contractual duties. That party also may use any one of the following remedies: (1) sue for damages for breach of contract; (2) cancel or rescind the contract; or (3) compel specific performance of the contract. Depending on the type of contract breached, more than one of these remedies may be available.

In Problem 1, Liebman committed a breach of contract by failing to perform her obligations. Southern Electronics not only may treat the contract as ended but may also bring suit against Liebman. The purpose of the suit would be to collect any money loss suffered as a result of the breach.

Sue for Damages

> **2.** Referring to Problem 1, Southern Electronics had to hire another personnel manager because Liebman quit after six months. The firm had to pay the new manager $32,000 for the remaining six months of the year instead of the $25,000 it would have paid to Liebman. What are the firm's rights against Liebman?

Because of Liebman's breach, Southern Electronics suffered harm in the form of a money loss. As you learned in Chapter 4, the word *damages* is used to describe money compensation paid to an injured party who suffers a loss. The injured party is under a duty to **mitigate** (lessen) the damages if it is reasonably possible. The act of mitigating, or lessening, is called **mitigation.** In Problem 2, Southern Electronics could sue Liebman for damages. How much is the company entitled to collect? It may collect only

compensatory damages (what it actually lost) because of Liebman's breach. Per the facts in the problem, if Liebman had remained at her job for the remainder of the year, she would have earned another $25,000. Since the new personnel manager was paid $32,000 for this period, the firm sustained a money loss of $7,000. Ordinarily, the firm would be entitled to collect this sum as basic damages.

If the firm had paid the new manager $25,000 or less for the six months, it would not have been able to prove any actual loss. Thus, it would not have been entitled to damages. In cases such as these, courts will award the injured party **nominal damages.** These are damages in name only and usually amount to just a few cents or $1. Nominal damages are awarded when there is a breach of contract, but no money damages result from the breach.

When an employer breaches a contract of employment, the employee may recover as damages the salary fixed by the terms of the contract, *less any money earned from similar employment elsewhere.*

When a contract for the payment of money is breached, just what is the injured party entitled to recover? The amount recovered usually includes the full debt, interest at the legal rate from the due date of the debt to the date of payment, plus courts costs and sometimes attorney's fees. As a general rule, punitive damages are not given in contract actions.

Rescind the Contract

PROBLEM

> **3.** Patkin orally agreed to employ Inada for a period of two years. Inada was fired after working only two months. If he had not been paid for the two-month period, what are his legal rights?

Where a contract is breached and the injured party has partly performed the duties, it is not necessary that a suit be brought under the contract. This is the case in Problem 3. The injured party may rescind the contract and sue for the *reasonable value of the services actually performed.* The oral contract between Patkin and Inada is unenforceable under the Statute of Frauds because it can't be performed within a year from the time it was made. Inada would have to rescind the contract entirely and sue for the reasonable value of the work he performed during the two months.

An injured party must exercise the right to rescind a contract promptly after discovering the facts of the breach. Generally, **rescission** is not permitted for a slight or casual breach. It may be used as a remedy only for breaches that are so substantial and fundamental that they defeat the object of the parties in making the contract. In addition, the party seeking to cancel must not be in default.

LAW IN THE NEWS

Jackson, Promoter Settle Out of Court

(Reprinted courtesy of *The Boston Globe*)

Concert promoter Frank J. Russo's $20 million breach-of-contract suit against entertainer Michael Jackson, his brothers and sister has been settled out of court for an undisclosed sum, Russo announced yesterday.

Describing himself as "very, very satisfied with the settlement," the Providence-based promoter said he felt his position had been vindicated. As part of the settlement, he added, he agreed not to reveal the amount of the award. He hinted that the amount was sizable, exclusive of attorney's fees, and quipped that he wouldn't have to worry about financing college tuitions of his six children.

The suit, which would have been heard in Los Angeles early next month, had arisen out of Russo's claim that the Jacksons contracted for his services as promoter of their 1984 Victory Tour and then ousted him.

"I had set up an office as promoter in Los Angeles for seven weeks in 1984," said Russo, president of Concerts East Inc. "I routed the whole tour, which the Jacksons ended up using.

"We had a very strong case."

Russo originally filed the action in June 1984 in US District Court in Rhode Island. Listed as defendants were Michael, Marlon, Randy, Jackie, Tito, and Jermaine Jackson. After a court ruling changed the venue to Los Angeles County, Russo engaged the law firm headed by Melvin Belli to represent him.

The Victory Tour eventually went on the road with Charles (Chuck) Sullivan serving as promoter.

"We charged that we had a contract to promote the Victory Tour," Russo said. "They broke it."

–ERNIE SANTOSUOSSO

Compel Specific Performance

The law seeks to give the injured party a just and adequate remedy. In most cases, money damages are regarded as adequate. There are instances, however, when money damages will not compensate a party for a loss caused by breach of contract.

PROBLEM

> **4.** Canate signed a written agreement to sell her house to Brusseau for $92,000. Later, she changed her mind and refused to go through with the deal. What legal remedy does Brusseau have?

Problem 4 is an example of a breach that can't be adequately remedied by money compensation. When this type of breach occurs, the court will compel the party who committed the breach to perform the contract *specifically.* The party who committed the breach will be ordered to do what had been agreed on. In Problem 4, Brusseau may ask the court for an order to compel Canate to perform the contract as agreed. Brusseau wants the house, not money damages.

Specific performance is a special remedy. It will be granted in cases involving real property (see Chapter 41) and personal property that can't be obtained elsewhere (antiques, valuable paintings, jewels, and so forth). The remedy of specific performance has been expanded under the Uniform Commercial Code in contracts for the sale of goods (see Chapter 20).

STATUTES OF LIMITATIONS

When a contract is breached, the injured party may sue for any money loss sustained. Obviously, though, it would be unfair to permit the passage of an unreasonable time before bringing suit. As time goes by, it becomes increasingly difficult to prove the facts. Witnesses can't be located, they may have died, or they may have forgotten the facts. Evidence may be lost or destroyed. Keeping records indefinitely would involve expense and would seriously interfere with business.

To meet these difficulties, states have adopted **statutes of limitations.** These laws specifically limit the period during which suit may be brought.

PROBLEM

> **5.** Quan sold a refrigerator to Patz for $700. Patz gave Quan a 60-day note in payment, but he didn't pay the note when due. When did the breach take place? Within what time period may Quan bring suit against Patz?

Each state has its own statute of limitations. If a creditor fails to bring suit on a claim against a debtor within the time fixed by the statute, the right of action is barred. The debt itself is said to be **"outlawed."** The period of time within which suit must be brought varies by state. In more than half the states, the time within which an action must be brought on a simple contract (one not under seal) is six years. In the case of a formal contract (one under seal), the period allowed for bringing suit varies from ten to twenty years. Some states have abolished the distinction between sealed and unsealed contracts. In these states, the period of limitation is now six years for both types of contracts. The Uniform Commercial Code sets a four-year limitation on actions involving breach of sales contracts.

A statute of limitations begins to operate from the *date the breach occurs.* In Problem 5, the breach took place when Patz failed to pay the note after the expiration of 60 days. In many states, Quan would have six years from the date of the breach in which to bring an action against Patz.

Reviving a Barred Debt

> **6.** Osgood lived in a state having a six-year statute of limitations on simple contract actions. He borrowed $500 from Xenakis on April 5, 1982. On April 20, 1988, Osgood paid Xenakis $100 as a partial payment of the debt. No further payments were made. On June 5, 1988, Xenakis filed suit to collect the balance of the debt. Does she have the legal right to collect?

Statutes of limitations merely set a time limit for bringing suit on a debt. They do not *discharge* the debt. Rather, they prevent a party from taking advantage of the remedies for breach just discussed. Payment of part of the principal or interest of a debt after the debt has been barred by the statute of limitations revives or renews the debt. The statute then begins to run again for another statutory period. A debtor's written promise to pay a barred debt also has the same effect. In Problem 6, Osgood's payment of $100 revived the debt. Xenaxis's claim for the balance would not expire before the end of the statutory period beginning April 20, 1988.

> **7.** Pavao owed Mintz $2,000, and the statutory period for collection of this sum was about to expire. Pavao then left the state in which the debt was incurred and didn't return for three years. Is Mintz's claim barred by the statute of limitations?

If the parties to be sued have left the state, the period of their absence is not counted because they are beyond the court's jurisdiction. However, the statute begins to run again as soon as they return. Mintz's claim in Problem 7 is not barred if he files suit against Pavao promptly after Pavao's return.

This unit has given you a broad introduction to contracts. Because the rights and obligations acquired as a result of contracting are so fundamental, knowledge of contract law will serve you well. In Unit 3 you will learn more about sales contracts, the most common form of contract in which you are likely to be a party.

Chapter 16 Review

"YOU BE THE JUDGE" REVIEW

Look again at the "You Be the Judge" cases given at the beginning of this chapter. Would you decide them differently now, after your study of the chapter?

Correct Decisions

1. Dolan may sue for breach of contract to recover damages amounting to the $90,000 salary due for the remaining two years of her contract. If she obtains other employment, the amount she earns will be subtracted from the $90,000. In addition, Dolan is entitled to interest and court costs. She may also receive her attorney's fees.

2. Yes. You can obtain a court order of specific performance to compel Estevez to deliver the antique chair. This remedy is available in the case of a sale of realty or other property that can't be obtained elsewhere, where money damages will not compensate the injured party.

UNDERSTANDING WHAT YOU HAVE READ

1. Give an example of a breach of contract.
2. What purpose do damages serve?
3. Is the injured party discharged from performing obligations on learning that the contract has been breached?
4. What are the remedies for breach of contract?
5. When are nominal damages awarded?
6. What damages may an employee collect when wrongfully discharged from a position?
7. Under what circumstances may a party rescind a contract and then sue for the reasonable value of the services performed?
8. When is a party entitled to specific performance?
9. Why were statutes of limitations enacted?
10. How may a debt barred by the statute of limitations be revived?

BUILDING YOUR LEGAL VOCABULARY

From this list, select the legal term that belongs in the blank in each sentence below. Write your answers on a separate sheet of paper.

breach of contract
compensatory damages
mitigation
nominal damages

outlawed
punitive damages
reasonable value

rescission
specific performance
statutes of limitations

1. The cancellation of a contract is also called ▦▦▦▦▦▦▦.
2. To punish or to make an example of a wrongdoer, a court might order ▦▦▦▦▦▦▦ to be paid.
3. A debt that is barred by the statute of limitations from being recovered is said to be ▦▦▦▦▦▦▦.
4. Basic or ▦▦▦▦▦▦▦ are those awarded in the amount of the loss sustained by an injured party.
5. A failure to perform contractual duties is called a ▦▦▦▦▦▦▦.
6. When money damages are due an injured party under a contract, that party is responsible for the ▦▦▦▦▦▦▦ of the damages.
7. An injured party who has partly performed his or her contractual duties may cancel the contract and sue for the ▦▦▦▦▦▦▦ of the services actually performed.
8. When money damages won't adequately compensate an injured party, that party may request the remedy of ▦▦▦▦▦▦▦.
9. A party who has been injured by another party's failure to perform a contract, but who cannot prove any actual loss, may be awarded ▦▦▦▦▦▦▦ in the amount of $1.
10. Laws that limit the time during which suit may be brought are called ▦▦▦▦▦▦▦.

APPLYING LEGAL PRINCIPLES

1. Ewald agreed in writing to buy a used car from Montavo for $2,900. Delivery and payment were to be made in 30 days. On the day of performance, Ewald tendered the exact amount called for by the contract. Montavo refused to accept it, however, claiming that he had sold the car to someone else. Does Ewald have an action against Montavo for breach of contract?

2. Assume in Problem 1 that, because of Montavo's action, Ewald was forced to pay $3,500 for an identical model of car. What are Ewald's damages?

3. Paul had a written employment contract with Canas for one year at a salary of $36,000. Paul worked for five months, collected $15,000 in salary, and was then fired without cause. Within a few days he found another job at a lower

salary. Then he brought suit against Canas for breach of contract. How much money would a court normally award as damages?

4. O'Reilly contracted with Campbell & Co., stockbrokers, for the purchase of 100 shares of Northern Transportation common stock. The purchase price per share was $65.50. The next day, after receiving a confirmation of the stock purchase, O'Reilly told Campbell & Co. that she had changed her mind about buying the stock. In the meantime, the price of the stock had dropped to $63 per share. What are Campbell & Co.'s legal rights?

5. Fabrizio's debt to Meged was due April 4, 1985. On June 15, 1991, the debt still had not been paid. Meged filed suit against Fabrizio. Does Meged have the legal right to collect? (The statute of limitations in Meged's state is six years.)

6. Dirkson owed Ortega $510. After the statute of limitations for breach of contract had run out, Dirkson paid $50 on account. Ortega now seeks to collect the balance of $460. Dirkson claims that the debt is outlawed by the statute of limitations. Can Ortega collect?

7. Wynn resided in a state that had a six-year statute of limitations. He loaned $500 to Liew, a neighbor. Wynn repeatedly asked for payment, but no part of the debt was ever repaid. One year before the expiration of the statute of limitations, Wynn moved to another state and stayed there for five years. When Wynn returned to Liew's state, he immediately began an action against Liew to recover the $500. Liew claims that the debt is barred by the statute of limitations. Is Liew correct?

8. Monroy, an antiques dealer, agreed to sell Spar a rare Roman coin. Later, Monroy notified Spar that she was going to donate the coin to a museum. Therefore, the coin was no longer for sale. What legal remedy is available to Spar?

ANALYZING COURT CASES

1. Crommelin was a candidate in a primary election for a U.S. congressional seat. He entered into a contract with Montgomery Telecasters to televise three political speeches. The television company refused to allow Crommelin to make the scheduled telecasts. Crommelin lost the primary election and then sued for breach of contract. As damages, he claimed the following: (1) the money he had spent for campaign expenses; and (2) the salary he would have received as a congressional representative. Is Crommelin entitled to recover? (*Crommelin v. Montgomery Telecasters*, 194 So. 2d 548)

2. Gulf South Capital Corp. entered into a contract to buy a motel from Brown. There was nothing in the written contract about paying off any mortgage or other claims against the property. When Gulf delivered the down payment, the check specified that all mortgage and other claims against the stated property above a certain amount were to be removed or paid off by the seller. Brown returned this check and contracted to sell the motel to another buyer. Gulf sued Brown for breach of contract. Is Gulf entitled to judgment? (*Gulf South Capital Corp. v. Brown*, 183 So. 2d 802)

3. While preparing for a special sale of new and used cars, Morristown Lincoln-Mercury entered into a written contract with R. N. Lotspeich Publishing Co. Lotspeich was to insert an ad for the sale into its newspaper, and the ad was to run for three days. At the request of one of the auto dealer's competitors, Lotspeich canceled Morristown Lincoln-Mercury's ad. As a result, Morristown had to reduce its order for new cars from 30 to ten. The auto dealer estimated that the potential profit from the sale of 20 cars amounted to $6,000, a sum the dealer might have made if Lotspeich had not canceled the ad. Morristown Lincoln-Mercury brought suit against Lotspeich for loss of the expected profits. Should it be successful? (*Morristown Lincoln-Mercury, Inc. v. R. N. Lotspeich*, 298 S.W. 2d 788)

BUYING AND SELLING GOODS

CHAPTERS

LEARNING OBJECTIVES

After you have studied this unit, you should be able to:

- Describe the meaning and purpose of the Uniform Commercial Code's provisions on sales of goods.

- Show how a binding sales contract is formed under the UCC.

- Define the term *ownership* or *title* and identify situations in which ownership passes from seller to buyer.

- Show that you understand sales warranties and product liability.

- Describe the rights and responsibilities of buyer and seller under a sales contract.

- Describe the legal remedies available for breach of a sales contract.

CHAPTER 17

Nature and Formation of Sales Contracts

Think about these cases.
If you were the judge, how would you decide each case?

1

You sold your five-year-old car to a friend for $1,600. When you tried to deliver the car and collect the money, your friend refused to accept the car. She claimed that since the contract was not in writing, she wasn't liable on it. Is she liable?

2

Ortiz agreed to trade his video camera for Silverman's personal computer. Later, they argued about the transaction. Ortiz claimed that it was a sale of goods, while Silverman claimed that it wasn't. Who is right?

THE UNIFORM COMMERCIAL CODE

Many of the problems we have studied thus far have dealt with buying and selling personal property in the form of goods. In fact, buying and selling goods are the most important economic activities in today's society. These activities are carried out through an exchange of legally binding promises or contracts.

PROBLEM

> **1.** Oppermann offered to sell an antique lamp to her neighbor, Agnew, for $250. Agnew agreed to buy the lamp at that price. Did Oppermann and Agnew enter into a binding contract?

PROBLEM

> **2.** Niven & Co., importers of foreign shoes, received an order for a stated quantity of men's shoes. The goods were to be shipped to Ott & Sons within ten days. Niven & Co. sent a letter of confirmation, agreeing to ship the shoes within ten days. Is there a binding contract?

Usually, the general principles of contract law apply to sales of goods. Judges have found it necessary, however, to supplement these rules with special rules relating to sales transactions. Many of these special rules are now included in the Uniform Commercial Code. The UCC attempts to standardize throughout the country all the rules governing the rights and duties of both buyers and sellers of goods. The Code recognizes the changing business customs and practices of a class of buyers and sellers known as *merchants.* According to the UCC, a **merchant** is a professional buyer or seller who usually has a specialized knowledge of certain goods and of the business customs and practices common to his or her line of business. By contrast, an ordinary consumer is a *nonmerchant.*

In Problem 1, there is a binding contract between two nonmerchants or consumers. Problem 2 is an example of a contract for a sale between two professional merchants. Because the UCC changes simple contract law and adds rules for the benefit of merchants in sales transactions, it is important to keep this distinction in mind. These changes and additions are contained in code sections relating to the formation of the sales contract, the Statute of Frauds, and the rights and duties of the parties. These sections will be discussed in the chapters that follow.

THE SALES CONTRACT

The parties involved in a sale of goods are the seller, known as the **vendor,** and the buyer, called the **vendee.** Both must be competent parties to make the contract legally binding. The subject matter of a sales contract is tangible personal property or goods.

LIVING UNDER THE LAW

The Uniform Commercial Code

Every state except Louisiana (which has enacted all but Article 2) has adopted the Uniform Commercial Code. This adoption represents the most sweeping codification of business law in our history.

A *code* is a collection of several separate but related areas of a single field of law into one law. The chief function of a *commercial code* is to provide the basic legal framework needed to control the flow of goods from producer to consumer.

Briefly, the UCC is designed to supersede all earlier uniform statutes relating to business law. Among others, those earlier laws included the Uniform Sales Act and the Uniform Negotiable Instruments Act.

The UCC consists of ten articles dealing with the legal principles that govern various phases of a commercial transaction. However, there are only five articles with which you need to be concerned. Those articles deal with sales and with commercial papers such as drafts, promissory notes, checks, and certificates of deposit.

Perhaps the most important lesson to be learned from a study of the UCC is the Code's "good faith" provision. This aspect of the UCC aims to place dealings between buyers and sellers on a high ethical plane. Because of its importance, you will find the UCC's "good faith" provision emphasized repeatedly in this book.

PROBLEM

3.   Cardona, a dealer in antique coins, agrees to sell a fifteenth-century Spanish coin to Shih for $4,500. Shih maintains that the sale of a rare coin is a sale of "goods" under the UCC. Cardona is equally certain that it is in a different classification. Who is legally correct?

The UCC uses the term **goods** to mean all things that are movable at the time they are identified as the subject matter of the sales contract. The term includes specially manufactured goods, the unborn young of animals, growing crops, and things such as timber and minerals that may be taken from land. The term does not include money used to pay for the goods, investment securities such as stocks and bonds, or assignments of contract rights. The money used to pay for goods is known as the **price,** or the consideration for the sales contract. Rare coins, however, when used as the subject matter of a sale as in Problem 3, *are* considered goods under the Code. Stocks and bonds are governed by a separate section of the UCC.

Under the provisions of the Code, the price may be payable in money, goods, services, realty, or some other consideration. In return for the price, the seller transfers ownership of or title to the goods to the buyer.

Present Sale and a Contract to Sell

Any contract entered into by a seller and buyer will be either a **present sale** of goods or a **contract to sell** goods at a future time. In a present sale, the seller transfers ownership or title to the goods to the buyer immediately when the contract is made. But in a contract to sell, the agreement is to transfer the title at some future time. Unless otherwise stated in the Code, the rights of buyer and seller are the same whether the contract is a present sale or a contract to sell.

Shubow bought a power mower from a lawn-and-garden equipment dealer and paid the dealer $220 for it. He also agreed to buy $75 worth of accessories a month later. Shubow's purchase of the mower is a present sale within the definition of the UCC. His agreement to buy the accessories at a future time is a contract to sell.

Firm Offers

We have seen that an offeror usually retains the power to revoke an offer at any time before the offeree accepts. If the offeree pays some consideration to keep the offer open (an option), the offeror gives up the power of revocation for a stated time period. In the absence of an option agreement, the offeror's unlimited power to revoke an offer is often contrary to the real intentions of the parties. It is also contrary to accepted business customs and practices.

4. Nihan & Co., wholesale toy merchants, offered in writing to sell 500 toys at $9 each to Wilson Toy Shops. The offer included this statement: "You may have 30 days in which to consider this offer. During that time, we shall not revoke the offer." May Nihan & Co. revoke its offer before the stated time expires?

Business people regard promises to hold offers open as **firm** (irrevocable) **offers** for the stated time, with or without consideration. Because of this fact, courts have tried by various legal devices to uphold certain firm offers. These include firm offers that are made in writing and signed by the offeror and that state they will not be revoked for a specific time period. Following the courts' actions, the UCC now makes firm offers irrevocable *during the* *time stated, or if no time is stated, for a reasonable time.* The Code further provides that a firm offer for a period beyond three months binds the offeror for a three-month period only. For nonmerchants, the common law rules of offer and acceptance apparently still apply. In Problem 4, Nihan & Co. may not revoke its offer for 30 days.

Counteroffers

> **5.** Sills, a fertilizer manufacturer, offered by mail to sell 500 bags of fertilizer to Bartlett, a landscape contractor. The price of each 100-lb. bag was $5. Bartlett immediately wired an acceptance: "Accept your offer. Ship by Friday. Will send check in payment next week." Did Bartlett's reply constitute an acceptance of Sills' offer?

Under the common law, an acceptance that materially changes the terms of the offer does not ordinarily create a contract. It is regarded as a qualified acceptance or counteroffer that terminates the original offer. This rule often results in hardships to merchants who are under the impression that they have created a binding contract. This is especially true when forms are used in buying and selling goods. When ordering goods, the buyer may use a form stating that the order is subject to certain conditions. The seller may respond by using a form that "accepts" the order subject to another set of conditions. The forms, of course, are in conflict. As a result, no contract is formed under the common law. Under the UCC, however, a contract has been created. This is because both parties have used "contract" forms specially drafted for the purpose and recognized by the business community. The Code provides that "additional or different terms are to be regarded as proposals for addition to the contract and *between merchants* become part of the contract unless they materially change it or notice of objection to them is given within a reasonable time, or the offeror expressly limits acceptance to the terms of the offer." Thus, in Problem 5, Sills will be bound by Bartlett's acceptance unless, within a reasonable time after receiving the acceptance, Sills objects to the conditions affecting *shipment date* and *date of payment.*

Communication of Acceptance

> **6.** Cacera, a dealer in scrap steel, mailed an offer to buy a quantity of steel from Brody Supply. Brody replied by sending a telegram accepting the offer. The telegram never reached Cacera. Is there a contract between the parties under the UCC?

We learned earlier that when an offer is made by mail, telegram, or other agency, and the offeror fails to state how the acceptance is to be made, an acceptance left with the offeror's agent is binding. This is true even if the acceptance never reaches the offeror. If the acceptance is delivered to an agency other than the offeror's, however, it is not binding until it is delivered to the offeror. This rule is no longer true in sales transactions under the UCC. The Code provides that an offer to buy or sell goods may be accepted in *any manner and by any medium that is reasonable under the circumstances.* For example, suppose that an offer is made by mail and the acceptance is made by telegram. Under the UCC, the acceptance in sales transactions is complete when the telegram is *sent.* A contract will arise even though the acceptance is never received by the offeror. In Problem 6, therefore, Brody's acceptance of Cacera's offer creates a binding contract if the courts find that an acceptance by telegram is reasonable under the circumstances.

Acceptance by Shipment of Goods

> **7.** Yasuro, Inc., makers of women's sportswear, sent an order for 15,000 yards of cotton goods to Walton Mills. Yasuro asked that the goods be shipped within ten days. On receipt of the order, Walton immediately wired: "Your order will receive our prompt attention." May Yasuro regard this telegram as an acceptance of its offer?

Under the common law rule, an acceptance must agree exactly with the terms of the offer. In this event, Walton's reply in Problem 7 would not create a contract. Under the UCC, however, a binding contract would result. This is so because the Code permits sellers to accept orders or other offers *either by actually shipping the goods or by a prompt promise to ship them.* The statement, "Your order will receive our prompt attention," in Problem 7 is such a promise. A seller who elects to *ship* the goods instead of *promising to ship* them must notify the buyer within a reasonable time that the offer has been accepted in this manner.

Sales Contracts and the Statute of Frauds

> **8.** Krikorian agreed to buy a TV and a VCR from Telectron Co. for $850. Because Telectron didn't have the particular models in stock that Krikorian wanted, she was not required to sign any papers or to make any payment. Telectron later received a shipment of the goods and attempted to hold Krikorian to her agreement to buy them. Is she liable?

As you know, certain contracts must be made in writing to be enforceable. In addition to those mentioned earlier, the Statute of Frauds section of the UCC requires that contracts for the sale of goods priced at $500 or more must be in writing to be legally enforceable. The agreement in Problem 8 was for more than $500 and was not in writing. Therefore, it is not enforceable under the Statute of Frauds.

Under the Code, a party, whether a merchant or a nonmerchant, seeking to enforce a contract for the sale of goods priced at $500 or more may satisfy the Statute of Frauds in one of several ways. The party may

1. produce a written contract or memorandum of the transaction; or
2. supply oral proof that (a) all or part of goods were received and accepted by the buyer; or (b) full or part payment was made by the buyer; or (c) the goods were specially made for the buyer and couldn't be sold to others. Also, if the party being sued admits in court that an oral sales contract with the other party had been formed, the sales contract will be enforced.

The Written Memorandum

For purposes of satisfying the Statute of Frauds, the Code states that any memorandum providing reasonable proof of an existing contract to buy or sell goods priced at $500 or more is sufficient. The memorandum must show enough of the contractual terms to enable a court to render justice properly in the event of a breach. The writing does not have to take any special form. It may consist merely of a series of related letters or telegrams that have passed between the parties. It must be signed by the party to be held liable, but the signature doesn't have to be handwritten and need not appear at the end of the memorandum. A typed, printed, or stamped name that appears in any part of the memorandum will serve as a valid signature.

The minimum UCC requirements as to the content of the writing are these: (1) it must contain evidence of a contract for the sale of goods; (2) it must be signed; and (3) it must specify the *quantity* of the goods that form the agreement's subject matter.

EXAMPLE

Assume that Krikorian, in Problem 8, had signed an order form. The form read, in part: "The purchaser agrees to purchase one Model 300 color television set, $575, and one Model 9263 VCR, $275, total $850. (Signed) Teresa Krikorian." The memorandum meets the minimum requirements of the Statute of Frauds. Therefore, it is enforceable against Krikorian.

PROBLEM

9. Lippman, a fabric manufacturer, ordered a quantity of goods by phone from Milbank Company. The price of the goods was $1,200. Immediately after the phone conversation, Milton sent a letter to Lippman confirming the order and promising to ship the goods within ten days. Later, Lippman canceled the order and stated that he wasn't liable on the oral contract. Is his claim correct?

The Code provides an exception to the rule that the memorandum must be signed by the party to be held liable. Between merchants, a written **confirmation** (acknowledgment of an order) is a memorandum sufficient to satisfy the Statute of Frauds. This is true unless the party who received the goods objects in writing within ten days to the confirmation's contents. Under the UCC, Lippman in Problem 9 would be liable if he failed to object to the contents of the confirmation within ten days.

Receipt and Acceptance of Part of the Goods

PROBLEM

10. Assume in Problem 8 that Telectron delivered the TV to Krikorian, who accepted it. Later, when the firm tried to deliver the VCR, Krikorian refused to accept it. When sued, she pleaded the Statute of Frauds as her defense. Is her defense legally correct?

Under the UCC, an *oral* contract for the sale of goods of $500 or more may be proved by showing that the buyer received and accepted all or part of the goods. Both *receipt* and *acceptance* of the goods must be shown. When a buyer receives an article, examines it, rejects it, and sends it back to the seller, the Statute of Frauds is not satisfied. The buyer's actions constitute only a receipt of the goods, not acceptance of them. Acceptance takes place when the buyer indicates a willingness to become the owner of the goods.

Suppose that a buyer receives and accepts part of the goods under an oral contract. May the buyer be held liable for the remaining goods? Under the Code, the buyer is liable *only for the portion of the goods received and accepted.* If the goods can't be separated into parts, the oral contract is unenforceable. In Problem 10, Krikorian is liable for the price of the TV but not for the price of the VCR.

Partial Payment

> **11.** Dugan, a building contractor, orally agreed to buy 400 yards of gravel from Hewes. The price agreed on was $19 a yard, and the gravel was to be delivered to Dugan's building site. Dugan made a partial payment of $1,900 at the time he entered into the oral agreement. Later, though, Dugan changed his mind and asked for his money back. He claimed that he wasn't liable on the oral contract. Is Dugan's claim legally correct?

Another way to enforce an oral contract covered by the UCC is to show that the buyer made either a full or a partial payment for the goods. But the Code states that the buyer is liable *only for the portion of the goods for which payment was made and accepted by the seller.* As with receipt and acceptance of part of the goods, the oral contract is unenforceable if the goods can't be separated into parts. A partial payment may be made by cash or check as well as by goods or services accepted by the seller. In Problem 11, Dugan may not get his money back. He is liable for the 100 yards of gravel he accepted and paid for. The balance of the contract, however, is unenforceable.

Goods Specially Manufactured for the Buyer

> **12.** Gamio had just remodeled her home to make it a bed-and-breakfast inn. She placed an oral order with a furniture manufacturer for three specially designed sofas to fit the lobby of the inn. The cost of the sofas was $3,600. After one sofa had been completed, Gamio canceled the order. Was she bound to accept and pay for the sofas?

If the goods ordered are manufactured specially for the buyer and are not suitable for sale to others, the oral contract is enforceable under the UCC. Oral proof of such contracts may be made regardless of the amount involved. It is important to note that the Code requires the seller to do something more than merely promise to make the goods. The seller must make a substantial beginning of the manufacture of the goods, as in Problem 12. Since the manufacturer in the problem had complied with the Statute of Frauds, it may enforce the *entire* contract against Gamio. The seller also may satisfy this requirement of the Code by contracting with another party to obtain the goods for the buyer.

Court Admission of a Contract's Existence

If a party being sued on an oral contract for a sale covered by the UCC admits in court that the contract exists, the contract is enforceable. The admission may be oral or written. Once the party admits there is a contract, its terms can be proved by oral testimony.

> Ninh sued Mirbeau on an oral contract for the sale of goods priced at $750. Mirbeau pleaded the Statute of Frauds as his defense. During the trial, Mirbeau took the stand to testify. He admitted during cross-examination that he had entered into an oral contract of sale with Ninh. Because of his admission, Mirbeau is bound to perform the contract or to pay damages to Ninh.

The Uniform Commercial Code and the Statute of Frauds, covered in this chapter, are critical to a study of business law. Because you will buy and sell goods throughout your life, it is important that you be familiar with the provisions of these laws. But it is also important that you understand the rights and duties that are transferred in sales contracts. We will study these topics in Chapter 18.

Chapter 17 Review

"YOU BE THE JUDGE" REVIEW

Look again at the "You Be the Judge" cases given at the beginning of this chapter. Would you decide them differently now, after your study of the chapter?

Correct Decisions

1. No. A contract for the sale of goods priced at $500 or more must be in writing to be enforceable.

2. Ortiz is correct. A barter transaction is regarded as a sale of goods under the UCC.

UNDERSTANDING WHAT YOU HAVE READ

1. What is the purpose of the Uniform Commercial Code?
2. Why is it important under the Code to distinguish between a merchant and an ordinary consumer?
3. What is the effect of a counteroffer in dealings between merchants?
4. Between sellers and buyers, how may an acceptance be communicated?
5. In dealings between merchants, how may an offer to buy goods for prompt or current shipment be accepted?
6. List four ways of satisfying the requirements of the Statute of Frauds for oral contracts covered by the UCC.
7. What information must the memorandum contain to satisfy the Statute of Frauds under the UCC?
8. What is the effect of each of the following on the Statute of Frauds:
   a. receipt and acceptance of part of the goods by the buyer?
   b. partial payment by the buyer?
9. Under what conditions is a contract to manufacture goods specially for the buyer enforceable under the UCC's provisions?
10. What is the legal effect of a defendant's court admission of the existence of a sales contract?

BUILDING YOUR LEGAL VOCABULARY

Match each of these legal terms with its correct definition from the list that follows. Write your answers on a separate sheet of paper.

confirmation	merchant	specially manufactured goods
contract to sell	present sale	vendee
firm offer	price	vendor
goods		

1. a merchant's written offer, stating that the offer will be held open
2. personal property that is the subject matter of a contract
3. a seller of goods
4. an expression indicating receipt of an offer or assurance of an understanding
5. the consideration for a sales contract
6. a professional buyer or seller who has a specialized knowledge of the goods
7. a sale in which ownership will pass sometime in the future
8. a buyer of goods
9. a sale in which ownership passes when the contract is made
10. goods made to order and unfit for sale to others

APPLYING LEGAL PRINCIPLES

1. Broadman contracted to sell a lot in the country to Jackowicz for $25,000. Would this transaction be governed by the Uniform Commercial Code?
2. Aguilar traded his electric drill to a neighbor for a band saw. Is this transaction considered a sale under the UCC?
3. You agreed to give your friend a radio in return for his repair of your motorbike. Is this transaction a sale under the UCC?
4. Moss entered into a written contract to sell 40 shares of American Widget stock to Bowen at $80 a share. Is this transaction a sale under the UCC?
5. Daoud, a wholesaler, mailed an offer to sell a quantity of goods to McDevitt, a retailer. The offer stated: "You may have ten days from the date of this letter to reach a decision. The offer will not be withdrawn during that period." Three days after receipt of the offer, McDevitt received a telegram withdrawing the offer. May Daoud withdraw the offer?
6. Kirschner, a truck manufacturer, agreed in writing to make twelve trucks of a certain type for Abbeson & Co. Before Kirschner began to make the trucks, Abbeson canceled its order. Abbeson

claimed that since the trucks weren't in existence when the contract was made, the contract was not enforceable. Is this claim valid?

7. Calabrese mailed a written order to Midwest Electric Co. on her own printed stationery. The order offered to buy a quantity of specific Weston refrigerators at $450 each. Midwest Electric immediately mailed a confirmation of the order, promising to ship the required quantity. However, the confirmation also stated: "Due to conditions over which we have no control, the price of the model you ordered has been increased. You will be billed at the new price of $470." Calabrese did not object to this statement and accepted delivery of the refrigerators. She refused, though, to pay more than $450 per unit. She claimed that she was not bound by the additional terms inserted by Midwest Electric. Is Calabrese's claim correct under the UCC?

8. Hess Company mailed an offer to Acosta Corp. to sell Acosta certain goods at specified prices. Acosta Corp. wired an acceptance of the offer, but the telegram never reached Hess Company. Was there a contract?

9. Foss, a furniture retailer, orally agreed to buy five dining-room sets at $1,200 each from Hardwood Furniture Co. Before the furniture was shipped, Foss notified Hardwood that he would not accept the furniture and was not liable on the oral contract.

   a. Is Foss's claim legally correct?
   b. If the total purchase price of his transaction had amounted to $450, would Foss be bound on the oral contract?

   c. Suppose that Foss had paid $3,600 on account. To what extent would he be liable on the oral contract?
   d. Assume that Foss had received and accepted three dining-room sets, but then refused to accept the last two. To what extent, if any, would he be liable on the oral contract?

10. Fenton signed the following memorandum, which she gave to Nobuharu:

    > I hereby agree to purchase from Emily Nobuharu one Magna 25-inch color TV set, Model 256A, for the sum of $720, C.O.D.
    >
    > *Carol Fenton*

    Fenton later refused to accept the TV, claiming that the memorandum was insufficient to satisfy the Statute of Frauds. Is she legally correct?

11. A hotel manager orally ordered eight specially made chandeliers, suitable only for the dining room of a specific hotel. Before the seller contracted to obtain the fixtures for the hotel manager, the manager canceled the contract. The seller sued. As a defense, the manager pleaded the Statute of Frauds. Is this defense valid under the UCC?

12. Assume in Problem 11 that the seller had made two of the fixtures before the manager canceled the contract. In that event, would the manager's defense of the Statute of Frauds be valid under the UCC?

13. Jacobs was a defendant in an action for breach of an oral contract for the sale of goods of $900. During the trial, she admitted in writing that she had entered into a sales contract with the plaintiff. What is the legal effect of her admission on her liability under the oral contract?

ANALYZING COURT CASES

1. Kaufman & Chernick, Inc., a tire dealer, advertised an offer of one free gallon of Zerex antifreeze with every purchase of a tire. E. I. DuPont Company, makers of Zerex, sought legal action to prevent Kaufman & Chernick from selling its product on such terms. DuPont claimed breach of contract. The tire dealer, however, contended that Zerex wasn't being sold to buyers of tires but was merely being offered to them as a gift. Do you agree with this contention? (*E. I. Du-Pont v. Kaufman & Chernick, Inc.*, 148 N.E. 2d 634)

2. Swanson ordered tulip bulbs from Van Meeruwen, to be delivered the following year. No price was mentioned. When delivery was refused the following year, Swanson brought suit for breach of contract. Van Meeruwen claimed that there was no binding contract between the parties because no purchase price had been specified. Was Van Meeruwen's claim legally valid? (*Van Meeruwen v. Swanson*, 141 N.W. 112)

3. In a single transaction, Standard Wallpaper Company orally sold to Towns two lots of wallpaper. The purchase price of either lot was below the $500 minimum required by the Statute of Frauds. The total price for both, however, exceeded the minimum price. Towns refused to accept the wallpaper when it was delivered, claiming the Statute of Frauds as a defense. Standard Wallpaper claimed that the Statute of Frauds did not apply in this case because the transaction consisted of two separate sales of wallpaper, with each sale under the $500 minimum. Whose claim is legally correct? (*Standard Wallpaper Company v. Towns*, 56 A. 744)

CHAPTER 18

Transfer of Ownership and Risk of Loss

Think about these cases.
If you were the judge, how would you decide each case?

1

MacIntosh stole your 15-speed bike and sold it to Cruz, an innocent buyer. Can you get the bike back from Cruz?

2

Pinto bought a microwave oven from Roberti's Discount Center. The oven was to be delivered to Pinto the next day, but it was destroyed in a fire at the store before delivery. Who stands the loss?

WHAT IS OWNERSHIP?

A buyer acquires a number of legal rights when a purchase is made. Some of these rights are (1) the right to possess the goods, (2) the right to enjoy the use of the goods, and (3) the right to dispose of the goods when desired. These rights to possess, use, and dispose of goods constitute a person's **ownership,** or **title,** to the goods. Actually, the term *title* refers to the *evidence* of ownership in goods. For practical purposes, however, the word *title* is used interchangeably with the term *ownership.*

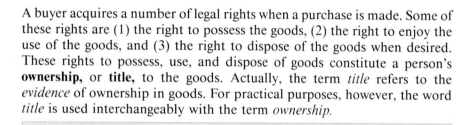

1. Evesham allowed her son to use her new car. The son drove the car negligently and injured a pedestrian. May the pedestrian hold both Evesham and her son liable for his injuries?

While ownership includes certain rights, it also implies acceptance of certain risks and responsibilities. If the goods are damaged, lost, destroyed, or stolen, ownership will determine to some extent who may sue third parties for loss or injury to the goods. The risks that may be acquired with ownership are jointly known as the **risk of loss.**

In about half the states, a car owner who allows a family member to use the car in such a way as to interfere with the rights of others will be held legally responsible. In Problem 1, the pedestrian may legally hold both Evesham and her son liable for his injuries.

Documents Indicating Ownership

Mere possession of goods is not conclusive proof of ownership. A person who borrows goods has possession but no title. A thief or someone who finds goods has possession but is not the owner of the goods. How can one prove ownership of goods? The most effective way to do this is to furnish a written **document of title.** There are two types of title documents mentioned by the Uniform Commercial Code. One is a **warehouse receipt** and the other is a **bill of lading.**

Warehouse Receipts

When goods are stored in a warehouse, the warehouse operator issues a warehouse receipt. This business paper serves as a receipt for the goods stored and as a contract for their storage. The receipt may take one of two forms. If the stored goods are to be delivered only to the person named in the document, a nonnegotiable (nontransferable) form is used. If the goods are deliverable to the bearer of the receipt or to a named person, a **negotiable instrument** (document) is issued. This document may be transferred if it is indorsed (signed on the back) and delivered. When the negotiable form of receipt is used, the owner may sell the goods while they are in storage. This is done by endorsing the warehouse receipt and giving it to the buyer. The buyer then has the right to delivery of the goods by the warehouse operator. A negotiable warehouse receipt is evidence of ownership of goods. (Negotiable instruments will be discussed in more detail in Unit 7.)

Bills of Lading

According to the UCC, a bill of lading is "a document evidencing the receipt of goods for shipment issued by a person engaged in the business of transporting or forwarding goods, and includes an airbill" (a document for air transportation). A bill of lading is not only a receipt for goods delivered to a carrier but also a contract for shipment of the goods. Like warehouse receipts, bills of lading are of two kinds. One is a **straight bill of lading** (see Figure 18.1), and the other is an **order bill of lading.**

A straight bill of lading is nonnegotiable. For example, a bill of lading that states that the goods are to be delivered to "John Duncan" is a nonnegotiable straight bill of lading. In contrast, a bill of lading that states that the goods are to be delivered to "the order of John Duncan" is a

Figure 18.1
A Straight Bill of Lading

STRAIGHT BILL OF LADING
ORIGINAL-NOT NEGOTIABLE

CAROLINA
FREIGHT CARRIERS CORPORATION
(CFCC)

FORM OP 297 9/85
SINGLE SHIPMENT PICKUP [X]

PLACE PRO LABEL HERE

SHIPPER NO. 895
CARRIER NO. BC 1354
DATE 1/10/--

TO: (CONSIGNEE)		FROM: (SHIPPER)	
Martinez Hardware Company		Benlo Lock Company	
STREET: 280 Central Avenue		STREET: 155 Third Street	
CITY, STATE: Havasu City, AZ	ZIP CODE: 86403	CITY, STATE: Miami, FL	ZIP CODE: 33015
ROUTE: I-95 to I-40			VEHICLE NO. 10

BILL TO:

NUMBER SHIPPING UNITS	HM	KIND OF PACKAGING, DESCRIPTION OF ARTICLES, SPECIAL MARKS AND EXCEPTIONS	WEIGHT (SUBJECT TO CORRECTION)	RATE	CHARGES (FOR CARRIER USE ONLY)
10		Cartons combination locks	450 lbs.	$29.83/ 100 lbs.	$134.24

REMIT C.O.D. TO
ADDRESS

NOTE—Where the rate is dependent on value, shippers are required to state specifically in writing the agreed or declared value of the property.
The agreed or declared value of the property is hereby specifically stated by the shipper to be not exceeding.
$ ______ per ______

C O D AMT: $

Subject to Section 7 of the conditions, if this shipment is to be delivered to the consignee without recourse on the shipper the shipper shall sign the following statement:
The carrier shall not make delivery of this shipment without payment of freight and all other lawful charges.
(Signature of Shipper)

C.O.D. FEE PREPAID [X] $
COLLECT [ ]

TOTAL CHARGES $ 134.24

FREIGHT CHARGES:
FREIGHT PREPAID except when box at right is checked
Check box if charges are to be collect [ ]

RECEIVED, subject to the classifications and tariffs in effect on the date of the issue of this Bill of Lading, the property described above in apparent good order, except as noted (contents and condition of contents of packages unknown), marked, consigned, and destined as indicated above which said carrier agrees to carry to its usual place of delivery at said destination, if on its route, otherwise to deliver to another carrier on the route to said destination. It is mutually agreed as to each carrier of all or any of said property over all or any portion of said route to destination and as to each party at any time interested in all or any of said property, that every service to be performed hereunder shall be subject to all the bill of lading terms and conditions in the governing classification on the date of shipment.
Shipper hereby certifies that he is familiar with all the bill of lading terms and conditions in the governing classification and the said terms and conditions are hereby agreed to by the shipper and accepted for himself and his assigns.

This is to certify that the above named materials are properly classified, described, packaged, marked, and labeled and are in proper condition for transportation, according to the applicable regulations of the D.O.T.

CARRIER: **CAROLINA FREIGHT CARRIERS CORP. AGENT**

SHIPPER: Benlo Lock Company
PER: John McKay

PER: Antoinette Lauria
DATE: 1/10/--
TIME: 12:10 P.M.
PIECES: 10

EQUAL OPPORTUNITY CONDITION: This contract contains the provisions of Sec. 202 of Executive Order 11246, Paragraphs 1 through 7.

negotiable order bill of lading. John Duncan may sell the goods described in the order bill of lading while they are in the possession of a carrier. He can do this by signing the back of the instrument and delivering it to the purchaser. An order bill of lading also serves as evidence of ownership of goods.

Bills of Sale

A **bill of sale** is a mere receipt issued by a seller to a buyer. It transfers to the buyer title to the goods described in the instrument. It is not a contract or a bill for the goods sold. A bill of sale may be used in any sale of personal property. It is especially important as evidence of the sale of a car because the buyer in some states can't get license plates without a bill of sale.

Who May Transfer Title?

A seller who has a clear title may transfer that title to a buyer. If a seller has a defective title or no title, the buyer is in no better position than the seller. This is true even though the purchase was made in good faith and for value.

Stolen Goods

> **2.** If you unknowingly buy a watch from someone who has stolen it, do you obtain a valid title?

Ordinarily, goods can't be sold by a person who isn't the owner. A thief, therefore, cannot transfer title to goods because the thief has no title to transfer. It is immaterial whether the buyer obtains the goods directly from the thief or from someone who bought the goods in good faith from the thief. The title to the stolen goods has never left the true owner. In Problem 2, you would not obtain a valid title to the watch.

Lost Goods

> **3.** Would you obtain a valid title if the watch in Problem 2 had been lost and then sold to you by the finder?

A finder of lost property gets possession but does not acquire title to the goods. Title still remains with the true owner. The finder does have a right of possession. That right is good against anyone except the true owner. If the finder sells the goods, the true owner may recover them even from a buyer who bought the goods from the finder in good faith and for value. In Problem 3, you would have a better right to the watch than anyone except the true owner.

Defrauded Buyers

PROBLEM

> **4.** Belluomini, relying on fraudulent statements made by the seller, bought a large quantity of aluminum cans from Pell Can Co. Shortly thereafter, Belluomini sold the cans to Xavier, an innocent buyer. Did Xavier obtain a good title to the cans?

A buyer who purchases goods through fraud or trickery practiced by the true owner obtains a *voidable* title. The buyer may avoid this type of sale when the true facts are discovered. Suppose, though, that the defrauded buyer resells the goods to an innocent third party. In that case, the third party obtains a good title. Where one of two innocent parties must suffer as a result of fraud, the loss should fall on the one who made the fraud possible. In Problem 4, therefore, the loss will fall on Belluomini. Xavier has obtained a good title.

TITLE AND RISK OF LOSS UNDER THE CODE

As you know, ownership sometimes includes responsibility for damaged, lost, destroyed, or stolen goods. In such situations the owner suffers the loss unless it can be proved that the loss was caused by another party who is legally liable. But ownership does not always determine who has the risk of loss. Under the Code, the determination of title and risk of loss depends on the agreement between the parties. However, if the parties have not mentioned either of these, the Code provides specific rules for their determination.

Generally, before title can pass from seller to buyer, the goods must be both *existing* and *identified*. Goods that aren't both existing and identified are called **future goods.** Future goods cannot be the subject matter of a present sale, as noted in Chapter 17. They can form the subject matter only of a contract to sell. **Existing goods** are those that have been grown, processed, manufactured, or packed. They must not only be in existence under the Code, but they also must be identified to the particular contract. This identification must take the form of proper marking, labeling, tagging, and crating.

A contract for sale may require the seller to do something in addition to identifying the goods to the contract. It may require that the goods be placed in the hands of a carrier for delivery to the buyer. If the goods *are* in the hands of a carrier, the seller may then have to deliver a negotiable document of title to the buyer. This document will allow the buyer to obtain possession of the goods. Finally, if delivery of the goods to a carrier is not required, special UCC rules govern the passing of title and risk of loss. Figure 18.2 summarizes when title and risk of loss transfers occur in some of the most common sales transactions.

Type of Sale	Transfer of Title Occurs	Transfer of Risk of Loss Occurs
Shipment contract (F.O.B., F.A.S., and C.I.F.)	At time and place of shipment	On delivery to carrier at shipping point
Delivery contract (F.O.B. destination, ex-ship, no arrival, no sale, buyer's place of business)	When goods are tendered at destination	When goods are tendered at destination
Ordinary sales by merchants and nonmerchants	At time and place of contracting	On receipt of goods from a merchant; on tender of goods by a nonmerchant
Sales on approval	When the buyer signifies approval or after a reasonable time	Borne by the seller until approval is indicated
Sales with privilege of return	At time and place of contracting	Same as for ordinary sales
Delivery of title document only	At time and place of delivery of document by seller	On buyer's receipt of negotiable title document
Goods held by bailee, without title document	At time and place of contracting	At time of bailee's acknowledgment of buyer's right to possession

Figure 18.2
Transfer of Title
and Risk of Loss

Delivery to the Shipping Point

A contract may require the seller to ship existing and identified goods by carrier but not to deliver the goods at a destination. In this event, the *title and risk of loss pass to the buyer at the time and place of shipment.* The shipment requirements include (1) delivery of the goods to the carrier at the shipping point, (2) forwarding the necessary documents of title to the buyer, and (3) promptly notifying the buyer of the shipment. Risk of loss is on the buyer even if the goods haven't been paid for, or even if the seller still has to do something to put the goods in the condition specified in the contract.

EXAMPLE

Corbin in Chicago orders a freight container of goods from Grimm & Co. of Fall River, Ohio. The goods are shipped "F.O.B. Fall River." Grimm & Co. must then deliver the goods to the carrier at Fall River, forward the original copy of the bill of lading, and notify Corbin of the shipment. Once this has been done, title to the goods and risk of loss will pass to Corbin. If the goods are lost or damaged in transit, the loss will fall on the buyer.

Under the Code, mercantile shipping symbols such as **F.O.B.** (free on board), **C.I.F.** (cost, insurance, and freight to a named destination), and **F.A.S.** (free alongside ship) are all title points. Title to the goods and risk of loss pass to the buyer at these points unless the seller breaches the contract. If that occurs, the loss will be the seller's.

Delivery to the Destination

A contract may require that existing and identified goods be delivered to a named destination. In this case, *title and risk of loss pass to the buyer on tender of the goods at the destination.* The goods must be tendered at a reasonable hour and with sufficient notice to the buyer to permit receipt of the goods. The seller also must deliver any document of title the buyer needs to obtain possession of the goods.

Suppose that the goods in the preceding example were shipped "F.O.B. Chicago." In that case, title and risk of loss would pass to Corbin when the goods arrived in Chicago and Corbin was notified to take delivery.

Goods in the Possession of Another

The goods to be sold may have been left in the possession of another party for a particular purpose. This is a contractual arrangement called a *bailment* (see Unit 5). The party with whom the goods have been left may be a warehouse, a garage, or a repair person. That party is called a *bailee.* If a sales contract doesn't require that the goods be transported and the goods are held by a bailee, the UCC provides these rules for the transfer of title and risk of loss:

1. When the contract requires the seller to deliver a negotiable document of title to the buyer, *title to the goods and risk of loss pass to the buyer at the time when and place where the seller delivers that document.*
2. When the contract does *not* require the seller to issue a negotiable document of title to the buyer and the goods are in the hands of a bailee, *title and risk of loss pass when the bailee acknowledges that the goods are being held for the buyer.*

Hirsch, a wholesaler, bought some furniture from Grand Furniture Co. and stored it in a warehouse. She received a negotiable warehouse receipt made out to her order. If Hirsch wants to sell the furniture, all she has to do to pass title and risk of loss to the buyer is indorse the warehouse receipt and deliver it to the buyer.

LIVING UNDER THE LAW

Establishing a Credit History

Nieman, eighteen, had just graduated from high school. Before going to college, he decided to get some business experience. After answering several "Help Wanted" ads, Nieman found a job that paid a good beginning salary. Nieman then felt that he could afford to buy a used car from Steve's Motors. The car was priced at $4,950 and could be bought with a surprisingly low down payment. The balance was to be paid in equal installments over a 24-month period. Nieman was about to write a check for the down payment when the salesperson said, "We'll have to check your credit record before completing this deal." Nieman replied, "I've never bought anything on credit before. I don't have a credit record." "In that case," the salesperson said, "you'll need a cosigner—a parent, relative, or friend."

Does Nieman's experience sound unusual? It's not unusual at all. Some creditors are reluctant to grant credit to consumers who have not established a "track record" with other creditors first. Building a good credit history is important, according to the Bureau of Consumer Protection of the Federal Trade Commission. The Bureau suggests that young people who do not have credit histories should begin to build them. They may begin to do this by applying for credit with a local business, such as a department store. Or they might borrow a small amount of money from a bank or credit union where they have a checking or savings account. Whichever method is used, the Bureau advises that before applying for credit, people should ask whether the creditor reports credit history information to local credit bureaus. Such reporting builds one's credit history.

What happens when an application for credit is rejected? In that event, the Bureau advises that the applicant should find out why. There may be reasons other than a lack of a credit history. The Bureau also cautions applicants to wait six months after a rejection before submitting another application. Finally, if an applicant still cannot get credit, the Bureau recommends that the person obtain a cosigner who has an established credit history. Once the debt is repaid, the applicant should try again to get credit on his or her own account.

Ordinary Sales by Merchants and Nonmerchants

In ordinary sales, the seller may be required to deliver the goods to the buyer. The contract may require, however, that the buyer must pick up the goods at the seller's place of business or some other location. In either case, title passes *at the time and place where the contract was made.* If the seller is a *merchant,* the seller bears the risk of loss until the buyer *receives* the goods. If the seller is a *nonmerchant,* the risk of loss passes to the buyer when the seller *tenders* the goods to the buyer to enable the buyer to take delivery.

EXAMPLE

> Barrone bought several shirts in a sale at Nordman's, a department store. Barrone personally selected the shirts from a display counter and agreed to pick them up the next day. Before he called for the shirts, they were destroyed in a fire at the store. Who bears the loss? The loss falls on Nordman's, whether it is a merchant or a nonmerchant seller. Because there has been no *delivery* or *tender of delivery,* Barrone will not be liable for the price.

SPECIAL RULES FOR TRANSFER OF TITLE

Most sales transactions that involve transfer of title are governed by the rules just discussed. There are, however, some instances where the passing of title requires special rules. These rules may be found in the Uniform Commercial Code.

Cash Sales

PROBLEM

> 5.   Madero paid cash for a dress at Marny's Boutique. The dress was handed to her, properly packed. When did Madero acquire title to the dress?

People who buy goods on a cash basis usually acquire title to them only when the price of the goods is paid in full. This rule protects the seller from buyers who have no established credit standing with the seller. In Problem 5, Madero acquired title to the dress when she paid the purchase price.

C.O.D. Sales

The letters **C.O.D.** (collect on delivery) merely indicate that the seller intends to retain control of the goods until the buyer pays for them. Under the UCC, when the seller is required to deliver the goods to a carrier for a

C.O.D. shipment, the *title passes to the buyer at the time of delivery to the carrier.* By means of the C.O.D. clause, the seller is deemed to reserve a security interest in the goods. This interest protects the seller's right to collect payment. However, when the seller's employees must deliver the goods, the letters C.O.D. may be taken as evidence that a cash sale was intended. In this event, no title passes until the goods are delivered and paid for.

> Masuro ordered a set of books from a publisher in Chicago. The books were to be delivered by an express shipper, and the terms were C.O.D. The books were shipped immediately. Title passed to Masuro as soon as the books were given to the express company for delivery to Masuro.

Sales with Privilege of Return

A buyer may purchase goods with the option of returning them if they can't be resold. In this event, *title and risk of loss pass at the time of delivery* if the seller is a merchant. If the seller is a nonmerchant, *title and risk of loss pass at the time of tender of delivery.* The title may revert to the seller, however, if the buyer returns the goods within an agreed time. If no definite time is agreed on, the goods must be returned within a reasonable time. The UCC states that the option to return extends to all or part of the goods. The return of the goods is at the buyer's risk and expense.

> VanBuren, a jewelry manufacturer, shipped five dozen necklaces to Kai Jewelers. The shipment was made under a written agreement allowing Kai Jewelers to pay for the necklaces it sold and to return any unsold necklaces. Title to the necklaces passed on delivery to Kai Jewelers. When Kai returns the unsold necklaces, title to them will revert to VanBuren.

Sales on Approval

> **6.** Emmett selected a pearl ring at a jewelry store. He intended to give the ring to his wife for her birthday. The jeweler agreed to let Emmett take the ring home *on approval.* If Emmett's wife didn't like the ring, he could return it. When does title to the ring pass to Emmett? When does the risk of loss pass to him?

A sale on approval can be advantageous in the purchase of expensive jewelry.

A buyer may receive goods *on approval* or *on trial.* In this case, *title and risk of loss will not pass to the buyer until, by word or conduct, the buyer has signified approval and acceptance.* If a buyer retains the goods beyond the agreed time, or beyond a reasonable time if no time is stated, the title passes to the buyer. Title also passes to a buyer who expressly states an intention to keep the goods. In Problem 6, title to the ring passes to Emmett when he shows approval by words or conduct. Risk of loss also passes to him then.

The UCC provides that acceptance of any part of the goods is equivalent to acceptance of all the goods. The Code further states that a buyer must *notify* the seller of an intention to return the goods. Otherwise, acceptance will be assumed. The return of the goods is at the seller's risk and expense.

The agreement between the seller and the buyer usually determines whether the parties intended a sale on approval or a sale with privilege of return. Sometimes, the parties fail to make their intentions clear on this point. In these cases, the Code provides that it is a sale on approval if the goods were bought for *use by a consumer.* If the goods were bought for *resale by a merchant,* it is a sale with privilege of return under the UCC. Since the risk of loss is on the seller until the buyer approves, this rule obviously favors the buyer in a sale on approval.

Auction Sales

An auction sale is complete when the auctioneer so announces by the fall of the hammer or in another customary manner. *Title passes to the successful bidder at that time.*

Bulk Sales

Under the UCC, a **bulk sale** is any transfer, not in the ordinary course of the seller's business, of a major part of the seller's stock and business fixtures. By "major part," the UCC means more than half of the business's goods. Sales such as these usually occur when a business is being sold to a new owner. Between the buyer and the seller, *title to the stock and fixtures passes when the contract is made.* However, if the UCC's provisions aren't carefully observed, the seller's creditors may have the sale set aside. An important provision of this law is that the buyer must give the creditors ten days' notice of the sale, by registered mail. Creditors have six months in which to set aside the sale if the provisions of the Bulk Sales Law are not observed.

EXAMPLE

Mullen, owner of a computer store, sold her entire stock of merchandise and fixtures to Morita. Mullen gave Morita an inventory of the goods and a list of her creditors. Shortly after the sale, Palazzo, a creditor to whom Mullen owed $900, sued Morita. Palazzo wanted to have the sale set aside on the ground that he hadn't been notified of the sale. Palazzo also claimed that the merchandise should be used to pay his debt. Palazzo will be successful. Morita violated the UCC's Bulk Sales Law, which requires the buyer of a major part of a business to notify the creditors at least ten days prior to the sale. A creditor who is not notified may have the sale set aside.

Obviously, questions regarding title and risk of loss are fairly complex. It's likely, though, that some of these questions will arise in your personal or business sales dealings. It is even more likely that you will buy goods that carry sellers' warranties. We will study warranties next, in Chapter 19.

Chapter 18 Review

"YOU BE THE JUDGE" REVIEW

Look again at the "You Be the Judge" cases given at the beginning of this chapter. Would you decide them differently now, after your study of the chapter?

Correct Decisions

1. Yes. No title passes through theft. Mac-Intosh had no title and cannot pass title to Cruz.

2. Roberti's Discount Center stands the loss. Risk of loss is on the seller if the seller is a *merchant* and the goods haven't been delivered to the buyer.

UNDERSTANDING WHAT YOU HAVE READ

1. What is meant by *title* or *ownership?*
2. What risks or responsibilities does title carry with it?
3. Can a thief or a finder of goods pass title to them? Can one with a voidable title pass a good title?
4. What business papers or documents may a person have as evidence of ownership of goods?
5. What is the difference between a negotiable and a nonnegotiable warehouse receipt?
6. What is the difference between a negotiable and a nonnegotiable bill of lading?
7. What is the purpose of a bill of sale?
8. For each of the following, explain when title and risk of loss pass to the buyer:
   a. existing and identified goods to be delivered to a shipping point
   b. existing and identified goods to be delivered to a destination
   c. existing and identified goods in the possession of a bailee
   d. ordinary sales by merchants and nonmerchants
9. When does title pass in each of the following situations? (a) Cash sale (b) C.O.D. sale (c) sale with privilege of return (d) sale on approval (e) bulk sale (f) auction sale
10. What does each of these terms mean? (a) F.O.B. (b) C.O.D. (c) C.I.F. (d) F.A.S.

BUILDING YOUR LEGAL VOCABULARY

Choose the legal term that will correctly complete each definition below. Write your answers on a separate sheet of paper.

1. The purchase agreement that allows a buyer to take back the goods if a resale isn't possible is a
   a. bailment.
   b. negotiable instrument.
   c. sale with privilege of return.
2. A transfer of a major part of a business (not in the ordinary course of business) is a
   a. sale on approval.
   b. bulk sale.
   c. sale with privilege of return.
3. The business paper that serves as proof of ownership is a/an
   a. bailee.
   b. document of title.
   c. airbill.
4. A negotiable document that is both a contract to ship and a receipt for goods delivered to a carrier is a/an
   a. order bill of lading.
   b. warehouse receipt.
   c. straight bill of lading.
5. Goods that have been grown, processed, manufactured, or packed as well as marked or labeled are known as
   a. future goods.
   b. goods held by a bailee.
   c. existing and identified goods.

APPLYING LEGAL PRINCIPLES

1. Alizio bought some sterling silverware from Campi for $350. Later, Duffy claimed the silverware had been stolen from him and demanded that Alizio return it. If Alizio is an innocent buyer, must she give up the silverware?
2. Boone bought a camera from Hodge. A month later, Hance claimed the camera, saying that she had lost it. Can Hance recover the camera?
3. Luciano fraudulently induced Dalton to sell him a ski boat. Three months later, Luciano sold the boat to Rosetti, an innocent buyer. Dalton sued Rosetti to get back the boat, claiming that Rosetti never obtained title because of Luciano's fraud. Do you agree with Dalton's claim?
4. Glenn, a business person located in Burlington, Vermont, ordered some tractors. The tractors were to be delivered F.O.B. Detroit. While the goods were in transit, lightning struck the freight train. A resulting fire destroyed the tractors. Does Glenn suffer the loss under the Uniform Commercial Code?

5. a. If the terms of the sale in Problem 4 had been F.O.B. Burlington, would your answer have been the same?

   b. If in Problem 4 the terms had been C.O.D., who would have suffered the loss?

6. Acme Store had 200 pairs of jeans that it offered to Bell for $12 a pair. The terms of the sale were net, 30 days. Bell accepted the offer and said that she would send for the jeans the next day. On receiving Bell's acceptance, Acme packed the jeans in boxes, tagged each box with Bell's name, and tied the boxes together. Then Acme placed the boxes in its "pickup" room. During the night, the Acme building caught fire and the jeans were destroyed. On whom does the loss fall?

7. Cafua ordered a bike that was advertised to be sold "on ten days' trial." Cafua was preparing to return the bike within the agreed time when it was stolen. Is Cafua liable for the purchase price?

8. On December 6, Stay Manufacturing sold and delivered three motors to Morgan. Payment was to be made within 30 days. Morgan was given the privilege of returning the motors any time within fifteen days. On December 12, one motor was damaged by fire, through no fault of Morgan. Must Morgan stand the loss?

9. Iwata, a rancher, agreed to sell ten sheep to Quellette. The sheep were to be selected from a flock of 300. The entire flock perished in a blizzard before Quellette selected the sheep. Iwata claimed that Quellette suffered part of the loss. Do you agree?

10. Marcus sold her record and tape store to Heileman, including all the stock, furniture, and equipment, and goodwill. Barzini, a creditor of Marcus, sought to set aside the sale. He claimed that, as a creditor of Marcus, he was entitled to notice of the sale. Is Barzini correct?

ANALYZING COURT CASES

1. Peters, a citrus-fruit grower, contracted with Macchiaroli for the sale of his entire crop of fruit. The contract set a price for each class of fruit on a "packed-out-box" basis. Macchiaroli gave Peters a deposit of $2,000. The contract provided that the deposit was "to be applied on the purchase of citrus fruit. If fruit taken does not equal deposit, a refund must be made." After Macchiaroli had picked 1,536 "packed-out-boxes" of fruit, a killing frost ruined the remaining fruit in the orchard. Macchiaroli had picked all the matured fruit, but some immature fruit still remained. Peters claimed that the property of all the fruit in the orchard had passed to the buyer, Macchiaroli, and that he must stand the loss. Is Peters legally correct? (*Peters v. Macchiaroli*, 243 P. 2d 777)

2. Radloff, a poultry dealer, sold his entire flock of turkeys to Bragmus. The flock consisted of about 100 turkey hens and

60 turkey toms at stated prices for specified grades. Bragmus was to call for the turkeys on an agreed date. Two days before Bragmus was required to take possession of the turkeys, a blizzard killed about half of them and damaged the remainder. Bragmus refused to accept or pay for any of the turkeys. Radloff claimed that title to the turkeys had passed to Bragmus and that he must stand the loss. Do you agree with Radloff? (*Radloff v. Bragmus*, 7 N.W. 2d 491)

3. In late August, Stowe contracted to sell Dimos a cooling unit for $1,365. The unit was to be installed in Dimos's cafe. Dimos was to have the privilege of trying the unit for one week before accepting it. After the unit was installed, the weather turned cool. Stowe agreed to extend the trial period until the weather became warm. During the winter, Dimos made up his mind that he didn't intend to keep the cooling unit. However, he failed to notify Stowe of his decision. When warm weather arrived, Dimos wrote to Stowe saying that he didn't want the unit and requested that Stowe remove it. Stowe refused to do so and sued for the purchase price. Should Stowe succeed? (*Dimos v. Stowe*, 71 S.E. 2d 186)

CHAPTER 19

Warranties

YOU BE THE JUDGE

Think about these cases.
If you were the judge, how would you decide each case?

1

Toscano, a chemist, ordered by letter a metal container from Stanford Products. In her letter, Toscano stated that the container had to be capable of withstanding certain temperatures. After she had tried the container at those temperatures, Toscano found it totally unusable. Was Stanford Products liable for breach of warranty?

2

As a result of eating a piece of cream pie in a restaurant, a man became seriously ill. Does he have the right to sue the restaurant?

WHAT IS A WARRANTY?

Sellers often make promises and representations to induce buyers to enter into sales contracts. Those statements may be based on *facts* such as those relating to age, identity, or quality of the goods. If a buyer relies on one of these promises or statements, the representation is legally known as a **warranty.**

Express Warranties

> **1.** (a) "This shirt won't shrink or fade." (b) "Bower preferred stock will yield a profit of $10 a share within the next six months." (c) "This car is the best buy in the city." (d) "This is a sample of the new Generation III computer." Which of these representations constitute warranties?

Under the Uniform Commercial Code, warranties in contracts for sale may arise in several ways. They may stem from oral or written statements of fact, from description, or from exhibition of samples of the goods. A warranty created by one of these methods is known as an **express warranty.** However, a seller's promises and representations may not be based on fact, but may be mere *expressions of opinion.* In this case, the promises or statements are usually referred to as **seller's talk,** or *puffs.* These promises are not regarded as warranties.

In Problem 1(a), a statement that a shirt won't fade or shrink is a factual statement. Because it can be proved, it constitutes a warranty. In Problem 1(b), though, the statement that the stock will show a profit within six months is merely an expression of the seller's opinion. This statement does not legally constitute a warranty. The same is true of Problem 1(c). In Problem 1(d), the exhibition of a sample or model is part of the basis of the bargain between the parties. It therefore creates an express warranty that the goods purchased shall conform to the sample or model.

An express warranty may be given while a contract for sale is being entered into or before the contract is made final. In either case, the price paid for the goods serves as the consideration for both the goods and the warranty. A warranty also may be made as a separate contract or after the sales contract is complete. In this event, the UCC provides that a *new* consideration is *not* necessary to make the warranty binding. This rule has considerably expanded the consumer's express warranty protection.

> Fortunato bought and paid for a suit costing $240. Two days later, she took the suit back to the store and questioned the wool content of the fabric. The store owner said, "I warrant that the suit contains at least 50 percent wool." The oral warranty is binding under the UCC without a new consideration.

The **Consumer Product Warranty and Federal Trade Commission Improvement Act** has been very helpful to consumers. This law requires all companies offering warranties with products costing $5 or more to state the terms of the warranty in complete and simple language. A warranty for a product costing more than $10 must be labeled either as a **full warranty** or as a **limited warranty.** A full warranty must provide for the repair of a defective product without cost to the consumer. If several repair attempts fail, a full warranty must offer the consumer the choice of a refund or a replacement. The conditions of a full warranty apply not only to the original buyer but also to any consumer who buys the product secondhand or receives it as a gift during the warranty period. A limited warranty has to spell out, in clear language, exactly what parts or labor it covers, and for how long. Figure 19.1 is a sample of a limited warranty. A particular product can carry both types of warranty, but the difference must be plain. A car, for example, might carry a "full, one-year warranty" as well as a limited warranty, covering only certain parts for a longer period. Parties who issue false or deceptive warranties may be subject to legal action by the federal government.

Figure 19.1
A Limited
Warranty

LIMITED ONE-YEAR WARRANTY

These car stereo components are warranted to be free of defects in material and workmanship for a period of ONE YEAR from the original date of purchase. This warranty excludes:

1. Voltage conversions.
2. Defects covered by the warranty that are not disclosed in periodic checkups.
3. Components whose serial numbers have been defaced, modified, or removed.
4. Damage resulting from:
   a. installation or removal of the product.
   b. accident, misuse, abuse, neglect, unauthorized repair or modification, or failure to follow instructions contained in the owner's manual.
   c. installation of parts or accessories that do not conform to the quality or specifications of the original parts or accessories.
   d. shipment. (Shipper must handle claims.)
   e. defective magnetic tapes.

We will pay all labor and material expenses for covered items.

Limitation of Implied Warranties

All implied warranties, including warranties of merchantability and fitness for purpose, are limited to one year from date of original retail purchase.

Exclusions

Our liability for a defective product is limited to the repair or replacement of said product, at our option. We are not liable for incidental or consequential damages of any kind. Some states do not allow limitations on how long an implied warranty lasts or the exclusion or limitation of incidental or consequential damages, so the above limitations and exclusions may not apply to you. This warranty gives you specific legal rights, and you may also have other rights which vary from state to state.

NEW GENERATION ELECTRONICS
13966 Silicon Road
Silicon Valley, CA 94411

Implied Warranties

Unless the parties to a contract for sale agree otherwise, the law will protect the buyer by imposing warranty obligations on the seller. The buyer often needs warranty protection imposed by law because he or she has no chance to examine the goods. In these cases the buyer is forced to rely on the seller's honesty.

2. Goldfarb bought a chair at a furniture store's warehouse sale and paid cash for it. The sales tag on the chair stated: "Price reduced to $199. Sale AS IS." Did this statement exclude any implied warranties?

A warranty imposed by law is known as an **implied warranty.** Sellers assume the same responsibility for these warranties as for express warranties. However, when the purchaser agrees to buy goods marked "as is" or "with all faults," the seller is not liable for any implied warranties except for the implied warranty of title. This is the situation in Problem 2.

The usual implied warranties are (1) warranty of title, (2) warranty of merchantability, and (3) warranty of fitness for a particular purpose.

The Code makes a distinction between a merchant-seller and a nonmerchant or casual seller. It also provides for a greater range of warranties in the case of the merchant-seller.

Warranty of Title

> **3.** Murray sold a tractor to Fidalgo for $2,200. Shortly after taking possession of the tractor, Fidalgo was forced to surrender it to the true owner. The tractor had been stolen from the owner and sold to Murray, who had no knowledge of the theft. What are Fidalgo's rights?

Under the UCC, a buyer in good faith has a right to acquire a good, clean title, lawfully transferred. In order to protect that title, the buyer should not have to sue or be sued. If events after the sale indicate that the seller did not possess a good title, the buyer may hold the seller liable for breach of the implied **warranty of title.** This is true whether the seller is a merchant or a nonmerchant. In Problem 3, Fidalgo may sue Murray for breach of the implied warranty of title. Of course, Murray may in turn sue the person who sold him the tractor for breach of the same warranty.

Warranty of Merchantability

> **4.** Yanni bought an outboard motor from a dealer in marine supplies. After she had attached the motor to her boat, she found that it wouldn't run. The motor had been stored in a warehouse so long that it was unfit for use. May Yanni claim a breach of an implied warranty?

A **warranty of merchantability** is implied in sales *by merchants* who regularly deal in the goods that are the subject of the sale. This warranty makes sellers liable for goods that are not of fair, average quality and fit for the *ordinary purposes* for which such goods are used. In other words, the goods must be "salable" in the ordinary course of business. On this basis, Yanni in Problem 4 may sue the dealer for breach of the implied warranty of merchantability.

This warranty includes sales of food and drink, to be consumed on the premises or elsewhere, and sales of drugs and cosmetics. It is important to remember that a nonmerchant or casual seller is not responsible for the implied warranty of merchantability. However, both merchant-buyers and final consumers may claim protection under this warranty.

Preventing Problems with Warranties

"This sleeping bag will keep you warm even in zero-degree weather," said the friendly sporting goods salesperson. On the strength of this promise, you bought the sleeping bag. In effect, you relied and acted on a factual statement that the law considers to be an express warranty.

Warranties vary in the amount of coverage they provide. So, just as you compare style, price, and other features of competing products before you buy, you should compare their warranties. The Magnuson-Moss Act passed by Congress in 1975 requires sellers' warranties to be available for you to read before you make a purchase.

There are precautions you can take to minimize the chances of having problems with goods you buy. The Federal Trade Commission recommends that you take these steps before you buy warrantied goods.

- Research the reputation of the company offering the warranty. A simple phone call to your local or state consumer protection offices or the Better Business Bureau will give you some valuable information about the firm. Remember, a warranty is only as good as the company that offers it.
- Read the warranty carefully. See exactly what protection it gives you.
- Save the sales slip and file it with your warranty. You may need it to document the date of your purchase. If a warranty is limited to first purchasers, you may need the slip to prove that you were the original buyer.
- Make sure to perform any maintenance or inspections required by the warranty.
- Use the product according to the manufacturer's instructions. Abuse or misuse of the product may cancel your warranty coverage.

Warranty of Fitness for a Particular Purpose

5. Monteiro ordered an electric pump. In his order he stated that the pump had to supply his summer camp, which served 150 people, with sufficient water under normal conditions. When the pump was installed, Monteiro found that it could not supply the required quantity of water. What are Monteiro's legal rights?

If the buyer informs the seller that she is relying on the seller's skill and judgment, there is an implied warranty that the item is fit for the purpose.

An implied **warranty of fitness for a particular purpose** arises in sales situations, such as in Problem 5. In these cases, a buyer informs the seller of a particular purpose for which the goods are needed. The buyer then relies on the seller's skill and judgment in supplying suitable goods. In the problem, the pump ordered by Monteiro did not supply the water needed under normal conditions. Therefore, Monteiro would have an action against the seller for breach of the implied warranty of fitness for a particular purpose.

The buyer doesn't have to make sure that the seller has actual knowledge of the particular purpose for which the goods are intended. It is sufficient if the circumstances give the seller reason to know the intended purpose, and to know that the buyer is relying on the seller to select proper goods. Suppose a buyer asks for an article by its patent or trade name. This would seem to indicate that reliance is being placed on the buyer's own judgment as to the capability of the article rather than on the seller's skill and judgment. However, a sale of a patented or trade-name article is treated the same as any ordinary sale in which a warranty of fitness for the purpose is implied. If, in fact, the buyer insists on a selected brand or trade name, it is obvious that there is no reliance on the seller's skill and judgment. Therefore, there is no implied warranty of fitness for purpose.

EXAMPLE

Allard went to Drennan's pharmacy and asked for Bright's toothpaste. Since Allard asked for the article under its patent or trade name, she did not rely on the seller's skill and judgment. There is no implied warranty of fitness for a particular purpose in this case.

Very often, the implied warranties of merchantability and fitness for a particular purpose overlap. This will result in a breach of both warranties.

> Rubin sold a TV to Warfield, but the set couldn't project a picture on its screen. This situation results in a breach of both implied warranties. The set isn't merchantable because it isn't of average quality. Neither does it fit the particular purpose for which Warfield bought it—viewing TV shows.

Exclusion of Warranties

Sellers usually know a great deal more about their products than the consumer does. This can result in an unequal bargaining position between sellers and buyers. Courts recognize this and often disregard clauses in sales contracts by which sellers try to take unfair advantage of unsuspecting buyers. If this weren't so, buyers would be left without any warranty protection if they bought defective products. The Uniform Commercial Code tries to follow the courts' policy. The Code states that sellers may be relieved from liability for express and implied warranties only if they comply with certain conditions.

> **6.** Willomen bought a dishwasher from Altmeyer, a dealer in household appliances. The written contract contained this clause: "There are no warranties that extend beyond the description on the face hereof." Does this statement exclude all implied warranties?

If sellers seek to exclude or modify the implied warranty of merchantability, the language they use must *specifically mention* merchantability. In case of a writing, the mention must be **conspicuous** (written so that a reasonable person would notice it). Again, if sellers wish to exclude or modify the implied warranty of fitness for a particular purpose, they may do so by using specific and conspicuous written language. The Code also states that sellers may exclude *all* implied warranties of fitness. This is done by means of a statement such as, "There are no warranties that extend beyond the description on the face hereof." This was the case in Problem 6.

As noted earlier, the Code allows exclusion of all implied warranties except of title where the language used includes "as is," "with all faults," or similar wording. The rule of **caveat emptor** ("let the buyer beware") still applies in many situations. These include situations where a buyer fails to notice observable defects before entering into a sales contract—whether after examining the goods, a sample, or a model, or after refusing to examine the goods.

Feldman bought a carload of tomatoes from Pao after inspecting several crates. Later, Feldman found that many crates contained overripe tomatoes that had to be thrown away. Feldman sued Pao for breach of the implied warranty of merchantability. Feldman cannot claim the benefit of any implied warranty. Because he had examined the tomatoes before buying them, the rule of caveat emptor applies.

Warranty Benefits for Third Parties

7.   Urbano bought a stuffed animal for her infant daughter from a local toy store. While playing with the toy, the daughter chewed on the animal's nose and became very sick from the chemicals used in the toy's manufacture. Is the toy store owner liable to the daughter for breach of an implied warranty?

Toys, food, and other consumer products go through many hands as they move from manufacturer or producer to final consumer. The consumer, the final link in the chain, usually deals directly with a retailer and has no dealings with the producer. If the purchased goods prove to be defective and a warranty has been breached, who is legally responsible to the consumer? Is the retailer who sold the goods liable? Or is the manufacturer who produced the goods liable?

At common law, the rule was that the buyer could hold only the immediate seller liable for breach of warranty. The reasoning for this was that the immediate seller was the party with whom the consumer had contracted. The manufacturer or producer, as a remote party, had no warranty liability to the final consumer. Gradually, courts began to realize the absurdity of this rule. This was especially true when producers actively participated in the selling process by means of packaging, labeling, and advertising practices aimed directly at consumers. Courts began to hold producers liable when they made inaccurate statements to consumers or manufactured their products so negligently as to cause injury or property damage to consumers. The courts' concern for the safety and interests of remote buyers is known today as **product liability.** Under product liability, consumers may sue the manufacturers and producers of defective products directly. The earliest product liability cases dealt with sales of food and drugs.

The authors of the Uniform Commercial Code took a neutral stand on the question of recognizing product liability suits by consumers. They did, however, extend warranty protection to a new class of consumers. That class is "any natural person who is in the family or household of the buyer or who is a guest in his home if it is reasonable to expect that such a person may use, consume, or be affected by the goods and who is injured in person by breach of the warranty." This provision would apply to Urbano's injured daughter in Problem 7. Most courts would permit the Urbanos to sue the local toy store owner for breach of the implied warranty of merchantability. Under the Code, however, they cannot sue the remote manufacturer of the toy. They would have to rely on the law of their own state. The UCC does not permit a seller to exclude the extended warranty protection to third parties.

A manufacturer's or producer's liability to a remote buyer may result from the *negligent manner* in which the goods were made. A manufacturer's failure to use reasonable care in making an article that is safe for its intended purpose will render the maker liable to injured users. Generally, injured parties choose to sue the manufacturer for breach of warranty rather than filing a tort action for negligence. This happens because a tort action is more difficult to prove.

Strict Liability

PROBLEM

8. Yagoda was injured when a crane he was running on a construction job for his employer failed to operate properly. He sued the maker of the crane for damages on the ground that the crane was defective. Can Yagoda hold the manufacturer liable?

A person who is injured by a defective or dangerous product may sue the manufacturer or distributor, regardless of any warranty or negligence on the seller's part. As noted in Chapter 4, this is known as **strict liability.** It developed out of product liability to protect injured users of a product. The person who brings suit may be a buyer, a consumer, an employee, or a third person such as a bystander or a pedestrian. Thus, Yagoda in Problem 8 should be successful in his suit against the maker of the crane. Yagoda has only to show that the product was defective or dangerous. The party suing does not have to have had any contractual relations with anyone in order to have this protection. It is important to remember that strict liability extends to claims for both personal injuries and property damage. Finally, strict liability applies to any transfer of goods. The transfer may involve a sale, a free sample distribution, or commercial leasing of goods. However, it does not cover a sale of *services.*

The last three chapters have discussed many of the rights and duties of the parties to a sales contract. But we have not yet talked about the parties' rights to performance or the remedies available if a sales contract is breached. We will study these topics in Chapter 20.

Chapter 19 Review

"YOU BE THE JUDGE" REVIEW

Look again at the "You Be the Judge" cases given at the beginning of this chapter. Would you decide them differently now, after your study of the chapter?

Correct Decisions

1. Yes. This was a sale in which the buyer relied on the seller's skill and judgment in selecting the goods. In this type of sale, there is an implied warranty that the goods will be reasonably fit for the purpose.

2. Yes. The man may sue the restaurant's owner for breach of implied warranty of merchantability.

UNDERSTANDING WHAT YOU HAVE READ

1. What is a warranty?
2. Give an example of an express warranty.
3. Give an example of an implied warranty.
4. What implied warranty is made with regard to the seller's title?
5. What implied warranty is made with regard to the merchantability of goods?
6. Who is liable for an implied warranty of merchantability? Who may benefit from this warranty?
7. What implied warranty is made with regard to goods sold for a particular purpose?
8. When does the principle of caveat emptor apply?
9. How may a seller avoid liability for warranties?
10. Under the Uniform Commercial Code, how may third parties benefit from warranties? from product liability?

BUILDING YOUR LEGAL VOCABULARY

Match each of these legal terms with its correct definition from the list that follows. Write your answers on a separate sheet of paper.

"as is" sale   express warranty   limited warranty   strict liability
caveat emptor   implied warranty   product liability
conspicuous   full warranty   seller's talk

1. a seller's guarantee stemming from a statement of fact, a description, or from exhibition of samples of the goods
2. the rule "let the buyer beware"
3. a manufacturer's or distributor's responsibility for injuries caused by a defective or dangerous product
4. statements of opinion to promote sales
5. a guarantee the law imposes on sellers
6. easy to be seen
7. a warranty that requires a defective product to be repaired or replaced without cost to the consumer
8. the courts' concern for the safety and interests of remote buyers
9. a purchase in which the buyer takes the risk as to the quality of the goods
10. a warranty that covers some parts or labor for a certain time period

APPLYING LEGAL PRINCIPLES

1. Queally sold Nolte a car and told him it was the best used car on the lot. Queally also stated that the car was worth $200 more than the price Nolte was paying. Nolte soon discovered the car needed major repairs and was not worth as much as he'd paid for it. May Nolte avoid the contract for breach of warranty?
2. Appel bought some carpeting from Apex Carpet. Appel relied on the seller's statement that the carpeting was colorfast and would not fade. Two months after the carpeting was installed, Appel discovered it was not colorfast. Does Appel have a claim for breach of warranty?
3. Three days after Quesada bought a sewing machine, she said to the dealer, "I don't think this machine is reliable. It'll probably need repairs soon." The dealer replied, "I guarantee the machine will run without repairs for at least two years." Shortly after, the sewing machine broke down and needed major repairs. Quesada claimed there was a breach of warranty. Was her claim legally valid?
4. Yuko bought a used Piper airplane from Deasy. Later, Yuko discovered that Domestic Finance Company held a proper lien against the plane. Yuko brought suit against Deasy for breach of warranty. Should she succeed?

5. Reiser bought a cake at a local bakery. After eating some of the cake, Reiser suffered serious injuries to his mouth from small glass particles in the cake. Reiser sued the bakery for his medical expenses. Was he entitled to collect?

6. Assume all the facts stated in Problem 5 except that the cake was eaten by a guest in Reiser's home. Would the guest have a legal claim against the bakery?

7. Pham sold a jet ski to Koniski "as is." Later, Koniski discovered that the motor contained worn-out parts and wouldn't operate properly. Does Koniski have a claim for breach of warranty against Pham?

8. Gaither was shopping at a supermarket and took a bottle of soft drink from a shelf. Suddenly, the bottle exploded in Gaither's hand. She sued the Better Beverage Company, which had bottled the drink, to recover damages. She claimed breach of warranty arising out of the sale of food or drink. Will Gaither succeed?

ANALYZING COURT CASES

1. Webster was served some fish chowder while she was dining at the Blue Ship Tea Room. Although she looked at each spoonful, she failed to notice a fish bone. The bone lodged in Webster's throat, causing a painful injury. Webster brought an action against the restaurant to recover damages for breach of the implied warranty of merchantability. Should she succeed? (*Webster v. Blue Ship Tea Room, Inc.*, 198 N.E. 2d 309)

2. Fairbanks, Morse & Co., manufactured electrical equipment. The firm sold a generator to Consolidated Fisheries Co. The generator was described in the sales contract as Model #1-1420 (1136 kilowatts). The sales contract also contained a clause that the seller "makes no warranties which extend beyond the description of the generator on the face of the contract." After the generator was installed, Consolidated Fisheries found it was incapable of generating 1136 kilowatts of electricity. Consolidated sued Fairbanks, Morse & Co. for breach of express warranty. Fairbanks maintained the description of the generator constituted an implied warranty that was ineffective because of the disclaimer clause. Whose contention was upheld by the courts? (*Fairbanks, Morse & Co. v. Consolidated Fisheries Co.*, 190 F. 2d 817)

3. Greenberg bought a can of salmon from Pelham Dairies. Lorenz owned and operated the store. When Greenberg's daughter ate the salmon, she injured her teeth and mouth because of a sharp, pin-shaped metal fish tag concealed and imbedded in the salmon. Sheila and her father brought an action against Lorenz for breach of the implied warranty of fitness for human consumption. Lorenz defended the action by claiming he had made the contract for sale with Sheila's father and that Sheila had no right to sue him. Was Lorenz's defense valid? *Greenberg v. Lorenz*, 173 N.E. 2d 773)

CHAPTER 20

Rights and Remedies of the Parties

Think about these cases.
If you were the judge, how would you decide each case?

1

Rotko bought a freezer from Farad Appliances. After the freezer was delivered, Rotko discovered that it wasn't freezing foods. Farad's repair person told Rotko that the defect could be corrected if he took the freezer to Farad's repair shop. Rotko refused to allow this and canceled the sale. Was she entitled to do so?

2

You bought an all-terrain vehicle. On the first day you used it, you noticed that the starter switch was defective. In spite of the problem, you kept using the ATV and made several installment payments on it. Six months later, you decided to return the ATV and recover the payments you had made. Will you succeed?

PERFOR-MANCE OF SALES CONTRACTS

In every sale, the seller must permit the transfer of possession of the goods to the buyer. This does not always include a physical delivery of the goods by the seller. Whether the seller is to send the goods or the buyer is to call for them depends on the contract terms. If nothing is said about delivery, the place of delivery is usually the seller's place of business. If the seller has no place of business, the place of delivery is the seller's residence. If the goods are at some other location and the parties knew of that location when the contract was made, then that place is the place of delivery. If no time for delivery is agreed on, a reasonable time is understood.

> **1.** Jaffee agreed to sell Buitrago 200 bolts of fabric. There were to be 50 yards per bolt, at a specified price per yard. The fabric that Jaffee delivered measured only 40–43 yards per bolt. When Buitrago refused to accept and pay for the goods, Jaffee sued him for breach of contract. Is Jaffee entitled to collect damages from Buitrago?

It is also the seller's duty to deliver the exact quantity of goods noted in the contract. If less is delivered, the buyer may reject the shipment. Thus, Buitrago in Problem 1 may reject the fabric shipment because Jaffee failed to deliver the correct quantity.

The buyer has a duty to accept and pay for goods that are correct according to the contract. A buyer's acceptance may be indicated by express words or by conduct.

> A buyer received goods and used them for more than a year without trying to return them. The court said that the buyer's continued use of the goods for more than a reasonable time indicated acceptance.

Usually, the buyer is allowed a reasonable time to inspect the goods before payment and acceptance. Unless otherwise agreed, delivery of the goods and payment of the price are to occur at the same time. A buyer does not have to pay for partial deliveries unless the contract requires such payment.

REMEDIES OF THE SELLER

Buyers sometimes wrongfully reject the goods or refuse to carry out a sales contract *before* the goods are delivered. When this happens, the Uniform Commercial Code makes certain remedies available to the seller.

PROBLEM

2. Nama, an electrical appliance manufacturer, sold 100 air conditioners to Stabile. Stabile was to make payment within 30 days. Before delivery of the units, Stabile notified Nama that he would not accept them and that the contract was canceled. What are Nama's legal rights?

If a buyer breaches a sales contract before delivery, the seller may (1) withhold delivery of the goods, (2) stop delivery if the goods are in transit, (3) resell the goods if possible and recover damages; if the goods can't be resold, recover the purchase price, or (4) recover damages for nonacceptance of the goods. In Problem 2, Nama may use any of these remedies, depending on the circumstances.

Withholding Delivery

If an unpaid seller has possession of the goods, delivery to the buyer may be withheld. This right is known as an **unpaid seller's lien.** A seller may exercise this lien (1) when goods are sold for cash and the purchase price has not be paid, (2) when goods are sold on credit and the credit terms expire before delivery, or (3) when the buyer becomes *insolvent* before delivery. **Insolvency** is the inability to pay debts when they become due.

EXAMPLE

Bueller sold a sailboat to Stiller for $4,500. Stiller gave Bueller a 30-day promissory note in payment of the full purchase price. As part of the agreement, Bueller began to install new equipment on the sailboat. For that purpose, Bueller was to keep the boat in his possession without charge. If Stiller fails to pay the note, Bueller may exercise a right of lien and hold the sailboat until the note is paid. The same result would follow if Stiller became insolvent before the boat was delivered to her.

The unpaid seller may lose a lien when (1) the goods are surrendered to the buyer, (2) the goods are given to a carrier for delivery to the buyer, (3) the right of lien is *waived* (given up) by extending credit to the buyer, and (4) the buyer offers to pay or tenders the price.

Stopping Delivery

If the goods have been given to a carrier for transportation, the seller may order the carrier not to make the delivery. This remedy may be used in the event of a buyer's breach, fraud, or insolvency. The right to stop goods in transit may be exercised even when the goods are possessed by a warehouse operator.

Usually, goods are no longer considered in transit if they have been delivered to the buyer or to the buyer's agent. After the seller has stopped the goods, the seller's rights are the same as if a delivery had never been made.

> Armas shipped a large quantity of toys to the Plastic Toy Co. While the shipment was in transit, Armas learned that Plastic Toy was in bankruptcy. Armas could notify the carrier to stop the shipment and redeliver the toys to her.

Right to Reclaim the Goods

If the goods have been delivered to an insolvent buyer, the seller has lost the chance to withhold the goods or stop them in transit. It is too late for either remedy, and there is no point in suing an insolvent buyer for the price. What the seller needs is a right to *reclaim* the goods—to regain possession of them. The Code gives the seller this right. The UCC provides that any goods received by a buyer on credit *within ten days of insolvency* may be reclaimed by the seller. If the buyer innocently or fraudulently claims to be solvent within *three months* of delivery, the ten-day limitation does not apply. The representation, however, must be in writing.

> Ferrer filed a bankruptcy petition five days after receiving goods on credit from LaForge. LaForge was totally unaware of Ferrer's financial condition. Under the UCC, LaForge may recover the goods because Ferrer received them within ten days of becoming insolvent. LaForge could disregard the ten-day limitation if he could show that, at least three months before delivery of the goods, Ferrer had stated in writing that he was solvent.

Recovery of Damages

A seller who has regained control of goods because of the buyer's breach, fraud, or insolvency is entitled to money damages for any loss suffered.

Resale Plus Damages

The Code permits the seller to make a reasonable resale of the goods and to recover damages. These damages will be *the difference between the resale price and the contract price, together with any incidental damages the seller has suffered.*

> Before shipping goods to Jenkins at the agreed price of $5,000, Arkin, the seller, learned that Jenkins was insolvent. Arkin resold the goods at a private sale and notified Jenkins. The goods were sold for $4,000. The expenses incurred in handling and storing the goods were $100. Arkin may hold Jenkins liable for damages of $1,100 ($1,000 loss on the sale plus incidental damages of $100).

A seller may not be able to resell the goods after making a reasonable attempt to do so. In this case, the seller may hold the buyer liable for *the entire purchase price* plus incidental damages.

Damages for Nonacceptance

The seller is not required to resell the goods that have been withheld or stopped in transit. Instead, the seller may sue the breaching buyer for damages for nonacceptance of the goods. This remedy is desirable if the market for the goods is expected to rise. It allows sellers to both collect damages and hold the goods to sell later at a higher price. A seller who sues for damages for nonacceptance may recover *the difference between the market price at the time and place of tender of the goods to the buyer and the unpaid contract price,* plus any incidental damages.

> Yoshido wrongfully rejected a shipment of plumbing supplies amounting to $2,000. The seller chose to sue Yoshido for damages for nonacceptance. If the current market price of the plumbing supplies is $1,600 at the time and place of tender of the goods, the seller may collect damages of $400 from Yoshido. This amount represents the difference between the current market price and the unpaid contract price. The seller may also collect any incidental expenses incurred because of Yoshido's breach.

Recovery of the Price

Suppose the seller's right to stop the goods in transit has ended because the buyer accepted the goods, or the goods were destroyed after risk of loss had passed to the buyer. May the seller sue for the purchase price in this event? The UCC states that the seller *may* recover the purchase price in both cases, if the goods conformed to the contract. As well as the price, the seller may recover incidental expenses such as commissions or shipping charges paid when making the sale. The Code also states that if the seller can't resell the goods at a reasonable price, the contract price may be recovered from the buyer.

CAREERS IN LAW

Judge

Historically, judges were honored and respected because they created laws and decided the fate of others. Today's judges are still subject to public scrutiny. Now, though, rather than creating laws, the primary duty of judges is to apply and interpret laws so that justice can be achieved. Judges are also responsible for assuring that proper court procedures are followed.

All federal court judges are required to be lawyers. They are appointed by the President of the United States and confirmed by the Senate. The American Bar Association provides a recommendation to the President and the Senate regarding each nomination. In the recommendation, the nominee is rated as being very qualified, qualified, or not qualified for the position.

At the state level, judges are appointed by the governor and confirmed by the state legislature. Local judges are usually elected to office for a stated term. If a vacancy occurs between election terms, the governor will appoint a local judge to serve for the remainder of the term. A recent law in California requires all newly appointed or elected judges in that state to be lawyers. This trend is beginning to spread across the country.

REMEDIES OF THE BUYER

Unless otherwise agreed, a buyer does not have to accept delivery of goods that fail in any way to conform to (match) the goods described in the contract.

PROBLEM

> **3.** Akito, a builder, contracted to buy 1,000 red tapestry bricks from Eton Supply. Eton delivered 1,000 red common bricks to the building site. What legal remedies are available to Akito?

The UCC allows a buyer who receives nonconforming goods to cancel the contract. In addition, the buyer may (1) accept or reject all or part of the goods, (2) sue for damages, (3) sue for damages for nondelivery, or (4) sue for damages for breach in regard to accepted goods. In Problem 3, Akito may use whichever of these remedies is to his advantage.

Acceptance or Rejection

Under the Code, a buyer who receives the wrong goods may reject or accept all of the goods, or accept part and reject the rest. Any rejection must occur within a reasonable time after delivery. The buyer may recover damages for the breach by giving notice of rejection to the seller. With one exception, the buyer must not exercise ownership of the rejected goods. The exception is that, in the absence of instructions, the buyer must make a reasonable effort to sell perishable goods or goods that may decline rapidly in value. If the buyer does not receive proper instructions from the seller, the buyer may reship the goods to the seller at the latter's expense.

Recovery of Damages

When a buyer rightfully rejects the goods or the seller fails to deliver, the buyer may (1) cancel the contract and recover the price paid, or (2) **cover** and collect damages. The right to cover is the buyer's legal right to go out on the open market and buy goods to substitute for those not received. Under the Code, a buyer who exercises a right to cover and suffers a loss may collect from the seller *the difference between the cost of cover and the contract price,* as well as incidental damages. Consumer-buyers may also exercise the right to cover. The remedy is not intended for use only by merchant-buyers.

Bullock, a retail grocer, contracted with Davidoff, a wholesaler, to buy 1,000 large cans of tomato sauce. Bullock was to pay 50 cents per can, and the goods were to be delivered within ten days. At the time of delivery, the tomato sauce was selling at 60 cents a can on the open market. Davidoff delivered the wrong tomato sauce, and Bullock rightfully refused to accept the goods. Bullock may cancel the contract with Davidoff. Then she may cover by buying 1,000 cans at 60 cents in the wholesale market. Bullock can then sue Davidoff for damages. The damages would include the difference in price plus any incidental expenses Bullock incurred in the transaction.

Damages for Nondelivery

Instead of covering, the buyer may elect to collect damages for nondelivery. In that case, the buyer may collect *the difference between the market price at the time the breach is discovered and the contract price,* together with any incidental damages. The market price is the same as the buyer would have paid if he or she had chosen to cover.

Damages for Breach in Regard to Accepted Goods

A buyer who accepts goods before discovering that they are not as represented may sue the seller for damages for breach of warranty. The buyer must give notice to the seller, however, that the goods do not conform to the contract.

4. Kennedy bought a rug from Doherty for $2,900. Doherty warranted the rug to be a genuine Sarouk. Later, Kennedy discovered that the rug was a cheap imitation, worth about $150. What amount of damages may Kennedy collect?

The measure of damages for a seller's breach discovered after acceptance is *the difference at the time and place of acceptance between the value of the goods accepted and the value they would have had if they had conformed to the contract.* In Problem 4, Kennedy may recover the difference between the actual value of the rug he accepted ($150) and the price he paid for it ($2,900). Thus, his basic damages would amount to $2,750. Also, as in the other remedies discussed, the buyer may recover incidental damages. A buyer who has not yet paid the full purchase price may deduct the damages from any remaining payments. However, notice of the deduction must be given to the seller.

Specific Performance or Replevin

PROBLEM

> **5.** Costa contracted with Alcon Products for the manufacture of a stated number of patented pipe fittings made only by Alcon. Shortly after the contract was signed, Alcon canceled it and refused to perform. Costa sued for specific performance. Will she succeed?

Under the UCC, a buyer may sue for specific performance if the goods are unique or if the buyer will otherwise suffer hardship. **Unique goods** are not only heirlooms or priceless works of art, as under the common law. Also, uniqueness is not the sole basis of the remedy of specific performance. The remedy may be granted in cases where damages won't fully compensate the buyer, or where the buyer is unable to obtain the product elsewhere (cover). This is the situation in Problem 5. Costa may sue Alcon for specific performance of the contract.

Replevin is the term used to describe a court action to obtain possession of goods. A buyer may be granted replevin if the goods can't be obtained by means of cover. It does not have to be shown that the buyer has title to the goods.

STATUTE OF LIMITATIONS

Under the Code, an action for breach of contract for the sale of goods must be brought within four years after the breach occurs. An original agreement between the parties may reduce this period to not less than one year, but it may not extend the period beyond four years.

EXAMPLE

> As a result of a breach of contract for delivery of certain goods, Kazan chose to sue the seller for damages for nondelivery. Kazan must bring suit within four years after the breach occurred unless the parties agreed to a shorter time period.

Buying and selling goods, as you now know, can be simple or complex activities. The results of those activities can vary, too, depending on the circumstances of the sales. In this unit we have expanded our understanding of the rights and responsibilities of buyers and sellers. In Unit 4 we will learn how the law protects consumers by assuring that the responsibilities assumed with a sale are carried out.

Chapter 20 Review

"YOU BE THE JUDGE" REVIEW

Look again at the "You Be the Judge" cases given at the beginning of this chapter. Would you decide them differently now, after your study of the chapter?

Correct Decisions

1. No. A seller must be given a reasonable opportunity to correct a legitimate defect in the goods. Rotko's refusal will result in a loss of her right to cancel the sale.
2. No. The seller is not required to take the ATV back. You continued to use the vehicle with knowledge of the defect and let an unreasonable time pass before notifying the seller of the defect. Thus, you have lost your right to claim damages for breach of warranty and must pay the contract price.

UNDERSTANDING WHAT YOU HAVE READ

1. List the seller's duties with regard to delivery of the goods to the buyer.
2. What are the buyer's duties if conforming goods are delivered by the seller?
3. What are the buyer's rights if nonconforming goods are delivered by the seller?
4. What rights may a seller exercise before and after the delivery of goods to a buyer who is insolvent or who has breached the contract?
5. If a seller has rightfully withheld goods or stopped them in transit, what may legally be done with them?
6. What is the measure of damages if a seller chooses to resell the goods? Give an example.
7. What is the measure of damages if a seller chooses to sue the buyer for non-acceptance of the goods?
8. When may a seller bring an action against the buyer for the price?
9. What action may be taken by a buyer who discovers, after acceptance, that the goods don't conform to the contract? How are damages measured?
10. What remedies are available to the buyer if the seller refuses to perform the contract and the goods aren't available elsewhere?
11. When is an action for breach of a sales contract barred by the statute of limitations?

BUILDING YOUR LEGAL VOCABULARY

From this list, select the legal term that belongs in the blank in each sentence below. Write your answers on a separate sheet of paper.

conforming goods	replevin	stoppage in transit
cover	specific performance	unique goods
incidental damages	statute of limitations	unpaid seller's lien
insolvency		

1. Goods that are rare, unusual, or obtainable only from one source are called ▨▨▨▨▨.
2. Inability to pay debts as they become due is the state of ▨▨▨▨▨.
3. ▨▨▨▨▨ are expenses reasonably incurred as the result of another's breach of contract.
4. The remedy of ▨▨▨▨▨ is a court order telling a party to do exactly what a contract calls for.
5. Goods that correspond exactly to or match those described in a sales contract are said to be ▨▨▨▨▨.
6. ▨▨▨▨▨ is a seller's right to stop delivery of goods to a breaching buyer while the goods are in the hands of a carrier or other bailee.
7. The buyer's right to ▨▨▨▨▨ is the right to go out on the open market and buy goods to substitute for those the seller failed to deliver.
8. The court action to obtain possession of goods is called ▨▨▨▨▨.
9. The law that sets a time period within which a suit may be brought on a contract for sale is called the ▨▨▨▨▨.
10. An ▨▨▨▨▨ is a seller's right to retain possession of goods until the price is paid.

APPLYING LEGAL PRINCIPLES

1. Koen, a paint and hardware dealer, contracted with Paragon Paint Co. to buy $2,000 worth of paint and varnish. Before the goods were delivered, Koen notified Paragon that he wouldn't accept the shipment. The shipment had been placed in the hands of a railroad firm for delivery to Koen. What action should Paragon take now against Koen?
2. Assume in Problem 1 that the railroad company redelivered the shipment to Paragon. What legal remedies are now available to Paragon?
3. Assume in Problem 1 that Paragon was unable to resell the paint and varnish after making a reasonable attempt to do so. What legal remedy may the company now use?
4. Six days after delivering a shipment of goods to Glick Golf Supply, the seller discovered that Glick was insolvent and couldn't pay for the goods. What legal remedy is open to the seller?

5. Goods arrived at their destination and temporarily were stored in a warehouse before delivery to the buyer. Before delivery, the seller learned that the buyer was insolvent. What legal remedy is open to the seller?

6. The seller stopped a shipment of goods in transit because of the buyer's insolvency. The buyer had agreed to pay $4,000 for the goods, but the seller got only $2,800 for them on resale. Shipping expenses amounted to $185; storage and handling totaled $65; and commissions were $84. Calculate the seller's damages.

7. Two months before buying a load of iron ore from Atlas Mining, D'Amico, the buyer, had made favorable written representations about his financial status. Actually, D'Amico was insolvent and nearly bankrupt. When Atlas discovered the true facts after delivery of the ore to D'Amico, the firm sought to recover the ore. If D'Amico had not yet disposed of the ore, would Atlas be entitled to get the shipment back?

8. Marks, a contractor, ordered 1,500 linear feet of oak flooring, Grade #1. The goods were to be delivered to a building site within ten days. When the shipment arrived by truck, Marks noticed that the flooring was Grade #2 oak. This was a lower grade of flooring that sold for 30 cents a linear foot less than Grade #1. What legal remedies are available to Marks?

9. Fishman bought a woodcarving that the seller had represented as the work of a famous sculptor. Shortly after receiving the carving, Fishman discovered that it had actually been made by a group of "starving students" and was worth about a tenth of what she had paid for it. What legal remedies are available to Fishman?

10. Esposito contracted to buy a book of poems originally owned by George Washington. What legal remedy may Esposito use if the seller refuses to deliver the book?

11. On January 26, 1989, Demko brought an action against Chau for breach of a sales contract. The contract was dated January 5, 1984, and the breach occurred on January 25, 1984. Chau's defense was that the action was barred under the UCC by the statute of limitations. Do you agree with Chau?

ANALYZING COURT CASES

1. Lynch ordered 100,000 cellophane bags from Paramount Paper Products Co. for use in packaging mint candies sold to retail stores. A sample bag, with which the bags were to conform, was submitted with the order. The entire order was delivered to Lynch, and 25,000 bags were used during the first few days. Shortly thereafter, the bags were found to be unsatisfactory. Lynch notified Paramount that the bags did not conform to the sample and were unsuitable. He also said that he wanted to return the unused bags. Paramount refused to ac-

cept the unused bags, claiming that Lynch's use of a substantial number of the bags without complaint was an effective acceptance of the entire order. Whose claim is legally correct? (*Paramount Paper Products Co. v. Lynch*, 128 A. 2d 157)

2. Singer bought a TV/stereo from Campbell Music Co. for $771.40. He made a down payment of $20, and five weeks later he paid another $400. After having the set for more than fifteen months and before completing payments, Singer sued to cancel the contract and to recover the $420 he had paid to the seller. He claimed that the set had never operated properly and that Campbell had guaranteed its performance to his personal satisfaction. Is Singer entitled to judgment? (*Campbell Music Co. v. Singer*, 97 A. 2d 340)

3. Alver and Willman entered into a contract in which Willman agreed to buy 7,200 100-lb. bags of popcorn. The bags were to be delivered in twelve monthly installments of 600 bags each, beginning the following October. The agreed price was $9 per 100 pounds. During the month of October, the market price of popcorn fell. Willman asked Alver to lower the price to $8 per 100 pounds. No agreement was reached between the parties on the price reduction, but Alver did agree to cancel the deliveries for the last six months of the contract. Willman refused to accept and pay for any popcorn. Alver brought suit to recover for breach of contract. Should he succeed? (*Willman v. Alver*, 252 F. 2d 895)

UNIT 4

CONSUMER PROTECTION AND CREDIT

CHAPTERS

LEARNING OBJECTIVES

After you have studied this unit, you should be able to:

- Understand the reasons for consumer protection laws.

- List the rights and remedies of consumers, sellers, and lenders under the major consumer protection laws.

- Identify advertising and sales practices that tend to harm consumers.

- Understand the concept of credit and the rights and duties credit imposes on consumers and sellers.

- Describe the main provisions of the Truth-in-Lending Law.

- Describe the meaning and effect of a secured credit sale.

CHAPTER 21

Laws for the Consumer

Think about these cases.
If you were the judge, how would you decide each case?

1

A manufacturer advertised that a face lotion it produced could make a remarkable improvement in the buyer's personal appearance. The manufacturer's claims proved to be impossible. Has the manufacturer violated a law?

2

You bought a box of candy as a gift for a friend. The box label bore a large slogan that said: "A pound's worth of love." The fine print on the label, however, showed that the box contained only twelve ounces of candy. Is the slogan so misleading as to be illegal?

WHAT IS CONSUMERISM?

Changes in the competitive market for sales of goods are occurring constantly, even though they are subtle. The term **consumerism** reflects today's focus on the rights and interests of consumers rather than of merchants. Historically, the principle of **caveat emptor** ("let the buyer beware") has governed sales of goods. This principle makes buyers responsible for their own interests when considering the claims manufacturers or sellers make about their goods. The caveat emptor rule has been a central feature of the economic law of supply and demand, which keeps sellers from charging too much for their goods or selling goods of poor quality.

Products today are often quite sophisticated. In order to make valid comparisons, consumers may need more product knowledge than they can reasonably be expected to have. Also, modern packaging makes direct comparison or full disclosure on a product's labeling impractical. These problems pointed up the need for some defined standards to regulate sales of goods.

The federal government has enacted statutes that protect unwary or unsuspecting buyers from the fraudulent practices of some sellers. Sales of goods are no longer controlled merely by the "let the buyer beware" principle. Consumer protection laws have been created in several primary areas. Consumer credit is one of those areas, and we will discuss credit and its effect on purchasing separately in Chapter 22. The other areas that have been the focus of federal, state, and local consumer protection laws are all product-related. They include product safety and performance, product packaging and labeling, advertising practices, and sales practices.

Product Safety and Performance

Some of the federal statutes that apply to product safety and performance are the Product Safety Act, the Magnuson-Moss Warranty Act, and the National Traffic and Motor Vehicle Safety Act. The name of each of these laws is helpful because it clearly describes the purpose of the act and the protection it gives.

The Product Safety Act

The Product Safety Act requires products to meet reasonable safety standards when used in the manner in which they are intended to be used. For instance, a baseball bat should be expected to withstand batting practice without splintering. However, it would be unreasonable to expect that the same bat would not splinter if it were used to hammer fenceposts into concrete.

The Magnuson-Moss Warranty Act

All consumer goods are bought for an *intended purpose.* The Product Safety Act requires those goods to be safe when used as intended. In the same manner, the **Magnuson-Moss Warranty Act** requires that the goods *perform*

Product Liability

Before the Industrial Revolution, goods produced for sale to consumers were simple products. Buyers were expected to examine the products and rely on their own judgment as to possible defects. Caveat emptor ("let the buyer beware") was the policy of the common law. A buyer who was injured by a defective or dangerous product was not allowed to sue the manufacturer unless the purchase was made directly from the manufacturer. Since most purchases were made through retailers, injured consumers were denied recovery of damages.

This feudal rule began to change in the United States with the decision in the leading case of *MacPherson v. Buick Motor Co.* In that case, Justice Cardozo laid down the principle that a product's manufacturer had the duty to make the product carefully, and that this duty extended even to users other than the purchaser. In other words, a third person could sue a manufacturer for negligence even though there

was no contract between that person and the manufacturer. Courts have since enlarged this principle. Today, an injured party may sue manufacturers, wholesalers, and retailers under product liability theories. These theories allow suits to be brought not only for negligence and breach of warranty but also in strict liability in tort. This latter action is imposed by the law when defective products have caused an injury. The term *strict liability* was given its name because the plaintiff does not have to prove "fault" as in negligence actions. Also, since this type of action does not depend on the existence of a warranty, it is said to be strictly in tort.

The earliest applications of strict liability were in cases involving food and drink. Today, however, it may be claimed for any product—from animal food to planes—sold in the condition (or substantially the same condition) in which it is expected to reach the ultimate user or consumer.

as implied when used properly. Certain products must be guaranteed to perform as implied for a specified period of time. Most appliances, for example, are warranted for one year from the date of purchase. Although food products are perishable and treated differently under the law, more and more food labeling now states a "use by" or "good if used before" date to assure the buyer of consumable goods.

Motor Vehicle Safety Laws

Cars and other motor vehicles are subject to especially severe federal standards because of the nature of the goods. A consumer who buys a motor vehicle can't be expected to know the vehicle is safe, even after a careful inspection. In order to protect the buyer and others who could be harmed if the vehicle were defective, laws such as the **National Traffic and Motor Vehicle Safety Act** have been enacted. These laws require makers and sellers of vehicles to adhere to very strict testing and documentation standards.

Product Packaging and Labeling

Recent packaging techniques, such as vacuum sealing and shrink-wrapping, prevent consumers from checking the contents of packages before purchase. Because of this, packages are now required by laws such as the **Fair Packaging and Labeling Act** to bear exterior labels that describe the contents of the packages. These descriptions must indicate the quantity of goods in the packages. For food, this is generally a weight or volume. For children's toys, the quantity might be the number of blocks or puzzle pieces.

If a product is not for general use, its labeling must indicate the appropriate users of the product. For example, many toys carry labels that state an age range of the children for whom the toy is appropriate. Other toy labeling carries a statement such as "Not for use by children under 3 years of age." These statements provide important information to parents of small children. They warn parents when packages contain something that is small enough to be swallowed or that might be toxic if an infant ate it. Some food labeling carries warnings such as "Not for use by people on salt-restricted diets." These warnings prevent harm to unsuspecting consumers.

PROBLEM

> **1.** Warm 'n' Wooly, Inc. made wool coats and sold them in interstate commerce. The coats did not bear labels showing the percentage and kind of wool used in them. Has the manufacturer violated a law?

A variety of federal laws have been designed to give consumers accurate information about particular products. For example, the **Wool Products Labeling Act** governs the sale of wool goods in interstate commerce. These goods must be labeled to indicate the percentage of (1) new and virgin wool, (2) reprocessed wool, and (3) reused wool. In Problem 1, the manufacturer of the wool coats has violated the provisions of the Wool Products Labeling Act. The maker is guilty of a misdemeanor.

There are a number of other federal laws that protect the consumer from being misled by the labels and packaging of specific products. One of the most important of these laws is the **Food, Drug, and Cosmetic Act.** This law is administered by the federal **Food and Drug Administration (FDA).**

2. The maker of a nonprescription diet capsule advertised it as a safe way to lose weight. Later, it was shown that extensive use of the diet capsule could cause cancer. The manufacturer didn't know of the side effects before beginning to advertise and sell the product. Is the maker liable to people who get cancer after using the diet capsule?

The federal Food, Drug, and Cosmetics Act requires packaged foods and drugs to bear the manufacturer's name and address, as well as a statement of the quantity or weight of the contents. It also requires every drug label to contain (1) the generic (common) name of the drug, (2) adequate directions for use, (3) cautions against uses that may be unsafe for children or dangerous to the consumer's health, and (4) a warning of any habit-forming properties of the drug. The Food and Drug Administration requires all drug makers to keep files of research data to support all claims made on behalf of a drug. In Problem 2, the manufacturer would be liable to a victim who could prove that use of the diet capsule had caused cancer.

Many states and cities have enacted their own laws to protect the consumer's health and welfare. For example, some state or local laws require businesses that dispense foods to undergo periodic inspections. These businesses include restaurants, bakeries, and meat markets. Some local and state laws require doctors, accountants, pharmacists, dentists, chiropractors, and many other providers of personal services to be licensed. These laws prevent incompetent people from offering their services to unwitting consumers.

Frisbee was about to complete a pharmacy course at Brookfield School of Pharmacy. Immediately after graduation, she planned to open her own drugstore. Frisbee must pass a licensing exam and obtain a state license to practice her profession before she will be able to dispense drugs.

The manufacture of goods that contain recycled or secondhand materials is often governed by consumer protection laws. These goods include mattresses, cushions, and upholstered furniture. Other health-related state and local consumer laws relate to the use and maintenance of swimming pools, the purity of drinking water, the operation of clinics and barber shops, and the inspection of meat and milk.

Some laws adopted by states and cities protect the safety of consumers' lives and property. Among these are laws prohibiting false or misleading advertising and regulating weights and measures. Some laws control the activities of insurance companies, state banks, building and loan associations, and personal finance companies. Other laws prohibit the sale of certain drugs without prescription, or require theaters to maintain proper fire and safety equipment. All of these laws, and many more, are designed specifically to benefit the consumer.

Advertising Practices

Since the days of traveling patent-medicine salespeople, consumers have been victimized by people who use false and misleading advertising. Usually, this advertising consists of misrepresentations and false claims made concerning a product. False **endorsements** (public recommendations), exaggerations, and **bait advertising** used to be common practice. For example, a seller might have claimed that a new business was an "old, established firm." Another seller might have exaggerated a product's durability by claiming it to be "indestructible" or "everlasting." Still another seller might have paid a prominent person to endorse a product while giving the impression that the praise was given voluntarily. And yet another seller might have baited customers into buying. Typically, this was done by actions such as falsely stating that the proceeds of a sale would go to charity, or advertising a special sale without having enough stock to meet reasonable customer demands.

To protect the public against such false and misleading advertising, federal, state, and local governments have passed many laws. The federal agency principally responsible for enforcement of these laws is the **Federal Trade Commission (FTC).** This agency examines advertising contained in newspapers, magazines, catalogs, and radio and TV broadcasts to detect false or misleading claims. The FTC is more concerned with protecting the consumer from being misled by advertising than with the advertiser's evil or fraudulent intent. The agency requires advertisers to maintain files of data in support of the claims they make in their ads, and it reserves the right to examine those files.

Victims who suffer loss through fraudulent advertising may obtain money damages in civil suits. In many cases, they may have the offender prosecuted criminally. In cases covered by federal laws, victims may request a hearing before the Federal Trade Commission. If the FTC finds that a seller is violating the laws dealing with advertising, it may issue a **cease-and-desist order** or require the seller to pay a fine. A cease-and-desist order requires the offender to stop its fraudulent practices immediately.

Sales Practices

Because selling practices often have made victims of consumers, special laws have been enacted to govern the methods sellers use to obtain sales agreements.

Agreements Unfair to the Buyer

Uninformed buyers may be victimized by sellers who require consumers to sign unfair, harsh, or oppressive sales contracts. Legally, these are called **unconscionable contracts.** A buyer also may be induced by a seller to assign his or her wages to the seller in payment of a debt.

> **3.** Gao ordered an encyclopedia from a sales representative who was selling the books at a street fair. Gao signed an installment sales contract that stated the price of the encyclopedia. The encyclopedia was delivered, and Gao made several installment payments. Then she discovered that the price she was paying was about two-and-a-half times the reasonable market value of the books. Gao stopped making payments on the installment contract, and the encyclopedia company sued her for the balance. Will the company succeed?

Unconscionable Contracts.   Both the Uniform Commercial Code and the Uniform Commercial Credit Code (UCCC) provide protection for consumers who are the victims of harsh and oppressive contracts. If a contract or any part of it is found to have been unfair at the time it was made, the court may refuse to enforce the entire contract. The court also may enforce part of the contract but rescind the clause or the part that is unconscionable. In Problem 3, most courts would consider the contract between Gao and the encyclopedia company to be one-sided and unfair. Gao would be allowed to avoid the agreement, return the books, and get back any money she had paid to the encyclopedia firm.

Agreements to Assign Wages.   Consumers have often assigned the rights to their earned wages to creditors in payment of debts. This type of assignment is now forbidden by the UCC and by the UCCC. However, this law does not prevent installment payments being made from a consumer's salary as long as the consumer has the power to revoke the agreement at will.

Door-to-Door Sales

> **4.** Orozco bought a vacuum cleaner from a door-to-door salesperson for $325. He made a down payment of $50 and agreed to pay the balance in installments. The next day, Orozco discovered that the machine was unsatisfactory. May he cancel the contract?

Door-to-door salespeople sometimes misrepresent the quality of the goods they are selling while using high-pressure sales tactics. A practical remedy is now available by law for unwary consumers who agree to buy goods or services offered on a door-to-door basis. The consumer may cancel such a contract within three days after the date of the transaction. The seller must give the buyer a written contract and also must inform the buyer of the

right to cancel the contract. If the seller doesn't do this, the right to cancel continues beyond the three-day period until such time as the buyer is notified. In Problem 4, Orozco may cancel the contract within three days of signing it. In addition, he is entitled to a refund of his down payment. Of course, he must return the vacuum cleaner to the seller.

Unordered Goods

Less reputable firms sometimes send out unordered goods. The firms hope that the receiver will choose to keep and pay for the items or will return them. Many consumers are intimidated into believing that they must pay for these goods, or they pay for them because they don't want to go to the trouble of returning them. When unordered goods are shipped through the mail, the receiver may consider them to be a gift and is under no obligation to pay.

EXAMPLE

> Through the mail, Hildebrandt received a set of gourmet pans that he had not ordered. He threw away the invoice but kept the pans. The manufacturer of the pans sued Hildebrandt for the price of the goods. Because the goods were unordered and sent through the mail, Hildebrandt may keep them without paying for them. The manufacturer's suit to recover the price of the goods will not be successful.

In·this chapter you have seen the kinds of benefits we have received from government regulation of sales and purchases. In the next chapter we will look at the impact of credit on the relationship between buyers and sellers. We also will learn about the laws that govern credit transactions.

Chapter 21 Review

"YOU BE THE JUDGE" REVIEW

Look again at the "You Be the Judge" cases given at the beginning of this chapter. Would you decide them differently now, after your study of the chapter?

Correct Decisions

1. Yes. False claims or exaggerations constitute a violation of a federal statute.
2. Yes. The package contains 25% less candy than is advertised in the slogan. This degree of inaccuracy of measurement is illegal.

UNDERSTANDING WHAT YOU HAVE READ

1. Name five areas in which consumer protection laws have been created.
2. Briefly describe the requirements of the Product Safety Act, the Magnuson-Moss Warranty Act, and the National Traffic and Motor Vehicle Safety Act.
3. How has modern technology affected a consumer's ability to obtain information about a product?
4. What kind of labeling must be carried by a product that is not for general use? Give an original example.
5. What four statements are required by the Food, Drug, and Cosmetics Act to be on every drug label?
6. What remedies are available to a buyer who suffers a loss through fraudulent advertising?
7. What two types of agreements unfair to the consumer are addressed by both the UCC and the UCCC?
8. What remedy does the law now provide for consumers who buy goods or services from door-to-door salespeople?
9. If you receive unordered goods through the mail, what is required of you?
10. After studying this chapter, do you believe consumers need more or less protection from sellers? Explain your answer.

BUILDING YOUR LEGAL VOCABULARY

Choose the legal term that will correctly complete each definition below. Write your answers on a separate sheet of paper.

1. Today's focus on the rights and interests of nonmerchant buyers rather than of merchants is called
   a. caveat emptor.
   b. consumerism.
   c. the law of supply and demand.
2. A contract that is unfair, harsh, or oppressive to one party is called a/an
   a. unconscionable contract.
   b. exaggeration.
   c. contract for sale.
3. A public recommendation made about a product is called a/an
   a. misrepresentation.
   b. assignment of wages.
   c. endorsement.

4. A court's or regulatory agency's instruction to a party to stop doing something is called a/an
   a. warning.
   b. cease-and-desist order.
   c. unconscionable contract.
5. False claims made by a seller to lure a buyer to purchase goods or services are called
   a. warranties.
   b. door-to-door sales.
   c. bait advertising.

APPLYING LEGAL PRINCIPLES

1. A toothpaste manufacturer claimed that its product would eliminate mouth odors. It was proved that mouth odors stem from gastric problems and a variety of infections and that the toothpaste had no effect at all on such causes. Did the manufacturer violate any federal law?
2. The Federal Trade Commission issued a complaint against Scuba-Do Company. The FTC claimed that the firm had made misrepresentations in its ads for scuba-diving equipment the firm manufactured. The company claimed that the FTC must prove fraudulent intent on

the company's part. Do you agree with Scuba-Do's claim?
3. A clothing manufacturer attached labels to slacks claiming that they were made of 100% virgin wool. The actual wool content was only 50%, and the remaining fiber content was 50% rayon. Which federal law did the manufacturer violate?
4. The maker of a cold remedy sold it in interstate commerce. Although the remedy was habit-forming, the label on the bottle contained no information to that effect. Was this a violation of a federal law?

5. The Lyttleton Drug Co. sent samples of a new drug to doctors around the country. The drug was not intended for use by anyone taking any other medicine. Although this was mentioned in the booklet accompanying the samples, the drug containers themselves merely stated "See booklet." Is this a violation of federal requirements?

6. Scilliani bought some living room furniture. The sales contract she signed provided that part of her wages would be assigned to the seller for two years to pay for the furniture. The contract also stated that it was "irrevocable." A month after delivery of the goods, Scilliani found that she couldn't afford to continue the assignment of part of her wages and tried to return the furniture to the seller. The seller, however, refused to accept the return and pointed out the "irrevocable" clause in the contract. Was this contract legal? Why?

7. Campos was visited by a door-to-door sales representative. The salesperson showed Campos a new door lock that could be installed in his home. The representative guaranteed that the device would be burglar-proof. After watching the demonstration, Campos signed a contract for installation of the device.

The total price was $150. The next day, Campos changed his mind and decided to cancel the contract. Is he legally allowed to do so?

8. A dealer in electronic equipment sold a VCR to Glendon for $700. The price was twice as much as that of similar VCRs sold by other dealers. At the time of the sale, the dealer knew that Glendon was supporting herself and four children on welfare payments and food stamps. Glendon sought to cancel the contract due to her inability to pay. Does she have a defense against the dealer's demand for payment?

9. Immediately after receiving his degree in architecture, Santiago opened his own architecture practice. He then drew up plans for the construction of a condominium complex for a fee of $7,000. If Santiago resided in your state, would he be allowed to do so?

10. Castlewood Country Club bought 30 tables from TipTop Table Co. The firm's advertisements stated that the tables were "impossible to break." The purchase contract had a "no refund" policy. After the tables were used twice, a number of them broke. May the country club obtain a refund if it returns the tables?

ANALYZING COURT CASES

1. Three women were killed when the car in which they rode exploded on impact after being rear-ended. The state prosecuted Ford Motor Company, the car's manufacturer, for criminal negligence and homicide. The state claimed that Ford knowingly and recklessly allowed cars with dangerous design flaws to remain on the road. Can the company be held criminally liable for the deaths of the women? (*State v. Ford Motor Co.*, Indiana Super., Elkhart Co. No. 5234)

2. Heinz, a service station operator, had a limited education. He signed a lease of a service station from Danfurth Oil Company. One clause in the lease provided that Danfurth would not be liable for its own negligence. It further stated that if Danfurth were negligent and an injury occurred, Heinz would have to reimburse the company for any money it spent. These terms were not explained to Heinz when he signed the lease. Later, one of Danfurth Oil's employees sprayed gasoline on Heinz, causing him to suffer severe burns. Heinz brought suit against Danfurth to recover for his injuries. Will he succeed? (Based on *Weaver v. American Oil Co.*, 276 N.E. 2d 144)

3. The Federal Trade Commission began a proceeding against a leading cigarette maker who advertised cigarettes that were "low in tar." The FTC claimed that this statement was too general and thus misleading to the public. It demanded that the maker cease advertising in this manner unless it stated exactly what the tar content was in each package. Do you agree with the FTC's position? (In re: *American Brands, Inc.*, Consent Order, FTC Docket 8799)

CHAPTER 22

The Debtor/Creditor Relationship

YOU BE THE JUDGE

Think about these cases.
If you were the judge, how would you decide each case?

1

A retail store advertised personal computers for sale. The ad included this statement: "$100 down, $10 per week." The ad contained no indication of the total price of the computers. Does this advertisement violate the provisions of the federal Truth-in-Lending Act?

2

First Bank claimed it was the only bank to offer no-fee credit cards. Gerard was told she would get a card only if she opened a fee-based checking account. Gerard said this constituted a card use fee. The bank said the fee was for the checking account and the card was free. Who is correct?

WHAT IS CREDIT?

As we learned in the last chapter, a number of federal and other statutes have been enacted to protect consumers. Those laws include protections regarding credit practices. The term **credit** refers to an extension of time given by a seller or lender for payment for goods, services, or loans. In a way, credit is the measure of trust granted by a merchant or lender who allows a party to use goods, services, or money now and pay for them later. Those payments are usually made in a series of payments called **installments.** The party who extends the credit is called the **creditor.** The party who receives the credit is clearly in the debt of the creditor, and so that party is called the **debtor.** In this chapter we will deal with the consumer as a debtor, or as an investor or borrower of funds.

A number of federal statutes have been enacted to regulate the use of credit. Among the most important of these is the **Consumer Credit Protection Act (CCPA).** Several states have adopted the broader Uniform Consumer Credit Code (UCCC), which was intended to expand the scope of consumer protection offered by various federal and state laws. In addition, various government agencies, such as the Federal Trade Commission, have widened their activities to control deceptive and misleading credit practices.

THE TRUTH-IN-LENDING LAW

Title I of the Consumer Credit Protection Act is the Truth-in-Lending Act. As noted in Chapter 12, the main purpose of this law is to assure that consumers know the cost of credit.

PROBLEM

> **1.** Vatalaro bought a car stereo and told the dealer that he would pay her for it in "a couple of weeks." After two months, the dealer still had not received payment. She then billed Vatalaro for the price of the stereo, plus interest for the two months' credit. When Vatalaro received the bill, he immediately paid the principal amount owed. He refused to pay the interest, however, since there had been no written credit agreement. Is Vatalaro required to pay the interest?

The Truth-in-Lending Act requires lenders and sellers who provide credit to give each borrower or buyer a detailed statement of the actual cost of credit. The cost must be stated both in terms of dollars and cents and of the **annual percentage rate (APR)** of interest paid for the use of the credit. The annual percentage rate is the fee for use of credit, stated as a percentage of the amount borrowed. This information is important because in most types of consumer credit, true costs are often much more than the actual amount borrowed. A consumer who knows the cost of credit is able to shop

Declaring Personal Bankruptcy

During the Middle Ages, a bankrupt was considered a criminal—someone who hid from creditors or took other actions to defraud lenders. A bankrupt who refused to turn over all his or her goods to creditors was imprisoned.

Fortunately, we have come a long way from this barbaric treatment of luckless debtors. The basic concepts of our latest bankruptcy law include, among others, provisions that (1) prorate the bankrupt's assets among creditors in a fair and suitable manner; (2) give honest debtors relief from their debts in order to try to "rehabilitate" the debtors; and (3) exempt certain property from the reach of creditors so the debtor can make a fresh start.

Declaring personal bankruptcy has certain positive sides as well as negative sides. On the positive side, the declaration keeps creditors away. No one can foreclose on the debtor's home or repossess the family car while the bankruptcy proceeding is taking place. But declaring bankruptcy has its costs. It can be quite difficult to re-establish credit after declaring bankruptcy. This problem is not helped by the fact that credit agencies keep a record of the bankruptcy for ten years. Also, although bankruptcy doesn't carry the stigma it did in the past, many people view the proceeding as a blow to their self-image.

Bankruptcy is not the only method of dealing with a debt problem. There are alternatives that a debtor may find more advantageous. Some of these include settling with creditors out of court, asking creditors to reduce payment amounts, getting help from a consumer credit counselor, or paying debts by selling or borrowing on assets.

around for the best credit terms. In Problem 1, Vatalaro is not required to pay interest. The dealer had not provided a written agreement detailing the cost of the credit.

Lenders Subject to the Law

People or businesses that regularly extend credit to consumers are called **lenders.** Banks, savings and loan associations, retail stores, auto dealers, credit unions, and finance companies are commonly lenders. Even doctors, plumbers, and other service providers may be lenders if they regularly extend or arrange for credit for customers.

Types of Credit Covered

The Truth-in-Lending Act applies to consumer credit as well as to real-estate credit.

PROBLEM

> **2.** Foo borrowed $3,000 from her credit union in order to pay some medical bills. She agreed to repay the credit union in three equal payments, at an APR of 10.9%. Is this loan subject to the provisions of the Truth-in-Lending Act?

The consumer credit must be for personal, family, household, or agricultural purposes and may not exceed $25,000. It must also be credit on which a **finance charge** (the fee for use of credit, stated in terms of dollars and cents) is imposed, and by agreement it must be payable in more than *four* installments. In Problem 2, Foo's loan agreement is not covered by the Truth-in-Lending Act. It is not payable in more than four installments.

Credit cards, which may be used to purchase many kinds of goods and services, are included under the Truth-in-Lending Act. The act covers the loss or theft of credit cards.

If a credit card is lost or stolen, the act states that a cardholder is not liable for more than $50 in unauthorized charges made before the holder notifies the issuer of the loss. Once the issuer has been notified, the cardholder is not liable for any unauthorized charges. An issuer who fails to comply with all the provisions of the act forfeits the right to collect even the $50.

The issuer of a credit card must (1) inform the cardholder of his or her potential liability in case of the card's loss or theft; (2) supply the cardholder with a self-addressed, postage-paid notice to be mailed to the issuer if the card is lost or stolen; and (3) provide a method by which the cardholder can be identified as the authorized user.

Real-estate credit in any amount is covered by this law, except for credit granted in first mortgages on homes. Also excluded is commercial or business credit (unless the business purpose is agriculture) and credit to government agencies.

Information Lenders Must Furnish

As mentioned, the most important disclosures required of lenders are (1) the cost of the loan in terms of dollars and cents, and (2) the annual percentage rate of the finance charge.

EXAMPLE

> Muller borrowed $5,000 from a bank, repayable over three years in monthly installments of $162.51. The bank stated that the interest rate was 10.5% a year. The annual percentage rate was actually 17%, however, because it was compounded over three years. The Truth-in-Lending Law requires the bank to tell Muller the total cost of his loan ($162.51 × 36 months = $5,850.36 − $5,000 principal = $850.36 interest). The bank also must tell Muller the annual percentage rate (17%).

The required information must be clearly printed, typed, or written on the credit agreement. Finance charges usually include interest as well as service charges, investigation fees, and perhaps insurance premiums. The annual percentage rate need not be stated if the finance charge is $5 or less or on loans of $75 or less. If a customer borrows more than $75 and the finance charge is $7.50 or less, the finance charge need not be stated.

Credit Advertisements

In advertisements that offer credit, the lender must tell "the entire truth" about the credit transaction, not just what the lender wants the borrower to know. All financing details must be spelled out regardless of the advertising media used. Vague terms such as "no money down" or "take years to pay" are prohibited. No advertisement may spell out a specific term unless all other terms are also clearly stated.

Cancellation Provisions

Under the Truth-in-Lending Act, some real-estate credit transactions may be canceled. Individuals who pledge their residences as **collateral** for a real estate loan of any amount may cancel the transaction within three business days of making the agreement. Collateral is property pledged to protect the lender if the borrower fails to repay. This provision does not apply, however, to commercial loans or to first-mortgage loans.

OTHER CREDIT REGULATIONS

In addition to the Truth-in-Lending Act, several other important federal laws regulate credit transactions. These include the Fair Credit Billing Act, the Fair Credit Reporting Act, the Equal Credit Opportunity Act, and the Fair Debt Collection Practices Act.

The Fair Credit Billing Act

The **Fair Credit Billing Act,** an amendment to the Truth-in-Lending Act, covers disputes between parties in credit agreements.

Sellers and lenders must spell out all financing details in their advertisements.

NEW TRUCKS IN STOCK!!!

RANGERS

$95 DOWN $129 PER MONTH

Stk. #'s: 26038, 26036, 26039, 26035, 26096, 26030. $128.98 per month, cash price $5936, dwn. pymt. $95 cash or trade. Annual percentage rate 11.68 for 60 months with bank approved credit. Amt. financed $5841, Interest $1897.80, deferred payment price $7833.80. Total of payments $7738.80. Six available at this price. Others available at different payments and prices.

BARROS FORD
1991 Broadway – Exit 26A off Route 80
932–4090

In the event of a billing dispute, a consumer has 60 days to notify a creditor of a billing error on a credit account. The creditor then has 30 days to acknowledge receipt of the dispute notice, and another 90 days to correct the account or explain a correct billing. A creditor must tell the consumer the names of any parties to whom the creditor reports a delinquent account.

The Fair Credit Billing Act also prohibits a credit card issuer from sending a card to someone who hasn't applied for it.

The Fair Credit Reporting Act

Title VI of the Consumer Credit Protection Act is called the **Fair Credit Reporting Act.** This law protects consumers against the circulation of inaccurate or obsolete information. It also ensures that credit bureaus or agencies exercise their duties to consumers fairly. The act states that a person who has been denied credit, insurance, employment, or government

The Fair Credit Reporting Act gives a consumer the right to know the contents of his or her credit file.

licenses or benefits has a right to know the reason for the denial. The consumer has a right to be told the name of the credit bureau that issued the unfavorable report, and then to know the contents of his or her file with the bureau. If the file's contents are found to be wrong or obsolete, the credit bureau must send correction notices to anyone who received the unfavorable information.

The Equal Credit Opportunity Act

The **Equal Credit Opportunity** Act allows everyone equal access to the credit market. It states that creditors may not discriminate against applicants on the basis of sex, marital status, race, religion, national origin, or age. A party who is denied credit must be notified within a reasonable time, and the reasons for the denial must be stated.

The Fair Debt Collection Practices Act

Another important aspect of the credit process is the collection of past-due accounts. The **Fair Debt Collection Practices Act** forbids collection agencies to use threats of violence, late-night phone calls, and misrepresentations when collecting debts. Except for finding out where a debtor lives or works, a collector may not communicate with third parties about a debt without a court's permission, unless that party is a spouse, parent, or financial advisor. A collector may not contact a debtor at work if the debtor's employer objects. Also, a collector may not deposit a postdated check before the date on the check.

This law applies only to debt-collection agencies. It does not apply to banks, department stores, and businesses that collect their own debts.

PENALTIES FOR SELLERS OR LENDERS

A seller's or lender's willful violation of the Truth-in-Lending Act can bring a maximum criminal penalty of $5,000, a year in jail, or both. A buyer or borrower also may sue the seller or lender for twice the amount of the finance charge. However, this amount may not be less than $100 or more than $1,000, plus court costs and reasonable attorney's fees.

REMEDIES OF SELLERS OR LENDERS

Buyers sometimes fail to keep up their installment payments. When this happens and collection efforts are unsuccessful, there are several remedies available to sellers.

PROBLEM

> **3.** Theissman entered into an installment contract to buy a stereo system from Barton-Hale Co. The price was $900, payable in monthly installments of $100. After paying $300, Theissman defaulted. Barton-Hale then repossessed the stereo system and resold it for $400. Is Theissman required to pay Barton-Hale any more money?

A seller is usually entitled to **repossession** of the goods if a buyer has defaulted on the payment contract covering the purchase of the goods. After taking back the goods, the seller may resell them and obtain a **deficiency judgment** against the defaulting consumer. A deficiency judgment is a court award equal to the difference between the amount due under the original contract and the amount the seller actually collects from a resale. The UCCC has changed this rule when it applies to consumer credit sales under $1,000. In a sale such as this, a seller must choose between repossessing the goods and suing the buyer for the balance of the purchase price. Since the original sale in Problem 3 involved only $900, Barton-Hale would have to make this choice.

If the contract price is over $1,000, the seller may repossess and resell the goods and obtain a deficiency judgment. These rules also apply in loans of money.

You can see that credit is an important influence on consumer buying power. While it may be necessary to "buy now and pay later," the net result is that credit makes the things we buy cost more. Credit is based on trust, and merchants are reluctant to trust consumers without some kind of guarantee of repayment. As a result, sellers often require buyers to provide some insurance for their interests. The sales agreements resulting from this are called *secured credit sales,* which we will explore in Chapter 23.

Chapter 22 Review

"YOU BE THE JUDGE" REVIEW

Look again at the "You Be the Judge" cases given at the beginning of this chapter. Would you decide them differently now, after your study of the chapter?

Correct Decisions

1. Yes. Under the Truth-in Lending-Act, an advertisement must contain all the terms of an agreement if it states any term or terms. This advertisement failed to state the price of the computers, the annual percentage rate of interest, the duration of the loan, and the finance charge.

2. Technically, although a fee-based checking account is required to obtain the credit card, the use of the credit card is free. If the bank's advertisements specify that the card's use is "free to all our checking account customers," the claim is legitimate.

UNDERSTANDING WHAT YOU HAVE READ

1. Why do goods, services, or loans cost more if they are obtained on a credit basis?
2. What is the main purpose of the Truth-in-Lending Act?
3. What are the two important disclosures required of lenders under the Truth-in-Lending Act?
4. What types of credit does the Truth-in-Lending Act cover?
5. If a consumer's credit card is lost or stolen, what procedure should the consumer follow? What is the consumer's liability for unauthorized charges?
6. What must a credit-card issuer provide to the cardholder?
7. What types of credit transactions may be canceled?
8. What are the main provisions of the Fair Debt Collection Practices Act?
9. What penalties do sellers or lenders face if they violate the Truth-in-Lending Act?
10. What remedies are available to a seller when a buyer defaults on his or her installment payments?

BUILDING YOUR LEGAL VOCABULARY

Match each of these legal terms with its correct definition from the list that
follows. Write your answers on a separate sheet of paper.

annual percentage rate (APR)
collateral
credit
debtor

Equal Credit Opportunity Act
Fair Credit Reporting Act
finance charge

installments
lender
repossession

1. the federal law that prohibits discrimination against credit applicants on the basis of sex, marital status, race, religion, national origin, or age
2. a series of regular payments for goods, services, or loans
3. a creditor's right to take back goods from a buyer who defaults on payments
4. the federal law that protects consumers against the circulation of inaccurate or obsolete information and ensures that credit agencies exercise their duties to consumers fairly

5. the fee for use of credit, stated as a percentage of the amount borrowed
6. property pledged to protect a lender if a borrower fails to repay
7. a party who receives credit
8. an extension of time given by a seller or lender for payment for goods, services, or loans
9. one who regularly extends or arranges for credit
10. the fee for use of credit, stated in terms of dollars and cents, and including other applicable charges

APPLYING LEGAL PRINCIPLES

1. Deluca, a farmer, obtained a $30,000 loan from National Growers' Bank. Deluca needed the money to buy ten acres of land on which to expand his farming business. Is this loan covered by the provisions of the Truth-in-Lending Act?
2. MacIntyre, a stockbroker, obtained a personal loan of $27,500 from a savings and loan association. She needed the money to buy a restored 1951 Rolls Royce for her husband. Is this transaction covered by the Truth-in-Lending Act?

3. The FTC accused Cady Store, Inc. of regularly extending credit to its customers without complete disclosure of credit terms, as required by the Truth-in-Lending Act. Cady argued that only "a few" of its customers were allowed to make installment payments. As such, the store claimed, it was not technically a lender. Upon investigation, it was shown that 34% of Cady's customers had extended-payment agreements with the store. In whose favor would you decide this case?

4. The Home Loan Company published a brochure noting that it offered 30-day loans repayable in two payments at 15-day intervals. The brochure neither gave an example of such a loan nor indicated any cost of credit. The local Better Business Bureau accused the loan firm of failing to fully disclose its credit terms in its advertisements. Home Loan defended itself by stating that, since these loans were repayable in two installments, they were exempt from the provisions of the Truth-in-Lending Act. Is the loan firm's claim correct?

5. Seeward lost his Gull Oil Co. credit card but didn't realize he had lost it until three weeks later, when he received a bill from the oil company. The statement showed that someone had charged a set of four truck tires to Seeward's account, in the amount of $280. Seeward immediately notified the oil company of the loss of the card and of its unauthorized use. The company claimed that since Seeward had not notified the firm immediately after the card was lost, he was liable for payment of the full $280. Is the oil company's claim correct?

6. Hong was interested in acquiring a second mortgage on her home. What advice would you give her about comparing the terms of credit?

7. Rhein Furniture placed an ad for a special sale in the local paper. The ad stated that people who bought furniture during the sale would receive "free credit for six months." In fact, the amounts of the purchases accrued interest until payments were to begin after six months. Does this advertisement constitute a violation of the Truth-in-Lending Act?

8. Esguerra signed a purchase agreement for a $30,000 lakefront lot. He put up his home as collateral for the agreement. Two days later, Esguerra decided not to buy the lot and canceled the sale. The salesperson who handled the transaction then sued Esguerra for the loss of her commission on the sale. Will the salesperson be able to collect?

9. Murchison Auto Sales, Inc. bought a series of 30-second spot ads to be aired by WKRZ Radio. The ads' jingle stated: "$99 down, $99 a month for a brand new Olds '99." No additional terms were stated in the ads. Do these advertisements comply with the requirements of the Truth-in-Lending Act?

10. Plak bought a computer for personal use. The price of the computer was $1,800. Plak paid 20% down and borrowed the balance from a bank. The loan was to be repaid in equal installments of $127 a month for one year. What was the principal amount of the loan? What was the finance charge?

11. Dellman applied for a charge account at Famoso Department Store, but her application was rejected. What are Dellman's rights under the Fair Credit Reporting Act?

12. Bolotin entered into an installment-sales agreement to buy $2,300 worth of exercise equipment from Fitness Supply. He made payments totaling $660, and then he defaulted on the payments. When its collection efforts failed, Fitness Supply repossessed the goods and resold them for $1,300. What amount has Fitness Supply lost on the resale? What are Fitness Supply's rights with respect to Bolotin?

ANALYZING COURT CASES

1. Adams obtained credit cards from United Oil Company for himself and his wife. The card stated, "This card is valid unless expired or revoked. Named holder's approval of all purchases is presumed unless written notice of loss or theft is received." Later, Adams returned his card to the company with a letter stating that he was canceling his account. He also stated that he could not return the card in his wife's possession because they had separated. Subsequently, United Oil sued Adams for purchases made by his wife on the credit card in her possession. Adams defended on the ground that he had canceled the contract. United Oil claimed that the contract was not revoked until both cards were surrendered. Had Adams effectively revoked or canceled the contract? (Based on: *Socony Mobil Oil Co. v. Greif*, 197 N.Y.S. 2d 522)

2. A door-to-door salesperson representing an appliance dealer sold the Westermans a refrigerator. The cash price of the unit was $899.98. With all finance charges, the total amount due was $1,229.76. The amount was to be paid in 36 monthly installments of $34.16. The Westermans made payments for a period of time, but then stopped paying. They claimed that the unit was so greatly overpriced that the contract was unconscionable and therefore unenforceable. An independent appliance dealer valued the unit at $350 to $400. The appliance dealer maintained that the Westermans had willingly signed the contract and must therefore complete their payments. Are the Westermans liable for payment of the full amount to the dealer? (*Toker v. Westerman*, 113 N.J. Super. 452; 274 A. 2d 78)

3. A bank held an insolvent deceased's note for $3,000. The bank convinced the widow of the deceased to sign a new note for the amount in exchange for the old note. Later, the widow maintained that the old note was not valuable consideration for the new one and that she was not a debtor since there can be no contract without mutual consideration. Can the bank as creditor require her to pay? (*Newman & Snell's State Bank v. Hunter*, 243 Mich. 331; 220 N.W. 665)

CHAPTER 23

Secured Credit Sales

YOU BE THE JUDGE

Think about these cases.
If you were the judge, how would you decide each case?

1

The Rakovics were farmers who lived on a small farm in Nebraska. When they needed money to meet their bills for the winter, they applied at a local bank for a loan. As collateral for the loan, they offered their next season's corn crop. Is this considered valid collateral for a loan?

2

The owners of Knudson Corner Photocopy applied for a loan, offering their photocopying equipment as security for the loan. Can the lender agree to make the loan against the equipment?

WHAT IS A SECURED CREDIT SALE?

A person who lends money or sells goods on credit relies on the debtor's honesty and ability to pay. If the debtor repays the debt, the creditor has no cause for concern. If a debt is not repaid, however, the creditor often has to sue to collect it. These lawsuits are time-consuming and expensive, and they often yield unsatisfactory results.

In order to give sellers and lenders greater protection, today's business has devised the **secured credit sale.** The law governing secured credit sales is found in Article 9 of the UCC. A secured credit sale results from an agreement in which the seller retains a **security interest** in goods in the buyer's possession. The security interest gives the seller the right to re-possess, or take back, the goods if the buyer fails to pay for them. In other respects, a secured credit sale is like an ordinary sale of goods in which title and risk of loss pass to the buyer. Figure 23.1 is an example of a **conditional** (installment) **sale contract,** a common example of a secured credit sale.

PROBLEM

1. Sandweg visited Norton Piano Company's showroom and chose a piano costing $3,500. The price was more than she could pay in full at the time of the purchase. The dealer agreed to sell her the piano under a written agreement providing for a down payment of $350, with the balance payable in monthly install-ments over twelve months. Was this a secured credit sale?

The written agreement in a secured credit sale is known as the **security agreement.** The subject matter of the agreement (goods or money) is the collateral. As you learned in Chapter 22, collateral is property pledged to protect a creditor's interests if a debtor fails to repay. The seller or lender is known as the **secured party,** and the buyer or borrower is the debtor. In Problem 1, Sandweg and the Norton Piano Company entered into a secured credit sale. Norton Piano is the secured party and Sandweg is the debtor. The collateral in which Norton Piano has a security interest is the piano. Sandweg also has certain rights in the piano.

Types of Collateral

Collateral may consist of **consumer goods**—goods used or bought for use for personal, family, or household purposes, as in Problem 1. It may also consist of crops, livestock, and products such as wool, milk, and eggs. These are known as *farm products.* Another form of collateral under the UCC is known as *inventory.* This consists of goods held by a person for sale or lease and supplies used in performing service contracts. A fourth type of collateral is known as *equipment.* Equipment consists of goods used primarily in business (including farming or a profession). Thus, furniture, fixtures, and office machines would be equipment if used for business purposes.

Figure 23.1
A Conditional
Sales Contract
(page one)

CONDITIONAL SALE CONTRACT — CREDIT SALE OF VEHICLE
INCLUDING DISCLOSURES REQUIRED BY FEDERAL LAW

CONTRACT DATE _____

CONTRACT NO. _____

Seller, _____, California is a creditor under provisions of the Truth-in-Lending Act (Regulation Z), and subject to the terms and conditions below and on the reverse side hereof, sells and Buyer, _____
　　Name of Dealer　　　　　　　Address　　　　　　　　　　　　　　　　　　　　　　　　Name of Buyer

California hereby buys and accepts for the price set forth the following described goods:

ANNUAL PERCENTAGE RATE The cost of your credit as a yearly rate.	FINANCE CHARGE The dollar amount your credit will cost you.	Amount Financed The amount of credit provided to you or on your behalf.	Total of Payments The amount you will have paid after you have made all payments as scheduled.	Total Sale Price The total of your purchase on credit including your downpayment of $
% $	$	$	$	$

Your payment schedule will be

No. of Payments	Amount of Payments	When payments are due

SECURITY: You are giving a security interest in the goods or property being purchased.

LATE CHARGE: If payment is over 10 days late, you will be charged 5% of the payment.

PREPAYMENT: If you pay off early, you may be entitled to a refund of part of the finance charge.

Read this contract for additional information about non-payment, default, any required repayment in full before the scheduled date, prepayment refunds and penalties and security interests.

Seller hereby sells and buyer hereby buys and accepts for the price and subject to the terms and conditions set forth below and on the reverse side the following described property:

	YEAR	MAKE/TRADE NAME		MODEL NUMBER	CYLS.
☐ NEW ☐ USED					
BODY TYPE (tonnage if truck)		SERIAL OR I.D. NUMBER		LICENSE NUMBER	

ACCESSORIES

☐ VINYL TOP ☐ AM-FM RADIO ☐ TAPE ☐ AUTO. TRANS. ☐ 5 SPEED TRANS.
　　　　　　　　　　　　　　　　　　　　　　　　　　　　MILEAGE
☐ POWER STR. ☐ CUST WHEELS ☐ PWR. WIND. ☐ A/C
ANY OTHER ACCESSORIES　　　　COLOR　　　　KEY NUMBER

ITEMIZATION OF AMOUNT FINANCED OF $ _____

1. Cash Price
　— Vehicle Price (net of any Seller rebates) $ _____
　— Seller Documentation Fee (not a governmental fee) $ _____
　— Sales Tax on above amounts $ _____
　— Service Contract $ _____
　Total Cash Price $ _____
2. Amount Paid to Public Officials
　— License $ _____
　— Certification of Title $ _____
　— Registration $ _____
　Total of Official Fees $ _____
3. Amount Paid to Insurance Companies $ _____
4. Amount Paid to _____ for Smog Certificate $ _____
5. Subtotal (sum of 1, 2, 3 and 4) $ _____

CREDIT INSURANCE

Neither Credit Life nor Credit Disability Insurance are required in connection with this sale. No charge will be made for such insurance and none will be provided unless the Buyer to be insured thereunder signs and dates the statement below. The cost of Credit Life Insurance will be

$ _____ and the Credit Disability Insurance will be

$ _____ for the term of the credit. As such buyer I certify that I have not reached my 65th birthday.

I desire ☐ Credit Life Insurance ☐ I do not desire Credit Life or Disability Insurance
☐ Credit Disability Insurance

DATE _____　　SIGNATURE OF BUYER TO BE INSURED

STATEMENT OF INSURANCE

Coverage	Deduct. or Limit	Mo.	Term Expires Before Cont.	After Cont.	Premium
Comprehensive					$
Fire and Theft					$
Combined Add'l Coverage					$
Deductible Collision $					$
Other (describe)					$
Credit Life		Expires with Contract			$
Credit Disability					$
TOTAL GROSS PREMIUM					

NOTICE: No person is required as a condition precedent to financing the purchase of an automobile that any insurance be negotiated or purchased through a particular insurance agent or broker. Buyer may choose the person through which any insurance to be written in connection with this sale is obtained. The cost of insurance to be obtained through Seller and charged for in this Contract is indicated above.

Buyer's signature (to be insured)

Seller

By

WARNING — UNLESS A CHARGE IS INCLUDED IN THIS AGREEMENT FOR PUBLIC LIABILITY OR PROPERTY DAMAGE INSURANCE, PAYMENT FOR SUCH COVERAGE IS NOT PROVIDED BY THIS AGREEMENT.

Buyer's signature

SERVICE CONTRACT (OPTIONAL)

Company	Price
Buyer	Term Mos.

SELLER-ASSISTED LOANS

To be completed in the event Seller assists Buyer in obtaining a loan from a third party if the loan is used directly or indirectly as payment upon the vehicle purchase order or conditional sale contract. Amount of loan.

$ _____

FINANCE CHARGE $ _____

TOTAL $ _____ PAYMENT SCHEDULE _____

AUTO CONDITIONAL SALE CONTRACT (Rev. 11/83)

The Security Agreement

If the buyer is in possession of the collateral, the security agreement must be in writing. It also must be signed by the buyer. It must contain at least a general description of the collateral (see Problem 3).

Protecting the Secured Party

A buyer who is in possession of the collateral may be in a position to take advantage of the secured party. This occurs when a dishonest buyer sells the goods to someone who has no knowledge of the security interest.

Figure 23.1
A Conditional
Sales Contract
(page two)

6. Amount of Your Downpayment
— Trade-in (year, make
and model _____

_____)

Gross Value $ _____
Current Liens $ _____
Net Agreed Value $ _____
— Deferred cash downpayment (pick-up payment)
(due_____) $ _____
— Deferred cash downpayment (pick-up payment)
(due_____) $ _____
— Assigned Manufacturer's Rebate $ _____
— Cash paid by buyer at or before
contract signing $ _____
Total of Downpayment $ _____

7. Amount Financed (5 less 6) $ _____

The Buyer may be required to pledge security for the loan which security must be mutually agreed to by the Buyer and the lender. Security (describe)

Notice to the buyer: If Seller Assisted Loan is described above you are obligated for the installment payment on both the Conditional Sale Contract and the loan.

$ _____ from the proceeds of this loan is included in ☐ Cash Downpayment ☐ Deferred Downpayment

CO-OWNER

By signing this contract, I agree only to those provisions which relate to the security interest to be retained by the Seller. I do not assume any personal liability for repayment of the indebtedness secured by the vehicle described herein.

Co-owner's Signature

SELLER'S ACCEPTANCE

Acceptance of this contract and delivery of property is conditioned upon credit approval.

Seller _____
Business
Address _____

By _____ Title _____

NAMES AND ADDRESSES OF ALL PERSONS TO WHOM NOTICE OF INTENT TO SELL IS TO BE SENT.

NOTICE TO BUYER: (1) Do not sign this Agreement before you read it or if it contains any blank spaces to be filled in. (2) You are entitled to a completely filled-in copy of this agreement. (3) You can prepay the full amount due under the agreement at any time and obtain a partial refund of the finance charge if it is $1 or more. Because of the way the amount of this refund will be figured, the time when you prepay could increase the ultimate cost of credit under this agreement. (4) If you default in the performance of your obligations under this agreement, the vehicle may be repossessed and you may be subject to suit and liability for the unpaid indebtedness evidenced by this agreement.

NOTICE (Traducción en Inglés)

By signing this notice and the accompanying consumer credit contract, you become responsible for the debt even if you are not to receive any property, services or money pursuant to the terms of the contract. You may be sued for payment even though you received no property, services or money, and although the person who receives such property, services or money is able to pay. This notice is not the contract which obligates you to pay the debt. Read the contract for the exact terms of your obligation.

AVISO (Spanish Translation)

Firmando este aviso y el contrato de crédito para consumidor adjunto, usted se hace responsable por la deuda aún si usted no vá a recibir ninguna propiedad, servicios ni dinero bajo los términos de este contrato. Usted puede ser demandado para que pague, aunque Ud. no reciba ninguna propiedad, servicios o dinero y aún cuando la persona que recibe dicha propiedad, servicios o dinero esta capacitada para pagar. Este aviso no es el contrato que lo obliga a pagar la deuda. Lea el contrato para las condiciones exactas de su obligación.

Buyer acknowledges that: (1) Buyer has read this contract, including the Terms and Conditions on the reverse side. (2) It contains all of the agreements between Buyer and Seller, including any promissory notes, or any other evidences of Indebtedness. (3) Prior to signing this contract Buyer received a fully completed copy and a copy of any purchase order, credit statement or other document which Buyer has been asked to sign in connection with this sale.

Buyer's Signature _____ Date _____   Buyer's Signature _____ Date _____

This document is only a general form which may be proper for use in simple transactions and in no way acts, or is intended to act, as a substitute for the advice of an attorney. The printer does not make any warranty, either express or implied, as to the legal validity of any provision or the suitability of these forms in any specific transaction.

PROBLEM

2. Assume in Problem 1 that before completing her payments to the piano dealer, Sandweg sold the piano to Ellers. Ellers was not aware of the dealer's security interest. Could the dealer enforce a security interest in the piano against Ellers?

To protect the secured party from the claims of innocent third parties, the UCC requires the secured party to file the security agreement or a **financing statement** in a public office. Figure 23.2 is an example of a financing statement. The place where the document is filed is usually the office of the clerk in the county or town where the buyer lives. This filing gives the secured party a **perfected security interest** in the goods. If the buyer is a nonresident, filing should be made in the county or town where the collateral is located. If the secured party fails to file, a third person buying consumer goods for personal use may acquire title that is free from the security interest. However, a secured party who files has a perfected security interest. A third person is bound by that security interest even if its existence wasn't known. In Problem 2, the dealer failed to file either the security agreement or a financing statement. Thus, Norton Piano cannot recover the piano from Ellers.

Suppose, though, that Sandweg sold the piano to a dealer in used pianos rather than to Ellers, and that dealer listed the instrument among the inventory of goods to be resold. The dealer's ownership of the piano would then be subject to the security interest held by the original dealer, and the original dealer could recover the piano from the used-piano dealer. This is true even though the original dealer hadn't filed the security agreement or a financing statement.

Figure 23.2
A Uniform Commercial Code Conditional Financing Statement

Uniform Commercial Code — FINANCING STATEMENT — Form UCC-1

IMPORTANT — Read instructions on back before filling out form

This FINANCING STATEMENT is presented to a filing officer for filing pursuant to the Uniform Commercial Code.

4. Filed for record in the real estate records.	5. Debtor is a Transmitting Utility.	6. No. of Additional Sheets Presented.
1. Debtor(s) (Last Name First) and address(es)	2. Secured Party(ies) and address(es)	3. For Filing Officer (Date, Time, Number, and Filing Office)
Ochi, Sheila M. 18925 Marquard Court Dallas, TX 75019	The First National Bank of Dallas 1400 Southwest Parkway Dallas, TX 75006	

7. This financing statement covers the following types (or items) of property:

One (1) 6108A Century 4-door sedan, Model Number 2119

☐ Products of Collateral are also covered.

Whichever is Applicable (See Instruction Number 9)	Sheila M. Ochi Signature(s) of Debtor (Or Assignor)	The First National Bank of Dallas By: Russell P. Vargo Signature(s) of Secured Party (Or Assignee)

Filing Officer Copy — Alphabetical
STANDARD FORM — UNIFORM COMMERCIAL CODE — FORM UCC-1 Rev. Jan. 1980 *Forms may be purchased from Hobbs & Warren, Inc., Boston, Mass. 02101*

In some states, a security interest in a car will be noted on the certificate of title.

Filing is not required in a secured credit sale of a car if a state law provides for security interests to be noted on the car's certificate of title. The notation on the certificate protects the seller's security interest as effectively as if a filing had been made.

A **chattel mortgage** is another familiar example of a secured credit sale. A chattel mortgage is formed when the owner of consumer goods borrows money and gives a security interest in the goods to a bank or private party. Under the UCC, the secured party in a chattel mortgage must file to perfect a security interest against third parties. In a chattel mortgage, the collateral is always personal property or goods rather than realty.

Kapoor borrowed $250 from Diggs and gave Diggs a security interest in a VCR that Kapoor owned. Diggs failed to file a financing statement or the security agreement (chattel mortgage) in a public office. If Kapoor sold the VCR before paying Diggs, an innocent third-party buyer would hold the VCR free and clear of Diggs's security interest.

In a sale of inventory goods, a security interest is perfected by filing. Since these goods are bought for resale purposes, a person who buys them from the debtor in the ordinary course of business obtains a clear title. This is true even if the existence of the security interest is known. A security interest in a sale of equipment is perfected by filing a financing statement in the proper public office. Filing is not required when the collateral is in the possession of the secured party.

EXAMPLE

Merritt borrowed $100 from Ishida. As security or collateral for the loan (pledge), Merritt gave Ishida her watch. Since Ishida has possession of the collateral, she does not have to file a financing statement to protect her rights against third parties.

Goods for sale can serve as collateral.

The Financing Statement

To be effective, a financing statement must be signed by the debtor. It must give the address of the secured party from whom information about the security interest may be obtained. It also must give the debtor's mailing address and contain a statement describing the collateral.

3. A financing statement described the collateral as "passenger and commercial automobiles." However, the statement failed to mention the cars' engine or serial numbers. Was the description sufficient to identify the property?

As in the case of a security agreement, any description that reasonably identifies the collateral is sufficient. The description given in Problem 3 is sufficient to satisfy the requirements of the Code, even though further inquiry may be needed to determine exactly which cars are subject to the seller's security interest. Instead of filing a financing statement, the secured party may file a copy of the security agreement if it is signed by the debtor and contains the required information.

A filing of a security agreement or financing statement is effective for five years from the date of filing. It may be renewed for another five-year period if necessary.

Default of the Buyer

Debtors sometimes fail to make installment payments when due or to comply with some of the terms of security agreements. If this occurs in a security agreement for the sale of *consumer goods,* all the installment payments become due and payable immediately. The purchaser is said to be *in default.* Some remedies for this situation may be contained in the security agreement itself. In addition to those remedies, the Code provides that the secured party may repossess the goods from the defaulting party if this can be done without breaching the peace. If the debtor will not willingly give up the property, the secured party must take legal action to regain possession.

4. Alemian bought a wide-screen TV for $1,800. He made a down payment of $300 and agreed to pay $100 a month until the full price was paid. The dealer retained a security interest in the TV. After Alemian had made three payments, he defaulted on the contract. The dealer then repossessed the TV. Could Alemian insist that the dealer resell the TV?

Hints for Installment Buyers

Obedo bought a used car from a dealer. The purchase was made on the installment plan. Obedo trustfully signed a blank contract, leaving the terms of the agreement to be filled in by the dealer. When filling in the terms, the dealer raised the price of the car above the figure that Obedo had orally agreed to pay. Was Obedo bound by the contract?

Without witnesses, Obedo would have a hard time convincing a court that the dealer had changed the agreed terms. It simply doesn't make sense to sign a blank contract that is to be filled in later by the other contracting party. This isn't the only practice, though, that causes installment buyers to suffer. These consumers often are guilty of many other practices that cost them dearly in legal fees and court costs when they seek redress. Here are some useful hints to avoid trouble with installment sales.

DOs

- Consult your Better Business Bureau, Chamber of Commerce, or local bank if in doubt about the seller's honesty.
- Insist on a plainly worded contract that clearly indicates all extra charges.
- Find out what penalties you face if you are late in making payments.
- Find out whether you'll earn a bonus if you pay off your balance before the end of the stated credit period.
- Notify the seller before the next installment payment if you run into unexpected money troubles.

DON'Ts

- Don't let the seller rush you. Take your time in installment buying. *Be sure you understand the contract.*
- Don't sign a contract containing blank spaces that the dealer says will be filled in later. An unpleasant surprise may await you.
- Don't grant too much security and thereby overprotect the seller. An example is a contract allowing the seller of a stereo to repossess the car in which the stereo was installed.
- Don't sign a contract containing an "add-on" sales clause unless you're sure that you are dealing with a reputable firm. For example, don't buy a baby carriage and add its cost to a contract you already hold for buying furniture on time. Get separate contracts.
- Don't sign a contract that calls for a big ("balloon") final payment.

If a debtor defaults when *less than 60 percent* of the purchase price of the goods has been paid, the UCC allows the secured party to keep the goods in full satisfaction of the debt. In this case, the debtor must be notified of the secured party's intention. If the debtor objects within 21 days, the goods must be sold at either a public or private sale. In Problem 4, Alemian may insist that the dealer resell the TV, even though he has paid the dealer less than 60 percent of the purchase price. If the debtor has paid *60 percent or more* of the purchase price, the goods *must* be resold within 90 days after repossession. If a loss results from the sale, the secured party may sue the debtor to collect the deficiency. If a profit results, however, the debtor is legally entitled to any sum remaining after payment of the balance of the debt and any expenses of the sale or repossession.

The Termination Statement

Under the UCC, certain steps must be followed to discharge a security interest.

PROBLEM

> **5.** Ginsberg completed all payments on some kitchen appliances. She wanted to have the dealer's security interest removed from the public records. What procedure must she follow?

A debtor who has completed all payments required under a security agreement is entitled to a written discharge of the obligation. The debtor may demand a written statement from the secured party, certifying that the secured party no longer has a security interest in the subject matter. This statement is known as a **termination statement.** It must be sent to the debtor within ten days after a proper demand has been made. A penalty of $100, payable to the debtor, is imposed on a secured party who fails to furnish such a statement. The debtor must then present the termination statement to the public office where the security agreement or financing statement is on file. After payment of the required filing fee, the financing statement or security agreement will be marked "terminated" and returned to the secured party. In Problem 5, Ginsberg should follow this procedure in order to have the dealer's security interest removed from the public records.

You've learned in this unit about the many protections the law gives to consumers and to the people who fill consumers' needs. Thus far, our study of the contracts made by consumers has focused primarily on sales of goods. However, consumer sales transactions also include other types of purchases. Let's move on to Unit 5, where we will study *bailments—* consumer purchases of services.

Chapter 23 Review

"YOU BE THE JUDGE" REVIEW

Look again at the "You Be the Judge" cases given at the beginning of this chapter. Would you decide them differently now, after your study of the chapter?

Correct Decisions

1. Yes. Farm products may be used as collateral for loans.

2. Yes. A lender may agree to use a debtor's equipment as security for a loan.

UNDERSTANDING WHAT YOU HAVE READ

1. What is meant by a secured credit sale?
2. How does such a sale benefit the seller? the buyer?
3. What may the collateral in a secured credit sale consist of?
4. Must the collateral mentioned in the security agreement be specifically described?
5. Describe the procedure a secured credit seller must follow to be protected from the claims of innocent third-party buyers.
6. What information must the financing statement contain?
7. If a financing statement or a security agreement is filed in a public office, for how long is the filing effective?
8. What are the legal rights of the secured party and the buyer if the buyer defaults on a secured sales contract?
9. What procedure must a debtor follow after receiving a termination statement?
10. Your friend is about to buy a boat from a dealer on the installment plan. List ten things your friend should consider before signing the contract.

BUILDING YOUR LEGAL VOCABULARY

From this list, select the legal term that belongs in the blank in each sentence below. Write your answers on a separate sheet of paper.

chattel mortgage
conditional sale contract
consumer goods
financing statement

perfected security interest
secured credit sale
secured party

security agreement
security interest
termination statement

1. An agreement in which the seller retains a security interest in goods in the buyer's possession is called a ▓▓▓▓▓▓▓▓▓▓▓▓.
2. A secured party who has filed a security agreement or financing statement with the appropriate public office has a ▓▓▓▓▓▓▓▓▓▓▓▓ in the goods.
3. An installment or ▓▓▓▓▓▓▓▓▓▓▓▓ is a common example of a secured credit sale.
4. In a secured credit sale, the seller or lender is the ▓▓▓▓▓▓▓▓▓▓▓▓.
5. A ▓▓▓▓▓▓▓▓▓▓▓▓ is the seller's right to repossess goods if the buyer fails to pay for them.
6. A ▓▓▓▓▓▓▓▓▓▓▓▓ is formed when the owner of consumer goods borrows money and gives a security interest in the goods to the lender.
7. A secured party's written certification that he or she no longer has a security interest in the subject matter of a sale is called a ▓▓▓▓▓▓▓▓▓▓▓▓.
8. The written agreement in a secured credit sale is called a ▓▓▓▓▓▓▓▓▓▓▓▓.
9. Things used or bought for use for personal, family, or household purposes are called ▓▓▓▓▓▓▓▓▓▓▓▓.
10. To protect the secured party from claims of innocent third parties, the UCC requires the secured party to file the security agreement or a ▓▓▓▓▓▓▓▓▓▓▓▓ in a public office.

APPLYING LEGAL PRINCIPLES

1. Mapes, an appliance dealer, sold a professional kitchen range to Probst for the latter's personal use. Mapes retained a security interest in the range. Would the range be classified as consumer goods?
2. Arguello, owner of a beauty salon, bought a stereo on the installment plan for the entertainment of his customers in the waiting area. Would the stereo be classified as consumer goods?
3. Kilmer borrowed $28,000 from the First National Bank and gave the bank a chattel mortgage on her cabin cruiser. In addition, Kilmer and the bank manager signed a financing statement that was filed in the town clerk's office. Did

the bank have a perfected security interest in Kilmer's cabin cruiser?

4. Deng bought a used automatic dishwasher from Vespucci, a neighbor, for installation in Deng's home. Jasper Appliance Corporation had originally sold the dishwasher to Vespucci, retaining a security interest in the equipment. Jasper Appliance failed to file a copy of the security agreement or a financing statement. Vespucci still owed Jasper Appliance $100 as an unpaid balance. Jasper now seeks to repossess the dishwasher from Deng. Is it legally entitled to do so?

5. Would your answer to Problem 4 be the same if Jasper Appliance had filed a financing statement before Vespucci sold the dishwasher to Deng?

6. Assume all the facts stated in Problem 4, except that Vespucci sold the dishwasher to a local country club for use in the club's kitchen. Could Jasper Appliance repossess the dishwasher from the country club?

7. Myren's Discount Store filed in the proper public office a financing statement signed only by the store's manager. Would such a filing give the store a perfected security interest in the goods sold?

8. Would your answer to Problem 7 be the same if Myren's had filed a copy of the security agreement signed only by the manager instead of a financing statement?

9. Cooper Motors repossessed a car it had sold to Ko on the installment plan. Ko had paid 45 percent of the purchase price before defaulting on her contract. Cooper notified Ko that it intended to accept the car in full payment of the balance due and to make no further claims against her. What legal rights does Ko have?

10. What legal rights would Ko have in Problem 9 if she had paid 60 percent of the purchase price at the time of repossession?

ANALYZING COURT CASES

1. Each of the following secured purchases was classified by a court as either consumer goods, inventory, or equipment. Classify each one as you believe the court would have.
   a. a boat purchased by farmers (*Atlas Credit Corp. v. Dolbrow*, 165 A. 2d 704; 193 Pa. Super. 649)
   b. a cash register bought under a bailment lease arrangement (In re: *Tops Cleaners, Inc.*, 20 Pa. D&C 2d 264)

   c. cars bought by a dealer from a manufacturer for purposes of resale (*Girard Trust Bank v. Lepley Ford, Inc.*, 12 Pa. D&C 2d 351)
   d. purchase of a household laundry dryer (*U.G.I. v. McFalls*, 18 Pa. D&C 2d 713)

2. Reitz bought a tractor and shovel and gave the National Dime Bank a security interest in the property. Thereafter, the bank filed a proper financing statement

to protect its security interest. Later, before completing the balance of the payments, Reitz traded the tractor and shovel to Cleveland Brothers Equipment Co., which resold the equipment to another party. National Dime Bank brought an action in conversion to recover the value of the equipment. In its defense, Cleveland claimed that the bank had no security interest in the equipment because it had failed to sign the original security agreement with Reitz. Was this defense proper? (Based on: *National Dime Bank v. Cleveland Brothers Equipment Co.*, 20 Pa. D&C 2d 511)

3. Parker sold office furniture to Wayside Realty Company, Inc. The parties entered into a security agreement in which Parker had a security interest in the furniture. The security agreement stated that the collateral was "furniture as per attached listing." However, no listing was attached to the security agreement, and no listing was included in the financing statement. Wayside Realty Company, Inc. sold the furniture to Yale Realty Company. Does Parker have a security interest in the furniture? (Based on: *J. K. Gill Company v. Fireside Realty, Inc.*, 499 P. 2d 813)

UNIT 5

BUYING SERVICES— BAILMENTS

CHAPTERS

LEARNING OBJECTIVES

After you have studied this unit, you should be able to:

- Distinguish between a bailment of goods and a sale of goods.
- Classify bailments and state the legal characteristics of each type.
- State the legal rights and duties of the parties in various bailment contracts.

- Show the legal differences between an ordinary and an extraordinary bailment relationship.
- Describe the liability of bailees such as common carriers of goods and hotelkeepers.

CHAPTER 24

Nature of Bailments

YOU BE THE JUDGE

Think about these cases.
If you were the judge, how would you decide each case?

1

Tavares borrowed Napoli's car to drive east to Englewild, a distance of 25 miles. Instead, Tavares drove west to Millersburg. Although Tavares exercised great care, the car was damaged in an accident. Is Tavares liable to Napoli for repairs to the car?

2

A tailor's shop was broken into during the night. Floyd's graduation dress, which had been altered, was stolen. The shop had been securely locked. The shop owner sent Floyd a bill for $45 for the alterations to the dress. Is Floyd legally obligated to pay the bill?

WHAT IS A BAILMENT?

If I leave a book or a watch with you and ask you to keep it for me temporarily, a legal relationship between us has been formed. As you learned in Chapter 18, that relationship is called a *bailment.*

> **1.** Blair, preparing to take a trip around the world, arranges to do the following:
> a. Leave her dog in the care of a neighbor.
> b. Have her furniture stored in a warehouse until her return.
> c. Let a friend use her car during her absence.
> Which of these arrangements can be considered bailments?

The person who transfers possession of the goods is known as the **bailor.** The person who accepts temporary possession is the **bailee.** You become a bailor when you lend things to your friends, when you check your coat in a restaurant, or when you take your camera to a camera shop for repair. Whenever you borrow books from the library, borrow things from your friends, or rent a bike or a typewriter, you are legally a bailee. In fact, bailments occur *whenever a bailor transfers possession of goods to a bailee for some special purpose, with the goods to be returned to the bailor or otherwise disposed of in accordance with the bailor's instructions.* In Problem 1, all the arrangements made by Blair before her trip are bailments.

How Is a Bailment Created?

A bailment is usually created by agreement between the bailor and the bailee. Ordinarily, this agreement is followed by an actual delivery by the bailor and acceptance of the goods by the bailee. In most cases, the agreement will constitute a contract if it is supported by a valuable consideration.

> **2.** Tayag saw a backpack containing textbooks lying on a field where a baseball game was being played. Since no one nearby seemed to be the owner, Tayag picked up the backpack. Is he legally a bailee?

A bailment relationship arises in an agreement to lend an article to another. However, this agreement is based only on the *consent* of the parties, without consideration. Sometimes, as in Problem 2, the law will create a bailment relationship. Since Tayag voluntarily picked up the backpack, the law will regard him as a bailee for the true owner. This also would be true if Tayag had mistakenly taken someone else's backpack instead of his own. Legally, even a thief is regarded as a bailee of stolen property.

3. To try on a coat on sale at a department store, Green took off her own coat. She laid it on the counter in the presence of a salesclerk. Is the salesclerk responsible for the old coat as a bailee?

The law also will create a bailment under the circumstances described in Problem 3. It is legally recognized that a customer must lay aside an old coat in order to try on a new one. In these cases, the salesclerk assumes the responsibility of a bailee although he or she doesn't actually take possession of the old coat. Sometimes store owners or managers refuse to become bailees by posting public notices stating that they will not be responsible for personal property.

Characteristics of a Bailment

There are five important characteristics of a bailment.

1. *Personal property.* The subject matter of a bailment must be some form of personal property or goods. This **bailed property** may consist of money, shares of stock, bonds, and other securities. It also may consist of familiar goods such as books, jewelry, cars, and so forth. Real property cannot be the basis of a bailment relationship.

EXAMPLE

Shea allowed his friend Allman to stay in his summer cottage while Shea was out of town on business. Since the subject matter of the agreement was realty, there was a landlord-tenant relationship between the parties rather than one of bailor and bailee.

2. *Bailor's possession.* The bailor is usually the owner of the property, but ownership is not required. Any person who has possession of personal property may be a bailor. The possession may be lawful or unlawful, so that either a finder or a thief may be a bailor.

3. *Retention of ownership.* We saw earlier that in a sale of goods, the seller usually parts with the title and possession of the goods. In a bailment contract, though, there is only a transfer of possession. Title does not pass to the bailee. If this weren't true, the contract would be a contract for sale. Actual physical possession isn't always necessary to create a bailment. A symbol that controls possession of the goods is sufficient. For example, giving another person the keys to a car is equivalent to a transfer of possession.

4. *Delivery and acceptance.* The subject matter of the bailment is usually delivered to and accepted by the bailee. Sometimes a person may have the obligations of a bailee without a formal delivery of the property. Someone who finds goods is that kind of bailee.

5. *Return of the bailed property.* The bailee's possession is only temporary. He or she must return the goods to the bailor when the purpose is accomplished. This doesn't mean that the bailee must return the article in the same form, however. It is sufficient if the identical article is returned or disposed of per the bailor's instructions, either in the same or in an altered form.

Concannon's TV had been damaged in a fire. She sent the set to Georgi's TV Service for servicing and replacement of the cabinet. Because the identical TV is to be returned in an altered form, this transaction is a bailment.

CLASSIFICA-TION OF BAILMENTS

Bailments often are classified according to the *benefits* given to the parties. A bailment may be (1) for the sole benefit of the bailor, (2) for the sole benefit of the bailee, or (3) for the mutual benefit of bailor and bailee, with some consideration passing between bailor and bailee.

An example of a bailment made for the sole benefit of the bailor is the delivery of an animal to a neighbor to be cared for, without charge, while the owner is away. When one neighbor loans tools temporarily to another, without charge, the bailment is for the sole benefit of the bailee. Renting a car, repairing a watch, storing furniture in a warehouse, and pledging shares of stock to a lender as security for a loan are all examples of bailments made for the mutual benefit of bailor and bailee.

This bailment is for the sole benefit of the bailee.

What type of bailment is represented by each of these situations?

Bailments also may be classified according to the duties imposed on the bailee by law. If the bailee is subject to unusual duties, either at common law or by statute, the bailment is known as an **extraordinary bailment.** Hotelkeepers and common carriers of goods are bailees in extraordinary bailments. Any other bailment is known as an **ordinary bailment.**

You've learned that some bailments may arise without consideration. This type of bailment is classified as a **gratuitous bailment.** It provides for services relating to the bailed article without consideration or benefit to one of the parties, either the bailor or bailee. Every other bailment may be classified as a **contract bailment,** or a bailment relating to services purchased from a bailee. This classification may be represented as follows:

1. Services obtained without charge (gratuitous bailments)
   a. bailment for the sole benefit of the bailor
   b. bailment for the sole benefit of the bailee
2. Services purchased from bailees (contract bailments)
   a. bailments for the benefit of both parties
   b. extraordinary bailments

Bailment for Sole Benefit of Bailor

A bailment for the sole benefit of the bailor is created when goods are delivered to another who is to hold them or perform another service without receiving payment. This is a gratuitous bailment.

> **4.** Aviles obtained permission to tie his sailboat to Babson's dock for the day. Without Aviles's knowledge or consent, Babson and his friends used the sailboat. Did Babson have a legal right to do so?

Although consenting to perform services without payment, the bailee is not legally relieved of all obligations arising out of the bailment. In fact, an important obligation of the bailee is not to use the property without the bailor's permission except if the use is reasonable and necessary to protect or preserve the goods. In Problem 4, Babson is liable for any damages to the sailboat resulting from the unauthorized use of the boat.

The bailee also assumes responsibility for exercising reasonable care in protecting the property from harm or injury. In a **sole-benefit bailment,** *reasonable care* means the type of care an ordinary person would exercise in a similar situation. To judge whether a bailee has used reasonable care in a given situation, the courts have used some of these tests: (1) Was the bailment for the sole benefit of the bailor or the bailee? Obviously, a bailor who derives the entire benefit can't expect the bailee to exercise the same degree of care of the property as in a bailment for the bailee's sole benefit. (2) What is the value or cost of the bailed property? A string of natural pearls requires greater care than a bridge table. (3) What is the nature of the property? A breakable item requires greater care than a nonbreakable one.

In a bailment for the sole benefit of the bailor, the bailor is obliged to warn the bailee of any defects in the goods that are likely to injure the bailee. This includes not only defects known to the bailor but also defects that a reasonable investigation by the bailor would disclose. If a bailee suffers any harm as a result of defects that the bailor knew about or could have discovered after a reasonable examination, the bailor is liable.

Bailment for Sole Benefit of Bailee

When goods are delivered to a bailee for his or her sole benefit and convenience, a bailment for the sole benefit of the bailee arises. This usually results from borrowing articles from others.

> **5.**   Goldwyn loaned a video camera to Zhen, who was attending a World Series game. Without asking Goldwyn's permission, Zhen allowed her friend Riseman to use the camera. Riseman damaged the camera. Is Zhen liable for the damage?

As in a bailment for the sole benefit of the bailor, the absence of consideration in a bailment for the sole benefit of the bailee makes this a gratuitous bailment. However, the bailee does assume certain obligations as a result of the bailment. One of these is the duty to use the borrowed article in accordance with the understanding with the bailor. A bailee who borrows an article for personal use does not have the right to lend the article to others without the bailor's consent. In Problem 5, Zhen would be liable to Goldwyn for the damage to the video camera.

The bailee is also bound to take reasonable care of the article in accordance with the circumstances of the bailment. Of course, as noted earlier, an important circumstance relating to the bailee's liability is the fact that the bailment was for the bailee's sole benefit. Greater care is required of the bailee in this type of bailment than if the bailment were for the sole benefit of the bailor.

> Paxson borrowed Scalata's racing bike. After Paxson rode the bike, he left it in front of his garage overnight. In the morning, Paxson discovered that the bike had been stolen. Paxson failed to take reasonable care of the bike and is liable to Scalata for the loss.

As in a bailment for the sole benefit of the bailor, the bailor must warn a borrower of any known defect in the bailed article that is not known or

What to Do if You're in an Auto Accident

State law requires the driver of any vehicle involved in an accident to stop immediately at the scene of the accident. Leaving the scene without stopping may, under certain circumstances, result in serious consequences. After stopping, make sure that you're not blocking traffic any more than is necessary.

The following suggestions should help you to get through the early phases of the accident:

- Help the injured. If someone is seriously hurt, get an ambulance, a paramedic service, or a doctor immediately. Unless you're trained in first aid, don't try to treat the victim(s).
- Note the position of the vehicles involved in the accident. Use flares, flashlights, or your four-way flashers to warn other drivers of the accident.
- Notify the police. This should be done as soon as possible after determining whether there are any injuries.
- Exchange the required information. Give the other driver your name, address, and vehicle registration number, and show the driver your license. You're entitled to the same information from the other driver. Copy the other person's license number as well as his or her name and address.
- Don't comment on the accident. Don't admit that you were wrong or careless. There's time for that after the facts are determined and clearly indicate that you were wrong.
- Try to obtain witnesses. Get the names and addresses of as many witnesses as you can find. Ask them to write or at least state what they saw.
- Take notes. Draw a diagram of the scene, calculate distances, and note skidmarks, broken glass, relative positions of the vehicles, and the damage incurred. If you happen to have a camera with you, take a photo of the scene.
- Consult a doctor. Get an examination as soon as possible. Serious injuries don't always show up immediately.
- Inform your insurance company. If you fail to do so, the company may not honor your policy.
- Don't rush into a settlement. Select your own lawyer and don't yield to attempts to solicit you as a client.

obvious to the bailee. However, unlike a bailment for the bailor's benefit, a bailor is not required to examine the goods or to look for unknown defects. If a bailee is harmed because of a defect known by the bailor and not communicated to the bailee, the bailor is liable for damages.

> Starr loaned her car to Donsky. Starr knew that the brakes were defective but failed to warn Donsky. As a result of an accident caused by the faulty brakes, Donsky was injured. Starr is liable for failure to warn Donsky of the defective brakes.

Bailee's Right to Reimbursement

In a bailment for the sole benefit of the bailor, a bailee may incur reasonable expenses while taking care of the property for the bailor.

> Trevor asked Medina to take care of his dog for a few days. Just after the dog was delivered to Medina, it became sick and Medina took it to a veterinarian. The vet's bill for treatment amounted to $120, and Medina paid the fee. This fee is properly chargeable to Trevor.

Other examples of reimbursable expenses incurred by bailees include the cost of feeding the bailor's animal or the cost of renting a safe-deposit box while caring for securities of the bailor. If these expenses should have been paid by the bailor, the bailee is entitled to reimbursement. It's important to remember, though, that in a bailment for the sole benefit of the bailee, the bailee is entitled to reimbursement only for unusual or extraordinary expenses.

> Igoe borrowed Swenson's car and spent $14 of her own money to fill the car's gas tank. Igoe is not entitled to reimbursement for this ordinary expense because the bailment is for her sole benefit. If, however, the fuel pump broke through no fault of Igoe's and she had to buy a new one, Igoe would be entitled to reimbursement from Swenson for this extraordinary expense.

This chapter has covered sole-benefit bailments in some detail. Now let's move on to Chapter 25, where we'll study **mutual-benefit bailments.** These agreements deal with services, repairs, work for hire, storage, and pledges of security for loans.

Chapter 24 Review

"YOU BE THE JUDGE" REVIEW

Look again at the "You Be the Judge" cases given at the beginning of this chapter. Would you decide them differently now, after your study of the chapter?

Correct Decisions

1. Yes. Tavares is liable because he deviated from the contract to drive to Englewild. Therefore, he is guilty of a breach of contract. The fact that he exercised great care does not change the result.

2. Floyd must pay the bill. As a mutual-benefit bailee, the shop owner took reasonable care of the graduation dress and is not guilty of any negligence. Ordinarily, the shop owner's insurance would compensate Floyd for her loss.

UNDERSTANDING WHAT YOU HAVE READ

1. What type of transactions usually result in bailment relationships?
2. Discuss the importance of the requirement of delivery and acceptance of the property by the bailee.
3. Explain how a bailment may result without the owner's actual delivery of the goods to the bailee.
4. How would you distinguish between a bailment contract and a contract for the sale of goods?
5. How does an ordinary bailment differ from an extraordinary one?
6. Classify each of these as a bailment for the sole benefit of the bailor, a bailment for the sole benefit of the bailee, or a bailment for the mutual benefit of bailor and bailee; as an ordinary or extraordi-

nary bailment; and as a gratuitous or contract bailment.
   a. Vincola leaves his motorcycle at an auto mechanic shop for a tune-up.
   b. Saco lends her computer printer to a neighbor.
   c. Kline finds a suitcase belonging to Jason.
   d. Hartung borrows a card table and chairs from his neighbor, Menachi.
   e. Tan takes her telephone to a phone store for repair.
   f. Kaplan rents a room at the Seaside Inn for an overnight stay.
   g. Alou ships some furniture by train to a distant city.
7. a. In a bailment for the sole benefit of the bailor, under what circumstances

may the bailee use the bailed property? Give a specific example.

b. In a bailment for the sole benefit of the bailee, under what circumstances may the bailee use the bailed property? Give a specific example.

8. In bailments for the benefit of either party, what important factors are considered in determining whether the bailee took reasonable care of the bailed property?

9. In both types of bailments, the bailor is under a duty to warn the bailee of any defects in the article that are likely to cause harm to the bailee. In what respects does this duty differ in the two types of bailments?

10. Discuss the bailee's right of reimbursement in each of the following types of bailments: (a) a bailment for the benefit of the bailor and (b) a bailment for the benefit of the bailee.

BUILDING YOUR LEGAL VOCABULARY

From this list, select the legal term that belongs in the blank in each sentence below. Write your answers on a separate sheet of paper.

bailed property
bailee
bailment
bailor

contract bailment
extraordinary bailment
gratuitous bailment

mutual-benefit bailment
ordinary bailment
sole-benefit bailment

1. A bailment that arises without consideration is classified as a ▓▓▓▓▓▓▓▓▓.
2. The party to whom goods are transferred in a bailment is called the ▓▓▓▓▓▓▓▓▓.
3. If a bailee is subject to unusual legal duties, such as the duties of common carriers or hotelkeepers, the agreement between the parties is known as an ▓▓▓▓▓▓▓▓▓.
4. A bailment that benefits both parties to the agreement is called a ▓▓▓▓▓▓▓▓▓.
5. Goods that form the subject of a bailment are known as ▓▓▓▓▓▓▓▓▓.
6. If a bailee's duties are not unusual, the agreement between the parties is known as an ▓▓▓▓▓▓▓▓▓.
7. The party who delivers goods in a bailment agreement is the ▓▓▓▓▓▓▓▓▓.
8. A ▓▓▓▓▓▓▓▓▓ occurs whenever one party temporarily transfers possession of personal property to another party for a special purpose.
9. A bailment that relates to services purchased from a bailee is classified as a ▓▓▓▓▓▓▓▓▓.
10. A bailment that benefits only one of the parties to the agreement is called a ▓▓▓▓▓▓▓▓▓.

APPLYING LEGAL PRINCIPLES

1. Cole borrowed a ladder from her neighbor, Arlin.
   a. Why is this a bailment?
   b. What type of bailment is it?
2. Vierra left her cat with her friend Solomon while she went out of town for the weekend.
   a. Did this arrangement result in a bailment?
   b. If so, what type of bailment is it?
3. Murrell, who was planning a trip to Japan, stored his car with Martini Storage at a monthly charge of $85.
   a. Was this a bailment?
   b. If so, what type of bailment is it?
   c. Did Martini Storage obtain title to the car?
4. Ruchel borrowed a dozen sheets of binder paper from her classmate, Nuon. Ruchel promised to return a dozen sheets to Nuon the next day. Is this a bailment? Why or why not?
5. Tree Preservation Co. of Hillsdale agreed to spray O'Donnell's trees and shrubs for $75. Was this a bailment? Why or why not?
6. Brewer found a package lying on a public park bench. Is Brewer a bailee? Explain, giving a legal reason for your answer.
7. Itoh obtained permission to store his car in Marino's garage for a week without charge. Without Itoh's permission, Marino used the car. Although he exercised proper care, the car was damaged in a collision with another car. Is Marino liable to Itoh for the damages?
8. Assume in Problem 7 that Marino kept his garage locked but that vandals broke into the garage and damaged the car.
   a. Is Marino liable to Itoh for the damage?
   b. Would your answer in (a) be the same if Marino had left the garage door closed but unlocked?
9. Jarvis borrowed a lawnmower from his neighbor, Gillis. Jarvis was injured because of a defective blade in the mower. Gillis knew of the defect but had failed to warn Jarvis. Is Gillis liable to Jarvis?
10. Hobart borrowed Dyott's car to drive to Oxford, a neighboring city. Within ten miles of Oxford, the oil pump on the car broke. Hobart had the car towed to a nearby filling station. The total bill for towing and installing a new oil pump came to $210, which Hobart paid. Is Hobart entitled to reimbursement from Dyott?

ANALYZING COURT CASES

1. Winger borrowed a Piper-Pacer 125 plane from the Pottawatomie Airport and Flying Service to fly from Manhattan to Clay Center, Kansas. Winger's own plane was being repaired in Clay Center. Although a strong wind was blowing from the north, Winger attempted a landing at Clay Center—a landing with the wind instead of against it. As a result the plane failed to stop in the runway. It ran through a wire fence to a short distance south of the runway, causing damage of about $3,900 to the plane. In an action to recover for the damage to the plane, the flying service contended that Winger was responsible for the damages. It claimed that he had failed to exercise the high degree of care and diligence required by the circumstances. Do you agree with this contention? (*Pottawatomie Airport and Flying Service v. Winger*, 271 P. 2d 754)

2. The Home Savings Bank permitted Sherwood to deposit valuable papers and silverware in its vault for safekeeping. Sherwood was a customer of the bank, but the deposit of his valuables was without charge and purely for his accommodation. Subsequently, the bank building and its contents, including Sherwood's property, were destroyed in a fire. Was the bank liable as a bailee of Sherwood's papers and silverware? (*Sherwood v. Home Savings Bank*, 109 N.W. 9)

3. Mickey went to a store to make some purchases. He was carrying a briefcase containing a sum of money. Mickey left the briefcase on the loading platform at the store, where it was found by employees of the store and held for him until he picked it up the next day. When he opened the briefcase, Mickey found that the money was missing. He brought an action against the store, claiming that it had failed to take proper care and was liable as a bailee. The store, however, claimed that it had no knowledge of the contents of the briefcase and took reasonable care of it under the circumstances. Who is right? (*Mickey v. Sears, Roebuck & Co.*, 76 Atl. 2d 350)

CHAPTER 25

Services Purchased from Bailees

Think about these cases.
If you were the judge, how would you decide each case?

1

Pascal parked his car in the parking lot of a sports stadium. He locked the car and took the keys inside with him. There were no attendants stationed at the parking area. When he returned, he found that thieves had taken his car stereo and battery. Pascal claimed the stadium operators were responsible. Is he legally correct?

2

Halaby employed Nguyen to take care of and watch her apple orchard during the summer season. Nguyen was to receive a weekly salary of $215. Was this arrangement a bailment for hire?

319

MUTUAL-BENEFIT BAILMENTS

Many bailment relationships benefit both the bailor and the bailee. When you rent a truck, for example, the rental firm receives a benefit in the form of a money payment. You receive a benefit from the use of the truck. Since both parties receive benefits, a mutual-benefit bailment is created.

Mutual-benefit bailments always arise as a result of a contract. In a bailment of this type, the bailee has the right to the exclusive use of the article during the bailment period. The bailee must use the article only in accordance with the terms of the contract. When the goods are returned to the bailor or disposed of per the bailor's instructions, the bailment relationship ends. Mutual-benefit bailments may be classified as bailments for repairs and services, bailments for hire, bailments for storing and safekeeping, and bailments as security for loans (pledges).

CAREERS IN LAW

Clerk of the Court

Basically, the nature of a court and the kinds of proceedings it handles determine the duties of the clerk of the court. One duty common to most court clerks is responsibility for the court schedule, or docket. The clerk is consulted any time a judge needs to schedule a proceeding.

As a court employee, the clerk is responsible for making sure that the jury selection process flows smoothly. This person also keeps records of the exhibits entered as evidence in trial proceedings.

Although no standard exists among different courts for selection of court clerks, the requirements are usually quite extensive. Many applicants have college degrees or several years of experience working within the court system. Court clerks need to have knowledge of civil, criminal, juvenile, and statutory law. They must be familiar with legal terminology and procedures and often must pass a comprehensive written test to be considered for employment.

In some instances, court clerks are selected and paid by the county in which the court has jurisdiction, making the position technically civil service. In all cases, however, the clerk of the court serves "at the pleasure of the court," meaning these clerks must maintain the standards of the court to keep their jobs.

If you are well organized and enjoy being in charge or keeping schedules, consider a career as a clerk of the court.

Bailments for Repairs and Services

A mutual-benefit bailment arises when a person delivers an article to another to be repaired or serviced. The bailee may be required to furnish the materials for the repairs, or the original article may be returned to the bailor in an altered form. Regardless, a mutual-benefit bailment exists.

PROBLEM

> **1.** Nemirov left a grandfather clock at a furniture refinishing shop to have the clock restored to its original condition. Through no fault of the refinishing shop's owner, a fire damaged the shop and Nemirov's clock. Is Nemirov entitled to recover for the damage to her clock?

In a mutual-benefit bailment, the bailee is required to take reasonable care of the property. *Reasonable care* in a mutual-benefit bailment means the ordinary care a prudent person would take in similar circumstances. If the property in the bailee's care is damaged, stolen, or destroyed and the bailee has exercised ordinary care, the loss falls on the bailor. Thus, in Problem 1, Nemirov (the bailor) would have to stand the loss unless the risk was covered by insurance. The damage to the clock occurred without any fault on the part of the refinishing shop's owner. When property is accepted for repair, the bailee must exercise ordinary care and diligence in safeguarding that property. Failure to exercise the required skill will make the bailee liable for any loss or damage to the goods resulting from an unskilled performance.

The bailee who is not paid for services has a right to retain possession of the goods until reasonable charges are paid. Legally, this is known as a **right of lien.** A bailee cannot exercise a right of lien if he or she has previously agreed to perform the services on credit. Also, the right can't be exercised if the bailee voluntarily permits the bailor to regain possession of the property without payment of the charge.

The goods may be destroyed or stolen, through no fault of the bailee. In this event, the bailee is entitled to be paid for services performed on the goods before the destruction or theft took place.

EXAMPLE

> A jeweler cleaned and repaired Barboza's watch for a total charge of $48. Before Barboza picked up the watch, the shop was burglarized through no fault of the jeweler. Barboza's watch was one of the articles stolen. The jeweler is entitled to collect for the work performed prior to the theft.

Bailments for Hire

A mutual-benefit bailment for hire arises only by contract. Both parties benefit because the bailee receives the use of the hired or rented article and the bailor receives payment for its use. As in a bailment for repairs, the bailee has the right to exclusive use of the article during the contract period. In addition, the bailee must exercise ordinary care and use the article only in accordance with the terms of the contract.

2. Otis rented an electric drill from We-Rent-It, Inc. A defect in the mechanism caused the drill to go out of control and injure Otis's hand. Is We-Rent-It liable for Otis's injury?

In a bailment for hire, the bailor impliedly warrants that the article is reasonably fit for the purpose for which it is to be used. This implied warranty of fitness for the purpose is founded on the same principles as the fitness warranty discussed in the law of sales. The bailor is obligated to inspect the bailed article for dangerous defects. Then the bailor must either make the article safe for the bailee's use or warn the bailee of any unsafe condition. In Problem 2, We-Rent-It is liable for Otis's injury. The rental firm failed to warn Otis of the defect in the electric drill's mechanism.

In a mutual-benefit bailment for hire, the bailee is responsible for repairs to the bailed property resulting from ordinary wear and tear. Repairs that are extraordinary in nature and not due to the neglect or fault of the bailee are usually the bailor's responsibility.

A person who rents a car, in the absence of an agreement to the contrary, would be responsible for gas and oil consumed in using the vehicle. The bailor would be responsible for extraordinary repairs, such as replacement of the battery or carburetor.

Bailments for Storing and Safekeeping

When goods are delivered to a warehouse for storage or safekeeping, a mutual-benefit bailment is created. The bailee, or warehouse operator, is one who is in the business of storing goods for profit. As you learned in Chapter 18, the written contract between that person and the bailor is a *warehouse receipt.* The UCC states that in order to obtain possession of the goods, a bailee (or someone who has bought the goods from the bailee) must give the warehouse receipt to the bailor and pay the storage charges. If the proper charges aren't paid, the warehouse operator may exercise a right of lien and keep the goods until payment is received.

3. Neng, a warehouse operator, stored Arden's frozen cream pies near some frozen seafood. When the pies were delivered to Arden, she discovered that they smelled like fish and were unsalable. Is Neng liable to Arden?

A warehouse operator must exercise ordinary care of the bailed property while it is in his or her possession, in accordance with the circumstances of the bailment. In Problem 3, Neng failed to use ordinary care in safeguarding the pies from contamination. Therefore, he is liable in damages to Arden.

When money is deposited in a bank, the relationship between the bank and the depositor is one of debtor and creditor. It is not a bailor-bailee relationship. However, if a bank receives funds from or for a customer on an agreement to return the identical funds to the depositor, a bailment results. The funds are considered a special deposit.

Most courts regard a bank's rental of a safe-deposit box to a customer as a mutual-benefit bailment. However, because the box can't be opened without the use of two keys—one in the renter's possession and the other in the bank's possession—some courts hold that the relationship is one of landlord and tenant. The written contract between the bank and the

Disclaimer of liability by a possible bailee is not always permitted by law.

customer often defines the nature of the transaction and contains provisions regulating the bank's liability in case of loss.

If a person parks a car in a parking lot, locks the car, and keeps the keys, the transaction is usually regarded as a temporary lease of parking space, not a bailment. However, if the car is given to a lot attendant to park and return when it is called for, possession and control of the car rests with the parking-lot operator. In this case, a bailment contract is created. Garage keepers and parking-lot operators are not liable for the loss of articles left in cars stored with them unless they've been notified of the presence of the articles. Some proprietors of garages or parking lots disclaim liability for loss of cars by printing disclaimers on claim checks or posting disclaimer notices. Statutes in some states prevent these disclaimers where the proprietor failed to take proper care of the bailed article.

Bailments as Security for Loans

Personal property may be deposited with another as security for the payment of a debt or for the performance of an obligation. When this occurs, a mutual-benefit bailment known as a **pledge** is created. The subject matter of a pledge may be any personal property, including securities such as stocks and bonds. The person who borrows the money and transfers possession of personal property is known as the **pledgor.** The one receiving possession is known as the **pledgee.**

PROBLEM

> **4.** Costello, a dentist, pledged her X-ray machine with Gee, another dentist, as security for a loan of $3,000. The loan was to be repaid within six months, with interest at 11%. Without Costello's permission, Gee used the machine on his own patients. Did Gee have a legal right to do so?

Under the provisions of the UCC, the pledgee, as a mutual-benefit bailee, must take ordinary care of the pledged property. The property may not be used without the consent of the pledgor. Thus, Gee, in Problem 4, had no legal right to use Costello's X-ray machine. He would be liable in damages if the machine were damaged in any way. The pledgee has a lien on the property and is entitled to retain possession of it until the debt is paid. The pledgee is obliged to redeliver the pledged article to the pledgor on receiving payment of the debt.

If the pledgor fails to pay the debt, the pledgee has the right to sell the pledged property. Before the sale takes place, however, the pledgee must make a proper demand on the pledgor for payment and must give sufficient notice of the sale. If the amount received from the sale is greater than the debt (including interest and the expenses of the sale), the excess must be paid to the pledgor. If it is less than the debt, the difference must be paid by the pledgor. The pledgor has a right to redeem the property at any time before the sale takes place.

People whose business is to lend money at interest on a pledge of personal property (other than securities) are known as **pawnbrokers.** Because pawnbrokers often deal with financially unfortunate people, their business is usually regulated by statute. Statutes commonly provide that a pawnbroker must (1) obtain a license to do business, (2) post a bond, (3) keep required records of all pledges (for police purposes), (4) issue receipts, known as **pawn tickets,** for pledged goods, (5) charge only statutory rates of interest on loans, and (6) refrain from selling the goods of defaulting pledgors unless they remain unclaimed (in some states) for at least a year. The requirements for notice of sale and division of the proceeds are generally the same as for ordinary pledges.

As you can see, many of our ordinary daily activities make us parties to mutual-benefit bailments. Certain mutual-benefit bailments, however, are not standard or ordinary in the eyes of the law. In Chapter 26 you will study special bailment relationships—those in which hotelkeepers and carriers of goods and passengers serve as bailees.

Chapter 25 Review

"YOU BE THE JUDGE" REVIEW

Look again at the "You Be the Judge" cases given at the beginning of this chapter. Would you decide them differently now, after your study of the chapter?

Correct Decisions

1. No. If a person parks a car in a parking lot, locks it, and keeps the keys, the transaction is usually regarded as a temporary lease of parking space, not a bailment. Therefore, the stadium operators are not liable for the theft.

2. No. The subject matter of the contract was not personal property. The relationship was that of employer-employee, not bailor-bailee.

UNDERSTANDING WHAT YOU HAVE READ

1. How does a mutual-benefit bailment differ from a sole-benefit bailment?
2. How may mutual-benefit bailments be classified?
3. In the case of a mutual-benefit bailment, what is meant by *reasonable care?*
4. a. What is a bailee's lien?
   b. When does a bailee lose the right of lien?
5. In a mutual-benefit bailment for hire:
   a. What does the bailor warrant?
   b. What are the rights and obligations of the bailee?
6. What are the rights and obligations of a warehouse operator?
7. What is the legal relationship between a bank and its depositors?
8. a. How do most courts regard the legal relationship between a bank and a renter of a safe-deposit box?
   b. Mention one legal argument against this view.
9. Under what circumstances may parking a car result in a bailor-bailee relationship?
10. a. How does a pledge differ from other mutual-benefit bailments?
    b. Mention six provisions generally included in statutes regulating the business of a pawnbroker.

BUILDING YOUR LEGAL VOCABULARY

Choose the legal term that will correctly complete each definition below. Write your answers on a separate sheet of paper.

1. The written contract between a bailor and a person who is in the business of storing goods for profit is known as a/an
   a. simple contract.
   b. warehouse receipt.
   c. extraordinary bailment.
2. The party who transfers possession of personal property as security for the payment of a debt or performance of a duty is the
   a. pledgor.
   b. bailee.
   c. pledgee.
3. A person whose business is to lend money at interest on a pledge of personal property is known as a
   a. warehouse operator.
   b. pledgor.
   c. pawnbroker.
4. An unpaid bailee's right to keep bailed goods until payment for services or repairs is made is called a
   a. pledge.
   b. right of lien.
   c. bailment for hire.
5. A mutual-benefit bailment in which personal property is left with another as security for payment of a debt or for the performance of an obligation is known as a
   a. bailment for repairs or services.
   b. pledge.
   c. bailment for storing and safekeeping.

APPLYING LEGAL PRINCIPLES

1. Polk left a ring with a jeweler to have the stones reset. The jeweler stored the ring in a safe overnight. Thieves blew the safe open and stole the entire contents, including Polk's ring. Is the jeweler liable to pay Polk for the ring?
2. Flores rented a car from U-Drive-It Company. Although Flores exercised extreme care, the car was damaged as a result of another driver's carelessness. Is Flores liable for the damage to the rented car?
3. Gau rented an electric sander from Mastercraft for one week. Because of a defect in the tool, Gau was injured. In a suit against Mastercraft, Gau claimed that the firm was liable for his injury because the sander wasn't fit for its intended purpose. Is Gau legally correct?
4. Douyon left a chair with an upholstery shop to be reupholstered. When she called for the chair, Douyon was told that it had been destroyed in a fire after it had been reupholstered. The fire was

not caused by the carelessness of the upholsterer. A bill for $160 was handed to Douyon for the upholsterer's services.
   a. Is the upholsterer liable to Douyon for the value of the chair?
   b. Is Douyon liable to the upholsterer for the $160 charge?

5. Alberti parked his car in an outdoor enclosed parking lot. Attendants were on duty at the lot at all times, day and night. One of the attendants collected a parking fee of $5 from Alberti and gave him a numbered claim check. Alberti was also required to leave his keys in the car and the doors unlocked. When Alberti called for the car later, he learned that it had been stolen. Is the owner of the parking lot liable to Alberti?

6. Braz took her car to an auto repair shop to have some engine work done. When she called for the car, the shop manager refused to release it until Braz paid the repair bill, amounting to $225. Braz claimed that she was entitled to her car even though the bill had not been paid. Is she legally correct?

7. Assume that, in Problem 6, the repair shop released the car to Braz without receiving payment for the repairs. What are the legal rights of the parties?

8. Caplan pledged his wristwatch with a pawnbroker as security for a loan of $50. Caplan failed to repay the borrowed money. What are the pawnbroker's legal rights? What are Caplan's legal rights?

9. Ellner stored her furniture in Danh's warehouse at an agreed charge of $85 per month. Ellner paid one month's storage in advance but didn't make any more payments. After three months, Ellner called for her furniture. Danh refused to release it to Ellner until the two months' charges were paid. Was Danh within his rights in refusing to release the furniture? Why or why not?

10. Kaminsky, a kennel operator, agreed to keep and care for Briscoe's dog while Briscoe spent a year in Europe on business. Briscoe agreed to pay a fee of $1,800 for the service. After one month, annoyed by the dog's lack of discipline, Kaminsky enrolled the animal in an obedience school. When Briscoe returned, Kaminsky handed her a bill for $1,800 plus expenses of $720: $420 for dog food and $300 for obedience-school tuition. The contract had said nothing about feeding expenses or training. Briscoe offered Kaminsky a check for $1,800, but Kaminsky refused to take it or to release the dog. What are the rights of the parties?

ANALYZING COURT CASES

1. Aircraft Sales & Service Company ran a flight school in which students were trained as airplane pilots. Gantt, a student at the school, was making a practice flight when he discovered that the controls weren't operating properly. Gantt tried to land, but the plane crashed and he was injured. An inspection of the wrecked plane disclosed that a screwdriver was lodged between the floorboard and the bottom surface of the plane. The screwdriver could have come into contact with the controls. Gantt sued the company to recover for his injuries. Should he succeed? (*Aircraft Sales & Service Company, Inc. v. Gantt*, 52 So. 2d 388)

2. Starita left his car with Campbell, a parking-lot owner. Starita paid the required parking fee, received a numbered parking ticket, and was told to leave the car unlocked with the key in the ignition. Campbell failed to tell Starita that the lot would be left unguarded after 10 P.M., or whatever hour he, Campbell, chose to leave the lot. When Starita called for the car at 10:30 P.M., he found the car missing and Campbell gone for the night. What are Starita's legal rights against Campbell? (*Starita v. Campbell*, 52 A. 2d 303)

3. Lippincott Distributing Company, wholesale grocers, delivered a large quantity of groceries to Union Grocers, Inc. The delivery was made subject to an agreement that Lippincott was to be paid as and when the groceries were sold. The agreement also stated that title to the groceries was not to pass until they were sold by Union Grocers. On receiving the shipment, Union Grocers placed the goods in a warehouse and received a negotiable warehouse receipt made out to its order. Later, Union Grocers pledged the negotiable warehouse receipt with Peoples Commercial and Savings Bank as security for a loan of $28,250. When Union Grocers failed to repay the loan, the bank seized the shipment of groceries in the warehouse. The bank also refused to surrender the goods to Lippincott. Lippincott sued the bank, claiming that it had never parted with title to the goods. How should the court decide the case? (*Lippincott Distributing Company v. Peoples Commercial and Savings Bank*, 30 N.E. 2d 691)

CHAPTER 26

Special Bailees— Carriers and Hotelkeepers

YOU BE THE JUDGE

Think about these cases.
If you were the judge, how would you decide each case?

1

You left your suitcase with the desk clerk at the Memphis Hotel and told him you would register as soon as you made an important phone call. When you returned to the desk to register, you were told your suitcase had been stolen. You, as a hotel guest, claim the hotel is liable for the suitcase and its contents. Is the hotel liable?

2

Your friend Lenihan, an electronics assembler, drove his car to and from work five days a week. Usually, three of Lenihan's co-workers rode with him each day. Each of them paid $1 a day to help cover Lenihan's expenses. Did this arrangement make Lenihan a public carrier?

WHAT IS A CARRIER?

Transportation of goods and people is one of the most important of our economic activities. Any individual or firm engaged in this activity is known as a **carrier.**

PROBLEM

1. Mallory Steamship Co. operated a fleet of cargo ships between New York City and various South American ports. The company carried freight for any person or firm that might wish to employ it. What kind of carrier is Mallory?

PROBLEM

2. Lena Trucking, Inc. operated several delivery trucks for the transportation of women's apparel. The firm was under contract with several clothing manufacturers to make local deliveries for them and not for any other manufacturers. What kind of carrier is Lena?

Shipping lines that offer their services to the public are considered common carriers.

Carriers who will accept any kind of goods for transport, offering their services to anyone, are known as **common carriers.** Railroads, shipping lines, trucking firms, and airlines are leading examples of common carriers. In contrast, carriers who agree to transport goods under individual contracts but do not offer their services to the public are known as **private** or **contract carriers.** Moving-van companies, individual truckers, and private delivery services transport goods as private or contract carriers. The distinction between common and private carriers is important because a common carrier is a special or extraordinary bailee with special rights and duties. A private carrier who transports goods for others is a mutual-benefit bailee. In Problem 1, Mallory Steamship Co. is a common carrier. In Problem 2, Lena Trucking, Inc. is a private carrier.

The party who delivers goods to a carrier for transportation is known as the shipper or **consignor.** The party to whom the goods are to be delivered is known as the **consignee.**

Obligations of Common Carriers

Common carriers of goods must furnish facilities that are adequate for transporting goods in the ordinary course of business. They must receive and carry the goods of anyone who applies for their services. However, consider the facts in this problem.

PROBLEM

> **3.** McVay delivered a truckload of uncrated office furniture to the freight agent of a railroad. McVay asked to have the furniture shipped to a city 250 miles away. Was the railroad required to ship the goods?

The carrier is excused from its duty to serve all customers if the shipper fails to comply with the carrier's reasonable rules. Those rules usually apply to the following goods:

1. *Goods that the carrier is not equipped to transport.* A carrier is not required to transport cattle, for example, if it has no cattle cars suitable for the purpose. Likewise, a shipper doesn't have to transport perishable fruits and vegetables if it has no refrigeration facilities.

2. *Goods that are not offered for shipment at the proper time and place.*

3. *Goods that are not properly crated and packed.* Thus, in Problem 3, the freight agent could properly refuse to accept McVay's uncrated furniture for shipment.

4. *Goods that are dangerous or injurious to public health.* A carrier is not obligated to transport dynamite, nitroglycerin, or similar goods.

If the shipper complies with the carrier's reasonable rules and the carrier then refuses to accept the goods, the carrier will be liable to the shipper for damages resulting from the refusal.

Rights of Common Carriers

Common carriers who transport goods across state lines (interstate commerce) are regulated by the **Interstate Commerce Commission (ICC).** This federal regulatory agency has the authority to fix the freight rates that carriers may charge for interstate shipments. The ICC also requires that carriers provide transportation facilities adequate for the communities they serve and continuous and uninterrupted service to all who apply. Carriers who transport goods within state lines (intrastate commerce) are regulated by state railroad, public utility, or public service commissions. These commissions perform the same functions in regulating intrastate shipments as the ICC performs in interstate shipments.

PROBLEM

4. The Midland & Western Railroad notified Gata, the consignee, of the arrival of a shipment of goods. The notice contained a request that Gata unload the freight car within 24 hours. The document also stated that failure to unload the goods would result in a special charge for detention of the freight car. Gata failed to comply with the notice and called for the goods three days later. Was she liable for the special charge?

In addition to governmental regulation, common carriers may make necessary and reasonable regulations for the conduct of their business. First, they may charge rates for their services that yield a fair profit on the investment (subject, of course, to a regulatory commission's approval). Second, they may impose a special payment, known as a **demurrage charge,** on either the consignor or the consignee for failure to load or unload goods within a reasonable time. Thus, in Problem 4, the Midland & Western Railroad was within its legal rights in imposing a demurrage charge on Gata. Third, they may enforce a **carrier's lien** on the goods in their possession to secure the payment of outstanding charges. In Problem 4, the carrier has a lien on the goods if either the transportation or service (demurrage) charges are not paid. If a carrier extends credit for the payment of its charges or voluntarily gives up possession of the goods, it loses its right of lien. A carrier's lien may be enforced by public or private sale of the goods.

Liabilities of Common Carriers

While goods are in transit, they are under the complete control of the carrier. Because of the great power it has over the goods in transit, the carrier is liable as an *insurer* (a guarantor of the safety of the goods).

PROBLEM

> **5.** A freight car containing a shipment of crated machinery was destroyed by fire while en route. The fire was caused by a bolt of lightning that struck the car. Was the carrier liable for the loss?

There are several exceptions to the general rule that a carrier is liable as an insurer of goods in transit. A common carrier is not liable for losses caused by any one of the following:

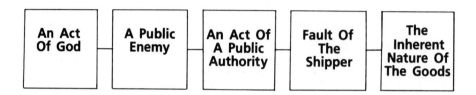

| An Act Of God | A Public Enemy | An Act Of A Public Authority | Fault Of The Shipper | The Inherent Nature Of The Goods |

1. *An act of God.* Loss or damage to goods as a result of an act of God is due to natural causes that humans could neither foresee nor avoid. Floods, earthquakes, tornadoes, and lightning are considered acts of God. Loss or damage to goods as a result of a fire caused by lightning, as in Problem 5, is an act of God. The carrier is not liable for the resulting loss. However, even though a loss is due to an act of God, the carrier will be liable if it could have prevented the loss through proper care and diligence.

EXAMPLE

> A common carrier delays shipping some goods temporarily left at a railroad siding in a city threatened by floods. If the goods are damaged by the flood waters, the carrier is liable for failing to take measures to prevent the loss.

2. *Act of a public enemy.* A common carrier is not liable for loss caused by the seizure or destruction of goods by the military forces of an opposing government. The term "public enemy" also includes pirates at sea. However, a carrier is liable for any loss caused by ordinary robbers, mobs, rioters, or strikers.

3. *Act of public authority.* If the goods are taken from the carrier by public authorities, the carrier is not liable. For example, health officers might remove a contaminated shipment of cheese or fish. The carrier also is not liable if goods are stopped in transit by the shipper.

4. *The fault of the shipper.* A common carrier is not liable for loss due to (a) improper packing by the shipper, (b) fraudulent labeling of the contents or concealment of the true value of the goods, and (c) improper addressing so that goods are lost.

EXAMPLE

In shipping goods by freight, Feld stated that their value was under $100 in order to get a lower rate. The goods were destroyed in transit. Feld filed a claim for $500, the true value of the goods. The carrier is liable only for the stated value of $100 because Feld concealed the true value from the carrier.

5. *The nature of the goods.* The nature of the goods may cause losses for which a common carrier is not liable. For example, fruits and vegetables may decay, liquids may evaporate or ferment, or animals may be injured while in transit. All of these are natural events for which a common carrier is not liable.

Limitation of a Carrier's Liability

A carrier may, by contract, limit its liability as insurer of the safety of the goods. The contract between the shipper and the carrier is in the form of a bill of lading. Therefore, the limitation of the carrier's liability is usually included in this document.

Although a carrier may *limit* its liability for loss of the goods, it is not allowed to *exempt* itself from liability resulting from negligence.

6. Arkin shipped goods worth $500 under an agreement that limited the carrier's liability for loss to $250. Because of this limitation, Arkin paid a lower shipping rate. The goods were lost in transit. Was Arkin bound by the carrier's limitation of liability?

Any clause in a bill of lading that limits the carrier's liability must be fair and reasonable. It must be based on a valuable consideration, such as the lower shipping rate mentioned in Problem 6. Because Arkin received a lower rate, he is bound by the contract provision limiting the carrier's loss liability to $250. The carrier must give the shipper a chance to ship the goods without any limitation of liability. In that case, though, the carrier may charge the regular or an even higher shipping rate.

A shipper who suffers a loss is usually required to file a claim for damages, in writing, with the carrier. It is commonly stated in the bill of lading that such a claim must be filed within nine months after delivery of the goods or after a reasonable time for delivery.

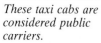

These taxi cabs are considered public carriers.

Termination of a Carrier's Liability

The liability of a common carrier as an insurer begins on receiving the goods for immediate transportation. If the carrier delays shipping the goods for some reason, its liability for loss or damage of the goods is that of an ordinary bailee in a mutual-benefit bailment.

> **7.** Marr received a notice of arrival of goods consigned to him from Zinman Co. of Salt Lake City, Utah. Ten days after receiving the notice, Marr went to the freight depot to remove the goods. He was told that they had been destroyed in a fire. Was the common carrier liable?

A common carrier also may be a mutual-benefit bailee of the goods after they have reached their intended destination. This occurs when the consignee fails to remove the goods within a reasonable time after receiving a notice of arrival from the carrier. Thus, in Problem 7, the carrier is liable for the destruction of the goods only if it has failed to use the ordinary care required of a mutual-benefit bailee under the circumstances of the bailment.

WHO ARE PUBLIC CARRIERS OF PASSENGERS?

A party who transports all people from one place to another for hire is a **public carrier.** The people being transported are legally known as **passengers.** Many carriers serve both as public carriers of passengers as well as common carriers of goods.

> **8.** Gimenez owned a minivan that could carry eight people. She agreed to drive several co-workers to their office every weekday for a weekly fare of $5 per person. Gimenez could choose her passengers. Was she a private or a public carrier?

> **9.** Parven, a licensed cab driver, hung a "Public Cab" sign in his car window. Then he parked at the local airline terminal. Is Parven a private or public carrier?

Public carriers of passengers must transport all people who request their services. They may not discriminate except that they are not required to carry anyone who is objectionable. Objectionable people are those who are likely to annoy or endanger the lives of the other passengers or those who refuse to pay the required fare. Railroads, ferries, buses, taxicabs, ships, and airlines are examples of public carriers of passengers.

A private carrier, also known as a contract carrier of passengers, is a party who transports people for hire under individual contracts. This type of carrier may select those with whom he or she wants to contract. Gimenez in Problem 8 is a contract carrier. A private carrier also may be a company that transports its own employees and doesn't serve others. For example, some firms operate shuttles to transport their employees from bus or train terminals to their workplace. Since Parven, in Problem 9, holds himself ready to transport anyone who may apply, he is considered a public carrier of passengers.

Who Are Passengers?

When a person seeks transportation and enters the carrier's premises, a legal relationship of carrier and passenger exists. The relationship exists even though the person hasn't yet bought a ticket or paid the required fare.

10.   Watley bought a train ticket at the train terminal and then left the terminal to do some shopping. While returning to the terminal, Watley was struck by a car and injured. Was Watley a train passenger at the time of the accident?

11.   Suri boarded a passenger train in order to sell refreshments to the passengers. She did not have the railroad company's permission to board the train. Is she a passenger?

A person who travels on a free pass issued by the carrier is regarded as a passenger. However, a person who enters a carrier's vehicle without permission, in order to sell goods to the passengers, is not legally regarded as a passenger. In Problem 10, Watley was not a passenger at the time he was injured. He had left the carrier's premises, and the accident happened in a place not subject to the carrier's control. In Problem 11, Suri is not a passenger. She entered the carrier's vehicle without permission and did not intend to become a passenger.

Liabilities for Passengers' Injuries

A public carrier of passengers must exercise reasonable care as soon as passengers enter the carrier's premises. Once the passengers are aboard, the carrier must take the utmost care to protect them from injury. A carrier who is guilty of even slight negligence will be held liable for passengers' injuries. In the absence of negligence, however, the carrier will not be liable for the passengers' injuries. Passengers, unlike goods, have an intelligence and free will of their own. For the safety of passengers, therefore, the carrier is not liable as an insurer, as in the case of goods. If a passenger's negligence causes him or her to be injured, the carrier cannot be held liable.

EXAMPLE

> Molina was riding to school on a public bus. As the bus neared the school, Molina jumped off without waiting for the bus to come to a stop. She fell and was badly hurt. The carrier is not liable for Molina's injuries because she was hurt as a result of her own negligence.

In some states, railroads may limit their liability for passenger injuries if the passenger pays less than the regular fare for the trip. The ticket or pass expressly provides that because of the reduced fare, the passenger assumes the risks of accident to his or her person or property. A number of states, however, refuse to allow the carrier to escape liability, even when transportation is at a reduced rate.

A railroad is a public carrier of passengers.

Liability for Passengers' Baggage

The contract to carry a passenger includes the duty of transporting a reasonable amount of baggage without extra cost.

PROBLEM

12. Stevens planned a weekend trip to the mountains. He packed a number of articles in a suitcase and checked it with the carrier. He received a baggage check as his receipt. When he reached his destination, Stevens's suitcase couldn't be found. Is the carrier liable?

A passenger's baggage consists of goods the traveler needs for pleasure, convenience, comfort, or for the ultimate purpose of the trip. Only the articles carried for the passenger's *personal use* are regarded as baggage. Articles such as sales samples or securities carried by a passenger are not properly considered baggage. What is or isn't baggage is sometimes a question of fact to be determined by a jury from the circumstances of a particular case.

If a passenger's baggage is checked, the carrier's liability is the same as that of an insurer of goods. The carrier may limit its liability for the loss of or damage to the baggage. However, the limitation of liability must be brought to the attention of the passenger. Typically, a passenger is notified of a carrier's limitation of liability by means of a notice posted on the back of the passenger's ticket, as shown in Figure 26.1. In problem 12, the carrier would be liable to Stevens for the suitcase and any goods in it that properly constituted baggage.

Figure 26.1
An Airline's Notice of Limitation of Liability

ADVICE TO INTERNATIONAL PASSENGERS ON LIMITATION OF LIABILITY

Passengers on a journey involving an ultimate destination or a stop in a country other than the country of origin are advised that the provisions of a treaty known as the Warsaw Convention may be applicable to the entire journey, including any portion entirely within the country of origin or destination. For such passengers on a journey to, from, or with an agreed stopping place in the United States of America, the Convention and special contracts of carriage embodied in applicable tariffs provide that the liability of certain carriers, parties to such special contracts, for death or personal injury to passengers is limited in most cases to proven damages not to exceed U.S. $75,000 per passenger, and that this liability up to such limit shall not depend on negligence on the part of the carrier. The limit of liability of U.S. $75,000 above is inclusive of legal fees and costs except that in case of a claim brought in a state where provision is made for

separate award of legal fees and costs, the limit shall be the sum of U.S. $58,000 exclusive of legal fees and costs. For such passengers traveling by a carrier not a party to such special contracts or on a journey not to, from, or having an agreed stopping place in the United States of America, liability of the carrier for death or personal injury to passengers is limited in most cases to approximately U.S. $10,000 or U.S. $20,000.

The names of carriers, parties to such special contracts, are available at all ticket offices of such carriers and may be examined on request. Additional protection can usually be obtained by purchasing insurance from a private company. Such insurance is not affected by any limitation of the carrier's liability under the Warsaw Convention or such special contracts of carriage. For further information please consult your airline or insurance company representative.

NOTICE OF BAGGAGE LIABILITY LIMITATIONS

Liability for loss, delay, or damage to baggage is limited unless a higher value is declared in advance and additional charges are paid. For most international travel (including domestic portions of international journeys) the liability limit is approximately $9.07 per pound for checked baggage and $400 per passenger for unchecked baggage. For travel wholly between

U.S. points federal rules require any limit on an airline's baggage liability to be at least $1250 per passenger. Excess valuation may be declared on certain types of articles. Some carriers assume no liability for fragile, valuable or perishable articles. Further information may be obtained from the carrier.

> **13.** Suppose that Stevens, in Problem 12, had taken his suitcase with him and placed it above his seat. The suitcase was then stolen from above the seat. Is the carrier liable for the loss?

If the passenger's baggage is not checked but is kept in the passenger's custody, the carrier's liability is not that of an insurer. The carrier is responsible for the loss of baggage in the passenger's custody only when the loss is caused by the carrier's negligence in providing reasonable protection of the baggage.

WHO ARE HOTELKEEPERS AND HOTEL GUESTS?

Hotelkeepers are extraordinary bailees because of the special nature of their business. That business requires them to serve the public without discrimination. Specifically, a **hotelkeeper** is someone regularly engaged in the business of providing living accommodations to all *transient* people who arrive in proper condition and who are willing to pay for the services furnished. A hotelkeeper may operate a hotel, motel, bed-and-breakfast inn, tavern, or a similar establishment. A **guest** is a transient who seeks temporary lodging at the hotel. The term "temporary lodging" as applied to transients implies either a short or a long stay, but one that may be terminated at any time. People who enter a hotel to attend a dance, banquet, or meeting, or to use facilities supplied to the public without charge, are not guests.

> **14.** Lightfoot was an army officer permanently stationed at Fort Lane in Virginia. His family lived at the Hotel Lorraine in Cleveland, Ohio. Lightfoot visited his family frequently, staying for short periods of time. During one of his visits, Lightfoot's military uniform and his wife's jewelry were taken from the family's hotel suite. Was the hotel liable for the loss?

A guest or a transient seeks temporary lodging at a hotel. An individual who contracts for more permanent accommodations, usually for a definite period of time, is known as a **boarder** or **lodger.** Legally, it is important to distinguish between the relationship of hotelkeeper and guest and boarding-house keeper and boarder. A hotelkeeper must usually receive all transients or guests. A boardinghouse keeper, however, is free to accept or reject people in accordance with his or her own judgment. Of course, this right is subject to the provisions of the **Civil Rights Act** of 1964, which prohibits discrimination against anyone because of race, creed, color, or national origin. A hotelkeeper is an extraordinary bailee with a special liability for the guests' property. A boardinghouse keeper is a mutual-benefit bailee, liable only if reasonable care is not taken of the lodger's belongings. In Problem 14, since Lightfoot's stay was of a temporary nature, he is regarded as a guest. The hotel is responsible for the loss of his uniform. However, since his wife is a permanent resident or boarder, the hotel is not liable for the loss of her jewelry unless failure to exercise reasonable care can be shown.

> **15.** Noda arrived at a local airport after a flight from Chicago. She gave her luggage to a porter from the Langley Hotel who met her at the airport. After transacting some business near the airport, Noda went to the hotel to register. She was informed that her luggage hadn't arrived at the hotel and was lost. Was the hotel liable?

A transient who requests accommodations and signs the register immediately becomes a guest of the hotel. One may become a guest before arriving at the hotel, however, as in Problem 15. Noda became a guest of the hotel as soon as she delivered her luggage to the hotel porter. Therefore, the hotel was liable for the value of her belongings.

Once established, the relationship of hotelkeeper and guest continues until the bill is paid and the guest departs, or until the guest ceases to be a transient and becomes a lodger or boarder.

Obligations of Hotelkeepers

The legal responsibilities of a hotelkeeper fall into three broad groups:

1. *To receive all proper persons who apply for accommodations if they are available.* Failure to do so may result in liability for damages to the person or persons rejected. However, a hotelkeeper has a right to exclude those who are unfit, such as intoxicated people, known criminals, or people who aren't dressed in accordance with the hotel's reasonable requirements.

2. *To exercise reasonable care in providing for the personal safety of the guest.* If a guest is injured while in the hotel, the hotelkeeper is not liable unless personally at fault. The hotelkeeper is not liable for an injury caused by a fire in the hotel if the hotelkeeper wasn't negligent in starting the fire.

> **16.** Metaxas, a guest at the Noble Hotel, notified the management that her wristwatch had been stolen from her hotel room. Was the hotel liable for Metaxas's loss?

Should You Buy Travel Insurance?

Your Great-Aunt Emily arrives in Vienna, but the airline mistakenly sends her luggage to Rome. Or suppose Aunt Emily gets sick or hurt while overseas and doesn't have enough cash or traveler's checks to pay for medical care. Does her medical insurance cover overseas illnesses? Would she be protected by a travel insurance policy bought from a travel agent before she left home? Surely, if Aunt Emily is on Medicare, no payment will be made for medical bills incurred outside the United States, except for limited payments for Canada and Mexico. And if she bought travel insurance, the extent of her coverage would be determined by the type of policy she purchased.

Generally, there are three types of travel insurance, sold primarily through travel agents: accident and medical policies, baggage policies, and trip cancellation or interruption policies. Travel agents report that 90% of travelers who buy special accident and medical plans for overseas travel already have their own health insurance policies that cover overseas travel. They also report that interest in baggage insurance is decreasing because more people are fully protected against baggage loss through their homeowner's insurance policies. Obviously, these people don't need the extra coverage. Yet trip cancellation is the fastest growing area of travel insurance. A simple illustration will show why it is so popular.

Let's say that Cory, an uninsured traveler, plans to fly to Mexico on June 15. A death in the family occurs on June 12, however, and Cory is unable to take her trip. If Cory cancels the trip at such a late date, she'll get only a partial refund from the carrier or tour agency. However, if Cory had bought cancellation insurance, the insurance company would have reimbursed her for the full amount of her down payment or for the cost of the trip, whichever was paid in advance.

At any rate, in the words of a veteran travel agent, "Purchase of travel insurance gives one peace of mind."

3. *To safeguard the guest's property.* As an extraordinary bailee, the hotelkeeper is an insurer of the goods placed in his or her care by a guest. This liability originated in early times when traveling was dangerous. The highways were infested with thieves who often operated with the help of innkeepers. In Problem 16, the Noble Hotel, as insurer, would be liable for the value of Metaxas's watch.

A hotelkeeper is not liable for property losses due to an act of God, the actions of a public enemy, the nature of the goods, or the fault of the guest.

EXAMPLE

> Berdeja, a guest of the Arlington Motel, left his room unlocked. As a result, all of his personal belongings were stolen from his room. Since the loss was due to Berdeja's carelessness, the motelkeeper was not responsible for the loss.

Delivery of baggage to a porter makes one a guest of the hotel.

In most states, hotelkeepers may limit their common-law liability as insurers. They may do this either by contract with the guest or by complying with special statutes. These statutes usually require the hotelkeeper to maintain a safe where guests may deposit their money, jewels, or other valuables for safekeeping. The hotelkeeper must post notices on the doors

of the rooms and in other public rooms of the hotel stating that such safekeeping facilities are provided for the guests' use. If the guests fail to deposit in the hotel safe the type of valuables described in the notice, the hotelkeeper is relieved from liability where the loss is not due to the hotelkeeper's fault. Usually, guests aren't required by these statutes to deposit with the hotelkeeper articles necessary for daily use. These goods include clothing, watches, luggage, and similar property.

A silver comb-and-brush set was stolen from the room of a motel guest. The motelkeeper was held liable for the loss as an insurer. The set was not regarded as jewelry, which must be checked, but as an article needed for everyday use.

Unless a special agreement is made for a higher valuation, a dollar limit usually applies to the hotelkeeper's maximum liability for loss of valuables deposited in the hotel safe. Statutes that limit the hotelkeeper's liability do not apply to people who aren't guests of the hotel.

A Hotelkeeper's Right of Lien

A hotelkeeper may require payment in advance for accommodations furnished to guests. The usual practice, however, is to present a bill when the guest checks out and to receive payment then.

17. Gulden, a registered guest of the Alton Hotel, prepared to leave without paying her bill. The hotel manager refused to let Gulden take her luggage out of the hotel. Did the manager have a legal right to do so?

If a guest fails to pay, a **hotelkeeper's lien** may be placed on the property the guest brought into the hotel. This lien gives the hotelkeeper the right to hold the guest's property until the bill is paid, as in Problem 17. The lien doesn't apply, however, to clothing worn by the guest. The right of lien is lost if the hotelkeeper allows the guest to take the property away without paying the bill. A similar lien is now given by statute to boardinghouse keepers in some states. If a guest fails to pay within a reasonable time, the hotelkeeper may sell the guest's property and pay the hotel charges.

Sales of goods and purchases of services (bailments) form a major part of our economic activity as consumers. However, consumers commonly make another type of purchase with respect to property. That purchase is insurance, which we will study next in Unit 6.

Chapter 26 Review

"YOU BE THE JUDGE" REVIEW

Look again at the "You Be the Judge" cases given at the beginning of this chapter. Would you decide them differently now, after your study of the chapter?

Correct Decisions

1. Yes. One may become a hotel guest even before registering. This may occur when a person delivers luggage to the hotel porter or desk clerk.
2. Lenihan is not a public carrier because he doesn't offer his services as a carrier to anyone who applies. "Where the owner of a motor car accepts a sum of money which is in effect a share of the expenses of a trip taken for the mutual advantage of the travelers . . . and where the journey is incidental to the main business or purpose of the operator of the vehicle," the owner cannot be regarded as a common carrier of passengers or even as a contract carrier. (Based on: *Chauncey v. Kinnaird*, 279 S.W. 2d 57)

UNDERSTANDING WHAT YOU HAVE READ

1. What is the legal difference between a common and a private carrier?
2. List three regulations that common carriers usually follow when conducting their business.
3. a. List three duties for which common carriers are held responsible.
   b. A common carrier is under a duty to serve all applicants for its services without discrimination. Provide four instances where a carrier is excused from this duty.
4. How may a common carrier limit its liability for loss or damage to the goods it transports?
5. How does a public carrier differ from a contract carrier of passengers?
6. What is a public carrier's liability for passenger injuries
   a. when a passenger is being transported on a reduced-fare ticket?
   b. when a passenger is being transported on a free pass?
   c. when a person boards the carrier's vehicle without permission in order to sell refreshments?

7. What is a public carrier's liability for loss of baggage
   a. when passengers check their baggage with the carrier?
   b. when passengers keep their baggage in their custody?
8. List three of a hotelkeeper's obligations to the general public.

9. List four exceptions to the rule that a hotelkeeper is legally regarded as an insurer of the guests' property.
10. How may a hotelkeeper's common-law liability as insurer of a guest's property be limited?

BUILDING YOUR LEGAL VOCABULARY

Match each of these legal terms with its correct definition from the list that follows. Write your answers on a separate sheet of paper.

carrier's lien	demurrage charge	lodger
common carrier	guest	passenger
consignee	hotelkeeper's lien	private carrier
consignor		

1. a person who is transported by a public carrier
2. a party to whom goods are transported by a carrier
3. the right to keep a guest's property until the charges for living accommodations are paid
4. a party who offers services for transportation of goods to anyone
5. a service fee imposed on a consignor or consignee for failure to load or unload goods within a reasonable time
6. a person who contracts for fairly permanent living accommodations, usually for a definite period of time
7. the right to retain possession of goods that have been transported until the transportation charges are paid
8. the party who delivers goods to a carrier for transportation
9. a party who agrees to transport goods or people under individual contracts but doesn't offer services to the general public
10. a guarantor of safety

APPLYING LEGAL PRINCIPLES

1. Breitner, a cotton farmer, asked the M & H Railroad Company to provide a freight car in which to ship baled cotton. The company denied Breitner's request because he had refused to grant the company a right-of-way through his farm for a new railway line. As a result, the company had been forced to obtain the right by legal process. May the railroad company refuse to give Breitner service?

2. A firm that manufactured explosives offered a quantity of its goods, carefully packed, to a common carrier for shipment. The carrier refused to accept the goods. Must the carrier accept the shipment?

3. While in transit, a shipment of skateboards was broken open by thieves and 50 of the boards were stolen. The consignee filed a claim with the railroad for the shortage. The railroad claimed that it used every precaution to safeguard the goods and that it wasn't liable for the theft. Was the railroad company liable for the loss?

4. The Iowa Central Railroad was transporting cattle for Randers. Government health officials seized and destroyed some of the cattle because they were diseased. Was the carrier liable for the loss?

5. A common carrier accepted a shipment of goods in Chicago for delivery to a buyer in Boston. While the goods were in transit, they were destroyed by a fire caused by the negligence of an employee of the carrier. Should the carrier be held liable for the value of the goods?

6. The Ghazi Contracting Company used a tugboat to transport its workers to an island where a hospital was under construction. Was the company a public carrier of passengers?

7. Lema, a news vendor, boarded a train without the railroad's permission in order to sell newspapers to the passengers. Was Lema a passenger?

8. Morales rented a room at the Parker Hotel for three months at a rental of $315 per week. His brother, who was in town for an overnight stay, rented a room at the same hotel at the rate of $70 a night. Are both of these men guests of the hotel?

9. Sandino, a hotel guest, caught her foot in a hole in the stairway carpet. She fell and was injured. The defect in the carpet was known to the hotel manager because several guests had complained about it earlier. Is the hotel liable for Sandino's injuries?

10. Ting was a guest at a hotel. While she was out of her room, a thief picked the lock on the door and stole Ting's luggage. The luggage contained $600 worth of clothing and personal items. Is the hotel liable?

11. LePage was a guest of the Crescent Hotel. The hotel provided a safe for the deposit of valuable articles. Proper notice of this service was posted on the door of each hotel room, per state law. LePage ignored this notice and kept possession of his valuables. They were stolen from his room during the day. Is the hotel liable?

12. Tessier failed to pay his motel bill when he checked out of the Motel Continental. The motel manager seized Tessier's luggage and refused to give it up until Tessier paid the bill. Did the manager have a legal right to do so?

ANALYZING COURT CASES

1. Hoffman was a guest at a hotel owned by the defendant, Louis D. Miller & Co. For safekeeping, Hoffman deposited a diamond ring valued at $1,800 with the desk clerk. The hotel, in compliance with a state law, had posted notices that limited its liability for articles accepted for safekeeping to $500 unless a special written agreement was made with the hotelkeeper. The ring was lost through the negligence of the hotel's employees. Hoffman sued, claiming that the hotel was liable for the full value of the ring. The proprietor of the hotel maintained that the hotel's liability was limited by statute to $500. Whose claim is legally correct? (*Hoffman v. Louis D. Miller & Co.*, 115 A. 2d 689)

2. Hallman and his family were driving to Florida. They stopped for the night at the New Colonial Hotel in Washington, D.C. When Hallman registered with the desk clerk, he asked if the hotel had parking facilities. The clerk told Hallman that the bellhop would take care of the car. The bellhop drove the car to an open parking lot, independently owned and operated by Federal Parking Services, Inc. Later, the bellhop gave Hallman a parking-lot receipt on which the name of the lot appeared, together with the stamped name, "New Colonial." At the parking lot the car was locked by an attendant, who kept the keys. The next morning, Hallman found that a side window of the car had been broken and the glove compartment had been forced open. Personal property valued at $557 had been removed from the car. Hallman sought to hold the hotel liable as insurer of his family's belongings. The hotel claimed that it was not negligent and was not responsible for the loss. Is Hallman's claim legally correct? (*Hallman v. Federal Parking Services, Inc.*, 134 A. 2d 382)

3. Ozark White Lime Co. shipped lime from Arkansas by the St. Louis–San Francisco Railway. The shipment was stopped at McBride, Oklahoma, by a landslide that blocked the tracks. The car containing the shipment was placed on a spur line several feet lower than the main tracks. The lime was then destroyed by flood waters from the Grand River. The lime company sued the railroad for the loss. At the trial, the lime company showed that the railroad had had an engine available to take cars from the spur track up to higher ground and that it had taken other cars beyond the reach of the flood waters. The railroad failed to explain why it had not moved the lime company's shipment. Will the lime company be successful in its suit? (*St. Louis–San Francisco Railway Co. v. Ozark White Lime Co.*, 9 S.W. 2d 17)

UNIT 6

INSURANCE

CHAPTERS

350

LEARNING OBJECTIVES

After you have read this unit, you should be able to:

- Explain the nature and purpose of insurance.

- Show that you understand the basic principles of law underlying the insurance contract.

- Describe the kinds of protection given by personal and property insurance contracts.

- Identify different types of life insurance policies and the contractual rights and duties of the parties.

- List the various types of auto insurance available.

- Explain the concepts of financial responsibility, no-fault auto insurance, and compulsory auto insurance.

- Describe the various forms of social insurance that protect citizens.

CHAPTER 27

Nature and Types of Insurance

Think about these cases.
If you were the judge, how would you decide each case?

1

Wyzinski bought a car when she turned 16. After an auto accident in which she was driving her car, Wyzinski filed a claim with her insurance company for the damages to the car. The company tried to deny the claim on the grounds that Wyzinski was an unreasonable risk because of her age. Was the firm's claim correct?

2

When Vao's fourteen-year-old son took up competitive platform diving, Vao wanted to take out a life insurance policy on his son. Does he have an insurable interest in his son's life?

WHAT IS INSURANCE?

Before studying the various kinds of insurance contracts, it is important to understand the purpose of insurance. Everyone constantly faces risks. A serious accident or an illness may result in a disability that prevents someone from earning a living. Death may remove the family breadwinner. Fire may destroy homes and personal belongings. An auto accident may involve considerable financial loss.

1. The Leite family consists of Mr. and Mrs. Leite and their two young children. Both Mr. and Mrs. Leite are employed, although Mr. Leite's income is the family's primary source of support. The family owns a home and two cars. The Leites are worried about their future. They are afraid that Mr. Leite may suddenly become unable to work and that a fire could damage their home and cause considerable loss. What advice would you give the Leites?

Insurance, of course, can't prevent these risks from becoming realities. The best it can do is soften the blow when it falls. It does this by providing an **indemnity**—a money payment—to make up for what was actually lost. That is the real purpose of insurance—protection against financial loss. In other words, the purchase of insurance transfers the risks to someone else, usually an insurance company organized for that purpose. Insurance companies are able to assume these risks and to compensate in case of loss because they do the same thing for many people. The company receives contributions from each person who buys insurance. These contributions are adequate to cover the losses of a few contributors. In this chapter and in Chapters 28–30, we'll study the various types of insurance that people purchase directly and individually. In Chapter 31 we will look at social insurance. Social insurance is partially purchased by taxpayers and workers and partially provided by the government and employers.

Insurance may be defined as a contract in which one party, for a consideration, agrees to **indemnify** (protect from harm) another for stated losses. In Problem 1, the Leites would be financially unable to cover their risks with their own funds. Therefore, they should take out insurance to provide for the family in case of emergency.

THE INSurance CONTRACT

Like other contracts, the insurance contract must contain the essentials of mutual assent, competent parties, legal purpose, and consideration. In many states, these requirements are modified. In some states, for example, a minor fifteen or older may enter into a binding life insurance contract.

LAW IN THE NEWS

Insurer Halts Coverage of Football Players

(Reprinted courtesy of *The Boston Globe*)

The major insurer of professional and college athletes has declared a moratorium on writing policies on football players this year, according to the cover story in the Dec. 1 issue of New England Business magazine.

Worcester-based State Mutual Life Assurance Company of America and American Sports Underwriters Inc. of Woburn provide coverage for more than 75 percent of the franchises and 42 percent of the athletes employed by those clubs.

Edward A. Dipple, president of American Sports Underwriters, says his company has "stepped away" from writing contracts on professional football players because of increasing injury rates, the use of steroids and the insurers' resulting failure to make underwriting profits, the story says.

Hazards in the insuring process, increasingly important in player contracts, are the heavier and faster players,

who cause more severe injuries, an inability to find an underwriter who will write a disability contract that is worthwhile and, at the college level, premiums that are affordable to institutions wishing to avoid lawsuits when a college athlete is disabled, the story says.

Lifestyles also play a role, according to the story. Says Dipple, "Is (the player) a drug taker, a drinker, a driver of fast cars?"

Mutual Assent

To purchase insurance, the buyer usually tells an agent of the insurance company the amount and kind of insurance desired. The buyer also gives the agent any other information the company needs to investigate the risk before assuming it. Thus, the person who desires insurance protection makes an offer to the company, in either written or oral form. Before a valid insurance contract arises, there must be an acceptance of this offer.

PROBLEM

2. Brennan phoned the local agent of an insurance firm and ordered an auto insurance policy. After giving the agent all the necessary information, Brennan was told that the company would insure the car. That night, because of Brennan's negligence while driving the car, he seriously injured a pedestrian. Does Brennan have any claim against the insurance firm for protection?

In property insurance, the agent or broker of the insurance company may orally accept a buyer's offer on behalf of the firm. The agent usually is given authority to bind the insurance firm during the period between making the application and the acceptance of the application by the firm. Therefore, in Problem 2, the insurance agent's oral acceptance of Brennan's offer created a binding contract over the phone. Normally, however, the agent binds the company by issuing a memorandum form to the applicant. This is a temporary acceptance of the risk. It is effective from the time the form is made out until the issuance of the formal policy, or until the company refuses to issue the policy. This memorandum is called a **binder.** The use of a binder is recommended as a means of avoiding disputes.

Competent Parties

Usually, anyone who may enter into an enforceable contract may obtain insurance. The party who takes out insurance is called the **insured.** The party who agrees to issue the insurance is called the **insurer** (the insurance company). The party who will receive benefit from the insurance contract is the **beneficiary.**

Legal Purpose

The subject matter of a contract of insurance is the assumption of a risk and the payment of compensation to one who has an **insurable** (financial) **interest** in the property or life insured. If the financial interest is not present, the contract is a mere wager and is illegal.

Consideration

The **premium** is the consideration the insured pays to the insurer in return for acceptance of the risk. The premium may be paid in one payment or in installments. The nature and character of the risk determine the amount of the premium in property insurance. For life insurance, the premium amount depends primarily on the age and general health of the insured at the time the contract is made.

Form of Contract

The written contract of insurance is known as a **policy.** Except in a few states, an insurance contract does not have to be in writing to be enforceable. But the ordinary insurance contract is a written contract. When the amount to be paid in the event of a loss is fixed on the face of the policy and doesn't depend on determination after loss, the policy is called a **valued policy.** (A life insurance contract is an example of a valued policy.) If the amount to be paid is to be determined by **appraisal** (evaluation) after the loss has occurred, the policy is called an **open policy.** (A fire insurance contract usually is an open policy.)

Figure 27.1
Principal Kinds
of Insurance
Contracts

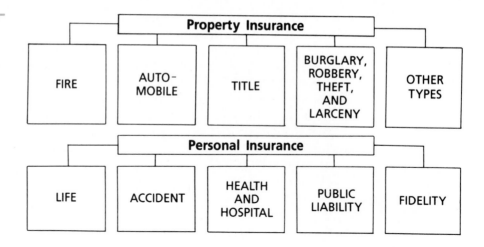

Merlo bought a mobile home and took out insurance in the amount of $50,000 to cover loss from fire and other perils. A fire caused damage to the home amounting to $6,000. Merlo will collect only this sum—her actual loss—although the policy was written for $50,000.

KINDS OF INSURANCE CONTRACTS

There are many kinds of insurance contracts. Coverage is available for almost any risk that may arise in personal or business life. As shown in Figure 27.1, the principal kinds relate either to property or personal protection. In later chapters, each type and the risks assumed by insurance firms will be discussed in more detail.

Insurable Interest in Property

To have a right to the benefits of insurance, one must have an insurable interest in the person or property that is insured. Otherwise the contract would be a wager, and in the event of loss the insured would obtain nothing under the policy.

3. Feigelman, a builder, agreed to construct a cottage, for which he was to be paid $52,000. All the materials were to be furnished by the builder. May Feigelman insure the materials while the cottage is being built?

Any person who would suffer *direct financial loss or liability* if certain property were damaged, destroyed, or lost has an insurable interest in the property. That person need not be the owner. For example, a bailee has an insurable interest in property. One who has a mortgage or lien on property has an insurable interest in the property for the protection of the mortgage or lien. One who sells goods under an installment contract has an insurable interest in the goods until the conditions of the sales contract have been met and title has passed. In Problem 3, Feigelman does have an insurable interest in the materials. If they were damaged or destroyed, he would have to replace them at his own expense. Thus, he may purchase a builder's risk policy of insurance. That policy will protect Feigelman from loss or damage to the materials to be used in the construction of the building.

Insurable Interest in a Life

Every person has an insurable interest in his or her own life. Anyone can insure his or her own life, and the insurance can be made payable to anyone the person chooses.

PROBLEM

4. To meet the claims of her creditors, VanDorn borrowed $20,000 from Tien. To protect her interest, Tien thought it wise to take out an insurance policy on the life of VanDorn. Does Tien have an insurable interest in VanDorn's life?

One person has an insurable interest in the life of another if the first person would suffer a financial loss if the second person died. In Problem 4, it is clear that Tien would suffer a financial loss if VanDorn died before the $20,000 was repaid. It follows, therefore, that a creditor has an insurable interest in the life of a debtor. But a creditor may not take out insurance on the life of a debtor if the amount of insurance is unreasonably greater than the amount of the debt. If that were the case, the policy would be a gamble or wager and void. A wife and a husband each has an insurable interest in the life of the other. Parents have insurable interests in the lives of their minor children. Employers have insurable interests in the lives of their employees. And businesses have insurable interests in the lives of their executives.

Duration of Insurable Interest

In *property* insurance, the insurable interest of the one who will benefit from the insurance must exist *at the time the loss occurs.* As soon as the insured's title to the property is transferred to another, the insurable interest ceases.

Parents have insurable interests in the lives of their minor children.

EXAMPLE

> Hitt had insured his car against loss by fire. He sold the car to Brimmer. Two days after the sale, some wiring in the engine caught fire and the car was destroyed. Hitt can't collect on his insurance policy because his insurable interest ceased when title to the car passed to Brimmer.

When insured property is sold, the insured should ask the insurance company to cancel the policy and refund the premium for the unexpired portion of the term.

In *life* insurance, it is sufficient that the insurable interest existed at the time the contract *went into effect.* The insurable interest does not have to exist at the time of loss. Suppose in Problem 4 that VanDorn had paid her entire debt to Tien and then died. Tien would be entitled to the benefits of the policy since she had an insurable interest in VanDorn—the loan —when the policy was issued.

Now that you understand the purpose of insurance and who may purchase it, let's look at the various kinds of insurance in more detail. In Chapter 28, we'll begin our detailed study with property insurance.

Chapter 27 Review

"YOU BE THE JUDGE" REVIEW

Look again at the "You Be the Judge" cases given at the beginning of this chapter. Would you decide them differently now, after your study of the chapter?

Correct Decisions

1. No. Wyzinski is able to contract for insurance since she has an insurable interest in the car. Since the company was willing to issue the policy to her, it must indemnify her for the loss.

2. Yes. Parents have insurable interests in their minor children.

UNDERSTANDING WHAT YOU HAVE READ

1. What is the purpose of insurance?
2. What is property insurance? List four types of property insurance.
3. What is personal insurance? List four types of personal insurance.
4. a. What is a premium?
   b. How is the premium determined?
5. a. What is a binder?
   b. What is the effect of a binder? Give an example.
6. a. What is an open policy? Give an example.
   b. What is a valued policy? Give an example.
7. Must an insurance contract be made in writing?
8. Give an example of an insurable interest in property.
9. Who may have an insurable interest in the life of another?
10. Must an insurable interest exist at the time of loss to entitle the insured to recovery under any kind of insurance?

BUILDING YOUR LEGAL VOCABULARY

From this list, select the legal term that belongs in the blank in each sentence below. Write your answers on a separate sheet of paper.

binder	insurance	policy
indemnify	insurer	premium
indemnity	open policy	valued policy
insurable interest		

1. The party who agrees to issue insurance is the ||||||||||||||||||||||.
2. A |||||||||||||||||| is a written contract of insurance.
3. An insurance agent's temporary acceptance of risk is issued in a memorandum known as a ||||||||||||||||.
4. |||||||||||||||||| is a contract in which one party, for a consideration, agrees to indemnify another for stated losses.
5. A |||||||||||||||||| is an insurance contract that carries on its face the amount to be paid in the event of a loss and doesn't depend on determination after loss.
6. To protect another for specific losses is to |||||||||||||||||| that party.
7. The |||||||||||||||||| is the consideration the insured pays to the insurer in return for acceptance of the risk.
8. A financial interest in the property or life of another is called an ||||||||||||||||||||.
9. When the amount to be paid is determined by appraisal after the loss has occurred, the insurance contract is known as an ||||||||||||||||||||.
10. The money payment provided by insurance to make up for what was actually lost is an ||||||||||||||||||||.

APPLYING LEGAL PRINCIPLES

1. Claudio called an insurance agent and asked that his new car be insured against loss by collision, fire, and theft. Claudio told the agent the value of the car and described it fully. The agent stated that the matter would be taken care of at once. That night, the car was stolen. Is Claudio protected by insurance?

2. Haug insured the life of Amico, her partner, and obtained a policy from an insurance company. A year later, the partnership was dissolved. Six months after that, Amico died. Can Haug collect the insurance if she has paid all of the premiums?

3. Benoit bought a car from Harrison Motors under a conditional sales contract. Before completing her payments, Benoit took out a collision, fire, and theft insurance policy on the car. Did she have a right to do so?

4. Assume in Problem 3 that Harrison Motors insured the car against collision, fire, and theft while it was in Benoit's possession. Did it have a legal right to do so?

5. The Berks took out a fire insurance policy on their house. Before the policy expired, the Berks sold their house to Macy. When a fire destroyed the house, the Berks sought to collect on the policy. Were they legally entitled to do so?

6. Ferraz obtained a $100,000 life insurance policy on her husband's life. After she had paid premiums for four years, the husband died. When Ferraz sought to collect on the policy, she was told that she had no insurable interest in her husband's life and that the policy was void. Was she entitled to collect on the policy?

7. Antell made an offer to buy a certain house. After his offer was accepted but before title to the house was transferred to him, he obtained a fire insurance policy on the house. Sometime later, the house was damaged by fire. The insurance company refused to pay for the loss, claiming that Antell had no insurable interest when the policy was issued. Was the company legally correct?

8. Wong loaned $5,000 to Janar, a friend. Because Janar's job as a construction worker carried high risks, Wong was nervous about being repaid. He took out an insurance policy on Janar's life in the amount of $25,000. When Janar died in a construction accident, the insurance company denied Wong's claim. Was the insurance company justified in doing this?

9. Biancarlo bought a special insurance policy to protect her jewelry against loss. The policy was designed to replace the items if they were stolen. A fire, however, ruined several of the pieces of jewelry. The insurance company agreed to have the damaged jewelry cleaned and reset or repaired but would not replace it. Is Biancarlo entitled to collect the full value of her policy?

10. Janeiro played professional football. When he was sidelined for the season because of a back injury, the team management filed an insurance claim for the payment of the disabled player's wages. Can the team management collect?

ANALYZING COURT CASES

1. A number of people contributed to the common fund of a certain burial association. The association issued a membership certificate to each contributor. The certificate stated the sum payable for funeral expenses on the death of any member. The Superintendent of Insurance in the state in which the association was located contended that the association had failed to comply with the state's insurance laws. The burial association maintained that its activities did not constitute an insurance business. Who is right? (*Indiana v. Willets*, 86 N.E. 68)

2. Baynes phoned Venturo, an agent of Bond Indemnity Insurance Co., and made a contract for car insurance. The policy was to cover bodily injury liability to third persons. While driving her car shortly thereafter, Baynes struck and injured Pell. Pell sued Baynes but couldn't collect a judgment he recovered in the action. Pell then sued Bond Indemnity, who denied liability on the ground that there was no written contract of insurance. The firm also claimed that its agent, Venturo, had no authority to make an oral contract of insurance over

the telephone. Do you agree with this contention? (Based on: *Bankers Indemnity Insurance Co. v. Pinkerton*, 89 F. 2d 194)

3. Galati rented a car from an auto leasing agency for a period of two years. The rental contract contained a provision that gave Galati an option to buy the car at an agreed price, less a portion of rent paid. In addition, Galati was required to insure the car in his own name and for his own benefit. Accordingly, he insured the car with New Amsterdam Casualty Co. Eight months later, with the consent of the leasing company, Galati exercised his option to buy the car and immediately sold it to his aunt. The auto insurance policy, however, was neither assigned nor canceled. Two days after she had taken possession of the car, the aunt was involved in an accident, and the car was demolished. Galati sued the insurance company on the policy, and the company set up lack of an insurable interest as a defense. Was the defense proper? (*Galati v. New Amsterdam Casualty Co.*, 381 S.W. 2d 5)

CHAPTER 28

Property Insurance

YOU BE THE JUDGE

Think about these cases.
If you were the judge, how would you decide each case?

1

The Schalls insured their house against loss by fire. A clause suspended the coverage if the house remained unoccupied for more than 60 days. The Schalls were gone for 71 days, during which the house was unoccupied. Shortly after, the house was damaged by fire. The insurance company claimed the policy was void. Is the firm legally correct?

2

Chesbro Paint Co. stored a highly explosive chemical in its warehouse. Although the warehouse and its contents were insured, the paint company had failed to inform its insurance company of the presence of the explosive chemical. Can the insurance company deny the claim?

363

NATURE OF PROPERTY INSURANCE

Under property insurance contracts, the insured is indemnified for losses due to fire, breakage, theft, and other damaging and destructive causes.

PROBLEM

> **1.** Tillman insured his office building and its contents, valued at $210,000, with Empire Insurance Company. Six months after the insurance policy was issued, Tillman's building was damaged by fire. The amount of the damage was $24,000. Tillman claims that the insurance company must pay him the amount on the face of the policy ($210,000). Is his claim legally correct?

In property insurance, the insured is entitled only to be placed in the position that existed before the loss occurred. Thus, the insured is compensated for the *exact* amount of a loss, regardless of the value of the property. In Problem 1, Tillman's claim is incorrect. He is legally entitled to recover only $24,000, the amount of the actual damage to his office building. However, if the insured's actual loss exceeded the amount of insurance carried, the insurer would be liable only for the face amount of the policy.

KINDS OF PROPERTY INSURANCE

In Chapter 27, we classified property insurance as (1) fire, (2) automobile, (3) burglary, robbery, theft, and larceny, (4) title, and (5) other types. These other types include marine, inland marine, and casualty insurance.

Fire Insurance

Most states have adopted standard fire insurance policies. These policies protect the insured against direct damage by fire and lightning. For an additional premium, the insured may obtain **extended coverage.** This coverage gives protection against loss caused by windstorm, hail, explosion, riot, smoke, and falling aircraft. The standard fire insurance policy will be discussed in more detail later in this chapter.

Automobile Insurance

A typical auto insurance policy covers property damage, bodily injury, and collision. It also covers loss or damage due to fire, lightning, theft, glass breakage, robbery, and pilferage. Auto insurance is discussed in Chapter 29.

Burglary, Robbery, Theft, and Larceny Insurance

The usual homeowner's or renter's policy covers any loss suffered by the insured or a member of the insured's household. However, the policy does not cover property owned by a person who is not related to the insured and who pays board or rent to the insured. The policy also doesn't cover loss of motorcycles, aircraft, cars, samples of goods for sale, animals, or loss by fire. Protection usually covers losses caused by the theft of property that the insured has placed in a bank, safe-deposit box, or public warehouse for safekeeping.

Title Insurance

Title insurance protects owners of realty from claims made against them, arising out of a defective title to the real estate.

Other Types

Marine insurance protects the owner of a boat for vessel, cargo, and other property loss or damage caused by storms and other perils of the sea.

Inland marine insurance protects the insured from all loss or damage to personal property, except loss from risks specifically excluded by the policy. The cause of the loss and place where it occurred are immaterial. Inland marine policies are generally known as **floaters** or **all-risk policies.** The term "all-risk" is used because the cause of loss is not significant when filing a claim under inland marine insurance. These policies cover loss of property such as furs, jewelry, laundry, goods in transit, musical instruments, neon signs, cameras, goods sold on the installment plan, and personal effects carried by travelers.

The term **casualty insurance** usually relates to commercial policies. However, it is also a sort of "umbrella" term used to refer to the liability portion of a homeowner's, renter's, or auto owner's insurance policy. These policies indemnify the insured against expenses resulting from bodily injuries or property damage suffered on the insured's property or as a result of an auto accident involving the insured's car. We will discuss bodily injury and property damage insurance further in Chapter 29.

STANDARD FIRE INSURANCE POLICIES

Risks Covered

Standard fire insurance contracts protect the insured from loss caused directly or proximately (very near) by a "hostile" fire. A hostile fire is a fire that has escaped its natural bounds. A fire insurance policy won't protect the insured from damage to furniture that is placed too close to a stove and becomes scorched. A fire that remains in a stove is considered a "friendly" fire. But if the furniture begins to blaze, the fire is then considered to have escaped from the stove to the furniture. Thus it has become a hostile fire, and recovery under the policy would be permitted.

Under a policy of fire insurance, the insured is indemnified for what is actually destroyed by a fire or by falling parts of a burning building.

Payment also may be made for cracking, scorching, and soot damage caused by a hostile fire; for damage from the water and chemicals used to put out a fire; and for loss due to the removal of property from the burning building or from premises endangered by the fire. The insured, however, must take all reasonable precautions and do everything possible to limit the property damage.

Under an ordinary fire insurance policy, the insured is not indemnified for indirect or remote fire damage. For example, losses from theft or from confusion of property removed from the burned premises are remote or indirect losses. These may not be covered by the insurance contract.

Removal of Property

The policy usually states that personal property located at a certain place will not be covered if it is moved to a new location. In order for the insurance to remain in force, a **notice of removal** must be given to the insurer. Also, the insurer's consent to the removal must be obtained.

Vacancy

When premises are unoccupied or vacant, the risk of loss increases. The policy generally provides that coverage will be suspended when the premises are left vacant or unoccupied beyond a period of 60 consecutive days. **Vacant premises** are those from which the customary furniture or other contents have been removed. **Unoccupied premises** are temporarily uninhabited, but they still contain the personal property they normally contain. If the premises are allowed to be vacant in violation of the policy, there is a breach of a material condition. The insurer doesn't have to pay for any loss, even though the breach in no way caused the loss. The coverage is reinstated, however, when the premises are occupied.

If these premises are vacant, the risk of loss increases.

Homeowners' and Tenants' Responsibility for Injuries to Third Persons

As a homeowner, you generally have a legal duty to protect anyone who comes onto your property from injury. As the renter of a home, your duty is basically the same. Legally, however, a renter or tenant of an apartment has a slightly different position. If a guest is injured in the lobby, hallway, or elevator of an apartment house, the guest has an action against the apartment building's owner. But the moment the guest enters the host's apartment, the latter may or may not be responsible for the guest's injuries. Responsibility for the injuries will be determined by the circumstances of each case. A wise precaution for those who own or rent dwellings of any kind is to get liability insurance!

You may be surprised to learn that under most conditions, owners and renters are not legally responsible for injuries to guests. This is because the law considers a guest to be on an equal footing with the members of your family. The guest must accept your home or apartment as he or she finds it, subject to the ordinary hazards of modern life. So if a guest trips over a carpet that is in good condition, the courts would be likely to decide that the accident was the guest's fault and deny any recovery. However, if there is an unusual danger—a broken tile or step, an uninsulated wire, and so forth—that you are aware of, you must warn the guest of the danger.

How about business visitors or "invitees," such as mail carriers, delivery people, and repair people? They have a right to expect that you have taken "reasonable care" to make your premises safe for them. Accordingly, you must inspect the premises for dangers and warn them of all that you discover. But you are not responsible if you made a careful inspection and found nothing.

To uninvited guests such as trespassers, you owe almost no protection. They enter your property at their own risk. However, if you were to see a trespasser approaching an open sewer, it would be your duty to warn that person of the danger.

Children have been favorites of the law since time began. They are deemed not to have the good judgment of adults. A host may be held strictly accountable for any injuries suffered by children on the host's property.

Additional Insurance

The standard fire insurance policy does not prohibit additional insurance covering the same property. The company limits the amount of such insurance, though, by means of a **rider.** A rider is a statement attached to and made part of the policy. The right to limit other insurance is deemed necessary in order to prevent overinsurance. Suppose, for instance, that an insured takes out a fire insurance policy with each of two different companies, covering the same property. In the event of a loss by fire, each company will pay its proportionate share of the loss.

> Urakami insured her home against fire with Continental Insurance Co. for $50,000 and with Empire Insurance Company for $30,000. Her home was damaged by fire to the extent of $4,800. Continental Insurance will pay $3,000 (5/8 of $4,800) as its proportionate share of the loss. Empire Insurance will pay $1,800 (3/8 of $4,800) as its share of the loss.

Increase in Risk of Loss

If the risk of loss increases by any means within the control or knowledge of the insured, without the insurer's consent, the insurance is suspended until the increased risk is removed. The insurer is not liable for a loss that occurs while the increased risk exists, even though the fire was not caused or affected by the increased risk. Thus, if the insured wants to keep flammable material on the premises, thereby increasing the risk of loss, the insurance company's written consent must be obtained.

Cancellation of Policy

Standard policies provide that either party may cancel a fire insurance contract at any time. If the policy is canceled by the insured, a refund of the premium paid for the unexpired term of the policy may be made. This refund is based on rates given in a table included in the policy. If the insurer cancels the policy, the insured is entitled to the full amount of the unearned premium.

> Ebersole paid a premium of $450 on a three-year fire insurance policy. At the end of the first year, he canceled the policy. He is entitled to receive something less than $300 at the rate stated in the policy. If the cancellation were at the company's request, Ebersole would receive exactly $300 as a return premium.

Coinsurance

Coinsurance provisions require the insured to carry an amount of insurance that totals a certain percentage of the value of the insured property. If the property is insured for less than the required amount, the insured must sustain a portion of any loss that occurs.

A merchant insured her goods with AB Insurance Co. for $24,000. The policy contained a coinsurance clause providing that the merchant must at all times carry insurance that covers 80% of the value of the merchant's stock. The insurance could be carried either with AB Insurance or another insurance company. A fire occurred when the merchant's stock of goods was valued at $40,000. The merchant had not increased her insurance. If the actual loss amounted to $16,000, the merchant would be able to collect only $12,000 from the company. She herself would have to sustain $4,000 of the loss.

$$\left(\frac{\text{Insurance Carried}}{80\% \text{ of Value of Property}} \times \text{Fire Loss} \right) = \left(\frac{\$24,000}{\$32,000} \times \$16,000 \right) = \$12,000$$

If the merchant's stock were completely destroyed, she would collect only the face amount of insurance carried ($24,000).

Assignment of Policy

The personal element is important in property insurance. The risk assumed by the insurer depends to a great extent on the character and conduct of the insured. An insurance company will refuse a policy to a person whose reputation is unsatisfactory. Therefore, a property insurance contract usually can't be assigned before a loss occurs without the insurer's consent.

The Crandalls sold their house to Fortes for $125,000. The Crandalls transferred their fire insurance policy on the house to Fortes without obtaining the consent of the insurance company. If a fire occurs while Fortes owns the house, the company would not be liable for the damage. The insurer's consent must be obtained to make the assignment valid.

Notice and Proof of Loss

Fire insurance policies usually provide that immediate written notice must be given to the insurer in the event of a loss. Immediate notice is interpreted to mean notice within a *reasonable time,* considering all the circumstances.

In addition to notice, the insured is required within a specified period (usually 60 days) to furnish the company with proof of loss. The insurer may expressly or by actions waive the failure of the insured to give notice of loss.

> A fire in Jia's home on New Year's Day caused damage amounting to $6,000. Jia notified the company of the fire loss on April 15 of that year. Jia's claim may be disallowed by the company for failure to give notice within a reasonable time.

Subrogation

Policies usually require the insured to assign to the insurer all rights of recovery against any party for loss or damage to the extent of the insurer's payment for damages. This is known as the **right of subrogation,** and it exists in property insurance. Suppose, for example, that a third party's wrongful or negligent act results in a fire that damages insured property. The insurance company indemnifies the insured for the loss. The company then has the right to stand in the place of the insured in recovering from the party whose wrongful act caused the loss.

> A fire insurance company paid World Steel Products $5,000 for fire damage caused by the negligence of employees of a chemical company located next door. On payment of the claim, the fire insurance company is subrogated to the rights of World Steel Products against the owner of the chemical company. The insurance firm may sue the owner of the chemical company for negligence in causing the loss.

Additional Coverage

For an additional premium, the insured may obtain additional protection against loss. This might include protection against loss from windstorm, hail, explosion, riot and civil commotion, fallen aircraft, vehicle damage, and smoke damage. The added protection is provided by means of an **indorsement,** or rider, attached to the fire insurance policy. The indorsement is called an **extended-coverage indorsement.**

Representations of the Insured

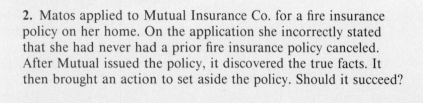

2. Matos applied to Mutual Insurance Co. for a fire insurance policy on her home. On the application she incorrectly stated that she had never had a prior fire insurance policy canceled. After Mutual issued the policy, it discovered the true facts. It then brought an action to set aside the policy. Should it succeed?

A fire loss must be reported immediately.

The applicant for insurance must in good faith reveal all material or important facts concerning the risk. This enables the insurer to decide whether to accept the application and issue the policy. If the applicant conceals or misrepresents any material facts, innocently or intentionally, the insurer may avoid the policy. In Problem 2, the fact that Matos had a previous fire insurance policy canceled is material to the risk. The misrepresentation misled the insurance company, regardless of the intent of the insured. The company could avoid the policy.

If a statement made by an applicant is not material to the risk, the misrepresentation will have no effect on the insurance contract. Also, a statement won't affect the validity of the contract if it is based on the applicant's belief, opinion, or judgment rather than on fact. A representation is not part of the policy itself. It is a separate matter that merely leads up to or induces an insurer to issue a policy.

Warranties

When a statement of fact is made a *part* of the insurance contract, it is considered to be a *warranty*. Legally, a warranty is presumed to be material to the risk assumed by the insurance company.

PROBLEM

3. A fire insurance policy contained a clause providing that gasoline would not be stored on the premises covered by the policy. The insured building was destroyed by fire. An investigation proved that gasoline stored on the premises caused the fire. Can the owner collect on a claim for insurance?

If the warranty isn't true in every respect, the contract is voidable on the part of the insurer. Obviously, this strict attitude on the part of the law regarding warranties often causes severe hardship to an insured who acts in good faith but mistakenly makes inaccurate statements to the company. Courts today tend to regard factual statements made by the insured to be representations rather than warranties. Some states have passed statutes abolishing the differences between representations and warranties. In Problem 3, the insured was guilty of a breach of a material warranty. Therefore, the building's owner can't collect for the loss.

Property insurance exists in order to protect us from financial loss if our belongings are stolen, lost, damaged, or destroyed. Automobile insurance is a special form of property insurance that protects us in a number of special ways. We will discuss auto insurance next, in Chapter 29.

Chapter 28 Review

"YOU BE THE JUDGE" REVIEW

Look again at the "You Be the Judge" cases given at the beginning of this chapter. Would you decide them differently now, after your study of the chapter?

Correct Decisions

1. No. Insurance coverage is suspended during a period of vacancy or unoccupancy that violates the policy. However, the coverage is reinstated when the premises are no longer vacant or unoccupied. Since the fire occurred after the coverage was reinstated, the company is liable for the loss.

2. Yes. The insurer is not liable for a loss that occurs while an increase of risk, of which the insurer has no knowledge, exists. The insurance coverage is suspended during that time.

UNDERSTANDING WHAT YOU HAVE READ

1. Explain this statement: "A contract of property insurance is one of indemnity."
2. What is the difference between marine insurance and inland marine insurance?
3. What is meant by a standard fire insurance policy?
4. Briefly explain each of the following clauses that are usually included in a standard fire insurance policy:
   a. risks covered
   b. vacancy or unoccupancy clause
   c. additional insurance clause
   d. increase of risk clause
5. What is the purpose of coinsurance?
6. Who benefits from a subrogation clause in a property insurance policy?
7. Distinguish between a representation and a warranty.
8. What is the effect of a material misrepresentation in fire insurance?
9. What is the effect of a breach of a material warranty?
10. What is meant by the statement, "In the absence of fraud, all statements made by the insured are construed as representations, not warranties"?

BUILDING YOUR LEGAL VOCABULARY

Choose the legal term that will correctly complete each definition below. Write your answers on a separate sheet of paper.

1. An insurer's assumption of an insured's right to collect payment for damages caused by a third party is called a/an
   a. right of subrogation.
   b. notice of removal.
   c. indorsement.

2. The type of property insurance that covers damage or loss to a boat, its contents, or other property as a result of perils of the sea is
   a. title insurance.
   b. inland marine insurance.
   c. marine insurance.

3. An attachment that adds protection against loss to a fire insurance policy is called a/an
   a. coinsurance provision.
   b. warranty.
   c. extended-coverage indorsement.

4. Inland marine policies are usually known as
   a. riders.
   b. floaters.
   c. indorsements.

5. Insured premises that are temporarily uninhabited but contain their usual items of personal property are called
   a. assigned premises.
   b. unoccupied premises.
   c. vacant premises.

APPLYING LEGAL PRINCIPLES

1. Kulick, a retail merchant, carried a standard fire insurance policy on her stock of goods. A fire erupted in a neighboring building, and Kulick's goods were badly damaged by smoke and water. Can Kulick collect damages under her policy?

2. During a fire in Rhuda's jewelry store, firefighters carried some of the goods out of the store to save them from the flames. Later, Rhuda found that $2,000 worth of his merchandise had been stolen. Is the insurer liable for the loss?

3. Ardley took out fire insurance on his household furniture. Shortly thereafter, he went out of town for six months on business. He stored some of his furniture in a friend's home. Was this furniture covered by Ardley's fire insurance contract?

4. Continental Fire Insurance Company canceled Guilfoyle's one-year fire insurance policy. Guilfoyle had paid the annual premium of $240. At the time of cancellation, the policy had been in force for five months. How much should

Guilfoyle receive from the insurer as a refund of premium?

5. Jhin, the owner of a home valued at $120,000, insured it against loss by fire to the extent of $72,000. Her fire insurance policy contained a coinsurance clause requiring insurance to the extent of 80% of the value of the property. A fire in Jhin's home caused a loss of $48,000. Jhin claims that she is entitled to recover $48,000. Do you agree with her?

6. The Fajardos insured their home against fire for $88,000. They sold the house to the Cushmans but didn't notify the insurance company of the change of ownership. Several weeks later, the house was damaged by fire. Can the Fajardos collect for the loss?

7. During a severe storm, a large tree fell and damaged Borofsky's home. Borofsky claimed that the fire insurance policy covering his home should protect him from the damages caused by the falling tree. Under what circumstances would this claim be true?

8. Colborn's house had been set on fire twice within a month. Without disclosing this fact to the insurance company, she obtained a policy of fire insurance. How would the fact that this information wasn't made known to the insurer affect the contract?

9. In his application for fire insurance, Varros stated that he didn't keep gasoline or any other flammable material on his premises. There was a small quantity of gasoline on the premises, although Varros wasn't aware of it. The company issued the policy. When a fire occurred, the company sought to avoid liability on the ground that Varros kept gasoline on the premises. Will the company succeed?

10. a. Suppose, in Problem 9, that the policy issued to Varros contained a clause providing that gasoline would not be stored on the premises. Although there was no gasoline on the premises at the time the policy was issued, Varros did keep some on his premises later. Would the company be able to avoid liability in the event of a fire?

    b. Would your answer be the same if the fire had not been caused by gasoline?

ANALYZING COURT CASES

1. Youse insured his diamond ring against loss, including "all direct loss or damage by fire." The insurer was Employers Fire Insurance Company. Youse accidentally threw the ring into a trash burner, where it was badly damaged by fire. When Youse tried to collect for the damage, the insurance company denied liability on the ground that the damage was caused by a friendly fire. Was the insurance company's contention legally correct? (*Youse v. Employers Fire Insurance Company*, 238 P. 2d 472)

2. A milk and egg processing firm insured its plant against fire. Smoke from a fire near its plant was absorbed by its egg powder. Cans of the powder delivered to the United States government were rejected as contaminated. The milk and egg processing company sued its insurance company for a total loss. The insurance company claimed that there had been no fire involving the insured property and therefore no total loss. Was the insurance company's claim legally correct? (*Marshall Produce Co. v. St. Paul Fire & Marine Insurance Company*, 98 N.W. 2d 280)

3. A merchant owned a stock of goods insured against loss by fire. The merchant sold the entire stock to Fuller and delivered the fire insurance policy to the latter. A written indorsement on the policy read, "For value received, pay the within in case of loss to J. Fuller." Later, a fire destroyed the goods. The insurance company refused to pay the loss on the ground that the policy couldn't be assigned without the company's written consent. Was the insurance company's defense proper? (*Fogg v. Middlesex Mutual Fire Insurance Co.*, 64 Mass. 337)

Automobile Insurance

Think about these cases.
If you were the judge, how would you decide each case?

1

Ahlstrom, who carried bodily ly injury insurance, loaned her car to her friend Leone. Leone ran a red light and struck a pedestrian. The pedestrian sued Ahlstrom's insurance company for the expenses of his injuries. Is the insurance company liable, if Ahlstrom wasn't driving her car when the accident occurred?

2

The Salazars' house was damaged when fourteen-year-old Yeaman hit a wall of the house while on a joyride in his parents' car. Can the Salazars recover the damages from the Yeamans' insurance company?

NATURE OF AUTOMOBILE INSURANCE

Driving an automobile today involves serious risks, regardless of the operator's driving skill. Statistics show that tens of thousands of people are killed in cars accidents in this country each year. Several million more are injured. Traffic safety experts estimate that many millions of cars are damaged every year in accidents. It's not surprising, therefore, that more laws have been passed to regulate the operation of automobiles than any other mechanical objects. These laws govern the ownership and use of cars, their licensing and registration, insurance requirements, and traffic violations. In this chapter, we'll deal only with insurance requirements.

PROBLEM

1. As a result of Gwon's negligence while driving, his car collided with one driven by Cerbi. Cerbi suffered severe injuries. The accident occurred in Gwon's state, where a financial responsibility law had been adopted. Gwon carried no insurance on his car. What are the rights of the parties?

Some states have compulsory insurance laws. By statute in those states, a person can't get a driver's license without having liability insurance. All states and the District of Columbia have passed some form of **financial responsibility laws.** The purpose of these laws is to keep those drivers off the highways who can't pay for the damage or injuries they cause. The laws apply to instances where an accident causes property damage of a specified amount or where a car owner is convicted of certain traffic violations. In these situations, financial responsibility laws require the owner to deposit with the state evidence of financial responsibility in the form of money or securities. When a standard liability insurance policy is in force at the time of the accident, the law makes it unnecessary to post such proof or evidence. Failure to submit proof of financial responsibility, regardless of fault, results in suspension of the driver's license as well as the registration (license plates). Often, proof of financial responsibility covering possible future accidents is also required. In Problem 1, if Gwon is unable to submit evidence of financial responsibility (money, property, or a liability insurance policy), his driver's license and car registration will be suspended until he fulfills the requirements. He also is subject to a suit for damages by Cerbi.

This situation is different in states that have adopted **no-fault insurance** laws. Under no-fault insurance, the injured party's own company pays rather than the company of the driver who caused the accident. For a further discussion of no-fault insurance, see pages 382 and 385. Also, refer to your state's statutes to see if it has adopted a no-fault law.

Figure 29.1
A Summary of
Basic Automobile
Insurance
Coverages

Type Of Coverage	Where Coverage Applies
	Persons
Bodily injury liability	Persons other than insured
Uninsured motorist	The insured, including family
Medical payments	The insured, including family Persons other than insured
	Property
Collision	The insured's car
Comprehensive physical damage	The insured's car
Property damage liability	Cars other than insured's Property other than cars

KINDS OF AUTOMOBILE INSURANCE

Insurance companies usually offer six basic types of insurance coverage:
1. Bodily injury liability insurance
2. Property damage liability insurance
3. Medical payments insurance
4. Collision insurance
5. Comprehensive physical damage insurance
6. Uninsured motorist insurance

Figure 29.1 summarizes the coverage provided by each of these types of auto insurance. We'll study the various kinds of coverage in the next few pages.

Bodily Injury Liability Insurance

Bodily injury liability insurance is the most important form of auto insurance offered to car owners and operators. Under this policy, the insurer agrees to pay, within the policy's limits, all amounts legally collectible from the insured as a result of bodily injuries suffered by another person. These expenses may include the injured party's medical bills, court costs, and loss of wages. This type of insurance is sometimes known as **public liability insurance.**

PROBLEM

2. Burton took out an automobile bodily injury insurance policy with "15/30 limits." Later, while driving through a busy intersection, he struck and injured Abreu. Abreu filed suit to recover damages for her injuries and was awarded a verdict of $19,500 against Burton. What is the liability of the insurance company?

A typical coverage for bodily injury is $15,000 for death or injury to one person, with a $30,000 limit on damages for death or injury of all individuals in a single accident. This plan is familiarly known as bodily injury insurance with "15/30 limits." Greater coverage, such as "25/50 limits" or "50/100 limits," costs just a little more in light of the extra protection it gives.

It's important that the insured learn the minimum limits under the financial responsibility laws of his or her state. In some states, "10/20" is sufficient. Other states, however, have higher limits.

The bodily injury insurance policy usually protects the insured in case of an accident that occurs when the car is driven by another person or by a member of the insured's family, with the insured's express or implied consent. However, policies often provide that the insured is not protected if the car is driven by a person under the legal age for driving. Usually, a higher premium is charged if the car is driven by a person under 25. In Problem 2, since Burton carried only "15/30 limits" and only one person was injured in the accident, the insurance company is liable only for $15,000. Burton would have to pay the remaining $4,500 out of his own funds.

Property Damage Liability Insurance

Property damage liability insurance protects an insured car owner or operator who is liable for damages to the property of *another.* It does not protect against loss or damage to the insured's *own* car. The minimum property damage limit is $5,000 for any one accident, regardless of the number of claims. This limit may be increased, however, for an additional premium.

> Tell carried an auto insurance policy with Excelsior Insurance Company. The property damage limit on her policy was $10,000. In an auto accident, Tell negligently damaged two other cars. The repairs to one car were estimated to be $2,400; the repairs to the second car were estimated to be $3,800. Excelsior Insurance is liable for the payment of both claims, totaling $6,200, because Tell carried a $10,000 limit on her property damage insurance.

Property damage policies usually provide that written notice of an accident must be given to the insurer or to the insurer's authorized agent as soon as is reasonably possible. The notice should contain information regarding the time, place, and circumstances of the accident. It should also contain the names and addresses of any injured parties and of any available witnesses.

The policy also provides that the company is not liable for damages caused by an operator under the minimum legal age for driving. The insurance protection under such a policy, as well as under the bodily injury policy, meets the requirements of the financial responsibility law of any state in the country.

Medical Payments Insurance

> **3.** Your father is driving you and a friend to a softball game when you are involved in an auto accident. As a result of the accident, your friend is injured and hospitalized for two weeks. Does your family's auto insurance policy cover the costs of your friend's medical bills?

Medical payments insurance protects the insured and all members of the insured's immediate family, whether they are riding in the family car or in *any other* car. Passengers and guests riding in the insured's car also are covered. Payment is made regardless of who is responsible for the accident. The insured may choose the limits for this coverage, and the limits apply to

No-Fault Automobile Insurance

Katz, a bicyclist, ran a stop sign and was hit by a car. The driver of the car was covered by liability insurance. Katz's medical bills were very costly. Because the driver who struck Katz was not at fault, none of the bills would have been covered under liability insurance. However, under a no-fault insurance law in Katz's state, her medical bills were paid regardless of fault.

No-fault insurance is designed to provide prompt payment of medical expenses and income loss regardless of who caused the accident. It's also designed to cut down on costly lawsuits by limiting the right to sue. To make this work, the law says that every owner of a car (except certain commercial vehicles) must carry insurance.

A recent federal survey of no-fault insurance in several states concluded that

1. no-fault provides more adequate and equitable benefits than the liability system, especially for seriously injured victims and for victims of single-car accidents where no second person could be blamed (as in Katz's case);

2. payments for financial losses are made promptly under no-fault insurance;

3. the backlog of court cases involving auto accident claims is substantially reduced by no-fault laws; and

4. overpayments for minor injuries are also reduced by these laws.

The federal Department of Transportation says, "No-fault auto insurance works."

each person injured in the accident. Medical payments insurance is important for all insured, especially those who often carry several passengers. In Problem 3, your family's auto insurance policy would cover your friend's medical bills.

Collision Insurance

Property damage liability insurance protects the insured against claims resulting from damage to the property of others. **Collision insurance** protects the insured against any damage to his or her *own* car when the damage is caused by a collision with another car or object. The collision must be the fault of the *insured* and not someone else.

4. Geng took out an auto insurance policy containing collision coverage. His policy had a $250 deductible for collision damage. Geng's car was damaged in an accident he caused, and Geng notified the insurance company as required. The repair costs for Geng's car were estimated to be $1,750. What is the insurance company's liability for collision damages to Geng's car?

Collision coverage is usually issued on a **deductible** basis. This means that the insurance company will pay for all collision damages *except* those in the amount of the deductible. The insured pays for collision damages in the amount of the deductible. In Problem 4, for example, Geng would be entitled to collect $1,500 from his insurance company. Geng himself would be liable for $250. Because the deductible feature lowers the insurance company's risk of loss by the amount of the deductible, it also lowers the insured's premium payment for the coverage.

As in the case of bodily injury and property damage insurance, the insured is under a duty to give prompt notice to the insurer. The insured also must give the insurer a chance to determine the extent of the damage to the car before making any repairs.

Comprehensive Physical Damage Insurance

Comprehensive physical damage insurance in an auto insurance policy usually protects the insured's car against losses due to fire, windstorm, flood, riot, glass breakage, theft, and vandalism.

5. Pawling insured her car with Lenox Casualty. Her policy contained a comprehensive clause covering damage to the car caused by fire, vandalism, and theft. Several packages were stolen from Pawling's car while it was parked in front of her apartment building. What is the insurance company's liability?

In case of loss, the insured must notify the company as soon as possible. In the event of theft of the car or a part of the car, a prompt report must also be made to the police. A sworn proof of loss must be submitted to the insurance company. Policies usually require the insured to state the location or place where the car is to be kept. This statement may constitute a warranty, and a breach of the statement may void the policy. For example, an insured may state that the car is kept in a private garage. Later, without the knowledge or consent of the insurer, the car is moved to a public garage. In this event, the insurer will not be liable for any claims.

Most insurance companies offer many types of auto insurance.

The maximum liability of the insurer is the actual cash value of the car at the time of loss. This amount may not exceed the stated liability on the face of the policy. Comprehensive coverage also is issued on a deductible basis.

The theft coverage under a comprehensive clause does not include the theft of property left in the car. Neither does it include tools and repair equipment unless the entire car is stolen. Thus, in Problem 5, Pawling's insurance company is not liable for the value of the packages stolen from her car.

The comprehensive clause, however, does cover loss of use of the car in the event of theft. The insured is reimbursed for money actually spent—not exceeding a stated sum per day—for transportation or for renting another car. However, no payment is made for a certain period of time (often 48 to 72 hours) after the theft is reported to the insurer and to the police.

Uninsured Motorist Insurance

Uninsured motorist insurance protects the insured and the insured's family against uninsured and hit-and-run drivers. This protection covers injuries to the extent of coverage that would have been available if the uninsured driver had been insured. The uninsured driver must be legally liable for the injuries suffered by the insured. In most states, this coverage doesn't apply to damage to the insured's car, which is available through collision insurance.

One of the most important advantages of this type of coverage is the immediate payment from the injured party's insurance company for medical costs. This is particularly helpful where recovery from the uninsured driver is doubtful, as in the case of an uninsured driver who is unemployed.

Harkness was injured when her car was forced off the highway by a car driven by Poole. The accident was caused solely by Poole's negligence. Later, it was discovered that Poole was an uninsured driver and was unemployed. If Harkness has insurance coverage against uninsured drivers, she will collect immediately for her medical costs under her auto insurance policy.

No-Fault Insurance

6. Hurley's auto insurance policy contained no-fault coverage. In an auto accident, Hurley suffered severe cuts and bruises. His hospital expenses and loss of wages amounted to $1,900. From whom is Hurley entitled to collect?

Under a no-fault insurance law, the injured party's insurance company pays for the injuries rather than the insurer of the driver who caused the accident. This means that the insured will collect regardless of who was at fault in the accident. The law is intended to reduce the number of costly lawsuits that arise from auto accidents.

Briefly, no-fault insurance laws require that each driver carry liability insurance to cover medical payments and loss of wages from accidents involving the insured and any passengers in the insured's car. Most plans allow each claimant to collect a maximum of $2,000 for medical expenses, lost wages, and incidental costs. But if a person suffers damages that come to more than $2,000, that person must go back to the old system and claim actual damages from the person who caused the damages. Since Hurley, in Problem 6, claimed total damages of $1,900, he would be entitled to collect this sum from his own insurance company.

A wise consumer purchases the protection needed—and often required by law—to minimize the risks involved with owning and operating a car. In today's society, the value of automobile insurance is growing every day. There are other forms of insurance purchases, however, that also provide valuable protection to consumers. One of those forms of insurance is personal insurance, which we will discuss next in Chapter 30.

Chapter 29 Review

"YOU BE THE JUDGE" REVIEW

Look again at the "You Be the Judge" cases given at the beginning of this chapter. Would you decide them differently now, after your study of the chapter?

Correct Decisions

1. Yes. The typical bodily injury liability insurance policy protects the insured in case of an accident that occurs when the car is driven by another person with the insured's consent.
2. No. Property damage liability coverage usually provides that the insurance company is not liable for damages caused by an operator under the minimum legal age for driving. The Salazars will have to file a civil action against the Yeamans to attempt to recover the damages to their house.

UNDERSTANDING WHAT YOU HAVE READ

1. Why should a car owner carry automobile insurance?
2. Explain what is meant by a financial responsibility law.
3. What protection is included in a bodily injury liability policy?
4. What is the purpose of property damage liability insurance?
5. What is the purpose of medical payments insurance?
6. What is protected by collision insurance?
7. Describe the risks covered by a comprehensive physical damage automobile insurance clause.
8. Why is it important to carry protection against uninsured drivers?
9. What is the purpose of no-fault insurance?
10. If a person incurs injuries exceeding the maximum allowable by a no-fault insurance law, what procedure must be followed to collect the damages?

BUILDING YOUR LEGAL VOCABULARY

Match each of these legal terms with its correct definition from the list that follows. Write your answers on a separate sheet of paper.

bodily injury liability
  insurance
collision insurance
comprehensive physical
  damage insurance

deductible
financial responsibility laws
medical payments
  insurance
no-fault insurance laws

property damage liability
  insurance
public liability insurance
uninsured motorist
  insurance

1. insurance that protects the insured's car against damage due to fire, windstorm, flood, riot, glass breakage, theft, and vandalism
2. regulations that require the injured party's insurance company to pay for injuries rather than the insurer of the driver who caused the accident
3. another name for bodily injury liability insurance
4. a policy that protects the insured's *own* car against damage caused by a collision
5. the amount of damages to be paid by the insured under the terms of collision and comprehensive insurance clauses
6. auto insurance coverage under which the insurer agrees to pay all amounts legally collectible from the insured as a result of another person's physical injuries
7. insurance that pays for the treatment of injuries of the insured and the insured's family, whether they are injured in the insured's car or in any other car, as well as of guests injured in the insured's car
8. insurance that protects the insured and the insured's family against damages caused by drivers who have no insurance or by hit-and-run drivers
9. coverage that pays for damages that an insured driver or owner causes to the property of others
10. regulations requiring drivers to submit proof of their ability to pay damages if they have no liability insurance

APPLYING LEGAL PRINCIPLES

1. Conforti carried insurance on his car with coverage for property damage. During a collision, the grille and front fenders of Conforti's car were badly damaged. What is his insurance company's liability?

2. Goldin's comprehensive automobile insurance covered loss by fire, lightning, and theft. A set of golf clubs Goldin left in her car was stolen. Is the insurance company liable for this loss?

3. Ronca took out a bodily injury liability policy with "10/20 limits." As a result of an accident, Ronca injured several people riding in another car. The injured people filed suit against Ronca for their injuries. A jury awarded them verdicts amounting to $35,000. What is the insurance company's liability?

4. Would the insurance company in Problem 3 be liable if the accident occurred while Ronca's husband was driving the car?

5. Assume in Problem 3 that only one passenger was injured as a result of the accident. For what sum would Ronca's insurance company be liable?

6. Arcila's two-year-old car was covered by collision insurance. The car was totally wrecked in an accident. After notifying his insurance company of the accident, Arcila filed a proof of loss. On the form he listed the car's purchase price as $8,950. The company offered to pay him $5,300, which represented the actual cash value of the car at the time of the accident. Arcila claims that the company owes him $8,950, the price of a new car. Who is right?

7. Patel's car was struck by a hit-and-run driver, and a business associate who was a passenger in Patel's car was hurt. What insurance coverage would protect Patel from claims for the passenger's injuries?

8. Kole's car struck a cement median strip on a road and overturned. The damage to the car was estimated at $4,200. Kole's collision coverage included a $250 deductible. For how much is the insurance company liable?

9. Nol was injured in an accident while riding in McPherson's car. Nol's family automobile insurance policy contains medical payments coverage with a $5,000 limit. Nol filed a claim with her insurance firm, showing these expenses: ambulance service, $175; X-rays, $350; hospital room, $3,200; doctors' fees, $1,300; prescriptions, $98. The total came to $5,123. Is the insurance company liable for all the items listed?

10. Charlton's car was stolen and then recovered. It was returned to him in damaged condition. Is the insurer liable for damages to the car under comprehensive coverage?

ANALYZING COURT CASES

1. A father allowed his son to use the family car but told him not to drive it. The son had his friend drive the car. The father's automobile insurance policy provided coverage for the insured and any "other driver" who was driving with the insured's permission. While driving the car, the friend ran into another car. The insurance company refused to pay, claiming that the father had not given permission to the friend to drive the car. Therefore, the company claimed that the friend was not an "other driver" within the protection of the policy. Was the insurance company justified in its claim? (*Esmond v. Liscio*, 224 A. 2d 793)

2. Northern Casualty Company issued an automobile collision insurance policy to Solon. While she was driving at a normal speed, Solon tried to stop the car when she thought she saw a warning signal light at a railroad crossing. The car skidded and spun completely around, causing the right wheel to collapse. When the insurance company denied liability for the damage to the car, Solon brought suit to recover on the policy. Should she succeed? (Based on: *The Great Eastern Casualty Co. v. Solinsky*, 263 S.W. 71)

3. Cuellar bought a car and obtained a theft policy from an insurance company. An employee of the dealership that sold the car to Cuellar agreed to teach him how to drive and to give him several lessons. Cuellar took a driving lesson one morning and asked the employee to return with the car in the afternoon for a second lesson. During the interval, the employee drove the car in the country for pleasure, was involved in an accident, and damaged the car. Cuellar had no knowledge of this action on the employee's part and sued the insurance company to recover for the theft of the car. The company claimed that the car had not been stolen. Was the company legally correct? (Based on: *Ledvinka v. Home Insurance Co.*, 115 A. 596)

Personal Insurance

Think about these cases.
If you were the judge, how would you decide each case?

1

Kellogg wanted to protect her young children in case of her death. She had a low-paying job, and little extra money to spare each month. Her life insurance agent advised her to purchase an endowment life insurance policy. Is this in Kellogg's best interests?

2

When Guevarra died, he owed a large debt to one creditor. The creditor claimed that it was entitled to the benefits of Guevarra's life insurance policy. Guevarra had named his children as beneficiaries of the policy's proceeds. Will the creditor be able to collect the proceeds?

WHAT IS PERSONAL INSURANCE?

In Chapter 27 we classified personal insurance as (1) life, (2) accident, (3) health and hospital, (4) public liability, and (5) fidelity. This classification shows the wide variety of risks that insurers cover when issuing personal insurance contracts. The insured and the insured's family may protect themselves against financial loss arising from a number of sources. Those sources include accidents, illness, death, claims for injuries sustained by others, and dishonesty of the insured's employees.

PROBLEM

1. Mallon's dog bit a neighbor's child. The neighbor spent $90 for medical treatment of the child's wounds. Mallon carried public liability insurance. Is she protected under the policy from her neighbor's claim?

A life insurance contract is intended to protect the dependents of the insured in case of the insured's death. In addition, the insured often seeks to build a reserve fund for his or her retirement years. Accident insurance and health and hospital insurance help the insured through the financial troubles caused by long illnesses and inability to work. A public liability policy protects the insured against claims arising in the home, on its grounds, or even away from home. For example, if a roofer fell while installing a new roof on the insured's home, a liability policy would protect the insured against the roofer's claim for damages. In Problem 1, Mallon would be protected by her public liability insurance against her neighbor's claim. A fidelity insurance policy protects employers from liability for the dishonest acts of their employees.

Life Insurance

People buy life insurance for various reasons. Some want financial protection for members of their family. Others are interested in making an investment and assuring financial protection. The type of life insurance policy one should purchase will depend on the person's age, income, and responsibilities, and on the purpose the insurance is to fulfill.

PROBLEM

2. Yeung was 29, married, and had two small children. His wife was unemployed, and the family's total income was Yeung's salary of $24,000 per year. One evening, Yeung was discussing life insurance with his father-in-law. The older man said, "I've just taken out a 20-year endowment life policy. I think it's a good buy. You should buy one too." Was this good advice?

Figure 30.1
A Comparison of
Property and Life
Insurance Contracts

	Property	**Life**
Parties	Insured and insurer	Insured, insurer, and beneficiary
Acceptance	By company or by authorized agent with binder; may be oral	By company; usually effective when first premium is paid
Insurable Interest	At time the loss occurs	At time contract is made
Payment of Insurer	Indemnity: amount determined by loss	Fixed amount: the amount agreed on when contract was made
Assignment by the Insured	Only with consent of the insurer	Insured free to assign, except when there is a beneficiary with a vested interest
Termination	By either party at any time before a loss	By insurer, if given right by policy or by law By insured at any time on proper action, unless there is a beneficiary with a vested interest

Young married people, such as Yeung in Problem 2, need to protect their families in case of the sudden death or disability of a wage-earner. Since Yeung's earnings are modest compared with his responsibilities, he needs the maximum amount of insurance at the lowest possible cost. For Yeung, term insurance is a better choice than endowment insurance. Yeung's father-in-law, however, who no longer has dependents to protect, can afford an expensive investment form of insurance like endowment. At any rate, the father-in-law's advice to Yeung is not good. This doesn't mean that Yeung would be locked into term insurance for the rest of his life. After his children have become self-supporting and his income has increased, Yeung can convert the term insurance into other forms of life insurance with investment features. These forms will be discussed later in this chapter.

A life insurance contract differs from a property insurance contract in several important ways. These differences are shown in Figure 30.1. Study the information on this chart carefully before continuing in this chapter.

Kinds of Life Insurance

The usual types of life insurance are (1) straight, or ordinary, life, (2) limited-payment life, (3) endowment, and (4) term policies.

Straight Life Policy

A **straight life policy,** also known as a *whole life policy,* is one for which the insured pays a definite yearly premium as long as he or she lives. The premium usually doesn't change as the insured grows older. On the insured's death, the face value of the policy is paid to the beneficiary named by the insured.

A recent outgrowth of the straight life policy is the **universal life policy.** This type of insurance is described in the "Living Under the Law" feature on page 396.

Limited-Payment Life Policy

A **limited-payment life policy** is one under which the insured pays only a certain number of premiums. The insurance is then fully paid up, but the amount of the policy is not paid until the insured dies. Premiums are usually higher than those for a straight life policy.

Endowment Policy

An **endowment policy** provides insurance for a stated period, such as 20 or 30 years. If the insured survives the period, the amount of the policy is paid to the insured. If the insured dies during the period, the amount of the policy is paid to the beneficiary. This type of policy combines life insurance protection with a savings plan. Therefore, it is more expensive than either straight life or limited-payment life insurance.

Term Policy

A **term policy** protects the insured only for a limited period of time, such as 5 or 10 years. The premium is calculated to remain the same during the term of the policy. However, as the insured grows older, premiums increase upon renewal of the policy. When the policy expires, there is no cash value. It offers pure life insurance protection for the stated period, at a low premium. It usually isn't available to people over the age of 65 or 70. Many term policies contain **conversion provisions.** These allow the insured to change to a straight life or endowment policy at a higher premium rate, but without a physical exam.

Standard Provisions in Life Insurance Contracts

In many states, life insurance contracts are subject to strict statutory regulation. This is done for the protection of the insured. As in fire insurance, standard provisions are provided by statute and must be included in all life insurance policies. Some of the more important provisions—such as those relating to change of beneficiary, misstatement of age, suicide, incontestability, grace period, and so on—will now be discussed in detail.

Change of Beneficiary

Usually the insured may change the beneficiary at will, on written request to the insurer. Some policies, however, have no provision for a change of beneficiary. In these contracts, a beneficiary has a legal interest that can't be taken away without the beneficiary's consent—not even by the insured's creditors. If a policy is payable to the insured's estate, however, creditors may obtain the proceeds to satisfy their claims.

> Yamaguchi took out a straight life insurance policy on her life. She named her husband as beneficiary. On Yamaguchi's death, her estate did not have enough funds to pay off all of her creditors. Yamaguchi's husband is entitled to collect the face value of the policy, free from the claims of his wife's creditors.

Misstatement of Age

A misstatement of age by the insured is a material misrepresentation, since it directly affects the insurer's risk. By statute, however, a misstatement of age usually doesn't wholly avoid the insurance company's duty of payment. The company generally must pay the amount of insurance that the premiums would have purchased if the insured's age had been properly stated.

> Fox, 35, applied for a 20-year endowment insurance policy. In the application he gave his age as 28. The policy is not void when the insurance company learns of the misrepresentation. The insurer would calculate the amount of insurance that the premiums Fox paid would have purchased for a 35-year-old person. That sum would then be payable on Fox's death or when the policy expired.

Suicide

If a policy is obtained by a person who intends to commit suicide, there can be no recovery under the policy. A life insurance policy usually provides that "death of the insured by his or her own hand" will avoid the payment of the policy. If the insured commits suicide while insane or by accident, however, the policy is not affected. Many states have statutes limiting the effectiveness of this provision for a period of one or two years immediately following the policy's issuance. Thereafter, the death of the insured by suicide will not defeat the claims of the beneficiaries.

Incontestability

> **3.** Wulff stated in her application for life insurance that she had never suffered from cancer. As a matter of fact, Wulff had been treated for cancer several years prior to her application. The disease had been arrested. Three years after the policy was issued, Wulff's disease became active again and she died. Can the insurance company refuse to pay Wulff's beneficiary because of the insured's misrepresentation?

Generally, both statutes and a life insurance policy provide that the policy shall be **incontestable** (not open to dispute) after it has been in force for a period of time. That period is often two years. Under these provisions, the insurer agrees to pay the beneficiary in spite of false representations and warranties made by the insured when the policy was issued. In Problem 3, Wulff's insurance company cannot avoid payment on her life insurance contract because the policy had been in force for more than two years. The incontestable clause doesn't apply, though, when the insured fails to pay the premiums or misrepresents his or her age.

Days of Grace

Statutes usually provide that after the first year, an insured is entitled to a **grace period** of 30 or 31 days after the premium is due in which to make a payment. During this period the insurance will remain in full force. The unpaid premium, however, may be deducted from any claim that may arise within that period.

> Almada paid the premium on his life insurance policy on March 18. The premium had been due on January 25. Because the grace period (30 days) had expired, Almada's policy lapsed.

Cash Surrender Value

The laws of most states provide a minimum **cash surrender value** for a life insurance policy after the second or third year of the policy's existence. This cash surrender value is somewhat less than the premiums that have been paid. A number of states have statutes requiring a table of cash surrender values to be included in the insurance policy. The table shows the cash surrender value of the policy at each successive year.

Buying Life Insurance—Whole, Term, or Universal?

Many differences separate the available types of life insurance. The kinds most commonly sold are whole life insurance and term life insurance.

Whole life insurance requires a relatively high premium but also provides significant benefits. As you pay for your whole life coverage, you also build a form of savings account. The premiums accrue interest and have a growing cash value. Also, a whole life policy is guaranteed to stay in force, regardless of changes in your health, for as long as you continue to pay the premiums.

Term life insurance is the most economical kind of life insurance. However, it expires after the short term stated in the policy, and it becomes more expensive and more difficult to obtain as you age.

Several years ago, a new kind of life insurance began to be marketed. It's called *universal life insurance.* Universal life insurance is considered highly speculative; that is, it involves a higher element of risk in return for the possibility of a higher payoff. The additional risk is incurred because the premiums and payoff amount are tied into the current interest rate or Federal Reserve Board money rate. As interest rates rise, both the premium payments and the value of the payoff increase. But as interest rates fall, premiums decrease as does the value of the payoff.

Many financial advisors still consider whole life insurance to be the wisest life insurance investment. When considering what kind of life insurance to buy, think about your own attitude toward financial investments and expenses. Also, be sure to consult more than one insurance agent or company.

EXAMPLE

Doan finds herself in financial difficulties. She has a limited-payment life policy that has been in force for fifteen years. If she desires, she may surrender the policy to the insurance company and collect its cash surrender value.

Loan Value

Most policies provide that the insured may apply to the insurance company for a loan of an amount equal to the cash surrender value of the policy. The rate of interest charged for this loan is usually lower than the rate other lenders would charge.

Lapse and Reinstatement

The insured's failure to pay premiums when they are due causes the policy to lapse and the contract to terminate. However, all policies provide that the insured, on application within a reasonable time, may have the policy reinstated if the insured is still an insurable risk.

Because of the savings feature of life insurance policies, they can't be forfeited. In other words, the insured can't lose his or her savings even though premium payments are stopped. Life policies usually provide that if a policy lapses due to failure to pay premiums, the insured may take advantage of several options. The insured may (1) receive the cash surrender value, (2) obtain a reduced paid-up insurance policy, (3) convert the policy to extended-term insurance, or (4) obtain an automatic premium loan. Of course, these options are available only if the policy has a cash value.

Warranties and Representations

The principles governing warranties and representations discussed with respect to property insurance generally apply with equal force to life insurance. Some states have abolished the distinction between warranties and representations in the absence of fraud in a life insurance contract. In those states, all of the insured's statements are regarded as representations, regardless of whether they are part of the policy.

PROBLEM

> **4.** Fogg completed and signed an application for life insurance. In the application, Fogg answered "No" to the question, "Have you, within the past five years, had medical or surgical treatment or any departures from good health? If so, state when, what, and duration." In fact, Fogg had been hospitalized for a heart attack only four months earlier. Eight months after receiving the insurance policy, Fogg died of a heart attack. May the insurance company avoid the policy?

Any *material false statements* made by the insured in an application, whether intentional or unintentional, will make a life insurance policy voidable. This is the case in Problem 4. The test of the "materiality" of a false statement is whether the insurer, with the full and correct information, would have refused to accept the risk. If so, the false statement is material.

Does the nature of a person's work affect that person's ability to obtain insurance?

Accident Insurance

Accident insurance is an important form of personal insurance. When an insured is injured in an accident, this type of policy will pay the insured a specific amount of money (often paid monthly) for a stated length of time. Some companies refer to privately purchased policies of this nature as **disability insurance policies.**

Health and Hospital Insurance

Because of the high cost of medical care today, health and hospital insurance is a very valuable form of personal insurance. Most health and hospitalization policies pay a percentage (commonly 80%) of all of the insured's medical expenses incurred in a calendar year, after the insured pays a deductible for the year. These policies typically have a **stop-loss clause.** This clause states that the insurance company will pay 100% of the insured's medical expenses after the insured has paid a predetermined amount. Some familiar carriers of health and hospital insurance are Blue Cross and Blue Shield.

In recent years, the concept of the **Health Maintenance Organization (HMO)** has rapidly gained popularity as an alternative to traditional health and hospital insurance. Under an HMO plan, an insured has access to a specific group of participating doctors, hospitals, and other health-care providers located in the area covered by the plan. The insured pays "dues," or small fees, for health care given under the plan. Because they focus on trying to keep members healthy, HMOs have developed a good record of health care nationwide.

Public Liability Insurance

Public liability insurance protects the insured against claims for any injuries to others for which the insured is legally liable. The injuries may arise on the insured's property or even while the insured is traveling. Commonly, liability insurance is included in a homeowner's, renter's, or automobile insurance policy rather than purchased separately.

EXAMPLE

> Levitz, who lived in an apartment in New York, purchased a renter's insurance policy that contained public liability coverage. While on vacation in Georgia, Levitz rented a bicycle for a ride through a park. As she rode down a path, Levitz struck and injured a pedestrian. Under the public liability coverage of her renter's policy, Levitz is protected against liability for the pedestrian's injuries.

Fidelity Insurance

Fidelity insurance is also known as **bonding.** It protects employers from liability for the dishonest acts of their employees. Employers often require that employees who handle cash or negotiable instruments be bonded.

There are two primary types of bonding policies. The **commercial blanket policy** bonds all employees in a company up to a maximum dollar amount. A **blanket position policy** indemnifies an employer against the dishonest acts of any employee who fills a certain position with the firm.

As you can see, personal insurance has a number of valuable benefits. It serves to protect us from financial troubles and allows us to maintain or improve the quality of life of those who survive us. But social insurance is yet another way in which we are protected from financial harm. We'll take a look at social insurance next, in Chapter 31.

Chapter 30 Review

"YOU BE THE JUDGE" REVIEW

Look again at the "You Be the Judge" cases given at the beginning of this chapter. Would you decide them differently now, after your study of the chapter?

Correct Decisions

1. No. In light of Kellogg's financial situation, she should purchase term insurance rather than endowment life insurance. The premiums for term insurance are low because this type of insurance has no cash value when it is paid up. However, it does provide life insurance for the term stated in the policy. Endowment life insurance, in contrast, is more expensive than term insurance. It combines life insurance with a savings plan, which Kellogg can ill afford.

2. No. Guevarra's children will receive the policy's proceeds because they were named in the policy as beneficiaries. Had Guevarra named his estate as the beneficiary, however, the creditor would have been able to collect the policy's proceeds.

UNDERSTANDING WHAT YOU HAVE READ

1. List at least five ways in which a life insurance contract differs from a property insurance contract.
2. How does an endowment policy differ from a straight life policy?
3. How does a limited-payment life policy differ from a straight life policy?
4. What is term insurance?
5. Under what circumstances is an insured prevented from changing a beneficiary?
6. What are the effects of a misstatement of age made in an application for life insurance?
7. How is an insurer protected by a suicide clause?
8. What are the usual provisions of an incontestability clause?
9. Explain the grace-period clause typically found in life insurance contracts.
10. How do courts regard the warranties and representations made by an insured in an application for life insurance?
11. What options are available to an insured whose life insurance policy lapses due to a failure to pay premiums?

BUILDING YOUR LEGAL VOCABULARY

Choose the legal term that will correctly complete each definition below. Write your answers on a separate sheet of paper.

1. A person who is named in a life insurance policy as the receiver of the proceeds of the policy is called a/an
   a. beneficiary.
   b. insured.
   c. insurer.
2. A life insurance policy that provides insurance for a stated period, such as 20 or 30 years, and has a cash value is known as a/an
   a. term policy.
   b. limited-payment life policy.
   c. endowment policy.
3. A life insurance policy that protects the insured only for a limited period of time, such as five or ten years, and has no cash value when it expires is called a/an
   a. term policy.
   b. straight life policy.
   c. blanket position policy.

4. The type of insurance that protects the insured from financial loss arising from accidents, illness, death, claims for injuries sustained by others, and dishonesty of employees is
   a. property insurance.
   b. personal insurance.
   c. automobile insurance.
5. The clause in a term insurance contract that gives an insured the right to change to another form of life insurance without a physical examination is known as a
   a. stop-loss clause.
   b. conversion provision.
   c. suicide clause.

APPLYING LEGAL PRINCIPLES

1. Parkinson carried a comprehensive personal-liability insurance policy. The contract gave Parkinson coverage of $25,000 and medical payments to each person injured up to $1,000. While playing golf, Parkinson injured another player. Would his policy cover a claim made against him by the injured person?

2. Sanger took out an insurance policy on the life of her husband. Three years later, she and her husband were divorced and Sanger remarried. She continued to pay premiums and kept the policy in force. Could she collect on the policy on the death of her first husband?

3. Flores took out a 20-year endowment policy on his own life, naming Regan as his beneficiary. The policy contained a provision that allowed Flores to change the beneficiary. Two years after the policy was issued, Flores changed the beneficiary from Regan to Obregon. On Flores' death, both Regan and Obregon claimed the insurance. Who is legally entitled to it?

4. Assume in Problem 3 that Flores had made his estate the beneficiary of the policy. Then, before his death, he had become heavily indebted. Could his creditors claim the insurance proceeds in payment of the debts?

5. In her application for life insurance, Pizzarro stated that she was 27 years old. Six months later, Pizzarro was killed in an explosion at her place of employment. On investigation, the insurer discovered that Pizzarro was actually 33 years old. Can the insurance company refuse to pay the beneficiary the proceeds of the policy?

6. Correll took out a 20-year limited-payment life policy for $50,000. The policy contained a clause that read, "If the insured dies by his or her own hand or act within two years from the date of issue of this policy, the Company shall be liable only for the amount of premiums actually paid on this policy." Three years after taking out the policy, Corell committed suicide. The policy's beneficiary sought to recover from the insur-ance company. Was the beneficiary enti-tled to recover the proceeds of the policy?

7. Lam failed to pay the premium on his life insurance policy when it became due. What rights does Lam have under the policy?

8. Samson obtained a straight life policy that contained a two-year incontesta-bility clause. Three years later, Samson died. An investigation showed that she had misrepresented her physical con-dition at the time she applied for the policy. Can the company refuse to make payment?

9. In applying for life insurance, VanHorn stated that his father had died at the age of 91. Actually, the father had died at the age of 90. The statement was made in good faith, but the policy provided that all statements made in the applica-tion were to be regarded as warranties instead of representations. On Van-Horn's death, the insurance company refused to pay, claiming breach of war-ranty. Is the insurance collectible?

10. When Varela applied for a life insurance policy, he stated in good faith that he was in excellent health. Within three months after the policy was issued, Va-rela died of cancer. When Varela's doc-tors determined that he must have had cancer for at least a year, the insurance company refused to pay the beneficiary. Can the beneficiary collect?

ANALYZING COURT CASES

1. Davis was insured under a plan of the Chicago Truck Drivers Union. The policy provided that it was not binding if the insured died by suicide. Davis committed suicide while insane. It was claimed that the policy wasn't binding because Davis knew what he was doing when he committed suicide. Was this a valid defense? (*Davis v. Chicago Truck Drivers*, 3 Ill. App. 2d 256, 121 N.E. 2d 353)

2. DeBellis applied for a policy of life insurance. Although he was a truck helper, he falsely stated in the application that he was a medicine salesperson. Would this false statement void the policy? (*DeBellis v. United Benefit Life Insurance Co.*, 372 Pa. 207, 93 A. 2d 429)

3. Boardman obtained a life insurance policy from Equitable Life Assurance Society. The face of the policy was to be paid to him at the end of twenty years. If Boardman died sooner, the policy was to be paid to his mother as beneficiary. The policy didn't contain a provision authorizing a change of beneficiary. Boardman was declared bankrupt. Haskell, the trustee in bankruptcy, sued the insurance company for the cash surrender value of the policy. Was the trustee entitled to judgment? (*Haskell v. Equitable Life Assurance Society*, 181 Mass. 341, 63 N.E. 899)

CHAPTER 31

Social Insurance

YOU BE THE JUDGE

Think about these cases.
If you were the judge, how would you decide each case?

1

Lee and Rico retired after working together for 30 years. Lee was 62, and Rico was 65. Lee objected when she discovered that her retirement benefits were less than Rico's. They had both worked the same length of time and had earned the same amount of wages. Should Lee receive the same benefits as her co-worker?

2

Jacobsen died in an accident, leaving his 38-year-old wife and three children under 18 without a source of income. Jacobsen had not purchased life insurance on his own life. Are there any insurance benefits available to Jacobsen's family?

WHAT IS SOCIAL INSURANCE?

All of the forms of insurance we have discussed in the last few chapters have been offered by private insurance carriers. They are types of insurance that are purchased by consumers. In some cases people can't afford to pay for necessary protections from financial loss. This was particularly true during the Great Depression in the United States in the late 1920s and 1930s. At that time, laws were passed to provide public protection for those who couldn't afford to purchase private insurance. These governmentally subsidized programs are known as **social insurance.** Both the federal government and state governments are involved in social insurance programs.

In 1935, the federal government enacted the **Social Security Act.** The purpose of this act was to provide a continued income for people whose incomes were reduced or lost through death, disability, or old age. After the **social security program** became effective, states began providing worker's compensation insurance, unemployment insurance, and state disability insurance. Because all of these forms of insurance are expensive to provide, their cost is shared by federal and state governments and by employers and employees. Figure 31.1 shows the kinds of protection given by social insurance programs.

Figure 31.1
The Protection Provided by Social Insurance

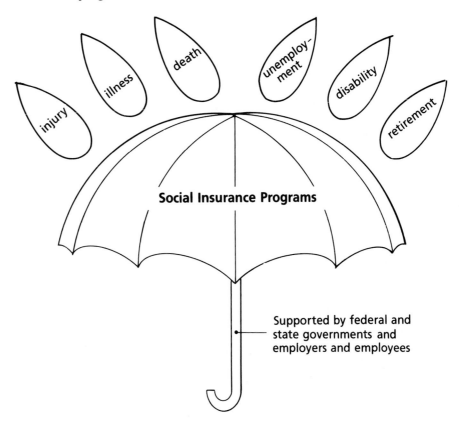

injury illness death unemployment disability retirement

Social Insurance Programs

Supported by federal and state governments and employers and employees

Social Security

Social security is funded in part by contributions of workers, in part by contributions of employers, and in part by the federal government. The **Social Security Administration (SSA)** oversees the government's social security programs. Before being able to work, each person applies for a social security card that bears a number. Figure 31.2 is a sample of a completed application form. Once a worker has a social security number and begins to earn wages, the worker's employer withholds part of the worker's wages to send to the SSA. The employer also contributes an amount equal to that withheld from the worker's wages. A self-employed worker contributes a larger amount of social security taxes because there is no employer to match that contribution.

In order to collect social security benefits, a worker must have contributed earnings to the system for a certain period of time. The SSA keeps records of the contributions made to the worker's numbered social security account. For every $250 earned in a calendar year, the SSA credits the worker with "one quarter" of credit, up to four quarters per year. This credit is granted regardless of whether the worker is employed full-time or part-time. The number of credits needed to receive a full social security benefit is 40, or the equivalent of working for ten calendar years. The government contributes to the worker's social security fund when the benefits are paid out.

Social security benefits are paid by four different types of federal social insurance: retirement, Medicare, disability, and survivor's insurance.

Retirement Insurance

Retirement insurance, sometimes called *old-age insurance,* pays a limited monthly income to people who work until they are either 62 or 65 and then retire. The theory behind this program is that these people have earned the right to a rest after a lifetime of work. The insurance is provided because some employers and individuals don't provide for the future. Retirement benefits are payable to a qualified worker as well as to his or her spouse, if the spouse is 62 or over. They also are payable to unmarried children of the worker who are under 18 (or under 22 if they are full-time students), or spouses of any age who are caring for dependent children.

PROBLEM

> **1.** Gani worked as a substitute teacher in the same school district for 32 years. When she retired at the age of 66, she was denied retirement benefits because she had been "just a temporary substitute." Should Gani be able to collect retirement benefits?

Figure 31.2
A Sample
Application for a
Social Security
Number Card

DEPARTMENT OF HEALTH AND HUMAN SERVICES
SOCIAL SECURITY ADMINISTRATION

Form Approved
OMB No. 0960-0066

FORM SS-5 — APPLICATION FOR A SOCIAL SECURITY NUMBER CARD (Original, Replacement or Correction)

Unless the requested information is provided, we may not be able to issue a Social Security Number (20 CFR 422-103(b)).

| INSTRUCTIONS TO APPLICANT ▶ | Before completing this form, please read the instructions on the opposite page. Type or print, using pen with dark blue or black ink. Do not use pencil. SEE PAGE 1 FOR REQUIRED EVIDENCE. |

NAA NAME TO BE SHOWN ON CARD — First | Middle | Last

NAB **1** FULL NAME AT BIRTH (IF OTHER THAN ABOVE) — First | Middle | Last

ONA OTHER NAME(S) USED

STT **2** MAILING ADDRESS — (Street/Apt. No., P.O. Box, Rural Route No.)

CTY CITY (Do not abbreviate) | **STE** STATE | **ZIP** ZIP CODE

CSP **3** CITIZENSHIP (Check one only)
☐ a. U.S. citizen
☐ b. Legal alien allowed to work
☐ c. Legal alien not allowed to work
☐ d. Other (See instructions on Page 2)

SEX **4** SEX
☐ MALE
☐ FEMALE

ETB **5** RACE/ETHNIC DESCRIPTION (Check one only) (Voluntary)
☐ a. Asian, Asian-American or Pacific Islander (Includes persons of Chinese, Filipino, Japanese, Korean, Samoan, etc., ancestry or descent)
☐ b. Hispanic (Includes persons of Chicano, Cuban, Mexican or Mexican-American, Puerto Rican, South or Central American, or other Spanish ancestry or descent)
☐ c. Negro or Black (not Hispanic)
☐ d. Northern American Indian or Alaskan Native
☐ e. White (not Hispanic)

DOB **6** DATE OF BIRTH — MONTH | DAY | YEAR | **AGE** **7** PRESENT AGE | **PLB** **8** PLACE OF BIRTH — CITY (Do not abbreviate) | STATE OR FOREIGN COUNTRY (Do not abbreviate) | **FCI** ☐

MNA **9** MOTHER'S NAME AT HER BIRTH — First | Middle | Last (Her maiden name)

FNA FATHER'S NAME — First | Middle | Last

PNO **10** a. Has a Social Security number card ever been requested for the person listed in item 1? ☐ YES(2) ☐ NO(1) ☐ Don't know(1) b. Was a card received for the person listed in item 1? ☐ YES(3) ☐ NO(1) ☐ Don't know(1)

▶ **IF YOU CHECKED YES TO A OR B, COMPLETE ITEMS C THROUGH E; OTHERWISE GO TO ITEM 11.**

SSN c. Enter the Social Security number assigned to the person listed in item 1. ☐☐☐ — ☐☐ — ☐☐☐☐

NLC d. Enter the name shown on the most recent Social Security card issued for the person listed in item 1 | **PDB** e. Date of birth correction (See Instruction 10 on page 2) — MONTH | DAY | YEAR

DON **11** TODAY'S DATE — MONTH | DAY | YEAR | **12** Telephone number where we can reach you during the day. Please include the area code. — HOME | OTHER

ASD WARNING: Deliberately furnishing (or causing to be furnished) false information on this application is a crime punishable by fine or imprisonment, or both.

IMPORTANT REMINDER: WE CANNOT PROCESS THIS APPLICATION WITHOUT THE REQUIRED EVIDENCE. SEE PAGE 1.

13 YOUR SIGNATURE | **14** YOUR RELATIONSHIP TO PERSON IN ITEM 1 ☐ Self ☐ Other (Specify)

WITNESS (Needed only if signed by mark "X") | WITNESS (Needed only if signed by mark "X")

DO NOT WRITE BELOW THIS LINE (FOR SSA USE ONLY)		
DTC (SSA RECEIPT DATE)	NPN	DOC
NTC CAN	BIC IDN	ITV ☐ MANDATORY IN PERSON INTERVIEW CONDUCTED
TYPE(S) OF EVIDENCE SUBMITTED		SIGNATURE AND TITLE OF EMPLOYEE(S) REVIEWING EVIDENCE AND/OR CONDUCTING INTERVIEW
		DATE
	DCL	DATE

FORM **SS-5** (1-85) 5/84 edition may be used until supply is exhausted   3

The amount of social security benefits one receives every month depends on the amount of the worker's annual earnings for a period of years before retirement. There are other factors, too, that influence the amount of the monthly payment.

1. If a retired worker continues to earn income over certain limits (from sources other than investments, savings, royalties, or insurance), that person's benefits will be reduced. After age 70, however, a worker's outside income does not influence the amount of the monthly payment.

2. A worker who retires at the age of 62 rather than 65 receives a smaller benefit because he or she will collect for a longer period of time.

In Problem 1, Gani is entitled to collect retirement benefits, beginning immediately, because she is over 65. The fact that she worked part-time has no bearing on her eligibility to receive benefits.

Medicare

Medicare is a government program that provides protection from medical and hospital expenses. Medicare is available to anyone over the age of 65 or who has been disabled for two or more years. The protection is divided into two categories: hospital insurance and medical insurance.

Hospital Insurance. This part of the social security program is automatically included for everyone. It is paid for by premiums paid into the social security system. Medicare **hospital insurance** is known as a *compulsory* program because an individual has no choice about whether to collect these benefits. The insurance covers expenses incurred during hospitalization and some of the extended or outpatient care needed after a hospital stay.

Medical Insurance. The medical insurance feature of Medicare is optional. A person who wants to take advantage of these benefits must apply for them and pay an additional premium in order to get them.

PROBLEM

2. Xenos, 83 years old and very ill, was being cared for at home by his family. When he became unable to feed, bathe, and dress himself, his family decided that they needed help to care for him. Will Medicare cover the cost of professional in-home health care for Xenos?

Even though premiums must be paid, Medicare medical insurance is still much less expensive than private medical insurance. The federal government subsidizes 70 percent of the entire program. After a small deductible has been met, benefits are paid at 80 percent of the cost of the services rendered to the recipient. Medical services covered include X-rays, doctors' fees, emergency room charges, hearing aids, special orthopedic equipment such as wheelchairs and braces, and a period of nursing-home

LAW IN THE NEWS

Trims in Medicare, Medicaid Proposed

Washington Post

WASHINGTON–A new round of Medicare and Medicaid cuts and revisions designed to reduce projected program outlays by about $90 billion over five years has been proposed by the Office of Management and Budget for President Reagan's fiscal 1988 budget, administration sources said yesterday.

If enacted by Congress, the cuts—$68.8 billion in Medicare and $21.6 billion in Medicaid—would dwarf any previous retrenchments in the two programs. Some of the changes would eliminate benefits. Others would cut payments to hospitals and doctors and others would increase taxes or payments by beneficiaries or workers.

"That size cut would be an absurd distortion of national priorities and threaten the quality and access of care for the aged and the poor," said Michael D. Bromberg, director of the Federation of American Health Systems, spokesman for more than 1,000 for-profit hospitals.

John Rother, legislative director of the American Association of Retired Persons, the nation's largest such group, said, "The Medicaid cuts and some of the Medicare changes would constitute a breach of faith with the old and poor."

The OMB decided on the reductions in the middle of last week after reviewing the tentative budget proposals of the Department of Health and Human Services for fiscal 1988, the sources said.

Unless the secretary of health and human services, Dr. Otis R. Bowen, appeals to the president successfully against some of the cuts, the OMB proposals will be included in the 1988 budget.

In addition to its proposals for the Medicare and Medicaid programs, which currently spend more than $100 billion a year for benefits to 30 million Medicare and 23 million Medicaid recipients, the OMB also decided on:

–A cut of about $600 million from the fiscal 1987 level in new funds for the National Institutes of Health.

–A cut in funds for the Alcohol, Drug Abuse and Mental Health Administration from $1.36 billion in fiscal 1987 to $1.1 billion in 1988.

–An increase in funds for AIDS from $411 million in fiscal 1987 to $471 million.

care. However, Medicare does *not* pay for the services of people who provide professional in-home health care. Thus, in Problem 2, the cost of employing someone to help with Xenos's in-home care would not be covered by Medicare medical insurance. His family would have to bear that expense.

Disability Insurance

An important benefit of the Social Security Act is the protection the act provides for workers under 65 who are seriously ill or injured and therefore unable to earn a living wage. These workers can receive payments from **disability insurance.** Disability insurance will pay amounts similar to those that would have been paid under retirement benefits if the worker had retired at the age of 65. To receive full disability benefits, workers over 31 years of age must have accrued five years of credits. Younger disabled workers need fewer quarters of credit to receive benefits.

Disability insurance benefits are paid to people who have a sickness or injury that is expected to make them unable to work for at least a year. Because the benefits don't begin until six months after an illness or injury occurs, it is important to inform the local Social Security office of the illness or injury as soon as it occurs. Failure to report a disability quickly can result in a denial of benefits, since the circumstances of the disability must be thoroughly investigated. Disability benefits also can be paid to the family of a disabled worker.

Survivor's Insurance

The dependents of a wage earner who dies can receive monthly payments of **survivor's insurance.** These payments are made on the assumption that the survivors aren't able to support themselves. Figure 31.3 shows who may receive the benefits payable under the survivor's insurance provisions of the Social Security Act.

Figure 31.3
Beneficiaries of Survivor's Insurance

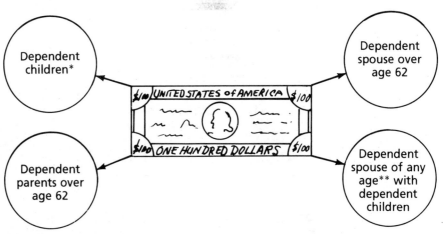

*Children are considered dependents if they are under age 18, or if they are under age 22 and are full-time students.

**A dependent spouse under age 62 with dependent children may collect benefits until the youngest child becomes ineligible due to age. Payments to the spouse then stop until the spouse is age 62, when benefits begin again.

State Social Insurance Programs

Although state-run social insurance programs must meet certain federal requirements, each state is free to administer its own programs. The three major programs most often associated with social insurance at the state level are worker's 1) compensation insurance, 2) unemployment insurance, and 3) state disability insurance.

Worker's Compensation Insurance

Worker's compensation insurance is designed to pay for the medical care and lost wages of people who are injured while at work. Some states provide compensation to workers who become ill because of certain occupational diseases. In the event of a death due to accident, the family or estate of the deceased worker usually receives a lump sum or payments for a fixed time. Compensation is based on wages earned and on the type of injury sustained.

The benefits of this insurance are payable out of a fund collected from employers by a state worker's compensation agency. The federal government has its own fund for its employees. The employers' payments are, in effect, premiums that pay for the cost of the benefits when injuries occur. These benefits are payable regardless of fault unless the injured worker was extremely careless, failed to follow standard safety rules, or was under the influence of mind-altering drugs (including alcohol) when injured.

Hanson started a small painting business and employed two painters. Hanson made regular payments to his state's worker's compensation agency for himself and his two employees. One of the painters was badly hurt when she fell off a ladder, even though she had followed all of the usual safety rules. The worker's medical expenses and any wages she loses while recovering from her injuries will be paid by worker's compensation insurance.

A worker's injury should be reported immediately to the state worker's compensation agency, because failure to do so may result in the loss of the benefits.

An employee insured at work is eligible for worker's compensation.

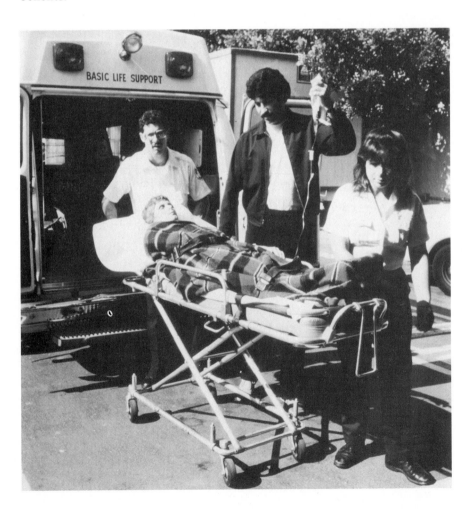

Unemployment Insurance

Each state has an agency that oversees **unemployment insurance.** Employers are required by law to contribute a percentage of all regular employees' wages to the unemployment insurance fund. A worker who is laid off from a job through no fault of his or her own is entitled to apply for unemployment benefits. In most states, a waiting period of a week is required before benefit payments are made. The maximum period during which benefits may be received varies from state to state, but it is often six months. In some cases benefits may be paid for a year. Workers who quit or are fired for gross misconduct are not eligible for unemployment insurance. Also, workers who are out of work because of labor disputes may not be eligible for unemployment insurance.

Actually, the goal of a state unemployment agency is to *keep* people working. An applicant for unemployment benefits must register for a job at a public employment agency and file a claim for benefits. The worker must have worked previously on a job covered by the state law—usually for a firm employing four or more people for a certain number of days per year. The worker also must have a certain amount of wage credits, or pay for work on covered jobs during the year or two prior to the layoff. In addition, the unemployed person has to be able to work and available for work. The agency keeps records of the kind of work each unemployed worker can perform, and about the general area in which the unemployed person could work. Then, if a job for which that worker is qualified becomes available in that area, the unemployed worker is required to apply for the job. Once a job has been offered to a worker, unemployment benefits are suspended—whether or not the worker takes the job. This rule helps to motivate unemployed people to take available jobs.

State Disability Insurance

State disability insurance (commonly known as *SDI)* protects workers who are disabled as a result of injuries or illnesses that aren't related to employment. Because workers in this situation can't collect worker's compensation or unemployment insurance, SDI provides them with an income for up to six months. If a worker is still disabled after six months, the federal social security disability program picks up the payments.

In this unit you have seen how insurance—whether privately purchased or supplied by government—protects us. Insurance is an important part of today's society, but many legal questions can arise from insurance-related problems. One good way to be sure you are well protected from financial loss is to study new trends in insurance and learn how changes in the law affect insurance protection. Also, if you are considering the purchase of insurance, you should "comparison shop" for a knowledgeable agent, coverage that suits your needs, and premium rates that you can afford.

Let's move on now to Unit 7, where we'll study *commercial paper*—the documents we use to meet our financial obligations.

Chapter 31 Review

"YOU BE THE JUDGE" REVIEW

Look again at the "You Be the Judge" cases given at the beginning of this chapter. Would you decide them differently now, after your study of the chapter?

Correct Decisions

1. No. A worker who retires at the age of 62 rather than 65 receives a smaller monthly payment of social security benefits. The government assumes that a worker who retires at the age of 62 will receive the benefits for a longer period of time than a person who retires at 65.

2. Yes. Jacobsen's wife and children would be eligible for the survivor's benefits payable under the Social Security Act.

UNDERSTANDING WHAT YOU HAVE READ

1. What is the name of the federal social insurance program? When did it take effect? What agency oversees the program?
2. What are the three main types of state social insurance?
3. List the four categories of protection provided by the federal social insurance program.
4. At what age may a worker begin to collect retirement benefits?
5. How can a retired worker earn money and still receive maximum social insurance benefits?
6. Briefly describe the two divisions or features of Medicare.
7. How is a disabled worker guaranteed constant protection under social insurance?
8. Who can collect survivor's insurance?
9. Why is it important to have a social security number?
10. What circumstances could prevent the payment of worker's compensation benefits to someone who is injured on the job?

BUILDING YOUR LEGAL VOCABULARY

From this list, select the legal term that belongs in the blank in each sentence below. Write your answers on a separate sheet of paper.

disability insurance
hospital insurance
Medicare
retirement insurance

social insurance
Social Security Act
state disability insurance

survivor's insurance
unemployment insurance
worker's compensation insurance

1. Workers who are laid off from their jobs can receive ||||||||||||||||||||| from their states.
2. Social security provides ||||||||||||||||||||| for people who are unable to work for at least a year due to illness or injuries.
3. The federal law passed in 1935 to protect the public from income losses is the |||||||||||||||||||||.
4. Certain relatives of a worker who dies can collect ||||||||||||||||||||| from the federal government.
5. Government-subsidized programs of ||||||||||||||||||||| are intended to protect those who can't afford to purchase private insurance.
6. The ||||||||||||||||||||| portion of Medicare is a compulsory program.
7. Employer contributions pay for ||||||||||||||||||||| for people who are unable to work as a result of causes that are not job-related.
8. The ||||||||||||||||||||| program pays for the hospital and medical bills of people over the age of 65 and people who are disabled for two or more years.
9. A worker injured on the job can get benefits from |||||||||||||||||||||, regardless of whose fault caused the event.
10. The social security program that provides a limited income for people who quit working at the age of 62 or 65 is called |||||||||||||||||||||.

APPLYING LEGAL PRINCIPLES

1. Nuan cut herself badly while chopping wood in her backyard. She applied for worker's compensation benefits to provide her with income while she was recovering at home. Will she be able to collect worker's compensation?

2. Mendoza was a truck driver for a soft-drink distributor. One day, he left his regular route and drove the truck across town to have lunch. As he pulled away from the restaurant, Mendoza was injured when his truck was struck by a car. Is he entitled to collect worker's compensation benefits?

3. Buxton worked as a waiter over the summer. When he went back to high school in the fall, he applied for unemployment insurance. Can he collect?

4. Chow retired at the age of 73 after teaching for 40 years. She continued to do consulting work and made $30,000 in the year after her retirement. The social security office denied Chow's claim for social security benefits because she made too much money. Is the social security office's denial correct?

5. Sokolski died, leaving her two young children, ages 8 and 6, in her sister's care. The sister applied for survivor's insurance, and the children were granted benefits. Should the sister also receive benefits?

6. Lundgren worked as a housekeeper for Symonds for twelve years. Every week, Lundgren was paid in cash. At the end of twelve years, Symonds laid off Lundgren. Lundgren applied for unemployment benefits, but the state unemployment agency denied her application. The agency claimed that no unemployment tax had ever been paid by Lundgren's employer. Can Symonds be forced to pay for Lundgren's unemployment benefits?

7. Gesner was disabled in a car accident at the age of 31. His doctors told him that he would never walk again. Gesner then applied for full disability benefits. His application was denied, however, because he had only 20 quarters of credit. Is this denial correct?

8. Rogers failed to report an industrial injury until three months after it happened. The doctor who treated Rogers told her that the injury would heal in four to six months. Can Rogers still collect disability benefits?

9. Winthrop stayed in the hospital for a day after his doctors released him because his apartment was being painted. Will Medicare cover the cost of the extra stay?

10. At the age of 55, Salieri retired from his job as a highway construction crew chief. Immediately after his retirement, he applied for retirement benefits from social security. When will he be able to begin collecting benefits?

ANALYZING COURT CASES

1. As a self-employed painting contractor, Le Khoi paid social security taxes at the higher rate required of self-employed workers. He also had employees. Le Khoi regularly withheld social security taxes from his employees' paychecks and paid matching funds to the Social Security Administration. After changing the legal status of the business from a sole proprietorship to a corporation, Le Khoi continued to pay the self-employment tax rate for himself. Under the rules of incorporation of a small business, everyone—including the owner of the business—is considered an employee of the corporation. Was Le Khoi entitled to a refund of the excess social security taxes he had paid for himself since the business was incorporated? (Based on a ruling of the Social Security Administration, 1981)

2. Rawitzer became ill. When she learned that she would be unable to work for eight months or more, she applied for disability insurance. Her application was rejected because she had been having symptoms of the illness for six months before she became too ill to work. Is Rawitzer entitled to disability benefits? (Based on the Social Security Act of 1935)

3. Garza, a construction worker, drove his own car to a grocery store on his lunch hour to buy groceries for use at his home. At the same time he bought a jar of coffee for use at his employer's office. While returning on a direct route to a restaurant where he often ate lunch, Garza was killed in an auto accident. Was Garza's widow entitled to collect a death benefit under a worker's compensation law? (Based on: *Tompkins v. Rinner Construction Company*, 398 P. 2d 578)

UNIT 7

COMMERCIAL PAPER

CHAPTERS

LEARNING OBJECTIVES

After you have studied this unit, you should be able to:

- Identify the negotiable instruments that substitute for money in our economy.

- Show that you understand the legal differences between negotiable instruments and other contracts.

- Describe how negotiable instruments are transferred and the legal effect of those transfers.

- State the rights and duties of original and secondary parties to negotiable instruments.

- Explain the rights and duties of bank depositors and their banks.

CHAPTER 32

Nature of Negotiable Instruments

Think about these cases.
If you were the judge, how would you decide each case?

1

You wrote a promissory note by typing the necessary information on a printed form. Then you signed the form with a rubber signature stamp. Is the instrument negotiable?

2

Collazo gave a note, payable on demand, to Sinar. Later, Collazo claimed that the note wasn't negotiable because it wasn't payable on a certain day. Was the note negotiable?

WHAT IS A NEGOTIABLE INSTRUMENT?

Business today couldn't be conducted without the use of **commercial paper**—documents such as checks, promissory notes, drafts, and certificates of deposit. Checks are used in nearly every business transaction, both by business people and by consumers. Promissory notes, whose origin may be traced to ancient times, are used by large and small businesses and by consumers. Drafts, of which the check is a specialized form, are widely used to settle business debts. Certificates of deposit, actually forms of promissory notes, are types of savings accounts. A bank agrees to repay the amount of the certificate with interest at a specified time. These commercial papers are often called *instruments* because they represent written expressions of legal acts and proof of such acts.

PROBLEM

> **1.** What function does commercial paper serve in these situations?
> a. Kihara buys goods from Newberger and pays for them by check.
> b. Perelli buys goods from Roque and gives her a promissory note, payable in 60 days.

The chief feature of a commercial paper is that it is a *negotiable* (transferable) *instrument* if it meets certain requirements. We'll discuss those requirements in this chapter. Because they are readily transferable, negotiable instruments serve as (1) substitutes for money and (2) instruments of credit. In Problem 1(a), when Kihara gave Newberger a check in payment for the goods, he used the check as a substitute for money. In Problem 1(b), Perelli used the promissory note as an instrument of credit. She gained 60 days' time in which to pay for the goods.

Since negotiable instruments circulate so freely, their use is strictly governed by statute law—namely, the Uniform Commercial Code (Article 3). Article 3 has been adopted in all the states. In later chapters we will study the principles that govern the use of negotiable instruments, including the rights and duties of the parties concerned.

The negotiable instruments in common use today are (1) promissory notes, (2) checks, (3) drafts, and (4) certificates of deposit.

Promissory Notes

A **promissory note** is an unconditional written promise to pay a stated sum to the order of a specific person, or to the bearer, at a definite time or on demand. The party who issues and signs a promissory note is legally known as the **maker**. The party to whom payment is promised is the **payee**. If the payee is in possession of the instrument, he or she is also known as a **holder**. In Figure 32.1, John G. Rosario, the maker, promises to pay $1,000, with interest, to the order of Jennifer K. Noble, on August 31, 19—.

$ 1,000.00   New York, NY   August 1 19 --

_____ Thirty days _____ after date __I__ promise to pay to

the order of _____ Jennifer K. Noble _____

One thousand and no/100--------------------- Dollars

at __Phoenix National Bank, Phoenix, AZ__

Value received with interest at __12%__.

No. __59__ Due 8-31, 19 --   *John G. Rosario*

Checks

A **check** is an unconditional written order to a depositor's bank. It directs the bank to pay on demand a specified sum of money to the order of a third person or to the bearer. Checks, unlike promissory notes, involve three parties. In Figure 32.2, Jill Tracer, the **drawer,** directs her bank, Citizens Bank, the **drawee,** to pay $32.40 to the order of The Fabric Farm, the payee of the check. A bank is always the drawee of a check.

JILL TRACER
6789 ROUND TOP DRIVE
LOS ANGELES, CA 90065   0002

Dec. 9 19 --   16-66
                        1220

PAY TO THE
ORDER OF *The Fabric Farm* _____ $ *32.40*

Thirty-two and 40/100 _____ DOLLARS

Citizens Bank

WILSHIRE PLACE, LOS ANGELES, CALIFORNIA 90005

MEMO *material* _____   *Jill Tracer*

⑈⑈ 1 2 2 0 0 0 6 6 4 ⑈⑈ 0 0 0 2 ⑈ 5 7 2 3 0 7 2 6 2 ⑈⑈

Drafts

A **draft** is similar to a check except that the order to pay is not on a bank but on a third party, who is named in the instrument. In Figure 32.3, Walter Carlin, the drawer, directs that Linda Rabkin, the drawee, pay $200 to the order of Christopher Quay, the payee.

Figure 32.3
A Draft

$ <u>200.00</u>   <u>Indianapolis, IN</u>   <u>May 1</u>, 19 <u>--</u>

<u>AT SIGHT</u>

Pay to the order of <u>CHRISTOPHER QUAY</u>

<u>Two hundred and no/100----------------------</u> Dollars

Value received and charge same to the account of

To <u>Linda Rabkin</u>   *Walter Carlin*

Address <u>Gary, IN</u>

Certificates of Deposit

The Uniform Commercial Code defines a **certificate of deposit** as "an acknowledgment by a bank of receipt of money with an engagement to repay it." A person who wants to make a temporary bank deposit against which checks are not to be drawn may obtain a certificate of deposit from the bank. The instrument is negotiable and acknowledges that the bank has received the money as a special deposit. It also contains the bank's promise to pay the sum noted on the certificate, with or without interest, to the depositor on demand or at a definite time.

How a Negotiable Instrument Differs from Other Contracts

In Chapter 14 we learned that contracts involving rights to money or property may be assigned. We also learned that an assignment may be oral or written and that the *assignee obtained no better title through the assignment than the assignor had.* Although this is true of contracts in general, it is not true of negotiable instruments.

PROBLEM

2. Fidalgo sold an air-conditioning unit to Gargill and warranted that it wouldn't rust. Gargill gave Fidalgo a promissory note in payment. Fidalgo then indorsed the note and gave it to Dooley, to whom he owed money. When the note came due, Dooley asked Gargill to pay it. Gargill refused, however, claiming that Fidalgo had defrauded him in the deal because the air conditioner had rusted. Must Gargill pay Dooley?

The fact that these instruments are *negotiable* means that a person who receives one in a legal manner may acquire a better title to the instrument than the person who transferred it had. Contracts in general may be in oral or in written form and assigned in that manner. However, a negotiable instrument *must* be in writing and is usually negotiated by indorsement plus delivery. In other words, the person who transfers it signs the back of the instrument and delivers it to another person. In other contracts, notice of assignment must be given to the debtor. In negotiable instruments, no notice of negotiation has to be given to the maker.

Another important difference between contracts in general and negotiable instruments relates to the requirement of consideration. With negotiable instruments, consideration is assumed or understood to exist unless it can be proved otherwise. In other contracts, consideration is not assumed to exist and must be shown. Figure 32.4 is a summary of the differences between ordinary contracts and negotiable instruments.

In Problem 2, Dooley received the promissory note by negotiation and knew nothing of the warranty made to Gargill. Thus, he is entitled to collect from Gargill. Through negotiation, Dooley received a better title to the promissory note given for the defective air conditioner than Fidalgo had.

Figure 32.4
Ordinary Contracts vs. Negotiable Instruments

	Ordinary Contracts	**Negotiable Instruments**
Form	May be made orally, in written form, or implied from the actions of the parties.	Must be made in writing.
Consideration	Must be present for the contract to be valid.	Need not be shown—it is presumed to exist.
Transfer	May be assigned in oral or written form.	Must be negotiated by (1) delivery alone or (2) delivery plus indorsement.
Notice	Assignee of the contract must give notice to the party obligated to perform the contract.	Notice of negotiation is not required.
Title	Assignee gets no better title than the assignor had.	Holder may obtain a better title than the transferor had.

FORM OF NEGOTIABLE INSTRUMENTS

The instruments studied in this chapter may or may not be negotiable.

> **3.** Helen Carr gave this typed instrument to Barry Woods.
>
> > I promise to pay 100 bushels of wheat to the order of Barry Woods.
> > August 24, 19—
> >
> > Helen Carr
>
> Is the instrument negotiable?

To be negotiable, an instrument must comply with five specific requirements of the Uniform Commerical Code. These requirements relate to (1) written form and signature, (2) unconditional promise or order, (3) payment to order or to bearer, (4) payment of a sum certain in money, and (5) payment on demand or at a definite time. An instrument that satisfies all five of these requirements is negotiable, and it may pass freely from hand to hand. The instrument shown in Problem 3 is nonnegotiable because it isn't payable in a sum certain in money.

Written Form and Signature

A negotiable instrument must be in writing. Any writing is sufficient to meet the statutory requirement. It may be handwritten in ink or pencil, typed, printed, or stamped. It's not a good idea to use pencil, though, because pencil can easily be changed.

> **4.** A promissory note looked like this:
>
> > I, Carmen Oliva, promise to pay to Charles Burkhardt or order, $450 on September 15, 19—.
>
> Was the instrument properly signed by its maker?

A promissory note or certificate of deposit must be signed by the maker, and a draft or check must be signed by the drawer. The maker or drawer usually signs in the lower right-hand corner of the instrument. However, a signature that appears in some other part of the instrument may still be regarded as a proper signature. The signature may consist of a name, a mark such as "X," initials, or a trade name. It may appear in written, typed, or printed form. In Problem 4, Carmen Oliva's signature appearing at the beginning of the promissory note is a valid signature.

Unconditional Promise or Order

5.   Kohl issued a promissory note that read as follows:

> I promise to pay the sum of $1,000 to the order of James
> Fiato if I inherit my aunt's property.
>   Theodore Kohl

Is this note negotiable?

If a negotiable instrument is to circulate freely as a substitute for money, it must contain a promise or order to pay absolutely—that is, without any conditions attached. In Problem 5, Kohl promised to pay if he inherited his aunt's property. For various reasons, Kohl may never inherit the property. Therefore, his promissory note is not payable unconditionally as required by the UCC.

Not only must the promise or order to pay be without conditions but the wording of the instrument also must show that the maker or drawer actually promises or orders the payment to be made. If an instrument reads, "I owe to bearer $500," or "Due John Doe $500," it is clear that these are mere admissions that a debt exists. They aren't promises or orders to pay money.

Under the UCC, a promise or order is not conditional merely because it "indicates a particular account to be debited or any other fund or source from which reimbursement is expected."

A promissory note contains this statement at the bottom: "Bookkeeper—Charge this note to petty cash." This statement doesn't make the note a conditional promise to pay merely because it indicates a particular account to be charged or debited.

If, however, the promise or order to pay depends solely on the existence of a *particular fund* rather than the general credit of the maker or drawer, the instrument is conditional and nonnegotiable.

An instrument read, "Payable out of my share of the profits of XYZ Company." This is a nonnegotiable instrument, even though there may be sufficient profits to pay it when it comes due.

Payment to Order or to Bearer

The UCC requires that an instrument, to be negotiable, must be payable to order or to bearer. These are known as **order instruments** or **bearer instruments.** This doesn't mean that equivalent words can't be used in place of "order" or "bearer." For example, "Pay to holder" may be used instead of "Pay to bearer." An instrument may be made payable to "the order of Joan Doe" or "to Joan Doe or order." However, if the instrument reads "Pay to Joan Doe," it is nonnegotiable because the words of negotiability (*order of* or *bearer*) are not included.

> **6.** Santos issued a check that contained all the requirements of negotiability, except that it was payable to "Cash." Is the instrument payable to order or to bearer?

Under the UCC, an instrument is payable to bearer when by its terms it is payable to (1) bearer or the order of bearer, (2) a specified person or bearer, or (3) cash or the order of cash, or any other indication that doesn't designate a specific payee. Therefore, the check issued by Santos in Problem 6 is payable to bearer and negotiable.

The Code also provides that an instrument may be made payable to the order of an estate, partnership, or unincorporated association. Such instruments are to be regarded as order rather than bearer instruments. An instrument may be made payable to the order of one person, to two or more persons jointly or in the alternative, or to one of several persons but not in succession. An instrument also may be made payable to an office or holder of an office, such as "Treasurer of the City Club." In either case, it is payable to the holder of the office and the successors of that official.

Payment in Money

For an instrument to be negotiable, the UCC requires that it be payable in money and that its sum be certain.

> **7.** Julianne Chen gave Henry Ash this promissory note:
>
> > I promise to pay to Henry Ash, or order, 80 British pounds, two months after date. Value received.
> > September 1, 19—
> >
> > *Julianne Chen*
> > Julianne Chen
>
> Is the note negotiable?

Is an instrument payable in commodities negotiable?

A sum is considered negotiable if the holder is able to determine the amount due from the instrument itself, with any necessary computation. Thus, a demand note bearing interest at twelve percent is negotiable. The Code defines money as "a medium of exchange authorized or adopted by a domestic or foreign government as part of its currency." For purposes of negotiability, this definition implies that money is more than legal tender. Under the UCC definition, an instrument payable in the currency of another country is payable in the number of dollars that the foreign currency would purchase on the instrument's due date. Thus, Julianne Chen's note in Problem 7 is payable in money and the sum is certain. However, an instrument payable in commodities (goods)—such as agricultural products—is not negotiable because it is not payable in money.

The sum to be paid is regarded as certain under the UCC even though the maker promises to pay it (1) with interest or discount, (2) in stated installments, (3) with exchange or less exchange charges, and (4) with costs of collection or an attorney's fees, or both, on default in payment at **maturity** (the due date). The sum payable is also certain if there is a conflict between the amount written in words and the amount expressed in figures. It is the amount written in words that will be paid.

Payment on Demand or at a Definite Time

> **8.** Is this note a negotiable instrument?
>
> > March 1, 19—
> > I promise to pay five hundred dollars to the order of Ellen
> > Eisen one year after my death. Value received.
> > Sonia Held

Under the UCC, an instrument must be payable on demand or at a definite time. A definite time includes payment (1) on or before a stated date, (2) at a fixed period after a stated date, or (3) at a fixed period after sight (after presentation to the drawee). A promise to pay on the happening of a stated event that is sure to take place, although the exact time isn't known (as in Problem 8), is not payable at a definite time. Therefore, the instrument in which the promise is made is nonnegotiable. An instrument's negotiability is determined as of the time it is issued and can't be changed by the happening of a later event. Under the Code, an instrument is payable at a definite time even though the holder has an option to extend the date of payment.

> A promissory note payable on March 1 states that its maturity date may be extended at the option of the holder. This statement does not affect the negotiability of the instrument since it gives the holder a right that belonged to him or her without the statement.

If the extension of the time for payment is at the option of the maker or drawee of a draft, a *definite time limit* must be stated, or the instrument will not be negotiable.

> A draft reads, "Payable on March 1 or April 1, 19—, at the option of the drawee." The insertion of April 1 makes the instrument payable at a definite time and therefore negotiable.

Instruments payable on demand include those payable at sight (on presentation to the drawee), and those in which no time for payment is stated.

Terms Not Essential to Negotiability

PROBLEM

9. Which terms in this instrument are not essential to the instrument's negotiability?

> Iowa City, Iowa
> November 1, 19—
> On demand, I promise to pay $1,000 (One Thousand Dollars) to the order of Jeffrey Hinn, at the First National Bank of Iowa City. Value received.
>
> *George P. Barns*
> George P. Barns

The negotiability of an instrument is not affected by the omission of certain items. These include (1) the place where the instrument is drawn or payable, (2) a statement of the consideration, or (3) the date of issue.

Place Where Drawn or Payable

A negotiable instrument does not have to state the place where it is drawn or payable. It is advisable to include this information, however, in order to make transfer of the instrument easier and to avoid possible confusion. In Problem 9, the items "Iowa City, Iowa" (place where drawn) and "First National Bank of Iowa City" (place where payable) may be omitted without affecting the note's negotiability.

Statement of Consideration

A negotiable instrument does not have to state that it is issued for value. It is customary, however, to include the words "value received" or similar wording. In Problem 9, omission of the words "value received" wouldn't affect the note's negotiability.

Date of Issue

A negotiable instrument is valid even though it isn't dated. If the date has been omitted, the holder of the instrument may insert the true date, which is the date of issue. In Problem 9, omission of "November 1, 19—" wouldn't affect the negotiability of the instrument. An instrument may be *antedated* (dated back) or *postdated* (dated ahead) without affecting its negotiability.

It's important to know that every time you sign a commercial paper, you have entered into a valid contract. This chapter has shown you how commercial paper can become negotiable or transferable. In Chapter 33 we'll study two forms of commercial paper—promissory notes and drafts—in detail.

LIVING UNDER THE LAW

How Negotiable is "Negotiable"?

Are some commercial papers and securities more negotiable than others?

Take the case of stock certificates that were stolen in a daring Jesse James type of robbery. The certificates were registered in the name of a Wall Street brokerage house. To transfer them would require the official stamped indorsement of the brokerage firm. Thus, it would be virtually impossible for the robbers to negotiate the "negotiable" stock.

So what is the most negotiable instrument currently being circulated? Checks, you say? Wrong. Hard cash is the most negotiable of all instruments. But even with cash, the larger the denomination of the bill, the lower the degree of negotiability. For example, one-dollar and five-dollar bills are more readily negotiated than, say, a thousand-dollar bill. Of course, rare coins and old bills as well as foreign money have very limited transfer possibilities.

Coupon (or bearer) bonds issued by private firms, cities, states, and other governmental bodies rank next to cash in order of negotiability. Checks, if properly indorsed, are widely accepted, but they are not as negotiable as cash. Mortgages, deeds, leases, and similar instruments may be assignable, but they are certainly nonnegotiable. Warehouse receipts and bills of lading have limited negotiability or are nonnegotiable.

We may conclude that negotiability depends on the amount of paperwork needed to change ownership. If instruments require indorsements or some proof of ownership, their negotiability is substantially reduced.

Chapter 32 Review

"YOU BE THE JUDGE" REVIEW

Look again at the "You Be the Judge" cases given at the beginning of this chapter. Would you decide them differently now, after your study of the chapter?

Correct Decisions

1. Yes. An instrument may be handwritten in ink or pencil (although ink is preferred), typed, or printed. The same rule applies to signatures.

2. Yes. To be negotiable, an instrument must be payable on demand or at a definite time. Collazo's note was payable on demand.

UNDERSTANDING WHAT YOU HAVE READ

1. What four types of commercial paper are in common use?
2. What are the chief functions of negotiable instruments?
3. Name the parties involved in
   a. a promissory note
   b. a check
   c. a draft
   d. a certificate of deposit
4. How do negotiable instruments differ from other contracts?
5. List five requirements of a negotiable instrument.

6. What kind of writing will satisfy the statutory requirement that a negotiable instrument be written?
7. Under the UCC, when is an instrument regarded as payable to bearer?
8. How does the Code define the term "money"?
9. What does the requirement of payment at a definite time include?
10. List the terms that are not essential to the negotiability of an instrument. Give an example of one of those terms.

BUILDING YOUR LEGAL VOCABULARY

Choose the legal term that will correctly complete each definition below. Write your answer on a separate sheet of paper.

1. An unconditional written order to a bank to pay a stated sum of money on demand to a third person or the bearer is a
   a. promissory note.
   b. check.
   c. certificate of deposit.
2. The party who issues and signs a promissory note is the
   a. maker.
   b. payee.
   c. drawee.
3. The due date on a negotiable instrument is also known as the date of
   a. issue.
   b. negotiation.
   c. maturity.

4. The medium of exchange authorized or adopted by a government as part of its currency is known under the UCC as
   a. a bearer instrument.
   b. an order instrument.
   c. money.
5. The commercial paper in which the order to pay is on a third party named in the instrument rather than on a bank is known as a
   a. certificate of deposit.
   b. draft.
   c. promissory note.

APPLYING LEGAL PRINCIPLES

1. a. What type of instrument is shown here?
   b. Name the parties and describe their relationships to one another.

> **First Depositor's Trust of Concord, Massachusetts**
>
>   July 6,19—
>
> This is to certify that Vittoria Hassan has deposited the sum of Fifty Thousand Dollars, payable one year from date with interest at 7.25%, upon return of this certificate at maturity, properly indorsed.
>
>   John Allende
>   Cashier

2. a. Identify this commercial paper.
   b. Identify the *drawer,* the *drawee,* and the *payee* in the document.

>   Kansas City, KS
>
> At sight, pay to the order of Harold Gerber Three Hundred Dollars ($300).
>
> To: Patrick Murphy   *Amanda Burstin*
>   Manhattan, KS   Amanda Burstin

3. a. What type of instrument is this?
   b. Identify the parties.

>   May 1, 19—
>
>   Thirty days after date, I promise to pay to Bearer the sum of Five Hundred and No/100 Dollars. Value received.
>
>   
>   Charles Galloway

4. What requirements of a negotiable promissory note are shown in this instrument?

$ 1,000	Houston, Texas	August 1 ,19 --

               30 days   after date _I_ promise to pay to

the order of   Joseph Ko

One thousand and 00/100---------------------- Dollars

at   The State Bank

Value received with interest at _12%_

No. _31_ Due _8-31_,19 --   *Barbara Insero*

5. State whether the instrument in Problem 4 would have been negotiable under the following circumstances. Give legal reasons for your answers.
   a. If Barbara Insero had not signed the note.
   b. If Barbara Insero had written, "I, Barbara Insero, promise to pay to the order of Joseph Ko," and so forth, but had not written her name at the bottom of the note.
   c. If the note had been written in pencil.
   d. If the words "order of" had been omitted.
   e. If the words "Value received with interest at 12%" had been omitted.
   f. If the date of the note had been omitted.

6. Are these negotiable promissory notes? State your reason in each case.
   a. "I.O.U. $500. J. Windsor."
   b. A written document, signed by Costa, stating, "Due Michael Losh, $150."
   c. "Pay Margaret Grabau and Bradley Grabau, or order."
   d. "This amount to be paid out of our profits on the Jackson Avenue construction job."
   e. "I promise to pay to the order of Daniel Grady $400 and a ton of coal."
   f. "Pay to bearer, Mary V. Cusick."

7. State which of these notes are negotiable. Give legal reasons for your answers.
   a. "On demand, I, Louise Glicksman, promise to pay to the order of Karen Feng, Fifty Dollars."
   b. A promissory note payable one month after the death of the maker.
   c. A promissory note payable one month after date with interest at 11%.
   d. A check payable to the "Vice President of the Njoku Company."
   e. A check payable in Mexican pesos.
   f. A promissory note payable "out of the money in your hands belonging to the estate of Samuel Noah."
   g. A draft payable to the order of "Minturn or McNeese."
   h. A promissory note payable on "May 25, 19—, or at a later date at the option of the holder."

8. Would this instrument be negotiable in each of the following situations? Give legal reasons for your answers.

$250.00   Glen Falls, Montana.
                      March 15, 19—
On demand, I promise to pay to Frank Kabarra or order Two Hundred and Fifty and No/100 Dollars at my office, 100 Glen Street.
Value received.   Deborah Heroux

   a. If the place where the instrument was drawn—Glen Falls, Montana—had been omitted.
   b. If the words "Two Hundred and Fifty and No/100 Dollars" had been omitted.
   c. If, instead of "On demand," the wording read, "On the day of my marriage."

ANALYZING COURT CASES

1. Hatcher bought a car from White. In payment, Hatcher gave White several negotiable promissory notes, payable on different dates. All of the notes contained this provision:

> In default of payment on any of the said notes, the whole shall become due and payable.

Hatcher claimed that this provision made the notes nonnegotiable. Is his claim legally correct? (*White v. Hatcher,* 188 S.W. 61)

2. Reilly issued a promissory note in the sum of $1,000, payable to the order of Piebes. This statement appeared in the bottom left-hand corner of the instrument:

> The face of the note is payable by the transfer of an equivalent amount of the common stock of the Armex Corporation now owned by the undersigned.

A subsequent holder of the note sued Reilly to collect the $1,000. Reilly claimed that the note was nonnegotiable. Was that claim legally correct? (Based on: *Markley v. Rhodes,* 12 N.W. 775)

3. As heir of F. J. Salta, Moore was sued by O'Rourke on this written document:

> Pay to L. O'Rourke—$1,000
>
> *F. J. Salta*
>
> (signed) F. J. Salta

Moore contended that the instrument was nonnegotiable. Do you agree? (*O'Rourke v. Moore,* 98 So. 2d 903)

CHAPTER 33

Promissory Notes and Drafts

YOU BE THE JUDGE

Think about these cases.
If you were the judge, how would you decide each case?

1

Comeau accepted a draft payable to Nally on which the name of Suto, the drawer, was forged. Can Nally collect from Comeau when the draft reaches maturity?

2

Lek, in Los Angeles, California, issued a draft payable to Grace, in London, England. The drawee was Pineiro. When the draft was dishonored on presentment for payment, Grace immediately telephoned Lek. Is Lek now liable on the instrument?

Figure 33.1
A Promissory Note

$ __750__   Raleigh, North Carolina, June 6, 19 --

__One month__   after date __I__ promise to pay to

the order of __Brenda J. Farro__

Seven Hundred Fifty and 00/100 ——— Dollars

at __Third State Bank, Raleigh, N.C.__

Value received

No. __237__ Due July 6 19 --   __Hector Munon__

PROMISSORY NOTES

The instrument shown in Figure 33.1 is a promissory note. You'll remember from Chapter 32 that a promissory note is negotiable if it contains all the requirements for negotiability. An instrument is negotiable if it contains an unconditional promise in writing, signed by the maker, to pay to the order of a designated payee or to bearer, a sum certain in money at a definite time.

---

1. Is the instrument shown in Figure 33.1 negotiable?

In order to negotiate or transfer a promissory note to another person, the payee simply writes his or her name on the back and delivers the note to the other person. This person is called the **indorser**. The person who receives the note is known as the **indorsee** or the *holder.* In answer to Problem 1, the instrument shown in Figure 33.1 is a negotiable promissory note because it contains all of the essentials of negotiability. In order to negotiate it, Brenda J. Farro, the payee, would write her name on the back of the note and deliver it to another person.

Kinds of Promissory Notes

Individuals, businesses, and governmental bodies make use of the usual type of promissory note as well as of special types of promissory notes.

---

2. Marlin issued a promissory note, payable to Mohr. The note contained this statement: "In case of default in payment, I hereby authorize the holder of this instrument to enter judgment against me in any court of record in Ohio." What type of promissory note did Marlin issue to Mohr?

A certificate of deposit is one of the special types of promissory notes. There are two other special types, as well: judgment notes and collateral notes.

Judgment Notes

The maker of a promissory note may agree that the note's holder may enter judgment against the maker without a trial if the maker fails to pay the note at maturity. This type of promissory note is known as a **judgment note.** In Problem 2, Marlin issued a judgment note in favor of Mohr. The note entitled Mohr to obtain judgment against Marlin under the conditions stated. This type of note is widely used because it allows the holder to obtain a judgment against the maker quickly and inexpensively.

Collateral Note

A **collateral note** is a promissory note that contains a description of the property, such as stocks and bonds, pledged as security for payment of the note. The note usually provides that the security behind it may be sold if the note isn't paid at maturity. If the note *is* paid, the security is returned to the borrower or maker of the note.

Liability of the Maker

PROBLEM

> **3.** Harlan issued a promissory note payable to Saldi. At maturity, Saldi failed to present the note to Harlan for payment. Harlan claims that she is no longer liable on the note. Is her claim legally correct?

The maker of a promissory note is absolutely required to pay it on the due date. If the maker fails to do so, the holder may then look to the indorsers for payment. The holder of the note does not have to notify or present the instrument to the maker in order to hold the maker liable. Therefore, Harlan's claim in Problem 3 is legally incorrect. If payment of the note is not made at maturity, the holder may sue the maker to recover the amount of the note. If the note is interest-bearing, the maker is liable for the face amount plus the interest. If the rate of interest isn't mentioned and the note is interest-bearing, the legal rate of interest will be understood.

Presentment of a Note for Payment

The UCC defines **presentment** as a demand for payment from the party primarily liable on the instrument. That party is the maker.

PROBLEM

4. Carson was the holder of a note issued by San Marco and indorsed by Nolan. At maturity, Carson failed to present the note to the maker, San Marco, for payment. Because of this, Nolan claims that he isn't liable on the note. Is his claim legally correct?

Any demand for payment is regarded as a presentment, no matter where or how it is made. A failure by the holder of a note to make a presentment to the maker for payment at maturity will discharge any indorsers from liability. It is important, therefore, to make proper presentment of the instrument to the maker on or before the instrument's due date. In Problem 4, Carson's failure to present the note to San Marco for payment discharges Nolan, and he is correct in claiming that he isn't liable. San Marco, however, is not discharged from liability.

The Code excuses presentment if (1) presentment is *waived* (given up) by the indorsers, (2) the maker is dead or insolvent, and (3) presentment can't be made after the holder exercises reasonable diligence. Presentment may be made *in person, by mail,* or *through a clearinghouse.* A **clearinghouse** is usually a Federal Reserve Bank that clears checks for its member banks.

Presentment of a note for payment must be made at a reasonable hour. If the note is presented at a bank, it must be during its banking day. A note payable on Saturday or on a legal holiday is payable on the next full business day for both parties.

EXAMPLE

A promissory note is payable on March 1, which falls on a Saturday. The holder must present this note for payment on Monday, March 3, the next full business day for both parties.

To determine the date an instrument is due, the starting date is excluded and the date of payment is included. Thus, an instrument dated September 3 and due in 30 days is due on October 3 (27 days in September plus 3 days in October).

Presentment must be made at the place specified in the instrument. If the place of business isn't specified, the presentment must be made at the maker's place of business or home. If the maker or the maker's authorized agent can't be found there, the presentment is excused under the UCC.

A holder's failure to comply with these requirements makes the presentment invalid. However, the person presenting has a reasonable time within which to comply. Presentment may be made to any one of two or more makers, or to any person who has authority to make or refuse payment of the instrument.

Electronic Fund Transfers

Today, many consumers use electronic fund-transfer (EFT) terminals for banking and shopping. Those consumers can save themselves money and headaches if they know their rights and possible liabilities under a recent federal law.

The law covers any transfer of funds through an electronic terminal or by phone, computer, or magnetic tape. Transfers at automated teller machines (ATMs), point-of-sale terminals in stores, airport cash dispensers, and other transfer devices are included. Under the law, financial institutions must tell holders of EFT cards what rights they have and what liabilities they assume. Validated EFT cards can't be distributed unless they are requested in writing by the consumer. Of course, the lender verifies the consumer's identity before issuing the card. The consumer must be told how to dispose of the card if it is no longer needed.

When the consumer accepts an EFT card, the lender must disclose these facts: (1) the consumer's liability for unauthorized transfers; (2) who is to be contacted in case of an unauthorized transfer; (3) what kinds of transfers the consumer can make and what charges may be imposed; (4) how errors will be corrected; and (5) the extent of the lender's liability to the consumer.

An important provision of the law relates to the consumer's liability for unauthorized transfers. The consumer's liability is limited to $50 if the lender is notified within two working days of an unauthorized transaction. The liability increases to $500 if the consumer waits beyond this period. If the consumer waits longer than 60 days, the liability is unlimited.

EXAMPLE

Elbaum and Hernon signed a promissory note as comakers. At maturity, the holder presented the note for payment to Elbaum and payment was refused. Hernon claims that she isn't liable on the note because it wasn't presented to her. Her claim is invalid. Presentment to one of two or more makers is sufficient to satisfy the UCC's requirements.

Dishonor of a Promissory Note

> **5.** Nizam was the holder of a promissory note on which Gelin's name appeared as maker and Arlett's as indorser. After proper presentment was made to Gelin, the instrument was dishonored. What procedure must Nizam follow to hold Arlett liable on the instrument?

If a maker is unable or refuses to make payment on a note that it properly presented, the note is said to be a **dishonored instrument.** The holder of the dishonored instrument must then give notice to all parties who may be liable for payment, unless they have earlier waived such notice. If the holder fails to give notice of a dishonor, the indorsers will be relieved of their liability.

The UCC provides that notice of dishonor must be given within a definite period of time. A bank must give notice of dishonor before midnight of the next banking day following the day of dishonor. Any other person must give such notice before midnight of the third business day after dishonor or receipt of notice of dishonor. In Problem 5, Nizam must notify Arlett within this statutory period of time in order to hold Arlett liable on the instrument.

The usual procedure in case of dishonor is for each indorser to notify the preceding indorser. However, the UCC allows any party who may be liable on the instrument to send notice of dishonor to any other party who may be liable on it.

> A promissory note is made payable to Borsini by Ajami, the maker. Borsini indorses the note to Chan, and Chan indorses it to Douros. At maturity, Ajami dishonors the note. Douros may send notice of dishonor to Borsini instead of to Chan. Borsini could then notify Chan. In fact, Borsini may send a notice of dishonor to Chan without waiting for a notice to come from Douros.

Notice may be given orally or in writing. Written notice is effective *when sent,* although *not received.* Notice of dishonor to one partner is notice to each, although the partnership may have been dissolved. When any party is dead or incompetent, notice may be sent to the party's last known address or given to the party's personal representative. An indorser may waive presentment and notice of dishonor by indicating this fact in writing and signing it.

Figure 33.2
A Draft

```
$ 1,200.00          Kittery, ME              March 5, 19 --
_____
                      At sight
_____
Pay to the order of ___ Richard Close _____
        One thousand two hundred and no/100 _____ Dollars
_____
Value received and charge same to the account of

To ___ Tanya Autilio _____        Atlantic Sales Co.
Address _ Santa Fe, New Mexico __
```

DRAFTS

The draft, or **bill of exchange,** is a commonly used business paper. Figure 33.2 is an example of a draft.

> **6.** Is the draft shown in Figure 33.2 negotiable?

You'll remember that a draft, like a promissory note, must contain the essentials of negotiability in order to be negotiable. A promissory note contains an *unconditional promise* to pay, but a draft contains an *unconditional order* to pay. Three parties are involved in a draft; only two are involved in a promissory note.

The instrument in Problem 6 (Figure 33.2) is fully negotiable. Atlantic Sales Co. is the drawer (the party who signed and issued the draft). Richard Close is the payee (the party to whom payment is ordered). Tanya Autilio is the drawee (the party who is ordered to pay the draft).

Kinds of Drafts

Drafts may be classified as (1) sight drafts and (2) time drafts. A **sight draft,** such as the draft shown in Figure 33.2, is payable immediately on presentation by the holder or payee to the drawee. A **time draft** is payable on a stated date, at a stated time after the date of the draft, or at the end of a designated time after sight. A time draft payable "sixty days after sight" is called a **time-after-sight draft.** Figure 33.3 is an example of this type of time draft. It must first be presented to the drawee for acceptance in order to fix the date of payment. The 60-day period begins to run from the date the drawee sees the instrument. If the drawee accepts a time-after-sight draft, it

Figure 33.3
A Time-After-Sight Draft

$ <u>900.00</u>   <u>Jackson, MS</u>   <u>August 13</u> , 19 <u>--</u>

At <u>sixty days</u> _____ after sight pay to the order of

----------------------Ourselves----------------------

-----------Nine hundred and no/100----------- Dollars

Value received and charge same to the account of

To <u>Carlton Norris</u>

Address <u>Denver, CO</u>   *Jensen and Hall Co.*

becomes in effect a promissory note payable to the payee or holder. A time draft payable "sixty days after date" is called a **time-after-date draft** (see Figure 33.4). This draft need not be presented to the drawee for acceptance because the date of payment can be determined by counting 60 days from the date of the instrument.

Figure 33.4
A Time-After-Date Draft

$ <u>3,000.00</u>   <u>Flint, MI</u>   <u>July 25</u> , 19<u>--</u>

Sixty days after date pay to the order of Leona Hailu

----------Three thousand and no/100---------- Dollars

Value received and charge same to the account of

To <u>Allen Jones & Company</u>

Address <u>Chicago, IL</u>   *James S. Jones*

When Are Drafts Used?

7. Mica, a retail merchant, owed $500 to Kalb, a wholesaler, for some goods Mica bought from Kalb. The debt was long overdue, and Mica had ignored Kalb's requests for payment. What may Kalb do to collect the debt?

Drafts are often used by sellers of goods to collect money due from buyers on either current or overdue accounts. In Problem 7, since Mica has ignored Kalb's requests for payment, Kalb might draw a sight draft on Mica and have it sent to a bank in Mica's city for collection. It's unlikely that Mica would fail to pay the local bank, because her credit standing and her reputation as a business person would suffer as a result.

Often, a seller of goods uses a sight draft attached to an order bill of lading in making a C.O.D. freight shipment. Both the sight draft and the bill of lading are forwarded by the seller's bank to a bank in the buyer's city. The local bank then notifies the buyer, who must pay the sight draft before the bill of lading—and ultimately, the merchandise—can be obtained.

Presentment of a Draft for Acceptance and Payment

8. Standen, the drawee of a draft payable "30 days after sight," refused to accept it when the holder presented it to her for acceptance. Is she legally obligated to do so?

Certain drafts must be presented to the drawee for both acceptance and for payment. The procedures for the presentment of promissory notes also apply to the presentment of drafts for acceptance and payment. A time draft must be accepted by a drawee before the drawee can be liable on the instrument. A drawee can't be forced to accept the draft, however, because there is no contractual obligation. In Problem 8, therefore, Standen need not accept the draft when it is presented to her. In order to be held liable, a drawee must indicate a willingness to assume the liability. The word "Accepted" or a similar word may be written across the face of the draft in addition to the drawee's signature. Figure 33.5 is an example of an accepted time draft. Under the Code, though, an acceptance is complete and binding if only the signature of the drawee appears on the instrument.

Giunta accepted a draft drawn on him by Kohn. At maturity, the holder presented the draft to Giunta for payment. Giunta refused to pay on the ground that the drawer, Kohn, was a minor. Giunta's claim is invalid. When he accepted the draft, he warranted that the drawer had capacity to issue the instrument.

The drawee's liability after acceptance is the same as that of a maker of a promissory note. By accepting, the drawee becomes primarily liable on the instrument. The drawee also admits (1) the existence of the drawer, (2) the genuineness of the drawer's signature, (3) the drawer's capacity to draw the instrument, (4) the existence of the payee, and (5) the capacity of the payee to indorse the instrument.

Figure 33.5
Accepted Time
Draft

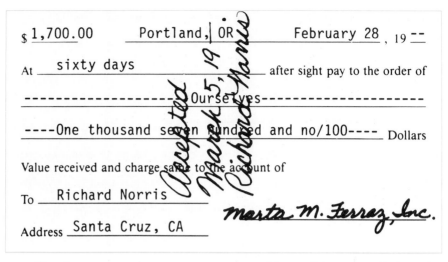

The drawee may postpone acceptance without dishonor until the close of the next business day following presentment. If the instrument isn't accepted within this time or is destroyed because the drawee doesn't want to accept it, the instrument is regarded as dishonored.

Dishonor of a Draft

> **9.** Takebe is the holder of a draft payable "60 days after sight." The draft was presented to the drawee for acceptance, but acceptance was refused. What legal steps may Takebe take to hold the drawer liable on the instrument?

If the drawee refuses to accept a draft that is properly presented, the instrument is said to be dishonored. The holder doesn't have to wait until the maturity date to proceed against the drawer and indorsers. In fact, the holder's right to collect from them is fully protected when due notice of dishonor is given, as in the case of promissory notes. In Problem 9, Takebe must give notice of dishonor to the drawer in order to hold the drawer liable on the instrument.

When a bank is the drawee, the UCC requires the bank to give a notice of dishonor before its midnight deadline. Any other person must give notice before midnight of the third business day after dishonor or receipt of notice of dishonor. Failure to give proper notice releases the drawer and indorsers only to the extent that such omission financially injures them.

Special Kinds of Drafts

There are a number of special kinds of drafts. These include trade acceptances, cashier's checks, bank drafts, money orders, and traveler's checks.

Figure 33.6
A Trade
Acceptance

No. 37	Boston, MA March 1, 19--
To Beverly Sturges	New Haven, CT
On March 31, 19-- *Pay to the order of*	Ourselves
Twenty-five hundred and no/100 *Dollars* ($ 2,500.00)	

Accepted at New Haven *on* March 10, 19--

Payable at First National Bank   Benton Brothers, Inc.

Beverly Sturges   *By John Benton*

Trade Acceptances

A **trade acceptance** (see Figure 33.6) is a special form of draft that is drawn by a seller on the buyer of goods. Sellers use trade acceptances often because they can *discount* (sell) these drafts at a bank. This is one way sellers can get the funds needed to carry on business.

Cashier's Checks

PROBLEM

10. Gould, who lives in Florida, wants to buy some appliances sold by Midwest Appliance of Chicago. Because the sellers don't know Gould, they refuse to ship the goods unless they are paid in cash or with some negotiable instrument that can be accepted as the equivalent of cash. What form of negotiable paper can Gould send?

Figure 33.7
A Cashier's Check

THE FIRST NATIONAL BANK OF SOUTH MIAMI

1000 North Main Street
South Miami, Florida

CASHIER'S CHECK   No. 66623

63-587 / 631

Date   June 6, 19--

Jillian Patterson

_____
$10,000 or over requires two signatures

PAY $400dols00cts

TO THE ORDER OF   LINCOLN GOULD

⑈063⑈058⑆⑈ ⑈998 530 4⑈

```
C U S T O M E R S   D R A F T
CN-202 11-82

[F] First
    Interstate
    Bank

                                    Sacramento _____ CALIFORNIA,___ June 6 ____19--
                                    _____
PAY TO THE
ORDER OF _____ Lincoln Gould-----------------------------------------------$ 100.00 _____

___ One Hundred and 00/100-------------------------------------------------- DOLLARS
            VALUE RECEIVED AND CHARGE SAME TO ACCOUNT OF              WITH EXCHANGE

TO _ The American Trust and Savings Bank _____
         (NAME OF BANK, FIRM OR INDIVIDUAL DRAWN ON)
     Sacramento, California _____
                                        ┌─────────────────────────┐
                                        │ ACCOUNT NUMBER          │
                                        │    03 678 9458          │
                                        └─────────────────────────┘
```

Figure 33.8
A Bank Draft

The credit given to a check is determined by the reputation of the drawer. Often, sellers don't know the credit standing of their buyers. When this occurs, sellers are justified in asking for payment in cash or in the form of a check that, by certification and other means, carries with it the certainty that it will be honored by payment.

A bank depositor may make use of the bank's credit. On request, the bank will issue to the depositor its own check, signed by its cashier, in return for the depositor's personal check. A check drawn by a cashier on the cashier's own bank as drawee is known as a **cashier's check** (see Figure 33.7).

Cashier's checks are frequently used in situations such as the one in Problem 10. The check is made payable to the depositor, Gould. Gould then indorses the check to the party to whom it is being transferred, Midwest Appliance.

Bank Drafts

Banks in one city carry funds deposited by banks in other cities. A depositor bank draws on its funds in other banks by means of a **bank draft** (also called a *bank check*). A bank draft is an order drawn by one bank on another bank in which the drawer bank has funds on deposit (see Figure 33.8).

Bank drafts are used when it's necessary to transfer funds to distant places. Individuals may buy them from banks to meet the needs of a situation such as that in Problem 10. Travelers often use bank drafts, traveler's checks, and letters of credit (which may be purchased at any bank) as a means of keeping themselves supplied with funds without carrying cash.

Figure 33.9
A Traveler's Check

Money Orders

Money orders can be bought at post offices, banks, express companies, and other places. They're particularly useful for people who want to make payments by mail but who don't have checking accounts. Money orders are readily accepted in payment of debts. Payees usually deposit them as if they were checks.

Traveler's Checks

People who don't feel it is safe to carry large sums of cash often buy **traveler's checks** (see Figure 33.9). These checks may be bought at banks, large travel agencies and ticket offices, and at express firms. They're usually issued in denominations of $20, $50, and $100. Each traveler's check is numbered serially and indorsed on its face by the buyer for identification purposes. The traveler indorses it again on its face before offering it in payment for goods or services. The person to whom the check is given examines both indorsements to see that they are alike. Traveler's checks should never be indorsed the second time except in the presence of the person to whom they are to be transferred.

Traveler's checks are acceptable in all parts of the world. It's a good idea for buyers to keep a record of the checks' numbers and of the numbers of the checks used. Then, if the checks are lost or stolen, the agency that issued the checks should be notified promptly. New checks will be issued to replace the missing ones.

As you can see, promissory notes and drafts are convenient tools to use to transfer funds from one party to another. There is an even more common instrument of negotiation of funds, however. That is the check, a form of draft that will be covered in detail in Chapter 34.

Chapter 33 Review

"YOU BE THE JUDGE" REVIEW

Look again at the "You Be the Judge" cases given at the beginning of this chapter. Would you decide them differently now, after your study of the chapter?

Correct Decisions

1. Yes. By accepting the draft, Comeau warranted that the signature of Suto, the drawer, was genuine.

2. Yes. A notice of dishonor may be given orally or in writing (UCC Sec. 3-305[3]).

UNDERSTANDING WHAT YOU HAVE READ

1. List the types of promissory notes and drafts in common use.
2. How does a promissory note differ from a draft?
3. Discuss the liability of each of the following parties:
   a. the maker of a promissory note
   b. the drawer of a draft
   c. the drawee of a draft (1) before acceptance and (2) after acceptance
   d. the indorser of a promissory note
4. How should presentment for payment of a promissory note or a draft be made?
5. What conditions must a holder fulfill in order to bind an indorser?
6. What is the effect of a failure to present an instrument in accordance with UCC requirements?
7. When is presentment excused?
8. When an instrument is dishonored, what steps should a holder take?
9. A draft dated July 12 is payable "30 days after sight." It is accepted by the drawee on July 15. When is the draft due?
10. A traveler plans to spend a month in Europe and doesn't want to carry cash to cover her expenses. The traveler has an account at a Texas bank. What options are available to the traveler?

BUILDING YOUR LEGAL VOCABULARY

Match each of these legal terms with its correct definition from the list that follows. Write your answers on a separate sheet of paper.

bank draft   indorser   sight draft
cashier's check maker   time draft
collateral note   presentment trade acceptance
dishonored instrument

1. a check drawn by a bank on itself, payable to a named payee
2. one who is primarily liable to pay an instrument
3. one who signs an instrument other than as a maker or drawer
4. a draft that is payable a stated number of days after the date on the instrument
5. a note that contains a description of the property pledged as security for its payment

6. a demand for payment from the party primarily liable on the instrument
7. notice given to all parties secondarily liable that an instrument was not paid
8. a special type of draft drawn by a seller of goods on a purchaser
9. a draft drawn on the funds one bank has on deposit at another bank
10. a draft payable immediately on presentation by the holder to the drawee

APPLYING LEGAL PRINCIPLES

1. Talero made a proper presentment of a promissory note to the maker, Volk. Volk, however, dishonored the note. What must Talero do in order to hold the indorsers liable?
2. A note payable on demand was presented to the maker for payment three years from the date of the instrument. The maker refused payment. Was the holder entitled to collect from the indorsers?

3. An instrument dated November 8 and payable three months after date was presented for payment on February 10 of the next year. Was the presentment made on time?
4. Neale was the holder of a promissory note he had received by indorsement from the payee, Toomey. On the day the note was due, Neale met the maker of the note on the street and asked for payment. Was this a proper presentment in order to hold Toomey liable if the maker refuses to pay?

5. The holder of a dishonored note gave oral notice of dishonor to the indorsers. The indorsers claimed that the notice was improperly given and refused to pay. Is the indorsers' claim correct?

6. Levitsky, the holder of a dishonored promissory note, sent notice of dishonor to Marwin, an indorser. The notice was mailed to Marwin's home, although Marwin's place of business was in another city. The instrument itself didn't indicate where notice of dishonor was to be sent. Did Levitsky give proper notice of dishonor?

7.
> At sight, pay to the order of Joel Cutler $100 and charge same amount to the account of Shu-Li Fong.
>
> K. A. Boehm

   a. Is the instrument shown above a negotiable sight draft? Why or why not?

   b. When is it due?

   c. Must the drawee pay this draft when it is presented?

   d. Suppose the draft read, "at ten days' sight." When would it be payable?

8. A draft payable 30 days after sight was presented to the drawee for acceptance. If the drawee refuses to accept it, what are the holder's legal rights?

9. Rohach presented a sight draft to Keefer, the drawee, for payment. Keefer refused to pay the instrument. A year later, Rohach gave notice of dishonor to Dolben, the drawer. Is Dolben liable to Rohach?

10. a. At maturity, an accepted draft was presented again to the drawee for payment. The drawee refused to pay, claiming that the drawer had no authority to draw the instrument. Is the drawee's claim correct?

   b. Assume in Problem 10(a) that the drawee refused to pay because the drawer's signature was a forgery. Is the drawee liable on the instrument?

11. Puzon accepted a draft payable "at 30 days' sight" by writing her full name, "Josefina Puzon," across the face of the instrument. Is this sufficient to constitute an acceptance?

12. Shalhoub presented a draft to Fisher for acceptance. Fisher destroyed the draft because he didn't want to accept it. When Shalhoub learned of Fisher's action, she sought to hold Fisher liable as an acceptor of a draft. Will Shalhoub succeed?

ANALYZING COURT CASES

1. A draft in the sum of $7,200 drawn on General Finance Corporation was deposited with Home Savings Bank for collection. General Finance orally promised to honor the draft, then refused to do so. In an action by Home Savings Bank to collect the draft, the question of whether an oral acceptance of a draft is binding on the drawee arose. How should the court decide this case? (*Home Savings Bank vs. General Finance Corp.*, 103 N.W. 2d 117)

2. A negotiable instrument contains the words, "payment guaranteed." It is claimed that these words make it unnecessary to present the instrument to the maker at maturity and to give notice of dishonor to the indorsers if the maker fails to pay it. Is this claim correct? (UCC Sec. 3-416[5])

3. Richards sold $800 worth of merchandise to Keenan. To obtain payment for the goods, Richards drew a draft on Keenan, dated January 5 and payable ten days after date to the Third National Bank. When the draft was presented to Keenan, he indorsed on the face of the instrument, "Accepted, payable February 15. J. Keenan." Could Richards treat the draft as dishonored by nonacceptance? (UCC Sec. 3-412[1])

Checks
and
Banking

YOU BE THE JUDGE

Think about these cases.
If you were the judge, how would you decide each case?

1

You were the holder of a check drawn by Firenza. You had it certified at Firenza's bank. The next day, the bank suspended payments. Is Firenza liable on the check?

2

Ely was the payee of a check. After several indorsements, Levy became the holder and presented the check for payment, but it was dishonored. Levy later presented the check again, and payment was again refused. Levy then notified all secondary parties of the dishonor. Is Ely, the original payee and indorser, liable for payment to Levy?

WHAT IS A CHECK?

In Chapter 32 we said that a check is a special form of draft, drawn on a bank and payable on demand. It is the most common form of draft in use today. The right to draw checks results from a contract between the depositor and the bank. Under this contract, the bank agrees to pay all checks properly drawn by its depositor. Failure of a bank to honor such checks makes it liable for injury to the drawer-depositor's credit standing and business reputation.

PROBLEM

---

1.   Is this instrument a check?

> Pocatello, ID   May 1, 19--
>
> At sight, pay to the order of ___*myself*___
> $400.00 ___*Four hundred and no/00*___ Dollars
> Value received and charge same to the account of:
> Amy Schimmer
> Rock Springs, WY
>   *Donna G. McBride*
>   Donna G. McBride

A check differs from other drafts in several important ways:

1. A check is always payable on demand.
2. A bank is always the drawee of a check. The instrument in Problem 1 is not a check because it is drawn on an individual rather than on a bank. Therefore, it is a draft.
3. Under the UCC, a check must be presented for payment within a time period that differs from the statutory periods of other drafts. This time limit will be discussed later.
4. Issuing a check when the drawer has no funds in the bank or insufficient funds on deposit is a criminal offense in many states.

Figure 34.1 is an example of a check.

Advantages of Using Checks

It is safer and more convenient to use checks rather than coins or currency when paying bills or withdrawing money on deposit in a bank. Checks may be sent through the mail at almost no risk to the sender. If they're lost, destroyed, or stolen, and the bank is properly notified, the payment will not be made. **Canceled checks** (checks that have been paid by a bank) serve not only as records of payments but also as receipts for bills paid.

Figure 34.1
A Check

National Bank of Boston	0089

LEXINGTON OFFICE
35910 GOUSHA BLVD., LEXINGTON, MA 02173

Dec 22 19 — — 5-39/110

PAY TO THE ORDER OF *Gary's Service Station* — $ | 49.90 |

Forty-nine and 90/100 ————————— DOLLARS

DENIS KELLEHER
1776 Spring Street
Lexington, Massachusetts 02173

Denis Kelleher

⑆0⑆⑆000 39X⑆: 0089⑈092226700⑈ ⑈0000003000⑈

Presenting Checks for Certification

2. Quiroga bought a valuable bracelet for her daughter and offered to pay for it by check. The jeweler, Tye, didn't know Quiroga. However, Tye agreed to accept Quiroga's check if she would have it certified. Quiroga had the check certified and gave it to Tye. How is Tye protected by the certification?

The drawee of a draft or check isn't liable on the instrument until he or she has agreed in writing to become liable. In a draft this agreement is known as an acceptance. In the case of a check, the agreement to be liable is known as **certification.** Certification, like acceptance, must be written on the check itself. A bank is under no legal obligation to certify a check.

Certification Obtained by the Drawer

To have a check certified, the drawer presents it to an officer of the bank. The officer deducts the amount of the check from the drawer's account and sets this amount aside for payment of the instrument. The word "Certified" and a bank official's authorized signature are written or stamped across the face of the check. The words "accepted" or "good" may be used instead of "certified."

The certification of a check obtained by the drawer protects the payee or any subsequent holder in several ways. It assures that (1) the check is genuine, (2) there are sufficient funds in the bank to pay the check, and (3) the bank is obligated to honor the check when it is presented for payment. *When the drawer obtains the certification, the drawer and the bank are liable for payment of the check.* In Problem 2, Tye receives these three protections because of the certification obtained by Quiroga.

Certification Obtained by the Payee or Holder

The payee or holder, instead of the drawer, may have a check certified. In doing so, the holder intends to take payment at a future time rather than at the present. By obtaining certification, the holder makes the bank the only debtor and discharges the drawer and any prior indorsers from liability. The legal effects of certification vary, depending on whether the drawer or the holder obtains the certification. If a bank becomes insolvent and unable to pay a check certified at the drawer's request, the drawer continues to be liable on the check. But *if a check has been certified at the holder's request and the bank then suspends payment, the loss is the holder's.* The drawer and any indorsers have been discharged.

> Assume that Tye, in Problem 2, had taken Quiroga's check to the bank for certification. Then, before the check was presented for payment, the bank became insolvent. In this case, Quiroga would no longer be liable for payment.

Presenting Checks for Payment

The period of time within which checks must be presented for payment or collection differs from that of other drafts and promissory notes.

> **3.** A check dated June 1 is presented to the bank for payment on July 15. The bank on which the check was drawn had become insolvent, however, on July 10 and had suspended all payments. What is the drawer's liability to the holder?

The UCC provides that an uncertified check that is drawn and payable within the United States must be presented for payment or for bank collection within 30 days after the date it was drawn or the date of issue to a holder or remitter, whichever is later, in order to hold the drawer liable. The Code holds that an indorser is liable for seven days after the date of the indorsement. If a holder fails to present a check within the Code's time limit, the indorsers are completely discharged. The drawer, as in Problem 3, is discharged from liability if the drawer's rights against the insolvent bank are assigned to the holder. The Code also provides that a bank isn't obligated to pay a check more than six months old unless it is certified. An

Laws to Cut Check Bouncing

Bouncing a $25 check in California and Oregon can cost the writer $125 plus court costs. Similar laws in more than a dozen states now allow merchants to sue bad-check writers in small claims court. The merchants can recover the amount of the original check plus a penalty of several times that sum. A few states are even sending check bouncers to classes! There, in eight-hour Saturday sessions, the bad-check writers are supposed to learn how to mend their ways. The curriculum ranges from a discussion of what is right and wrong to practical exercises in balancing one's checkbook.

How are these laws working out? Despite the laws, Americans still bounce more than a million checks a day. According to the American Bankers Association, this represents one percent of all checks written. Grocery stores in California say that their losses due to bad checks amount to 100 million dollars a year. But some states report success with their new laws. In Colorado, for example, the occurrence of bad-check writing dropped twenty percent after passage of a triple-damage law. Montana reports a drop in bad-check losses. In Illinois, the threat of triple damages has convinced many bad-check writers to settle up before lawsuits are filed. A county attorney in Texas, who doubted that the classroom requirement would do any good, now reports that bad-check complaints have fallen by 40% since the Texas law was enacted. Few graduates of bad-check courses are caught bouncing another check.

It's a known fact that most check bouncers aren't hardened criminals. Many aren't aware of their actual checkbook balances when they write checks. As a result, they overdraw their accounts. These check writers just need to be given enough education and publicity not to err again.

uncertified check more than six months old is regarded as *stale.* However, a bank may pay such a check without being liable to its customer. Suppose a check is presented for payment by the holder and payment is refused. In that event, the holder must give notice of dishonor to the drawer and indorsers. Failure to do so will discharge them from liability.

Stopping Payment on Checks

When properly ordered to do so, a bank must refuse to pay an uncertified check issued by a depositor. The depositor must first issue a **stop-payment order** to the bank. Under the UCC, the stop-payment order must be given before payment or certification of the check. In any event, it must be given before midnight of the day after the check is issued.

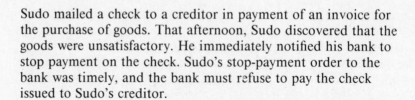

Sudo mailed a check to a creditor in payment of an invoice for the purchase of goods. That afternoon, Sudo discovered that the goods were unsatisfactory. He immediately notified his bank to stop payment on the check. Sudo's stop-payment order to the bank was timely, and the bank must refuse to pay the check issued to Sudo's creditor.

A stop-payment order may be oral until the depositor has a reasonable opportunity to put it in writing. An oral stop-payment order is valid for fourteen days, but it may be confirmed in writing within that period. A written stop-payment order is effective for six months but may be renewed in writing. A bank is liable to the drawer if it fails to comply with a stop-payment order. It's important to remember that a drawer can't stop payment after a check has been certified.

Postdated Checks

4. Lakis issued a check on May 1 and dated it June 1. Is the instrument negotiable?

A check is payable on demand. A postdated check is a mere promise to pay at a future date. Since the instrument in Problem 4 was postdated, it can't be presented for payment until June 1. It is a draft payable at a future time rather than a check. Its validity, however, is not in any way affected by the postdating. Under the UCC, negotiability is not affected by the fact that an instrument is undated, antedated, or postdated.

Who is liable for payment of a check on which the signature has been forged?

Alteration of Checks

5. Gottlieb carefully wrote a check for $18, payable to bearer. The payee raised the amount to $1,800, cashed the check at the bank on which it was drawn, and disappeared. Who must suffer the loss?

The Code defines an **alteration** of an instrument as any change in the contract of a party, brought about by adding or removing parts of the signed writing or by changing the number or relations of the parties to the contract. Because the bank alone has the chance to inspect a check at the time of payment, the bank is liable for payment of an altered check. However, if the drawer carelessly writes a check so that it can easily be altered and the bank is not negligent, the drawer must bear the loss. In Problem 5, the bank would be liable to Gottlieb for $1,782—the difference between the raised amount and the original amount of the check.

Forged Signatures and Indorsements

A *forgery* occurs when the depositor's name is signed by someone who has no authority to do so and with the intention of defrauding the depositor.

PROBLEM

> **6.** When Evans received her canceled checks with her bank statement, she found that one of the returned checks bore a forged signature. Evans promptly notified the bank. Is the bank liable for the loss?

Usually, a bank is liable if it pays a check on which the depositor's signature has been forged. However, a depositor's negligence may have been responsible for the forgery or alteration. In this event, the bank is not liable if it made the payment in good faith and exercised ordinary care. The Code requires that a depositor examine his or her bank statement and canceled checks with reasonable care and notify the bank promptly of any forgery or alterations on a check. If the depositor fails to do so and the bank can prove that it has been harmed by the depositor's failure to give prompt notice, the bank isn't liable for payment. In Problem 6, since Evans promptly notified the bank of the forgery, the bank would be liable for the loss.

Regardless of who is negligent, a drawer who fails to report a forged signature or alteration within *one year* after receiving the canceled check must bear the loss. It is important to remember that the one-year limitation applies only to checks on which the depositor's *signature* was forged or the amount raised. It does not apply to a forged *indorsement.* For a forged indorsement, the Code provides a three-year period.

Death of the Depositor

PROBLEM

> **7.** Satut died on February 5. Three days before his death, he had issued a check to Zaslow in payment of a debt. The bank on which the check was drawn paid it to Zaslow on February 13. The bank had no knowledge of Satut's death. Was the payment of the check valid?

The death of a depositor ends the bank's authority to pay the depositor's checks. If a bank honors a depositor's checks without knowing that the depositor has died, however, it isn't liable for the payments made. This is the case in Problem 7. Under the UCC, even if a bank knows of a drawer's death or incompetence, it has *ten days* after the date of death or the court ruling of incompetence in which to pay or to certify checks drawn on or before the date of the drawer's death or incompetence.

Checks, other drafts, and promissory notes are used daily in the business transactions of consumers and business people. Their purpose is to transfer and negotiate funds. In Chapter 35, the specifics of transfer and negotiation will be presented.

Chapter 34 Review

"YOU BE THE JUDGE" REVIEW

Look again at the "You Be the Judge" cases given at the beginning of this chapter. Would you decide them differently now, after your study of the chapter?

Correct Decisions

1. No. If the certification is obtained by the holder or payee, the bank becomes the only debtor. The drawer and prior indorsers are discharged from liability.

2. No. Payment must be made before the close of business on the day of presentment in order to avoid dishonor. Secondary parties should have been notified after the first presentment.

UNDERSTANDING WHAT YOU HAVE READ

1. a. What is a check?
   b. List four ways in which a check differs from other drafts.
   c. What are some of the advantages of using checks?
2. a. What is the legal effect of certification of a check at the request of the drawer?
   b. What is the legal effect of certification of a check at the request of the holder or payee?
3. Under the UCC, when must an uncertified check be presented for payment in order to hold the drawer liable? the indorsers?
4. Under the UCC,
   a. when must a stop-payment order be given to a bank?
   b. how may a stop-payment order be made?
   b. for how long is a written stop-payment order effective?
5. a. What is the difference between postdating and antedating a check?
   b. What is the legal effect of postdating a check?
6. Discuss the liability of a bank for payment of an altered check.

7. Discuss the liability of a bank for payment of a check containing a forged signature of the drawer.
8. What duty does the UCC impose on depositors when they receive their canceled checks from the bank?
9. Under the UCC, how much time does a depositor have to report to the bank

    a. a forgery of the depositor's signature on a canceled check?
    b. a forgery of an indorsement on a canceled check?

10. Discuss the bank's liability if it pays a check drawn by its depositor just before death.

BUILDING YOUR LEGAL VOCABULARY

Choose the legal term that will correctly complete each definition below. Write your answers on a separate sheet of paper.

1. A depositor's oral or written request to a bank not to pay a check is called a
    a. presentment.
    b. judgment note.
    c. stop-payment order.
2. The unauthorized signing of another's name with intent to defraud is known as
    a. forgery.
    b. dishonoring an instrument.
    c. indorsing an instrument.
3. A bank's written agreement to become liable for payment of a check is called
    a. certification.
    b. negotiation.
    c. acceptance.

4. Checks that have already been paid by a bank are known as
    a. stale checks.
    b. canceled checks.
    c. certified checks.
5. Any change in an instrument brought about by adding or removing parts of the signed writing or changing the number or relations of the parties is called a/an
    a. alteration.
    b. forgery.
    c. cancellation.

APPLYING LEGAL PRINCIPLES

1. Detwiler drew a check payable to David Giudice. Giudice presented it to the bank for payment. The teller refused to cash the check because Giudice couldn't furnish satisfactory identification.
   a. Must the bank cash the check for Giudice?
   b. Has Detwiler any claim against the bank?
2. Trulio received a check for $6,000 from Comenos, drawn on the Fidelity Trust Company. Instead of cashing the check, Trulio had it certified at Comenos's bank. Shortly afterward, Fidelity Trust Company became insolvent and suspended payments. Trulio now claims that Comenos should pay her the $6,000. Is Trulio's claim correct?
3. Would your answer to Problem 2 be the same if Comenos had had the check certified and then mailed to Trulio?
4. Benjoya issued a check to the Diebold Company on January 5. Diebold Company didn't present the check for payment until August 10. Benjoya's bank refused to pay it, claiming that the check was stale. Was the bank obliged to accept the check for payment?
5. Sung forgot to deposit a check and carried it in his pocket for more than a month.
   a. Is the drawer released from liability on the check?
   b. If the bank became insolvent and suspended payments during the month, what would the result be?
6. Jester bought some goods and paid for them by check. When she examined the goods, she found that she'd been defrauded. She stopped payment on the check. Under what circumstances is Jester allowed to do this?
7. McGrory wrote a check for a small amount, payable to bearer, and gave it to a repair person. The latter negotiated it by delivery to Grinberg. Grinberg raised the amount on the check and cashed it at the bank. What are the liabilities of the parties?
8. Montes discovered that a canceled check returned in her end-of-month bank statement contained a forged signature.
   a. Is the bank liable to Montes for paying the check?
   b. What must Montes do to protect her legal rights against the bank?
   c. Would your answers be different if Montes discovered a forged indorsement instead of a forged signature?
9. The drawer of a check for $50 delivered it to the payee. The payee negotiated it to Woo. Woo fraudulently altered the check by raising it to $500. She then negotiated it to Fogel. Can Fogel collect $500 from the drawer?
10. On September 15, the State Bank paid a check that had been drawn by a depositor on August 29. The bank had been notified on September 1 of the depositor's death on that day. Is the bank liable for an improper payment of the check?

ANALYZING COURT CASES

1. J. W. Jones, as drawer, issued a check payable to E. P. Kash. The check was for $200, payable at the People's Bank and Trust Company of Seattle. More than four years later, Kash presented the check to Jones for payment, but payment was refused. An action was brought against Jones on the check. He pleaded that the check had never been presented to the bank for payment and that he hadn't received proper notice of dishonor. Will the court agree with Jones's contention? (Based on: *Fick v. Jones*, 55 P. 2d 334)

2. Plau instructed McLean, an employee, to draw a check on Pacific National Bank, payable to McLean, for $50.20. McLean wrote the check in his own handwriting, leaving space to the left of the amount. After Plau signed the check, McLean raised the amount of the check to $550.20. When McLean presented the check at the bank, he received the raised amount. Plau brought an action against the bank to recover the raised amount. Should she succeed? (Based on: *Goldsmith v. Atlantic National Bank*, 55 So. 2d 804)

3. Blodgett drew a check on the National Exchange Bank, payable to the order of Miller Corporation. At the request of the corporation, the bank certified the check. Before the check was paid, a dispute arose between Blodgett and the corporation as to the amount due the corporation. The bank then refused to honor the certified check. The Miller Corporation brought an action against the bank, claiming that a bank couldn't refuse to pay a certified check. Do you agree with this claim? (Based on: *Fiss Corp. v. National Safety Bank & Trust Co.*, 77 N.Y.S. 2d 293)

Transfer and Negotiation

Think about these cases.
If you were the judge, how would you decide each case?

1

Schiff received a check from Halas, indorsed "Halas." Above Halas's indorsement, Schiff wrote: "Pay to the order of Armand Schiff." Did Schiff's act destroy the negotiability of the check?

2

You are the payee of a check. You transferred the check by a blank indorsement. Are you now primarily liable on the instrument?

TRANSFER OF A NEGOTIABLE INSTRUMENT

Transfer is the act of delivering an instrument to another with the intention of passing one's rights in the instrument to that party. Legally, transfer may take place either by assignment or negotiation. Under the UCC, an instrument is considered *negotiated* when the maker or drawer transfers it to the payee with the intention of making the payee a holder. As you learned in Chapter 33, a holder is a person to whom an instrument has been issued or indorsed and who has possession of it. It is the transfer of the instrument from one party to another, beginning with the maker or drawer, that constitutes the process of negotiation. In accordance with statutory requirements, negotiation may take place in two ways: (1) by indorsement and delivery or (2) by delivery alone.

Indorsement and Delivery

> **1.** Kelly issued a promissory note payable to the order of Shirley Saito. What must Saito do if she wants to transfer the note to a third party?

An instrument that is payable to order may be negotiated only by indorsement and delivery. The party who negotiates the instrument in this manner is the indorser. The party to whom the instrument is negotiated is the indorsee, or **holder.** In Problem 1, if Saito wants to negotiate the promissory note payable to her order, she must indorse it and deliver it to the third party. This is the only method that Saito may use to transfer her rights in the note to another so as to make that person the instrument's legal owner.

An indorsement must be in writing. Although usually written in ink, an indorsement may be made with a rubber stamp or typed. It may be written either on the instrument itself or on a paper firmly attached to it (an *allonge*). The instrument must be indorsed by the owner or by someone with authority to indorse it for the owner. An indorsement is effective for negotiation only when it transfers the entire instrument, or any unpaid balance if the instrument has been partially paid.

> Borges is the payee of a promissory note in the amount of $800. He indorsed the note to Vicks to the extent of $400. The negotiation of part of the amount can't be made unless the $400 represents the unpaid balance on the note.

CAREERS IN LAW

Paralegal

A relatively new career to the field of law is that of paralegal. The prefix *para-* means "close to," "subsidiary," or "alongside of." A paralegal works closely with one or more lawyers and performs many of a lawyer's functions. However, a paralegal does not have the extent of legal training that an attorney has.

Like paramedics, who perform some limited medical procedures, paralegals perform some limited legal procedures. They prepare many kinds of legal documents, research cases, and draw up briefs. They perform much of the routine legal work that their attorney-employers would otherwise have to do.

The difference between paralegals and legal secretaries (see page 143) is sometimes difficult to determine. The paralegal profession developed because legal secretaries found that their duties and knowledge extended far beyond the requirements of standard secretarial positions. A grass-roots movement began as well-qualified and professional legal secretaries demanded more respect for their abilities—as well as larger salaries. Today, many corporate legal counsels and large law firms make wide use of paralegals.

A number of local, county, and state organizations as well as many two- and four-year colleges offer paralegal training that leads to certification. However, there is not yet a standardized list of qualifications and requirements for this profession. Therefore, neither the American Bar Association nor any state bar association is affiliated with or recognizes these training groups.

Delivery Alone

A negotiable instrument payable to bearer or to "Cash" or "Expense" may be negotiated by delivery, without any indorsement. The person who negotiates the instrument by this method is known as a **transferor.** The party to whom it is delivered is known as the **transferee.** Although the law allows these negotiations, as a practical matter, bearer instruments are usually indorsed before they are delivered to another party. This is done because the indorsement gives the holder additional protection with regard to the payment of the instrument. The UCC states that an instrument payable to bearer may be changed to an order instrument by means of a special indorsement. Then the instrument must be indorsed again and delivered before it can be negotiated further. We'll discuss this special indorsement later in this chapter.

KINDS OF INDORSE-MENTS

Five kinds of indorsements are commonly used: (1) blank, (2) special, (3) qualified, (4) restrictive, and (5) accommodation.

Blank Indorsements

> **2.** A check payable to Lucy Noravong was indorsed by her as follows:
>
> *Lucy Noravong*
>
> Noravong then mailed the check to Glasberg, but it was lost in the mail. A finder cashed the check, and the money wasn't recovered. Who bears the loss?

By writing only her name on the back of the check, Noravong used a **blank indorsement.** This indorsement changes the instrument from one payable to order to one payable to bearer. Since bearer paper may be negotiated by delivery alone, Noravong made it possible for anyone—even a finder or a thief—to negotiate the check and obtain payment. Since Noravong's lack of knowledge or carelessness made this loss possible, she must legally stand the loss. To protect herself from the loss, Noravong should have used a special indorsement.

Special Indorsements

> **3.** Instead of using a blank indorsement, Noravong indorsed the check as follows:
>
> *Pay to the order of*
> *Terrence Glasberg*
> *Lucy Noravong*
>
> What protection does this indorsement give to Glasberg?

A **special indorsement** (also known as a *full indorsement*) specifies the person to whom or to whose order it makes the instrument payable. Any instrument specially indorsed is payable to the order of named indorsee. The instrument *may not be negotiated further without that person's indorsement.* By making the instrument payable to the order of Terrence Glasberg, only Terrence Glasberg can transfer title to the instrument. In fact, because of a UCC rule, both Noravong and Glasberg will be protected against loss or theft of the check. The UCC rule permits a holder of an instrument indorsed in blank to change the blank indorsement to a special indorsement. This is done by writing a statement above the signature of the blank indorser, making the instrument payable to the holder.

Clanton received a promissory note indorsed in blank by the payee, Jerrier. Clanton may write above Jerrier's indorsement, "Pay to James Clanton," or "Pay to the order of James Clanton." This addition converts the blank indorsement to a special indorsement. To negotiate the instrument further, Clanton must indorse it again.

When the holder of an order instrument converts a blank indorsement to a special indorsement, the instrument is changed from bearer paper back again to order paper.

Qualified Indorsements

4. Gomes, the payee of a check, indorsed it this way:

> Pay to the order of
> Cynthia Bauer
> without recourse
> Ronald Gomes

What is the legal effect of this indorsement?

A party who indorses a negotiable instrument "without recourse" is using a **qualified indorsement.** The indorser, such as Ronald Gomes in Problem 4, is transferring his or her right or title in the instrument. However, the transfer is *qualified* by the indorser's express statement that he or she does not agree to pay the instrument if the maker fails to pay. The indorsement does *not* release the qualified indorser from all liability on the instrument. Under conditions described later in this chapter, the indorser may be held responsible for payment. This type of indorsement is used in special situations where the qualified indorser has no personal interest in the transaction out of which the negotiable instrument arose.

In settling a lawsuit, Mancini, an attorney, received a check payable to his order. The payment actually belonged to his client. Mancini didn't want to assume the liability of a regular indorser. Therefore, he indorsed the check "without recourse" and turned it over to his client. If the drawer of the check fails to pay it because of financial troubles, the attorney can't be held liable as an indorser.

Restrictive Indorsements

5. Gentile, the payee of a promissory note, wanted to transfer the note to her bank for collection at maturity. She indorsed the note as follows:

> *Pay to the First National Bank*
> *for collection*
> *Antonia Gentile*

What is the legal effect of this indorsement?

The UCC considers an indorsement to be a **restrictive indorsement** in three instances: (1) If the indorsement is conditional (payable only on the occurrence or nonoccurrence of a stated event), it is restrictive. For example, "Pay to the order of Milton Di Santo on completion of repairs to my building" is a restrictive indorsement. (2) If the indorsement makes the indorsee the agent of the indorser for a specific purpose, it is restrictive. "Pay to the First Federal Bank for deposit only" is a restrictive indorsement because it makes the bank the indorser's agent for a specific purpose. (3) An indorsement that states it is for the benefit or use of the indorser or of another person is a restrictive indorsement. For example, the indorsement "Pay to Melanie Quail for support and education of Jennifer Quail" is restrictive.

The Code states that *a restrictive indorsement does not affect the negotiability of the instrument.* The most common use of the restrictive indorsement is to make the indorsee the agent of the indorser. This is the case in Problem 5, where the instrument is indorsed to a bank for collection purposes only. A restrictive indorsement "for deposit only" or "for collection only" is often used when depositing checks and other commercial paper by mail. If these papers carry the restrictive indorsement and are stolen or lost, they can't be used for cash or for any other purpose.

Accommodation Indorsements

6. Hayashi wants to borrow $5,000 from a bank. The bank, however, says that Hayashi's credit standing isn't adequate to warrant the loan. How may Hayashi assure the bank that she'll repay the loan?

A person who wants to borrow money may be unknown to the lender or may have a credit standing that fails to meet the lender's requirements. To meet these requirements, the borrower may seek help from someone whose credit standing is satisfactory and who will lend credit to the borrower without consideration. Such a person is known as an **accommodation party.** In Problem 6, Hayashi would have to obtain the signature of a financially responsible person in addition to her own signature on a promissory note. This type of indorsement is called an **accommodation indorsement.** The accommodation party would be liable on the note to the bank or to any holders who paid value for it. That party would not be liable to Hayashi. If called on to pay the instrument, the accommodation party may recover the amount from Hayashi.

Is an indorser liable to pay an instrument issued by a minor?

OBLIGATIONS OF INDORSERS AND TRANSFERORS

Anyone who indorses an instrument without qualification and receives consideration for that indorsement assumes two legal obligations. First, the indorser enters a contract to pay the instrument under certain conditions if the maker or drawee fails to pay. Second, the indorser enters a contract of warranty.

Contract to Pay

There are two sets of circumstances under which an unqualified indorser agrees to pay if an instrument isn't paid at maturity. First, if the instrument is properly presented for payment (or for acceptance and payment in the case of a draft payable after sight), the indorser must pay the instrument. Second, if due notice of dishonor has been given to the indorser in case of refusal of acceptance or payment, the unqualified indorser must pay the instrument.

Contract of Warranty

PROBLEM

> **7.** Weitz indorsed a promissory note by special indorsement to Colon. At maturity, Colon presented the note to the maker for payment. The maker claimed that her signature was a forgery and refused to pay. Colon now claims that Weitz is liable for payment of the note. Is Colon's claim legally valid?

Anyone who transfers an instrument by delivery and indorsement and receives consideration makes five warranties to the transferee and to any subsequent holder. The indorser warrants (1) that the transferor has good title to the instrument; (2) that all signatures are genuine or authorized; (3) that the instrument hasn't been materially altered; (4) that no defense of any party is good against the transferor; and (5) that the transferor has no knowledge of any insolvency proceeding against the maker or acceptor or the drawer of an unaccepted instrument.

In Problem 7, Colon could hold Weitz liable for breach of the warranty that all signatures are genuine. Obviously, if the maker's signature was forged, Weitz as an indorser is liable. The same would be true if the maker pleaded incapacity to issue negotiable instruments because of minority. In that case, however, the indorser's liability would be under the warranty that no defense of any party is good against the indorser. This warranty would also make the indorser liable if the maker pleaded illegality as a defense against the holder. The illegality may stem from a note issued as a result of a usurious or gambling transaction made illegal by local or state law. A person who transfers a bearer instrument by delivery alone makes the same five warranties. These warranties are made to the *immediate transferee,* however, not to subsequent holders.

Unqualified Indorser	Qualified Indorser	Transferor without Indorsement
An unqualified indorser who receives consideration warrants to the immediate transferee and to any subsequent holders that:	A qualified indorser who receives consideration warrants to the immediate transferee and to any subsequent holders that:	Transferor without indorsement who receives consideration warrants *only to the immediate transferee* but not to any subsequent holders that:
1. the transferor has good title to the instrument.	1. the transferor has good title to the instrument.	1. the transferor has good title to the instrument.
2. all signatures are genuine or authorized.	2. all signatures are genuine or authorized.	2. all signatures are genuine or authorized.
3. the instrument hasn't been materially altered.	3. the instrument hasn't been materially altered.	3. the instrument hasn't been materially altered.
4. no defense of any party is good against the transferor.	4. he or she has no knowledge of any defense good against the transferor.	4. no defense of any party is good against the transferor.
5. he or she has no knowledge of any insolvency proceeding against the maker or drawer.	5. he or she has no knowledge of any insolvency proceeding against the maker or drawer.	5. he or she has no knowledge of any insolvency proceeding against the maker or drawer.

Figure 35.1
Warranties of Indorsers and Transferors

Someone who transfers an instrument by means of a qualified indorsement (without recourse) makes the same warranties as a regular indorser except as to Warranty 4. Instead of warranting that no defense of any party is good against the transferor, the qualified indorser warrants that he or she has no knowledge of any defense that may be good against the transferor. The warranties of a qualified indorser, like those of a regular indorser, extend to all subsequent holders of the instrument who acquire it in good faith. Figure 35.1 highlights the features of the warranty contract entered into by indorsers and transferors of negotiable instruments.

This chapter has focused on the role played by indorsers and transferors in the negotiation of commercial paper. As you know, the parties to whom negotiable commercial papers are transferred are known as *holders*. The special rights of holders will be the focus of Chapter 36.

Chapter 35 Review

"YOU BE THE JUDGE" REVIEW

Look again at the "You Be the Judge" cases given at the beginning of this chapter. Would you decide them differently now, after your study of the chapter?

Correct Decisions

1. No. A holder may convert a blank indorsement to a special or full indorsement without affecting the negotiability of the instrument or the liability of the parties.

2. No. As an indorser, you are secondarily liable.

UNDERSTANDING WHAT YOU HAVE READ

1. How would you define *negotiation?*
2. How does negotiation differ from a mere transfer?
3. How may bearer paper be negotiated?
4. How may order paper be negotiated?
5. Give an example of each of the following indorsements: (a) blank, (b) special, (c) restrictive, (d) accommodation, (e) qualified.
6. Which indorsement in Problem 5 gives the indorser the least amount of protection?
7. Which type of indorsement should be used
   a. when you want to mail a negotiable instrument to a bank for deposit?
   b. when a payee wants to mail a check to a creditor in payment of a debt?
   c. when you're cashing a check at a bank?
   d. when you want to transfer an instrument so that it can be used only for a particular purpose?
8. a. When does one become an accommodation indorser?
   b. What is the liability of an accommodation indorser?
9. What warranties are given by transferors of bearer instruments?
10. List the warranties made by indorsers of order instruments.

BUILDING YOUR LEGAL VOCABULARY

From this list, select the legal term that belongs in the blank in each sentence below. Write your answers on a separate sheet of paper.

accommodation indorsement	qualified indorsement	transfer
accommodation party	restrictive indorsement	transferee
blank indorsement	special indorsement	transferor
holder		

1. One who negotiates an instrument by delivery, without indorsement, is known as a ▓▓▓▓▓▓▓▓▓▓▓.
2. The indorsement that transfers the instrument "without recourse" is a ▓▓▓▓▓▓▓▓▓▓▓.
3. An indorser makes a ▓▓▓▓▓▓▓▓▓▓▓ simply by writing his or her name on the back of an instrument.
4. The act of delivering an instrument to another with the intention of passing one's rights in the instrument to that party is called ▓▓▓▓▓▓▓▓▓▓▓.
5. An ▓▓▓▓▓▓▓▓▓▓▓ is a person with a good credit standing who helps a borrower by agreeing to co-indorse a loan instrument.
6. An indorsement that is conditional, makes the indorsee the indorser's agent for a certain purpose, or states that it is for the specific benefit of another is known as a ▓▓▓▓▓▓▓▓▓▓▓.
7. A person to whom an instrument has been issued, transferred, or indorsed and who has possession of it is called a ▓▓▓▓▓▓▓▓▓▓▓.
8. An ▓▓▓▓▓▓▓▓▓▓▓ is the indorsement of a financially responsible party on the loan instrument of someone who can't meet the lender's credit requirements.
9. An indorsement that specifies the person to whom or to whose order it makes the instrument payable is a ▓▓▓▓▓▓▓▓▓▓▓.
10. The party to whom a bearer instrument is transferred by delivery is called a ▓▓▓▓▓▓▓▓▓▓▓.

APPLYING LEGAL PRINCIPLES

1. Laird refused to accept a promissory note from Kung because Kung had indorsed the note with a rubber stamp. Was Laird's action legally justified?
2. Ott was the payee of a promissory note in the amount of $500. She transferred the note by special indorsement to Niro in the sum of $200. When the note was due, Niro tried to collect $200 from the maker. Was she entitled to do so?
3. A holder of a check payable to "Bearer" mailed it without indorsement to Salvato, a creditor. Was the check transferred by assignment or by negotiation?
4. A promissory note payable to the order of James Vargo was transferred without

indorsement to Roberta Fulton. Was the note assigned or negotiated to Fulton?

5. A business person accepted a check from a customer, payable to "Cash." She transferred the check to a creditor by delivery without indorsement. If the drawer of the check were unable to pay, would the business person be liable for payment?

6. Esquivel issued a promissory note payable to Salton or bearer. The note was transferred by delivery to Fenig without being indorsed by Salton. Fenig later sued Esquivel to recover on the note. Esquivel claimed as his defense that the instrument had not been negotiated to Fenig. Do you agree with Esquivel?

7. Son made out a promissory note payable to bearer and put it in his pocket. The note fell out of Son's pocket and Ravech found it. Ravech negotiated the note by delivery for value to Yagoda. Yagoda didn't know how Ravech had obtained possession of the note. On the due date, Yagoda presented the note to Son for payment, which was refused. Yagoda then sued Son. Who is entitled to judgment?

8. Fusco received a promissory note indorsed in blank by the payee, Tirelli. Fusco wrote above Tirelli's name, "Pay to the order of Benjamin Fusco." When Fusco presented the note for payment on the due date, the maker refused to pay him. The maker claimed that Fusco had no right to change the indorsement. Was the maker's claim legally correct?

9. Nathan, payee of a promissory note, indorsed it to Theodoros as follows:

> *Pay to Stephen Theodoros*
> *without recourse*
> *Sally Nathan*

By special indorsement, Theodoros negotiated the instrument to Wasser. When Wasser was unable to collect on the note from the maker, he brought suit against Nathan. Is Nathan liable?

10. When she made a deposit at the National Bank of Winchester, Serret used the indorsement, "Pay to the order of the National Bank of Winchester, for deposit, (signed) Isabel Serret." Serret claimed that this indorsement made the instrument nonnegotiable. Do you agree?

11. Verdone presented a note to the maker, Esmail, for payment at maturity. The maker claimed that she was only sixteen years old and therefore wasn't liable on the instrument. Could Verdone look for payment from the indorsers from whom he had purchased the instrument?

12. Assume in Problem 11 that the maker pleaded illegality as a defense and refused to pay the instrument. Could Verdone hold the indorsers liable?

13. Vance loaned money to Kenyon and received a 60-day note in return. The note was dated October 1, payable to the order of Vance, and signed by Kenyon. Beale's signature also appeared on the note as an accommodation indorser. The note was due November 30.
   a. State why Vance wanted Beale's signature on the note.
   b. Suppose Kenyon fails to pay the note on November 30 and Beale is forced to pay it. Does Beale have a claim for reimbursement from Kenyon?

ANALYZING COURT CASES

1. Simpson signed and delivered his promissory note for $1,500, payable to the order of Benton Bank & Trust Company. The bank negotiated the note to Federal Credit Bank but failed to indorse it. Federal Credit Bank later filed an action against the maker, Simpson, to recover the payment of the note. Simpson pleaded that the Federal Bank was not a holder of the instrument. Was Simpson's plea legally correct? (Based on: *Federal Intermediate Credit Bank v. Carolina Petroleum Company*, 151 S.E. 738)

2. A negotiable interest-bearing note was delivered to Elias, the payee. She indorsed the note to Whitley but kept it in her possession so she could collect the interest until her death. She intended that Whitley should have the note after her death. After Elias died, her executor found the note and refused to deliver it to Whitley. The executor maintained that Whitley had no legal right to the note because of a lack of delivery while Elias was alive. Was Whitley entitled to the note? (Based on: *Cartwright v. Coppersmith*, 24 S.E. 2d 246)

3. Pitts signed and delivered his negotiable promissory note, payable to the order of Stepp. Stepp indorsed the note in this way:

> "I hereby transfer my rights to this note over to W. E. McCullough. (signed)
>
> William C. Stepp"

Stepp then negotiated the note to McCullough. The note was not paid when due, and McCullough sued Stepp as indorser of the instrument. As his defense, Stepp claimed that it was his and McCullough's intention that the instrument be transferred without any liability on the part of Stepp for payment, as indicated by his indorsement. Was Stepp's defense legally sound? (*McCullough v. Stepp*, 85 S.E. 2d 159)

CHAPTER 36

Rights of Holders and Defenses of Makers

YOU BE THE JUDGE

Think about these cases.
If you were the judge, how would you decide each case?

1

Falzon paid $375 for a $400, nine-month promissory note, fifteen days before the note was due. On this information alone, does Falzon qualify as a holder in due course?

2

Janik, the payee of a $100 note, changed the amount to $1,000. Janik then negotiated the note to Isler, a holder in due course. Is Mota, the drawer, liable to Isler for $1,000?

RIGHTS OF HOLDERS

As you learned earlier, a *holder* is someone in possession of an instrument that has been issued or indorsed to him or her. A holder may be an indorsee, a transferee, or a payee of the instrument. A holder may have the same rights as any assignee of a simple contract or may enjoy *superior* rights to those possessed by the former holder or owner of the instrument.

> **1.** Farren gave his nephew a promissory note for $500 as a token of his affection. The nephew negotiated the note to Meers. Meers didn't know how the nephew had obtained the note but paid the nephew full value for it. At maturity, the uncle refused to pay Meers because the note had been issued to the nephew without consideration. Is the uncle's claim legally valid?

A holder who has rights superior to those of the former holder or owner is known as a **holder in due course.** The superior rights allow the holder to collect payment on the instrument when one who isn't a holder in due course wouldn't be able to do so. The reason for this rule is to encourage the free circulation of negotiable instruments. In Problem 1, the nephew is simply a holder of the note. Meers, however, is a holder in due course. If the nephew sought to collect on the note from his uncle, he would be unsuccessful because he had paid no value to obtain it. But as a holder in due course, Meers would be entitled to collect.

In order to become a holder in due course, a person must satisfy the requirements of the Uniform Commercial Code.

Requirements of a Holder in Due Course

The UCC states that a holder in due course is one who takes the instrument (1) for value, (2) in good faith, and (3) without notice that it is overdue or has been dishonored or of any defense or claim to it on the part of any person.

For Value

To qualify as a holder in due course, a person actually must have given value for the instrument. In Problem 1, the nephew received the note as a gift. Since he didn't pay value for it, he wasn't a holder in due course. Meers, in contrast, meets all of the statutory requirements and is a holder in due course. Under the Code, value actually must be paid to satisfy the requirement. A mere promise to pay value won't make a person a holder in due course.

The Law Merchant

The common law was feudal in origin. Thus, neither its principles nor its procedures were suitable for the settlement of mercantile disputes. Most medieval judges were ignorant of the special customs of merchants, and few judges made an effort to learn those customs. Chief Justice Mansfield was one exception. He was on familiar terms with people who knew mercantile customs and soon learned those customs himself. It was through the efforts of Lord Mansfield and his successors that the early law merchant developed. And from the law merchant, the law of negotiable instruments arose.

Prior to the 1600s, the law merchant was a body of special law enforced in special courts for special people. The special law was based on the customs of merchants relating to sales, bills of exchange (drafts), insurance, partnerships, and related topics. The special courts were called *mercantile courts* and were located along the seacoast of western Europe. The special people were merchants. Nonmerchants could not sue or be sued in the mercantile courts.

Gradually, the law merchant was merged into the common law. Today's Uniform Commercial Code owes much to the law merchant, one of the most valuable contributions ever made to the development of English common law.

Good Faith

2. Arnel purchased a promissory note on which there were clear signs of erasures. Later, Arnel learned that the amount had been raised from $100 to $500. Is Arnel a holder in due course?

Good faith means honesty in fact in the conduct or transaction concerned. A holder who knows that the payee obtained the instrument from the maker by dishonest means can't qualify as a holder in due course because of bad faith. Courts look to the mind of the particular holder who is claiming to be a holder in due course. They don't consider what the state of mind of a prudent person would have been under the circumstances.

Regardless of state of mind, a holder who fails to make proper inquiries about any suspicious circumstances (such as obvious erasures) may be guilty of bad faith. In Problem 2, Arnel would not be a holder in due course because of the obvious alteration of the instrument.

Without Notice

> **3.** An instrument payable on demand is presented for payment by the holder seven months after the date of issue. Is the holder considered a holder in due course?

A holder in due course must take the instrument without notice that it is overdue or dishonored. If an instrument is payable on demand and the purchaser has reason to know that more than a reasonable time has passed since the date of issue, the purchaser isn't regarded as a holder in due course. What is a reasonable time is a question of fact. It will be decided by the nature of the instrument, the customs of the trade, and the particular facts of the case. In Problem 3, the holder would not usually be considered a holder in due course because the demand instrument is seven months old. When an instrument is payable at a fixed time, its due date is definite. A transfer of such an instrument on the day of maturity is considered a transfer before the instrument is overdue.

DEFENSES OF MAKERS

The parties primarily liable (maker and drawer) may claim certain defenses against the holder in due course when the holder seeks to enforce payment. These defenses may be classified as (1) personal defenses and (2) real defenses.

Personal Defenses

A **personal defense** is one that can't be used against a holder in due course. It may be used only between the immediate parties to an instrument or against a person who doesn't qualify as a holder in due course.

> **4.** Go gave a promissory note to an antique dealer in payment for a chair that she was told was once owned by Andrew Jackson. She later found out that she had been defrauded in the deal. Meanwhile, the antique dealer had negotiated Go's note to a holder in due course. Must Go pay the holder in due course when the note becomes due?

The personal defenses are (1) fraud in the inducement, (2) duress and undue influence, (3) nondelivery of a complete or incomplete instrument, (4) payment before maturity, (5) lack of consideration, and (6) counterclaim.

Fraud in the Inducement

In Problem 4, the antique dealer could not collect on the note from Go because of the fraud practiced on Go. However, a holder in due course would be entitled to collect. *The maker of a negotiable instrument may not claim the personal defense of **fraud in the inducement** against a holder in due course.*

Duress and Undue Influence

A maker or drawer may sign a negotiable instrument while under threat of bodily harm or as a result of improper persuasion. A party who obtains an instrument in this manner is not allowed to collect on it. However, a holder in due course *may* enforce payment. *Duress and undue influence are personal defenses that a maker may not use against a holder in due course.*

Nondelivery of an Instrument

A negotiable instrument that is complete or incomplete may be lost or stolen and then transferred to a holder in due course. In this event, the holder may enforce payment against the maker or acceptor. *Nondelivery of a complete or incomplete instrument may not be used as a defense against a holder in due course.*

Duress in the signing of a negotiable instrument is usually a personal defense.

> Derkin lost a check payable to "Cash" while she was on her way to the bank. The finder negotiated the check to a holder in due course. The holder may enforce payment on the instrument. Even if the check were incomplete but signed by the drawer, a holder in due course would be able to collect if the check were completed and negotiated to the holder.

Payment Before Maturity

The maker of a negotiable instrument may have paid the instrument on or before the due date but failed to take it away from the holder for cancellation. If that instrument is later negotiated to a holder in due course, the holder may compel the maker to pay it again. *Payment before maturity is a personal defense that can't legally be claimed against a holder in due course.*

> Erhardt paid his promissory note in favor of Duval ten days before the date of maturity. Erhardt left the note in Duval's possession. Duval negotiated the note to Catler, a holder in due course. Catler may compel Erhardt to pay the note again.

Lack of Consideration

In Problem 1 at the beginning of this chapter, the nephew couldn't collect on his uncle's promissory note without any consideration. However, since the nephew had transferred the note for value to Meers, a holder in due course, Meers could enforce payment. This is true because *lack of consideration is a personal defense that the maker may not claim against a holder in due course.*

Counterclaim

The maker of a promissory note may not use the personal defense of counterclaim against a holder in due course.

> **5.** Michaels, a plumber, repaired the hot-water heater in Espadero's dental office. Dr. Espadero paid Michaels with a 30-day promissory note for $110. Two weeks later, Dr. Espadero performed dental services amounting to $65 for Michaels. Meanwhile, Michaels had negotiated the note to Irvin, a holder in due course. Is Irvin entitled to collect $110 from Dr. Espadero?

In Problem 5, Dr. Espadero's claim against Michaels is legally considered to be a **counterclaim.** Since Michaels owed Dr. Espadero $65, he was entitled to collect the difference between this sum and the face of the promissory note. However, Dr. Espadero's counterclaim against Michaels is a personal defense and may not be used against a holder in due course. Irvin may collect $110 from Dr. Espadero.

Real Defenses

A maker's **real** (absolute) **defense** is one that prohibits a holder in due course from collecting on a negotiable instrument.

Forgery

Forgery is an absolute defense that the maker may claim against anyone, even a holder in due course.

> Pinckney, a holder in due course, presented a promissory note to the maker, Feldman, for payment. Feldman claimed forgery and proved that the signature on the note was not hers. Since Feldman didn't sign the note, no contract arose. Pinckney can't collect from Feldman but may hold the indorsers, if any, liable on the warranty that the signature was genuine.

Incapacity of the Maker

If a minor or an insane person signs a negotiable instrument, he or she can't be held liable on it by a holder in due course. *A holder in due course may not collect from a maker who pleads the real defense of **incapacity** against such a holder.*

> Suppose that Feldman, the maker of the note in the last example, had claimed minority as a defense. In this case, Pinckney would not be able to collect on the instrument.

Illegality

Most states have enacted laws covering the validity of negotiable instruments issued as a result of illegal transactions.

> **6.** Bulatti, the maker of a promissory note, proved that she had issued the note to pay a gambling debt. Could Gibbs, the holder in due course, collect on the note?

Illegality as declared by statute—as when a note is issued to cover a gambling debt—is an absolute defense.

If a negotiable instrument is given in payment of a gambling debt, neither the payee nor a holder in due course may enforce payment on it. Gambling makes a contract void, and any negotiable instrument issued as a result of a gambling transaction is also regarded as void. In Problem 6, Gibbs may not collect on Bulatti's promissory note. *Illegality is an absolute defense that may be claimed against a holder in due course.*

Alteration

A material alteration of a negotiable instrument may affect the date, the sum payable, the rate of interest, or the place of payment.

PROBLEM

7. Masimba, the maker of a promissory note, claimed that the note had been altered to raise the amount from $180 to $1,800. Would Masimba be liable to a holder in due course for $1,800?

If a material alteration is made without the consent of prior parties to the instrument, those parties are discharged from liability. The person who altered the instrument may not legally recover even the original amount. However, the UCC allows the holder in due course of an altered instrument to recover the original amount. In Problem 7, the holder in due course would be entitled to collect $180 from Masimba. *A holder in due course may collect only the original amount of a negotiable instrument when the maker claims the real defense of material alteration.*

Fraud in the Execution

Fraud in the execution of an instrument is an absolute defense that may be used by the maker against anyone, even a holder in due course.

EXAMPLE

> Ruzik sold a car to Gokita and handed Gokita a paper to sign. Gokita examined the paper and found it to be a properly drawn duplicate bill of sale. As he prepared to sign it, Ruzik, by trickery, substituted a negotiable promissory note. Gokita unknowingly signed the note instead of the bill of sale. Ruzik indorsed the note to Widoff, making Widoff a holder in due course. Because Gokita signed what he thought was a duplicate bill of sale, no contract came into existence. Widoff, although a holder in due course, can't collect on the instrument.

Figure 36.1 is a summary of the personal defenses and real defenses that apply to negotiable instruments.

Figure 36.1
Defenses of the
Maker or Drawer
of a Negotiable
Instrument

Personal	Real or Absolute
Good against the payee but not good against a holder in due course	**Good against anyone**
Duress or undue influence	Incapacity
Fraud in the inducement	Fraud in the execution
Lack of consideration	Forgery
Counterclaim	Illegality, making a contract void
Payment before maturity	Material alteration
Nondelivery of an instrument	

Holders in Due Course in Consumer Sales

Suppose you unknowingly bought a defective appliance from a dishonest merchant. You signed an installment contract and a promissory note in payment. After you discovered the defect in the product, you notified the seller that you would withhold payments on the note until the problem was corrected. Legally, can you do this? Yes, because you have a personal defense—breach of warranty or breach of contract on the part of the seller. You may plead this defense if the seller sues you. But what if the seller has already negotiated the note to a bank or a finance company, presumably a holder in due course? Under the traditional holder-in-due-course principle, you would have to pay the note in full. A personal defense is ineffective against a holder in due course.

In order to protect consumers in such cases, some states have adopted laws limiting or completely eliminating the holder-in-due-course rule. Also, the Federal Trade Commission has issued regulations governing consumer credit contracts. These rules require that a consumer credit contract must contain a special notice, printed in bold type. The notice must state that any holder or assignee of the consumer's note or installment contract is subject to all the defenses that the consumer could have set up against the seller. This ruling effectively eliminates the holder-in-due-course principle in most retail consumer sales on credit.

DISCHARGE OF NEGOTIABLE INSTRUMENTS

Under the UCC, instruments may be discharged in various ways. The discharge methods may include (1) payment, (2) cancellation, (3) fraudulent or material alteration, or (4) other means.

Discharge by Payment

A negotiable instrument is usually discharged by the payment of money to the holder by the party primarily liable on the instrument. A discharge also may take place by the payment of a consideration other than money. In that event, the holder to whom payment is made must agree to accept the offered consideration.

EXAMPLE

> At maturity, Zuniga presented an accepted draft to the drawee for payment. The drawee offered to pay the draft with the equivalent value in merchandise. Zuniga accepted the goods, and the draft was marked "Paid in Full." The instrument was discharged by payment.

If an instrument is paid before maturity, the person making the payment should obtain possession of the instrument. If this isn't done and the instrument is later negotiated to a holder in due course, the party primarily liable may have to pay the instrument again.

Discharge by Cancellation

The Code allows the holder of a negotiable instrument to discharge any party from obligation to pay by cancellation, even without consideration. Specifically, the Code allows a holder to cancel the instrument or a party's signature by destruction or mutilation or by striking out the party's signature. Cancellation also may occur when the holder surrenders the instrument or gives up the right to collect it (*renounces* it) by a signed writing delivered to the party obligated to pay. Title to the instrument isn't affected unless the instrument is surrendered at the time of cancellation or renunciation.

A negotiable instrument is discharged by cancellation when the holder destroys it.

Jarmon was the holder of a promissory note on which Nihan's name appeared as maker. At maturity, Jarmon wrote to Nihan: "Enclosed please find your promissory note with your signature removed. Payment of this instrument will no longer be required." The promissory note was effectively discharged by cancellation and surrender of the note.

Discharge by Fraudulent or Material Alteration

To constitute a discharge of an instrument, an alteration must be material or made with a fraudulent purpose. A **material alteration** is one that changes the contract of a party to the instrument. Despite the fact that an instrument is discharged by alteration or fraud, the holder in due course may enforce it according to its original terms.

Hendrickson, the indorsee of a negotiable instrument, altered it by advancing the date of payment from three months to one month. The instrument was discharged as to Hendrickson. If she transferred the altered instrument to a holder in due course, the holder could enforce payment according to the original terms of the instrument.

Discharge by Other Methods

A negotiable instrument may be discharged in other ways mentioned in the Uniform Commercial Code. For example, the discharge may be by means of any agreement that would ordinarily discharge a simple contract for the payment of money. Other methods mentioned in the Code were discussed earlier. They relate to discharge of the obligations of the parties in case of certification of checks and unexcused delay in presentment or notice of dishonor.

This unit has explained how commercial paper helps us to transact business efficiently. Because they substitute for money, negotiable instruments are extremely valuable in today's economy. It's important to know that they are true contractual agreements and that they carry with them special rights and duties.

Thus far, our study of business law has focused on the business dealings of individuals who are acting for themselves. The next unit will explain how business is carried on by people who represent others. Those people are known as *agents* and *employees.*

Chapter 36 Review

"YOU BE THE JUDGE" REVIEW

Look again at the "You Be the Judge" cases given at the beginning of this chapter. Would you decide them differently now, after your study of the chapter?

Correct Decisions

1. Yes. The value paid for the note indicates good faith in effecting the transaction. If the other requirements of a holder in due course are met, Falzon does qualify as a holder in due course.

2. No. Mota is liable only for the original amount of $100. Material alteration is a real or absolute defense that the maker or drawer can use against a holder in due course. The maker or drawer is liable, however, for the original amount of the instrument.

UNDERSTANDING WHAT YOU HAVE READ

1. How does a holder in due course differ from an ordinary holder?
2. What is a personal defense?
3. Name six defenses that a maker may claim against an ordinary holder but not against a holder in due course.
4. What is a real or absolute defense?
5. Name five absolute defenses that a maker may claim against a holder in due course.
6. A maker who refuses payment of a note to a holder in due course might use any of the following defenses. In each case, explain fully whether or not the holder would succeed in collecting from the maker.

   a. The maker was a minor at the time the note was signed.
   b. The maker had given the note in payment of a gambling debt.
   c. The maker's signature on the note had been forged.
   d. The maker had merely signed a blank piece of paper, and someone had inserted a promissory note above the maker's signature.
   e. The car the maker had contracted to buy for the note had never been delivered, and the seller had disappeared.
   f. The note had been issued for $25, and it had been raised to $2,500.

g. The maker had been tricked into signing a promissory note instead of a bill of sale.

h. The maker had paid the note before maturity and had received a receipt for the money paid. At the time of payment, the payee had stated that he had left the note in the vault, but he had assured the maker that the note would be destroyed.

i. The maker had issued the note without receiving any consideration.

j. The maker had signed the note under threat of bodily harm.

7. Explain four ways in which a negotiable instrument may be discharged.

BUILDING YOUR LEGAL VOCABULARY

Match each of these legal terms with its correct definition from the list that follows. Write your answers on a separate sheet of paper.

counterclaim
forgery
fraud in the execution
fraud in the inducement

good faith
holder in due course
incapacity

material alteration
personal defense
real defense

1. the act of signing another's name with intention to defraud

2. a defense that prohibits a holder in due course from collecting from a maker on an instrument

3. fraud practiced by one party while another party is in the process of negotiating an instrument

4. the inability of a maker to sign a negotiable instrument because of lack of majority or insanity

5. a claim made in response to another party's claim

6. a party to a negotiable instrument who has superior rights to those of a former holder or owner

7. a change to a negotiable instrument that affects the date, the sum payable, the rate of interest, or the place of payment

8. honest conduct in a transaction

9. a defense that can't be used against a holder in due course

10. fraud practiced while persuading another to negotiate an instrument

APPLYING LEGAL PRINCIPLES

1. Drohan gave her daughter a 60-day promissory note for $1,000 as a college graduation gift. The daughter discounted the note at a bank where she was a depositor. The bank didn't know that the note had been issued as a gift. On maturity of the note, Drohan refused to pay the bank. As her defense, she claimed lack of consideration. Should the bank succeed in collecting on the note?

2. How would you have answered Problem 1 if the daughter hadn't negotiated the note to the bank but instead had held it to maturity and then sought to enforce payment?

3. Ouk sold his car to Notini for $3,950. Notini gave Ouk a 60-day promissory note for the purchase price. Later, Notini discovered that Ouk had made false statements about the car to induce him to buy it. Notini then offered to return the car and notified Ouk that he wouldn't pay the note. Ouk sued Notini on the note. Will Ouk succeed?

4. Athey induced Cespedes, a blind man, to sign a paper that Athey represented to be a contract to lease a house. However, the paper was actually a promissory note. Athey negotiated the note to Bordon, a holder in due course. Does Bordon have a legal right to collect the amount of the note from Cespedes?

5. Before maturity, Levene paid a note she owed to Fanger. Fanger promised to deliver the note to Levene the next day. Instead, Fanger negotiated the note to Kane, a holder in due course. Can Kane collect on the note from Levene?

6. Kee borrowed $550 from Falkner, signing a four-month note. Later, Kee painted Falkner's garage, and Falkner was to pay him $300. When Kee's note became due, it was presented for payment by the bank to which Falkner had negotiated it. Kee refused to pay the entire $550, claiming that he owned Falkner only $250. Did Kee have a valid defense against the bank?

7. Kritz, a holder in due course, presented a promissory note to McLean, whose name appeared as the maker, for payment. McLean proved that her signature had been forged. Can Kritz collect from McLean?

8. A check made payable to bearer and signed by Kanai was stolen from Kanai's safe by Bard. Bard negotiated the check to Ransom, a holder in due course. Ransom deposited the check in his bank. In the meantime, Kanai had stopped payment on the check. Is Kanai liable to Ransom?

9. O'Leary, age 17, wrote a 90-day promissory note for $250 to Rickson, in payment of a debt. The note was negotiated several times in the usual course of business. At maturity the note was in the hands of Langdon, a holder in due course. When Langdon demanded payment, O'Leary refused to honor it and pleaded her minority as a defense. Was O'Leary within her legal rights?

10. Moldave bought a color TV for $600. He gave the seller a promissory note for $600 in payment. The seller erased the original amount, which had been written in ink, and typed in a much larger

figure. The erasure could easily be seen on the face of the note. The seller then indorsed the note to Jandreau, who claimed to be a holder in due course. Do you agree?

ANALYZING COURT CASES

1. Standfield bought a 20-year, six-percent road bond through a reputable brokerage firm. The bond was payable to bearer and negotiable. By state law, the bond could be used by the owner in payment of taxes. When Standfield offered the bond in payment of county taxes, she was told that she couldn't do so because of a rumor that the bond had been stolen. Standfield sued the county. During the trial, the evidence showed that the bond had, in fact, been stolen. In whose favor should a judgment be given? (Based on: *Stricker v. Buncombe County*, 172 S.E. 188)

2. Stephens employed Hunter, a lawyer, to represent him in a case and gave him a note in payment. When the case came up for trial, Hunter failed to perform. Later, Heller told Stephens that she wanted to buy the note from Hunter. Stephens explained the circumstances and advised Heller not to buy the note. Nevertheless, Heller bought it from Hunter. On the due date of the note, Stephens refused to pay it, and Heller brought suit to collect from him. Should Heller succeed? (Based on: *Heideman v. Stefano*, 291 S.W. 265)

3. The Welfare Department of the City of Danton mailed a monthly welfare check to Rita Jones. Another woman who had the same name got possession of the check, indorsed it with her name, and cashed it at her bank. The bank collected the amount of the check from the City of Danton. After learning the true circumstances, the City of Danton sued the bank that cashed the check for the return of the money. Will the City of Danton succeed? (Based on: *Fulton National Bank v. U.S.*, 197 F. 2d 763)

UNIT 8

AGENCY AND EMPLOYMENT

CHAPTERS

494

LEARNING OBJECTIVES

After you have studied this unit, you should be able to:

- Describe the agency relationship and its importance.

- Show that you understand the types of authority exercised by various agents and the agents' responsibility to principals and to third parties.

- Show that you understand the legal responsibilities of principals to agents and to third parties, and third parties to principals and to agents.

- Describe the rights and duties of employers and employees to each other and to third persons.

- Explain the nature and provisions of various laws passed for the protection of workers and employers.

CHAPTER 37

Creation of Agency

Think about these cases.
If you were the judge, how would you decide each case?

1

Comeau, a minor, appointed Winkler, an adult, as her stockbroker and financial advisor for a two-year period. The appointment was made in a written contract. After six months, Comeau discharged Winkler, claiming that her contract was voidable. Is Comeau liable for breach of contract?

2

This conversation took place between a husband and wife:

Husband: "Marriage alone doesn't make you my agent."

Wife: "I'm sorry, but it does."

Who is right?

WHAT IS AGENCY?

A special legal relationship is created when one person is authorized to act for another in business dealings with third parties.

> **1.** Ortiz needed to hire a traveling salesperson for his business. He inserted a "Help Wanted" ad in the newspaper, and a number of people applied for the job. What legal relationship will exist between Ortiz and the person he selects for the position?

The legal relationship that arises when someone is given authority to transact business for another is known as **agency.** The party who grants the authority is known as the **principal.** The one who receives the authority to act as a representative of the principal is called the **agent.** The party with whom an agent deals is known as the **third party.** The acts of the agent obligate the principal to third parties and give the principal rights against third parties.

At various times, all of us act as principals and as agents. If you ask a friend to buy a ticket for you to a basketball game or concert, you're acting as a principal and your friend is your agent. If your mother sends you to a store to buy a head of lettuce, you're acting as her agent. Similarly, business people transact most of their business through agents. Examples include selling goods through agents known as salespersons (as in Problem 1), buying goods through purchasing agents, hiring a lawyer to handle legal matters, and appointing a real-estate broker to buy or sell realty. Agency is important in everyday life. Therefore, everyone should know something about the legal principles that apply to this relationship.

Who May Be a Principal?

> **2.** In Problem 1, does Ortiz have the legal authority to appoint an agent?

Usually, anyone competent to act for himself or herself may appoint another to act as agent. In some states, minors may appoint agents to act for them, but the appointment is voidable on the part of the minor. If Ortiz, in Problem 2, is competent to act for himself, he may legally appoint another to act for him. Groups of people may appoint others to act for them. Corporations must act through agents.

Who May Be an Agent?

> **3.** In Problem 1, may Ortiz select any one of the applicants to be his agent?

Anyone who is authorized to act as an agent may be an agent. The principal may appoint a minor as an agent, because the resulting contract is not the minor's but the principal's. The minor is merely a go-between for the principal and the third party. In Problem 3, Ortiz may choose any one of the applicants. However, he should exercise care in his choice since he may be responsible for the agent's acts. Laws in most states require that certain agents, such as auctioneers or insurance or realty agents, be licensed. An agent may be a partnership or a corporation.

Agent, Employee, and Independent Contractor

An ordinary employee, unlike an agent, has no power to enter into binding contracts with third parties on behalf of the employer. Sometimes the same person may be both an employee and an agent.

> Stebbins was hired as a delivery person by Peskin Parcel. Her duties included driving a company delivery van for the purpose of making deliveries and securing new customers. When Stebbins drove the van and carried packages for her customers, she was acting as an employee of the firm. But when she secured new customers and agreed to deliver packages for them, she was acting as the agent of Peskin Parcel.

An **independent contractor** is someone who agrees to perform services for another in a situation in which the person who requested the services has no control over the contractor's performance.

> Brawley, a licensed plumber, agreed to install new bathroom fixtures in Martell's home for $3,200. Brawley was an independent contractor rather than Martell's agent or employee. He alone had full control over the means and methods used to produce a satisfactory result. He is usually considered to be an independent business person.

LIVING UNDER THE LAW

Legal Research by Computer

Computers are revolutionizing the art of legal research. In the late 1950s, the University of Pittsburgh began the initial efforts in computer-assisted legal research (CALR). These efforts focused on searching statutes by computer but were soon followed by case-law research efforts. However, it was the United States Air Force that developed the first major CALR system, known as *Legal Information Through Electronics* (later called *FLITE*).

Today, computer-assisted legal research systems are available commercially from publishers of electronic databases. Among the systems in common use are LEXIS, offered by Mead Data Central, and WESTLAW, offered by West Publishing Company. These systems provide the full texts of cases, statutes, letters, memo-

randa, and other research materials, as well as special topical files in areas such as tax, securities, and labor.

Briefly, a CALR system works as follows: A query (a legal question to be researched) is sent to a large, mainframe computer, using any of a number of compatible terminals and public telecommunications networks. The computer then transmits the desired information through the same network, and the information appears on the screen of the inquirer's terminal.

These systems are designed for use in conjunction with the more traditional tools of legal research. As the systems' publishers maintain, they are only a means—and not an end—to the total research effort.

HOW AN AGENCY RELATIONSHIP ARISES

There are several ways of creating an agency. These include (1) agency by appointment, (2) agency by ratification, (3) agency by estoppel, and (4) agency by necessity.

Agency by Appointment

4. In Problem 1, after Ortiz has chosen an applicant, what legal steps must be taken to create the agency?

The usual method of creating an agency is by express authorization. This is called an **agency by appointment.** No particular form of language is necessary. The contract of agency may be oral, written, or implied from the actions of the parties. It must contain all the essentials of a binding agreement, as discussed in earlier chapters. Also, *if the services of the agent can't be completed in less than one year from the time the contract is entered into, the contract must be in writing* under the Statute of Frauds. In some states, an agency to contract for or to make a sale or a lease of real property for a period over a year must be in writing. Figure 37.1 is a written agency agreement, called a **power of attorney,** to sell real property.

It's always advisable to have a written contract appointing an agent, even though the written form isn't required by statute. In Problem 4, Ortiz should enter into a written contract with the applicant he chooses.

Agency by Ratification

> **5.** Maye, without authority and in Allende's name, bought an antique coin for Allende. Maye thought Allende would like to add the coin to her collection. Could Allende be held liable on the contract?

Sometimes a person acts for another without having any authority to do so, or without having adequate authority. This is the situation in Problem 5. Unless Allende, with full knowledge of the facts, approves the purchase made on her behalf by Maye, the contract isn't binding on Allende. If Allende does approve, however, an **agency by ratification** (approval or confirmation) arises. In this event, both Allende and the seller of the coin are bound.

In an agency of this type, the ratification by the principal must be of the entire unauthorized act. The principal may not ratify only the part of the transaction that benefits the principal and reject the rest. Also, the action taken must have been done in the name of the principal and not on behalf of the person who acted as agent. The principal must have full knowledge of the facts, as well.

Agency by Estoppel

> **6.** Rego represented herself as Sarno's agent but had no authority from Sarno to do so. She entered into a contract to sell land for Sarno to Mittell. Sarno was present during the transaction but remained silent. Later, Sarno refused to carry out the contract. Can he be compelled to do so?

Figure 37.1
A Power of
Attorney to Sell
Realty

POWER OF ATTORNEY

KNOW ALL PERSONS BY THESE PRESENTS:

That I, Claire T. Kwon, of Jackson, Mississippi, do hereby constitute and appoint Louis J. Germaine, of Clinton, Mississippi, my true and lawful attorney, for me, and in my name,

(a) To grant, bargain, and sell all lands in and to which I am, or may be, in any way entitled or interested; and

(b) To make, execute, and deliver goods and sufficient deeds thereto; and

(c) To receive payment therefor.

IN WITNESS WHEREOF, I have set my hand and seal this 9th day of December, 19--.

Claire T Kwon   (L.S.)

In the presence of

Laura M. Carleo

A basic rule of agency law is that an agent without authority cannot bind the principal. However, if the principal misleads the third party into thinking that the agent does have authority, the principal will be bound. The agency created in this manner is called **agency by estoppel.** A principal who is guilty of a false "holding out" cannot use the defense of the agent's lack of authority when there is reasonable reliance on the part of the third party. In other words, the principal is *estopped,* or prevented from stating the true facts. In Problem 6, Sarno can be compelled to carry out the contract. By allowing Mittell to believe that Rego was his agent, Sarno created an agency by estoppel.

Agency by Necessity

PROBLEM

7. A husband failed to provide food and clothing for his dependent family. The wife, as agent for her husband, bought the required necessaries and charged them to her husband's account. Is the husband liable?

The law sometimes assumes that an agency relationship exists when the circumstances show that the assumption is reasonable and just. This type of agency is called an **agency by necessity.** Although the principal hasn't consented to the agency, it arises in the event of urgent or emergency situations.

Sometimes husbands and wives can be agents for each other.

EXAMPLE

While the owner of an auto dealership was out of the country, a water pipe burst in the dealership's showroom, threatening to destroy the cars in the showroom. In this situation, the employee left in charge of the business—who normally wouldn't have authority to order repairs—would become the owner's agent by necessity. In order to protect the principal from loss, the employee must contract for the repairs and obligate the owner to pay the bills.

Under the common law, a husband has a legal duty to furnish his dependent wife and children with the necessaries of life. Failure to do so gives the wife the authority to buy the necessaries and to pledge her husband's credit. This is the case in Problem 7. In many states today, either spouse may serve as a spouse's agent by necessity. An agency by necessity also is implied in the case of a minor who fails to receive necessaries from his or her parents or guardian.

This chapter has given you a foundation in the principles of agency. Agency relationships are extremely valuable, and even necessary, in most business dealings. When principals and agents properly perform their obligations to one another, business can be transacted efficiently. In Chapter 38, we'll take a closer look at the obligations of principals and agents.

Chapter 37 Review

"YOU BE THE JUDGE" REVIEW

Look again at the "You Be the Judge" cases given at the beginning of this chapter. Would you decide them differently now, after your study of the chapter?

Correct Decisions

1. No. In most states, an appointment of an agent by a minor is voidable by the minor or by his or her legal guardian.
2. The husband is right. Marriage by itself does not result in a principal-agent rela-tionship between a wife and husband. A dependent spouse may become an agent by necessity if necessaries such as food and clothing aren't provided by the other spouse.

UNDERSTANDING WHAT YOU HAVE READ

1. What is an agency relationship?
2. Who may be an agent?
3. Who may act as a principal?
4. How are an agent, an employee, and an independent contractor different from one another?
5. How may an agency be created?
6. When must an agency contract be made in writing?
7. What is a power of attorney?
8. What requirements must be met before an agency by ratification can arise?
9. Give an example of an agency by estoppel.
10. How does an agency by estoppel differ from an agency by ratification?

BUILDING YOUR LEGAL VOCABULARY

Choose the legal term that will correctly complete each definition below. Write your answers on a separate sheet of paper.

1. A written authorization to act as an agent is a/an
   a. power of attorney.
   b. accommodation indorsement.
   c. agreement to sell realty.
2. Someone who has full control over the services he or she performs for another is a/an
   a. third party.
   b. independent contractor.
   c. employee.
3. An agency that is created by express authorization, whether oral, written, or implied, is an
   a. agency by appointment.
   b. agency by necessity.
   c. agency by estoppel.
4. The party who grants the authority to transact his or her business to another is known as the
   a. agent.
   b. third party.
   c. principal.
5. The agency agreement that is created when one party approves or confirms acts performed on his or her behalf by an unauthorized agent is an
   a. agency by ratification.
   b. agency by estoppel.
   c. agency by necessity.

APPLYING LEGAL PRINCIPLES

1. Moeda asked his neighbor to buy him a pocket tape recorder costing not more than $50. The neighbor agreed to do so. Was the neighbor acting as Moeda's agent?
2. Coleridge, a manufacturer, appointed Petrakes, a minor, to be her purchasing agent. Petrakes contracted with Kotter to buy two delivery trucks for the factory. Was Coleridge bound?
3. Would your answer to Problem 2 have been the same if Coleridge had been a minor and Petrakes an adult?
4. The Omuras orally authorized Modica to find a buyer for their house and to enter into a written contract for its sale. Modica found a buyer and signed a contract as agent for the Omuras. Was the contract binding on the Omuras?
5. The Kohn Company orally gave Graffeo an exclusive right to sell its products on a commission basis for two years. Was the company bound on this contract?
6. A captain of a freighter contracted for emergency repairs to the vessel because of storm damage. Were the ship's owners liable for the repairs?

7. Without authorization, Hollins bought a famous portrait for Libman from the Classical Art Galleries. Hollins had represented herself as Libman's agent and made the purchase in Libman's name. Under what circumstances would Libman be liable for the purchase?

8. Gobel, without authority, contracted to buy a camcorder and VCR for Foy. When Foy learned of the transaction, she agreed to accept and pay for the VCR but refused to take the camcorder. Was Foy within her legal rights?

9. The owner of an imported goods store planned to leave on a 30-day trip to South America. Just before he left, he gave a written authorization to his assistant to manage the store and to sign all checks in payment of business debts. What type of agency was created?

10. DiRosa, a minor, was well supplied with clothes by her parents. However, she bought a jumpsuit at a department store and charged it to her mother's account. Was her mother liable on the contract?

ANALYZING COURT CASES

1. Jenkins, a soldier in the army, was stationed in West Germany. His wife lived in the United States while he was overseas, and she used his car for family purposes. Without consulting her husband, the wife traded the car for a new one. When Jenkins returned from overseas, he sued the auto dealer for the value of the car his wife had traded in. He claimed that his wife was not his agent and had no authority to sell his car. Was Jenkins's claim legally sound? (Based on: *Barber v. Carolina Auto Sales Co.*, 115 S.E. 2d 291)

2. Lewis was principal of Hapeville High School. He rented two station wagons from Dixie Drive It Yourself System in order to transport students to athletic activities. The rental contract was signed:

HAPEVILLE HIGH SCHOOL

John G. Lewis

John G. Lewis
Principal

The contract provided that the customer was responsible for any damage occurring to the vehicles while in the customer's possession. One of the station wagons was damaged in an accident, to the extent of $400. In an action by Dixie against Lewis, he set up as his defense the fact that he had signed the contract as agent for Hapeville High School. Was Lewis's defense valid? (*Dixie Drive It Yourself System v. Lewis*, 50 S.E. 2d 843)

3. Calley borrowed Berrios's car. Later that day, Berrios found herself without transportation. She called Calley and asked him to pick her up at a certain place. While Calley was driving to pick up Berrios, he collided with a car driven by Allard. Allard suffered severe personal injuries as a result of the accident and sued Berrios and Calley for his injuries. He contended that Berrios was liable because Calley was her agent or employee when bringing the car to pick her up. Was Allard's contention correct? (Based on: *English v. Dhane*, 294 S.W. 2d 709)

CHAPTER 38

Relations of Principal and Agent

YOU BE THE JUDGE

Think about these cases.
If you were the judge, how would you decide each case?

1

Wissman, a salesperson, drove a company-owned car for her employer, Rand Manufacturing. She was told not to drive faster than 30 mph when calling on customers in residential areas. While disobeying the instructions, Wissman ran into and injured Milano. Is Rand liable to Milano?

2

An agent received $2,750 from the sale of certain goods. He deposited the money in his personal bank account. Shortly thereafter, the bank failed and the principal sued the agent for $2,750. Should the principal succeed?

A PRINCIPAL'S OBLIGATIONS TO AN AGENT

A principal has the following three basic obligations to an agent: (1) compensation, (2) reimbursement, and (3) indemnity.

Compensation

> **1.** Fenester, a real-estate broker, was authorized to sell a house and lot for the Danhs. Nothing was said about paying for Fenester's services. After the house was sold, Fenester claimed that he was entitled to 10% of the sale price. The usual commission in that community was 6%. Are the Danhs required to pay the rate charged by Fenester?

A principal must pay the agent for services performed in accordance with the terms of their agreement. In Problem 1, the agreement fails to state a specific rate or amount of **compensation** (payment for services). In a case such as this, the agent is entitled to the customary compensation. Fenester, therefore, would be entitled to a commission of six percent of the selling price of the house. If there is no established rate of compensation, the agent may collect a reasonable sum for the work performed.

Reimbursement

A principal must *reimburse* (pay back) the agent for all expenses incurred by the agent while lawfully carrying out the assigned duties. This duty is called **reimbursement.** The principal doesn't have to reimburse the agent, though, if the expenses arose out of the agent's misconduct or carelessness.

> An agent transferred title to a certain property to the wrong person. The agent isn't entitled to reimbursement for any expenses incurred in correcting this error.

Indemnity

An agent has a right to assume that the principal's instructions are lawful. The agent also has a right to assume that he or she won't incur personal liability to third parties when carrying out the principal's instructions. An agent who does incur personal liability, without any fault on his or her part, is entitled to **indemnity** (protection against harm) from the principal.

A principal asked an agent to repossess a car. The car had been sold by the principal on a time-payment plan. Unknown to the agent, the principal had no legal right to repossess the car. In a suit brought by the buyer of the car against the agent, the agent was required to pay money damages. He is entitled to indemnity from the principal.

AN AGENT'S OBLIGATIONS TO A PRINCIPAL

An agent has five basic obligations to a principal: (1) obedience, (2) loyalty, (3) reasonable care, (4) the duty to account, and (5) personal performance of duties.

Obedience

2. Barquin was hired by Maher, a store owner, to manage the store. She was told to sell only for cash. She sold some goods to a customer on credit, and the debt couldn't be collected. Is Barquin liable to Maher?

An agent, acting with or without compensation, must obey all reasonable instructions. Barquin's failure to do so in Problem 2 makes her liable to Maher for any loss Maher incurs.

Someone who agrees to act as an agent without compensation is called a **gratuitous agent.** That person isn't legally obligated to fulfill his or her promise. However, if the agent undertakes to perform the act, he or she must follow instructions properly. Otherwise, the agent is liable for any resulting loss.

Loyalty

An essential part of every contract of employment is the employee's **loyalty** (sense of obligation) to the employer. Loyalty is particularly required of agents because they often act in a confidential capacity.

3. Duong offered Levinson a commission to sell her car, and Levinson quickly sold it to Carey. When Duong learned that Carey had commissioned Levinson to buy a car for him, Duong refused to pay Levinson. Was she legally justified?

Arbitration Can Be Better Than Litigation

"I'll sue you for every dollar you have!" said the irate and frustrated principal to the nonchalant agent. But litigation may not be the most sensible course for the principal to follow. It usually involves a long, drawn-out, costly, and exposed public procedure that may yield an unsatisfactory result for both parties.

In any contractual dispute, a simpler and less annoying procedure, if applicable, is for the opposing parties to refer the dispute to arbitration. There are two primary ways to do this. First, the contract between the parties may provide that in case of a dispute, the parties are required to submit the contract to arbitration. This requirement is made ". . . in accordance with the rules of the American Arbitration Association and judgment upon the award rendered may be entered in any court having jurisdiction thereof." Second, the parties may file a Submission Agreement with the association. This document outlines the facts behind the dispute and asks for a decision by an impartial third party.

Shortly after receiving the request for arbitration, the association sends each party a list of qualified arbitrators to judge the issues involved. Each party selects certain arbitrators and returns the list. In some cases, the parties agree to a panel of arbitrators. From the names submitted, the association chooses the arbitrator or panel.

A hearing is scheduled and held in quarters provided by the association. If they choose, the parties may be represented by attorneys. The hearing is less formal than a court proceeding. It is also much faster and not as strictly bound by the rules of evidence. Within 30 days or so after the hearing, the arbitrator must announce the award, which is legally binding. Arbitrators serve without compensation, and the cost of the entire proceeding is small compared with the cost of a court case.

If an agent learns any fact important to the subject matter of the agency, he or she must notify the principal immediately. The law considers the identity of the principal and agent to have been merged by the agency relationship. Therefore, notice to the agent is usually held to be notice to the principal. It follows that in conducting an agency, an agent's own personal interests may not be promoted. Without the principal's knowledge

An agent cannot be loyal to two competing principals unless both have consented.

and consent, an agent may not buy the principal's property. Also, an agent's property may not be bought for the principal without the principal's consent. For example, a stockbroker may not sell his or her own stocks to a customer without the customer's knowledge and consent. An agent can't be loyal when serving two competing principals unless both have consented. In Problem 3, neither principal had consented to Levinson acting for both of them. Therefore, Levinson isn't entitled to compensation from either.

Reasonable Care

> **4.** Zaman commissioned Melzer, a lawyer, to invest some money for him. Melzer used the money to buy bonds. Soon, the bonds were found to be worthless. Was Melzer liable?

An agent has the duty to exercise **reasonable care** in conducting the agency. In Problem 4, Melzer wouldn't be liable to Zaman for the loss if a reasonable person would have bought the bonds as a personal investment under similar circumstances. An agent must act with reasonable care but isn't required to guarantee the success of the undertaking.

Duty to Account

> **5.** Clafin was authorized to sell her principal's computer for $700. She sold it for $825. To whom does the extra $125 belong?

An agent must keep an accurate record of goods and monies received or issued in the conduct of the agency. The money or goods of the agent and principal must not be mixed together. If the money is kept in a bank, the agent must open a separate account. The account usually should be in the principal's name, with the agent also named on the account. If the agent's and principal's monies are mixed and the bank fails, the law assumes that it was the agent's money that was lost. The agent will be liable to the principal for the loss.

If an agent in a sale of goods obtains a price greater than the one authorized by the principal, the extra profit belongs to the principal and not to the agent. In Problem 5, Clafin should record and deposit the entire $825 for the principal and then pay the whole amount to the principal. Clafin's agreed compensation and any proper expenses should then be deducted. A principal also may recover any secret rebate or bonus the agent receives, even though the agent has acted entirely in the principal's interest.

An agent who violates his or her duties to a principal is liable for any resulting damages the principal suffers.

Personal Performance of Duties

> **6.** Osamu, a skilled trial lawyer, was employed by Sykes Corporation to conduct an important lawsuit. The suit involved the title to valuable property. Without the firm's consent, Osamu delegated the trial of the action to another lawyer. Could Osamu properly delegate this duty to another?

Some agency agreements are of a personal nature and require special knowledge, skill, or judgment on the part of the agent. In an agency such as this, an agent may *not* appoint a **subagent** to carry out his or her duties unless the principal expressly or impliedly consents. This is the case in Problem 6. The reason for this rule is that the principal is entitled to personal performance by the agent because of certain special qualifications. If the agent were permitted to shift his or her duties to another, the principal could suffer an injury. However, if the agent's duties are of a purely mechanical nature, they may be delegated. For example, an agent appointed to sell certain goods may delegate to a subagent mechanical duties such as preparing invoices, receipts, and bills of lading.

Figure 38.1
*A Principal's
and an Agent's
Obligations*

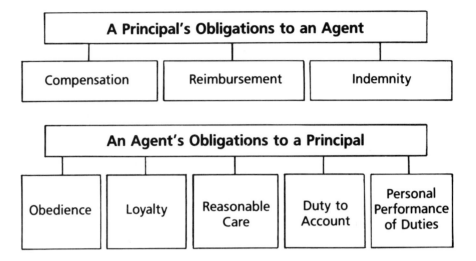

Argo was hired to manage a retail store. She was granted the right to hire more salespeople if needed. If Argo hired Vernick for this purpose, Vernick would not only be Argo's subagent but also an agent of the store's owner.

Figure 38.1 summarizes the obligations principals and agents owe to one another.
Like other contractual agreements, an agency agreement creates rights and obligations on the part of both parties. This chapter has explained the obligations that principals and agents owe to one another as a result of the agency relationship. Chapter 39 will explain how principals and agents relate to third parties.

Chapter 38 Review

"YOU BE THE JUDGE" REVIEW

Look again at the "You Be the Judge" cases given at the beginning of this chapter. Would you decide them differently now, after your study of the chapter?

Correct Decisions

1. Yes. The private instructions a principal gives an agent aren't binding on third parties who know nothing of such instructions. Wissman was engaged in furthering the interests of her principal. Rand, the principal, must stand the loss.

2. Yes. An agent should keep the principal's property and money separate from his or her own. If the funds can't be separated, the agent must bear any loss that occurs.

UNDERSTANDING WHAT YOU HAVE READ

1. What obligations does a principal owe to an agent?
2. Name five important duties that an agent owes to the principal.
3. Briefly explain each of the agent's duties.
4. What is the effect of an agent's failure to perform his or her duties?
5. If an agency agreement fails to state the agent's compensation, what is the agent entitled to collect?
6. What are the duties of a gratuitous agent?
7. May an agent act both for the principal and for the third party?
8. May an agent buy from or sell to a principal? Explain.
9. Under what circumstances is a principal liable for the acts of a subagent?
10. What test is used to determine whether an agent has exercised reasonable care in his or her duties?

BUILDING YOUR LEGAL VOCABULARY

Match each of these legal terms with its correct definition from the list that follows. Write your answers on a separate sheet of paper.

compensation   loyalty   reasonable care
duty to account   obedience   reimbursement
gratuitous agent   personal performance of duties   subagent
indemnity

1. a principal's obligation to protect an agent against harm
2. an agent's obligation to exercise the skill and diligence a reasonable person would use under similar circumstances
3. a person to whom an agent delegates the performance of the agent's duties
4. an agent's obligation to keep accurate records of goods and monies received or issued in the conduct of an agency
5. a principal's obligation to pay an agent for services performed in accordance with the terms of the agency
6. an agent's obligation to carry out agency duties that are of a personal nature and require special knowledge, skill, or judgment
7. an agent's obligation to notify the principal of any fact important to the subject matter of the agency and to act only in the interests of the principal
8. a principal's duty to pay back an agent for all expenses incurred by the agent while lawfully carrying out assigned duties
9. an agent's duty to follow all reasonable instructions of the principal
10. someone who agrees to act as an agent without compensation

APPLYING LEGAL PRINCIPLES

1. Kinney, an adult, hired Fadavi, age 16, to sell magazines on a commission basis. Kinney later refused to pay Fadavi the commission due her. Kinney claimed that because Fadavi was a minor, the contract was void. Was Kinney right?

2. Colyer engaged Lek, a realty broker, to sell a house and lot belonging to Colyer. Colyer authorized Lek to incur any advertising and other expenses that might be reasonably needed to sell the property. Lek spent $250 for advertising but failed to find a buyer. Is Lek entitled to reimbursement for his expenses?

3. Landau, acting under instructions from his principal, innocently distributed free samples of a new brand of toothpaste in a small town. Landau was fined $25 for violating a town ordinance prohibiting such distributions without a permit. Was Landau entitled to collect $25 from his principal?

4. DePina, a credit manager, was told by her employer not to extend more than $1,000 credit to any customer without the employer's approval. DePina allowed credit to Bellino, a customer who had always paid promptly, to the extent of $2,000. What rights does the employer have if Bellino fails to pay?

5. Cyr hired Amend, a licensed real-estate agent, to sell some land for him for $50,000. Without permission, Amend bought the property under a false name. A few days later, Amend resold the land for $75,000. Cyr later discovered these facts and sued Amend for the additional $25,000. Is Cyr entitled to collect this sum?

6. Vann gave her agent, Federico, $40,000 to invest in high-grade bonds. Instead, Federico bought a speculative common stock that soon proved worthless. Vann sued Federico for the $40,000. Is Federico liable for this sum?

7. Chan engaged Farrell to sell several pieces of property for her. Farrell was told to deposit the money received from the sales to Chan's account at the First National Bank. Farrell used the money to speculate in the stock market and lost all of it. May Chan recover damages from Farrell?

8. Fess was sent by his employer, Estevao, to paint Delapa's house. Fess became sick and, without Estevao's permission, sent a fellow painter, Todd, to do the work.
   a. Can Fess collect from Estevao for Todd's services?
   b. Can Todd collect from Fess for his services?

9. A registered letter reached the First National Bank of Nesbit. The letter stated that certain listed bonds had been stolen. A receiving clerk read the letter but failed to tell the bank manager of the letter's contents. A short time later, the bank manager accepted the bonds as security for a loan. The owner of the bonds brought suit against the bank, which pleaded that the manager hadn't received notice of the theft. Is the bank liable?

10. Boylan gave Pally $5,000, instructing her to buy a used car for Boylan for $4,500 and to keep $500 for her commission. Pally found a used car, bargained for it, and finally bought it for $4,300. Unknown to Boylan, Pally kept the extra $200. Should Boylan recover this sum?

ANALYZING COURT CASES

1. Steinberg leased a shop in which he ran a profitable business in women's clothing. He hired his brother and sister to help run the shop. Before the leased expired, he applied to the landlord for its renewal. During Steinberg's absence from the city and without his knowledge, his brother and sister leased the shop from the landlord on their own account. Steinberg brought an action in a court of equity to set the lease aside. Who should receive judgment? (*Steinberg v. Steinberg, et al.*, 206 N.Y.S. 134)

2. Whitney gave Martine money to loan for him. Martine loaned the money to an insolvent person. The loan was secured by a second mortgage on property that was scarcely worth the amount of the first and second mortgages put together. Whitney was unable to recover when the debt fell due and sued Martine for the loss. Will he be successful? (*Whitney v. Martine*, 88 N.Y. 535)

3. Dryden was a manufacturer of industrial chemicals. She instructed Alexander, a wholesale dealer in tanks and boilers, to order a certain type of tank for her. Alexander ordered the required tank in his own name. When the tank arrived, Dryden inspected it and refused to accept it. Because of Dryden's refusal, Alexander was forced to keep the tank and pay for it. Alexander brought suit against Dryden to recover the purchase price. Was Alexander entitled to collect? (Based on: *Clifton v. Ross*, 28 S.W. 1085)

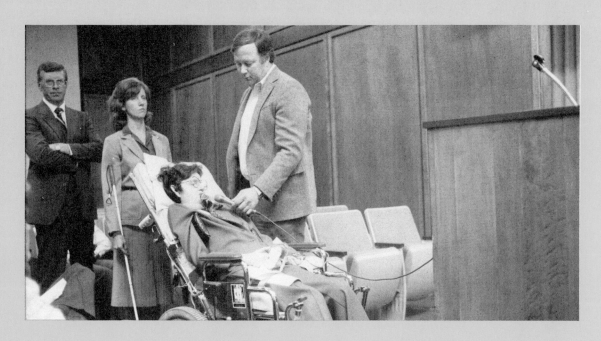

Relations of Principal, Agent, and Third Party

YOU BE THE JUDGE

*Think about these cases.
If you were the judge, how would you decide each case?*

1

Rintell was an agent for Foo Electronics Co. He signed a simple contract for Foo with Masi Supply Co. as follows: "Brad Rintell, agent." Can Masi Supply hold Rintell liable on the contract?

2

Mendona borrowed $2,500 from Pellagrino for the purpose of expanding her business. As a condition of the loan, Pellagrino was to manage the business until the debt was repaid. At the end of a month and before any of the debt was repaid, Mendona discharged Pellagrino. Can she legally do so?

SCOPE OF AUTHORITY

Scope of authority is the term used when an agent acts within the limitations or range of authority given by a principal.

> **1.** Boland was the purchasing agent for a chain of restaurants. She contracted to buy a very large quantity of melons in order to get a sizable discount. Is the principal bound on the contract?

In Problem 1, Boland was authorized to buy food for the restaurant chain. She was expected to use her judgment in determining the quantity needed and the price to be paid. When purchasing the melons, she clearly acted within the scope of her authority. Her principal is liable on the contract.

A principal's liability to third parties depends on the agent's actions. Therefore, it is important in all cases to know the agent's scope of authority. This authority may be *actual* or *apparent,* and the actual authority granted to an agent may be *express* or *implied.*

Express and Implied Authority

An agent may be authorized either orally or in writing to carry out certain duties. This is called **express authority.** In addition, the agent has **implied authority** to do things incidental and necessary for carrying out the express duties.

> In Problem 1, Boland has express authority to buy food supplies. She has implied authority to choose the suppliers with whom she will deal. Also, Boland has implied authority to determine the quality and quantity of goods to be bought, the prices to be paid, and the terms of payment.

Apparent Authority

Apparent authority is the authority that the principal, by words or conduct, has led third persons to believe the agent has. To be bound on the basis of apparent authority, the principal must act in such a way that the law won't permit the principal to deny that the agent was given authority.

> **2.** Pagano instructed the manager of his electronics store to hire two clerks to work on Saturdays. The manager hired three clerks. Is Pagano liable for the salary of the third clerk?

You and Your Agent

Suppose you hire a repair person to fix your roof. The repairer drops some roofing material on your neighbor's prize-winning rose garden. Are you liable for the repair person's act? In all likelihood, you are. Or suppose you ask a friend to drive your car and take your computer monitor to an electronics shop for repair. On the way, your friend runs down an elderly pedestrian. Are you responsible for the pedestrian's injuries? After all, you didn't cause the injuries. But that's not the way the law looks at the situation. You may be partially liable.

In both cases, you asked someone to act for you. Legally, what the roof repairer did, you did. And the same goes for the friend who was taking your computer monitor to be fixed. Each of them acted as your "agent," and the law says that you are a "principal." As such, you are responsible for your agents' acts.

The fact remains that agents do most of the world's business. Third parties who do business with you or with your agent have a right to expect you to stand behind the agent's word. If your agent follows your instructions, or if you allow third parties to think that someone is your agent, you are responsible for any deal the agent makes in your name.

The complexity of today's business world makes the law of agency extremely important. Because a dishonest agent can cause irreparable harm to the principal, great care must be taken when choosing an agent.

Apparent authority may be equal to, greater than, or even less than the agent's actual authority. A principal sometimes issues special instructions to limit the scope of the agent's authority. This fact will not release the principal from liability to innocent third parties who know nothing of such instructions and who rely on the agent's apparent authority. This is the situation in Problem 2. Pagano would have to pay the third clerk's salary. It's important to note that an agent's express and implied authority binds the principal both as to third parties and as to the agent. The apparent authority given to the agent binds the principal *only as to third parties.*

KINDS OF AGENCY

Agents are classified as *special agents* or *general agents* on the basis of the authority given to them by the principal.

Special Agents

PROBLEM

> **3.** An insurance agent called on Fonseca and took Fonseca's application for health insurance. The agent assured Fonseca that the policy would cover all hospital bills, without limit. When Fonseca received the policy, he didn't notice that it contained a maximum limitation on hospital bills covered. Later, Fonseca underwent surgery and spent time in the hospital. His hospital bills exceeded the maximum stated in the insurance policy. Fonseca sued the insurance company to recover the excess hospital bills, claiming that the company's agent had stated that the policy wasn't limited. Can Fonseca recover?

A person who is engaged to perform a single task, such as selling a car, after which the agency ceases, is known as a **special agent.** Also, someone engaged to perform a series of acts narrow in scope and specific in nature, such as those of a salesclerk in a shoe store, is a special agent. Because the agent is employed only to perform a single service or a series of specific acts, third parties are deemed to know that the agent's authority is limited. If an agent performs acts not usually part of the duties of similar special agents, the third party must inquire into the real scope of the agent's authority.

When using their express authority, special agents have implied authority to do only such acts as are needed or usually performed. For example, a mere agency to purchase usually gives the agent no implied power to buy on credit or to sign the principal's name to negotiable paper in payment for goods unless credit is needed to make the purchase. Likewise, a mere agency to sell usually gives the agent no authority to sell on credit unless that's the custom of the trade. An agent who doesn't possess the goods usually has no right to receive payment for them. However, an agent in possession of the goods usually does have that implied power. An agent who is authorized to sell goods ordinarily has the implied power to warrant title to the goods. Where warranties of quality are given by custom or usage in the business (a question of fact), the agent has an implied power to warrant quality.

In Problem 3, the insurance agent had no authority—either express, implied, or apparent—to represent that the policy was unlimited. The agent was a special agent merely to take Fonseca's application, and no more. The insurance company wasn't liable on the agreement between the agent and Fonseca.

General Agents

> **4.**   The manager of a supermarket hired two packers to help the cashiers at the checkout counters. She agreed to pay them at the rate of $5.00 per hour. Did the manager have the power to hire the packers?

An agent who represents a principal in dealings of a general, continuous nature and whose powers consequently are broad in scope is a **general agent.** A general agent has wider express authority than a special agent. Also, a general agent's implied powers are greater in number and extent than those of a special agent. In Problem 4, the supermarket manager had the implied power to hire the packers.

A PRINCIPAL'S LIABILITY TO THIRD PARTIES

The principal is liable to third parties on contracts made by an authorized agent while acting within the actual or apparent scope of authority. Even if the agent isn't authorized to act but the principal ratifies the contract, the principal is liable. Third persons may sue the principal on a simple contract made by an agent who fails to disclose the fact that another person is the principal. A principal whose name is not revealed in an agency transaction is called an **undisclosed principal.**

> **5.**   Howry was authorized to sell securities for Foran. After making false and fraudulent representations to Yang, Howry sold Yang five bonds. Upon discovering the fraud, Yang sued Foran for damages. Was Foran liable?

If an agent commits a tort or a fraudulent act while acting within the scope of actual or apparent authority, the principal is liable to the third party. In Problem 5, Foran is liable for the fraudulent representations made by her agent, Howry.

AN AGENT'S LIABILITY TO THIRD PARTIES

As stated earlier, when an agent acts within the scope of authority, the principal but not the agent is bound on the resulting contract. However, consider the facts in this problem.

6.   Geis contracted to sell to Rotermund a boat belonging to Avalos. Geis had no authority to act for Avalos, but she represented to Rotermund that she was Avalos's agent. Could Rotermund hold Geis liable on the contract?

In dealing with third parties, an agent may become personally liable in these instances:

1. People who assume to act for others without authority, or who exceed their authority, are personally liable to those with whom they are dealing. In Problem 6, Rotermund may hold Geis liable on the contract for the sale of the boat.

2. If an authorized agent's own name is used to make a contract and the principal's name is not disclosed, the agent becomes liable on the contract as if the agent were the principal. The third party may choose, however, to hold the undisclosed principal liable instead of the agent. In contrast, the undisclosed principal may sue the third party on a simple contract to enforce a contract made for the principal's benefit.

EXAMPLE

Eaton authorized Debarros to buy certain antiques without disclosing Eaton's name. Debarros bought the antiques from Imperial Importing as instructed by Eaton. When Debarros failed to pay for the goods, Imperial discovered that he was acting for Eaton. Imperial may choose to hold either Debarros or Eaton, but not both, liable on the contract.

3. If, during the performance of agency duties, an agent enters into a formal contract with a third party and signs a promissory note as the maker, the agent alone is liable for payment of the note. The agent can also sue the third person on the written instrument.

EXAMPLE

Assume that Debarros, from the preceding example, had signed and delivered a promissory note in favor of Imperial Importing in payment for the antiques. In this event, Debarros would be personally liable on the note. Eaton wouldn't be liable because her name didn't appear on the instrument.

4. An agent is personally liable for torts and crimes, whether committed within or outside the scope of employment. A principal isn't liable for

Who is liable for torts an agent commits within the scope of the agent's employment?

crimes committed by the agent unless the principal took part in the agent's acts.

> Berman was a candidate for a political office. His campaign treasurer made a false report of the campaign expenses. A state statute required the filing of such reports and made it a crime to make a false report. Berman was prosecuted for the false report made by the treasurer. At the trial, Berman proved that he knew nothing about the report and hadn't authorized its filing. The court upheld his plea and held the treasurer personally liable for the crime.

TERMINATION OF THE AGENCY

An agency contract may terminate either by the act of one or both of the parties, or by operation of law.

Termination by Act of the Parties

The principal and agent may voluntarily terminate the agency by (1) agreement, (2) revocation by the principal, or (3) abandonment by the agent.

By Agreement

The principal and the agent may include a termination provision in the agency contract itself. This clause may state that the agency is to end after a specified period of time, on the happening of an uncertain event, or after the agency's purpose has been accomplished. The parties also may terminate an agency by mutual agreement at any time.

By Revocation by the Principal

> **7.** Han loaned O'Hara $1,000. As security for the loan, O'Hara gave Han a certificate for 100 shares of Panex common stock with authority to sell the stock if O'Hara failed to repay the loan. Could O'Hara revoke Han's authority to sell the stock?

The agent's authority to act for the principal may be revoked by the principal at any time. However, if such revocation is wrongful, the principal is liable to the agent for breach of contract. Although a person can't insist on continuing as agent if the principal wants to end the agency, there is an important exception to this rule. If an agent has an interest in the subject matter of the agency itself and not a mere interest in being compensated for his or her agency services, an **agency coupled with an interest** arises. In this case, the principal cannot revoke the agency, and the law will not revoke it. In Problem 7, O'Hara can't revoke Han's authority to sell the stock because of Han's financial interest in the subject matter.

By Abandonment by the Agent

Usually, an agent who has no legal right to renounce or abandon the agency is liable in damages to the principal if the agency is abandoned. A party who abandons his or her agency duties may or may not be entitled to compensation for services rendered. An agent who was employed on a commission basis is entitled to any commissions that have been earned. An agent who was salaried is entitled to receive salary up to the time the agent quits the agency.

Termination by Operation of Law

> **8.** Barsamian, who owned a beauty salon, employed an unlicensed beautician to work in his shop. A law was passed requiring all beauticians to be licensed. How does this law affect the employment contract?

In spite of the intentions of the parties, the agency contract may terminate by operation of law. This may occur in these instances:

1. when either the principal or the agent dies or becomes unable to fulfill the agency agreement, except where the agency is coupled with an interest;
2. when a law passed after the creation of the agency makes illegal the work the agent was hired to perform;
3. when the subject matter of the agency contract is destroyed or no longer exists (for example, if a building the agent is to sell burns down); and
4. when either party becomes bankrupt.

In Problem 8, the employment contract between Barsamian and the unlicensed beautician was terminated by operation of law when the licensing law made the beautician's work illegal.

Notice to Third Parties

A notice of **revocation** to the agent terminates the agency as far as the principal and agent are concerned. However, a principal should take additional steps to protect himself or herself from liability to third parties.

9. Pawlak worked as a salesperson for Wholesale Grocers. One of her duties was to collect each week from the company's charge customers. Pawlak was discharged from her job because of inefficiency. Without the firm's knowledge, she collected from several customers after her discharge and failed to account for the money. Wholesale Grocers tried to collect a second time from its customers. Was the company entitled to do so?

When the agent's authority is revoked or abandoned, the principal should give actual notice of termination to anyone with whom the agent has been dealing on a credit basis. Failure to do so makes the principal liable for acts the former agent commits within the apparent scope of the agent's prior authority. Thus, Wholesale Grocers in Problem 9 isn't entitled to collect a second time from its customers. The company failed to notify its customers properly of the agency's termination.

Usually, a notice published in a general-circulation newspaper is sufficient notice to third parties who have dealt with the agent on a cash basis or who have never dealt with that agent before.

As you can see, an agency agreement is essentially a contract to make contracts. Agency contracts allow many people and organizations to transact their business efficiently. However, the employment contract is even more basic to the transaction of business today. We'll study the employment contract next, in Chapter 40.

Chapter 39 Review

"YOU BE THE JUDGE" REVIEW

Look again at the "You Be the Judge" cases given at the beginning of this chapter. Would you decide them differently now, after your study of the chapter?

Correct Decisions

1. Yes. An agent who fails to disclose his or her representative capacity is jointly and severally liable with the principal. Rintell should have indicated his agency capacity by writing the name of the principal and using the word "by" or "per" before his own signature. If he had done so, only Foo Electronics would have been liable on the contract.

2. No. An agency coupled with an interest can't be terminated by a discharge of the agent by the principal.

UNDERSTANDING WHAT YOU HAVE READ

1. What does the term *scope of authority* mean?
2. Why is it important to know the agent's scope of authority?
3. Distinguish between an agent's express and implied authority.
4. What is apparent authority? Give an example.
5. What is the difference between a general agent and a special agent?
6. When is an agent personally liable
   a. in contracts made with third parties?
   b. for torts and crimes committed when dealing with third parties?
7. Under what circumstances is a principal liable to third parties
   a. on contracts made on the principal's behalf by an agent?
   b. for torts and crimes committed by the agent?
8. How may an agency contract terminate?
9. What is an agency coupled with an interest?
10. Describe the types of notice of termination of an agency that a principal is required to give to third parties.

BUILDING YOUR LEGAL VOCABULARY

From this list, select the legal term that belongs in the blank in each sentence below. Write your answers on a separate sheet of paper.

agency coupled with an interest   implied authority   special agent
apparent authority   revocation   termination provision
express authority   scope of authority   undisclosed principal
general agent

1. A principal may discontinue an agent's authority by means of ▒▒▒▒▒▒▒▒ of the contract.
2. An agency in which the agent has an interest in the subject matter is called an ▒▒▒▒▒▒▒▒.
3. A ▒▒▒▒▒▒▒▒ is one who represents a principal in dealings of a general, continuous nature and whose powers are broad in scope.
4. A principal whose name isn't revealed in an agency transaction is known as an ▒▒▒▒▒▒▒▒.
5. A clause in an agency contract that states when the agency is to end is a ▒▒▒▒▒▒▒▒.
6. The power that a principal, by words or conduct, has led third persons to believe an agent has is called ▒▒▒▒▒▒▒▒.
7. The term that describes the limitations or range of an agent's power to act for a principal is ▒▒▒▒▒▒▒▒.
8. An agent's indirect power to do things incidental and necessary for carrying out express duties is the agent's ▒▒▒▒▒▒▒▒.
9. A person who is engaged to perform a single task or a series of specific tasks that are narrow in scope is known as a ▒▒▒▒▒▒▒▒.
10. The power given either orally or in writing to an agent to carry out certain duties is the agent's ▒▒▒▒▒▒▒▒.

APPLYING LEGAL PRINCIPLES

1. Hau, the general manager of a store, didn't have enough funds to pay the store's bills. She borrowed money at a local bank in her principal's name. Was the principal liable to the bank?

2. Demos was employed as a salesclerk in a stereo equipment store. He sold a customer a compact disc player for less than the regular price, at a loss to his employer. Can the employer collect the difference from the customer?

3. Baptiste, a restaurant owner, employed Kelley to manage the business. Baptiste gave Kelley a specific order not to buy supplies on credit. Banuelos, not knowing of Baptiste's order to Kelley, sold supplies to the restaurant on terms of 30 days. Can Banuelos hold Baptiste liable for the payment?

4. Rubin, without authority, represented herself as Spilka's agent in the purchase of a classic car. If Spilka affirmed the purchase, would he be liable as the principal?

5. Fisher, authorized to act as his father's agent, agreed to sell land belonging to his father to Reigler. Fisher didn't tell Reigler that he was acting as an agent. Later, the father refused to perform the contract made by his son. On learning that the father was the principal, Reigler sued the father to enforce the terms of the contract. Should Reigler succeed? Under what circumstances may Reigler hold the son liable?

6. Hammer was employed to book passengers for bus tours. To induce passengers to sign tour contracts, Hammer made fraudulent statements about the cost of the trip and places to be visited. After the tour was over, the passengers brought suit for failure to perform as per agreement. Can they recover?

7. Fay Textile Mills employed Folgueras as a sales agent. Folgueras obtained a large order for cotton goods that would have netted him a large commission. However, Fay Textile Mills arbitrarily revoked Folgueras's authority to act as agent. The agency contract still had six months to run. What are Folgueras's legal rights?

8. Abudi borrowed $5,000 from Gittes. As security for the loan, Abudi gave Gittes written authority to collect rents from the tenants of a building Abudi owned. May Abudi revoke Gittes's authority to collect the rents?

9. On May 1, Lubin engaged Junno to sell a house for her. On May 5, Lubin died. What was the effect of Lubin's death on the agency?

10. Okomo was employed by Prete Collection Agency as a collector of unpaid accounts. He was employed for a period of three years at $15,000 per year. At the end of two years, Prete discharged Okomo without cause.
   a. Was Okomo's authority to collect debts terminated?
   b. If Prete gave notice in a local newspaper of Okomo's discharge, would the notice be binding on people who had dealt previously with Okomo on a credit basis?
   c. Would the notice in (b) be binding on people who didn't know of the agency and failed to read the notice?

ANALYZING COURT CASES

1. In September, Dutra authorized Menke to act as agent for the express purpose of selling stock that Dutra owned in a certain mining company. The power of attorney given to Menke provided that it should be "irrevocable" for one year. In April of the following year, Dutra notified Menke that the power of attorney was terminated. Did this action by Dutra terminate the agency? (Based on: *Shumaker v. Hazen*, 372 P. 2d 873)

2. Isaksen carried bodily injury and property damage insurance on her car with Federal Mutual Insurance Co. She bought a new car and immediately called the home office of the insurance company, asking that the existing policy be changed to cover the new car. She was connected with Ma, an employee of the company. Ma assured Isaksen that the new car was insured as requested from that moment on. The next day, before any change had been made to Isaksen's policy, she was involved in an accident. When the insurance company refused to pay for Isaksen's damages, Isaksen sued the company. The firm defended on the ground that Ma was a mere clerk in the auto underwriting department and had no authority to make policy changes. Was Isaksen's new car covered by insurance? (Based on: *Farm Bureau Mutual Insurance Co. v. Coffin*, 186 N.E. 2d 180)

3. Mota was a sales agent for Arnold, a wholesale dealer in fertilizers and insecticides. Mota sold Steele, a commercial grower of lily bulbs, 200 gallons of "Shale Weed Killer No. 57." Before the sale, Steele had told Mota that he wanted a weed killer to use on a field in which he had planted lily bulblets. Mota expressly warranted that the weed killer could be safely used on the fields where the bulblets were planted. When Steele applied the weed killer to his fields, most of the lily bulblets were killed. Steele then sued Arnold for breach of warranty. Arnold contended that Mota had lacked the authority to warrant the weed killer. Was Arnold's defense legally correct? (Based on: *Start v. Shell Oil Co., et al.*, 273 P. 2d 225)

CHAPTER 40

The Employment Contract

YOU BE THE JUDGE

Think about these cases.
If you were the judge, how would you decide each case?

1

Shaw, an employee of Tan's Travel Service, was told to drive a company car to the post office to mail a package to a client. Shaw drove the usual route and negligently injured a pedestrian. Was the employer liable for the pedestrian's injuries?

2

Tse worked as an engineer for United Instrument Co. She showed the plans for a new United instrument to a friend who worked for a competitor. When United discovered this fact, Tse was discharged from her job. Tse then sued United for damages as a result of her discharge. Is she entitled to collect?

WHAT IS AN EMPLOYMENT CONTRACT?

You learned in Chapter 37 that one who represents another in a business transaction with a third party is known as an agent. Often, an agent also performs regular tasks for another that don't include making contracts with third parties. A person who performs those tasks is called an **employee.** The party under whose direction and control the employee works is known as an **employer.**

An employment contract may be a private, individual agreement between an employer and an employee. It also may be a formal group contract resulting from an agreement made between a union and an employer.

> **1.** Macchia asked Campos, a neighbor, to help move some furniture in her apartment. If Campos agrees, is she legally regarded as Macchia's employee?

An employment contract, like other contracts, must contain all the essentials studied earlier. In Problem 1, Campos is a mere volunteer who agrees to perform a "neighborly good deed." The parties had no intention of entering into an employment contract. Therefore, Campos is not legally regarded as Macchia's employee.

Form of Employment Contracts

An employment contract, like an agency contract, may be oral or written. It may be expressed or implied from circumstances, as when a person is allowed to perform services for which payment is expected or usual.

> **2.** Braga orally agreed to work for Dettman for a period of two years, at a weekly salary of $500. After six months, Braga quit his job. Dettman claims that Braga is bound by contract to work for him for two years. Is Dettman's claim legally correct?

Many individual employment contracts are made orally. However, group employment contracts resulting from employer-union agreements are usually in writing. When an employment contract can't be performed within a year from the time it is made, the Statute of Frauds requires that the contract be in writing to be enforceable. In Problem 2, Dettman's claim isn't legally correct. The contract he made with Braga should have been in writing. Regardless of the requirements of the Statute of Frauds, it is a good idea to make all employment contracts in writing to avoid any future problems.

Collective-Bargaining Agreements

Millions of workers in the United States are represented by **bargaining units** when employment contracts are negotiated with employers. A bargaining unit often is a union chosen by workers to represent them in dealing with employers.

PROBLEM

> **3.** Pimsburg Company was engaged in the manufacture and sale of farming machinery. The firm refused to negotiate for a new union contract with representatives of a majority of its employees. The employees claimed that this was a violation of the National Labor Relations Act. Is their claim legally correct?

A bargaining unit negotiates with employers about wages, hours, working conditions, pensions, and other matters included in group employment contracts. The resulting agreement is known as a **collective-bargaining agreement.** It must be approved by a vote of the rank-and-file union members before it becomes binding on union as well as on nonunion workers. This procedure must be in accordance with the provisions of the 1935 **National Labor Relations Act** (sometimes called the *Wagner Act*). This federal law was designed to encourage collective bargaining and to prohibit unfair labor practices by employers. For example, under this act employers may not (1) interfere with or dominate a union, (2) discharge an employee for union membership or activity, (3) refuse to bargain with the representatives of the majority of the employees, and (4) threaten to close the plant, replace workers with machines, or move the plant to another location to avoid the union. In Problem 3, Pimsburg Company is guilty of an unfair labor practice because it refused to negotiate with the representatives of the majority of its employees.

As time passed, many people felt that the Wagner Act gave labor an undue advantage over management. As a result, the **Labor-Management Relations Act** (Taft-Hartley Act) was passed in 1947. This act upheld all the provisions of the Wagner Act not repealed or amended by the new act. It also adopted a list of unfair labor practices in which unions were forbidden to engage. In 1959, both of these acts were supplemented by the **Labor-Management Reporting and Disclosure Act** (Landrum-Griffin Act). This act requires unions to disclose certain information about their financial conditions both to union membership and to the federal government.

These laws provide that the **National Labor Relations Board (NLRB)** will enforce the rights of both workers and management. Employers and employees who disagree with NLRB findings may appeal to the federal courts.

An Employer's Liability for Employees' Acts

An employer is liable for any careless or wrongful acts (torts) committed by an employee acting within the scope of the employment. The employer's liability is similar to that of a principal's liability for the torts of an agent. The injured person also may hold the employee personally liable for causing the injury. An employee alone is responsible for any torts committed while engaged in personal business and not the employer's business.

> Sarto, a truck driver, borrowed her employer's truck to take her son's soccer team to a game. The game was in a neighboring town. During the trip, Sarto struck and injured Carreio. Sarto's employer is not liable for Carreio's injury because Sarto wasn't acting within the scope of her employment when the injury occurred. She was engaged in her own personal business.

Termination of the Employment Contract

An employment contract may terminate in the same manner as any other contract. If a definite time is stated in the contract, the employment will terminate when that time expires. If no time is mentioned in the contract, it may be terminated by notice given by either party.

> **4.**   Gladden was under a three-year contract to manage a professional baseball team. He and the club's management agreed to end the contract at the end of the first year. Is the agreement to terminate binding on the parties?

An employment contract also may be terminated by mutual agreement, as in Problem 4.

An employee has the *power* to refuse to carry out the terms of a contract with an employer, because no one may be compelled to work for another against his or her will. But without the *right* to do so, the employee may be liable to the employer for damages for breach of contract.

> Artura, an actress, wrongfully abandoned an employment contract that had six more months to run. Artura's employer may sue her for money damages suffered as a result of the breach. While Artura had the power to quit her job, she had no legal right to quit.

When an employee under a contract is discharged by an employer *without cause,* the employer is liable for damages sustained by the employee. The employer may discharge an employee *for cause* without becoming liable for money damages. Causes that may justify such a discharge are disobedience, disloyalty, incompetency, fraud, and nonperformance of duties.

EXAMPLE

> Hendrix falsely represented on an employment application that she had five years' experience as a hotel accountant. After discovering the true facts, the employer discharged her. The employer was justified in firing Hendrix because she had practiced fraud in falsely representing her experience.

DISCRIMINATION IN EMPLOYMENT

The Civil Rights Act passed in 1964 prohibits discrimination in hiring, promotion, pay, or discharge of an employee because of race, color, religion, sex, or national origin. There also is a federal law prohibiting job discrimination against older workers. The purpose of these laws is to provide equal job opportunities for all citizens and to prevent economic loss because of job discrimination. Similar laws have been enacted in many cities and states.

PROBLEM

> **5.** As a condition of employment, an applicant either had to pass a general intelligence exam or present proof of a high school education. Neither requirement was directly related to successful performance on the job. Is this practice a violation of the Civil Rights Act?

The federal law applies to all employers of 25 or more workers, to employment agencies, and to unions that maintain hiring halls. Although the Civil Rights Act permits testing of job applicants, the test may not be used to prevent equal opportunity for employment. For instance, if a test contains questions that don't relate directly to the job for which the employee is to be hired, the employer is guilty of violating the law. In Problem 5, neither of the employer's requirements related directly to job performance. Thus, they were in violation of the Civil Rights Act. An employer who violates the act may face a civil suit for damages or a fine. Enforcement of anti-job-discrimination laws is usually entrusted to **fair employment practices commissions.**

Protecting Young Workers

If you take either a full-time or a part-time job while you are a minor, you should know which federal and state laws protect you as a young worker. These laws were enacted to ensure that you have adequate educational opportunities and also to keep you from getting hurt or doing work that is too hard for you.

Generally, child-labor laws apply to employment of minors under eighteen. These laws prohibit employers from hiring you for certain kinds of work and night work and regulate the number of hours you may work. In fact, some of these laws may keep you from getting jobs in certain industries. But you must remember that the "cannots" and "shall nots" for minors in labor laws are for your protection.

Which labor laws are we talking about? Well, for one, we're talking about the federal Fair Labor Standards Act. This law sets minimum ages for the employment of minors in interstate or foreign commerce. It also sets wage and hour standards for workers of any age who are engaged in interstate commerce. The minimum hourly wage is set by law, although it changes from time to time. Overtime pay of at least time and a half must be paid for all hours worked over 40 per week.

If you should be injured at work, your state worker's compensation law usually will pay for your medical care and give you cash benefits for the time you aren't able to work. States also have laws requiring safety measures, such as machine guards and maintenance of safe and healthful work places.

Finally, federal and state governments have laws prohibiting discrimination in hiring and employment practices because of race, creed, color, or nationality.

Be sure to watch the important laws introduced in your state legislature and in Congress. They affect you as a citizen, as a consumer, and as a worker.

LAWS REGULATING LABOR

Today, all states and the federal government have enacted laws to protect workers. Federal statutes apply only to workers engaged in interstate commerce. In Chapter 31, you learned of the protections provided by federal and state programs such as social security, worker's compensation, and unemployment insurance. In this chapter we'll deal with government's regulation of working conditions and safety, wages and hours, and the labor of minors.

Regulation of Working Conditions and Safety

The common law provided insufficient protection for employees in the areas of working conditions and safety. Under the common law, an employee who could prove injuries caused by the employer's negligence could recover for injuries suffered within the scope of employment. In spite of the employer's negligence, an employee who also was negligent could not recover damages (contributory negligence theory). Nor could the employee recover for injuries caused by the negligence of fellow employees. The common law also stated that certain employees, such as those working in explosives plants, coal mines, or lumber camps, assumed special occupational risks. If injuries were suffered in these risky occupations, the employer wasn't liable.

PROBLEM

> **6.** Grey worked at a furniture manufacturing plant. He was injured on the job when one of the machines he was using failed to work properly. The machine was known throughout the industry as a defective and dangerous type. It had been discarded by all other manufacturers. Could Grey hold his employer liable for his injuries?

The employer's negligence under the common law could be implied from (1) failure to furnish a safe place for employees to work; (2) failure to furnish safe tools and appliances, although they didn't have to be the latest models; (3) failure to furnish competent fellow employees or to exercise reasonable care in selecting employees; and (4) failure to enforce reasonable rules for the safe conduct of the business. In Problem 6, the employer violated the common law by failing to furnish safe tools with which the plant's employees could work.

PROBLEM

> **7.** The laws of a certain state required employers to provide guard rails around machinery to protect employees from dangerous contact with the moving parts on the machines. Braz was injured by a machine that was not properly protected by her employer. What are Braz's rights?

The health and safety of workers are now provided for by laws in every state. These laws usually deal with the proper construction, heating, ventilation, and lighting of buildings. Employers are required to maintain satisfactory standards of sanitation as well as adequate safeguards for those who use machinery. A machine that may cause injury must be protected by suitable guard rails, fencing, and the like. In Problem 7, Braz could sue her employer for damages. Also, the state could fine the employer for violating the law.

On the federal level, the **Occupational Safety and Health Act (OSHA)** has been enacted to protect workers. This law directs the Secretary of Labor to establish certain work-related safety and health standards. Businesses engaged in interstate commerce must observe these standards. Employers must furnish a place of employment that will not expose employees to a recognized risk of death or serious bodily harm. OSHA inspectors are required to inspect an employer's business premises and observe the working conditions at the work site. If violations are found, citations will be issued. A willful violation that results in the death of an employee can lead to a fine of up to $10,000 and/or imprisonment for up to six months. An important provision of the act requires employers of ten or more employees to keep certain records of all work-related deaths, injuries, and illnesses.

Regulation of Wages and Hours

> **8.** Hasegawa was employed as a stock clerk by Joffe Apparel Manufacturers. The firm shipped its goods to several states. Hasegawa was paid at the rate of $3.10 an hour. At the time of Hasegawa's employment, the federal minimum wage was $3.35 an hour. After working for Joffe for three months, Hasegawa quit and sued Joffe for back wages. He claimed that the firm had violated the minimum-wage provisions of the federal Wage and Hour Law. Is his claim correct?

In 1938, the federal government enacted the **Fair Labor Standards Act,** commonly known as the *Wage and Hour Law.* The purpose of this act was to provide maximum hours and minimum wages for all workers engaged in interstate or foreign commerce or with production of goods for such commerce. A minimum hourly wage was prescribed by the act, and that wage is revised periodically by Congress. The maximum hours are set at 40 per week. In Problem 8, Hasegawa's claim is correct. He received an hourly rate that was below the minimum rate prescribed by law.

Under the federal law, overtime wages must be paid at the rate of one and a half times the regular rate for each hour worked in excess of the maximum workweek.

> Hasset worked for International Electronics as a mechanical assembler. She worked 50 hours a week and was paid at the rate of $6.50 an hour, or $325 a week. Under the Fair Labor Standards Act, Hasset was entitled to be paid $357.50 per week. Her wages should have been calculated as follows: $260.00 (40 hrs. × $6.50 per hour = $260.00) + $97.50 (10 hrs. × $9.75 per hour = $97.50) = $357.50.

The provisions of this federal law don't apply to executives, managers, or administrators. The number of exempted occupations under the act is gradually diminishing as changes are made in covered jobs. In 1964 the Fair Labor Standards Act was amended by the **Equal Pay Act.** This law prohibits employers from discriminating on the basis of sex in the payment of wages for equal work. This prohibition applies to employees in the same firm who have similar working conditions and do equal work on jobs requiring equal skill, effort, and responsibility. Exceptions to this rule may occur if the wage differences are shown to be based on seniority, merit, a system measuring earnings by quantity or quality of production, or any other factor other than sex.

Arlington Laboratories employed Ravech as a research assistant. Her weekly salary was $350. McHoul worked as a research assistant in the same department. He was paid $375 a week for performing the same work. Under the Equal Pay Act, Ravech is entitled to the same rate of pay as McHoul.

Minimum wage and hour laws applicable to those engaged in intrastate commerce may be found in many states.

Regulation of the Labor of Minors

9. Levenson, sixteen, worked from 10 P.M. to 6 A.M. in the maintenance department of a manufacturing plant. Does this constitute a violation of the law?

The Fair Labor Standards Act prohibits the employment of people under sixteen years of age in certain occupations. Also, people under eighteen may not work in any nonagricultural job that the Secretary of Labor has declared to be especially dangerous. Minors of fourteen or fifteen may work outside school hours in a limited number of jobs, such as in office and sales jobs, and for a limited number of hours. Some states prohibit minors from working before 6 A.M. or after 10 P.M. In Problem 9, Levenson would be unable to continue with his job if the laws of his state prohibited night work by minors. Minors between the ages of fourteen and sixteen may work for their parents in jobs other than manufacturing or mining and may work in agriculture if the work doesn't interfere with their schooling. Federal laws governing the labor of minors apply only to work in interstate or foreign commerce. Provisions on the labor of minors also may be found in the federal Employers' Liability Act and the Public Contracts Act. They forbid the labor of minors under sixteen, with certain stated exceptions.

Minors are prohibited by law from working in certain dangerous jobs.

This study of agency and employment has explained many of the rights and duties one acquires when working for or directing the work of others. Because they allow people to accomplish a number of personal and business objectives, agency and employment contracts are very important.

All of you have already served as agents and principals in some manner, and many of you have already been employed. However, it's likely that most of you have not yet had personal experience with owning or renting real property. In the next unit we will study the legal aspects of renting and owning realty.

Chapter 40 Review

"YOU BE THE JUDGE" REVIEW

Look again at the "You Be the Judge" cases given at the beginning of this chapter. Would you decide them differently now, after your study of the chapter?

Correct Decisions

1. Yes. The employee was clearly acting within the scope of his employment when the accident occurred. If the employee is negligent, the employer is liable.

2. No. Tse was discharged *for cause.* The discharge was justified by Tse's disloyalty to her employer.

UNDERSTANDING WHAT YOU HAVE READ

1. How does an employee differ from an agent?
2. When must a contract of employment be made in writing?
3. What purpose was served by the passage of each of these laws:
   a. the National Labor Relations (Wagner) Act?
   b. the Labor-Management Relations (Taft-Hartley) Act?
   c. the Labor-Management Reporting and Disclosure (Landrum-Griffin) Act?
4. Under what circumstances is an employer liable for the wrongful acts committed by an employee?

5. How may an employment contract terminate?
6. a. In what areas does the federal Civil Rights Act of 1964 prohibit discrimination in employment?
   b. Do you think this law has achieved its purpose?
7. In what four ways could an employer's negligence be implied under the common law?
8. How do state and federal laws provide for the health and safety of workers?
9. What are some of the main provisions of the federal Fair Labor Standards Act?
10. How do the states and the federal government regulate the labor of minors?

BUILDING YOUR LEGAL VOCABULARY

From this list, select the legal term that belongs in the blank in each sentence below. Write your answers on a separate sheet of paper.

bargaining unit
collective-bargaining
   agreement
employee
employer

Equal Pay Act
fair employment
   practices commission
Fair Labor Standards
   Act

National Labor
   Relations Act
National Labor
   Relations Board
Occupational Safety
   and Health Act

1. The ▓▓▓▓▓▓▓▓▓ prohibits employers from discriminating on the basis of sex in the payment of wages for equal work.
2. Enforcement of anti-job-discrimination laws is often entrusted to a ▓▓▓▓▓▓▓▓▓.
3. The party under whose direction and control a worker performs his or her job is known as an ▓▓▓▓▓▓▓▓▓.
4. The ▓▓▓▓▓▓▓▓▓ is the federal agency that enforces the rights of both workers and management.
5. Often, a ▓▓▓▓▓▓▓▓▓ is a union chosen by workers to represent them in dealing with employers.
6. The ▓▓▓▓▓▓▓▓▓ is the federal law that provides maximum hours and minimum wages for all workers engaged in interstate or foreign commerce or with production of goods for such commerce.
7. The group employment contract resulting from a union's negotiations with an employer is called a ▓▓▓▓▓▓▓▓▓.
8. The law designed to encourage collective bargaining and to prohibit unfair labor practices by employers is the ▓▓▓▓▓▓▓▓▓.
9. The law that directs the Secretary of Labor to establish certain mandatory work-related safety and health standards for businesses engaged in interstate commerce is the ▓▓▓▓▓▓▓▓▓.
10. A person who performs regular tasks for another, not including making contracts with third parties, is called an ▓▓▓▓▓▓▓▓▓.

APPLYING LEGAL PRINCIPLES

1. On March 1, Bourso entered into an oral contract to work for Ashoka as superintendent of her paint factory. The contract was to run for one year from April 1. Bourso worked until July 15, when Ashoka discharged him. Bourso sued on the contract, and Ashoka pleaded the Statute of Frauds as her defense. Was this a good defense?

2. Novarro, a machinist employed by Harrison Tool Co., participated actively in organizing a union among his fellow employees. Because of his union activities, the company discharged Novarro. Did the firm violate the provisions of the National Labor Relations Act?

3. To avoid bargaining with the union representing his employees, Minehan moved his plant to Cedar Falls, 500 miles distant from the old location. The union contended that Minehan violated a provision of the National Labor Relations Act. Do you agree?

4. An employee of a carpet-cleaning firm, through carelessness, ruined Simkin's expensive wall-to-wall carpeting. Was the cleaning company liable for the damages?

5. Gantos was employed to make deliveries for a local merchant. After delivering a package to a customer within the city limits, Gantos drove the delivery van to the next town to visit a friend. While returning from this visit, Gantos struck and injured a pedestrian. Was her employer liable for damages?

6. A supermarket employed Favia as a packer. After he had been working for several weeks, Favia refused to continue with his assigned work. He expressed a desire to be a cashier. The management disagreed and discharged Favia. Is Favia entitled to damages for breach of contract by the management?

7. Otero, 60, applied for a position as a stockbroker. In spite of her previous experience, she was told that she didn't qualify because of her age. Was this a violation of a federal law?

8. Salten, the vice-president of a publishing firm, was employed under a written two-year contract. After a year, Salten had an argument with the president of the firm and quit. Is she legally entitled to do so?

9. Laas was the public relations manager of a cosmetics manufacturer. After a year of employment, Laas was discharged. At the time of the discharge, Laas's boss told him, "We feel that a woman would be more suitable in this position than a man." Has the employer violated the law? If so, what are Laas's legal rights?

10. Benetto Chemical Co., engaged in interstate commerce, employed May, fifteen, in its equipment maintenance department. Did the company violate any federal or state law?

ANALYZING COURT CASES

1. Fiedler shipped farm products from Florida to northern states by tractor-trailer. Nazarian, an employee, drove the truck. During one of the trips, Nazarian detached the trailer in Charlotte, North Carolina. She then drove to Morganton, 75 miles west of Charlotte, to visit her family and pick up some clothes. While driving to Morganton, she negligently struck and killed Thoms. An action for wrongful death was brought against both Fiedler and Nazarian. Who is liable? (Based on: *Travis v. Duckworth*, 75 S.E. 2d 309)

2. The duties of several office employees of the First State Abstract and Insurance Co. included preparing insurance policies and applications for insurance, reports, and other documents. These documents were intended for transmission in connection with the transaction of business for out-of-state insurance firms. First State Abstract had admittedly paid these employees less than the minimum hourly wage required by the Fair Labor Standards Act. The firm also had failed to pay them at the overtime rate for hours worked over 40 a week. The insurance firm claimed in its defense that the employees' duties didn't constitute interstate commerce. Therefore, it was claimed that the provisions of the Fair Labor Standards Act didn't apply. Was this claim legally correct? (*Wirtz v. First State Abstract and Insurance Co.*, 362 F. 2d 83)

3. An Ohio statute required employers to supply seats and cafeteria facilities for female employees. It also limited women's working hours and prohibited the employment of women in jobs requiring the lifting of weights over 25 pounds. The validity of this statute was challenged on the ground that it violated the federal Civil Rights Act of 1964 by not treating men and women employees alike. Was the statute valid? (*Jones Metal Products Co. v. Walker*, 267 N.E. 2d 814)

UNIT 9

OWNING AND RENTING PROPERTY

CHAPTERS

544

LEARNING OBJECTIVES

After you have studied this unit, you should be able to:

- Distinguish between real and personal property.
- Give examples of the ways in which ownership of real property is acquired and the legal limitations on such ownership.
- Describe the different kinds of tenancies and how they terminate.
- Describe the legal procedures of buying and selling a home.

- Discuss ways to avoid pitfalls when taking title to a home.
- Describe the legal characteristics of the lessor-lessee relationship.
- Explain the provisions commonly found in leases.
- Explain the essential elements of a valid will.
- Describe how property is transferred by wills and inheritance.

CHAPTER 41

Nature and Ownership of Real and Personal Property

YOU BE THE JUDGE

Think about these cases.
If you were the judge, how would you decide each case?

1

Quinto sold her house to Kim. After the sale, Quinto removed a dining-room chandelier. She had moved the chandelier from house to house on several other occasions. Kim claimed the chandelier was a fixture and belonged to her. Who was right?

2

A bicycle was stolen from Chinn's garage. The thief replaced the handlebars and put a new seat on the bike. If Chinn recovers the bike from the thief, must he pay the thief for the improvements?

THE NATURE OF REAL AND PERSONAL PROPERTY

In Chapter 18 you learned that anything people use, possess, enjoy, or transfer to others is known commonly as *property*. In a strictly legal sense, it's not the thing itself but the right of ownership in it that is their property. There may be many property rights in a single object of wealth. For example, one person may own a building and the right to the income derived from it. A second person may have the right to take the building from the owner if the owner fails to pay a debt for which the building stands as security. And a third person may have the right to possess the building and use it.

> **1.** Pineda, a high-school senior, made an inventory of the property he owned. He listed the following: (1) 50 shares of XYZ Corporation stock, (2) a 35-mm camera, (3) an AM/FM stereo cassette player, and (4) one acre of improved land he had inherited from his grandmother. How should Pineda's property be legally classified?

You also know that all property is classified as either *personal* or *real* property. **Personal property** refers to a movable thing or an interest or right in that thing. If the thing can be touched or felt, it is known as **tangible personal property**. In Problem 1, Pineda's camera and stereo may be classified as tangible personal property. Since his 50 shares of stock can't be touched, they are called **intangible personal property**.

Real property (realty) includes not only the surface of the earth but also everything beneath it (minerals, oils, gases, and so forth) and everything a reasonable distance above it. Therefore, if the limbs or roots of trees belonging to one person extend into the land of another person, the second person may cut them off. Land also includes **perennials** (crops that grow from year to year without replanting) such as grass, fruit, and berries. However, growing crops such as corn, wheat, and potatoes are called **annuals**. These crops, which are cultivated by human beings, are classified as personal property. Pineda's acre of land in Problem 1 is real property.

Fixtures

> **2.** Suppose Pineda's inventory included some bookshelves that were permanently attached to the wall of his bedroom. Are the shelves real or personal property?

Generally, permanent improvements to real property are regarded as **fixtures.** Fixtures are articles of personal property that have been attached to real property in such a manner that removal of them will result in injury to the realty. Pineda's bookshelves in Problem 2 are fixtures if removing them will damage the wall to which they're attached. Other examples of fixtures include air-conditioning systems, furnaces, pipes, and pumps.

ACQUIRING OWNERSHIP OF PERSONAL PROPERTY

There are several ways to acquire personal property. These include (1) acquisition by creation, purchase, or finding; (2) acquisition by gift; and (3) acquisition by accession.

Acquisition by Creation, Purchase, or Finding

A person who creates something, such as a sculpture, a painting, or a quilt, acquires ownership of that personal property. Such ownership also may be gained by buying the property or by inheriting it from another. A person also may acquire personal property by finding it, as discussed in Chapter 18.

Acquisition by Gift

Another method of obtaining personal property is by receiving it as a gift. The person who gives a gift to another is known as the **donor.** The person who receives a gift is known as the **donee.** There are two types of gifts of personal property. A gift made by a person during his or her lifetime is known legally as a **gift inter vivos.** A gift made by a person in danger of immediate death is known as a **gift causa mortis.** However, all gifts have three basic requirements. There must be (1) an *intention* by the *donor* to pass title; (2) *delivery* of the property or some symbolic act as a substitute for delivery, such as delivery of keys to a car or safe-deposit box; and (3) *acceptance* of the gift by the *donee.*

EXAMPLE

> Farver and Kopec had been dating for two years. Farver promised Kopec that she would give him a car for his birthday. Farver failed to keep her promise, and they later broke up. Kopec sued Farver to obtain the car. Since Farver failed to *deliver* the car to Kopec, the promise to make the gift wasn't binding. Also, as you learned in Chapter 10, the promise would be unenforceable because of lack of consideration.

Acquisition by Accession

> **3.** Lupo failed to make the installment payments on a car she had bought recently. The seller repossessed the car. Lupo then claimed that the new tires, which she had put on the car to replace the old worn ones, belonged to her. Was she legally entitled to them?

As a general rule, if something is added to personal property by labor or materials, or both, the owner of the original property becomes the owner of the additions or improvements. This is known as gaining title by **accession.** In Problem 3, suppose the owner had no knowledge of or hadn't consented to the replacement of the tires. The courts have said that under the principle of accession, the original owner (the seller) is entitled to the new tires. This is true because the old tires were no longer available, and the new tires couldn't be removed without seriously decreasing the value of the car.

A more difficult problem arises when personal property is stolen and the thief makes additions or improvements. In these cases, the courts say the original owner may recover the property in its improved form without compensating the thief.

FORMS OF OWNERSHIP OF REAL PROPERTY

Real property may be owned by one person alone or by two or more people at the same time. Ownership of property is legally known as a **tenancy.**

> **4.** Odom bought a six-room ranch home for himself and his widowed daughter. Odom wants the deed to state that, in case of the death of either of them, the other is to own the house. What form of ownership should Odom choose?

If title to property is in the name of a single person, that person is said to own *in severalty.* The ownership is a **tenancy in severalty.** If ownership is in two or more people, the law recognizes these tenancies: joint tenancy, tenancy in common, tenancy by the entirety, and community property.

Joint Tenancy

Joint tenancy is created when two or more people own *equal interests* in the *same property,* which they acquired *at the same time.* The chief feature of

LIVING UNDER THE LAW

Should You Own Property Jointly?

Millions of people in this country consider joint ownership of property—stocks, bonds, bank accounts, and homes—to be a simple way of beating the high costs and tedious delays of probate. *Probate* is the legal term that describes a court-supervised process of establishing the validity of a will and administering a decedent's estate. Property held jointly usually passes automatically to the survivor when one owner dies. This type of arrangement is so common that it is called the "poor person's will." However, experts state that there are distinct advantages and disadvantages in owning property jointly.

ADVANTAGES
- It's simple and convenient for a family of modest means.
- It develops trust between wife and husband—tangible proof that a marriage is a partnership of equal sharing.
- Death of one joint tenant (owner) makes the property immediately available to the survivor.
- Either party can withdraw funds from a bank account or write a check.
- It substantially reduces attorney's fees and other legal expenses incurred in a probate proceeding.

DISADVANTAGES
- Joint ownership isn't a substitute for a valid will. For example, if all joint tenants die in an accident at the same time and there are no wills, property will pass under state laws. This is undesirable, especially in second marriages where distant relatives of each decedent joint tenant inherit.
- Both spouses must consent for property transfers to be legally effective.
- It can be ended without the consent of all joint tenants, and even without their knowledge. This may defeat the survivorship intent of the joint tenancy.
- The surviving spouse may be inexperienced or incompetent in handling estate property.

this tenancy is that, upon the death of one of the joint tenants, his or her interest passes to the surviving joint tenant or tenants. The decedent's interest continues to pass until the last surviving tenant owns the property in severalty. In Problem 4, therefore, Odom and his daughter should take title to the house as joint tenants. If one joint tenant contracts to sell his or her interest to another, the joint tenancy ends.

The advantages and disadvantages of joint tenancy are discussed in the "Living Under the Law" feature in this chapter.

Tenancy in Common

Two or more people may acquire the same property by separate instruments or by a will or a deed that names the people as owners. In this case, a **tenancy in common** is created. Unlike a joint tenancy, a tenancy in common has no right of survivorship. If one tenant in common dies, the interest passes to his or her heirs, not to the cotenants. An individual tenant in common may dispose of his or her interest to an outsider without the consent of the cotenants. The buyer then becomes a tenant in common with the others.

EXAMPLE

> Sage and Lioz were tenants in common of a valuable piece of lakefront land. Lioz sold his interest to Murrin. Murrin then became a tenant in common with Sage.

Tenancy by the Entirety

PROBLEM

> **5.** A large commercial building was deeded to Rachel Odaka and her husband Peter. What kind of legal ownership was created?

A form of tenancy in use in many states is the **tenancy by the entirety.** This tenancy may be created only when the co-owners are married to each other. Basically, it's a joint tenancy with rights of survivorship. In Problem 5, the Odakas were regarded as tenants by the entirety. An important feature of this tenancy is its effect on the rights of creditors of either tenant. Unlike a tenancy in severalty or a tenancy in common, a tenant by the entirety holds the property free from the claims of creditors. Neither tenant by the entirety can sell or convey an interest in the property without the consent of the other.

Condominium Ownership

> **6.** Sapir and his wife bought a two-bedroom apartment in a condominium development for $85,000. They received a deed to the unit at the closing. What is the nature of their ownership?

A single owner of a condominium unit is an owner in severalty. The unit owner also is a tenant in common, along with the other unit owners, of the parts of the realty that aren't under the unit owners' supervision and control. If ownership of a condominium is vested in a husband and wife, as in Problem 6, they usually hold their unit as tenants by the entirety. They hold the remaining parts of the development as tenants in common. This type of ownership has become popular, especially among people who aren't interested in the chores connected with ownership of a single-family home.

Community Property

> **7.** Before her marriage, Lera owned a large ranch in New Mexico. After her marriage, she lived on the ranch with her husband. Does her husband have any co-ownership rights in the ranch?

Community property ownership prevails in several states, mainly those under Spanish influence before they were admitted to the Union. In this type of ownership, property acquired by a husband and wife through their joint or individual efforts during the marriage is regarded as community property. Each owns an undivided half-interest in such property, regardless of who earned it. The property that each owned individually at the time of the marriage or acquired by gift or inheritance during marriage is not community property. It is the separate property of the husband or wife. In Problem 7, Lera's husband is not a co-owner of community property. The ranch is Lera's separate property and isn't considered community property.

Certainly, you are already the owner of personal property. It's likely that you will own real property, too, at some time in your life. Because of this, it's important that you know the kinds of ownership recognized by the law. It's also important that you know *how* to acquire title to real property, and how that title may be limited. We'll study these topics in the next chapter.

Chapter 41 Review

"YOU BE THE JUDGE" REVIEW

Look again at the "You Be the Judge" cases given at the beginning of this chapter. Would you decide them differently now, after your study of the chapter?

Correct Decisions

1. Kim was right. Although Quinto intended to take the chandelier with her when she sold the house, she didn't disclose this fact to Kim. The chandelier is a fixture and part of the realty belonging to Kim.

2. No. Chinn is entitled to the improvements by *accession*—the increase in the value of the property by the addition of other property. As owner of the bike, Chinn also is entitled to the new seat and handlebars and doesn't have to compensate the thief for the new equipment.

UNDERSTANDING WHAT YOU HAVE READ

1. Define the term *property*.
2. Distinguish between real and personal property.
3. What is the basic difference between tangible and intangible property?
4. How do annuals differ from perennial crops? Give an example of each.
5. List five ways to acquire personal property.
6. What are the three basic requirements of a valid gift?
7. Explain how a joint tenancy differs from a tenancy in common.
8. a. What kind of ownership do a husband and wife acquire when they purchase a home in joint names?
   b. How does this type of ownership differ from an ordinary joint tenancy?
9. How does the community property principle work?
10. Briefly describe the kinds of ownership acquired with the purchase of a condominium.

BUILDING YOUR LEGAL VOCABULARY

Choose the legal term that will correctly complete each definition below. Write your answers on a separate sheet of paper.

1. The type of ownership of real property in which a husband and wife hold the property free from the claims of creditors is a
   a. tenancy in common.
   b. community property ownership.
   c. tenancy by the entirety.

2. A gift of personal property made by a person during his or her lifetime is a
   a. gift inter vivos.
   b. donee.
   c. gift causa mortis.

3. A movable thing that can be touched and felt, or an interest in that thing, is known as
   a. tangible personal property.
   b. intangible personal property.
   c. real property.

4. The type of ownership of real property that arises when two or more people own equal interests in the same property, acquired at the same time, with right of survivorship, is a
   a. tenancy by accession.
   b. tenancy in severalty.
   c. joint tenancy.

5. Articles of personal property that are attached to real property in such a way that removal will injure the realty are called
   a. perennials.
   b. fixtures.
   c. annuals.

APPLYING LEGAL PRINCIPLES

1. Oliva sold his home to Wein. After the sale was made but before Wein moved in, Oliva dug up a Japanese red maple tree that he had planted two years earlier. Was he entitled to do so?

2. O'Connor, a tenant, installed additional cabinets in her kitchen. The cabinets were fastened permanently to the wall and their removal would have damaged the wall. May O'Connor take the cabinets with her if she vacates the property?

3. Jemly, a marine, was sent overseas during an international crisis. Before leaving the United States, he gave his savings account passbook to his sister, saying, "If I don't come back, you can have it all." A month later, Jemly was killed in a bomb explosion at his base in a foreign country. Does his sister own his savings account?

4. Onishi, critically ill and believing she was about to die, gave a valuable ring to her niece. Shortly thereafter, Onishi recovered from her illness. A bit later, however, she was killed in an auto accident. The executor of her estate claimed that the ring belonged to Onishi's estate. Was the executor correct?

5. Kleinfeld and Palin, adjoining property owners, each owned a summer cottage on Lake Success. They also owned a speedboat together. Palin claimed that all the property was owned jointly. Kleinfeld, however, disputed this claim. Who was correct?

6. McGuill and Derr owned real estate as joint tenants. McGuill, without Derr's consent, sold her interest to Paone. Paone now claims that he and Derr are joint tenants of the property. Do you agree?

7. De Sousa and Hogan owned an office building as tenants in common. After Hogan died, De Sousa claimed that he was entitled to Hogan's share. Hogan's heirs disputed De Sousa's claim. Who is right?

8. Mustafa lived with her husband in a community property state. She inherited a large sum of money from her uncle's estate. Is her husband entitled to claim a one-half interest as community property?

9. Salzberg and his wife owned 100 acres of land as tenants by the entirety. Without his wife's consent, Salzberg sold 50 acres of the land to DeRota. Does DeRota have a valid title to the land?

10. Lubinski's house had been robbed. Shortly after the robbery, Lubinski gave his brother a cereal box containing $30,000 in cash. The box was tightly sealed with tape. Lubinski said to his brother, "Take this home with you." The brother did as requested and never opened the box. However, each time Lubinski visited his brother he took the box into a private room and returned the box to Jerome before leaving. After Lubinski died, the brother claimed that the money had been given to him. Do you agree?

ANALYZING COURT CASES

1. Yoder and his wife transferred title to a piece of land to Willard M. Short and his sister Emma. The deed delivered to Short and his sister provided that the property was transferred to them "jointly and not as common tenants, their heirs, and assigns forever." After Willard Short died, his sister Emma contracted to sell the property to the Milbys. Later, the Milbys refused to comply with the terms of the contract on the ground that Emma didn't have absolute title to the property. Emma Short brought an action in specific performance against the Milbys. Should she succeed? (*Short v. Milby, et al.*, 64 A. 2d 36)

2. Rojas gave Icaza an engagement ring. Before they were married, Rojas was killed in a plane crash. The executor of Rojas's estate demanded that Icaza return the ring. Was she entitled to keep it? (Based on: *Cohen v. Bayside Savings and Loan Association*, 309 N.Y.S. 980)

3. Frank Stammets opened a savings account at First National Bank in the name of "Frank Stammets or Lena Stammets." Lena was Frank's sister. The signature card stated that the account was owned by Frank and Lena as joint tenants with the right of survivorship. Only Frank signed the signature card, and all the money deposited was Frank's. On Frank's death, Lena claimed the bank account. Frank's executor claimed it on the ground that Lena had never signed the signature card. Who owned the bank account? (In re: *Stammet's Estate*, 148 N.W. 2d 468)

CHAPTER 42

Acquiring Title to Real Property

YOU BE THE JUDGE

Think about these cases.
If you were the judge, how would you decide each case?

1

Pinson, by deed, transferred title to certain real estate to her son. Before turning over the deed to her son, Pinson died. The son now claims to be the sole owner of the realty. However, his claim is disputed by other family members. Who is legally entitled to the realty?

2

Loy gave a written easement to his neighbor, Furey, to run a water ditch across Loy's property. The ditch was intended to irrigate Furey's land. Later, Loy sold his property to Pollack. Pollack had the ditch filled in because it was dangerous to her family. Furey then sued Pollack. Will he succeed?

WAYS TO ACQUIRE TITLE

Acquiring ownership in personal property is a fairly simple task in comparison with acquiring ownership in real property. Specific procedures must be followed when title to realty is transferred. Also, specific documents must be completed. We'll discuss these topics in this chapter.

> **1.** Tran inherited 250 acres of land located in a remote area of northern Montana. He never actually took possession of the land and paid no attention to it for 22 years. When Tran finally decided to take possession of the land, he found Helfrich occupying it, paying the taxes, and using it as grazing land for cattle. Did Helfrich acquire title to the land?

The ownership of real property may pass from one person to another in many ways. However, there are five common ways in which ownership in realty is acquired: (1) by purchase, (2) by gift, (3) by adverse possession, (4) by tax sale, and (5) by inheritance. The first two of these methods are accomplished by voluntary act of the owner. The last three are accomplished by operation of law.

Acquisition by Purchase

Most people who own real property acquire title by buying the property from a prior owner. This type of transfer is made by means of a contract that requires the delivery of a **deed.** A deed is a written instrument that conveys title to real property. Contracts for the sale of real property must be in writing under the Statute of Frauds. Also, they must contain all the essentials of a valid contract.

Acquisition by Gift

Property is transferred by gift when the owner (the donor) delivers a deed to another person (the donee). The deed must comply with the laws of the state in which the property is located. The document doesn't have to be delivered directly to the donee but may be given to a third party for the benefit of the donee. In any case, the gift of the property isn't valid unless the deed is actually delivered to the donee or to a third party for the donee's benefit.

> Lu executed a deed to her summer home in favor of her daughter. She delivered the deed to her attorney with instructions to turn it over to her daughter shortly after her death. This act on Lu's part created a valid gift of the realty to her daughter when the lawyer delivered the deed to her on Lu's death.

Acquisition by Adverse Possession

Title to real property may be acquired by **adverse possession** if a person holds land belonging to another without interruption and without the owner's consent for a statutory period. That period is usually five to fifteen years. In Problem 1, Helfrich acquired title by adverse possession because he complied with the statutory requirements. In addition, he occupied the land and paid the taxes on it.

Acquisition by Tax Sale

The procedure by which one acquires title as a result of a **tax sale** is entirely statutory. In most states, if the taxes assessed on real property aren't paid for a stated period of time, they become a lien on the property. If the lien isn't satisfied after a certain time has passed, the governmental body involved will sell the property at a public tax sale. A person who buys property at a tax sale obtains a valid title to the property.

Acquisition by Inheritance

The owner of realty has the right to dispose of it by means of a will (subject to conditions noted in Chapter 44). If the owner dies without a will, the property will descend to the owner's heirs according to the laws of the state where the property is located. When a property owner dies without a will and leaves no heirs, the property will **escheat** (return) to the state.

PROCEDURES FOR BUYING REALTY

The procedures for transferring title to real property are quite technical. For this reason, it's always a good idea for a prospective buyer of realty to be represented by a competent lawyer.

There are four basic steps in transferring title to realty. First, a contract of sale must be prepared. Second, a title search must be performed and an abstract of title must be furnished. Third, title must be closed. Fourth, the deed must be recorded. We'll look at each of these steps in detail in the next few pages.

Contract of Sale

PROBLEM

2. A contract for the sale of real property looked like this:

> January 8, 19—
>
> Received of Anton Ullsperger, $7,500 on said purchase of property at 1031 Milwaukee Avenue, Chicago, Illinois, at a price of $75,000.
>
> C. Meyer

Meyer refused to perform this contract. She claimed that the memorandum was insufficient to meet the requirements of the Statute of Frauds. Is she required to deliver a deed to Ullsperger?

The contract of sale, sometimes known as a **land contract,** is the most important instrument in buying and selling realty. It doesn't pass title to the property. Rather, it merely serves as evidence of an agreement to pass title at a definite future time. Also, it can't be enforced under the Statute of Frauds unless it is in writing and contains four specific components. The required components are (1) the names of the buyer and seller, (2) a description of the property sufficient to identify it, (3) the consideration, and (4) the signature of the party to be held liable, although usually both parties to the contract sign it. No particular form of contract is required. It may be in the form of one or more letters, or even receipts, provided they contain the elements required by the Statute of Frauds. In Problem 2, Meyer will have to deliver a deed to Ullsperger. The written memorandum is sufficient to meet the legal requirements.

Title Search and Abstract of Title

After the contract of sale has been signed, the most important step to be taken by the buyer is to determine whether the seller has good title to the property. In a large city it is customary to have a **title search** (title investigation) done by a title company rather than by a lawyer or public official such as a county clerk or registrar of deeds. The title company makes a report on the ownership of the property. This report is called an **abstract of title.** Unless the contract provides otherwise, the seller is required to furnish the buyer with an abstract of title. The abstract doesn't prove that the seller is the owner of the property. For this purpose the abstract should be given to a competent lawyer for examination. The attorney will be in a position to express an opinion on the validity of the seller's title.

In many large cities, buyers of realty can pay an extra fee to obtain a title insurance policy from the title company that made the search. This policy will protect the buyer against any flaws that may develop later in the title and for which the title company is liable.

Title Closing

The contract of sale states the date for delivery of the deed conveying title to the property and notes the purchase price paid. If the seller's title is found to be good, the parties with their lawyers will meet on the date agreed on. The **title closing** (the performance or closing of the contract) will be accomplished at this meeting. If all the conditions of the contract have been met, the buyer's lawyer will deliver a certified check for the balance of the purchase price. The seller's lawyer will deliver a properly executed deed to the property. The buyer will acquire title immediately on delivery of the deed. The deed is then recorded in the proper public office by the lawyer for the buyer or by the title company.

If any conditions have to be met by either the seller or the buyer before the deed is delivered, a special contract is prepared. It is known as an **escrow**

agreement. By the terms of this agreement, the deed to the property is delivered to a disinterested third party, often a title insurance firm. The third party holds the agreement until the conditions stated in the agreement have been met. Neither the buyer nor the seller may act as escrow holder.

Regulation of Title Closings

In 1974, a federal statute was enacted to regulate the practices involved with title closings. Before the passage of the **Real Estate Settlement Procedures Act (RESPA),** the amount of the settlement or **closing costs** often shocked buyers. Also, buyers were sometimes victimized by practices that harmed their interests. Briefly, RESPA has a three-fold purpose: (1) to educate the homebuyer, (2) to reduce closing costs, and (3) to eliminate practices abusive to buyers. The law covers all real estate sales that are financed by federally related loans such as Veterans Administration (VA) loans and Federal Housing Administration (FHA) loans. In these transactions, RESPA requires lenders to provide buyers with an information booklet prepared by the government. The booklet is intended to simplify the settlement process for both buyers and sellers. Buyers also receive advance disclosure of the settlement costs and are given a chance to "shop around" for better terms from other lenders.

Under the act, the party conducting the closing must complete a standard form known as a **Uniform Settlement Statement.** This form must show the closing costs that the parties to the sale will incur. Among the usual items disclosed are (1) real estate brokers' commissions, (2) loan origination fees, (3) **points** (service charges deducted from the mortgage loan), (4) appraisal fees, (5) credit report fees, and (6) attorneys' fees.

The act also prohibits certain practices that are harmful to the homebuyer, such as requirements to pay **kickbacks** or unearned fees. A kickback results from a secret agreement or from duress. Basically, it is a share in the amount received by another party. For example, a lender might be required to pay a real estate broker part of the lender's fees in return for the broker's services in referring the borrower to that lender.

Hurd signed a contract of sale to buy a home. Duchon, Hurd's real-estate broker, suggested that Hurd apply to First Federal Savings Bank for a loan to buy the home. Unknown to Hurd, Duchon had arranged with an officer of the bank to receive a percentage of the bank's fees for any loan made to a borrower recommended by Hurd. The bank's payment to Hurd in this instance is a kickback.

Criminal penalties of both fines and imprisonment are provided in RESPA for violations of its provisions.

Recording the Deed

The laws of all states require that deeds to real property be recorded. In fact, although an unrecorded deed is valid between the parties concerned, it is ineffective and void with respect to later innocent buyers of the same property. The reason for this rule is that buyers of land should be entitled to rely on the title as it appears in the public records. They should be protected against unrecorded deeds and other liens. It's important, therefore, that a buyer record the deed in the proper public office. This is usually the office of the county clerk or registrar of deeds. The recording should be done immediately after the title closing. If two innocent buyers of the same property both obtain deeds, the one who records the deed first has the better title.

Saraf conveyed his house and lot by deed to Heinz on August 15. Ten days later, he conveyed the same property to Clancy, an innocent buyer for value. Clancy immediately took possession of the property. Heinz then brought suit against Clancy for possession of the realty. At the trial, Heinz proved that she had recorded her deed at the county clerk's office on August 16. Her deed would have priority over Clancy's deed.

O'Neill sold a four-acre lot to Ford. Ford neglected to record his deed. Two weeks later, O'Neill sold the lot again to Inge, an innocent buyer, who immediately recorded his deed. Between Ford and Inge, both innocent buyers for value, Inge has the better title because he was first to record the deed.

KINDS OF DEEDS

Three types of deeds are in common use in this country. They are the quitclaim deed, the bargain and sale deed, and the warranty deed. The parties to a deed are the **grantor** (one who conveys title to realty) and the **grantee** (one to whom title is transferred).

3.   A contract provided for the transfer of certain realty from Kitsman to Fujiwara for a cash consideration. Nothing was said about the type of deed the seller was to deliver to the buyer. What type of deed should Fujiwara require of Kitsman?

Quitclaim Deed

A **quitclaim deed** merely releases the seller's or grantor's present interest in the property. This deed doesn't obligate the grantor in the least. If the grantor has good title to the property at the time of execution of the quitclaim deed, the deed is sufficient to pass ownership. If the grantor has no interest, none will be transferred to the buyer or grantee.

> After buying a house and five acres of land, Duzan discovered that a neighbor had a right to cross the land in order to reach a highway. Duzan offered the neighbor $2,500 to give up the right to cross the land. The neighbor may do so by signing and delivering a quitclaim deed to Duzan.

Bargain and Sale Deed

A **bargain and sale deed,** unlike a quitclaim deed, transfers title to real property. In this deed, however, the grantor does not warrant to the grantee that the title is complete and perfect. Unless the buyer specifically provides in the contract of sale for a warranty deed, he or she will be entitled to a deed that merely passes title. This is a bargain and sale deed. In Problem 3, Fujiwara will receive a bargain and sale deed from Kitsman unless he insists on a full-covenant warranty deed.

Warranty Deed

In a **warranty deed,** also known as a *full-covenant warranty deed,* the grantor warrants to the grantee that the grantor has complete and perfect title to the property except as to matters mentioned in the deed. The **covenants** (representations and promises that amount to warranties) usually found in warranty deeds are these:

1. *Title.* The grantor warrants that he or she is the owner of the realty and has a legal right to convey it.

2. *Against encumbrances.* The grantor warrants that there are no **encumbrances** on the realty, except as noted in the deed. Encumbrances are claims against the property, such as mortgage or tax liens.

3. *Quiet enjoyment.* The grantor guarantees that the grantee will not be evicted or dispossessed by anyone having a better title or lien.

4. *Further assurance.* The grantor agrees to obtain and to give to the grantee and the grantee's successors any legal documents that may be needed to perfect the title. An example of such a document might be a quitclaim deed from the heir of a deceased previous owner.

5. *Warranty.* The grantor guarantees the title. If any warranty is broken, the grantee may sue for its breach and recover any damages sustained as a result of the breach.

Figure 42.1 is a sample of a Warranty Deed.

Figure 42.1
A Warranty Deed

HOBBS & WARREN, INC.
PUBLISHERS STANDARD LEGAL FORMS
BOSTON · MASS.

EDGAR J. QUESADA and LUCIA M. QUESADA

of 156 Bedford Street, City of Lexington, Middlesex   County, Massachusetts,

being   married, for consideration paid, and in full consideration of   One Dollar ($1)

grants to   ANDREW P. NICOLAI and PETRA P. NICOLAI, Joint Tenants   *

of 2951 Bainbridge Avenue, Bronx, New York   with **warranty covenants**

all that certain lot or parcel of land, with the buildings and
improvements thereon, situated and lying in the town of Lexington,
County of Middlesex and State of Massachusetts, designated as Lot
Number 24 as laid out and surveyed by Wulff Engineering Co., Woburn,
Massachusetts, and filed in the Office of the Clerk of the County of
Middlesex on May 29, 1984, as Map Number 6357.
    TOGETHER with all rights, title, and interest in and to the land
lying in the streets in front of and adjoining said premises to the
center line thereof.

Witness their hands   and seals this........16th........ day of.....January............,19--

Edgar J. Quesada   *Lucia M. Quesada*

The Commonwealth of Massachusetts

ss.   January 16, 19--

Then personally appeared the above named   Edgar J. Quesada and Lucia M. Quesada

and acknowledged the foregoing instrument to be   their   free act and deed before me

Evelyn Cohen
Notary Public — Justice of the Peace

My commission expires ....June 15........... 19....

(*Individual — Joint Tenants — Tenants in Common.)

CHAPTER 183 SEC. 6 AS AMENDED BY CHAPTER 497 OF 1969

Every deed presented for record shall contain or have endorsed upon it the full name, residence and post office address of the grantee
and a recital of the amount of the full consideration thereof in dollars or the nature of the other consideration therefor, if not delivered
for a specific monetary sum. The full consideration shall mean the total price for the conveyance without deduction for any liens or
encumbrances assumed by the grantee or remaining thereon. All such endorsements and recitals shall be recorded as part of the deed.
Failure to comply with this section shall not affect the validity of any deed. No register of deeds shall accept a deed for recording unless
it is in compliance with the requirements of this section.

LIMITATIONS ON OWNER- SHIP OF REAL PROPERTY

An owner of property has the rights to possess, use, enjoy, and transfer it to another. But these rights are subject to three types of recognized limitations: (1) limitations created by contract (by the parties themselves), (2) limitations imposed by law, and (3) limitations created by real property liens.

Limitations Created by Contract

PROBLEM

> **4.** Willhaven College cut streets through its campus and allowed the public to use them. However, the college didn't want the public to have any permanent right to use these streets. What legal steps should the college authorities take to accomplish their purpose?

A seller sometimes writes restrictions into a deed of land. These restrictions often are intended to benefit not only the seller's property but also the property of adjoining neighbors. For example, a deed might provide that any building to be erected on the land must be of a certain type, below a certain height, or set back a certain distance from the street. Restrictions such as these usually "run with the land." This means that they are binding on future owners of the property.

Easements and licenses are two other forms of contractual limitations on real property sales.

Easements

A restriction sometimes included in a deed is one relating to the right to use the land of another owner for a special purpose. This right is legally known as an **easement.** The most common examples of easements are a right of way over the grantor's land or the right to a party wall or a common stairway, alley, or driveway. Easements also may be acquired by long, uninterrupted use (twenty years in some states and five to fifteen years in others) *without the consent of the owner.* For example, the public might walk across a certain parcel of land in order to reach a public street. If they do this for the statutory period of years, without interruption and without the owner's consent, an easement has been created. In Problem 4, the college authorities should prevent uninterrupted use by blocking the campus streets at least once in the course of the statutory period for creation of an easement.

Licenses

It's important to distinguish an easement from a license. As it applies to real property, a license is a right—granted either orally or in writing—to use the land of another for a stated purpose, but without granting any permanent interest in the land. A license differs from an easement in that

(1) it is personal and can be used only by the party to whom it is given; (2) it may be revoked at any time; and (3) it doesn't carry an interest in the land and therefore doesn't have to be in writing.

Cao and Lavin owned cabins on the opposite side of a private lake. Cao obtained permission to use Lavin's dock for fishing. This arrangement amounted to a license or personal privilege. Lavin could revoke the license at any time.

Limitations Imposed by Law

There are seven common limitations imposed by law on the sale of real property. These include (1) air rights, (2) water rights, (3) taxes, (4) assessments, (5) eminent domain, (6) zoning laws, and (7) public health and safety laws.

Air Rights

5. Eccles owned property next to an airport. She brought suit to prevent planes from flying over her land. Will she succeed?

Under the common law, an owner of land has exclusive ownership down to the center of the earth and "up to the sky." Under modern law, however, there is a right to fly planes for a lawful purpose over the land of another without prior permission. Rights such as this are known as **air rights.** The flight must be made at such a height that it doesn't damage or interfere with the use made of the land. In Problem 5, Eccles won't succeed if the planes fly above her land at an altitude at least as great as that set by law.

In addition to protection from low-flying planes, a landowner is also protected from air and noise pollution. Federal and state statutes set standards to reduce air and noise pollution mainly from cars, motorcycles, and planes.

Water Rights

6. Comenos drew water for farming purposes from a stream that flowed through his property. A landowner farther upstream built a dam across the stream, cutting off the entire flow of water. Does Comenos have any legal rights?

Transfers of real property are subject to limitation by **water rights.** For example, an owner of land next to a stream that isn't navigable has title to the soil to the middle of the stream. However, the owner doesn't have title or ownership rights in the water. The owner may use the stream to a reasonable extent, but must not diminish or interfere with the right of use of others who may be farther along the stream's course. Thus, in Problem 6, Comenos could obtain a court order requiring the upstream owner to remove the dam and stop interfering with the natural flow of the stream. If a waterway is a navigable river and forms a boundary between the land of two owners, each owner's land extends to the low-water mark.

Taxes

Taxes are charges imposed on citizens to raise funds for public purposes or government expenses. Realty taxes are based on official valuations of real property. Nonpayment by realty owners may lead to penalties and loss of the property.

Assessments

Assessments are charges against real property that has been benefited by a local improvement. These improvements might include the installation of a sewer system, the construction of sidewalks, or the paving of streets. Like taxes, assessments become liens if they aren't paid. If the liens remain unsatisfied, the consequences for nonpayment of assessments are the same as for nonpayment of taxes.

Eminent Domain

PROBLEM

7. Nzuyen owned a tract of land in a residential area. The local authorities wanted to acquire the site for construction of a school. If Nzuyen refuses to sell the property and no other suitable site is available, what may the authorities do?

The right of a government or a government subdivision to take private property for a public purpose on payment of just compensation is known as the right of **eminent domain.** When this right is exercised, a jury often is called on to determine the fair market value of the property taken. The proceeding by which the property is taken is known as a **condemnation proceeding.** Because of Nzuyen's refusal to sell in Problem 7, the local authorities would have to bring condemnation proceedings against him to obtain title to the tract.

Zoning Laws

Zoning laws regulate the use that may be made of real property in certain areas. The object of zoning is to insure an orderly physical development of the regulated area. Commonly, zoning laws divide cities into three zones —residential, commercial, and manufacturing. Commercial and manufacturing enterprises aren't permitted in residential zones. Courts usually enforce zoning laws if they are necessary and reasonable.

Public Health and Safety Laws

A community may restrict the use of real property to protect the health, safety, morals, and welfare of citizens. This is true even though it may result in the curtailment of private property rights. The community may require, for example, that buildings be constructed in a certain manner. Safety and health laws may require that buildings have safety devices to prevent and control fires or that they contain adequate waste-disposal facilities. In large cities, health, sanitation, and building departments supervise the enforcement of these laws.

Real Property Liens

PROBLEM

> **8.**   D'Errico owned a single-family home. She applied to Excelsior Savings and Loan Association for a loan of $28,000 to pay for the cost of remodeling her home. What security will the association require before making the loan?

Real property, as well as personal property, may be subject to liens. A lien on real property is a charge on the property, making it subject to sale in order to satisfy a claim against the owner. The chief real property liens are (1) mortgages, (2) judgment liens, and (3) mechanic's liens.

Mortgages

A **mortgage** is a lien created when the owner of realty borrows money and uses the property as security for repayment of the debt. The written evidence of the security for the debt is a document called a **real-estate mortgage.** In addition, the borrower usually assumes personal liability for the debt by giving the creditor a written promise to repay. This promise often takes the form of a bond or promissory note. Thus, the lender receives both a mortgage and a bond or note as security for the debt. In Problem 8, D'Errico will be required to deliver to the savings and loan association a bond or note and a mortgage before the $28,000 loan will be granted. The parties to a mortgage are the **mortgagor** and the **mortgagee.** The borrower or debtor is the mortgagor, and the lender or creditor is the mortgagee.

A realty mortgage should be in writing under the Statute of Frauds and should be executed with the same formalities as a deed. Statutes in many states usually require that mortgages be recorded in the proper public office.

Before Taking Title to Real Property

Assume that you have just signed a contract of sale for a piece of real property. Is there anything you can do to protect yourself before you take final title to the realty? Yes. You would be well advised to follow these suggestions.

- Be sure that the seller has clear title to convey. A title search may show that the seller isn't the legal owner or that there is some restriction on the seller's right to dispose of the property.
- Ask for a full-covenant warranty deed. The seller will then be responsible for any flaws in the title conveyed to you.
- Find out exactly how much you're paying for the property.
- Make sure that there aren't any liens or assessments outstanding against the property.

- Find out what your rights or restrictions will be as the owner of the property. Look for easements. They may restrict the area on which you can build or prohibit you from putting a fence around your property.
- Find out exactly what you are buying. Legal descriptions are often misinterpreted.
- Find out whether zoning laws and restrictive covenants will keep you from constructing the kind of building you want to build. Restrictive covenants frequently set a minimum price on the houses allowed in a neighborhood or require a certain type of architecture.
- When buying realty, never sign a contract of sale that hasn't been carefully checked by a competent lawyer.

The purpose of this requirement is to protect the mortgagee against claims by innocent buyers of the property and by creditors.

The mortgagor still owns an interest in the property and has the right to its possession. Therefore, he or she has practically the same control over the property as existed before the mortgage was made. The mortgagor may sell, lease, or assign the property. He or she also may place additional mortgages on the property if there is enough security remaining over and above the previous mortgages.

The mortgagee may require the mortgagor to pay the interest on the mortgage, insure the property, keep the property in good repair, and pay all taxes and assessments against the property. The mortgagee also may require that the principal be repaid either in installments or in a lump sum, as stated in the mortgage. The mortgagee may sell or transfer the bond and mortgage to a third party. However, the third party won't obtain a greater interest than the mortgagee had at the time of the transfer.

A mortgage is terminated by payment of the entire debt at or before the required time. A mortgagee can't be compelled, though, to accept repayment before the mortgage debt is due unless otherwise provided in the mortgage. When the debt is paid, the mortgagor should obtain a release, called a **satisfaction piece,** from the mortgagee. This document should be recorded in order to clear the mortgagor's title to the property.

A mortgagor may fail to perform contractual obligations such as making mortgage payments on time or paying taxes and assessments on the property. This failure will give the mortgagee a right to declare the entire debt immediately due and payable. By the terms of the mortgage, the mortgagee may cause the property to be sold at public auction to satisfy the claim. The legal procedure for exercising this right is known as **foreclosure.** If the amount realized at the foreclosure sale is less than the sum due on the foreclosed mortgage, a deficiency judgment may be entered against the mortgagor. This is due to the fact that the mortgagor is personally liable on the bond or promissory note for the entire debt. To avoid a deficiency judgment, mortgagors often offer the mortgagee a deed to the property.

At any time before the foreclosure sale, and in many states even after the sale, the mortgagor is given time to redeem the property on payment of all sums due, plus interest. The time allowed is usually one year. This legal right to redeem is known as the mortgagor's **right of redemption.**

Judgment Liens

PROBLEM

> **9.** Byers obtained a judgment against Lavigne for $25,000. Byers then filed a judgment lien against Lavigne's real property in order to satisfy the debt. Is Byers legally allowed to do so?

A person who obtains a court judgment against another for a sum of money becomes a judgment creditor. He or she may cause the judgment or a copy of it to be filed in a public office in the county in which the judgment debtor has realty. The filing or recording of the judgment creates a **judgment lien** on the real property in favor of the judgment creditor. In Problem 9, Byers is legally entitled to file a judgment lien against Lavigne. If the lien isn't satisfied, Byers may bring a proceeding similar to foreclosure of a mortgage lien to sell Lavigne's realty and apply the proceeds against the debt.

Mechanic's Liens

PROBLEM

> **10.** Santini, a carpentry contractor, furnished lumber and services amounting to $17,500 in the construction of a home for Eisner. If Eisner fails to pay Santini, what are Santini's legal rights against the property?

A **mechanic's lien** arises when a person performs services or furnishes materials, or both, in the improvement of another person's realty. If payment for these services and materials isn't made, the "mechanic" (the person who performed the services or provided the materials) may file a notice of lien against the realty of the party who failed to pay. The notice should be filed in the county clerk's office of the county where the realty is located. Filing this notice creates a lien against the real property. Like mortgage and judgment liens, the mechanic's lien also may be foreclosed if it isn't satisfied. In Problem 10, Santini may file a mechanic's lien against Eisner's realty.

Ownership of real property can bring many rewards, primarily in terms of providing you with financial security. However, the acquisition of real property is neither a simple nor an inexpensive process. Many people choose to rent real property rather than to buy it. It's very possible that you will rent real property, either as a place to live or as a place to work, at some time in the future. Let's move on, then, to learn some of the principles of landlord-tenant law.

Chapter 42 Review

"YOU BE THE JUDGE" REVIEW

Look again at the "You Be the Judge" cases given at the beginning of this chapter. Would you decide them differently now, after your study of the chapter?

Correct Decisions

1. Unless Pinson disposed of the realty by will, it will pass to her heirs as intestate property. The realty doesn't belong to the son because the deed was never delivered to him during Pinson's lifetime.

2. Yes. An easement runs with the land. Furey can't be deprived of the easement without his consent.

UNDERSTANDING WHAT YOU HAVE READ

1. Describe the contents of a written contract of sale for realty.
2. Briefly discuss five methods of acquiring real property.
3. What important steps must a buyer of realty take to effect the purchase?
4. Briefly describe each of these deeds:
   a. a quitclaim deed
   b. a bargain and sale deed
   c. a full-covenant warranty deed
5. What five covenants are usually included in a warranty deed?
6. What is the purpose of recording a deed?
7. Explain and give an example of each of the following:
   a. air rights
   b. water rights
   c. right of eminent domain
   d. easement
   e. license (as it applies to realty)
8. What is the difference between realty taxes and realty assessments?
9. What is the purpose of zoning laws?
10. a. What is a mortgage?
    b. What is the nature of another document that a lender may require a mortgagor to provide?
11. What six disclosures must the person handling a title closing make to the parties to the sale?
12. List five rights and five duties of a mortgagor of realty.

BUILDING YOUR LEGAL VOCABULARY

Match each of these legal terms with its correct definition from the list that follows. Write your answers on a separate sheet of paper.

abstract of title   escrow agreement   mortgage
easement   foreclosure   quitclaim deed
eminent domain   mechanic's lien   warranty deed
encumbrances

1. a special contract prepared in a sale of realty by which the deed to the property is delivered to a third party to hold until certain conditions have been met
2. a government's right to take private property for a public purpose on payment of just compensation
3. a document that merely releases the seller's present interest in a parcel of realty
4. a report on the quality of ownership or title of a piece of property
5. a lien created when the owner of realty borrows money and uses the property as security for repayment of the debt
6. a restriction in a deed that relates to the right to use the land of another owner for a specific purpose

7. a charge made against a landowner's real property by one whom the landowner has failed to pay for services or materials provided in the improvement of the owner's real property
8. claims, such as mortgage or tax liens, against realty
9. a document by which title to realty is conveyed and in which the grantor guarantees or covenants that he or she has complete and perfect title to the property except as to stated matters
10. the legal procedure by which a mortgagee exercises the right to cause the mortgaged property to be sold at public auction to satisfy a claim against the mortgagor

APPLYING LEGAL PRINCIPLES

1. Singer orally agreed to sell his summer home to Grozier. Later, Singer refused to deliver a deed to the property. He claimed that the contract wasn't binding because it wasn't in writing. Is his claim legally correct?

2. By deed, Borg transferred to Amara title to certain realty that she owned. Borg delivered the deed to her lawyer for safekeeping. The lawyer was instructed to send the deed back to Borg at the end of six months. Was the delivery of the deed to the lawyer a delivery in escrow?

3. Flores claimed title to land by adverse possession. He proved that for a period of more than twenty years, he had from time to time entered onto the land and cut and removed pine trees. Did Flores have title to the land?

4. Cullum sold a house and lot to Mayne and delivered a full warranty deed to Mayne. Before Mayne recorded the deed, Cullum fraudulently sold the property to Luong, an innocent buyer. Luong immediately recorded his deed in the proper public office. Shortly thereafter, Mayne recorded her deed. Who has legal title to the property?

5. While selling a building to Ono, McCloud discovered a cousin's potential claim against the building. The cousin was friendly toward McCloud and didn't want to interfere with the sale. What method may McCloud use to clear the title?

6. Salvucci bought a one-acre building lot in a new development. The deed she received at the closing provided that any house built on the lot must cost at least $100,000. Salvucci planned to build an $80,000 house. Can she be prevented from building the less expensive house?

7. For over twenty years, a neighbor passed over a corner of Altstein's land without Altstein's permission and without interruption. May Altstein now prevent the neighbor from doing so?

8. Braude owned her own home. She failed to pay real-estate taxes for a period of four years. What rights does the city have against the property?

9. Figueroa, a plumber, supplied labor and material amounting to $1,500 in repairing the heating system in Deakin's home. If Deakin fails to pay, what may Figueroa do?

10. City authorities installed new sewers on the street where Chinh's house was located. The city then sent Chinh a notice stating that her share of the cost of this improvement was $600. Was Chinh liable for payment?

11. The city of Aberdeen proposed to build a highway through property belonging to Osteen. Osteen refused to sell any of his land to the city for this purpose. What are the legal rights of the parties?

12. Janke bought a new home in an area zoned for single-family homes. In fact, the zoning laws provided that commercial enterprises were prohibited within a five-mile area. Janke soon learned that ten acres of land next to his home had been sold to a builder. The builder planned to build a shopping center on the site. What would you advise Janke to do?

13. Perham mortgaged his home for $75,000 as security for a debt. He failed to make the periodic payments of principal and interest. The mortgagee foreclosed the mortgage and the property was sold. Is it legally possible for Perham to regain title to the property?

14. A judgment was filed against Fruman by her creditors. What is the effect of this judgment?

15. For a number of years, Swope allowed a neighbor to keep a yacht tied up at Swope's private dock. Does Swope have the right to revoke this privilege?

ANALYZING COURT CASES

1. ADCO, an outdoor advertising firm, signed an agreement with a hotel owner. By the terms of the agreement ADCO was granted the exclusive right and privilege of maintaining an advertising sign on an outside wall of the hotel. ADCO installed the sign. Later, the hotel owner claimed the right to remove the sign during the agreed period. Do you agree? (*Baseball Publishing Co. v. Bruton*, 302 A. 2d 362)

2. Oliveira executed deeds to his property, naming his wife and children as grantees. He delivered the deeds to his wife and told his children of the transaction. The deeds weren't recorded until four years after Oliveira's death. McGraw, a creditor of Oliveira, claimed that the deeds didn't convey title to the property to the wife and children. Was McGraw's claim legally correct? (Based on: *McGuigan v. Heuer*, 268 N.W. 679)

3. A river flowing through Davenport's farm was navigable by canoes, rowboats, and other small craft. Occasionally, the river had been used for floating timber to market. Ogata entered the stream from a public road crossing, where she put a canoe in the river. She floated downstream, fishing as she went, until she got to the southern line of Davenport's farm. At that point, Davenport tried to stop Ogata. Did he have a legal right to do so? (Based on: *Elder v. Delcour*, 269 S.W. 2d 17)

CHAPTER 43

Renting Real Property

YOU BE THE JUDGE

Think about these cases.
If you were the judge, how would you decide each case?

1

Ogden rented an apartment in a building owned by Kravitz. One morning, while Ogden was out, a large patch of plaster fell from the ceiling of Ogden's kitchen. There was no provision for repairs in Ogden's lease, and Kravitz refused to fix the ceiling. Is he legally obligated to do so?

2

You own an unfurnished apartment building. One of your tenants has failed to pay her rent and is about to move out. You think you have the right to hold the tenant's piano as security for the unpaid rent. Are you legally entitled to hold the tenant's property?

WHAT IS A LEASE?

Owners of real property may permit others to have exclusive possession of the property. This is done by an express or implied contract known as a **lease.** The contract relationship created by a lease is generally known as that of **landlord** and **tenant** or **lessor** and **lessee.** The landlord (lessor) is the owner of the realty. The tenant (lessee) is the party who leases the realty from the owner. The consideration a tenant pays to a landlord for the use of the property is known as **rent.**

Like any other contract, a lease must be made for a lawful purpose. It may be in oral or written form. In most states, though, the Statute of Frauds provides that leases for a period longer than one year (three years, in some states) must be in writing to be enforceable. A lease for a period of one year or less may be made orally, despite the fact that the term of the lease is to begin at a future date. The term of a lease may range from one day to 99 years. Figure 43.1 is a sample of a typical written lease.

PROBLEM

> **1.** Thea had just bought a two-family house. She entered into two contracts: (a) She rented the upper apartment to Hook for one year at $800 a month. (b) She rented a furnished single room on the ground floor to Doaks for $125 a week. What legal relationship is created by each of the contracts?

The relationship of landlord and tenant differs from that of boarding-house keeper and boarder. A tenant is entitled to exclusive possession and control of the premises. A boarder or lodger, however, merely enjoys the use of the premises subject to the supervision of the boardinghouse keeper. A boardinghouse keeper has a lien on the lodger's belongings. In most states, a landlord has no lien on a tenant's possessions. In Problem 1(a), all the essentials of a valid lease are present. Thus, the legal relationship created is that of landlord and tenant. In Problem 1(b), however, the relationship created is that of boardinghouse keeper and boarder.

KINDS OF LEASES

A lease may run for a time period stated in the agreement, such as six months, one year, 21 years, or some other period. Legally, a lease for a definite term is known as a **tenancy for years.** In Problem 1(a), a tenancy for years was created because the lease was for a term of one year. However, when the parties fail to state how long the lease is to run but agree on a rent payable at fixed intervals, a **periodic tenancy** is created. A periodic tenancy may arise by the week, by the month, or so forth. It doesn't terminate until the end of any given period *after proper notice.*

Figure 43.1
A Typical Lease

HOBBS & WARREN, INC.
PUBLISHERS STANDARD LEGAL FORMS
BOSTON · MASS.

This Indenture, MADE the   15th   day of

August   in the year of our Lord one thousand nine hundred and --

Witnesseth, That   Patino Associates, Inc., 7230 Glenview Avenue, Plaza, NJ 07098, hereinafter called the Lessor,

do hereby lease, demise, and let unto George P. and Melinda S. Halas, 976 North Salem Road, West Orange, NJ 07052, hereinafter called the Lessees, the property known as Apartment No. 204 East on the second floor in the Parkview Building, situated at 7200 S.W. 83rd Street, Plaza, NJ 07098

To hold for the term of   one (1) year

from the   1st   day of September   nineteen hundred and --

                                                    total
yielding and paying therefore the/rent of   Nine thousand six hundred dollars ($9,600)

And said Lessees do   promise to pay the said rent in   advance in twelve (12) payments, the first payment of $800 on the 1st day of September, 19--, and continuing on the first day of each month thereafter for the full term of this lease.

and to quit and deliver up the premises to the Lessor, or its   attorney, peaceably and quietly at the end of the term, in as good order and condition, reasonable use and wearing thereof, fire and other unavoidable casualties excepted, as the same now are, or may be put in to by the said Lessor, and to pay the rent as above stated, during the term, and also the rent as above stated for such further time as the Lessees may hold the same, and not make or suffer any waste thereof; nor lease, nor underlet, nor permit any other person or persons to occupy or improve the same, or make or suffer to be made any alteration therein, but with the approbation of the Lessor thereto, in writing, having been first obtained and that the Lessor may enter to view and make improvements, and to expel the Lessees, if they shall fail to pay the rent as aforesaid, or make or suffer any strip or waste thereof.

And provided also,   that in case the premises, or any part thereof during said term, be destroyed or damaged by fire or other unavoidable casualty, so that the same shall be thereby rendered unfit for use and habitation, then and in such case, the rent hereinbefore reserved, or a just and proportional part thereof, according to the nature and extent of the injuries sustained, shall be suspended or abated until the said premises shall have been put in proper condition for use and habitation by the said Lessor, or these presents shall thereby be determined and ended at the election of the said Lessor or   its   legal representatives.

In witness whereof, The said parties have hereunto interchangeably set their hands and seals the day and year first above written.

Signed and sealed in presence of

Anne J. Hoe   *George P. Halas*

                                         Melinda S. Halas

Agent, Patino Associates, Inc.

Suppose in Problem 1(a) that the contract between Thea and Hook didn't mention the term for which it was to run. It merely stated that the rent was to be paid monthly at the rate of $800. In this event, the parties had created a periodic tenancy. It could be ended at the end of any month, after proper notice of termination.

If the parties enter into a lease for an indefinite term and the lease may be terminated *at any time* by either party, a **tenancy at will** is created. A tenancy at will also arises under an agreement that the tenant may remain in possession until the landlord sells the premises or constructs a new building. In most states, a landlord must give a tenant 30 days' notice if a tenancy at will is to be terminated.

IMPORTANT CLAUSES IN LEASES

There is no required form of lease. The agreement may be expressed in any words that clearly indicate the intention of the parties. Usually, a properly prepared lease contains (1) a description of the property, (2) the term or the length of time the lease is to run, (3) the amount of the rent, (4) an indication of when the rent is to be paid, (5) the date the lease is to commence, and (6) the signatures of the parties.

In addition, leases often contain clauses giving the parties legal rights and imposing on them various legal obligations. These clauses technically are considered to be covenants or conditions. However, the rights and duties of the parties also are governed by covenants not expressed in the lease but implied by law. Some of the more important covenants commonly found in leases are clauses relating to (1) quiet possession and enjoyment of the premises, (2) repairs and decorations, (3) assignment and subletting, (4) holdovers, (5) rent, (6) fire, (7) security deposits, and (8) fixtures.

Quiet Possession and Enjoyment of the Premises

2. Nieves was the lessee of an apartment under a written lease for a term of two years. He claimed that his apartment became uninhabitable when defective plumbing allowed sewer gas to escape into his apartment. After the lessor failed to remedy the defect, Nieves abandoned the apartment. Is he legally justified in doing this?

A landlord, either expressly or impliedly, makes a covenant that the tenant will enjoy undisturbed possession of the premises. A breach of this covenant is legally known as an **eviction**. A landlord may cause an eviction by direct action, such as by renting the premises to another and allowing the new tenant to possess the premises during the terms of the original tenant's lease. This results in ousting the original tenant from all or part of the leased premises. This kind of eviction is known as an **actual eviction.**

A **constructive eviction** arises when a lessor allows a certain condition to exist that interferes with the tenant's possession and makes the premises uninhabitable. In this case, the tenant may claim a constructive eviction and move out, as Nieves did in Problem 2. Thus, when a landlord fails to furnish heat as agreed or fails to remove rodents or insects from the leased premises, the courts have held that the tenant has been constructively evicted. The legal effect of a constructive eviction is that the tenant may consider the lease terminated and rightfully stop paying rent. The tenant also may bring an action against the landlord for breach of the covenant of quiet enjoyment of the premises. In the event of a constructive eviction, the tenant must vacate the premises promptly. A tenant can't claim to have been evicted while still in possession of the premises.

EXAMPLE

A tenant in an office building claimed that the air-conditioning system didn't work at night. The building was constructed with sealed windows that couldn't be opened. The tenant refused to pay rent, claiming constructive eviction. However, he did not move from the building. The court held that a tenant who continues in possession must pay rent and can't claim constructive eviction.

Repairs and Decorations

In the absence of a special agreement in the lease, the tenant must make ordinary repairs. When the lease expires, the tenant must surrender the premises in a condition as good as that at the beginning of the lease. Reasonable wear and tear and damage by the elements are exceptions to this rule. Some states have enacted statutes that impose on the lessor the duty to keep the premises in repair in certain cases. This duty generally can't be enforced by the tenant, however.

If a lease is for a part of a building, the lessor must repair the parts of the building that he or she can control, such as the roof and the stairways. If a building becomes unfit for occupancy because of a sudden act of the elements (rain, snow, and so forth), the tenant usually may surrender the premises and won't be liable for future rent.

In urban apartment buildings, landlords often do more than the lease requires because of local sanitation codes or state statutes. They paint rooms and keep floors in good condition to prevent buildings from becoming unsafe or unhealthful. They repair faucets to avoid wasting water, which might subject them to penalties.

When a landlord fails to remedy a condition that makes the premises uninhabitable, a tenant may consider the lease terminated.

EXAMPLE

Hovey owned an apartment building containing a number of apartments. The halls and stairways weren't properly maintained and needed repair. Since Hovey had control over these areas of the building, she had the legal duty to keep them in good repair. The tenants didn't have exclusive possession and control of these areas and therefore had no duty to keep them in repair.

Assignment and Subletting

PROBLEM

3. What kind of legal relationship is created by each of these two contracts?

    a. Otoya, a traveling auditor, leased a studio apartment from Matinez. The term of the lease was one year, and the rent was $525 per month. Six months after taking possession of the premises, Otoya assigned the lease to Gabler. Gabler agreed to occupy the apartment for the rest of the term at the same rental.

    b. Assume that Otoya in Problem 3(a) left on a two-month trip to South America. He agreed to let Gabler occupy the apartment during his absence at the same rental.

LIVING UNDER THE LAW

New Rights for Tenants

Laws governing landlord-tenant relationships evolved during feudal days. Until recently, landlords exercised near-feudal authority over tenants in most states. A tenant could be evicted for nonpayment of rent even though the landlord had failed to provide the tenant with safe and sanitary shelter.

Now that has changed by statute. Tenant organizations have been successful in challenging the common-law rights of landlords. As a result, extensive legal reform has occurred in most states. Do tenants take advantage of these hard-fought reforms? Many don't, according to tenant activists. They say that a widespread educational program is needed to acquaint tenants with their new rights. The following are some of the most important new tenant rights.

- **Implied Warranty.** Most states and the District of Columbia now recognize that it is the landlord's duty to comply with local housing codes and to furnish safe and habitable housing. Otherwise, tenants can sue for damages or use the warranty as a defense against eviction for nonpayment of rent.
- **Repairs.** After giving sufficient notice, the tenant in more than half the states is allowed to make minor repairs when the landlord refuses to do so. The tenant may recover the cost of the repairs by deducting the costs from future rent payments.
- **Tenant Deposits.** Laws in 80% of the states now require a prompt return of the security deposits tenants post when they move in. However, landlords are allowed to deduct, within limits, for damages caused to the premises by tenants. In some states, landlords must pay interest on the deposits.
- **Retaliation.** Tenants who report code violations or undue harassment by landlords are now protected from rent increases, utility shutoffs, or evictions. This is a far cry from what a landlord could do to an activist tenant under the common law.

In the absence of a prohibition in the lease, a tenant may assign the lease or may **sublet** all or part of the premises. To sublet is to agree to rent (or *let)* part of the remaining term of a lease.

When a lease is assigned, the tenant's *entire interest* in the premises is transferred to another, who becomes liable to the landlord. The tenant, however, remains liable to the landlord for the faithful performance of the lease by the assignee. In some states, an assignment of a lease for longer than one year must be made in writing. In Problem 3(a), Otoya transferred his entire interest in the leased apartment to Gabler. The legal relationship between the two parties was that of assignor and assignee.

When a tenant sublets the premises, *something less than the entire interest* is transferred to another. The original tenant becomes a sublessor or a landlord with respect to the subtenant or sublessee. However, the original tenant remains liable for the performance of the contract with the original landlord. In Problem 3(b), Otoya merely sublet his apartment for two months. At the end of that time, the premises were to be turned over to him again. The relationship created between Otoya and Gabler in this case was that of sublessor and sublessee.

Leases sometimes provide that a tenant may not assign or sublet a lease without the landlord's written consent. Tenants should read leases carefully to see whether assignment or subletting, or both, are prohibited.

Holdovers

When a tenant has a lease for a year or longer, the period of tenancy ends without notice on the last day of the term. If the tenant continues in possession, he or she is regarded as a **holdover.** Some courts say that if a tenant holds over even for a day, the lease is renewed for a similar period and on the same terms as the original lease. However, if the original lease was for more than a year, the holdover tenant is liable only for one more year on the lease. A tenant who can't move because of illness or some other uncontrollable reason isn't usually regarded as a holdover.

EXAMPLE

> Soong's three-year lease was to expire on July 31. Three months before July 31, Soong notified the landlord of her intention to terminate the lease. On August 1, however, Soong changed her mind and sent a check to the landlord for the August rent. The landlord deposited the check in her bank. The legal effect of the landlord's action was to renew Soong's lease for one more year.

Rent

The tenant's chief obligation is to pay the rent, which is usually a definite sum payable at a stated time. Leases often provide that the rent must be paid in advance. If they are silent on the subject, though, the rent is payable at the end of the period.

Fire

A lease usually provides that the tenant must give the landlord immediate notice of any fire and that the landlord must repair fire damage as quickly as possible. If the tenant remains in possession, the rent continues despite the fire. If the damage is so severe that the tenant is forced to move, however, the rent ceases until the property is restored to its former condition. If the building is totally destroyed by fire, the lease is no longer effective but rent is due up to the time of the fire.

Security Deposit

A landlord may require a tenant to furnish security for the faithful performance of the lease. This is called a **security deposit.** It is most often provided in the form of cash, but it also may take the form of negotiable securities or a bond that guarantees performance. Under the common law, security deposited with the lessor remains the property of the tenant. The lessor may not even use the security deposit unless the lease authorizes such use. Some states have passed laws making a lessor a trustee of the security deposit. If it is misused, the lessor is subject to criminal penalties.

Fixtures

PROBLEM

> **4.** DiSipio rented a service station and installed new fuel pumps at a considerable cost. When his lease expired, Jenkins wanted to move to a new location and to take the pumps with him. His landlord claimed that the pumps were fixtures and belonged to the realty. Is the landlord legally correct?

Tenants sometimes make improvements that are attached to the leased premises. If the improvements can't be removed without causing substantial damage to the property, the law will consider these improvements to be fixtures. Unless the lease provides otherwise, the tenant won't be permitted to remove the fixtures on termination of the lease. They are considered to have become part of the realty.

Exceptions to this rule include **trade fixtures, agricultural fixtures,** and **ornamental fixtures.** Trade fixtures are things such as bowling alleys, barber chairs, and theater seats. Agricultural fixtures consist of items such as tool sheds and henhouses. Ornamental fixtures are installed in order to make a dwelling or office more comfortable and attractive. These consist of things such as bookshelves, Venetian blinds, and chandeliers. In Problem 4, the fuel pumps installed by DiSipio were trade fixtures. Therefore, the landlord had no legal right to regard them as part of the realty.

To prevent misunderstandings, a tenant should insist on a lease clause stating that any improvements made by the tenant are to be regarded as his or her personal property. The tenant should then remove the fixtures before the lease expires. Failure to remove the fixtures may allow them to become the lessor's property.

OTHER RIGHTS OF THE LANDLORD

The landlord has the right to enter the premises to demand payment of rent. Often, the landlord also has the right to show the premises to prospective tenants. If the tenant abandons the premises, the landlord may enter them to take care of them. The landlord has the right to recover for any damages to the premises that aren't caused by normal wear and tear.

OTHER DUTIES OF THE TENANT

A tenant must use the leased premises in accordance with the terms of the lease. The tenant may not injure the property permanently. When the lease expires, the tenant must remove all of his or her personal property. Tenants are usually liable to third parties for injuries caused by the defective condition of premises that are under the tenant's control. Under certain conditions, such as when the landlord agreed to keep the premises in good repair, the tenant may recover from a landlord any damages he or she pays to a third party. However, a tenant should be sure to carry personal liability insurance as protection from the claims of third parties injured on the premises leased by the tenant.

TERMINATION OF THE LEASE

A lease, like any other contract, is usually terminated by the expiration of the period stated in the contract. Death of the lessor or tenant doesn't ordinarily terminate the contract. Leases also are terminated by (1) agreement, (2) breach of the lease by either party, (3) destruction of the premises by fire, and (4) operation of law. A lease may terminate by operation of law in cases when the state exercises the right of eminent domain or when the specified use of the premises becomes unlawful.

PROBLEM

> **5.** Kalomiris, a month-to-month tenant, was notified by her landlord on June 28 that she had to move by June 30. The landlord stated that the premises had been rented to someone else beginning July 1. Does Kalomiris have to comply with the landlord's demand?

In the case of a periodic tenancy, such as in Problem 5, the landlord must give the tenant sufficient notice, usually in writing, that the lease will be terminated. This notice must be given a certain number of days before the expiration of the tenancy. The time varies from seven to thirty days in the various states. Kalomiris's landlord isn't legally entitled to terminate the tenancy because he failed to give the required notice of termination. Kalomiris may stay at least another month.

Most landlord-tenant relationships are satisfying to all parties concerned. Because problems do arise in leases of real property, though, it's important that you know the basics of landlord-tenant law.

As mentioned in Chapter 42, inheritance is one method of acquiring real property. Inheritances often are granted in wills. In Chapter 44 we'll study the legal aspects of transferring property rights through inheritance and wills.

Chapter 43 Review

"YOU BE THE JUDGE" REVIEW

Look again at the "You Be the Judge" cases given at the beginning of this chapter. Would you decide them differently now, after your study of the chapter?

Correct Decisions

1. Yes. The landlord is required by statute to keep the premises fit for habitation. In some states an implied warranty of fitness pertains to residential premises.

2. No. A landlord does not have a lien on a tenant's personal property for unpaid rent unless an agreement or statute provides for such a lien.

UNDERSTANDING WHAT YOU HAVE READ

1. What is a lease?
2. Who are the parties to a lease?
3. What is the consideration for the lease contract?
4. What is the difference between a landlord-tenant relationship and a boardinghouse keeper–boarder relationship?
5. When must a lease be in writing?
6. Briefly describe each of the following:
   a. a tenancy for years
   b. a periodic tenancy
   c. a tenancy at will
7. What provisions should a well-drawn lease contain?

8. Briefly explain each of these clauses commonly found in leases:
   a. a clause on repairs and decorations
   b. a clause on assignment and subletting
   c. a quiet possession and enjoyment clause
   d. a rent clause
   e. a holdover clause
   f. a clause relating to fire on the premises
   g. a clause regarding a security deposit
   h. a clause dealing with fixtures
9. What is the difference between assigning a lease and subletting a leased premises?
10. How may a lease terminate?

BUILDING YOUR LEGAL VOCABULARY

Choose the legal term that will correctly complete each definition below. Write your answers on a separate sheet of paper.

1. Improvements such as theater seats and barber chairs that are attached to a premises leased for commercial purposes are known as
   a. ornamental fixtures.
   b. trade fixtures.
   c. agricultural fixtures.
2. The party who leases real property from an owner is called the
   a. lessee.
   b. lessor.
   c. holdover.
3. A lease that may be terminated at any time by either party and that runs for an indefinite term creates a
   a. periodic tenancy.
   b. tenancy at will.
   c. tenancy for years.
4. The process of forcing a tenant out of leased premises by failing to remedy a condition that interferes with the tenant's possession and makes the premises uninhabitable is called
   a. actual eviction.
   b. constructive eviction.
   c. subletting.
5. Cash, negotiable securities, or a bond left with a landlord by a tenant as assurance of the faithful performance of a lease is known as
   a. rent.
   b. damages.
   c. a security deposit.

APPLYING LEGAL PRINCIPLES

1. Recinos orally agreed to rent a seaside house from Eresian for the months of June, July, and August. On July 2, Recinos notified Eresian that she would leave the house on July 31 and wouldn't be able to use it during August. Eresian wasn't able to rent the house for the month of August. Was Recinos liable for the August rent?

2. Gemma Realty Co., as lessor, entered into a three-year written lease with Levesque. The rental unit was a one-bedroom apartment, and the rent to be paid was $600 per month. What type of tenancy did this lease create?

3. Nisi leased one apartment in a two-family house, and Gans leased the other. The landlord retained control of the basement. Rats entered all parts of the building, and the landlord made no attempt to exterminate them. Both tenants had given the landlord notice of the condition. May the tenants move out before their leases expire?

4. Kung, a wealthy importer, occupied a penthouse apartment under a five-year lease. With three more years of the lease to run, Kung died. The executor of Kung's estate, claiming that death automatically terminated the lease, refused to carry out the terms of the lease. Will the executor be able to sustain his position?

5. After Lazar's one-year lease expired, she continued to live in the rented house with her landlord's consent. The landlord informed Lazar that she had thereby renewed the lease for another year. Lazar claimed that she was now a month-to-month tenant. Do you agree with Lazar?

6. Thai rented an apartment for a period of two years. The lease required Thai to give the landlord three months' notice of his intention to move at the expiration of the lease. When the lease expired, no notice had been given to the landlord. Thai, however, sought to move out. The landlord notified Thai that the lease had been renewed for one more year under the terms of the original lease. What are the rights of the parties?

7. On March 1, Dennis signed a two-year lease, agreeing to pay $1,100 a month rent for a house owned by Cantares. On June 1, Dennis assigned her lease to Mollo and gave proper notice to Cantares. Mollo lived in the house until December 1 and then moved out while still owing two months' rent. The house remained unoccupied until March of the following year. Cantares, the lessor, then sued Dennis for $5,500, the rent due for the last five months of the lease. Was Dennis liable for this sum?

8. Mahmud rented a two-bedroom apartment from Rosoff under a two-year lease. Three months after Mahmud moved into the apartment, a fire of unknown origin totally destroyed it. Mahmud refused to continue to pay the rent. Was Mahmud within his legal rights?

9. A guest of Kanai was injured in a fall caused by a defective stairway in the apartment house where Kanai lived. The landlord claimed that Kanai was liable for the guest's injury. Is Kanai liable?

10. Osmer replaced her landlord's refrigerator with a newer model of her own. When the lease expired, she planned to put the original refrigerator back into the kitchen and take her own with her to a new apartment. The landlord claimed that the refrigerator installed by Osmer was a fixture and had become the landlord's property. Is the landlord legally correct?

ANALYZING COURT CASES

1. Stennett, the owner of land near a high-way, entered into a contract with Bor-ough Bill Posting Company. In the agreement Stennett gave the firm the ex-clusive right to erect a billboard on the land and to post advertising on the board. He reserved the right to cancel this privilege if the land was sold for building purposes. In that event, Sten-nett agreed to refund a part of the con-sideration that Borough had paid him. In a suit brought by Stennett against the firm, Borough claimed that a landlord-tenant relationship had been created. Is this claim valid? (Based on: *Stockholm v. Borough Bill Posting Co.*, 129 N.Y.S. 745, 144 A.D. 642)

2. Nova owned a building in a business district. On the ground floor she rented space to a dry cleaners and to a gift shop. The center door on the ground floor was at the top of an open stairway leading down into the basement. The door appeared to be part of a double door leading into the cleaners. There was no warning sign posted over the center door, and the door was unlocked. Dellorco, a customer, wanted to enter the cleaners but opened the center door by mistake. Before she realized her mis-take, she fell down the stairs and was injured. She sued Nova for her injuries. Was she legally entitled to collect? (Based on: *Trimble v. Spears*, 320 P. 2d 1029)

3. Rawana leased realty to Lubar. Lubar installed certain trade fixtures on the property. He had bought the fixtures on credit, and they were subject to a chattel mortgage in favor of Somol. Before the lease expired, Lubar abandoned the realty and the fixtures. Later, he claimed that he was entitled to remove the fix-tures. Was Lubar's claim legally correct? (Based on: *Rinaldi v. Goller*, 309 P. 2d 451)

CHAPTER 44

Transferring Property by Will and Inheritance

YOU BE THE JUDGE

Think about these cases.
If you were the judge, how would you decide each case?

1

Sloan, a widow, died without leaving a will. She had been nursed through her illness by her daughter. Sloan's daughter and two surviving sons agreed to divide their mother's estate by giving one-half to the daughter and one-fourth to each of the sons. Will the law allow such a division?

2

Benito's will contained a provision leaving $1 to his son. The father and son had quarreled on many occasions and hadn't been on speaking terms for years. After the father's death, the son claimed that the provision giving him a $1 inheritance was invalid. Is the son legally correct?

WHAT IS A WILL?

A person may dispose of property after death by a written document known as a **will.** Since a will doesn't take effect until after the maker's death, it may be revoked at any time. The maker can prepare a new will as often as desired.

---

1. Is this a valid will?

> I give to my wife, Geneve M. Givens, all of my real and personal property, wherever situated.
>
> June 2, 19—   Ronald T. Givens

In order for the courts to regard a will as valid, it must meet certain legal requirements. These requirements vary by state and are strictly governed by statute. As we shall see, one of the requirements is that a will be witnessed by competent witnesses. In Problem 1, Givens did not comply with this requirement. Therefore, he hasn't made a valid will.

The person making a will is known as the **testator.** All of the testator's property together is called that person's **estate.** If the testator disposes of personal property by will, the gift is legally known as a **bequest** or **legacy.** The person to whom the legacy or bequest is made is known as a **legatee.** When the testator disposes of real property by will, the gift is known as a **devise.** The person to whom it is made is called the **devisee.** In states that have adopted the **Uniform Probate Code,** all people who are given gifts through will are known as devisees. In these states, distinctions between legatee (personal property) and devisee (realty) are abolished.

A person who dies without making a will or who leaves an invalid will is said to have died **intestate.** The property of an intestate person is distributed in accordance with state laws. If a person dies intestate and leaves no relatives, the property *escheats* (passes) to the state.

WHO MAY MAKE A WILL?

The testator must be of a sound and "disposing" mind. This means that the testator must know the nature and extent of the property to be disposed of by will. The testator also must know his or her relationship to those who are to receive the property.

---

2. Kalter, eighteen and of sound mind, made a will leaving all of her personal belongings to her brother. Her brother was Kalter's only surviving relative. Was she legally competent to make a will?

In many states, a person who is at least eighteen years of age is legally competent to make a will disposing of personal or real property. If she met the age requirements of her state, Kalter in Problem 2 would be legally competent to make a will.

Although a testator may be of a sound and disposing mind and of legal age, he or she must also be free from fraud and undue influence. Usually, if fraud and undue influence are exercised on the testator, the entire will is invalid. The burden of proving fraud or undue influence rests with the party who seeks to have the will declared invalid.

REQUIRE-MENTS OF A VALID WILL

A person who has the proper qualifications for making a will also must comply strictly with the legal requirements that apply to preparing and executing wills. A will must be (1) in writing, (2) properly signed by the testator, and (3) properly witnessed. Figure 44.1 is an example of a typical will.

In Writing

The law doesn't require that any special form be used in preparing a will. Any language or wording that clearly sets forth the testator's intentions may be used. The will may be typed, handwritten, or printed. In some states, a will appearing entirely in the handwriting of the testator is valid even though it isn't witnessed. These handwritten wills are called **holographic wills.** In many states oral wills disposing of personal and sometimes real property may be made by military personnel in actual combat, or by others who think they are about to die. These are called **nuncupative wills.** These oral wills usually must have at least two witnesses. They become invalid and unenforceable on the expiration of a specified period after the military service ends.

Properly Signed by the Testator

A testator may place his or her signature anywhere on a will unless a state law provides otherwise. Usually, any mark of the testator will be a sufficient signature if the testator intends it to be a signature. Some state laws require that the testator sign at the physical end of the will. The signature should be exactly as it appears in other parts of the will. A testator should initial any page of the will that doesn't bear his or her signature.

Properly Witnessed

> **3.** How could Ronald Givens in Problem 1 have met the requirement that his will be properly witnessed?

Figure 44.1
A Typical Will
(first page)

LAST WILL AND TESTAMENT

I, JOSEPH ALBERT BENEVISTA, a resident of San Mateo County, State of California, being of sound mind, do hereby revoke any and all prior wills and codicils thereto heretofore made by me, and do make and publish this to be my Last Will and Testament.

FIRST: I direct that all my just debts, funeral expenses, and administrative expenses be paid as soon as practicable after my decease.

SECOND: All the rest, residue, and remainder of my estate, both real and personal, wheresoever situated, of which I may die seized or possessed, or to which I may in any manner be interested and entitled to at the time of my demise, I give, devise, and bequeath to my beloved wife, CYNTHIA JAMISON BENEVISTA.

THIRD: If my beloved wife shall predecease me, or she and I shall die under such circumstances that there is not sufficient evidence to determine who survived the other, then I give, devise, and bequeath all the rest, residue, and remainder of my property, both real and personal and wheresoever situated, of which I may die seized or possessed, or to which I may be entitled at the time of my death, to my beloved daughter MARIA JANE BENINO.

FOURTH: I hereby nominate, constitute, and appoint my wife, CYNTHIA JAMISON BENEVISTA, as EXECUTRIX under this my Last Will and Testament. In the event that my said wife shall predecease me or otherwise fail to qualify and to so serve, then I nominate, constitute, and appoint my beloved son-in-law, GEORGE PATRICK BENINO, as EXECUTOR in her place and stead.

Figure 44.1
*A Typical Will
(second page)*

FIFTH: I direct that no bond or undertaking be required of any EXECUTOR OR EXECUTRIX Under this Last Will and Testament in any court, place, or jurisdiction for his or her faithful performance of duties as EXECUTOR OR EXECUTRIX.

IN WITNESS WHEREOF, I have hereunto subscribed my name this 5th day of January, 19--.

Joseph Albert Benevista
JOSEPH ALBERT BENEVISTA

Subscribed by JOSEPH ALBERT BENEVISTA, the Testator named in the foregoing Last Will and Testament, in the presence of each of us, and at the time of making such subscription, the above instrument consisting of two pages was declared by said Testator to be his Last Will and Testament, and each of us, at the request of said Testator and in his presence and in the presence of each other, signed our names as witnesses thereto. In the opinion of each of us the said Testator was of sound mind and had the capacity to make said Last Will and Testament.

Witness	Address
Marilyn G. Hurley	103 Hacienda St. San Mateo CA 94403
Peter H. Hurley	103 Hacienda St. San Mateo CA 94403
Sarah M. Seto	236 Highland Ave. Palo Alto CA 94303

Anyone who can be sworn and can testify in court is usually a competent witness to a will. The testator should ask at least three competent people to act as witnesses. Preferably all should be younger than the testator. It's important that those selected be disinterested persons, unrelated to the testator and not mentioned in the will as beneficiaries. (In states that have adopted the Uniform Probate Code, interest does *not* disqualify a witness or invalidate a gift made under the will.) Witnesses should be shown the will and told that it is the testator's last will and testament. The testator should specifically ask the witnesses to sign the document as witnesses. While the witnesses look on, the testator should sign the will. The witnesses should then sign their names and addresses in the presence of one another and of the testator. No change should be made in a will after it has been properly executed. It isn't necessary that the witnesses know the contents of the will. Ronald Givens, in Problem 3, should have followed these steps in order for his will to have been properly witnessed.

A will may be revoked by tearing it up or burning it.

CHANGING OR REVOKING A WILL

A testator may tear up or burn an old will and prepare a new one. However, the same formal steps must be taken when preparing the new will as were taken when preparing the original will.

> Bianco prepared a will in the proper legal manner, leaving $10,000 to his daughter. A year later, Bianco tore up the will and properly prepared another one. In the new will, the daughter received the sum of $1. The first will was revoked, and the new will became Bianco's last will and testament.

There is still another method that a testator can use to change a will. An addition or supplement to the old will may be prepared. This is legally known as a **codicil.** The testator may note any desired changes in the codicil. It's important to remember, though, that the codicil also must be in writing, signed by the testator, and properly witnessed.

CARRYING OUT THE PROVISIONS OF A WILL

A will merely gives legal instructions as to how the testator's property is to be distributed. Someone must see that these instructions are carried out. The person who does this is called an **executor** (or an **executrix** if a woman). (The Uniform Probate Code refers to both executor and executrix as *personal representatives.*) The executor/executrix is usually chosen by the testator and named in the will. Anyone of legal age may serve in this capacity. The testator's husband or wife, sister, brother, lawyer, a bank, or even a friend may qualify. Of course, the person selected must be willing to accept the responsibility. If the person named is willing to serve, he or she will submit the will to a **probate court** or **surrogate's court** for **probate.** As mentioned in the "Living Under the Law" feature on page 550, probate is the process of establishing the validity of a will and administering a decedent's estate. The court will hold a hearing to determine the validity of the will. At the hearing, the witnesses to the will testify that they signed as witnesses at the testator's request. If the court is satisfied that the will is valid, the executor or executrix will receive **letters testamentary.** This document is a certificate of authority to act.

> **4.** Quen is appointed executrix under Priebe's last will and testament. What are Quen's duties?

Why You Should Make a Will

Many people resent any government interference with their private lives. However, many of those same people are content to let their state governments decide who gets their property after they die. Lawyers estimate that more than half of all citizens go to their graves without leaving wills.

Various reasons have been given to explain why people fail to express their intentions while they are fully able to do so. The reasons range from forgetfulness to naive confidence that the state's distribution of the property will reasonably reflect their own wishes.

What are some of the things a will can accomplish? Estate experts claim that these are the most important:

- You, not the state, decide who gets your property.
- You may name the estate executor or executrix (personal representative) of your choice.
- You may name the guardian of your minor children.
- You may make gifts, effective at or after your death, to charity.
- You may create a trust in your will whereby your estate or a portion of it will be kept intact, with income distribution for the benefit of those you name.
- You decide who bears any tax burden, rather than the law making that decision for you.

What happens if you fail to make a will?

- Your property will be distributed according to a formula fixed by law. The formula is rigid and makes no exceptions for parties who may be in need.
- The court appoints an administrator or representative whom you may or may not have known. Usually, this isn't the person you would have selected to manage your estate.
- The cost of probating your estate may be greater than if you had made a will.
- Your estate may be subject to greater court supervision.

It's entirely possible for a person to make his or her own will if it's a simple one. However, a substantial estate requires a will prepared by a trained professional.

Remember, everyone needs a will!

After receiving the letters testamentary, the executor or executrix must make an inventory of all the testator's property that has not been disposed of by bequest or devise. Then the property must be converted into cash. For example, the executor or executrix may sell the testator's stocks and bonds to pay legacies or to meet the testator's debts. Also, the executor/executrix must pay all taxes, administration expenses, funeral expenses, and other debts. The remaining property is then distributed according to the terms of the will. After submitting a report called an **accounting** to the probate court, the executor/executrix is discharged. These are the duties that will be required of Quen in Problem 4.

A personal representative, such as an executor or executrix, must submit an accounting to the probate court.

INTESTACY

The condition of being intestate is called **intestacy.** The property of a person who dies intestate (without a valid will) can't be distributed in the way that person actually intended. As a result, the real and personal property of that person will be distributed according to the state laws of descent.

PROBLEM

> **5.** Linsky owned a considerable amount of real and personal property. He died suddenly at the age of 40, leaving no will. His wife and his parents were his only surviving relatives. How will his property be distributed?

Because the states differ in the way they distribute intestate property, you should check your own state statutes on this topic. However, all states follow this common pattern:

1. When the deceased leaves only a wife or husband, the surviving spouse inherits all the property.
2. When the deceased leaves a spouse and children, the surviving spouse is entitled to one-third of the property. The remaining two-thirds is divided equally among the children. (In states that follow the Uniform Probate Code, the surviving spouse receives the first $20,000 in value plus half the remaining estate.)
3. When the deceased leaves only a spouse and both parents, the spouse receives one-half and the parents receive the remaining half of the estate. This is the distribution that will be made of Linsky's estate in Problem 5.

The probate or surrogate's court will appoint an **administrator** (*personal representative* under the Uniform Probate Code) to take charge of the intestate person's property. The administrator serves under the court's supervision. The certificate of authority issued to this party is known as **letters of administration.** Usually, the administrator is the decedent's surviving spouse. Before the letters of administration are issued, the administrator must post a bond. The bond guarantees that the administrator will perform his or her duties faithfully. These duties are essentially the same as those of an executor or executrix.

The Importance of a Will

Many people postpone making a will until it's too late. We've already seen that their property is distributed under state laws as intestate property. Property distributed in this way may be given to people for whom it had never been intended.

Any but the most simple of wills should be prepared by a lawyer.

Itturalde, a wealthy woman, died intestate. She left only a step-daughter whom she loved and a nephew whom she couldn't tolerate. Under the state's intestacy laws, the nephew was first in line for Itturalde's property. The stepdaughter was left without a cent.

If Itturalde had drawn up a proper will, her nephew would not have gotten her property. A competent lawyer should prepare all but the most simple wills.

A will should be left with the lawyer or with a bank. It shouldn't be left in the testator's safe-deposit box. After the testator's death, a court order is needed to open a safe-deposit box. This may cause undue hardship to the decedent's family and to the executor or executrix.

This unit has explained the legal aspects of owning and renting property. You've learned how to acquire property and how to dispose of it properly. You've also learned how to avoid some of the common problems that arise when you own, rent, or distribute property.

At this point in your study, you're quite familiar with the concept of ownership. However, there is still another kind of ownership that we haven't discussed. That is ownership of a business, which we'll address in Unit 10.

Chapter 44 Review

"YOU BE THE JUDGE" REVIEW

Look again at the "You Be the Judge" cases given at the beginning of this chapter. Would you decide them differently now, after your study of the chapter?

Correct Decisions

1. No. The three children will have to share their mother's estate according to the inheritance laws of the state in which their mother lived.

2. No. A parent may disinherit a child, especially where the intention to do so is clearly stated in the will.

UNDERSTANDING WHAT YOU HAVE READ

1. What is a will?
2. Who can make a valid will?
3. What are the requirements of a valid will?
4. Briefly describe how a will should be signed and witnessed.
5. How may a will be changed or revoked?
6. What is the purpose of a codicil? How must it be executed?
7. Why must a will be probated?
8. What are the duties of a personal representative under the Uniform Probate Code?
9. How is the property of an intestate person distributed?
10. Why is it important that everyone have a will?

BUILDING YOUR LEGAL VOCABULARY

From this list, select the legal term that belongs in the blank in each sentence below. Write your answers on a separate sheet of paper.

administrator

bequest

codicil

devise

executor/executrix

intestate

letters testamentary

nuncupative wills

probate

testator

1. An estate's ▨▨▨▨▨▨ is the party who sees that the instructions given in a will are carried out.
2. One who dies ▨▨▨▨▨ has died without leaving a will.
3. The maker of a will is known as the ▨▨▨▨▨▨.
4. A ▨▨▨▨▨ is a gift of personal property made by will.
5. Oral wills made by military personnel or by others who think they are about to die are called ▨▨▨▨▨.
6. ▨▨▨▨▨ is the process of establishing the validity of a will and administering a decedent's estate.
7. The person appointed by a court to take charge of the property of a decedent who had no valid will is called the ▨▨▨▨▨.
8. A gift of real property made by will is legally known as a ▨▨▨▨▨.
9. A ▨▨▨▨▨ is an addition or supplement that changes an existing will.
10. A probate or surrogate's court authorization to an executor or executrix to act in carrying out the provisions of a will is known as ▨▨▨▨▨.

APPLYING LEGAL PRINCIPLES

1. Corbin bought a printed form of will in a stationery store. Then she carefully filled in the blank spaces in her own handwriting, using a ballpoint pen. Later the document was properly signed and witnessed. Is it a valid will?

2. Shortly before his death, Soo wasn't able to recall how much real and personal property he actually owned. Also, he couldn't recognize his closest relatives, to whom he intended to give most of his property. Was Soo legally competent to make a will?

3. Hailer, who could neither read nor write, signed her will in the presence of witnesses with an *X*. Was this a proper signature?

4. Under the provisions of Floro's will, his daughter Alexis received a legacy of $5,000 in cash. The remaining property was left to Floro's wife. The daughter sought to have the will set aside on the sole ground that her share was inadequate. Is she legally entitled to do so?

5. Cass made a will in which she left a legacy of $25,000 to her son. Later, Cass tore up that will and prepared a new one, disinheriting her son. Did the second will revoke the first one?

6. Upon Chau's death, his safe-deposit box contained two properly executed wills. One was dated June 15, 1978, and the other was dated October 12, 1987. Each will left all of Chau's property to different friends and relatives. Which will should the court accept?

7. Clancy, named as a beneficiary in Wesson's will, was asked to witness the will. Was Clancy eligible to do so?

8. After Feliciano executed his will, he decided to give $1,000 to the Hillcrest Orphanage. He formally executed a codicil to his will to make this bequest. Was the codicil valid?

9. Lin died intestate. She was survived by her husband, two minor sons, and her father. The net amount to be distributed after payment of taxes, debts, and administration expenses was $150,000. How should the estate be distributed?

10. Mohr willed his estate, consisting of a piece of land worth $16,000, to his son. At the time of his death, Mohr was indebted to Bell for $5,000. The son claimed that he was entitled to the real property and that the $5,000 debt of his father had been canceled by death. Was Bell entitled to receive $5,000 from Mohr's estate?

ANALYZING COURT CASES

1. Kehr wanted to change her will, which was in her attorney's possession. She wrote the attorney, saying that she had changed her mind about the will he was holding for her and had canceled it. At the top of her unsigned carbon copy of the will, she wrote the words "null and void." Then she signed her initials underneath and put the copy with her personal belongings. After Kehr's death, the letter to the attorney couldn't be found. Had the will been revoked? (In re: *Kehr's Estate*, 95 A. 2d 647)

2. Snyder wrote the following one-line statement: "I give all that I possess to my beloved nephew, Hendley Jones." The writing was dated and signed. Upon her death the writing was admitted to probate as a valid will. Was the probate court's action proper? (*Poindexter v. Jones*, 106 S.E. 2d 144)

3. Ewing died intestate, and one of his brothers made the funeral arrangements. The estate's administrator refused to pay the funeral home's bill on the ground that the estate hadn't contracted for the funeral. Was the estate liable for the funeral bill, assuming that the bill was reasonable? (In re: *Ewing's Estate*, 14 N.W. 2d 663)

UNIT 10

OWNING
A BUSINESS

CHAPTERS

606

LEARNING OBJECTIVES

After you have studied this unit, you should be able to:

- Identify the types of business organizations recognized by law.

- Distinguish between a single proprietorship and a partnership.

- Show how a partnership operates, describe the rights of the partners, and explain their duties to each other and to third parties.

- Describe the ways a partnership terminates.

- Show that you understand the concept of stock ownership in a corporation and describe the various kinds of stock ownership.

- Explain the legal rights and duties of stockholders, directors, and officers of a corporation.

- Discuss government's role in regulating corporations.

CHAPTER 45

Sole Proprietorships and Partnerships

Think about these cases.
If you were the judge, how would you decide each case?

1	2
Ricardo, a partner in the firm of Ricardo & Stein, wants to sell her interest in a computer belonging to the firm. Can she legally do so without Stein's consent?	Ryan is a partner in a limited partnership. His name isn't included in the firm name. He invested $50,000 in the firm and agreed to keep the books on a part-time basis. Is Ryan a general partner?

THE MEANING OF BUSINESS

The word **business** has a variety of meanings today. Sometimes it's used to describe a person's work or occupation—what the person does to earn a living. More often, people use the term *business* to mean the act of exchanging goods and services for a profit, or an enterprise that exists for that purpose.

> **1.** Yeh and Reynard decided to raise money for the Huntsdale Community Chest. Yeh used his own car during the campaign and paid his own expenses. Reynard paid postage and advertising bills for the promotion of the drive. Together, they collected $11,000 for the fund. Were Yeh and Reynard engaged in a business enterprise?

The arrangement described in Problem 1 is not a business enterprise. It wasn't undertaken for the purpose of earning a living or making a profit. It was merely a voluntary association of people for a charitable purpose.

TYPES OF BUSINESS ORGANIZA-TIONS

The law recognizes many kinds of business organizations. In order to be legally recognized, a business must adopt a form of ownership that has legal approval. In all states, the law recognizes these businesses: (1) the sole proprietorship, (2) the general partnership, (3) the limited partnership, and (4) the corporation. Within recent years, a specialized organization known as the **professional service corporation** has been authorized by statute in many states. This enables doctors, dentists, lawyers, and other professional people to obtain some of the tax advantages enjoyed by corporations. We'll discuss corporations in Chapter 46.

There are other forms of business organizations that are sometimes used in special situations. These are the joint-stock company, the business trust, the joint venture, and the cooperative association. Because these types of organizations don't have equal recognition in the various states, we won't discuss them here.

Sole Proprietorships

The **sole proprietorship,** a business owned by one person, is the oldest and most familiar type of business organization.

> **2.** Devaney owned and operated a gourmet foods shop in the city of White Pines. She contracted to buy a competing shop located across the street from her own. May Devaney do so without obtaining the consent of the city or state authorities?

Anyone who is competent to make contracts may engage in business as a sole **proprietor** (owner). No formal permission is needed except where the law requires a license to do business. In Problem 2, Devaney needs no permission from the authorities to buy the competing shop. In general, a business may be operated in any manner the proprietor chooses as long as there is no interference with the rights of others. The proprietor, however, must observe federal, state, and local laws that relate to taxation, minimum wages, sanitation, and other matters.

Contracts with others are made by the sole proprietor or by agents in the proprietor's behalf. The sole proprietor retains all profits and bears the full loss from business operations. Liability to creditors for business debts extends to the proprietor's own property. Unlike some other forms of ownership, a sole proprietorship ceases to exist in the case of the death, imprisonment, or insanity of the individual owner.

General Partnerships

PROBLEM

> **3.** Seven people entered into an agreement to manufacture furniture. Their agreement provided that each member would have an equal voice in the management of the business. Also, the profits and losses were to be divided equally among the seven. Was this association a partnership?

The law of partnership as expressed in case law and in the **Uniform Partnership Act (UPA)** is founded on legal principles originating in the Roman civil law, the law merchant, and the English common law. The aim of the UPA is to improve the common law of partnership and to establish uniformity among state laws of partnership. A **partnership** is an association of two or more individuals to carry on a business for profit as co-owners. A **co-owner** is a person who not only shares in the profits but also has a voice in the business's management. This person may act as agent for the firm in the transaction of partnership business. The individuals in Problem 3 are conducting a business for profit as co-owners. Therefore, the association is a partnership.

A partnership form of organization has many advantages.

1. It is easily formed by agreement between individuals, and the state is not a party to that agreement.
2. It may operate in more than one state without having to comply with many legal restrictions.
3. Generally, each owner has an equal voice in the management of the business.
4. It is subject to less governmental regulation and supervision than a corporation.

A **general partnership** is one in which all of the partners have unlimited liability for the partnership debts and participate equally in running the business. They are known as **general partners.** This kind of partnership has many of the advantages of the sole proprietorship. In addition, it has the advantages of larger capital resources and specialized managerial skills. However, it also has certain disadvantages. First, a partner's liability for the debts of the partnership is unlimited. Second, a partnership is dissolved anytime a member withdraws or dies. Third, only a limited number of individuals may conduct a business in the partnership form.

Limited Partnerships

PROBLEM

4. Diedrich and Jabour wanted to enter the building construction business. Diedrich was an expert in the construction of apartment buildings but had no funds to invest. Jabour knew nothing about construction but was willing to contribute all the capital needed. What form of business organization should Jabour choose?

The distinctive feature of a **limited partnership** is that the liability of one or more partners is limited. However, there must always be at least one general partner in the firm who is subject to unlimited personal liability for the firm's debts. **Limited partners** contribute cash or property but *not services.* They may not participate in the management of the business or exercise any control over the business. If they do, they become liable as general partners, with unlimited liability. Limited partners have a right to receive a share of the profits and to inspect the financial records of the business. They are entitled to a return of their investment if the business is dissolved. A limited partnership can be formed only if a statute such as the **Uniform Limited Partnership Act (ULPA)** authorizes it. Most states have adopted the ULPA. Its purpose is to permit some investors to have limited liability for a partnership's debts in return for forsaking the right to participate in the firm's management.

A limited partnership may be formed by two or more people who sign and swear to a certificate setting forth the essential details of the partnership. These details include the name of the partnership; the nature and location of the business; the name and place of residence of each partner, whether general or limited; the amount of cash or property contributed by each partner; and the share of profit each limited partner is to receive. The **Certificate of Limited Partnership** must be filed in the county where the partnership has its principal place of business.

The limited partnership is used in many new businesses and especially in real-estate enterprises such as shopping centers and apartment buildings.

CAREERS IN LAW

Court Reporter

Of the many opportunities for careers in law, the most overlooked may be that of court reporter. A court reporter records everything that is said during a legal proceeding. The reporter or stenographer uses a special typing machine to record the transcript in a form of code called *machine shorthand*. Then the reporter transcribes the coded notes into typed pages and gives them to the clerk of the court. These typed pages become the court's official record of the proceeding and are usually available to the public.

Some court reporters are employees of the court, while many are self-employed. Those who are self-employed contract their services to the judicial system. They can be in control of their own time schedules and work as much or as little as they choose. The rate of pay varies, depending on the nature of the job and the court in which the work is performed. Generally, though, court reporters are well paid.

Reporters who can transcribe legal proceedings into foreign languages are in special demand. Fluency in a second language is a valuable asset in this field because some parties or witnesses in legal cases don't speak English.

Training in court stenography is available at many junior colleges and at vocational and business schools. The training period is often two years. A trainee must then pass a test to become certified as a court reporter. The training is fairly rigorous. As you can imagine, court reporters must be highly skilled and have excellent manual dexterity in order to capture every word spoken at a legal proceeding. However, the rewards of this career can be great.

The investor in such enterprises enjoys limited liability and certain income tax advantages. The general partners conduct the everyday business and assume responsibility for debts of the firm. In Problem 4, Jabour should choose the limited partnership form of business organization. This will limit her liability for debts to the extent of her investment.

FORMATION OF A PARTNERSHIP

A partnership doesn't exist if two or more people engage in a public or private enterprise without intending to earn or share profits. However, people who don't consider themselves partners may be conducting a business that is a legal partnership.

> **5.** Several people entered into an agreement to write and sell advertising. Their enterprise was known by different names at various times. Scott, one of the members, signed an agreement with her associates stating that she wasn't to be regarded as a partner. Profits and losses were to be divided equally among the members. Was this legally a partnership?

According to the Uniform Partnership Act, *a partnership exists when two or more people voluntarily combine their skill, labor, and usually their capital for the purpose of conducting as co-owners a business for profit.* In Problem 5, Scott is legally regarded as a partner in spite of her contrary intention. She is a co-owner of a voluntary association conducting a business for profit. The basic test is: Are the essential elements of a partnership present, including a share of the profits and losses and a voice in the management? If so, it's immaterial what the parties think or declare. An implied partnership exists, based on their actions and conduct. However, the mere fact that the parties call themselves "partners" doesn't legally create a partnership. The terms of the agreement must, in the eyes of the law, show that a partnership was intended and does in fact exist. Suppose someone receives a share of the net profits of a business in payment of a debt, wages, rent, or interest on a loan. Does that make the person a partner? The Uniform Partnership Act states that in such cases, a partnership agreement is not to be assumed.

> Conklin owned a factory building that he rented to Matsuda, a toy manufacturer. Their agreement provided that Matsuda was to pay Conklin ten percent of the profits of her business as rent. No partnership arose through the mere payment of some of the net profits as rent.

THE PARTNERSHIP CONTRACT

A partnership agreement may be made orally or in writing, or it may be implied from the actions of the parties. However, the essentials of a valid contract—mutual assent, competent parties, legal purpose, and consideration—must be present.

> **6.** Cameron and Schuyler orally agreed that each was to contribute $30,000 in cash toward purchasing and operating a hotel. Cameron was to be in charge during the day and Schuyler at night. The partnership was to last for a period of two years. All profits and losses were to be divided equally. Was the agreement binding?

To avoid misunderstandings, it's advisable that a contract of partnership be drawn up in writing. This contract usually is called **Articles of Partnership** or a **Certificate of Co-Partnership.** It contains provisions regarding the duties of each partner, salaries, division of profits, and the like. Figure 45.1 is a sample of fairly typical Articles of Partnership.

Remember, the Statute of Frauds states that a contract that can't be performed within a year from the time it is made must be evidenced in writing. This provision applies to partnership contracts and should be carefully observed by the partners. Thus, the oral agreement in Problem 6 isn't binding. Because the partnership relationship was to last for two years, the contract had to have been in writing.

Articles of Partnership usually specify the rights, powers, and duties of each partner. A general partner is publicly and actively engaged in transacting the firm's business. A partner who doesn't take an active part in conducting the business is known as a **silent partner.** A silent partner may or may not be known to the public as a partner. If unknown to the public, a silent partner is often called a **dormant** (sleeping) **partner.** A **secret partner** is one who takes an active part in the firm's management but isn't known to the public as a partner.

A minor who is a member of a partnership may withdraw from the firm at any time before reaching majority. However, the minor's investment in the firm can't be withdrawn if the withdrawal would make it impossible for the firm's creditors to collect what is due them.

Rights of Partners

The Articles of Partnership should state the rights of the individual partners. When no agreement exists, the partners' rights are governed by the Uniform Partnership Act and by the common law. Some of the important rights of partners include (1) sharing in the management of the business, (2) sharing profits and losses, (3) inspecting books and records, and (4) repayment of loans, with interest.

Figure 45.1
*Articles of
Partnership*

ARTICLES OF PARTNERSHIP

(1) Names of partners

(2) Nature of business

(3) Name of partnership

(4) Place of business

(5) Duration of partnership

(6) Duties of partners

(7) Contribution of capital

(8) Interest of partners

(9) Accounting

(10) Salaries of partners

(11) Drawing account

(12) Termination

ARTICLES OF PARTNERSHIP, made this 1st day of October, 19--, between ELIZABETH A. BORSOS, residing at 1129 Woodall Way, in the City of Boise, Idaho, and MICHAEL L. MAYO, residing at 529 Lightfoot Drive, in the City of Boise, Idaho, as follows:

THE ABOVE-NAMED PARTIES AGREE to become partners in the business of manufacturing and selling baked goods, and by these presents do agree to become partners under the firm name of Bread 'n' Bagels, at 301 North Second Street, City of Boise, Idaho, and that said partnership is to begin on the first above-mentioned date and to continue for two (2) years thereafter.

AND IT IS AGREED by and between the parties that at all times during the continuance of this partnership, they and each of them will give their entire time and attention to the business, and to the best of their endeavors and of their skill and power exert themselves for their joint interest, profit, benefit, and advantage in the aforesaid business.

AND IT IS AGREED by and between the parties that each shall contribute to the capital of the partnership the sum of Five Thousand Dollars ($5,000), the receipt of which is mutually acknowledged.

AND IT IS AGREED by and between the parties that they shall and will at all times during the continuance of said partnership bear, pay, and discharge equally between them all necessary expenses that may be required for the maintenence and management of said business, and that all profit and increase that shall arise by means of their said business shall be divided equally between them, and all loss that shall happen to their said business shall be equally borne between them.

AND IT IS AGREED by and between the parties that they shall have and keep at all times during the said partnership true books of account, and that the said partners shall render each to the other a true and perfect inventory and account of all profit and increase every six (6) months, or more often if necessary.

AND IT IS AGREED by and between the parties that each partner shall draw a salary of Nine Hundred Dollars ($900) a month, and shall be entitled to draw from the profits, beginning on the 15th day of April, 19--, and on the 15th of the month at each succeeding half-year, one quarter of the profits for the preceding period of six (6) months, or a greater equal proportion thereof, as may from time to time be agreed upon.

AND IT IS AGREED by and between the parties that at the end of the partnership they shall render complete accounts of all their dealings with the business, and all property of whatever kind or character shall be divided equally between them.

IN WITNESS WHEREOF, we have hereunto set our hands and seals this 1st day of October, 19--.

Elizabeth A. Borsos (L.S.)
Elizabeth A. Borsos

Michael L. Mayo (L.S.)
Michael L. Mayo

In the presence of:

Pierre L. Freeman

Sharing in the Management

Each general partner has an equal voice in the management and control of the business. However, the partners may provide in the Articles of Partnership for a division of authority and responsibility. In the absence of agreement, a majority of the partners can decide all matters except those that require unanimous consent.

Sharing Profits and Losses

PROBLEM

> **7.** Salza and DiCenso conducted a real-estate brokerage business as partners. Their partnership agreement didn't mention how profits and losses were to be shared. At the end of the year, the partnership books showed a profit of $16,000. How should the profits be divided?

Regardless of the amount of capital contributed, partners are entitled to share profits and losses *equally* unless they agree otherwise. In Problem 7, therefore, the $16,000 profit will be divided equally between Salza and DiCenso. Unless the partnership agreement provides for salaries, a partner isn't entitled to pay for services rendered. This is true even if a partner has to perform extra services because his or her copartner is ill.

Inspecting Books and Records

All partnership transactions must be fully and accurately recorded in the partnership books. These records must be available for inspection by any or all of the partners.

Repayment of Loans with Interest

Under the Uniform Partnership Act, a partner who advances money to the firm as a personal loan becomes a creditor of the firm. He or she is entitled to interest from the date of the loan until repayment is made, even if no interest payment is specified.

Duties of Partners

The relationship between partners is one of mutual trust and confidence. Each partner is an agent for the firm, acting within the scope of the partnership business. Thus, each partner has the power to bind the co-partners and to make them liable for the actions of individual partners. This liability is unlimited, extending even to the partners' personal assets. Therefore, when carrying out their duties, it is important that partners (1) exercise good faith and loyalty to each other, (2) use reasonable care and skill in performing their duties, and (3) render an accounting of all business transacted for the firm.

Good Faith and Loyalty

> **8.** Feldman, a partner in the firm of Feldman and Dwan, received a secret commission of five percent on all partnership purchases made during the year. Dwan claimed that the commissions belonged to the partnership and should be divided between them. Feldman disputed this claim. Who is right?

A partnership is a personal relationship that requires the highest degree of good faith and loyalty on the part of its members. This implies that a partner must not take advantage of the firm by making secret profits or commissions. A partner also should not use funds belonging to the firm for personal benefit. In Problem 8, Dwan is correct in his claim that the commissions secretly collected by Feldman belong to the firm. Feldman's failure to treat the commissions as partnership earnings constitutes a breach of good faith.

A partner must devote full time to the partnership business. He or she may not engage in business enterprises that might be in competition with the partnership or that prevent the partner from properly performing his or her partnership duties. Also, if a partner knows of any important matters that affect the firm's operations and fails to inform the copartners, it is regarded as a breach of good faith.

Reasonable Care and Skill

Partners must exercise reasonable care and skill in carrying out their partnership duties. They are liable for any loss suffered by the partnership if they are grossly negligent. They aren't liable, however, for honest mistakes or errors in judgment.

> Halliday was authorized by her copartners to invest some of the firm's money in corporate stock. On the recommendation of a stockbroker at a well-known brokerage firm, Halliday bought 200 shares of a certain common stock. The price of the stock soon declined, and the partnership sold it at a considerable loss. Halliday's copartners sought to hold her personally liable for the loss. Since Halliday acted with reasonable care and skill in selecting the investment, she can't be held personally liable.

Accounting of Firm Business

All partners must prepare and turn over to the partnership an accurate accounting of any business transactions made for the firm. The burden of proving the accuracy of each item in an accounting is on the partner who submitted the record.

Giordano and Klein were partners in a wholesale grocery business. Klein refused to account for any of the profits. He also refused to let Giordano inspect the books and records. Klein is under a duty to render a proper accounting to his partner and must allow Giordano to inspect the books.

A partner who has the duty of keeping the books and records for the partnership must do so in a proper manner.

Powers of Partners

Since a partner is an agent of the partnership for the transaction of its business, the principles of agency law apply to the partner's conduct. It follows, therefore, that each partner has the authority to bind the partnership to contracts relating to the firm's business. A contract that isn't actually or apparently related to the partnership's business isn't binding unless authorized by the remaining partners.

9.   Nocito and Madoff are partners in a law practice. Without Nocito's knowledge or consent, Madoff borrowed $7,000 from a loan company. She deposited the funds in the firm's bank account. At maturity, Nocito refused to pay the debt. He claimed that Madoff had no authority to borrow money for the partnership. Is the partnership liable?

The powers of partners are so extensive that a partner whose honesty or ability are in doubt shouldn't be accepted. Usually, the powers of a partner in a **trading partnership**—one that buys and sells goods—are much broader than those of a partner in a **nontrading partnership.** A nontrading partnership is one formed for professional purposes, such as the practice of law, medicine, or accountancy. The partnership in Problem 9 isn't liable for the $5,000 debt incurred by Madoff. A partner in a nontrading firm has no power to borrow money unless authorized by the other partners.

Trading Partnerships

In a trading partnership, partners may exercise these powers:

1. Buy on credit. Third parties have a right to rely on a partner's authority to make credit purchases of goods ordinarily dealt in by the firm. The fact that a partner wasn't actually authorized to do so has no effect on the rights of innocent third parties who know nothing of the partner's lack of authority.

2. Borrow money. In trading partnerships, it is customary for partners to borrow money. For this purpose they may make, accept, and indorse negotiable instruments in the firm's name.
3. Receive payment of debts due the firm.
4. Hire agents and employees to conduct the firm's business.
5. Sell all or part of the firm's stock of goods and give warranties in connection with sales.
6. Make binding contracts relating to the firm's business.

Nontrading Partnerships

A partner in a nontrading partnership usually has no power to bind the firm by purchasing on credit or borrowing money in the firm's name. This was the case in Problem 9. An agreement among partners to limit themselves in the exercise of these powers isn't binding on third parties who aren't aware of the agreement. An unauthorized act committed by a partner may be ratified (as in agency) by the remaining partners.

LIABILITIES OF PARTNERS

There are two forms of liability that apply to partnerships. The first is tort liability, and the second is contract liability.

Tort Liability

Under the Uniform Partnership Act, partners are liable jointly and individually for any torts committed by a copartner, agent, or employee acting within the scope of the firm's business.

EXAMPLE

> Silton was a partner in the firm of Jacobs and Silton. While driving the firm's delivery truck, Silton negligently injured Leiva who then sued both Jacobs and Silton to recover damages for his injuries. Jacobs claimed that she wasn't liable because she wasn't driving at the time of the accident. However, Silton's tort was committed while he was acting within the scope of the firm's business. Therefore, Jacobs also is liable for her partner's negligent acts. Leiva may elect to sue both partners jointly (together) or individually.

Contract Liability

Unless statutes provide otherwise, partners are liable jointly on partnership contracts. A partner doesn't agree to become individually liable on a partnership contract. Rather, he or she agrees to be liable *collectively* with all the other partners. Thus, a party who sues a partnership for breach of contract must sue all firm members and bring all of them into court. Otherwise, any partners not mentioned in the suit escape liability.

EXAMPLE

> The partnership of Appel, Birney, and Coan owed $5,000 to Dao. Dao brought suit against Appel alone and obtained a judgment against him. When she couldn't collect the full amount from Appel, Dao sought to bring another action against Birney and Coan for the balance. In most states, Dao wouldn't be allowed to do so. Partners must be sued jointly. Failure to do so will release the partners who weren't joined in the original suit.

People admitted as partners into an existing partnership are liable for all partnership debts incurred before their admission into the firm. However, under the Uniform Partnership Act, their liability extends only to the amount of their investment in the partnership.

DISSOLUTION OF A PARTNERSHIP

The Uniform Partnership Act defines a **dissolution** as the change in partners' relationships that occurs when a partner ceases to be associated with the firm or when a new partner is admitted. A partnership may be dissolved by (1) the acts of the parties, (2) the withdrawal of a partner, (3) death or bankruptcy, and (4) a court decree.

Acts of the Parties

A partnership is dissolved at the end of the period stated in the partnership agreement, or when the purpose for which the partnership was created has been performed. The partners also may dissolve the firm by an agreement made at any later time. If there is no agreement as to how long the partnership is to exist, any partner may lawfully dissolve the firm at any time.

Withdrawal of a Partner

A partnership is dissolved by the voluntary withdrawal of one of the partners. However, if the withdrawal violates the terms of the partnership agreement, the violating partner will be liable for damages for breach of contract.

Death or Bankruptcy

The death or bankruptcy of a partner or the bankruptcy of the partnership dissolves the firm unless the partnership agreement provides otherwise.

Court Decree

PROBLEM

> **10.** Molinda, a partner in the firm of Ming, Molinda & Co., was dishonestly transacting partnership business. His copartners discovered his dishonesty. What are the rights of the parties?

If a partner becomes insane or the business is being carried on at a heavy loss, a partnership may be dissolved by a **court decree** (ruling). Misconduct such as dishonesty and constant violation of the partnership agreement will entitle innocent partners to apply for dissolution by court decree. In Problem 10, Molinda's partners may request a court to dissolve their partnership.

WINDING UP PARTNERSHIP AFFAIRS

After dissolution, the partnership remains in existence until all its affairs have been wound up. No new contracts or business may be entered into during this period. The partners can't bind the firm by any new agreements except those needed to wind up the partnership affairs. If the dissolution is due to a partner's withdrawal, that partner remains liable for the debts due the old creditors of the firm. Unless personal notice of the withdrawal is given to the firm's old creditors, the withdrawing partner will become liable to any who, without knowing of the withdrawal, extend further credit to the firm. To be protected against new creditors of the firm, the withdrawing partner must insert a notice in a local general-circulation newspaper. This notice is called a **Public Notice of Dissolution,** as shown in Figure 45.2.

Figure 45.2
A Public Notice of Dissolution

Public Notice

NOTICE is hereby given that the partnership lately existing between Gary Foo and Ronald Josephson, under the firm name and style of Fojo's Cycle Shop, and carrying on a retail bicycle business at 196 South Acoma Boulevard, Havasu City, Arizona, was dissolved on the 2d day of April, 19—, by mutual consent. Gary Foo will carry on the business above alone and is solely authorized to settle all debts due to and from the said firm.

FOJO CYCLE SHOP
By GARY FOO

Dated: April 2, 19—

Even if the remaining partners agree to assume the partnership's liabilities, the withdrawing partner won't be released except as to creditors who consent to the arrangement.

When a partner dies, the surviving partners have the right to terminate the firm's affairs. The decedent's heirs have no authority to interfere with the remaining partners. Also, the heirs cannot represent the deceased partner in an attempt to carry on the business. The decedent's estate is entitled to a proper accounting after the surviving partners have had time to terminate the firm's affairs. The estate is entitled to payment in cash for the decedent's interest, as shown by the accounting. The surviving partners may claim a reasonable compensation for settling the partnership affairs.

Creditors' Rights on Dissolution

PROBLEM

> **11.** The firm of Reiner & Dominguez was declared bankrupt. The firm's assets amounted to $10,000 and its liabilities to $25,000. Reiner had personal assets amounting to $5,000 and personal liabilities of $5,000. Dominguez had personal assets of $18,000 and personal liabilities of $3,000. What rights did the partnership's creditors have as against the personal creditors of the partners?

If the firm's assets are insufficient to meet the claims of its creditors, the creditors have a legal right to collect from the partners' personal assets. The personal creditors of the partners, however, have first claim on the partners' personal assets. A partner who pays any of the firm's debts from his or her personal assets must be reimbursed by the copartners for any sums paid over and above that partner's actual share of the liability. Thus, in Problem 11, Reiner's personal creditors will receive full payment of their claims ($5,000). This will leave Reiner with no personal assets for the firm's creditors. On the other hand, Dominguez's personal creditors will be paid in full, and a surplus of $15,000 will be available to meet the claims of the firm's creditors. Reiner will owe Dominguez one-half of this sum as his share of the firm's debts.

Sole proprietorships and partnerships are important to our economy. Artists, beauticians, plumbers, electricians, bakers, writers, independent sales representatives, and many other people engaged in small business create these forms of business organizations. Because they are closely held by their owners, these businesses can operate with a great deal of freedom from any governmental constraints. The corporate form of business, however, is more closely watched by the government. You'll learn the reasons for this in the next chapter.

Chapter 45 Review

"YOU BE THE JUDGE" REVIEW

Look again at the "You Be the Judge" cases given at the beginning of this chapter. Would you decide them differently now, after your study of the chapter?

Correct Decisions

1. No. Partners own firm assets jointly. Individual partners don't possess any salable, assignable, or mortgagable interest in specific partnership property.

2. Yes. A limited partner who is active in the firm becomes a general partner. However, if Ryan had been paid a salary as an employee, he would still be regarded as a limited partner.

UNDERSTANDING WHAT YOU HAVE READ

1. What does the term *business* mean?
2. What are the primary features of each of the following forms of business organizations:
   a. a sole proprietorship?
   b. a general partnership?
   c. a limited partnership?
3. How does the Uniform Partnership Act define a partnership?
4. What basic test is used to determine whether an association of two or more people is a partnership?
5. What is the purpose of Articles of Partnership?
6. Under what conditions may a minor withdraw from a partnership?
7. What four rights does the law usually give to partners?
8. Briefly discuss each of the following duties of partners:
   a. good faith and loyalty
   b. reasonable care and skill
   c. accounting of business transactions
9. a. What is the liability of partners for contractual obligations incurred by a partner while engaged in the partnership's business?
   b. What is the liability of partners for wrongful acts committed by a copartner, agent, or employee while engaged in the partnership's business?
10. What liability does a new partner have for debts incurred by the partnership before he or she was admitted to the firm?

11. Briefly discuss each of the ways in which a partnership may be dissolved.
12. What should a withdrawing partner do to be protected against claims made by
    a. old creditors of the firm?
    b. new creditors of the firm?
13. If a partner dies,
    a. what are the rights of the remaining partners?
    b. what are the duties of the remaining partners?
    c. what are the rights of the deceased partner's heirs?
14. What are the rights of a partnership's creditors if the firm's assets are insufficient to meet their claims?

BUILDING YOUR LEGAL VOCABULARY

Match each of these legal terms with its correct definition from the list that follows. Write your answers on a separate sheet of paper.

Articles of Partnership
business
dissolution
general partner
limited partnership
partnership
Public Notice of Dissolution
silent partner
sole proprietorship
trading partnership

1. a partner who doesn't take an active part in conducting the business
2. a written contract of partnership
3. a business that has a single owner
4. one who has unlimited liability for the partnership's debts and participates equally in running the business
5. an association of two or more individuals to carry on a business for profit as co-owners
6. the act of exchanging goods and services for a profit, or an enterprise that exists for that purpose
7. a statement placed in a local general-circulation newspaper which informs the public that a partnership has been dissolved
8. a partnership that buys and sells goods
9. the change in partners' relationships that takes place when a partner ceases to be associated with the firm or when a new partner is admitted
10. a partnership in which the liability and participation of one or more partners is limited

APPLYING LEGAL PRINCIPLES

1. LaSelva obtained a position as manager of a bookstore. His salary was to be $450 per week. In addition, he was to receive a bonus of twenty percent of the net profits at the end of the year. Is LaSelva regarded as a partner if the bookstore is owned and operated as a partnership?

2. Yelin, a minor, became a partner in the firm of Mejia and Ravatt by investing $8,000 cash. Shortly thereafter, Yelin sought to withdraw from the firm and demanded the return of her investment. Under what circumstances would she legally be permitted to do so?

3. Searcy and Irrera orally agreed to form a partnership for a period of three years. After six months, Irrera refused to carry out the terms of the agreement. Searcy brought an action against Irrera for breach of contract. Will Searcy be successful?

4. Hu and Cline were partners in a grape-growing operation for a number of years. At the end of the last harvest, Hu sold his interest in the partnership to Beene. However, Cline refused to be Beene's partner. Beene claimed that Hu had a right to sell his interest and that when he did so, Beene automatically became Cline's partner. Was Beene legally correct?

5. Gerardin invested $40,000 and Mitchum invested $20,000 in a service business. At the end of the year, the profits realized from the business amounted to $12,000. Gerardin demanded two-thirds of this sum. Mitchum claimed that the profits should be divided equally, since the original agreement failed to provide for the division of the profits. Who was right?

6. While driving the firm's car on business, Ngo struck a car driven by Geswell and severely injured him. Ngo was a partner in the firm of Eason & Ngo. Geswell sued both Ngo and Eason to recover damages for his injury. Was Eason liable for Ngo's wrongful conduct?

7. Lordes and Sullivan were partners. Zopatti brought suit against them and obtained a judgment for $4,000. Because the partnership had no assets, Zopatti sought to collect the sum from Lordes's personal assets. Lordes refused to pay, claiming that she was liable for only half of the judgment. Was Lordes correct?

8. Werboff and Shimizu were partners in a firm that manufactured and sold jigsaw puzzles. Per the partnership agreement, Werboff's duty was to act as a sales representative and Shimizu was to be in charge of production and purchasing. Werboff bought a large supply of raw materials on credit from Cashman, who knew nothing of the agreed duties of the partners. Cashman now seeks to hold the partnership liable for the sum due. Can he do so?

9. Quizon, a partner in the trading firm of Quizon and Nolen, borrowed $5,000 from the bank to be used in the business. When the loan became due, the bank demanded the money from the firm. Nolen refused to pay, claiming that Quizon had no authority to borrow money for the partnership. Is the partnership liable?

10. Would your answer to Problem 9 have been the same if Quizon and Nolen had been lawyers and Nolen hadn't authorized Quizon to borrow money for the firm?

11. Brand and Normile were partners under an agreement that was to last for five years. They leased premises for that period. Before the lease expired, Normile negotiated with the landlord to renew it for herself. The lease was a valuable one, and Brand claimed that the renewal benefits belonged to the firm and not to Normile personally. Is Brand's claim correct?

12. Slote and Rabin were partners in a real-estate business. Slote was to conduct the selling and Rabin was to manage the office. Rabin became ill and had to stay away from the business for several months. During this time, Slote was forced to take care of the office as well as to continue his sales duties. At the end of the year, Slote sought to recover extra compensation for having performed the office duties. Was Slote entitled to extra compensation?

13. Marques invested $50,000 in the partnership of Marques and Lushan while Lushan invested $25,000. At the end of the year, Marques demanded interest on her investment. Is she entitled to it?

14. Berger withdrew from the firm of Berger, Kan, and Lind. At the time of her withdrawal she notified all the creditors that she was withdrawing. She also stated that Kan and Lind were going to pay all the firm's debts. Pooley, a creditor, sought to collect from Berger for some goods sold to the partnership before the dissolution. Is Berger liable to Pooley?

15. The firm of Morris & Oda became bankrupt. The firm's assets were $3,000, and its liabilities were $10,000. Morris had no personal assets, but Oda had personal assets of $12,000. May the creditors recover their claims in full? If so, how?

ANALYZING COURT CASES

1. J. L. Sidwell and his son Joseph were doing business under the firm name of J. L. Sidwell & Son. Joseph was only 15 years old at the time. J. L. Sidwell died while Joseph was still a minor. Joseph entered into a contract with the firm's creditors to settle all of the partnership's debts. The executor of the father's estate claimed that this agreement was invalid since Joseph was a minor and couldn't be a partner. Do you agree with this claim? (Based on: *Parker v. Oakley, et al.*, 57 S.W. 426)

2. A theatrical and motion-picture company entered into a contract with Jack Dempsey, a world heavyweight boxing champion, and his manager, Jack Kearns, to include both of them in a vaudeville show. Dempsey and Kearns were to be paid $4,000 a week and half of the profits of each performance over and above a stated sum. During a per-formance in Kansas City, Missouri, the box-office receipts were stolen from a safe in the office of Pantages, the theater manager. As a result, Pantages refused to pay the agreed amount to Dempsey and Kearns, claiming that the stolen funds were partnership funds. Was this claim correct? (*Dempsey-Kearns Theatrical & Motion Picture Enterprise, Inc. v. Pantages*, 267 P. 550)

3. Ettelsohn, Allen, and Levinson formed a limited partnership. All legal requirements for forming a limited partnership were complied with except that Ettelsohn, the limited partner, contributed goods instead of cash as specified by statute. In an action brought by Claflin, a creditor of the firm, it was claimed that Ettelsohn was a general partner. Was this claim valid? (*Claflin v. Sattler*, 43 N.W. 382)

CHAPTER 46

Corporations

YOU BE THE JUDGE

Think about these cases.
If you were the judge, how would you decide each case?

1

Lee and Carli each owned 100 shares of stock in a corporation they had formed. Lee wanted to transfer 50 shares to her daughter. Carli claimed that Lee couldn't do so without Carli's consent. If there were no prior agreement between them about transferring shares, could Lee legally do so if Carli objected?

2

A medical corporation sent a nurse-practitioner to a patient's home. In the course of the trip, the nurse struck and injured a pedestrian. Who is liable for the pedestrian's injury?

THE BUSINESS CORPORATION

A sole proprietorship or a partnership can be formed without meeting any special requirements of state or local authorities. However, the corporate type of business enterprise can't exist without the government's consent.

1. Loeb, Matlak, and Oshima owned 60 percent of the stock of Excelsior Realty Co. Upon Loeb's death, Matlak claimed that the corporation had been automatically dissolved. Oshima, however, claimed that the death of a stockholder had no effect on the life of a corporation. Who is legally correct?

Unlike a partnership, a **corporation** is looked on as an individual body, existing separately and apart from its membership or owners. It may sue and be sued in its own name, and corporate existence isn't affected by the death of a stockholder. In fact, a corporation may have a perpetual existence. In Problem 1, therefore, Oshima's claim is legally correct. A corporation is an artificial "person" created by law, separate and distinct from the persons who own it.

In addition to the fact that it is a legal entity with a perpetual life, a corporation has other important advantages.

1. It is the only type of business organization that can raise substantial capital from a large number of investors.
2. By virtue of its size, a corporation can finance itself by dividing its ownership into many small, salable units. These units are called **shares.** Collectively, the shares are known as **stock.**
3. The **shareholders** (investors or owners) have *limited liability* for corporate debts.
4. The shareholders can easily transfer their shares if they so desire.

However, a corporation also has some disadvantages.

1. The cost of organizing and maintaining a corporation, with its many formal procedures, is high.
2. It is subject to special taxes, such as license fees and franchise taxes, which partnerships don't have to pay.
3. It also must pay high taxes on its earnings.
4. It is closely regulated by government agencies.

Figure 46.1 offers a comparison of the features of corporations and partnerships. It may be helpful if you refer to this figure as you proceed through this chapter.

Character-istics	Corporations	General Partnerships	Limited Partnerships
Method of creation	Certificate of Incorporation or charter issued by a state	Agreement of the parties	Must file a Certificate of Limited Partnership with proper state official
Duration	May have a perpetual existence	Terminates by agreement, death, bankruptcy, withdrawal of a partner, or court decree	According to the terms provided in the certificate
Legal entity	A legal entity in all states for all purposes	Limited entity for such purposes as suing in firm name, owning property in firm name, and bankruptcy	Same as a general partnership
Management	Shareholders elect directors who are responsible for management	Equal voice in management by all partners	Management by general partners; limited partners have no voice except as permitted by statute
Transfer-ability of interest	Generally, stock is freely transferable unless otherwise provided between shareholders	Partners cannot sell or assign partnership *property* for their own purposes but can assign their partnership *interest* in profits and surplus	General partner has the same rights as in a general partnership; limited partnership interest is transferable
Liability of members	Limited liability of shareholders	Unlimited liability of partners	General partners—unlimited; Limited partners—limited

Figure 46.1
Corporations and Partnerships

THE PROFESSIONAL SERVICE CORPORATION

In the past, professional services such as those furnished by lawyers, doctors, and accountants could be performed only by individuals. The reason given for this restriction was that the relationship of the practitioner to the patient or client was highly personal. Statutes have now been passed in every state authorizing professional people to incorporate. By doing so, the members derive certain income tax advantages such as pension and profit-sharing plans. Neither of these advantages is available to private parties or to partnerships to the same extent as to corporations.

It's important to remember that the liability of a shareholder in a professional corporation is the same as that of a shareholder in an ordinary business corporation. However, each shareholder charged with malpractice is *individually* liable.

EXAMPLE

Hoskins and Benz were engaged in the practice of law as a professional corporation. The corporation was sued by a client for malpractice. The client claimed that Hoskins had represented her in a negligent manner in a suit for personal injuries. The suit against the corporation will be dismissed by the court. A professional corporation isn't liable for the malpractice of one of its members. Hoskins is personally liable for the acts that resulted in financial loss to the client.

FORMATION OF A CORPORATION

Corporations must obtain government's permission to do business.

PROBLEM

2. Robeson wants to form a stock brokerage business. Cohen and Chanh are willing to provide financial backing in return for being part-owners, and provided that the business is incorporated. How do they go about forming a corporation?

In most states, a person who has the capacity to contract may form a corporation. Some states require that at least three people serve as **incorporators,** although the Model Business Corporation Act, which has been adopted in more than half the states, requires only one incorporator. The incorporators prepare and sign a written document known as a **Certificate of Incorporation, Articles of Association,** or simply a **charter.** When all requirements have been met, including payment of the proper fees, the state accepts the Certificate of Incorporation. Upon its acceptance, the certificate forms the corporation's charter, authorizing its existence and stating its powers. These are the steps required in Problem 2 to form a corporation.

A corporation's charter usually contains (1) the name of the corporation, (2) the location of the corporation's principal place of business, (3) the purpose for which the corporation is formed, (4) the names, residences, and other statutory qualifications of the incorporators, (5) the duration of the corporation, (6) the amount of authorized capital stock, and (7) the names and addresses of the members of the board of directors for the first year. After the charter has been received and filed in a public office (usually that of the county clerk), the corporation may do business.

KINDS OF CORPORATIONS

EXAMPLE

Corporations may be classified as **public corporations** or **private corporations.** Public corporations are organized for governmental purposes. Cities, towns, school districts, and state universities are some examples of public corporations. Colleges, churches, social clubs, lodges, and private hospitals are examples of nonprofit private corporations.

> Three prominent educators wanted to organize a community college. The school was to be operated on a nonprofit basis. The college could be organized as a nonprofit private corporation.

Private business corporations for profit purposes can be found in many fields, including manufacturing, mining, finance, and service. In this book we'll study only private business corporations.

Corporations also may be classified as **domestic corporations** or **foreign corporations.** A corporation is a domestic corporation in the state in which it is incorporated. Everywhere else, it is considered a foreign corporation. A foreign corporation that complies with the laws of the state in which it wants to do business will be allowed to do so.

CAPITAL STOCK

PROBLEM

A charter authorizes a corporation to issue and sell shares of stock. Buyers or shareholders also may be called **stockholders.** The document that represents the buyer's interest in the corporation is known as a **stock certificate.** The certificate may have a value—called **par value**—printed on its face. This is a fixed, arbitrary value such as $1, $10, or $100. If the stock has no fixed value, it is known as a **no-par-value stock.** The corporation may sell no-par-value stock for any amount set by its board of directors.

> **3.** Ortiz owns 100 shares of the preferred stock of Kingston Corporation. What advantages does he have over owners of common stock?

The total number of shares of stock a corporation is allowed by its charter to issue is known as the corporation's **authorized capital stock.** If all or part of this stock is sold, it is known as the **issued and outstanding capital stock** of the corporation. The capital stock is often divided into two classes. When only one class of stock is authorized, it is known as **common stock.** Each share of common stock carries the same rights and privileges. When more than one class of stock is authorized, the classes are usually common stock and **preferred stock.** Owners of preferred stock, as in Problem 3, often are given preference over common stock owners when the corporation's profits are distributed. Other preferences, such as division of corporate assets upon dissolution and voting rights, may be provided for in the charter.

POWERS OF A CORPORATION

A corporation has only the powers that the state has granted to it. That grant gives the corporation the legal capacity to fulfill the purposes for which it was created. The sources of this power are the corporate charter and the state's corporation laws.

PROBLEM

> **4.** Jovano Electronics Corporation borrowed $50,000 in order to pay current debts. The corporation gave a promissory note in return for the loan. The charter contained no express authority for issuing such instruments. A stockholder of the corporation claimed that the firm had acted beyond its powers. Do you agree?

A corporation has these powers: (1) the *express* powers contained in the charter, (2) the *implied* powers that are needed to carry out the express powers and that vary by corporation, and (3) the *incidental* or *general* powers that every corporation must have in order to exist. There are seven of these general powers: (1) power to have continued existence for the period stated in the charter (even perpetual), (2) power to have a corporate name, (3) power to have a corporate seal, (4) power to make **bylaws** (rules for managing the business), (5) power to buy, own, hold, and sell property, (6) power to make charitable contributions, and (7) power to enter into contracts of every kind related to the business. Thus, borrowing money was necessary to carry out the express powers granted to Jovano Electronics Corporation in Problem 4. Therefore, the corporation had the implied power to borrow money and to issue promissory notes as security for debts.

The **Model Business Corporation Act** gives corporations broad powers to act. This law has been adopted by more than half of the states. Any act or contract that goes beyond the powers that a corporation can lawfully exercise is said to be an **ultra vires act.** In most states, if the ultra vires contract has been completely performed, neither party can cancel the contract because it was originally ultra vires. In contrast, if neither party has performed any of the contract's terms, the courts won't hold either liable for breach of contract.

MANAGE-MENT OF A CORPORATION

A corporation may act only through authorized representatives or agents. For this purpose, stockholders select **directors** and entrust them with the management of the corporation. The directors in turn select the **officers** of the corporation. The officers are responsible to the directors for the actual conduct of the business.

Directors

PROBLEM

> **5.** Cappielo, a director of Sun Television, Inc., entered into a contract on behalf of the firm to buy electronic components. Cappielo wasn't an officer of the corporation and hadn't been delegated by the board of directors to make the agreement. Is Cappielo's action binding on the corporation?

Under the Model Business Corporation Act, only one director is required. Some states, however, require a minimum of three directors. Unless a statute or the corporation's bylaws provide otherwise, a director need not be a stockholder. In fact, even a minor or a nonresident is eligible for membership on the board. Independent "outside" directors—presumably not obligated to the corporation's management—are estimated to form majorities on 90 percent of the boards of United States corporations today. The directors meet regularly. They resolve important questions, determine profits to be paid to shareholders, select officers, and establish and guide the policies of the corporation.

Actions taken by the board of directors usually are considered valid only if taken at a proper meeting. Directors can't act singly (as in Problem 5), but only as a body. Although the directors have the primary duty of exercising the powers of the corporation, they may delegate the power to perform acts that are purely mechanical or routine in nature. This type of performance may be delegated to one of their members, to an executive committee, or to a particular officer or agent.

Directors are liable for losses sustained by the corporation as a result of their unauthorized or negligent acts. These acts amount to a breach of trust. Certain important matters that affect the entire corporation must be decided by the stockholders and the directors. These matters might include placing a mortgage on the corporation's property, merging with another firm, or dissolving the corporation.

Directors today function under the supervision of the Securities and Exchange Commission and of vigilant study groups. They are answerable for the company's integrity in its relationships with shareholders, customers, and the general public.

Officers

PROBLEM

> **6.** Hansen, acting within her powers as president of Malbo Corporation, entered into a contract with Mirata. The contract resulted in a considerable loss for the corporation. Hansen had acted in good faith and had used her best judgment. Was she personally liable for the loss?

A director has no individual authority to bind the corporation to a contract. However, an officer of the corporation, acting within the authority granted by the corporation, may enter into contracts as the corporation's agent. Corporate officers are elected by the board of directors. Typically, they include a president, vice-president, secretary, and treasurer. One officer may hold two offices, such as secretary-treasurer.

The duties of the officers are contained in the bylaws. The president, as the chief executive officer, presides at stockholders' and directors' meetings. The secretary keeps the **minutes** (official records) of these meetings and has charge of the corporate records, such as the books in which stock certificates are recorded. The treasurer, as the chief financial officer, is responsible for all corporate funds and other assets. The treasurer pays all corporate debts and must keep accurate records of the corporation's financial dealings.

Officers are not personally liable for losses incurred by the corporation if they act in good faith and exercise reasonable care. In Problem 6, Hansen wouldn't be personally liable for the corporate loss.

RIGHTS OF STOCK-HOLDERS

A person doesn't acquire the rights of a stockholder until he or she is recognized as the legal owner of the stock.

PROBLEM

> **7.** Schofield owned a certificate for 500 shares of Huron Corporation stock. He sold the stock to Poicaro and assigned the certificate to her in proper form. Poicaro tried to attend a stockholders' meeting but was refused admission by an officer of the firm. Was the officer justified in this action?

When a stock purchase is made directly from the corporation, the buyer becomes a stockholder as soon as the subscription is accepted by the corporation. This is true even though the stock certificate hasn't yet been issued and the price hasn't yet been paid. However, when stock is bought from another stockholder, the purchaser isn't recognized by the corporation as a stockholder until the transfer is recorded on the corporate books. This is done by delivering the assigned certificate to the proper corporate officer or to a designated **transfer agent.** This person records the change in ownership, cancels the old certificate, and issues another in the name of the new owner. In Problem 7, the officer was justified in refusing admission to Poicaro. Until Poicaro's stock purchase is properly recorded, she can't be considered a stockholder.

When stock is bought through a stockbroker, as in most cases, the broker arranges to have the certificate issued in the buyer's name.

Ownership in a corporation entitles the stockholder to certain rights and privileges. These are (1) the right to a stock certificate, (2) the right to transfer stock, (3) the right to attend meetings and to vote, (4) the right to dividends, (5) the right to inspect the corporation's books, (6) the preemptive right to buy new issues of stock, and (7) the right to a share of the firm's net assets upon dissolution.

Right to a Stock Certificate

As evidence of stock ownership, a stockholder is entitled to a certificate issued in proper form. If the certificate is lost, stolen, or destroyed, the stockholder may get another certificate from the corporation by complying with certain UCC requirements. Keeping stock certificates in a safe-deposit box is the best guarantee of their safety.

Right to Transfer Stock

Ownership of stock impliedly gives a stockholder the right to transfer it. This right is sometimes subject to a restriction that the holder must not sell the stock to an outsider without first offering it for sale to the corporation. Under the UCC, this kind of restriction must appear on the face of the stock certificate. As mentioned in Problem 7, someone who buys stock from a stockholder must have the transfer recorded on the corporation's books.

Right to Attend Meetings and to Vote

PROBLEM

8. The bylaws of Yukon, Inc. provided for cumulative voting for members of the board of directors. The corporation had a total of 1,200 shares issued and outstanding. Hassan, a shareholder, owned 900 of the shares. Aarons owned the remaining 300 shares. If five directors were to be elected by the shareholders, how many could Hassan elect?

A stockholder's right to vote at stockholders' meetings is governed by (1) the charter, (2) the corporation's bylaws, and (3) state statutes. The right to vote is often given only to holders of common stock. Each stockholder is entitled to one vote for each share of stock owned. To give minority stockholders a chance to be represented on the board of directors, many states allow a system of voting known as **cumulative voting.** Suppose, as in Problem 8, that five directors are to be elected by cumulative voting. Hassan would have a total of 4,500 votes (900 shares × 5 directors to be elected). Aarons would have 1,500 votes (300 shares × 5 directors to be elected). Hassan could cast 1,125 votes, if he chooses, for each of four candidates. However, he can't elect all five directors. This is true because Aarons could cast all of her 1,500 votes for one candidate and elect that person to office. Under ordinary voting methods, Hassan with his 900 votes could elect the entire slate of five candidates because splitting votes among candidates isn't allowed.

A stockholder who can't attend a meeting to vote may designate another—not necessarily a stockholder—to attend that meeting and to vote. This is done by means of a written designation called a **proxy** (see Figure 46.2). Only stockholders, and not directors, may vote by proxy. Proxies are revocable without notice.

Figure 46.2
A Proxy

PROXY

Solicited by the Management of Vaisy Corporation

I (we) hereby appoint John Dare, Paul E. Karter, Richard I. Lane, and George T. Mackay as proxies with power of substitution to represent me (us) and to vote all my (our) stock in Vaisy Corporation held by me (us) on the Record Date, April 3, 19 —— , on all matters, including the election of directors, which may come before the Annual Meeting of the Stockholders to be held on Monday, the 23rd day of May, 19 —— , at 11 a.m. at United Hall, 803 Farmington Avenue, Hartford, Conn., and at any adjournment thereof.

> **The proxies shall vote this stock as specified below, or where no choice is specified, shall vote the stock FOR the following proposal.**

The Board of Directors recommends a vote FOR the resolution

Approving the selection of independent auditors for
the year 19 —   ☐ FOR   ☐ AGAINST

(SIGN ON REVERSE SIDE AND RETURN PROMPTLY)

Figure 46.2
A Proxy

Right to Dividends

PROBLEM

> **9.** Moreland owned 1,000 shares of Wabash Corporation stock. On July 15, the board of directors declared a quarterly dividend of 50 cents per share, payable August 15. On July 25, Moreland sold the stock to Desiato. Who is entitled to the dividend?

Dividends are payments made to shareholders out of the profits earned by the corporation. They are paid when and as the board of directors declares them. Usually they're paid in cash, although payment in stock or other personal property is allowed. Stockholders can't force the directors to declare a dividend unless they can prove that the directors are acting in an unreasonable or dishonest manner. Corporations usually declare their dividends payable to stockholders of record as of a certain date. This means that the stockholder whose name appears on the corporation's books on that day is entitled to payment of the dividend. Since Moreland in Problem 9 was the owner of the corporation's books on July 15, she is entitled to the dividend.

Right to Inspect the Corporation's Books

Most states have statutes giving a stockholder the right to inspect the books and records of the corporation. However, the demand for inspection must be in good faith and must be exercised only at a reasonable time and place. Also, the Model Business Corporation Act limits the right of inspection to prevent inspection of the documents for improper purposes, such as to obtain mailing lists for sales solicitations. Under the act, only stockholders who have owned stock for at least six months or who own at least five percent of the outstanding stock have the right of inspection. In addition, the MBCA requires that an inspection request be made in writing and that the purpose of the inspection be stated clearly.

Preemptive Right to Purchase Stock

A stockholder usually has a right to purchase new issues of corporate stock before such issues are sold to the general public. This is called a **preemptive right.** It helps existing stockholders to preserve their proportionate interest in the ownership of the corporation.

EXAMPLE

> Jeka owned ten percent of the capital stock of Hyland Films, Inc. If the stockholders voted to amend the charter by increasing the capital stock, Jeka would have the right to buy ten percent of the new issue. This would allow him to maintain his proportionate interest in the ownership of the corporation.

Recently, there has been a trend toward the abolition of the preemptive right. Statutes as well as court decisions have made many exceptions to this requirement.

Right to a Share of the Net Assets

Upon dissolution of the corporation, the corporate property is first used to pay debts. The remainder, or **net assets,** is then distributed among the stockholders in proportion to their stock ownership.

LIABILITY OF STOCKHOLDERS

Stockholders, unlike partners, have a limited liability. They usually aren't liable for the debts of the corporation beyond the amount they have invested in the firm. However, if a stockholder fails to complete payments on a purchase of stock from the firm, either the corporation or its creditors may hold the stockholder liable for the balance.

EXAMPLE

> Hadaya bought 100 shares of stock from Occidental Trading Corporation for a total price of $1,150. She had paid $350 on account when the corporation failed. Either Occidental Trading or its creditors may hold Hadaya liable for the payment of the $800 due on the stock purchase.

In some states, such as New York and Wisconsin, stockholders are personally liable for unpaid wages to employees if the wages can't be collected from the corporation.

DISSOLUTION OF A CORPORATION

Corporate existence may end either by voluntary or involuntary dissolution. When a corporation is organized to exist only for a limited number of years, a voluntary dissolution may result from the charter's expiration. Also, a voluntary dissolution may happen through surrender of the charter when *all* shareholders give their *written* consent. In addition, a resolution passed by the board of directors and approved by two-thirds of the shareholders may give rise to a voluntary dissolution.

PROBLEM

10.   The Nemitz Corporation, organized to manufacture auto parts and accessories, engaged in illegal transactions. May a shareholder bring an action to dissolve the corporation?

Involuntary dissolution may occur by means of (1) a suit for dissolution by the firm's shareholders and (2) forfeiture of the charter by the state.

If a shareholder can show a court of equity that the officers or directors are acting fraudulently or illegally, as in Problem 10, the court will order that the firm be dissolved. A corporation that misuses its corporate powers or fails to file annual reports or pay franchise taxes also may forfeit its charter. However, the forfeiture must be brought about either directly by the state or by shareholders and creditors acting through the proper authorities.

Often, a corporation is dissolved by **merger** or **consolidation.** For example, when two corporations are merged, one of the firms surrenders its charter and is absorbed by the other firm. In a consolidation, a new corporation comes into existence with the consent of the state and the stockholders of the corporations.

A dissolved corporation ceases to exist. It no longer has the power to enter into contracts, to sue and be sued, or to exercise any other powers granted by its charter. However, most states give the directors of a dissolved corporation a limited time within which to wind up the corporate affairs.

EXAMPLE

Bourdeau owed $5,000 to Aponte Corporation. The corporation's directors and shareholders voted to dissolve. Since Bourdeau had failed to pay his debt to the corporation, the corporation sued him to collect it. Bourdeau defended the suit by claiming that he was no longer liable because of the dissolution. Bourdeau will have to pay the $5,000. Liability to the corporation doesn't terminate on dissolution. The corporation has time to wind up its affairs, which includes collecting funds owed to the corporation.

LIVING UNDER THE LAW

Ways to Avoid Securities Fraud

The purchase of stocks, bonds, and other securities always carries with it an element of risk. The risk of fraud is one of the most serious. Here are some suggestions to help you avoid being trapped in a securities fraud.

- Think before buying.
- Deal only with a securities firm you know.
- Be skeptical of securities offered over the phone by any firm or sales representative you don't know.
- Guard against all high-pressure sales tactics.
- Beware of promises of quick, spectacular price rises.
- Be sure you understand the risk of loss.
- Get the facts. Don't buy on tips or rumors.
- Ask the person who is offering securities over the phone to mail you written information about the corporation. Save all such information for future reference.

- If you don't understand the written information, talk to someone who does.
- Give as much thought to buying securities as you would to buying any valuable property.

PROTECTING BUYERS OF SECURITIES

The federal government and most states have enacted laws to protect people against investments in speculative (risky) or fraudulent securities, including certain corporate stocks. As mentioned in Chapter 12, the Securities and Exchange Commission (SEC) is the most important federal agency for the regulation of security sales.

The Securities and Exchange Commission

The SEC is charged with enforcing the **Securities Act** of 1933. This act makes it illegal to use the mails or any means of transportation or communication in *interstate commerce* to sell or offer to buy a security unless (1) the security is registered with the SEC and (2) a proper prospectus is used. A **prospectus** is any circular, letter, or other communication that offers a security for sale to the public. In the public interest, the SEC may require changes to be made in a proposed prospectus. Under a law passed in 1934, the SEC also has the power to regulate the trading of securities on stock exchanges and in "over-the-counter" (nonexchange) markets. Under this law, no exchange may transact business unless it is registered or exempted from registration by the SEC. Violations of both laws are punishable by heavy fines, imprisonment, or both. The SEC doesn't guarantee or approve issues of securities. It merely requires public disclosure of information as to the actual value of securities offered for sale to the public. Prospective investors may apply directly to the SEC for information about a registered security. Also, complaints may be filed directly with the SEC.

The United States Postal Service

The **United States Postal Service** is an independent unit of the executive branch of the federal government. It enforces postal fraud laws, which attempt to prevent the use of the mails to carry out fraudulent schemes —especially "get-rich-quick" plans. Postal inspectors gather evidence and if fraud is detected, the Postal Service may issue a **fraud order.** The accused party must appear and explain the suspected activities. Failure to appear results in a cancellation of the party's privilege of receiving mail or cashing money orders. The Postal Service doesn't try to recover money lost by defrauded people. The victims must bring their own civil suits for that purpose. In certain cases the postal authorities may submit evidence to the United States Attorney General for criminal prosecution.

"Blue-Sky" Laws

Many states have enacted **"blue-sky" laws** to protect the investor from fraudulent schemes for the sale of securities. In general, they require (1) a public listing of securities, (2) submission of the prospectus for approval by the proper state officer or department, and (3) the filing of certain statements on the corporation's financial condition with the proper state authorities. After satisfactory compliance with state requirements, a corporation may be given permission to offer the securities for sale to the public in the state. Failure to comply with the state regulations may result in a fine, imprisonment, or both.

   In addition to federal and state laws regulating the sale of securities, local stock exchanges and brokerages have their own rules and regulations.

Chapter 46 Review

"YOU BE THE JUDGE" REVIEW

Look again at the "You Be the Judge" cases given at the beginning of this chapter. Would you decide them differently now, after your study of the chapter?

Correct Decisions

1. Yes. An outstanding characteristic of a corporation is the transferability of its shares of stock. No permission is needed for Lee to transfer some of her stock to her daughter.

2. The nurse-practitioner and the corporation are both liable for the pedestrian's injury. A shareholder wouldn't be liable for ordinary torts committed by others.

UNDERSTANDING WHAT YOU HAVE READ

1. What steps must incorporators take when forming a corporation?
2. What information does a corporate charter usually contain?
3. How may corporations be classified?
4. What is
   a. a share of stock?
   b. authorized capital stock?
   c. issued and outstanding stock?
5. Explain each of these types of corporate powers:
   a. express powers
   b. implied powers
   c. general powers

6. What are the powers and duties of the board of directors of a corporation?
7. What are the powers and duties of officers of a corporation?
8. What seven rights are usually granted to the stockholders of a corporation?
9. What is the liability of a stockholder?
10. How may a corporation be dissolved?
11. What is the function of the Securities and Exchange Commission?
12. How do the United States Postal Service and "blue-sky" laws protect buyers of corporate stock?

BUILDING YOUR LEGAL VOCABULARY

Choose the legal term that will correctly complete each definition below. Write your answers on a separate sheet of paper.

1. The total number of shares of stock a corporation is allowed by charter to issue is the firm's
   a. preferred stock.
   b. authorized capital stock.
   c. no-par-value stock.
2. A circular, letter, or other communication that offers a security for sale to the public is a
   a. charter.
   b. proxy.
   c. prospectus.
3. Payments made to shareholders out of the profits earned by a corporation are
   a. bylaws.
   b. minutes.
   c. dividends.

4. The authorized agents or representatives of a corporation who are entrusted with final authority for a corporation's management are its
   a. officers.
   b. shareholders.
   c. directors.
5. A small, salable unit of ownership in a corporation is a
   a. share.
   b. net asset.
   c. stock certificate.

APPLYING LEGAL PRINCIPLES

1. Two people who had operated their business as a partnership decided to convert it into a corporation. They changed the name of the firm and informed their customers and creditors that they had formed a corporation. Neither of them did anything further. Was a valid corporation formed?

2. Classify each of these organizations as a public corporation, a private business for profit, or a private nonprofit enterprise:
   a. Pennsylvania State University
   b. General Motors Corporation
   c. First Baptist Church
   d. Lion's Club
   e. San Antonio, Texas
   f. Eastman Kodak Corporation
   g. American Red Cross
   h. Ford Foundation

3. Dunlap owned 300 shares of voting stock of Zanco Corporation. At the annual meeting, three new directors were to be elected. How many votes would Dunlap have under the cumulative method of voting? Could she cast all of her votes for a single candidate?

4. The amended charter of Joshi Corporation permitted the company to issue an additional 1,000 shares of common stock at $100 a share. Sesto owned 200 of the 1,000 shares of outstanding stock. He claimed that the firm had to let him buy at least 200 shares of the new stock before the issue was offered to the public. Do you agree with him? Explain.

5. The board of directors of Minkin Chemical Corp. declared a dividend to holders of record as of April 15, payable on May 1. Houton owned 1,000 shares of the corporation's stock. On April 10, Houton sold his stock to Lai.

   a. Who is entitled to the dividend if Lai has the transfer registered on the books of the corporation on April 16?

   b. If Lai had the transfer registered on the corporation's books before April 15, to whom would the corporation pay the dividend?

6. Hanrahan Cycle Corporation had made profits since its organization. However, its directors had never declared a dividend. The firm's business was constantly growing. May Helfand, a stockholder, compel the corporation to pay a dividend?

7. Obi was a director of Commercial Housing Corporation but not an officer. She contracted for some landscaping and hired a superintendent for one of the firm's buildings. Is the corporation bound?

8. Would your answer to Problem 7 have been different if Obi had been president of the firm?

9. The officers of Genito Corporation, in good faith, entered into a contract to buy supplies for the firm. As a result of this action, the corporation suffered a substantial financial loss. Could the stockholders of the firm legally hold the officers personally liable for the loss?

10. Petras Corporation was organized for the purpose of transporting cargo from Seattle, Washington, to Long Beach, California. Actually, the firm operated gambling ships off the coast of California. What legal action may the stockholders take?

11. Garrido owed Excello Corporation $3,200 for stock she had bought from the firm on the installment plan. The firm became bankrupt and couldn't pay the claims of its creditors. What rights do the creditors have against Garrido?

12. The S&S Corporation failed. Does Pizer & Co., a creditor, have a legal claim against Dolbec, a paid-up stockholder?

ANALYZING COURT CASES

1. Cortez Corporation leased certain real estate from Sturm. The corporation experienced financial difficulties and failed. Sturm sought to hold the stockholders personally liable for the rent on the ground that the corporate structure was a sham. Were the stockholders personally liable for the corporation's debts? (Based on: *Shaw v. Bailey-McCune*, 355 P. 2d 321)

2. The directors of the Southwest Block Co. voted to go out of business. The corporation ceased functioning, and all its assets and liabilities were turned over by the board of directors to Larson. In a suit by Walters against Larson, the question of whether the corporation was then in existence was raised. How should this question be decided? (*Walters v. Larson*, 270 S.W. 2d 112)

3. November was a stockholder in National Exhibition Company. The firm owned a franchise for the operation of the New York Giants, a major-league baseball team. November sued the corporation to prevent it from moving its franchise from New York City to San Francisco. November claimed that the board of directors of the company acted improperly in authorizing the transfer of the franchise. The improper actions claimed were (1) waste and mismanagement of the corporate assets on the part of the directors and (2) lack of stockholder approval of such an extraordinary corporate act. Should November succeed in his action against the corporation and its directors? (*November v. National Exhibition Company*, 173 N.Y.S. 2d 490).

Glossary of Legal Terms

Because legal terminology is very specialized, it is important that you understand the meanings of the terms you encounter in your study of business law. This glossary contains brief, concise definitions of nearly 700 legal terms highlighted or encountered in the text. The definitions are provided here in order to give you the opportunity to refresh your legal vocabulary as you proceed through the text.

absolute liability Responsibility for injuries that result from legal but dangerous actions, in spite of precautionary measures and extreme diligence.

abstract of title A report on the history of the ownership of real property, often prepared by a title company.

acceptance An offeree's expression of willingness to be bound by the terms of an offer.

accession Acquisition of title to property by means of an increase or improvements made to existing property.

accommodation indorsement A method by which a financially responsible party helps a less credit-worthy party by cosigning a negotiable instrument, thereby assuming liability for payment of the instrument.

accommodation party A party who agrees to help a less creditworthy party obtain a loan by co-signing a promissory note, thereby assuming liability for payment of the note.

accounting A report or summary of financial dealings, required to be submitted by the party who has been handling the transactions.

actual eviction Direct action taken by a landlord to oust a tenant from all or part of a leased premises.

administrative law A class of laws enacted by regulatory agencies.

administrator A person appointed by a probate court to settle the estate of an intestate person.

adverse possession A method of acquiring title to real property by holding the property of another without interruption and without the owner's consent for a statutory period.

affirm To validate or confirm.

affirmance Validation or confirmation.

agency The legal relationship that arises when someone is given authority to transact business for another.

agency by appointment An agency created by express authorization.

agency by estoppel An agency created when a principal is estopped, or prevented, from claiming that an agent was unauthorized. Such an agency occurs if the principal has misled a third party into thinking that the agent did have authority.

agency by necessity An agency implied by law in urgent or emergency situations in which the agency relationship is reasonable and just.

agency by ratification An agency created when a principal, with full knowledge of the facts, approves or confirms another party's unauthorized act performed in the principal's behalf.

agency coupled with an interest An irrevocable agency relationship in which the agent has an interest in the subject matter of the agency itself and not a mere interest in being compensated for his or her agency services.

agent A party who receives authority to transact business for another.

agricultural fixtures Agricultural improvements, such as henhouses and tool sheds, which are attached by a tenant to leased property but remain the tenant's property.

air rights Ownership of the air space above the surface of land.

airbill A document that authorizes transportation of goods by air.

all-risk policy See *floater.*

allonge A paper attached to a negotiable instrument to receive further indorsements when there is no room for additional indorsements on the back of the instrument.

alteration Any fraudulent change in the contract of a party, brought about by adding or removing parts of a signed instrument or by changing the number or relations of the parties to a contract.

annual percentage rate (APR) The fee charged for use of credit, stated as a percentage of the amount borrowed.

annuals Cultivated crops that complete their life cycles in one season and are classified legally as personal property.

answer A court document in which a defendant responds to the plaintiff's charges.

antedate To date as of an earlier time than the present.

apparent authority Authority that a principal, by words or conduct, has led third persons to believe an agent possesses.

appellate court A court that reviews the decision of a trial court on the appeal of a dissatisfied party to the original action.

appellate jurisdiction Authority to review a decision of a lower court or administrative agency.

appraisal A valuation of property by an authorized party.

arbitration The process by which a dispute is settled out of court by an independent third party whose solution must be accepted by the disputing parties.

arbitrator An independent third party authorized by disputing parties to resolve their differences out of court.

arraignment A court appearance in which a defendant in a criminal action hears the charges or indictment and is offered a chance to enter a plea of guilt or innocence.

arrest The act of taking a suspected criminal into custody.

arson Willfully and maliciously setting a fire, usually causing damage to or destruction of a building.

Articles of Association See *charter.*

Articles of Partnership A written contract of partnership; a Certificate of Co-Partnership.

"as is" sale A sale in which the buyer takes the risk as to the quality of the goods.

assault Making a threat with the intention of causing bodily injury to another by force or violence.

assessment A charge against real property that has been benefited by a local improvement.

assignee A party to whom rights under a contract are transferred.

assignment Any act or words, whether spoken or written, which show an intention to transfer rights under a contract to another.

assignor A party who transfers rights under a contract to another.

auction A presentation of goods for sale to the highest bidder.

authorized capital stock The total number of shares of stock a corporation is allowed by its charter to issue.

authorized means of communication An approved or sanctioned method of communicating acceptance of an offer.

bail Money or property provided by someone accused of a crime in order to obtain a temporary release from custody.

bailee A party who accepts temporary possession of goods under a bailment contract.

bailiff A minor court official who performs messenger or ushering services for a court.

bailment A contract in which one party temporarily transfers possession of goods to another for some special purpose.

bailor A party who temporarily transfers possession of goods to another under a bailment contract.

bait advertising False claims made by a seller to lure a buyer to purchase goods or services.

bank check See *bank draft.*

bank draft An order drawn by one bank on another bank in which the drawer bank has funds on deposit, usually used to transfer funds to distant places.

bankruptcy The legal condition of a party whose property has been taken over by a court for settlement of debts owed to the party's creditors.

bar To prevent; to prohibit.

bargain and sale deed A deed that transfers title to real property but does not warrant that the title is complete and perfect.

bargaining unit A group that performs negotiating tasks for its constituents; often, a union chosen by workers to represent them in dealing with employers.

battery Unlawfully striking or touching another person.

bearer instrument An instrument payable to bearer or to the order of bearer, to a specified person or bearer, to cash or the order of cash, or to any other nonspecific payee or drawee.

beneficiary A party who will receive benefit from something, such as from an insurance policy or from a decedent's estate.

bequest A gift of personal property by will; a legacy.

bilateral contract A contract that arises through an exchange of mutual promises.

bill of exchange See *draft.*

bill of lading A document given by a common carrier that is both a receipt for goods shipped and a contract for the shipment.

bill of sale A written receipt issued by a seller to a buyer that transfers to the buyer title to the goods described in the instrument.

binder A written memorandum evidencing insurance coverage during the period between making an application for insurance and the acceptance of the application by the insurer; a temporary acceptance of an insurance risk.

blackmail See *extortion.*

blank indorsement A method of transferring one's rights in a negotiable instrument by signing the back of the instrument, making it payable to bearer and negotiable by delivery alone.

blanket position policy A type of fidelity insurance that protects an employer against losses caused by the dishonest acts of any employee who fills a certain position with the firm.

"blue-sky" laws State laws that protect investors from fraudulent schemes for the sale of securities.

boarder A person who contracts with a boardinghouse keeper for living accommodations for a definite period of time; a lodger.

bodily injury liability insurance Automobile insurance that protects the insured, within stated limits, against all amounts legally collectible from the insured as a result of bodily injuries suffered by another; public liability insurance.

bonding See *fidelity insurance.*

breach of contract Failure to perform contractual duties; a breaking of a contract.

bribery Giving something of value to another in order to influence that person's judgment or conduct.

brief A written argument that presents to an appellate court both the basic contentions of a party to a legal action and the supporting legal arguments.

bulk sale Any transfer, not in the ordinary course of a seller's business, of a major part of the seller's stock and business fixtures.

burden of proof Responsibility for establishing proof of claims in a legal action.

burglary Breaking into and entering a building with intent to commit a crime.

business The act of exchanging goods and services for a profit, or an enterprise that exists for that purpose; a person's work or occupation.

business law A group of laws that regulates the business transactions of individuals and business organizations.

bylaws Rules made by a corporation for its own government.

C.I.F. The mercantile shipping symbol for *cost, insurance, and freight* to a named destination.

C.O.D. The mercantile shipping symbol for *collect on delivery.*

canceled check A check that has been paid by a bank.

capacity to contract Ability to acquire legal rights and to assume legal responsibility for one's own acts.

carrier An individual or firm engaged in the business of transporting goods or people.

carrier's lien The right of a common carrier to retain possession of goods in order to secure payment of outstanding transportation charges.

case law The total of reported cases as forming a body of jurisprudence, or science of law.

cash surrender value An amount, less than the premiums that have been paid, payable to an insured by an insurer when a life insurance policy is surrendered by the insured.

cashier's check A check drawn by a bank cashier on the bank as drawee and issued to a depositor in return for the depositor's personal check.

casualty insurance The liability insurance protection provided under an insurance policy, usually related to commercial policies.

caveat emptor *(Latin)* Let the buyer beware.

cease-and-desist order A command, issued by a court or a federal agency, which requires a party to stop its unlawful practices immediately.

Certificate of Co-Partnership See *Articles of Partnership.*

certificate of deposit A negotiable instrument issued by a bank, certifying that a named person has deposited a stated sum of money payable to the order of the named person.

Certificate of Incorporation See *charter.*

Certificate of Limited Partnership The document that sets forth the essential details of a limited partnership and that, when signed, sworn to, and properly filed, creates a legally recognized limited partnership.

certification A bank's guarantee, written or stamped across the face of a personal check, that the bank will honor the check when it is presented for payment.

certified check A check that a bank has guaranteed will be honored when it is presented for payment.

charitable subscription A promise or pledge to make a gift to a charitable, religious, educational, or similar institution.

charter A document, prepared by incorporators and accepted by the state, which authorizes the existence of a corporation and states the corporation's powers; Articles of Association; a Certificate of Incorporation.

chattel mortgage A secured credit sale formed when the owner of consumer goods borrows money and gives a security interest in the goods to a bank or private party.

check An unconditional written order to a depositor's bank, directing the bank to pay on demand a specified sum of money to the order of a third person or to the bearer.

circuit A geographical area in which a United States Court of Appeals has jurisdiction.

citation A specific reference to a published court opinion.

civil death statutes State laws that prohibit convicted people from contracting for any purpose.

civil law The branch of law that governs disputes of a noncriminal nature between two or more parties.

Civil Rights Act A 1964 federal law that prohibits discrimination against anyone on the basis of race, creed, color, or national origin.

clearinghouse A Federal Reserve bank that clears checks for its members.

closing costs Expenses incurred during the settlement or performance of a contract for the sale of real property, often including brokers' commissions, loan origination fees, points, appraisal fees, credit report fees, and attorneys' fees.

co-owner One who shares ownership of something with another; a person who shares in the profits and management of a business.

Code Napoléon A collection of French laws completed during the rule of Napoléon Bonaparte and used today in the state of Louisiana.

codicil A formally executed addition to a will, by which the testator makes some addition, change, or retraction to the will.

coinsurance provision A clause in an insurance contract, requiring the insured to carry an amount of insurance that totals a certain percentage of the value of the insured property.

collateral Property pledged to protect a lender if the borrower fails to repay.

collateral note A promissory note that contains a description of property, such as stocks and bonds, pledged as security for payment of the note.

collective bargaining agreement An agreement that results from the negotiations of a bargaining unit with an employer on matters included in a group employment contract.

collision insurance Automobile insurance that protects an insured against any damage to his or her own car when the damage is caused by a collision with another car or object and the collision was the fault of the insured.

commercial blanket policy A type of fidelity insurance that protects an employer against losses caused by the dishonest acts of all employees in the firm.

commercial bribery Giving something of value to an agent in order to induce the agent to do business.

commercial paper A written document, such as a promissory note, a draft, or a check, which serves as evidence of a debt.

common carrier A carrier, such as a railroad, shipping line, trucking firm, or airline, which will accept goods for transport and offers services to anyone for a fee.

common law A system of law developed in England, based on customs and traditions and characterized by the practice of deciding cases by following precedent.

common stock A class of corporate stock in which each share carries the same rights and privileges.

community property ownership A form of property ownership, recognized in several states, in which a husband and wife each own an undivided half-interest in property acquired through their joint or individual efforts during the marriage.

comparative damages An award determined by the amount of negligence contributed by each party to a tort action.

comparative negligence Relative responsibility for fault of each party in a tort action for negligence.

compensation Payment or remuneration.

compensatory damages An award made to an injured party as compensation for the actual dollar amount of the loss suffered.

competent party A person capable of entering into a contractual agreement.

complaint A court document that states the cause of action against a named party; the original pleading in an action.

comprehensive insurance Automobile insurance that protects the insured's car against losses due to fire, windstorm, flood, riot, glass breakage, theft, and vandalism.

computer-assisted legal research (CALR) A system of locating cases, statutes, and other legal materials by means of accessing electronic databases.

condemnation proceeding The proceeding by which private property is taken under the government's right of eminent domain.

conditional sale contract An installment sale; a secured transaction under the UCC.

confirmation An acknowledgment; a written document acknowledging an order between merchants.

consideration Something of value given by both parties to a contract; the price bargained for and paid for a promise.

consignee A party to whom a carrier is to deliver goods that are being transported.

consignor A party who delivers goods to a carrier for transportation; a shipper.

consolidation A joining of two corporations in which both firms surrender their charters, becoming one new corporation with a new charter.

conspiracy An agreement between two or more parties to commit a criminal act.

constitutional law A class of laws that defines the powers and limitations of the federal and state governments.

constructive eviction Dispossession of a tenant from leased property as a result of a landlord's failure to remedy a condition that makes the premises uninhabitable.

Consumer Credit Protection Act (CCPA) A federal law that regulates the use of credit.

consumer goods Goods used or bought for use for personal, family, or household purposes.

Consumer Product Warranty and Federal Trade Commission Improvement Act A federal law requiring all companies offering warranties with products costing $5 or more to state the terms of the warranty in complete and simple language.

consumerism The focus on the rights and interests of consumers rather than of merchants in the competitive market for sales of goods.

contempt of court Willful disobedience to or disrespect for a judge or a court, subject to legal penalties.

contract A promise or an agreement that creates legal obligations enforceable at law.

contract bailment A bailment that provides for services relating to a bailed article, with consideration or benefit to one of the parties.

contract carrier See *private carrier.*

contract rate of interest The statutory maximum interest rate or charge that lenders may impose on borrowers.

contract to sell An agreement between a buyer and a seller to transfer the title to certain goods at some future time.

contracts The branch of civil law concerned with agreements that voluntarily create legal obligations.

contributory negligence Negligence contributed by the plaintiff in a tort action to the event in which the injury occurred.

Controlled Substances Act A 1970 federal law that makes certain drug- and alcohol-related activities illegal.

conversion The unlawful taking and use, destruction, or alteration of the personal property of another.

conversion provision A clause in a life insurance policy that allows the insured to change to another form of life insurance without undergoing a physical exam.

conviction A finding of guilt in a criminal action.

corporation A body formed and authorized by law to act as a single person, separate and distinct from its members or owners.

counteroffer An acceptance that differs from the terms of an offer and terminates the original offer.

court A place or an assembly where laws are interpreted and applied.

court decree A determination or ruling of a court.

court docket The schedule used by a court.

courts of equity Special courts developed under common law to fairly and justly compensate injured parties by means of an appropriate form of nonmonetary relief.

covenant A written representation or promise; a warranty.

cover To purchase, in good faith, goods to substitute for those due from a seller who has breached a sales contract.

credit An extension of time given by a seller or lender for payment for goods, services, or loans.

creditor A party who extends credit to another.

crime An act that directly or indirectly interferes with or tends to interfere with the fundamental rights of the community as a whole, and for which the law prescribes punishment.

criminal law The branch of law that protects society against public wrongs by providing punishment for those who commit the wrongs.

criminal mischief Deliberately causing damage to the property of another; vandalism.

cumulative voting A system of voting shares of stock that allows the splitting of votes in order to give minority stockholders a chance to be represented on the board of directors.

damages Awards allowed by law as compensation for an injury or loss caused by another.

debtor A party who receives credit from another.

decedent A person who has died.

declaration See *complaint.*

deductible A clause in an insurance policy that relieves the insurer of responsibility for an initial stated loss of the kind insured against.

deed A written instrument that conveys title to real property.

defamation A false and intentionally communicated statement that brings hatred, disgrace, ridicule, or contempt on another.

default A failure to perform or to fulfill an agreement.

defendant The party sued in a civil action or the party charged with a crime in a criminal action.

deficiency judgment An award made to a seller when a buyer has defaulted on a sales contract, in an amount equal to the difference between the amount due under the original contract and the amount the seller actually collects from a resale; a personal judgment entered against any person liable on a mortgage debt and due to the mortgagee after foreclosure.

delegation The act of entrusting a duty to another for performance.

demurrage charge A special payment imposed on a consignor or consignee by a common carrier for failure to load or unload goods within a reasonable time.

devise A gift of real property by will.

devisee A party to whom a gift of real property is made by will.

director One of a group of people chosen by stockholders to manage a corporation and to exercise its powers.

disability insurance Government-subsidized insurance that pays a limited monthly income to people under 65 who are unable to work because of serious illness or injury.

disaffirmance Annulment; the procedure by which a minor may avoid contracts that the law considers voidable.

discovery The pretrial exchange of information (facts and documents) between the parties to a civil action in order to eliminate the element of surprise in litigation.

dishonored instrument A negotiable instrument that a maker is unable or refuses to pay after it has been properly presented.

dissolution A change in the relationships of partners that occurs when a partner ceases to be associated with the firm or when a new partner is admitted.

district attorney The prosecuting officer of a judicial district.

dividends Payments made to shareholders out of the profits earned by a corporation.

document of title A document that proves ownership of property.

domestic corporation A corporation operating in the state in which it is incorporated.

donee A party who receives a gift from another.

donor A party who gives a gift to another.

dormant partner A partner who is not actively engaged in conducting the partnership and who is unknown to the public.

draft An unconditional written order to a party named in the instrument, directing the party to pay a specified sum of money to the order of a third party or to the bearer.

drawee A party who is ordered to pay the amount of a check or draft. In the case of a check, the depositor's bank is the drawee. In the case of a draft, a third party named in the instrument is the drawee.

drawer A party who orders the payment of the amount of a check or draft.

driving while intoxicated (DWI) Operating a motor vehicle while under the influence of alcohol (or, in most states, while under the influence of drugs).

drug-related crime The use, sale, transportation, or possession of illegal drugs.

due process of law The full protection of the law as afforded to a person accused of a crime, including a fair trial to determine guilt or innocence.

duress The prevention of exercise of one's will through the fear of injury.

easement A right or privilege, such as a right of way, which a party may have in another's land.

economic frustration The doctrine by which performance of contractual duties is excused when it can be done only at an unreasonable cost.

embezzlement The unlawful taking of money or property by someone who was entrusted to look after it.

eminent domain The right of a government to appropriate private property for public use on payment of just compensation.

employee A person who performs regular tasks for another, usually for wages or salary.

employer A party who directs and controls the regular tasks of another.

encumbrance A claim, such as a mortgage or tax lien, against real property.

endorsement A public recommendation, often made by a prominent person, to purchase a product or service.

endowment policy A life insurance policy that pays the amount of the policy to the insured after a stated period of time, such as 20 or 30 years, or that pays the face value of the policy to a named beneficiary if the insured does not survive the stated period.

enemy alien A foreign-born resident of the United States whose country of citizenship is at war with the United States.

Equal Credit Opportunity Act A federal law that prohibits discrimination against credit applicants on the basis of sex, marital status, race, religion, national origin, or age.

Equal Pay Act A 1964 amendment to the federal Fair Labor Standards Act that prohibits employers from discriminating on the basis of sex in the payment of wages for equal work.

equity law The branch of law that grants relief when there is no adequate remedy at law.

escheat Return (of real property) to the state if the owner dies without legal heirs.

escrow agreement A special contract prepared in connection with a conditional sale of real property, requiring a disinterested third party to hold the deed to the property until all conditions stated in the agreement are met.

estate All the property belonging to one party.

estop To prevent; to bar.

eviction Dispossession of a tenant from leased property.

executed contract A contract whose terms have been completely carried out by the parties.

execution The process by which a public official is ordered to seize property of a judgment debtor in order to satisfy the debt.

executor/executrix A person who is appointed in a will to carry out the terms of the will.

executory contract A contract in which some act remains to be done on the part of one or both parties.

exemplary damages See *punitive damages.*

exercise of ownership Actions that indicate one's intention to keep property or goods; an implied acceptance of another's offer of property or goods.

existing goods Goods that have been grown, processed, manufactured, or packed and that have been identified to a particular contract by means of proper marking, labeling, tagging, and crating.

express authority Oral or written authority, given by a principal to an agent, to carry out certain duties.

express contract A contract made by the direct or specific agreement of the parties.

express warranty A warranty created by a seller's written statements of fact, from description, or from exhibition of samples of goods.

extended coverage Expanded or extra insurance protection purchased by an insured for an additional premium.

extended-coverage indorsement A rider, attached to and made part of an insurance policy, which expands the insured's protection against loss and for which an additional premium is paid.

extortion Acquiring money, property, or other benefit from another through threat or the use of force; blackmail.

extraordinary bailment A bailment in which the bailee is an insurer of the goods in his or her possession and is subject to unusual duties, either at common law or by statute.

F.A.S. The mercantile shipping symbol for *free alongside ship.*

F.O.B. The mercantile shipping symbol for *free on board.*

Fair Credit Billing Act A federal law that regulates credit billing. The Act outlines the procedures to be followed in the event the credit-card holder disputes the accuracy of the statement of account.

Fair Credit Reporting Act A federal law that protects consumers against the circulation of inaccurate or obsolete credit information.

Fair Debt Collection Practices Act A federal law that regulates the debt-collection practices of collection agencies.

fair employment practices commission A government agency entrusted with the enforcement of anti–job-discrimination laws.

Fair Labor Standards Act A 1938 federal law enacted to provide maximum hours and minimum wages for all workers engaged in interstate or foreign commerce or with production of goods for such commerce; the Wage and Hour Law.

Fair Packaging and Labeling Act A federal law requiring packages of consumer goods to bear exterior labels that describe the contents of the packages and identify appropriate users of the product.

false arrest Unlawful detention of a person by a law enforcement official without probable cause for the detention.

false imprisonment Unlawfully detaining a person or forcing a person to remain somewhere against his or her will.

Federal Trade Commission (FTC) The federal agency that oversees methods of competition in interstate commerce in order to assure fairness. It also enforces consumer credit laws and various consumer protection acts.

felony A crime of a serious nature, for which the punishment is death or imprisonment in a state or federal prison for more than one year.

fidelity insurance Insurance that protects employers against losses caused by the dishonest acts of their employees; bonding.

finance charge The fee for use of credit, stated in terms of dollars and cents.

financial interest See *insurable interest.*

financial responsibility laws State laws requiring that a motor-vehicle owner who does not have automobile liability insurance must deposit money or securities with the state as evidence of financial responsibility for damages or injuries incurred as a result of operation of the vehicle.

financing statement A written document that a secured party in a secured credit sale must file in a public office in order to be protected from the claims of innocent third parties.

firm offer An irrevocable promise to hold an offer open for a stated time, with or without consideration.

fixture An article of personal property which has been attached to real property in such a manner that its removal will result in injury to the real property; a permanent improvement to real property.

floater An inland marine insurance policy; an insurance policy that covers loss of personal property regardless of the cause of the loss; an all-risk policy.

Food and Drug Administration (FDA) The federal agency that administers the Food, Drug, and Cosmetic Act and requires drug makers to keep files of research data to support all claims made on behalf of a drug.

Food, Drug, and Cosmetic Act A federal law requiring labeling on packaged foods and drugs to state the maker's name and address, the quantity or weight of the contents, the generic name of the drug, adequate directions for use, cautions against unsafe uses, and warnings of any habit-forming properties.

forbearance A refraining from the enforcement of something (a right, debt, or duty) that is due.

foreclosure The legal procedure by which a mortgagee or lender causes real property to be sold at public auction to satisfy a mortgage debt on which the borrower has defaulted.

foreign corporation A corporation operating in a state other than the state of its incorporation.

forgery Changing or creating a legal or valuable document in order to deceive another, often with intent to obtain the rights, money, or property of another.

formal contract A contract in writing and under seal.

fraud Intentional deception that causes loss to another.

fraud order An accusation of fraud issued by the United States Postal Service to a party suspected of using the mails to carry out a fraudulent scheme.

"friendly" fire The insurance term for a fire that does not escape its natural bounds.

full-covenant warranty deed See *warranty deed.*

full indorsement See *special indorsement.*

full warranty A product warranty that provides for the repair of a defective product without cost to the consumer, or for a refund or a replacement if several repair attempts fail, within a stated warranty period.

future goods Goods that are not both existing and identified.

gambling agreement An agreement that calls for a payment or transfer of something valuable to another on the happening of an uncertain event; a wagering agreement.

general agent A person employed to represent a principal in dealings of a general, continuous nature and whose powers are broad in scope.

general jurisdiction Authority of a court to hear a wide range of cases.

general offer of reward An offer addressed to the first member of the general public who, by performing the act required with knowledge of the offer of reward, creates an agreement.

general partners Co-owners of a partnership in which all partners have unlimited liability for the partnership debts and participate equally in running the business.

general partnership A partnership in which all the partners have unlimited liability for the partnership debts and participate equally in running the business.

General Release An instrument evidencing the surrender of a claim or a right of action to the party against whom the claim or right exists.

gift causa mortis A gift made by a person in danger of immediate death.

gift inter vivos A gift made by a person during his or her lifetime.

"good faith" provision A clause in the Uniform Commercial Code that aims to place dealings between buyers and sellers of goods on a high ethical plane.

goods All things that are movable at the time they are identified as the subject matter of a sales contract; personal property.

government A collection of people or an organization that is responsible for the direction and supervision of its citizens.

grace period A period, usually of a month, following the due date for the payment of an insurance premium, during which the insured may pay the premium.

grand jury A jury that examines accusations against people charged with serious crimes to decide whether the evidence will support the prosecution of the accused.

grantee A party to whom title to real property is transferred by deed.

grantor A party who transfers title to real property by deed.

gratuitous agent A party who agrees to act as an agent without compensation.

gratuitous bailment   A bailment that provides for services relating to the bailed article, without consideration or benefit to one of the parties.

guardian   A person appointed by a court to be legally responsible for the care of an incompetent or of the incompetent's property.

guest   A transient who seeks temporary lodging at a hotel, motel, bed-and-breakfast inn, tavern, or a similar establishment.

Health Maintenance Organization (HMO)   A medical insurance plan under which an insured pays small fees for services provided by a specific group of health-care professionals located in the area covered by the plan.

holder   A party in possession of and legally entitled to receive payment of a negotiable instrument.

holder in due course   A party who takes possession of a negotiable instrument for value, in good faith, and without notice that it is overdue or has been dishonored or of any defense or claim to it on the part of any person.

holdover   A tenant who retains possession of leased property after the term of the lease has expired, without the landlord's consent.

holographic will   An unwitnessed will that appears entirely in the handwriting of the maker.

"hostile" fire   The insurance term for a fire that has escaped its natural bounds.

hotelkeeper   A person regularly engaged in the business of providing living accommodations to all transient people who arrive in proper condition and are willing to pay for the services furnished.

hotelkeeper's lien   A hotelkeeper's right to retain possession of property brought by a guest into the hotel if the guest fails to pay the hotel's charges.

illegal agreement   A promise or an agreement that is neither recognized by law nor enforceable because of its harmfulness to society.

implied authority   An agent's inferred authority to do things incidental and necessary for carrying out the express duties of the agency.

implied contract   A contract in which the intentions of the parties may be judged from their acts rather than from written or spoken words.

implied warranty   A warranty imposed by law.

incidental damages   An award made to an injured party as compensation for expenses reasonably incurred as the result of the wrongful act of another.

incontestable   Not open to dispute or contest.

incorporators   People who form a corporation by preparing, signing, and filing the articles of incorporation with the proper state office.

indemnify   To protect against harm or loss.

indemnity   Security against harm or loss; a money payment made to compensate a party for a loss.

independent contractor   A person who agrees to perform services for another in a situation in which the party who requested the services has no control over the contractor's performance.

indictment   The formal accusation of a crime, prepared by a grand jury.

indorsee   A party to whom a negotiable instrument is transferred and delivered.

indorsement   An inscription on the back of a negotiable instrument, authorizing the transfer of the instrument; in insurance, a provision or a rider added to an insurance contract to alter its scope or application.

indorser   A party who signs his or her name on the back of a negotiable instrument with the intention of transferring rights in the instrument to another.

infant   See *minor.*

informal contract   See *simple contract.*

infraction   A minor violation of the law or a misdemeanor of a less serious nature.

injunction   A court order that forbids the performance of a certain act or requires the performance of a certain act.

inland marine insurance   Insurance that protects the insured from all loss or damage to personal property, except loss from risks specifically excluded by the policy.

insanity   Unsoundness of mind that prevents a person from having the mental capacity required by law to enter into certain relationships.

insolvency   Inability to pay debts when they become due.

installments   A series of payments, often made monthly, which together comprise a total debt.

insurable interest   An interest that arises when a party would suffer direct financial loss or liability if a certain life were lost or if certain property were damaged, lost, or destroyed; a financial interest.

insurance A contract in which one party, for a consideration, agrees to protect another party from stated losses.

insured A party who takes out insurance.

insurer A party who agrees to issue insurance; an insurance company.

intangible personal property A movable thing that cannot be touched or felt, or an interest or right in that thing.

interference with business relations and contracts Unlawful interference with another's fundamental right to engage in a trade or business.

international law A class of laws that regulates the conduct of one nation or its citizens toward another nation or its citizens.

interstate commerce Commerce between states.

Interstate Commerce Commission (ICC) The federal agency that regulates the activities of common carriers who transport goods across state lines.

intestacy The condition of being intestate.

intestate The condition of one who dies without leaving a valid will.

intrastate commerce Commerce within the borders of a state.

invasion of privacy Unlawful intrusion into another's private life, with the result of causing outrage, mental suffering, or humiliation.

issued and outstanding capital stock Authorized capital stock that has been sold.

joint tenancy Ownership of the same property by two or more people who acquired their equal interests at the same time, and in which the ownership interest of a decedent tenant passes to the surviving tenant(s).

judge The official who decides matters brought before a court and who guides court decisions.

judgment by default Judgment awarded to a plaintiff solely on the pleadings and evidence because the defendant has failed to answer the summons or to appear in the action.

judgment lien A creditor's right or charge against the realty of a debtor, created by the filing of a court judgment against the debtor for a sum of money.

judgment note A promissory note in which the maker agrees that the note's holder may enter judgment against the maker without a trial if the maker fails to pay the note at maturity.

jurisdiction Power and authority to hear and determine a legal controversy and to render judgment.

jury A group of impartial people chosen to determine questions of fact in a legal action, under the guidance of a judge.

jury foreman A jury member who acts as chairperson or spokesperson for the jury and announces the jury's verdict.

kickback A return of part of a sum received, often resulting from a secret agreement or duress.

kidnapping A form of extortion in which a person is unlawfully seized and detained or carried away by force or fraud, usually with a demand for ransom.

Labor-Management Relations Act A 1947 federal law enacted to protect employees by forbidding certain unfair labor practices by unions; the Taft-Hartley Act.

Labor-Management Reporting and Disclosure Act A 1959 federal law requiring unions to disclose certain information about their financial conditions both to union membership and to the federal government; the Landrum-Griffin Act.

land contract A contract for the sale of real property.

landlord An owner of real property who leases the property to another; a lessor.

Landrum-Griffin Act *See Labor-Management Reporting and Disclosure Act.*

larceny Taking someone's personal property with the intention of keeping it from its rightful owner; theft.

law The body of principles that governs our conduct with other individuals and with the government.

law merchant A kind of common law established among traders and merchants during the Middle Ages to govern business transactions.

lease A contract granting the use of real property for a definite period in consideration of the payment of rent.

legacy See *bequest.*

legal purpose Lawful reason for entering into a contract.

legal rate of interest The statutory interest rate or charge that lenders may impose on borrowers when the parties fail to state a rate to be charged.

legal tender All coins and currencies of the United States.

legatee A party to whom a gift of personal property is made by will.

lender See *creditor.*

lessee See *tenant.*

lessor See *landlord.*

letters of administration Authority granted by a probate court to a person to settle the estate of an intestate person.

letter of credit A letter issued by a bank, certifying that a named person is entitled to draw credit up to a certain sum.

letters testamentary Authority, granted by a probate court to a person named in a will as executor or executrix, to settle the decedent's estate and to carry out the provisions of the will.

liability Legal assignment of responsibility for a given act or omission.

libel An untruthful publication or writing that tends to injure the reputation of another.

lien A right or a charge against specific property as security for a debt or for performance of some act.

limited jurisdiction Authority to hear only one particular type of case.

limited partners Co-owners of a partnership in which the liability of one or more partners is limited.

limited partnership A partnership in which the liability of one or more partners is limited.

limited warranty A product warranty that spells out, in clear language, exactly what parts or labor it covers and for how long.

limited-payment life policy A life insurance policy in which the insured pays a limited number of premiums, and the face value of the policy is paid only when the insured dies.

litigation A court action or lawsuit.

locus sigilli (L.S.) *(Latin)* Place of the seal.

lodger See *boarder.*

lottery A supervised game of chance in which some consideration is paid for a chance to win a prize.

Magnuson-Moss Warranty Act A federal law requiring that goods perform as implied when used properly, usually for a stated period of time.

majority The status of a person who has reached the age at which full civil rights are granted; legal age.

maker A party who issues and signs a promissory note.

malpractice The negligence of a professional person, such as a doctor or lawyer, who fails to exercise an accepted degree of skill or care when rendering services.

marine insurance Insurance that protects owners of boats from vessel, cargo, and other property loss or damage caused by storms and other perils of the sea.

material alteration An intentional modification of an agreement that changes the rights or duties of the parties.

material fact A fact that is very important or consequential to an agreement.

maturity The time when a negotiable instrument falls due and becomes payable.

mechanic's lien A right or charge against the realty of a party who has failed to pay for services or materials provided in the improvement of the realty, in favor of the party who provided the services or materials.

mediation The process by which a dispute is settled out of court by an independent third party whose solution is subject to the disputing parties' approval.

mediator An independent third party authorized by disputing parties to find a resolution of their differences to which both disputing parties can agree.

medical payments insurance Automobile insurance that protects an insured and all members of the insured's immediate family against losses due to medical bills incurred as the result of an accident, whether they are riding in the family car or in any other car and regardless of who is at fault in the accident.

Medicare Compulsory hospital insurance and optional medical insurance provided under social security to people who are over the age of 65 or who have been disabled for two or more years.

mercantile courts Medieval courts that resolved disputes relating to the special customs of merchants.

merchant A professional buyer or seller who usually has a specialized knowledge of certain goods and of the business customs and practices common to his or her line of business.

merger A joining of two corporations in which one of the firms surrenders its charter and is absorbed by the other firm.

minor A person not of full legal age; an infant.

minutes The official record of a meeting.

Miranda decision A landmark 1966 United States Supreme Court decision in the case of *Miranda v. Arizona* that requires police to inform suspects of their rights, including the right to be silent and to have an attorney present during police questioning.

misdemeanor A crime that is less serious than a felony, usually carrying a penalty of a fine, a sentence to a local jail for less than one year, or both.

mistake An error or misunderstanding.

mitigate To lessen; to make less severe.

mitigation The act of mitigating or lessening.

Model Business Corporation Act A model statute prepared by the American Bar Association that it submits to states for adoption. It covers all phases of corporate law.

money order A form of draft issued by a post office, bank, express company, or telegraph company for payment of a specified sum of money.

mortgage A lien on property used as security for a loan.

mortgagee The lender or creditor in a mortgage.

mortgagor The borrower or debtor in a mortgage.

motion A request to obtain an order, a ruling, or a direction from a judge.

mutual assent The meeting of the minds of the parties to a contract; mutual agreement.

mutual-benefit bailment A bailment that benefits both the bailor and the bailee.

National Labor Relations Act A 1935 federal law enacted to encourage collective bargaining and to prohibit unfair labor practices by employers; the Wagner Act.

National Labor Relations Board (NLRB) The federal agency that regulates labor practices.

National Traffic and Motor Vehicle Safety Act A federal law that requires makers and sellers of vehicles to adhere to very strict testing and documentation standards in order to protect consumers from injuries caused by defective vehicles.

necessaries Goods or services needed to sustain the life and well-being of a minor or of a minor's dependent family, usually including food, clothing, medical care, shelter, basic education, and equipment with which to earn a living.

negligence Failure to use the skill or care necessary to prevent injury to other persons or property.

negotiable instrument A written and signed document that contains an unconditional promise or order to pay to order or to bearer a sum certain in money, on demand or at a definite time.

net assets All the property owned by a person or business after payment of all debts.

no-fault insurance Automobile insurance under which an accident victim is compensated for actual losses (property damage, medical bills, and lost wages) by his or her own insurance firm, regardless of who was at fault in the accident.

no-par-value stock Stock that has no fixed value.

nominal damages A court award, often amounting to a few cents or $1, given to a party whose legal right has been violated but who has not sustained any actual loss.

nonmerchant An ordinary consumer; a nonprofessional buyer or seller of goods.

nontrading partnership A partnership formed for professional purposes, such as the practice of law, medicine, or accountancy, rather than for purposes of buying and selling goods.

notice of assignment Notice given by an assignee to a debtor in order to protect the assignee from any fraudulent action on the part of the assignor.

notice of dishonor Notification that a holder of a dishonored instrument, in order to be protected from loss on the instrument, must give to all parties who may be liable for payment of the instrument.

notice of removal The notification an insured must give to an insurer to inform the insurer that insured personal property has been moved to a new location.

novation A new contract that arises when a new party is substituted for one of the original parties to a contract.

nuisance Unlawful interference with another's possession and enjoyment of property or with the health or comfort of another.

nuncupative will An oral will that is valid only when made by a person during his or her last illness or by a member of the military who believes that he or she is in immediate danger of death.

obstruction of justice An act that prevents or hinders justice from being accomplished.

Occupational Safety and Health Act (OSHA) A federal law directing the Secretary of Labor to establish certain work-related safety and health standards that must be observed by businesses engaged in interstate commerce.

offer A proposal; an offeror's promise that something shall be done or happen, or shall not be done or happen, if the offeree complies with the offeror's stated conditions.

offeree The party to whom an offer or proposal is made.

offeror The party who makes an offer or proposal to another.

officer An executive, elected by the board of directors of a corporation, who may make binding contracts for the corporation.

old-age insurance See *retirement insurance.*

open policy An insurance contract in which the amount to be paid in the event of a loss is to be determined by appraisal after the loss has occurred.

opinion A court's written expression of the legal reasons and principles on which a decision is based.

option A purchased right to hold an offer open for a given time.

option contract A contract in which an offeree purchases from the offeror the right to hold the offer open for a given time.

order bill of lading A negotiable bill of lading stating that certain goods are to be delivered to the order of a named party and serving as evidence of ownership of the goods.

order instrument An instrument payable to the order of a specified person.

ordinance A law or regulation passed by a local governmental body.

ordinary bailment A bailment in which the bailee is subject to the usual or standard duties of a bailee.

original jurisdiction Authority to hear a case for the first time.

ornamental fixtures Decorative improvements, such as bookshelves and chandeliers, which are attached by a tenant to leased property but remain the tenant's property.

out-of-court settlement The reconciliation of legal differences out of court.

ownership The rights to possess, use, and dispose of property; title.

par value A fixed, arbitrary value printed on the face of a stock certificate.

pari-mutuel A legal betting pool in which those who bet on competitors finishing in the first three places share the total amount bet, minus a percentage for the management.

parol Oral; by word of mouth.

parol evidence rule The legal principle prohibiting the introduction in court of oral evidence that tends to contradict the written terms of an agreement.

partnership An association of two or more individuals to carry on a business for profit as co-owners.

passenger A person transported by a public or private carrier.

past consideration A promise made or an act completed before any request is made for it.

pawn ticket A receipt for goods that have been pledged to a pawnbroker as security for a loan.

pawnbroker A person whose business is to lend money at interest on a pledge of personal property other than securities.

payee A party to whom payment of a promissory note is promised.

perennials Crops that grow from year to year without replanting and are classified legally as real property.

perfected security interest The interest in goods that a secured party obtains by filing with the appropriate public office a security agreement or financing statement evidencing a secured credit sale.

periodic tenancy A lease agreement for an indefinite term, with rent payable at fixed intervals.

perjury Willfully giving false testimony while under oath as to a material matter in a legal proceeding.

personal defense A defense that may not be used against a holder in due course in a legal action involving a negotiable instrument.

personal property A movable thing or an interest or right in that thing; personalty.

physical evidence Items (documents, photographs, or objects) submitted to a court as proof of fact in a court action.

plaintiff The party who brings an action in a court of law against another party.

pleadings Written statements of the claims and defenses of the parties to a legal action.

pledge A mutual-benefit bailment in which goods are left with another as security for the payment of a debt or for the performance of an obligation.

pledgee A party who receives possession of goods in a bailment as security for a loan.

pledgor A party who borrows money and transfers possession of goods to another in a bailment as security for the loan.

points Service charges deducted by a lender from a mortgage loan.

policy A written contract of insurance.

postdate To date as of a later time than the present.

power of attorney A written document in which a principal empowers an agent to make contracts and to act for the principal.

precedent A legal decision on which later decisions are based.

preemptive right A stockholder's right to purchase new issues of corporate stock before such issues are sold to the general public.

preferred stock A class of corporate stock in which each share carries special rights and privileges, especially with respect to distribution of the corporation's profits.

premium The consideration paid for insurance.

present sale A sale in which the seller transfers ownership or title to certain goods to the buyer immediately when the contract is made.

presentment A demand for payment from the party primarily liable (the maker) on a negotiable instrument.

pretrial hearing A meeting or session in which the issues of a legal action are finally determined before the trial of the action.

price The consideration for a sales contract; the money used to pay for goods.

principal A party who grants to another the authority to transact his or her business.

private carrier A carrier who agrees to transport goods under individual contracts but does not offer services to the public; a contract carrier.

private corporation A corporation organized for a nonprofit purpose as well as a business corporation for profit; a corporation whose ownership is restricted to certain individuals rather than offered to the general public.

probate The process of establishing the validity of a will and administering a decedent's estate.

probate court The court that directs the process of establishing the validity of a will and administering a decedent's estate; surrogate's court.

procedural law The set of rules that determines the process of enforcing the rights and duties of individuals.

process A court order, such as a summons, which notifies a defendant of a legal action and commands the defendant to appear in court or to answer.

product liability Responsibility of manufacturers for injuries caused by products that are defective as a result of the negligent manner in which they were made.

Product Safety Act A federal law requiring products to meet reasonable safety standards when used in the manner in which they are intended.

professional service corporation A corporation formed by a group of people, such as lawyers, doctors, or accountants, who render professional services.

promisee A party to whom a promise is made.

promisor A party who makes a promise to another.

promissory estoppel The principle that bars a party from taking back certain types of promises, such as charitable subscriptions, on which another party has relied.

promissory note An unconditional written promise to pay a stated sum to the order of a specific person, or to the bearer, at a definite time or on demand.

property Anything people use, possess, enjoy, transfer to others, or maintain a right of ownership in; the branch of civil law governing the possession and transfer of real property through gift, purchase, or inheritance.

property damage insurance Automobile insurance that protects an insured against liability for damages to the property of another.

proprietor   Owner.

prosecution   The party who begins or conducts criminal proceedings.

prospectus   A circular, letter, or other communication that offers a security for sale to the public.

proxy   The written instrument by which a stockholder of a corporation appoints another to represent or vote in the stockholder's place; the person with such authority.

public carrier   A party who transports people from one place to another for hire, offering services to anyone.

public corporation   A corporation organized for governmental purposes; a corporation whose ownership is offered to the general public.

public defender   An attorney appointed by a court to represent someone who cannot afford to hire a private attorney in a criminal action.

public liability insurance   See *bodily injury liability insurance.*

Public Notice of Dissolution   A notice inserted in a local general-circulation newspaper to inform new creditors of a partnership of the withdrawal of one of the partners, thereby protecting the withdrawing partner from any claims of the new creditors.

punitive damages   An award made to an injured party to make an example of or to punish the wrongdoer for an intentional tort; exemplary damages.

qualified indorsement   A method of transferring one's rights in a negotiable instrument by indorsing the back of the instrument and expressly stating that the indorser does not agree to pay the instrument if the maker fails to pay. However, the qualified indorser is liable for certain warranties.

quasi contract   An implied contract created by law to render justice to an innocent party.

quitclaim deed   A deed in which the grantor gives an interest in property to the grantee, whatever that interest may be, without covenants.

ratification   Approval of an act that previously had not been binding; the procedure by which a minor may approve a voidable contract on reaching majority.

real defense   A defense that may be used against a holder in due course in a legal action involving a negotiable instrument; a defense that prohibits a holder in due course from collecting on a negotiable instrument.

real-estate mortgage   A written document describing the security given for a mortgage debt.

Real Estate Settlement Procedures Act (RESPA)   A 1974 federal law that regulates the practices involved with title closings in real-estate sales financed by federally related loans.

real property   Land and anything permanently attached to land; land including not only the surface of the earth but also things beneath the surface, such as minerals, oils, and gases, and things a reasonable distance above the surface; realty; real estate.

realty   See *real property.*

receipt or possession of stolen property   Receiving or holding property believed to be stolen, with the intention of keeping the property from its rightful owner.

reimbursement   Restoration or payment of an equivalent; a principal's duty to pay back an agent for all expenses incurred by the agent while lawfully carrying out assigned duties.

rejection   The act of rejecting; an offeree's refusal to accept an offer.

remedy   The legal means, such as a court action, by which the violation of a right is prevented or compensated.

renounce   To give up something, such as a right.

rent   The consideration a tenant pays to a landlord for the use of real property.

replevin   A court action to recover specific personal property wrongfully taken or detained.

reply   A court document submitted by the plaintiff in a legal action in response to the defendant's answer to the complaint.

report   A published volume of court decisions or opinions.

repossession   The taking back or regaining of possession of goods by a seller or lender when a buyer has defaulted on a payment contract for the goods.

rescind   To cancel; to annul.

rescission   Cancellation or annulment.

restrictive indorsement   A method of transferring one's rights in a negotiable instrument by signing the back of the instrument and making it payable only under certain conditions, only to make the indorsee the agent of the indorser for a specific purpose, or only for the benefit or use of a named party.

retirement insurance Social security insurance that pays a limited monthly income to people who work until they are either 62 or 65 and then retire.

revocation The act of withdrawing or recalling a power previously conferred.

rider A statement, attached to and made part of a document, which modifies or supplements the document.

right of lien A bailee's right to retain possession of bailed goods until reasonable charges for the bailee's services are paid; a legal right in another's property as security for the performance of an obligation.

right of redemption A mortgagor's legal right to redeem property in the process of being foreclosed on payment of all sums and interest due.

right of subrogation An insurer's right to stand in the place of or to substitute for the insured to recover from a third party who caused a loss for which the insurer indemnified the insured.

risk of loss The risks (of damage, loss, destruction, or theft) that may be acquired with ownership.

robbery Taking away property from the immediate presence or possession of another by means of force or with the threat of harm.

sale on approval A sale in which title and risk of loss pass only when the buyer has signified approval and acceptance of the goods.

sale with privilege of return A sale in which a buyer purchases goods with the option of returning them if they can't be resold.

satisfaction piece A written document acknowledging that a mortgage debt has been satisfied.

scope of authority The range or extent of authority given by a principal to an agent.

secret partner A partner who takes an active role in the management of a partnership but who is not known to the public as a partner.

secured credit sale A sale in which a seller or lender retains a security interest in the goods that are the subject of the sale or loan until the buyer repays the debt.

secured party The seller or lender in a secured credit sale.

Securities Act A 1933 federal law that regulates the sale of securities.

Securities and Exchange Commission (SEC) The agency that administers federal laws dealing with stocks, bonds, and similar instruments.

security agreement A written agreement evidencing a secured credit sale.

security deposit Cash, negotiable securities, or a bond that a landlord may require a tenant to furnish as security for the faithful performance of a lease.

security interest An interest in personal property or fixtures that secures payment or performance of an obligation.

seller's talk Promises or statements made by a seller that are based on mere expressions of opinion rather than on fact.

shareholder An investor in or owner of a corporation.

share A small, salable unit of ownership in a corporation.

sight draft A draft payable immediately on presentation by the holder or payee to the drawee.

silent partner A partner not actively engaged in the conduct of the partnership.

simple contract An oral or written contract that is not under seal; an informal contract.

slander An untruthful oral statement that tends to injure the reputation of another.

social agreement A promise or an agreement of a nonbusiness nature that is not legally enforceable because it is not particularly important to society in general.

social insurance Government-subsidized insurance that protects citizens against financial loss.

Social Security Act A 1933 federal law enacted to provide a continued income for people whose incomes are reduced or lost through death, disability, or old age.

Social Security Administration (SSA) The federal agency that oversees the government's social security program.

social security program The federal program under which the provisions of the Social Security Act are carried out.

sole proprietorship A business owned by one person.

sole-benefit bailment A bailment that benefits only the bailor or the bailee.

special agent A person employed only to perform a single service or a series of specific acts narrow in scope, after which the agency ceases.

special indorsement A method of transferring one's rights in a negotiable instrument by signing the back of the instrument and specifying the person to whom or to whose order the instrument is payable.

specific performance The principle of equity law that requires an agreement to be carried out under its original terms.

standardized duties Contractual duties that are merely mechanical or do not involve special skill, knowledge, and judgment.

state disability insurance Protection for workers who are disabled as a result of injuries or illnesses that aren't related to employment.

statute law A class of laws passed by legislative bodies.

Statute of Frauds A law requiring that certain contracts be in writing to be enforceable.

statutes of limitations Laws that prevent the bringing of a legal action if the action is not begun within a certain time after the cause of action has accrued.

stipulated means of communication A specified or directed method of communicating acceptance of an offer.

stock The ownership element of a corporation, usually divided into units or shares.

stock certificate The document that represents an ownership interest in a corporation.

stock exchange A place where security trading is conducted according to an organized system.

stockholder See *shareholder.*

stop-loss clause A provision in a health and hospitalization insurance policy which states that the insurer will pay 100% of the insured's medical expenses after the insured has paid a predetermined amount.

stop-payment order A depositor's order to a bank to refuse to pay an uncertified check issued by the depositor.

straight bill of lading A nonnegotiable bill of lading stating that certain goods are to be delivered to a named party.

straight life policy A life insurance policy in which the insured pays a definite yearly premium as long as he or she lives, and the face value of the policy is paid to a named beneficiary after the insured's death; a whole life policy.

strict liability Responsibility of manufacturers, wholesalers, and retailers for injuries caused by defective products, regardless of fault.

subagent A party appointed by an agent to carry out the agent's duties.

sublet To agree to rent, or let, part of the remaining term of a lease.

subpoena A court order commanding a person to appear and testify in a legal action or proceeding.

substantial performance The doctrine by which a party's duties under a contract are considered to have been substantially carried out if defects in performance are minor and the performance was accomplished honestly and in good faith.

substantive law The set of rules that creates, defines, and establishes the rights and duties of individuals.

suicide clause A clause in a life insurance policy that relieves the insurer of the responsibility to pay the benefits under the policy in the event of the death of the insured by his or her own hand within a certain period of time (e.g., two years).

summons A court order which notifies a defendant that a legal action has been filed and commands the defendant to appear in court or to answer.

surrogate's court See *probate court.*

survivor's insurance Social security insurance that pays a limited monthly income to the dependents of a worker who has died.

Taft-Hartley Act See *Labor-Management Relations Act.*

tangible personal property A movable thing that can be touched or felt, or an interest or right in that thing.

tax sale A governmental body's sale of real property in order to satisfy an unpaid tax lien on the property.

taxes Charges imposed on citizens to raise funds for public purposes or for government expenses.

tenancy Ownership of real property.

tenancy at will A lease agreement for an indefinite term, with both parties having the option of terminating the lease at any time.

tenancy by the entirety Ownership of real property by co-owners who are married to each other, and in which neither tenant can sell or convey an interest without the other's consent.

tenancy for years A lease agreement for a definite term.

tenancy in common Ownership of real property by two or more people who acquired the same property by separate instruments or by a will or a deed, with no right of survivorship.

tenancy in severalty Ownership of real property by a single person.

tenant A party who leases real property from a landlord; a lessee.

tender An unconditional offer and readiness to perform an obligation under a contract.

term policy A life insurance policy that protects the insured for a limited period of time, such as five or ten years, and that has no cash value at the end of the term.

termination by performance Discharge of a contract by actual performance of the contractual duties by the parties.

termination statement A written document certifying that a secured party no longer has a security interest in the subject matter of a secured credit sale.

testator The person who makes a will.

testimony Oral statements of a witness in court, made under oath during a trial of an action or other legal proceeding.

theft See *larceny.*

third party A party with whom an agent deals.

time-after-date draft A draft payable at the end of the stated time after the date of the draft.

time-after-sight draft A draft payable at the end of a stated time after its presentation to the drawee for acceptance.

time draft A draft payable on a stated date, at a stated time after the date of the draft, or at the end of a stated time after sight.

"Time Price" doctrine A principle, developed by the courts, which exempts all sales credit transactions from general usury laws.

title Evidence of ownership in goods; ownership.

title closing The performance or closing of a contract for the sale of real property.

title insurance Insurance that protects owners of realty from claims made against them, arising out of defective title to the real estate.

title search An investigation undertaken by a buyer of real property to determine whether the seller has good title to the property.

tort A private or civil wrong committed against an individual rather than against society as a whole.

torts The branch of civil law dealing with private wrongs committed by one person against another or against another's property.

trade acceptance A special form of draft drawn by a seller on the buyer of goods.

trade fixtures Improvements, required by a tenant's trade, which are attached by a tenant to leased property but remain the tenant's property.

trading partnership A partnership formed for the purpose of buying and selling goods.

transcript The written record of a court proceeding.

transfer The act of delivering an instrument to another with the intention of passing one's rights in the instrument to that party.

transfer agent A party designated to record changes in stock ownership, to cancel old stock certificates, and to issue new stock certificates.

transferee A party to whom a negotiable instrument is delivered.

transferor A party who negotiates a negotiable instrument by delivery to another.

travel insurance Protection against financial losses (accident and medical, baggage, and trip cancellation or interruption) that may be incurred when traveling.

traveler's check A draft purchased from a bank or express company and signed by the purchaser at the time of purchase and again at the time of cashing as a precaution against forgery.

treason A serious crime consisting of commission of an act of war against one's country or of giving aid to the enemies of one's country.

trespass Unlawful interference with the person or property of another; unauthorized entry on and damage to the land of another.

trial court A court of original jurisdiction.

Truth-in-Lending Act A 1969 federal law that requires full disclosure of the terms of substantially all consumer credit transactions.

ultra vires act An act of a corporation beyond the scope of its powers.

unconscionable contract A contract that is unfair, harsh, or oppressive to one party to the agreement.

undisclosed principal A principal whose name is not revealed in an agency transaction.

undue influence Improper use of power over the mind of another, causing the latter to make contracts or gifts that he or she otherwise would not make; unfair persuasion.

unemployment insurance Government-subsidized insurance that pays a limited, temporary income to workers who are laid off from their jobs through no fault of their own.

unenforceable contract A contract that is not enforceable against either party because of lack of certain requirements, such as a writing.

Uniform Commercial Code (UCC) The collection of laws that attempts to standardize all the rules governing the rights and duties of buyers and sellers of goods, commercial paper, and documents.

Uniform Commercial Credit Code (UCCC) A uniform law drafted by the National Conference of Commissioners on Uniform State Laws that attempts to standardize state laws governing commercial credit transactions.

uniform laws Laws that are the same from state to state.

Uniform Limited Partnership Act (ULPA) A law adopted by states to establish uniformity among state laws governing limited partnerships.

Uniform Partnership Act (UPA) A law adopted by states to improve the common law of partnership and to establish uniformity among state partnership laws.

Uniform Probate Code A set of rules that attempts to standardize state laws governing the process of establishing the validity of a will and administering a decedent's estate.

Uniform Settlement Statement A form that itemizes the closing costs to be incurred by the parties to a real-estate sale, required to be completed by the party conducting the title closing.

Uniform Small Loan Law A law that allows loans in some states to be made at rates in excess of the usury rate if the lender is licensed and the amount and the length of time of the loan are limited.

unilateral contract A contract that arises by exchanging a promise for an act or an act for a promise.

uninsured motorist insurance Automobile insurance that protects the insured and the insured's immediate family against losses due to injuries caused by uninsured and hit-and-run drivers.

union A bargaining unit that represents a group of workers in their negotiations with an employer.

unique goods Goods that are rare, unusual, or obtainable only from one source.

United States Court of Claims The federal court that hears cases involving claims against the federal government.

United States Courts of Appeals Federal courts that have appellate jurisdiction in particular geographic circuits.

United States District Courts Federal courts that have geographically limited jurisdiction over cases involving a federal penalty, admiralty and maritime cases, cases arising under patent and copyright laws, and disputes involving more than $10,000 between residents of different states.

United States Postal Service An independent unit of the executive branch of the federal government that operates the federal mail system and enforces postal fraud laws.

United States Supreme Court The federal court of highest authority. This court hears appeals from lower federal courts and from state supreme courts in cases involving issues of great significance to the public or questions of constitutionality. Although it has original jurisdiction, the Supreme Court rarely exercises that jurisdiction.

universal life policy A life insurance policy whose premium and payoff amounts vary, depending on the current interest rate and the Federal Reserve Board money rate.

unoccupied premises A building or part of a building that is temporarily uninhabited but still contains the personal property it normally contains.

unpaid seller's lien The right of a seller who has not been paid for goods to withhold delivery of the goods to the buyer.

usury Charging a higher rate of interest on a loan than that permitted by law.

vacant premises A building or part of a building that is uninhabited and from which the customary furniture or other contents have been removed.

valid contract A contract that contains the essential elements of mutual assent, consideration, competent parties, and legal purpose; a contract that has legal strength or force and is binding.

valued policy An insurance contract in which the amount to be paid in the event of a loss is fixed on the face of the policy and does not depend on determination after loss.

vandalism See *criminal mischief.*

vendee The buyer in a sales transaction.

vendor The seller in a sales transaction.

verdict The decision of a jury.

versus *(Latin)* Against.

vicarious liability Responsibility for the wrongful acts or omissions of another.

void agreement An agreement that has no legal force or effect.

voidable contract A contract that may be rendered void at the option of one party.

Wage and Hour Law See *Fair Labor Standards Act.*

wagering agreement See *gambling agreement.*

Wagner Act See *National Labor Relations Act.*

warehouse receipt A document issued by a warehouse operator as a receipt for goods stored and as a contract for their storage.

warranty A seller's promise or representation of facts, on which a buyer relies when entering into a sales contract; in a sale of realty, the grantor's covenant that the grantee will have title to the property being transferred.

warranty deed A deed that transfers title to real property and in which the grantor warrants to the grantee that the grantor has complete and perfect title to the property except as to matters mentioned in the deed.

warranty of fitness for a particular purpose An implied warranty in which a seller guarantees that goods are suitable and fit for the purpose for which the buyer needs the goods.

warranty of merchantability An implied warranty that makes merchant sellers liable for goods that are not of fair, average quality and fit for the ordinary purposes for which such goods are used.

warranty of title An implied warranty that the seller of goods possesses a good, clean title to the goods and can lawfully transfer that title to the buyer.

water rights Rights to use waterways that flow through the property of another.

whole life policy See *straight life policy.*

will A written document disposing of property, to take effect after the death of the maker.

Wool Products Labeling Act A federal law that governs the sale of wool goods in interstate commerce.

worker's compensation insurance Government-subsidized insurance that pays for the medical care and lost wages of people who are injured while at work or who become ill as a result of certain occupational diseases.

writ of execution A court order that commands a court official to seize property of a judgment debtor in order to satisfy the debt.

wrongful death A wrongful act that results in the death of another, even without intention to kill.

zoning laws Laws regulating the use that may be made of real property in certain areas.

Index